D1247796

The Complete Guide
to Middle-Earth

From *The Hobbit* to *The Silmarillion*

The Complete Guide to Middle-Earth

From *The Hobbit* to *The Silmarillion*

ROBERT FOSTER

A Del Rey Book

BALLANTINE BOOKS · NEW YORK

A Del Rey Book
Published by Ballantine Books

Library of Congress Cataloging in Publication Data

Foster, Robert, 1949-
    The complete guide to Middle-earth.

    "A Del Rey book."
    Published in 1971 under title: A guide to Middle-earth.
    1. Tolkien, John Ronald Reuel, 1892-1973—Dictionaries, indexes,
etc. I. Title.
PR6039.032Z49 1978   823'.9'12   77-26825
ISBN 0-345-27520-9

This edition published by arrangement with Mirage Press.

Manufactured in the United States of America

First Ballantine Books Edition: August 1974

Revised and enlarged edition: March 1978 (hardbound)
Second Printing: April 1978

To the memory of my grandfather, Louis N. Feipel,
who gave me his love of words and books.

Contents

Introduction

With the appearance of *The Silmarillion,* the publication of J. R. R. Tolkien's mythopoesis is virtually complete. The reader can now appreciate the full scope and significance of the history of Aman and Middle-earth, the central stages in the great drama of the Creation of Eä. One can trace in detail the Light of Aman from the Two Trees on Ezellohar to the renewing power of the Phial of Galadriel in the stinking darkness of Shelob's Lair. The terror felt there by Sam Gamgee is better understood after reading of the Unlight of Ungoliant, and Boromir's desire for the Ring can be seen as a wisp of the Shadow of Melkor, who lusted after Light but created only Darkness. Not only do the great conflicts between East and West—from the First War and the Battle of the Powers to the Battle of Fornost and the War of the Ring—reveal the nature of good and evil and the immeasurable compassion of Ilúvatar, but also, the identity of the forces that intervene to give victory to the good suggests the progressive freeing of Man from the influence of both Valar and demons to work out his own destiny, known to Ilúvatar alone.

Writing this revised edition of my *Guide to Middle-earth* has enhanced my awareness of these correspondences, designs which are surely central to the joy of Faerie and which give Professor Tolkien's work its marvelous and profound coherence. But it has also made me aware of a difference between the conception and the realization of this cycle of myth and romance, between the "visionary scene" and its "frame," [1] between the Vision and the Text. The

[1] J. R. R. Tolkien, "On Fairy Stories," *Tree and Leaf* (all editions), p. 83.

ix

"seamless web of Story" [2] is indeed endless and without blemish, but books—and lives—alas, are not. In the first edition of the *Guide* I used any information available to me that I believed came from Professor Tolkien and had been transmitted accurately; I hoped that these details would ultimately appear in print. But now—faced with a plethora of revised texts, calendars, letters, illustrations, interviews, anecdotes, and reports of conversations, some containing contradictory information—I have come to believe that inconsistencies, sometimes deliberately maintained by Professor Tolkien, occur where the details of the Vision were not clear to him, where he was stymied by a single leaf on the Tree, not sure of "its shape, and its sheen, and the glistening of dewdrops on its edge," [3] not yet ready to fix it in the Text. Yet these inconsistencies, which can bulk large in an alphabetic treatment of Faerie, should not be allowed to detract from the general bloom of this lushly foliated Tree.

So this revised *Guide* is limited to the Text, to published works by Professor Tolkien in the latest editions available to American readers. The basic text for *The Lord of the Rings* is again the Ballantine paperback edition, with emendations from the revised Houghton Mifflin hardback edition; Appendix C contains a concordance between the two editions. British editions contain several further emendations, which I have not taken into account; of those I have heard of or seen, the most significant is the change of *d* to *dh* in *Galadrim* and *Caras Galadon,* which resolves the confusion (encouraged, it seems, by the Elves themselves, as Christopher Tolkien's comment in *The Silmarillion* on *Galadhriel* suggests) between Sindarin *galad* 'light' and *galadh* 'tree.' The three exceptions to this rule of Text are sources which seem particularly trustworthy: the Pauline Baynes map of Middle-earth displays a number of place-names evidently given her by Professor Tolkien; Clyde Kilby's intimate *Tolkien and the Silmarillion* contains intriguing hints of the End; so much of the information con-

---

[2] *Ibid.*
[3] J. R. R. Tolkien, "Leaf by Niggle," *ibid.,* p. 88.

tained in Professor Tolkien's letters to and conversations with my friend Dick Plotz has been corroborated by *The Silmarillion* that I feel confident in using other items.

In general, I hope that I have not forgotten the limits of a reference work. I count myself fortunate to have wandered in the Fairy-realm of Arda for fifteen years now, and while my tongue is certainly not tied, for the sake of my own delight I have learned not "to ask too many questions, lest the gates should be shut and the keys be lost." [4] This *Guide* is intended to be supplementary to the works of Professor Tolkien and no more; its value is that it can clarify deep-hidden historical facts and draw together scraps of information whose relation is easily overlooked, thus aiding the wanderer in Arda in his quest for its particular Truth. When matters are unclear in the Text I have tried to remain silent, but those places where I have been unable to restrain my conjectures are liberally sprinkled with "perhaps," "presumably," and such words. By now the entries which comprise this *Guide* represent the product of ten years of intermittent labor and frequent correction by myself and careful readers, until I can hope that the errors which remain are more mechanical than substantive.

There is one major deviation from this conservative treatment of the Text. Unlike *The Lord of the Rings,* whose Appendix B provides precise dates for the events of the Second and Third Ages, *The Silmarillion* contains little exact chronological information aside from sporadic indications of the passage of years ("But when Tuor had lived thus in solitude as an outlaw for four years") and rough dating from the first rising of the Sun. Desiring to make the information concerning the First Age more compatible with that for later Ages, I have taken it upon myself to coordinate these indications of time into a Chronology of the First Age (Appendix A). This Chronology may help to unify in the minds of readers the episodic sequence of events and personages in the Wars of Beleriand; by counting years, it also underscores the rapid collapse of Beleriand after Dagor Bragollach and the tragedies of the early deaths

[4] "On Fairy Stories," p. 3.

of Huor (at 31), Túrin and Nienor (36 and 27), and Dior (about 39). In addition, I must confess to having succumbed to the scholarly joys of writing an Appendix. The dates given for the First Age, therefore, both in the entries and in Appendix A, are strictly my own and should be taken as approximations rather than as completely trustworthy deductions; my derivation of these dates is fully explained in the Appendix.

The principles involved in determining entries are fairly simple. In general, any capitalized word or phrase receives a separate entry unless it is a clearly identified epithet or a translation of a name not used independently of the main name; thus there is an entry for *Súlimo* but not for its full translation, *Lord of the Breath of Arda,* and *Voronwë* as the epithet of Steward Mardil is not listed separately. In addition, certain noncapitalized items (mostly the names of species and objects, such as the great spiders and ithildin) have been included. Variant spellings (which in most cases reflect Professor Tolkien's further development of the Eldarin languages) are noted, but most variations in the use of accent marks have been ignored. Page references in main entries are to significant references only; cross-references usually cite the first occurrence only. Geographical entries do not always cite the maps on which the place in question is shown, and historical entries occasionally use dates given in Appendix B without citation; in both cases the references can easily be found. References to the various Indices are given only when they contain new information.

When entries are genuine forms in Middle-earth languages, I have indicated this, giving translations wherever I am sure of them. A question mark following a language identification or translation obviously indicates uncertainty. Translated Rohirric (Old English) forms are occasionally translated again into modern English; the language of other forms is indicated as "tr.—" wherever I felt there was a possibility of confusing them with Elvish or genuine Mannish forms. However, by and large I have not indicated the language of names and terms "Anglicized" into English, Germanic, or Celtic equivalents; as Appendix F suggests, most Adûnaic, Rohirric, Westron, Mannish, and Hobbitish forms have been so translated. In *The Lord of the Rings* I have assumed that English versions of Middle-earth names (e.g., *Treebeard* for *Fangorn*) represent Westron forms used by Men and Hobbits. But in *The Silmarillion* this is obviously not the case, since Westron did not develop until the late Second Age. Here I have assumed that the English versions, even though capitalized, are merely translations intended for the convenience of the reader, not translated Mannish names.

The perspective of the entries in the revised *Guide* is somewhat more confused than that of the first edition. Entries of First Age persons, places, and events receive the perspective of *Quenta Silmarillion,* familiar but somewhat removed. The Valar and the West are described in the present tense, except for geographical features changed at the fall of Númenor. For later Ages, because the historical materials appended to *The Lord of the Rings* ultimately derive from Gondor, entries adopt the point of view of a Dúnadan scholar of the early Fourth Age or (for Hobbit entries) that of a historically minded Took of the Great Smials or Fairbairn of the Tower. Thus, all entries not specifically limited in time refer to conditions during the Long Peace (for Beleriand) or the War of the Ring (elsewhere). Death dates for Elves refer, of course, only to the death of their bodies in Arda, and I have not given death dates for those who have gone over Sea, for they live still. It should be noted that Shire records state that Bilbo lived for one hundred and thirty-one years and seven days. References to months and days are those of Appendix B, and are thus in the Shire Reckoning. This difference between Hobbit and Dúnadan dates is no more than a day in the spring and summer, since 2 Yule equaled yestarë in the Stewards' Reckoning. However, following the Dúnedain I have made FO 1 equal TA 3021 (SR 1421), although in the Shire FO 1 equaled SR 1422.

In the course of ten years this *Guide* has profited from the assistance and friendship of many people. Dick Plotz encouraged me to write a *Guide* and gave me access to his correspondence with Professor Tolkien. Ed Meskys and

Felice Rolfe published an earlier version of these entries in their fanzine *Niekas,* and Ed put me in touch with Jack Chalker of Mirage Press, who published the *Guide* in 1971 and in turn contacted Ballantine Books. Among the people (not as many as I could have used) who have found errors in the first edition or whose linguistic research I have drawn on in preparing my translations, I must mention Jim Allan, Paula Marmor and other members of the Mythopoeic Linguistic Fellowship, Mark Mandel, and George Stadtmueller. Ann Barrett kindly reviewed the manuscript of the present version. Judy-Lynn and Lester del Rey, Owen Lock, and the staff at Ballantine Books have been extremely helpful in the preparation and editing of this revised version. Without the timely assistance of Cindy Wiitala I would still be typing away somewhere in the *R*'s, and without the strong voice and accurate eye of Sara Oswald numerous errors in the page references would not have been detected. Words are inadequate to express my gratitude to J. R. R. (and Christopher) Tolkien for the joy his labors have afforded me. The keen precision of his mind and pen recalls the harping of Sir Orfeo:

> In the world was neuer man born
> That euer Orpheo sat byforn,
> And he myght of his harpyng here,
> He schulde thinke that he were
> In one of the ioys of Paradys,
> Suche ioy and melody in his harpyng is.

SOURCES AND ABBREVIATIONS

LotR — *The Lord of the Rings,* revised Ballantine edition.
   I — *The Fellowship of the Ring*
  II — *The Two Towers*
 III — *The Return of the King*

  HM — first Houghton Mifflin edition of *LotR.*
RHM — revised Houghton Mifflin edition of *LotR.*
   H — *The Hobbit,* Ballantine edition.
   K — Clyde Kilby, *Tolkien and the Silmarillion,* Wheaton, Ill.: Harold Shaw, 1976.
   L — J. R. R. Tolkien, "Guide to the Names in the Lord of the Rings," *A Tolkien Compass,* ed. Jared Lobdell, La Salle, Ill.: Open Court, 1975.
  PB — the Pauline Baynes map of Middle-earth, 1971.
   R — *The Road Goes Ever On,* Boston: Houghton Mifflin, 1967.
  RP — information from Dick Plotz.
   S — *The Silmarillion,* Houghton Mifflin edition.
   B — *The Silmarillion,* Ballantine edition.[1]
  TB — *The Adventures of Tom Bombadil;* all American editions have identical text and pagination.

  Ad. — Adûnaic
 B.S. — Black Speech
Hobb. — Hobbitish
 Kh. — Khuzdul
  Q. — Quenya
Roh. — Rohirric
  S. — Sindarin
West. — Westron

[1] To be published in the spring of 1979.

gen. — genuine
tr. — translated
FA — First Age
SA — Second Age
TA — Third Age
FO — Fourth Age
SR — Shire Reckoning
WR — the War of the Ring

ABYSS The low places of the Timeless Halls (q.v.) of Ilúvatar. (S 17; B 5)

ACCURSED YEARS The Dark Years (q.v.). (III 72)

ADALDRIDA BRANDYBUCK (fl. TA 29th Cent.) Hobbit of the Shire, wife of Marmadoc Brandybuck. She was born a Bolger. (III 476)

ADALGRIM TOOK (TA 2880-2982) Hobbit of the Shire, son of Hildigrim Took. (III 475)

ADAMANTA TOOK (fl. TA 29th Cent.) Hobbit of the Shire, wife of Gerontius Took. She was born a Chubb. (III 475)

ADAN See: Edain.

ADANEDHEL (S.: 'man-elf') Name given to Túrin (q.v.) in Nargothrond because of his beauty and the nobility of his speech and bearing. (S 210, 313; B 258, 390)

ADELARD TOOK (TA 2928-FO 3) Hobbit of the Shire, son of Flambard Took. He was a guest at the Farewell Party, where he was given an umbrella by Bilbo. (I 64; III 475)

ADORN River in western Rohan, flowing westward from its source in the Ered Nimrais until it joined the Isen. (I 16; III 431)

ADRAHIL (fl. TA 30th Cent.) Dúnadan of Gondor, Prince of Dol Amroth. Adrahil was the father of Finduilas and probably the father or grandfather of Imrahil. (III 418)

1

ADUIAL   (S.) Undómë (q.v.). (III 485)

ADÛNAIC (Ad., from *adûn* 'west')   The common language of the Dúnedain of Númenor. In the days of the pride of Númenor (SA 2899-3319) Adûnaic was also used at the royal court.

In origin Adûnaic was the ancestral speech of the House of Hador, and thus it was related to the tongues of the Edain and the Men of the Vales of Anduin. Its development in the First Age was strongly influenced by Elvish as a result of contact with Moriquendi in the East and with the Eldar in Beleriand. In turn, Adûnaic was the major source of the vocabulary and grammar of Westron.

Also called Númenorean. (III 391-92, 507; S 141, 142, 148, 262, 267; B 168, 170, 177, 323, 330)

ADÛNAKHÔR, AR- (Ad.: 'west-lord')   (fl. SA 2899) Dúnadan, nineteenth King of Númenor (2899-?) and the first to take his royal name in Adûnaic. He persecuted the Faithful and punished the public use of Elvish.

The Quenya form of his name was Herunúmen. (III 390, 391-92, 454; S 267-68; B 330)

ADURANT (S.: 'double-course')   River in Beleriand flowing west from Ered Luin, the southernmost tributary of Gelion and southern boundary of Ossiriand. Tol Galen lay in the Adurant. (S 123, 188, 313; B 147, 229, 390)

ADVENTURES OF TOM BOMBADIL, THE A Buckland poem about Tom Bombadil, written probably before the WR. (TB 8-9, 11-16)

AEGLOS (S.: 'point-snow' or 'icicle')   The spear of Gil-galad, a famous weapon used by him in the Battle of Dagorlad.

Also spelled Aiglos. (I 319; RHM III 437; S 294, 313; B 364, 390)

AEGNOR (S.: 'fell fire')   (d. FA 455)   Noldorin Elf of the House of Finrod, fourth son of Finarfin. He returned to

Middle-earth with the host of Fingolfin because of his friendship with Fingon, and he settled on the northern slopes of Dorthonion with his brother Angrod. Aegnor was slain by the fires from Thangorodrim during Dagor Bragollach.

The Quenya form of his name was Aikanáro. (S 61, 84, 120, 150, 151, 305, 306, 314, 362; B 64, 94, 141, 180, 182, 379, 380, 390, 454)

A ELBERETH GILTHONIEL   Elven-chant sung in Rivendell, of which only the first stanza is recorded. Each line is written in iambic tetrameter; the seven-line stanza rhymes *aababcc*. The song is a hymn of praise and a prayer for aid, addressed to Varda.

It is subtitled *aerlinn in Edhil o Imladris,* 'aerlinn of the Elves of Imladris'; aerlinn may be the mode of composition. (I 312; R 62-67)

AELIN-UIAL (S.: 'lake-twilight')   Region of Doriath, the stretch of the River Sirion between the inflow of Aros and the Falls. The river here branched into many marshes and pools, through which the border guard of Doriath ran ferries.

Also called the Meres of Twilight and the Twilight Meres. (S 114, 122, 168, 217, 355; B 134, 145, 203, 267, 445)

AELUIN (S.)   Tarn in eastern Dorthonion, the headquarters of Barahir's outlaw band. It was said that its clear waters were hallowed by Melian. (S 162, 163, Map; B 195, 197)

AERANDIR (S.: 'sea-wanderer') (fl. FA 600)   Mariner, companion of Eärendil on his voyages. (S 248, 250; B 307, 309)

AERIE   Supposedly an Elven-realm, in Bilbo's poem *Errantry.* The name is merely an imitation of Elvish, and thus probably bears no meaning in terms of the geography of Arda. (TB 8, 25)

AERIN (S.) (fl. FA 473-96) Adan of the House of Hador. She lived in Dor-lómin and was married (probably after the Nirnaeth Arnoediad) to an Easterling named Brodda. Aerin aided Morwen and Túrin after the battle. (S 198, 215; B 243, 264)

AERLINN (S.: 'sea-song'?) See: *A Elbereth Gilthoniel*. (R 62)

AFTERCOMERS Men (q.v.). (S 83, 99; B 92, 114)

AFTERLITHE The seventh month of the Shire Reckoning (q.v.), coming after Lithe, and thus corresponding roughly to our July.
 Afterlithe was called Mede by the inhabitants of Bree. (III 478, 483)

AFTERYULE The first month of the Shire Reckoning (q.v.), coming after Yule, and thus corresponding roughly to our January.
 In Bree the name was Frery. (III 478, 483)

AGARWAEN (S.: 'bloodstained') Pseudonym used by Túrin (q.v.) in Nargothrond. (S 210; B 257)

AGLAROND (S.: 'glittering caves') The caverns of Helm's Deep, first worked by the Númenoreans and later used as a refuge and storage-place by the Rohirrim. During the Battle of the Hornburg, Gimli fought in the Aglarond and discovered their great beauty. After the WR, he settled in the caves with some Dwarves of Erebor and became the Lord of the Glittering Caves. The new gates of Minas Tirith were probably forged here, and the Dwarves of Aglarond did many great works for Gondor and Rohan.
 Called by the Rohirrim the Caverns of Helm's Deep and in Westron the Glittering Caves; the Glittering Caves of Aglarond was a bilingual (and redundant) name. (II 193-5; III 451; S 291; B 361)

AGLON (S.: 'narrow pass') Pass into Beleriand from

Lothlann between the hills of Dorthonion and Himring. Aglon was fortified by Celegorm and Curufin, but the pass was forced by Morgoth's armies during Dagor Bragollach. Maedhros soon retook Aglon, but when he fled from the north after the Nirnaeth Arnoediad the pass was left undefended. (S 123, 152-53, 314; B 147, 183-84, 390)

AHA (Q.: 'rage') The later name for the tengwa cl (number 11), adopted when this letter came to represent initial breath *h* and medial and terminal *ch*.
See: harma. (III 500)

AIGLOS Aeglos (q.v.). (I 319)

AIKANÁRO (Q.: 'sharp or fell flame') The original name of Aegnor (q.v.) (S 362; B 454)

AINULINDALË (Q.: 'Ainu-song—') The Great Music sung by the Ainur, the development of the three themes of Ilúvatar and thus an expression of the divine order. The first theme, created by Ilúvatar but developed by the Ainur, presented the form of Eä. This theme was marred by the discord of Melkor, but the second theme, probably indicating the shaping of Arda, defeated this discord and incorporated it into itself. The third theme, in which the Ainur did not participate, dealt with the creation of the Children of Ilúvatar and their history up to the Dominion of Men.
Also called the Music of the Ainur, the Great Music, the Music, and the Song. (S 15-20, 28, 41, 45-46, 68, 105; B 3-9, 21, 38, 43-44, 74, 121)

AINULINDALË Account of the Creation of Eä, said to have been written by Rúmil of Tirion in the First Age. This is probably the ultimate source of the Creation account in the Red Book of Westmarch. (S 314; B 390)

AINULINDALË Account of the Creation of Eä by Ilúvatar, the rebellion of Melkor, and the preparation of Arda by the Valar for the Children of Ilúvatar. Closely associated with *Quenta Silmarillion, Ainulindalë* was probably based on the account by Rúmil of Tirion and brought to Middle-earth by the Noldorin Exiles. It was preserved through Bilbo's *Translations from the Elvish* in the Red Book of Westmarch. (S 8, 15-22; B xiii, 3-13)

AINUR (Q.: 'holy ones') Angelic spirits, offspring of the thought of Ilúvatar. Most of the Ainur dwell with Ilúvatar, but some, the Valar and Maiar (qq.v.), have come to Eä to fulfill the Ainulindalë. Others, including Ungoliant and the Balrogs, came to Eä to hinder the Ainulindalë and conquer or destroy the Light; of these, some, notably Melkor and Sauron, have been cast out into the Void.

The Ainur have no innate forms, and the names by which the Valar and Maiar are known were probably given them within Eä. Although beings of spirit, they have kinship with each other and gender.

Also called the Holy Ones and the Great Ones. (S 15-22, 25-26, 314, 355; B 3-13, 17-18, 390, 445)

AINUR OF THE GREAT SONG Those of the Ainur who participated in the Ainulindalë. (S 205; B 251)

AKALLABÊTH (Ad.: 'the downfallen') Name given to Númenor (q.v.) by the Dúnedain after its destruction.

The Quenya equivalent is Atalantë, whence the Greek Atlantis. (K 23; S 281; B 347)

AKALLABÊTH The history of the founding and downfall of Númenor, probably composed by the Dúnedain early in the Third Age and preserved through a Gondorian manuscript copied for the Tooks and kept at Great Smials. (I 39; S 8, 259-81; B xiii, 319-49)

ALATÁRIEL Altariel (q.v.). (S 360; B 451-52)

ALCARIN, TAR- (Q.: 'the glorious') (fl. SA 28th Cent.) Dúnadan, seventeenth King of Númenor. (III 390)

ALCARINQUË (Q.: 'glorious') A star, wrought by

Varda in preparation for the awakening of the Elves. (S 48, 314; B 48, 391)

ALCARONDAS The flagship of Ar-Pharazôn, destroyed with the rest of the Númenorean fleet that sailed to Valinor.

Also called Castle of the Sea. The name should be Adûnaic, but its form seems Quenya. (S 278; B 343)

ALDA (Q.: 'tree') Name of the tengwa 𝄞 (number 28), used in Quenya for *ld* but in Sindarin and Westron frequently representing *lh*. (III 500)

ALDALÓMË (Q.: 'tree-shadow') A term used by Fangorn the Ent to refer to Fangorn Forest, perhaps part of the long name of the Forest. (II 91)

ALDAMIR (Q.: 'tree-jewel') (d. TA 1540) Dúnadan, twenty-third King of Gondor (1490-1540). He died a violent death. (III 395)

ALDARION, TAR- (Q.: 'of trees') (d. SA 1075) Dúnadan, sixth King of Númenor. He had tragic relations with his father, Tar-Meneldur, and with his wife, perhaps related to the fact that he left no male heirs. (III 390, 391; RP 9/12/66)

ALDARON (Q.: 'lord of trees') A title of Oromë (q.v.). (S 29, 314; B 22, 391)

ALDËA (Q.: 'tree-day') Quenya form of the Númenorean and Westron names for the fourth day of the enquië, named in honor of the White Tree. The Sindarin form was Orgaladh, and the Hobbitish Trewesdei.

See also: Aldúya. (III 484)

ALDOR (tr. Roh.: 'prince, old') (TA 2544-2645) Man, third King of Rohan (2570-2645). Aldor reigned for seventy-five years and completed the conquest of Rohan east of the Isen. In his time Harrowdale and other valleys in the Ered Nimrais were settled.

Aldor was known as the Old because of his long life and reign. (III 434)

ALDUDÉNIË (Q.: 'two trees lament') Account of the destruction of the Two Trees, composed by Elemmírë the Vana soon after the event and known to all the Eldar. (S 76, 314; B 84, 391)

ALDÚYA (Q.: 'trees-day') Quenya form of the Eldarin name for the fourth day of the enquië, named for the Two Trees. The Sindarin form was Orgaladhad. (III 484)

ALFIRIN (S.) A golden flower that grew, among other places, in the fields of Lebennin. (III 185)

ALMAREN (Q.) Island in the Great Lake of Middle-earth, dwelling-place of the Valar in the time of the Two Lamps. Almaren, and the dwellings of the Valar, were destroyed when Melkor cast down the Two Lamps.

Also called the Isle of Almaren. (S 35, 36, 37; B 30, 32)

ALPHABET OF DAERON The Angerthas Daeron (q.v.). (III 493)

ALQUALONDË (Q.: 'swan-haven') City and port in Eldamar on the coast north of the Calacirya, built by the Teleri when they came to Aman. Olwë was its lord. The harbor of Alqualondë was entered through a great natural arch.

Also called the Haven of the Swans and the Haven. (I 309; S 61, 86-87; B 65, 97-98)

ALTARIEL (Q.: alata 'radiance' + riel 'garlanded maiden') The original name of Galadriel, referring to her golden hair.

Also spelled Altáriel and Alatáriel. (R 58; S 360; B 451-52)

AMAN (Q.: 'blessed, free from evil') The great western continent lying between Belegaer and Ekkaia. Valinor lay in central Aman west of the great curve of the Pelóri. Eldamar comprised the narrow coastal strip east of the Pelóri near the Calacirya, while to the north and south stretched the great wastes of Araman and Avathar. Aman and Tol Eressëa were removed from Arda when Arda was made round at the destruction of Númenor.

Frequently called Aman the Blessed and the Blessed Realm. Also called the Ancient West. See also: the Undying Lands. (III 392; L 179; S 37, 51, 57, 62, 73, 74, 80, 101, 264, 279-80, 314; B 32, 51-52, 59, 66, 80, 81, 88, 116, 326, 346, 391)

AMANDIL, TAR- (Q.: 'lover of Aman') (fl. SA 6th Cent.) Dúnadan, third King of Númenor. (III 390)

AMANDIL (d. SA 3319) Dúnadan, last lord of Andúnië and the father of Elendil. He was the leader of the Faithful and resisted the seductions of Sauron, but at last, seeing that doom was fast approaching, he counseled his followers to take to their ships. Amandil himself sailed to Aman to beg the Valar for mercy; he was never heard from again. (III 391; S 271, 272, 275-76, 292; B 335, 336, 340-41, 362)

AMANYAR (Q.: 'those of Aman') The Eldar who completed the Great Journey, as opposed to the Úmanyar.
Cf.: the Calaquendi. (S 353; B 440)

AMARANTH BRANDYBUCK (TA 2904-98) Hobbit of the Shire, second child of Gorbadoc Brandybuck (III 476)

AMARIË (Q.) (FA-) An Elda of the Vanyar, loved by Finrod. She did not go into Exile with him. (S 130; B 155)

AMBAR (Q.: 'fate, doom') As a common noun, the fate of an individual. More generally, Ambar was used to refer to the fate of Eä, and thus (as in the vow of Elendil on his landing in Middle-earth) could be synonymous with Arda, Eä, and even the Ainulindalë. (III 303; S 223, 355; B 275, 445)

AMBARONA (Q.) A term used by Fangorn the Ent to refer to Fangorn Forest, perhaps part of the long name of the Forest. (II 91)

AMLACH (fl. FA 4th Cent.) Adan of the Third House, son of Imlach. At first he did not wish to join in the struggle against Melkor, but after being impersonated in a great council by Melkor or one of his servants, Amlach changed his mind and entered the retinue of Maedhros. (S 144-45; B 173)

AMLAITH OF FORNOST (S.) (d. TA 946) Dúnadan, first King of Arthedain (861-946). Amlaith was the eldest son of Eärendur, the last King of Arnor. (III 394)

AMON AMARTH (S.: 'mount doom') The name given Orodruin (q.v.) by the people of Gondor when it burst into flame before Sauron's attack on Gondor in SA 3429. (III 393; S 293; B 363)

AMON DÎN (S.: 'silent mount') Hill in Gondor east of Druadan Forest, site of the first of the northern beacon-towers of Gondor.
Called Dîn for short. (III 20, 130, 132)

AMON EREB (S.: 'lonely hill') The easternmost extension of the Andram, a hill standing alone within sight of the Gelion. Amon Ereb was of great strategic importance, for it was the southernmost fortified place in East Beleriand and guarded the northern approaches to Taur-im-Duinath.
Also called Ereb. (S 96, 122, 153, 315; B 110, 146, 184, 391)

AMON ETHIR (S.: 'hill of spies') Hill in Beleriand,

built by Finrod a league east of Nargothrond to watch the approaches to that city.

Also called the Hill of Spies. (S 217-18, 315; B 267-68, 391)

AMON GWARETH (S.) Hill in Tumladen on which was built the city of Gondolin. Its north side was the Caragdûr. (S 115, 125, 126, 239, 243; B 135, 149, 151, 296, 300)

AMON HEN (S.: 'hill of the eye') One of the three peaks at the southern end of Nen Hithoel, located on the western bank of the Anduin. The Seat of Seeing (q.v.) was built on the summit of Amon Hen.

Called in Westron the Hill of Sight or, less commonly, the Hill of the Eye. (I 509-26)

AMON LHAW (S.: 'hill of the ear') One of the three peaks at the southern end of Nen Hithoel, located on the eastern bank of the Anduin. A high seat, probably called the Seat of Hearing, was built on its summit.

Called in Westron the Hill of Hearing. (I 509-10, 526)

AMON OBEL (S.) Wooded hill in West Beleriand, the most prominent feature of Brethil. At the end of the 5th Century FA, the Haladin had a stronghold, Ephel Brandir, here. (S 200, 216; B 245, 266)

AMON RÛDH (S.: 'hill bald') Hill in West Beleriand between Talath Dirnen and Nivrim. The halls of the Noegyth Nibin were delved in Amon Rûdh.

Amon Rûdh was rocky and bare of vegetation save for seregon. (S 201, 202-03, 204; B 246, 248, 250)

AMON SÛL (S.: 'hill of the wind') Weathertop (q.v.). See also: the Tower of Amon Sûl. (I 250, 346; S 315; B 392)

AMON UILOS (S.: 'mount ever-snow-white') Sindarin name for Taniquetil (q.v.). (S 37; B 32)

AMPA (Q.: 'hook') Name for the tengwa ᛒ (number 14), used in Quenya for *mp* and often used in other languages for *v*. (III 500)

AMRAS (S.) (d. FA late 6th Cent.) Noldorin Elf of the House of Fëanor (q.v.), with his twin brother Amrod the youngest son of Fëanor. He swore to the Oath of Fëanor and accompanied his father to Middle-earth, where he lived with Amrod in the plains and forests of East Beleriand. Although the twins kept to themselves during the Siege of Angband, in times of war they fought alongside their brother Maedhros. Amras and Amrod were slain during the attempt of the sons of Fëanor to recover the Silmaril by force from Elwing at the Havens of Sirion.

Amras and Amrod were alike in appearance and temperament. They seem to have been among the more mild-mannered of the sons of Fëanor, and were great hunters. (S 60, 83, 124, 142, 153, 247, 305; B 63, 93, 148, 170, 184, 305, 379)

AMROD (S.) (d. FA late 6th Cent.) Noldorin Elf of the House of Fëanor (q.v.), twin brother of Amras (q.v.) (S 60, 83, 124, 142, 153, 247, 305; B 63, 93, 148, 170, 184, 305, 379)

AMROTH (Silvan) (d. c. TA 1981) An Elven-king who built the port of Dol Amroth. He was the lover of Nimrodel. When his white ship was blown out to sea without her, he jumped into the water to return to her and was lost.

Although Dol Amroth was in Belfalas, Amroth's high house was in Lórien, on Cerin Amroth. (I 441-42, 454; III 181, 506)

ANACH (S.) Pass in northern Beleriand between the Ered Gorgoroth and the Crissaegrim. Toward the end of the 5th Century FA, Orcs from Dorthonion built a road through the pass and used it to raid Dimbar. (S 200-01, 205, 206, 246-47; B 245-46, 251, 253, 305)

ANADÛNÊ (Ad.: '—western') Adûnaic form of Nú-menórë (q.v.). (S 261, 315; B 321, 392)

ANAR (Q.) The Sun (q.v.). (S 99; B 114)

ANARDIL (Q.: 'sun-lover') (d. TA 411) Dúnadan, sixth King of Gondor (324-411). (III 394)

ANÁRION, TAR- (Q.: 'of the sun') (c. SA 1200) Dúnadan, eighth King of Númenor. (III 390)

ANÁRION (d. SA 3440) Dúnadan, younger son of Elendil and, with his brother Isildur, second King of Gondor (3320-3440). He escaped from the wreck of Númenor with two ships, and he and Isildur established the kingdom of Gondor. Anárion's lands were named Anórien after him, and his chief dwelling was at Minas Anor.

When Sauron attacked Gondor in 3429. Anárion defended Osgiliath and the line of the Anduin, and later entered Mordor with the army of the Last Alliance. He was slain by a stone cast from the Barad-dûr. (I 319, 320; III 394, 401; S 272, 280, 291, 293, 294; B 336, 346, 361, 364, 365)

ANARRÍMA (Q.) A constellation formed by Varda from ancient stars in preparation for the awakening of the Elves. (S 48; B 48)

ANARYA (Q.: 'sun-day') Quenya form of the name of the second day of the enquië, named for the Sun. The Sindarin name was Oranor and the Hobbitish name Sunnendei. (III 484)

ANBORN (S.) (fl. WR) Dúnadan of Gondor, a Ranger of Ithilien. (II 359, 373-74, 377)

ANCA (Q.: 'jaws') Name for the tengwa ccl (number 15), used in Quenya to represent *nk*. (III 500)

ANCALAGON (S.: 'jaws-rushing') Greatest of the

winged dragons, slain by Eärendil in the Great Battle. The fall of his body broke Thangorodrim.

Also called Ancalagon the Black. (I 94; S 252, 355; B 312, 446)

ANCALIMË, TAR- (Q.: 'great-light') (fl. SA 1100) Dúnadan, seventh ruler and first Ruling Queen of Númenor (1075-?). She was the only child of the previous king, Tar-Aldarion. (III 390, 391, 410, 453)

ANCALIMON, TAR- (Q.: 'great-light) (c. SA 24th Cent.) Dúnadan, fourteenth King of Númenor. During his reign the factions of the King's Men and the Faithful developed. Tar-Ancalimon refused to give up his life before he decayed in body and spirit. (III 390; S 266; B 329)

ANCIENT DARKNESS The Void (q.v.). (S 271; B 335)

ANCIENT HOUSES The Three Houses of the Edain (q.v.). (II 127)

ANCIENT SPEECH, ANCIENT TONGUE Quenya (q.v.) (I 119, 124)

ANCIENT WEST Aman (q.v.), so called in the Third Age after its removal from Arda. (S 304; B 378)

ANCIENT WORLD The world of the First Age, so called by Aragorn. (I 460)

ANDAITH (S.: 'long-mark') Tehta showing vowel length, used optionally in the Mode of Beleriand. (III 499)

ANDO (Q.: 'gate') Name for the tengwa $\mathcal{P}$ (number 5), used for *nd* in Quenya, and frequently representing *d* in other languages. (III 500)

ANDOR (Q.?: 'gift-land') Name given to Númenor (q.v.) by the Dúnedain. (S 260; B 321)

ANDRAM (S.: 'long wall') The great escarpment of Beleriand, running from the Falas through Nargothrond and the Falls of Sirion to Ramdal and Amon Ereb. The Andram usually referred only to the portion between Nargothrond and Ramdal. (S 96, 122, 153; B 109, 146, 184)

ANDRAST (S.: 'long shore') The point of land, terminating in the Cape of Andrast, dividing the western end of the Bay of Belfalas from the Sea. (PB)

ANDROTH (S.: 'great—') Caves in Mithrim, probably in the Mountains of Mithrim. After the Nirnaeth Arnoediad some Sindar and Edain lived there in hiding, and later Tuor dwelt there as an outlaw. (S 238; B 294)

ANDUIN (S.: 'great-river') The greatest river of northwestern Middle-earth, flowing from its sources in the far north about 1500 miles to its delta in the Bay of Belfalas. Anduin and its many tributaries drained the area between Mirkwood and the Misty Mountains (known as the Vales of Anduin), and also Anórien, Ithilien, and much of Rohan and Lebennin. Its principal tributaries were the Gladden, Celebrant, Limlight, Entwash, Morgulduin, Erui, Sirith, and Poros.

Called in Westron the Great River.

See also: the Carrock, Sarn Gebir, Rauros, Nindalf, Nen Hithoel, Ethir Anduin, Cair Andros. (I 21, 483, 488ff.; S 54; B 55)

ANDÚNIË (Q.: 'west') City and port on the west coast of Númenor. At first Andúnië was the chief city of Númenor, for the Eldar of Eressëa sailed here. As the Shadow fell on Númenor, Andúnië was surpassed in size and importance by Armenelos, and its Faithful were forced to move to the east coast.

The Lords of Andúnië, descended from Valandil, son of

Silmariën, were the highest nobles of Númenor. (III 391; S 261, 268; B 321, 322, 331)

ANDÚRIL (Q.?: 'west-brilliance') The sword of Aragorn II, forged from the shards of Narsil (q.v.) by elvensmiths in Rivendell in TA 3018. On its blade was a design of seven stars (for Elendil) between a crescent moon (for Isildur) and a rayed sun (for Anárion), as well as many runes. Because of its heritage and its bearer, and because of its great brightness, Andúril quickly became a famous weapon.

Called in Westron the Flame of the West. Also known as the Sword that was Broken, the Sword Reforged, etc. (I 233, 362; II 147, 176; III 150; S 363; B 455)

ANDWISE ROPER (b. TA 2923) Hobbit of the Shire, first son of Roper Gamgee. Like his father, he was a roper in Tighfield.

Called Andy for short. (I 449; II 276; III 477)

ANFALAS (S: 'long-shore') Fief of Gondor, a coastal area between the Lefnui and the Morthond.

Called in Westron Langstrand. (I 16; III 50; S 358; B 449)

ANFAUGLIR (S.: 'great-thirst-jaws') Carcharoth (q.v.). (S 180, 197; B 218, 241)

ANFAUGLITH (S.: 'great-thirst-ash') Name given to Ard-galen (q.v.) after it was burned by the fires of Melkor during Dagor Bragollach. The plain remained a parched desert, except for the mound of Haudh-en-Nirnaeth.

Also called the Gasping Dust and Dor-nu-Fauglith. (S 151, 190-92, 197; B 181, 232-34, 241)

ANGA (Q.: 'iron') Name for the tengwa ᴄᴄ⎰ (number 7), usually used in Quenya to represent ɔɔ. (III 500)

ANGAINOR (Q.?: 'iron—') Chain made by Aulë to bind Melkor. (S 51, 252; B 52, 312)

ANGAMAITË (Q.: 'iron—') (fl. TA 1634) Dúnadan, great-grandson of Castamir and a leader of the Corsairs of Umbar. He and his brother Sangahyando led the raid on Pelargir in 1634 in which King Minardil of Gondor was slain. (III 407)

ANGAMANDO (Q.: 'iron-prison') Angband (q.v.). (S 356; B 446)

ANGARÁTO (Q.: 'iron-eminent man') The Quenya form of Angrod (q.v.). (S 356; B 446)

ANGBAND (S.: 'iron-prison') The great underground fortress, prison, barracks, mines, and factory of Morgoth, located 150 leagues north of Menegroth behind the southwestern corner of the Ered Engrin. Built by Melkor after he destroyed the Two Lamps, Angband was first held by Sauron and was intended to guard Utumno against assault by the Valar. Angband was destroyed after the Battle of the Powers, but its pits were not bared, and Balrogs and other of Melkor's servants hid there during their master's captivity.

After he returned to Middle-earth with the Silmarils, Melkor rebuilt Angband, raised Thangorodrim (q.v.) over it, and built a great tunnel under the Ered Engrin from Angband to Ard-galen. Angband served as Melkor's headquarters during the War of the Great Jewels, and here he bred his monsters. Although it was attacked a number of times, Angband was not taken until the Great Battle; it was, of course, destroyed in the breaking of Beleriand.

Called also the Hells of Iron. The Quenya form was Angamando. (I 260; S 47, 51, 81, 95-96, 118, 153, 179-82, 192, 252, 356; B 47, 52, 90, 109, 139-40, 185, 217-20, 234, 312, 446)

ANGBOR (S.: 'iron—') (fl. WR) Man of Gondor, probably a Dúnadan, lord of Lamedon at the time of WR. Angbor led the defense of Linhir against the Corsairs, and commanded the army that marched to Minas Tirith after that battle. (III 185, 187, 193)

17

ANGELICA BAGGINS (b. TA 2981)   Hobbit of the Shire, daughter of Ponto Baggins and a guest at the Farewell Party. Because of her vanity, she was given a convex mirror by Bilbo. (I 64; III 474)

ANGERTHAS DAERON (S.: 'long-runes of Daeron') A mode of the cirth (q.v.), the full development of the Certhas Daeron under the influence of the Tengwar. Although attributed to Daeron, the Angerthas was probably devised by the Noldor of Eregion, who used the system frequently. The Angerthas was adapted by the Dwarves of Khazad-dûm (see: Angerthas Moria), who gave it a cursive form.

Also called the Alphabet of Daeron and Daeron's runes. (III 493, 495, 501-04; S 95; B 108)

ANGERTHAS MORIA (S.: 'long rune-rows of Khazad-dûm')   Dwarvish adaptation of the mode of the Angerthas Daeron in use in Eregion, used by Durin's Folk in Khazad-dûm and Erebor. The Dwarvish changes, which were unsystematic, were basically a result of the need to represent Khuzdul sounds not occurring in Elvish, and of the desire to represent weak vowels. The Dwarves of Erebor further adapted this system; their changes showed a tendency to return to the original Elvish mode. (III 495, 501-04)

ANGHABAR (S.: 'iron-delvings')   Iron mine of Gondolin, discovered by Maeglin in the northern Echoriath. (S 138, 316; B 166, 393)

ANGLACHEL (S.: 'iron-flame')   Sword of meteoritic iron, one of a pair forged by Eöl, who gave it to Elwë in return for permission to dwell in Nan Elmoth. Despite Melian's warning that the malice of Eöl was in the sword, Beleg took Anglachel from the armory of Menegroth when he went to search for Túrin the second time, and Túrin unknowingly slew Beleg with it.

Túrin had the sword reforged in Nargothrond and renamed it Gurthang. With this blade Túrin (known as Mormegil) performed great deeds, but he also used it for rash and senseless murders, and in time he turned the blade on himself. Gurthang broke as it killed him, and the shards were laid next to Túrin's body.

Anglachel was black and very hard; the edges of the reforged Gurthang shone with pale fire. The sword was apparently sentient. (S 201-02, 207-10, 213, 216, 225, 226, 361; B 245-46, 255-57, 262, 266, 277, 278, 452)

ANGLE The land between the Mitheithel and the Bruinen. Between TA 1150 and 1350 many Stoors lived here, but left because of the threat of war and the terror of Angmar. At the time of the WR the Angle seems to have been largely deserted, except for the trolls of the Trollshaws. (III 396, 457)

ANGLE Egladil (q.v.). (I 450)

ANGMAR (S.: 'iron-home') Witch-kingdom on both sides of the northern Misty Mountains, north of the Ettenmoors, ruled by the Lord of the Nazgûl, who was then known as the Witch-king of Angmar. Its capital was Carn Dûm. Angmar was peopled with Orcs, Hill-men, and other such creatures.

Angmar arose about TA 1300 and, for the next 700 years, attempted to destroy the Dúnedain of the North. Cardolan and Rhudaur fell quickly, the former effectively destroyed by 1409 and the latter infiltrated even earlier, but Arthedain, aided by the Elves of Rivendell and Lindon, held out until 1974, although nearly defeated in 1409. In 1975, the Witch-king was defeated in the Battle of Fornost by armies from Lindon (led by Círdan and Eärnur and strengthened by the latter's army from Gondor) and Rivendell (led by Glorfindel); he was driven from the North and his servants west of the Misty Mountains slain or scattered. Those few who survived east of the Mountains were destroyed soon after by the Éothéod (q.v.). (I 270; III 397-400, 411-12, 429, 457-58)

ANGRENOST (S.: 'iron-fortress') Isengard (q.v.). (II 95)

ANGRIM (S.) (fl. FA 430)   Adan of the First House, father of Gorlim. (S 162; B 195)

ANGRIST (S.: 'iron-cleaver')   Knife made by Telchar of Nogrod. Beren took it from Curufin and used it to cut a Silmaril from the Iron Crown of Melkor. The blade snapped when he tried to cut out a second jewel.

As its name implies, Angrist was strong enough to cut iron easily. (S 177, 181; B 215, 219)

ANGROD (S.: 'iron-eminent one') (d. FA 455)   Noldorin Elf of the House of Finrod, the third son of Finarfin. Like his brother Aegnor, he returned to Middle-earth with the host of Fingolfin because of his friendship with Fingon, and he settled on the northern slopes of Dorthonion.

The first of the Exiles to enter Doriath, Angrod also was the one who finally told Elwë the full story of the rebellion of the Noldor. He was slain by the fires from Thangorodrim during Dagor Bragollach.

The Quenya form of his name was Angaráto. (S 61, 84, 111-12, 120, 128-29, 150, 151, 305, 306, 356; B 64, 94, 130-31, 141, 154, 180, 182, 379, 380, 446)

ANGUIREL (S.: 'iron—')   Sword forged by Eöl, the mate of Anglachel (q.v.). It was stolen from Eöl by Maeglin. (S 202; B 247)

ANNA (Q.: 'gift')   Name for the tengwa **ᴄ** (number 23). (III 500)

ANNAEL (S.) (FA)   Sindarin Elf of Mithrim, the foster father of Tuor. (S 238; B 294)

ANNATAR (S.: 'gift-lord')   Name assumed by Sauron in the Second Age when he sought to seduce the Elves of Middle-earth. (S 287; B 355)

ANNON-IN-GELYDH (S.: 'gate-of-the-Noldor')   Eastern entrance to a subterranean riverbed in the western hills of Dor-lómin; the tunnel led to Cirith Ninniach. Annon-in-Gelydh was built by Turgon when he dwelt in Nevrast. (S 238, 316; B 294, 393)

ANN-THENNATH (S.: 'long—') A mode of song among the Elves. The original version of the Lay of Leithian was composed in this form.

Spelled "ann-thannath" in the RHM Index; this spelling may be the correct one. (I 260; RHM III 437)

ANNÚMINAS (S.: 'tower of the west' or 'sunset-tower') City built by Elendil on the shore of Nenuial, the first capital of Arnor. Annúminas was deserted sometime between TA 250 and 861 because of the decline of Arnor, and the court removed to Fornost. Rebuilt at the beginning of the Fourth Age by Elessar, Annúminas became the northern capital of the Reunited Kingdom.

The chief palantír (q.v.) of the North was kept at Annúminas until its loss. (I 320; II 259; III 402; S 290, 292, 316; B 360, 362, 393)

ANÓRIEN (S.: 'sun-land') That part of Gondor north of the Erui, west of Anduin and east and south of Rohan, originally the demesne of Anárion. Anórien contained the Druadan Forest, and also much fertile farmland. Its capital and chief city was Minas Tirith.

Called in Rohirric Sunlending. Anórien was derived from the older Sindarin form Anóriend. (III 14, 19, 127; L 192)

ANSON ROPER (b. TA 2961) Hobbit of the Shire, son of Andwise Roper. He probably lived in Tighfield, and was probably a roper. (III 477)

ANTANI See: Atani. (III 506)

ANTO (Q.: 'mouth') Name for the tengwa ᑖ (number 13), used in Quenya to represent *nt* and frequently in other languages for *dh*. (III 500)

APANÓNAR (Q.: 'after-born') Name given to Men (q.v.) by the Eldar. (S 103; B 119)

APPLEDORE Surname used by Men of Bree (I 212; III 335)

AR- (Ad.: 'royal, king') Prefix attached to the royal names of those rulers of Númenor who took their names in Adûnaic. The Kings and Queens are entered in this *Guide* under the root of their royal names.
Cf.: Tar-. (III 390)

ARADAN (S.: 'king's man') (fl. FA 4th Cent.) Adan of the Third House, son of Marach. His birth-name was Malach, and in his youth he joined in the migration of his House from Eriador to Estolad. He soon left Estolad for Hithlum, where he spent fourteen years, probably in the service of Fingolfin, and received his Sindarin name. Aradan apparently ruled the large portion of his people that went farther west than Estolad. (S 143, 147; B 172, 177)

ARADOR (S.: 'royal—') (d. TA 2930) Dúnadan, fourteenth Chieftain of the Dúnedain of the North (2912-30). He was slain by hill-trolls in the Coldfells. (III 394, 420)

ARAGLAS (S.: 'royal-leaf') (d. TA 2455) Dúnadan, sixth Chieftain of the Dúnedain of the North (2327-2455). (III 394)

ARAGORN I (S.: 'royal-tree') (d. TA 2327) Dúnadan, fifth Chieftain of the Dúnedain of the North (2319-27), killed by wolves. (III 394, 401)

ARAGORN II (TA 2931-FO 120) Dúnadan, sixteenth and last Chieftain of the Dúnedain of the North (2933-3019), restorer of the Dúnedain kingdoms in Middle-earth and, as Elessar, first King of the Reunited Kingdom (3019-FO 120). As the heir of Isildur, he was raised secretly in Rivendell and was known as Estel until he was twenty, when Elrond revealed to him his lineage.

Aragorn then went off into the Wild; for nearly seventy years he fought against Sauron in many ways and learned the customs of various peoples, until he was the hardiest and the wisest Man of his time. During this period Aragon served in disguise Thengel of Rohan and Ecthelion of Gondor. In Gondor he was known as Thorongil because of the star of the Rangers that he wore; his greatest feat there was a raid on Umbar in 2980 in which he destroyed a large part of the fleet of the Corsairs. In 2956 he met Gandalf, and the two became close friends. In 3017, after thirteen years of intermittent searching at Gandalf's request, Aragorn captured Gollum. The next year, he met Frodo and his companions at Bree and helped them to get to Rivendell. Aragorn was one of the Nine Companions, and led the Fellowship after Gandalf fell in Khazad-dûm.

During the War of the Ring, Aragorn was one of the leaders of the defense at the Battle of the Hornburg; during his time in Rohan he and Éomer became fast friends. Then, accompanied by Legolas, Gimli, and a company of Rangers, Aragorn took the Paths of the Dead, acting on information gleaned from the palantír of Orthanc, which he wrested from the control of Sauron. As the heir of Isildur, Arogorn caused the Dead to obey him, and with their aid he defeated the Corsairs at Pelargir and captured their fleet. He then brought a large body of men from southern Gondor to Minas Tirith to turn the tide of the Battle of the Pelennor Fields. Later, he was captain of the Army of the West (q.v.).

After the WR, Aragorn became King of the Reunited Kingdom and Lord of the Western Lands as Elessar Telcontar and married Arwen, daughter of Elrond. During his 120-year reign he extended the borders of the Kingdom and re-established long-absent peace and prosperity.

In addition to the wisdom he gained through his long period of fighting Sauron, Aragorn possessed Elven-wisdom and the foresight of the Dúnedain. It was said with justice that in him the nobility of the Númenoreans of old was restored.

Aragorn met Arwen when he was twenty, just before he departed from Imladris. He loved her from that moment, and they plighted their troth in 2980. Elrond, however, would not consent to marry his daughter to any Man who was less than the King of both Arnor and Gondor, and so the two were not married until after the WR. Aragorn and Arwen had one son, Eldarion, and a number of daughters.

From the time of its forging in 3018, Aragorn bore the sword Andúril, and before then on occasion he bore the shards of Narsil.

Aragorn was called Elessar and Elfstone by Galadriel and the people of Gondor during the WR because of the emerald brooch he wore; he took this name, which was foretold for him, as his royal name. Called Strider in Bree before the WR, he took the Quenya equivalent of this name, Telcontar, as the name of his family. Also called Isildur's Heir, the Renewer, Longshanks and Wing-foot; the last name was given him by Éomer after the journey of the Three Hunters. (I 91, 231, 233, 313, 324, 332-33, 365, 387, 486; II 47, 254-55; III 150-52, 169-80, 284, 302, 394, 417-18, 420-28, 438, 461, 462; S 303; B 377)

ARAGOST (S.: 'royal-fortress') (d. TA 2588) Dúnadan, eighth Chieftain of the Dúnedain of the North (2523-88). (III 394)

ARAHAD I (S.: 'royal—') (d. TA 2523) Dúnadan, seventh Chieftain of the Dúnedain of the North (2455-2523). (III 394, 401)

ARAHAD II (d. TA 2719) Dúnadan, tenth Chieftain of the Dúnedain of the North (2654-2719). (III 394)

ARAHAEL (S.: 'royal—') (d. TA 2177) Dúnadan, second Chieftain of the Dúnedain of the North (2106-77). (III 394)

ARAMAN (Q.: 'outside or beside Aman') The great

northern waste of Aman, comprising all the land between the Sea and the Pelóri north of Eldamar. Araman was deserted and mountainous, and its northern extremes were bitterly cold.

See also: Helcaraxë, Oiomúrë. (S 80, 87, 89, 316-17; B 88, 98, 101, 394)

ARAN- (S.: 'royal') The royal prefix used by the Kings of Arthedain after Malvegil and by the Chieftains of the Dúnedain of the North to indicate their claim to all of Arnor. Unlike the Númenorean prefixes Ar- and Tar-, the element Aran- was an integral part of the name and was given at birth, as may be seen in the naming of Arvedui.

Sometimes shortened to *Ara-* or *Ar-*. (III 394, 410; S 356; B 446)

ARANARTH (S.: 'royal-realm') (d. TA 2106) Dúnadan, first Chieftain of the Dúnedain of the North (1974-2106). He was the elder son of Arvedui, the last King of Arthedain. (III 394, 398)

ARANEL (S.: 'royal-star' or 'royal Elf') The surname of Dior (q.v.) (S 188; B 229)

ARANRÚTH (S.: 'king's ire') The sword of Elwë in Doriath and also of the Kings of Númenor. (S 201, 317; B 246, 394)

ARANTAR (Q.) (d. TA 435) Dúnadan, fifth King of Arnor (339-435). (III 394)

ARANUIR (S.: 'royal—') (d. TA 2247) Dúnadan, third Chieftain of the Dúnedain of the North (2177-2247). (III 394)

ARANWË (Q.) (FA) Elf of Gondolin, father of Voronwë. (S 239; B 295)

ARAPHANT (S.: 'royal—') (d. TA 1964) Dúnadan, fourteenth King of Arthedain (1891-1964). During his reign contact with Gondor was renewed. (III 394, 409, 411)

ARAPHOR (S.: 'royal—') (d. TA 1589) Dúnadan, ninth King of Arthedain (1409-1589). In the year of his accession, while still a youth, with the aid of Círdan he drove the forces of Angmar away from Fornost and the North Downs. During Araphor's long reign Arthedain seems to have been at peace, since Angmar was temporarily subdued by the Elves of Lindon and Rivendell. (III 394, 397)

ARASSUIL (S.: 'royal—') (d. TA 2784) Dúnadan, eleventh Chieftain of the Dúnedain of the North (2719-84). In his time Eriador was troubled by Orcs. (III 394, 401-2)

ARATAN (Q.: 'royal man') (d. TA 2) Dúnadan, second son of Isildur. He fought with the Last Alliance and was slain in the Battle of the Gladden Fields (q.v.) (S 295; B 366)

ARATAR (Q.: 'the exalted') The eight chief Valar—Manwë, Varda, Ulmo, Yavanna, Aulë, Mandos, Nienna, and Oromë.
   Also called the Eight and the Holy Ones of Arda. (S 29, 317, 356; B 23, 394, 446)

ARATHORN I (S.: 'royal—') (d. TA 2848) Dúnadan, twelfth Chieftain of the Dúnedain of the North (2784-2848). He died a violent death. (III 394)

ARATHORN II (TA 2873-2933) Dúnadan, fifteenth Chieftain of the Dúnedain of the North (2930-33). He was slain by Orcs while fighting with Elladan and Elrohir.
   Arathorn married Gilraen in 2929; their only child was Aragorn II. (III 394, 420)

ARAVAL (S.: 'royal—') (d. TA 1891) Dúnadan, thirteenth King of Arthedain (1813-91). (III 394)

ARAVIR (S.: 'royal—') (d. TA 2319) Dúnadan, fourth Chieftain of the Dúnedain of the North (2247-2319). (III 394)

ARAVORN (S.: 'royal—') (d. TA 2654) Dúnadan, ninth Chieftain of the Dúnedain of the North (2588-2654). (III 394)

ARAW (S.) Oromë (q.v.). (III 29, 395)

ARCHET Village of the Bree-land on the northern edge of the Chetwood. (I 205, 245)

ARCIRYAS (Q.: '—ship') (TA 19th Cent.) Dúnadan, younger brother of Narmacil II of Gondor. He was an ancestor of Eärnil II. (III 410)

ARDA (Q.: 'region, realm') The Earth, intended by Ilúvatar to be the abode of his Children. As conceived in the Ainulindalë, Arda was to be temperate and symmetrical, but it was seriously marred by the malice of Melkor and the struggles between him and the Valar.

When the Valar had fulfilled as much of the Vision as they could, Arda was round and flat, encircled by Ekkaia, the Outer Sea, which in turn was enclosed within the Walls of the Night (q.v.). Arda contained at least two great continents, Aman and Middle-earth, separated by Belegaer (qq.v.). Beneath the field of Arda was a great expanse of rock, pocked with caves; it is not said if this rock rested on anything. Above was the Veil of Arda, the atmosphere.

At the Change of the World, Ilúvatar removed Aman from Arda and made Arda the spherical world in which we dwell. It is said that the original design of Arda will be restored at the End.

For various changes in Arda, see also: Beleriand, the Enchanted Isles, Ered Engrin, Tol Eressëa, Númenor, the Pelóri, the Two Lamps, Arda Marred, and the Bent World.

Also called the Earth and, when considered as a realm, the Kingdom of Arda, of Earth or of Manwë, and the Little Kingdom. (II 134; III 321; R 66; S 18, 19, 20-22, 25,

27

35, 37, 57, 62, 101, 102, 278-79, 281, 317; B 7, 8, 10-12, 17, 29, 31, 59, 66, 116, 118, 344-45, 348, 394)

ARDA Name for the tengwa 𝑦 (number 26), usually used to represent *rd* in Quenya and *rh* in Sindarin and Westron. (III 500)

ARDA MARRED The Earth, flawed by the evil of Melkor and those who do his will. (S 255; B 316)

ARD-GALEN (S.: 'region-green') The great plain lying north of Dorthonion, east of Ered Wethrin and south and west of Ered Engrin. Although fouled somewhat by the wastes of Angband, Ard-galen remained fair and grass-covered; during the Siege of Angband it was patrolled by the cavalry of Fingolfin and Maedhros.

Ard-galen was devastated by fire during Dagor Bragollach, and was known afterward as Anfauglith (q.v.). (S 106, 118, 119, 150-51, 317; B 124, 140, 141, 181, 394)

ÁRE (Q.: 'sunlight') Early name for the tengwa 𝑔 (number 31), originally áze and later esse (qq.v.). (III 500)

AREDHEL (S.: 'noble elf') (d. c. FA 330) Noldorin Elf, youngest child and only daughter of Fingolfin. She returned to Middle-earth with the Exiles and dwelt with her brother Turgon in Nevrast and Gondolin. About FA 300 she grew restless in Gondolin and left to visit the sons of Fëanor, who had been her friends in Eldamar. She was separated from her companions in Nan Dungortheb and given up for dead, but in fact she survived to be seduced by and wed to Eöl of Nan Elmoth.

Aredhel bore Eöl a son, Maeglin, who at length, desiring to be established as the heir of Turgon, persuaded her to flee from Nan Elmoth. Eöl followed them to Gondolin, and in a quarrel before the throne of Turgon, Aredhel was slain by a poisoned dart when she protected Maeglin with her body from the wrath of Eöl.

Aredhel was tall, had dark hair and a pale complexion,

and wore only silver and white. For this reason she was called Aredhel the White and Ar-Feiniel, the White Lady of the Noldor or of Gondolin. She liked to ride and hunt. (S 60-61, 131-38, 305, 358; B 64, 156-65, 379, 449)

ÁRE NUQUERNA (Q.: 'áre reversed') One of the names for the tengwa **ʒ** (number 32).
See: áre, áze nuquerna. (III 500)

AR-FEINIEL (S.?) Aredhel (q.v.). (S 60; B 64)

ARGELEB I (S.: 'royal-silver') (d. TA 1356) Dúnadan, seventh King of Arthedain (1349-56). On his accession, since no heirs of Isildur remained in either Rhudaur or Cardolan, Arthedain claimed lordship over all of Arnor. Rhudaur, which was controlled by Angmar, contested this claim. In the war that followed, Argeleb fortified the Weather Hills but was slain in battle. (III 394, 397)

ARGELEB II (d. TA 1670) Dúnadan, tenth King of Arthedain (1589-1670). In 1600 he gave permission to Marcho and Blanco to settle the Shire. (I 23; III 394, 398)

ARGONATH (S.: 'stones of the kings') The carved rocks at the upper end of the chasm at the northern entrance to Nen Hithoel, on Anduin. They were two immense and awesome statues of Isildur and Anárion, one on either side of the river. The Argonath was built by Rómendacil II about TA 1340 to mark the northern boundary of Gondor.
    Also called the Pillars of the Kings, the Gates of Argonath, the Gates of the Kings, and the Gates of Gondor; the first was probably the actual Westron name, although all were commonly used. (I 508-09; III 405; R 67; S 291; B 361)

ARGONUI (S.: 'royal-stony') (d. TA 2912) Dúnadan, thirteenth Chieftain of the Dúnedain of the North (2848-2912). (III 394)

ARIEN (Q.) Maia, a powerful spirit of fire devoted to

Laurelin and the golden flowers in the gardens of Vána. She was chosen by the Valar to guide the Sun (q.v.). (S 99-100, 356; B 114, 446)

ARKENSTONE   A great white jewel found deep beneath Erebor by Thráin I. The Arkenstone was the greatest treasure of the Kings of Erebor, but was left in Erebor when Smaug drove the Dwarves out in TA 2770. In 2941, while a member of Thorin and Company, Bilbo found it when he explored Smaug's hoard. The Arkenstone was used by him to attempt a reconciliation between Thorin and the Elves and Men besieging him, and was later buried with Thorin.

Also called the Heart of the Mountain. (III 439, 440; H 220, 225-26, 257, 275)

ARMENELOS (Q.: 'royal-heaven-fortress')   City of Númenor, built on a hill near Meneltarma. The Court of the Kings was located here, as was Nimloth and, later, the Temple built by Sauron. After the decline of Andúnië, Armenelos was probably the largest city in Númenor.

Also known as Armenelos the Golden. (S 261, 263, 273; B 322, 324, 337)

ARMINAS (S.: 'royal-tower')   (FA)   Noldorin Elf, a follower of Angrod. After Dagor Bragollach he dwelt in the Falas with Círdan. In the spring of FA 496 he and Gelmir carried Ulmo's warning of the peril of Nargothrond to Orodreth. (S 212; B 260)

ARMY OF THE WEST   The small army of Men of Gondor and Rohan, led by Aragorn, Gandalf, Imrahil, and Eomer, which during the WR marched on the Morannon to divert Sauron's attention from Frodo. The Army was on the brink of annihilation by Sauron's forces when the Ring was destroyed and Sauron's power broken. The Army then won a great victory over the Haradrim and Easterlings allied with Sauron, as well as over the now-leaderless Orcs and trolls.

Pippin, Legolas, Gimli, Beregond, Elladan, and Elrohir also marched with the Army.

Also called the Host of the West. (III 193-208, 278-80)

ARNACH See: Lossarnach. (III 152, 508)

ARNOR (S.: 'royal-land') The senior Dúnadan Kingdom of Middle-earth, founded in SA 3320 by Elendil, who ruled directly as its first king. At its greatest Arnor included all the lands between the Gwathlo-Bruinen and the Lhûn. Arnor's first capital was Annúminas, but before 861 the capital was moved to Fornost, the chief city of the country. Unlike Gondor, Arnor did not prosper, and the dwindling of the Dúnedain began with the disastrous Battle of the Gladden Fields (q.v.) in TA 2. However, throughout all its troubles, the descent of the rulers of Arnor, the Line of Isildur, was preserved.

When Eärendur, the tenth King, died in TA 861, Arnor was split among his three sons, the eldest becoming King of Arthedain (q.v.). The Dúnedain in the other two kingdoms, Cardolan and Rhudaur (qq.v.), quickly dwindled, and in 1349 Arthedain claimed lordship over all of Arnor. After this time, what was properly speaking Arthedain was sometimes called Arnor.

Angmar and Rhudaur used this claim as a pretext to attack Arthedain, and in 1974 the kingdom fell. The heirs of Isildur became the Chieftains of the few Dúnedain of the North, until after the WR, when Arnor was re-established by Elessar.

Also called the North-kingdom and the Northern Kingdom. (I 181, 320-21; III 394, 396-454, 456; S 290-91; B 361)

AROD (tr. Roh.: 'quick, swift') (fl. WR) A swift and fiery horse of Rohan, lent to Legolas and Gimli by Eomer. Arod bore them during the WR through Rohan and the Paths of the Dead, and probably also bore Legolas in the Battle of the Pelennor Fields. (II 51; III 70)

AROS (S.) River in Beleriand, flowing from Dorthonion

south and then west. It emptied into Sirion just above Aelin-uial. Its principal tributary was the Celon.

Aros formed the eastern and southern boundaries of Doriath. (S 124; B 147-48)

AROSSIACH (S.: 'Aros-ford') Ford on the upper Aros. Here the old road from Nan Dungortheb crossed Aros on its way to Himlad or to Nan Elmoth and the Dwarf-cities of the Ered Luin. (S 121, 132, 133; B 145, 158)

ARTAMIR (Q.: '—jewel') (d. TA 1944) Dúnadan of Gondor, son of King Ondoher. He was killed in battle with the Wainriders. (III 409)

ARTHAD (S.) (d. FA 460) Adan of the First House, one of the last twelve of the outlaws of Barahir in Dorthonion. (S 155, 162-63; B 187, 196)

ARTHEDAIN (S.: 'realm of the Edain') Dúnadan kingdom, one of the divisions of Arnor, founded in TA 861. Its capital was Fornost. Arthedain included the land between the Lhûn and the Brandywine, and also the land north of the Great East Road as far east as Weathertop. Arthedain had in its possession the two palantíri of the North kept by Men in the Third Age.

The Kings of Arthedain were descended from Amlaith, the eldest son of Eärendur, the last King of Arnor, and so in them the Line of Isildur was maintained.

In 1349, Argeleb I claimed lordship over all of Arnor because of the extinction of the royal families of Cardolan and Rhudaur; but Rhudaur, aided by Angmar, contested the claim and attacked Arthedain. Sometimes aided by Cardolan, Lindon, and Rivendell, Arthedain repulsed major attacks in 1356 and 1409, as well as various minor attacks, with waning strength. In 1974 Fornost was captured by Angmar; King Arvedui fled to the Ered Luin and then to Forochel, where he drowned the next spring. However, Angmar was defeated by the Elves of Lindon and Rivendell and the remnant of the army of Arthedain, aided by a large force from Gondor commanded by Eärnur. Arthedain was not re-established; Fornost was deserted and the Dúnedain of the North became a scattered people.

Although for most of its history Arthedain was estranged from Gondor, during the reign of King Araphant (1891-1964) contact between the two realms was renewed. Arvedui married Princess Fíriel, the daughter of Ondoher of Gondor, and although his claim to the throne was rejected in 1944, the realms remained friendly. Without Gondor's aid in 1975 Angmar could not have been defeated.

Also called the North-kingdom. (III 394, 396-400, 410-11)

ARVEDUI (S.: 'king-last') (d. TA 1975) Dúnadan, fifteenth and last King of Arthedain (1964-74). At his birth, Malbeth the Seer foretold that he was to be the last king, which is why Arvedui was given his name. In 1944, on the death of Ondoher of Gondor and his sons, Arvedui claimed the crown of Gondor because of his descent from Isildur, who was King of Gondor with Anárion, and because he was the husband of Fíriel, Ondoher's only surviving child, who was heiress to the throne by the laws of Númenor. Although Arvedui's claim was rejected, King Eärnil of Gondor promised to give him aid at need. Late in 1973, Arvedui asked for aid against Angmar, but before the fleet sent by Eärnil arrived, the Witch-king overran Arthedain. Arvedui sent his sons to Lindon, but he remained on the North Downs until the last. He then hid in the Dwarf-mines in the northern Ered Luin until forced by hunger to seek refuge with the Lossoth. In March of 1975, Círdan sent a ship to Forochel to rescue Arvedui. He and his men boarded the ship, but it was trapped in the ice and Arvedui was drowned. (III 394, 398-400, 409-11, 458)

ARVEGIL (S.: 'royal—') (d. TA 1743) Dúnadan, eleventh King of Arthedain (1670-1743). (III 394)

ARVELEG I (S.: 'royal—') (d. TA 1409) Dúnadan, eighth King of Arthedain (1356-1409). After his father's death, he drove the forces of Angmar and Rhudaur back from the Tower Hills, with aid from Lindon and Rivendell, and for fifty years Arthedain, together with Cardolan, maintained a frontier along the Weather Hills, Great East Road, and lower Hoarwell. In 1409, Arveleg was killed while unsuccessfully defending the Tower Hills against a massive assault by Angmar and Rhudaur. (III 394, 397)

ARVELEG II (d. TA 1813) Dúnadan, twelfth King of Arthedain (1743-1813). (III 394)

ARVERNIEN (S.) Land west of the Mouths of Sirion, so called late in the First Age when it became a haven for Elves and Men (including Eärendil and Elwing) who escaped from the ruin of Doriath, Gondolin, and the Falas. Arvernien was protected by Ulmo and by the mariners of Círdan, living on Balar (q.v.). (I 308; S 196, 237, 244; B 240, 293, 302)

ARWEN (S.: 'royal maiden') (TA 241-FO 121) Eldarin princess, daughter of Elrond and Celebrían. For nearly three thousand years she lived in contentment in Imladris and Lórien, until in 2951 she met Aragorn in Rivendell. In 2980 they plighted their troth on Cerin Amroth, and after the WR they were wed, and Arwen became Queen of Gondor. She bore her husband one son and a number of daughters. However, by marrying Aragorn she chose not to accompany her father over Sea at the end of the Third Age, and thus became mortal. After Aragorn died in FO 120, Arwen went to Lórien, where she died the next winter. Her grave was made on Cerin Amorth.

Arwen was noted for her dark beauty, which was said to resemble that of Lúthien. Because of this beauty, which was never again to appear among the Elves in Middle-earth, she was called Undómiel, or in Westron, Evenstar, and she was known as the Evenstar of her people. (I 299-300; III 310, 312, 421-28, 456)

ASCAR (S.: 'rushing, impetuous') River of Beleriand, the northernmost tributary of Gelion, rising near Mount

Dolmed and flowing into Gelion near Sarn Athrad. The Dwarf-road from Nogrod and Belegost ran along its banks.

Ascar was renamed Rathlóriel, the Goldenbed, when the treasures of Doriath were placed in its depths after Beren, Dior, and the Laiquendi recovered them from the Dwarves of Nogrod who had sacked Menegroth. (S 92, 123, 235, 318; B 104, 146-47, 291, 395)

ASEA ARANION (Q.: 'leaf of the kings') Athelas (q.v.). (III 172)

ASFALOTH (S.: '—blossom') (fl. WR) Glorfindel's swift white horse, which bore Frodo to Rivendell from the Ford of Bruinen. (I 279, 281-82, 284-86)

ASH MOUNTAINS, ASHEN MOUNTAINS The Ered Lithui (q.v.). (I 17; III 245)

ASPHODEL BURROWS (TA 2913-3012) Hobbit of the Shire, daughter of Gorbadoc Brandybuck and wife of Rufus Burrows. She was a guest at the Farewell Party. (III 476)

ASTA (Q.: 'month') The month of the various Dúnedain and Westron calendars. The asta usually contained 30 days, although two astar in the Kings' Reckoning had 31 days. (III 480-81)

ASTALDO (Q.: 'valiant') Surname of Tulkas (q.v.). (S 28; B 22)

ASTRON Fourth month of the Shire Reckoning (q.v.), corresponding roughly to our April.

Called Chithing in Bree. (III 478)

ATALANTË (Q.: 'perfective-down-fallen') Name given to Númenor (q.v.) by the Dúnedain after its destruction. (S 281; B 347)

ATANAMIR, TAR- (Q.: 'man-jewel') (fl. SA 23rd

Cent.) Dúnadan, thirteenth King of Númenor (2251-?). He rejected the counsel of the Messengers of Manwë, spoke openly against the Ban of the Valar, and was the first King to cling to his life when he began to age.

Because Númenor reached the zenith of its bliss during his reign, he was called Tar-Atanamir the Great. (III 390, 391, 454; S 264-66; B 326-28)

ATANATAR I (Q.: 'man-father') (d. TA 748) Dúnadan, tenth King of Gondor (667-748). (III 394)

ATANATAR II (d. TA 1226) Dúnadan, sixteenth King of Gondor (1149-1226). In his time Gondor reached the height of its power and splendor. Atanatar, however, loved luxury and did nothing to maintain the power of Gondor. The watch on Mordor was neglected, but the royal crown was replaced by a jeweled crown of precious metals.

Atanatar was known as Alcarin, the Glorious, because of the luxury and power of his realm. (III 395, 401, 402, 404)

ATANATARI (Q.: 'man-fathers') The Edain (q.v.). (S 103; B 120)

ATANI (Q.: 'second-ones') Name given to Men in the lore of Valinor, but in Middle-earth applied only to the Three Houses of the Elf-friends, the Edain (q.v.).

Spelled *Antani* on III 506. (III 506; S 41, 103, 143, 318; B 38, 119, 171, 395)

ATENDËA (Q.: 'double-middle') The leap-year of the Númenorean calendar system and of those derived from it, so called because the year was lengthened by doubling Loëndë, the middle day of the year. (HM III 386)

ATHELAS (S.: 'kingsfoil') A healing plant brought to Middle-earth by the Númenoreans, which grew only in places where they had lived or camped. Athelas had a heartening fragrance, and in the hands of the heirs of Elendil it had great powers for curing wounds and counteracting poisons and evil influences. Aragorn used athelas by crushing and boiling its leaves in water and then either washing his patient's wounds in the tincture or having the patient breathe the steam.

Called kingsfoil in Westron and asëa aranion in Quenya (I 266, 436-37; III 170-77; L 198)

AULË (Q.) Ainu, one of the Aratar; after Manwë, Varda, and Ulmo, the most powerful of the Valar. Aulë fashioned the substances of which Arda was composed and is the master of crafts and of the knowledge of substances. He delights in the nature of substances and in works of skill, but he is not concerned with possession or mastery. Besides the shaping of Arda, Aulë's greatest works were the Two Lamps of the Valar, the vessels of the Sun and Moon, and the Dwarves, whom he created out of impatience for the Children of Ilúvatar.

Despite his lordly skill, Aulë is humble and compassionate, and indeed the Dwarves survived only because Aulë submitted them to the will of Ilúvatar. His spouse is Yavanna, with whom he dwells in central Valinor.

Aulë was known as the Smith, the Maker, and (since he taught them much and shared their interest in crafts) the Friend of the Noldor. The Dwarves called him Mahal. (III 518, 519; S 19, 20, 25, 27, 29, 30, 35, 36, 39, 43-46, 78, 99, 260; B 8, 10, 18, 20, 23, 24, 29, 30, 35, 40-45, 87, 113, 321)

AUTHORITIES The Valar (q.v.). (I 33; RP 9/12/65)

AVALLÓNE (Q.: 'near Valinor') City and port built by the Eldar in the early Second Age on the eastern shore of Tol Eressëa. It had lamplit quays and a great white tower.

Also called the Haven of the Eldar. (III 390; S 260, 262-63, 282, 292, 318; B 320, 324, 349, 362, 395)

AVARI (Q. 'unwilling, refusers') Those Elves who refused the summons of the Valar and the Great Journey.

37

Probably the Avari are equivalent to the Silvan Elves (q.v.).

Also called the Unwilling. (S 52, 99, 286, 309, 318; B 53, 113, 355, 383, 395)

AVATHAR (Q.: 'shadows') The southern portion of Aman, a cold, dark, deserted, and ignored area lying between the southern Pelóri and the Sea. Avathar was the home of Ungoliant before she poisoned the Two Trees. (S 73, 74, 318; B 80, 81, 396)

AZAGHÂL (d. FA 473) Dwarf, Lord of Belegost. Azaghâl was slain by Glaurung during the Nirnaeth Arnoediad, but in return he severely wounded the dragon and forced him to leave the field. (S 193; B 236)

AZANULBIZAR (Kh.) The valley outside the Great Gates of Khazad-dûm, lying between two arms of the Misty Mountains. Azanulbizar contained the Kheled-zâram and the source of the Silverlode. In TA 2799 the Battle of Azanulbizar, the final and greatest battle of the War of the Dwarves and Orcs, was fought here.

Called Nanduhirion in Sindarin and the Dimrill Dale in Westron. (I 370, 432-34; III 442)

ÁZE (Q.: 'sunlight') Earliest name for the tengwa ℰ (number 31), used when the letter had the value z in Quenya. When the z-sound became merged with weak r, the name became áre or esse (qq.v.). (III 500)

ÁZE NUQUERNA (Q.: 'áze reversed') Earliest name for the tengwa ℨ (number 32). Its use paralleled that of áze (q.v.). (III 500)

AZOG (d. TA 2799) Orc, king of the Orcs of Khazad-dûm. His murder and defilement of Thrór in 2790 touched off the War of the Dwarves and Orcs. In the Battle of Azanulbizar, the final battle of the war, Azog led the Orkish forces. He killed Náin, but was in turn slain by Dáin II. (III 441-42, 443; H 37)

BACK-DOOR The stone door in the eastern side of the Misty Mountains through which Bilbo escaped from the Orcs who had captured him in TA 2941. The back-door was located west of the Carrock.

Also called the Goblin-gate. (H 12, 94-95, 100)

BADGER-BROCK The head of the Badger-folk in the Old Forest, in the poem *The Adventures of Tom Bombadil.* He—and they—were quite possibly fictional. (TB 12-13)

BADGER-FOLK A family of badgers living in the Old Forest, in the poem *The Adventures of Tom Bombadil.* (TB 13)

BAG END A dwelling in Hobbiton, built about **TA** 2880 by Bungo Baggins at the end of Bagshot Row. Bungo, Bilbo, and Frodo Baggins lived there. From September, 3018, until her imprisonment and his death, Lobelia and Lotho Sackville-Baggins lived in Bag End, and Saruman made it his headquarters in the Shire. After Frodo went over Sea, Sam Gamgee and his heirs lived there.

Bag End was a typical, if somewhat more luxurious than the ordinary, hobbit-hole.

Also spelled Bag-End. (I 43; III 356, 367-71, 376; H 15-20)

BAGGINS A well-to-do family of Hobbits, with members living all over the Shire. The Bagginses were connected with most of the aristocratic families of the Shire, as well as with the Chubb-Bagginses and Sackville-Bagginses.

The Bagginses were in general an unexceptionable (by Hobbit standards) family, their more eccentric members having a considerable portion of Took blood. (I 30; III 474)

BAGSHOT ROW Street in Hobbiton, running along the side of Hobbiton Hill below Bag End. Before the WR, the Gamgees lived at Number 3 Bagshot Row and Daddy Twofoot lived next door. During the WR, Bagshot Row was torn up by Saruman and made into a gravel and sand quarry. After the War, Bagshot Row was restored and named New Row. (I 44, 45; III 359, 366, 373-74; L 178)

BAIN (d. TA 3007) Man, second king of Dale (2977-3007). He was the son of Bard I and the father of Brand. (I 301; III 462, 463)

BALAN The birth-name of Bëor (q.v.). S 142; B 170)

BALAR (S.) Large island in the Bay of Balar. In origin it was a piece of Tol Eressëa, the floating island on which Ulmo transported the Eldar to Aman; this piece grounded in the Bay and broke off. In later years Ossë often visited Balar, and the island was controlled by Círdan and the Falathrim. After the Falas was overthrown, Balar became the chief Sindarin refuge in Beleriand; after the fall of Gondolin, Gil-galad ruled here as High King of the Noldor.

Many pearls were found in the shallows off its shores. Also called the Isle of Balar. (S 57, 92, 121, 196, 244; B 59, 105, 143, 239, 302)

BALBO BAGGINS (b. TA 2767) Hobbit of the Shire. He married Berylla Boffin; they had five children. (III 474)

BALCHOTH (S.: '—people') Tribe of Easterlings controlled by Sauron, who in the twenty-fifth century of the Third Age lived in Rhovanion east of Mirkwood. They frequently raided the Vales of Anduin south of the Gladden, and greatly distressed its inhabitants. As their power grew, the Balchoth began attacking Gondor's outposts on the Anduin. In 2510 they crossed Anduin and invaded Calenardhon. In the Battle of the Field of Celebrant, the

Balchoth, although aided by Orcs of the Misty Mountains, were annihilated by Cirion of Gondor and the Eothéod. After this battle the Balchoth passed from history. (III 415)

BALDOR (d. TA 2569)   Man of Rohan, eldest son of King Brego. At the feast held to celebrate the completion of Meduseld he vowed to tread the Paths of the Dead. During the WR, his body was found there by the Grey Company.

On III 459 the year of Baldor's death is given as 2570; unless he did not immediately fulfill his vow, or survived for a long time inside the Mountains, this may be an error. (III 71, 84, 315, 434)

BALIN (TA 2763-2994)   Dwarf of the House of Durin, King of Khazad-dûm (2989-94). Balin was a follower of Thráin, and later of Thorin, from the time of the War of the Dwarves and Orcs. Balin accompanied Thráin on the journey in 2841 that cost him his life, and a century later he was one of the members of Thorin and Company. After the death of Smaug he settled in Erebor, but in 2989 he went to Khazad-dûm with many Dwarves of Erebor and set up a Dwarf-colony there. Five years later he was slain by an Orc in Azanulbizar.

Balin and Bilbo became quite friendly in 2941; he seems to have been kindlier than many Dwarves. (I 316, 416, 418-19; III 445, 446, 450; H 21, 26, 286)

BALROGS (S.: 'power-terror' or 'demon of might')   Maiar who rebelled with Melkor, after Sauron the mightiest and most terrible of his servants. They were spirits of fire and bore whips of flame, but they were also cloaked in darkness. Their lord was Gothmog (q.v.).

Balrogs fought frequently in the Wars of Beleriand, but most were destroyed in the Great Battle. The few survivors hid deep underground, but in TA 1980 one was uncovered by the Dwarves at the root of the mithril-vein in Khazad-dûm. This demon, known in the Third Age as "the Balrog," killed two Kings of Durin's Folk in two years, and the Dwarves fled. About 2480 Sauron peopled Khazad-dûm with orcs and trolls; the Balrog ruled over these by his terror. The Balrog was destroyed by Gandalf in TA 3019 after a ten-day battle.

The Quenya name for them was Valaraukar, singular Valarauko. The Balrog of Khazad-dûm was also known as Durin's Bane (because of his murder of Durin VI) and the Terror. (I 423-25, 428-30, 461; II 134-35; III 439; S 31, 47, 251, 318; B 26, 46, 311, 396)

BAMFURLONG Farmer Maggot's farm, located in the Marish near the Bucklebury Ferry. Its major crop was mushrooms. (I 132-38; TB 21; L 178)

BANAKIL (gen. West.: 'halfling') See: Hobbits. (III 519)

BANAZÎR (gen. Hobb.: 'half-wise') See: Samwise Gamgee. (III 517)

BANDOBRAS TOOK (TA 2704-2806) Hobbit of the Shire, the second son of Thain Isengrim II. In 2747, he led the force that defeated an Orc-band in the Battle of Greenfields. His descendants included the North-tooks of Long Cleeve.

Bandobras was the third tallest hobbit in history; he was four feet five inches tall and able to ride a horse. He was nicknamed Bullroarer. (I 20, 25; II 402, 475; H 30)

BANKS Hobbit surname in Bree and in the Shire. (I 212; III 475)

BAN OF THE VALAR The one restriction placed on the Númenoreans by the Valar at the beginning of the Second Age, which was that the Dúnedain could never set foot on the Undying Lands or sail west out of sight of Númenor. Beginning in the reign of Tar-Ciryatan the Númenoreans began to speak against the Ban, which they thought deprived them of immortality, but when the Ban was broken by Ar-Pharazôn in SA 3319, the Valar laid down their guardianship of the world and Númenor was destroyed by Ilúvatar.

Also called the Ban of the Lords of the West. (III 390, 392; S 262-64, 278; B 323-26, 344)

BARAD-DÛR (S.: 'tower-dark') The fortress of Sauron, built by him with the power of the One Ring between SA 1000 and 1600. At the end of the Second Age it was besieged and captured (3434-41), but its foundations could not be destroyed while the Ring survived. Sauron began to rebuild the Barad-dûr in TA 2951, but it was destroyed in 3019 when the Ring was unmade.

The Barad-dûr was located at the southern end of a great spur of the Ered Lithui, and was the greatest fortress in Middle-earth in the Second and Third Ages.

Called in Orkish Lugbúrz and in Westron the Dark Tower. Also called the Great Tower (by its Lieutenant). (I 519; III 204, 245, 269-70, 276, 453, 455, 462; S 294; B 365)

BARAD EITHEL (S.: 'tower of the well') The fortress at Eithel Sirion, the greatest castle of Fingolfin and Fingon. Barad Eithel both guarded Hithlum from assault and enabled the Noldor to strike at Angband across Ard-galen. Because of its strategic importance, it was the site of many battles and sieges, and in the late First Age it was held by the House of Hador for the High Kings of the Noldor. Hador was slain here during Dagor Bragollach and his son Galdor seven years later. Barad Eithel no doubt fell after the Nirnaeth Arnoediad. (S 119, 152, 160, 191, 318; B 140, 170, 193, 233, 396)

BARAD NIMRAS (S.: 'white-horn tower') Tower built by Finrod during the Long Peace, located in the Falas on the cape west of Eglarest. Barad Nimras was intended to guard against attack by Morgoth from the sea. It was taken by a land attack in FA 474 and destroyed. (S 120, 196; B 142, 239)

BARAGUND (S.) (d. FA 460) Adan of the First

House, son of Bregolas and father of Morwen. Baragund was one of the last twelve of Barahir's outlaw band in Dorthonion. (S 148, 155, 162-63, 307; B 177, 187, 196, 381)

BARAHIR (S.: 'tower-lord') (d. FA 460)   Adan, lord of the First House (455-60), Elf-friend, son of Bregor, husband of Emeldir and father of Beren. During Dagor Bragollach, Barahir saved the life of Finrod, who vowed aid to his house and gave him the ring of Barahir (q.v.). After the battle Barahir returned to Dorthonion and fought a guerrilla war against the forces of Morgoth. His ever-dwindling band had a refuge at Aeluin, and Barahir was slain there when he was betrayed by Gorlim. (I 260; III 388, 400; S 148, 152, 154-55, 161, 162-63, 307, 359; B 177, 178, 182, 186-87, 194, 195-97, 381, 451)

BARAHIR (FO 2nd Cent.)   Dúnadan, grandson of Faramir. Barahir wrote *The Tale of Aragorn and Arwen.* He may have been Prince of Ithilien and Steward of Gondor. (I 38)

BARAN (FA 4th Cent.)   Adan, son of Bëor and lord of the First House. He dwelt in Estolad. (S 142, 143; B 170, 171)

BARANDUIN (S.: 'goldenbrown-river')   River flowing south and southwest from its source, Nenuial, into the Sea, so called because of its color. It was crossed by the Great East Road in the Shire by the Bridge of Stonebows.
   The original (and genuine) Hobbitish name for the river was Branda-nîn, 'border-water,' which was later corrupted to Bralda-hîm, 'heady ale,' its normal name at the time of the WR. The translated Hobbitish name was the Brandywine. (I 16; III 515, 520; S 290; B 360)

BARANOR (S.: 'tower-sun') (fl. WR)   Man of Gondor, father of Beregond. He came from Lossarnach. (III 36, 49)

BARAZ Barazinbar (q.v.). (I 370)

BARAZINBAR (Kh.: 'redhorn'?) One of the Mountains of Moria, the farthest west and north. Barazinbar had sheer, dull-red sides, and was topped with a silver crown of snow. The world's only mithril-vein was located beneath Barazinbar, and here the Balrog hid.

Called Barazinbar the Cruel by the Dwarves because of its bad weather. Called in Sindarin Caradhras and in Westron Redhorn. Also called Baraz.

See: Redhorn Gate, Redhorn Pass. (I 369, 370, 374-84, 413, 432; III 439)

BARD I (d. TA 2977) Man, a descendant of Girion of Dale and a noted archer. He was born and raised in Esgaroth, and in 2941 he organized the defense of the town against Smaug and killed the dragon. After this, Bard became the leading figure in Esgaroth; he led the army of Men that fought in the Battle of the Five Armies. Bard used his share of Smaug's hoard to rebuild Dale, and he also gave a considerable amount to the Master of Esgaroth for the rebuilding of that town. He became the first King of the re-founded Dale, and his heirs ruled after him.

Although Bard was somewhat grim of spirit and face, he was wise and an able leader.

Called Bard the Bowman and Bard the Dragon-shooter. (H 234-42, 250, 275-76, 286)

BARD II (fl. FO 1st Cent.) Man, fourth King of Dale (TA 3019-FO ?). With Thorin III, Bard led the army of Men and Dwarves that broke the siege of Erebor during the WR. (III 469)

BARDINGS The Men of Dale (q.v.). (I 301)

BAR-EN-DANWEDH (S.: 'house of ransom') The Dwarf-caves of Amon Rûdh, so named by Mîm because he sheltered Túrin there in return for his own life. (S 203, 204, 206, 356; B 248, 250, 252, 446)

BARLIMAN BUTTERBUR (fl. WR) Man of Bree, keeper of the Prancing Pony at the time of the WR and a friend of Gandalf. Physically, Barliman was short, fat, bald, and red-faced. Mentally, he was by no means quick-witted and had a bad memory, but he was good-hearted and perceptive in the long run.

Called Barley for short. (I 209 ff., 291, 345; III 333 ff.)

BARROW-DOWNS Downs east of the Old Forest. On the Barrow-downs were the Great Barrows, from which the Downs took their name. Because of the barrows the Downs were revered by the Dúnedain.

During the wars with Angmar, in TA 1409 the Dúnedain of Cardolan took refuge here. About 1636 the barrows were inhabited by evil Barrow-wights from Angmar, and the Barrow-downs became a place of great dread.

The Sindarin name was Tyrn Gorthad. (I 188-201; III 398)

BARROWFIELD The field outside Edoras where the Kings of Rohan were buried. At the end of the Third Age there were two groups of barrows, nine on the west side for the Kings of the First Line and eight on the east for the Kings of the Second Line. Simbelmynë grew on the west side of the mounds. (II 142; III 314, 436)

BARROW-WIGHTS Evil spirits from Angmar who infested the Great Barrows after TA 1636. The wights tried to entrap people in the barrows and then sacrifice them. (I 193-98, 347; III 398; TB 13-15)

BATTLE The Battle of Dagorlad (q.v.). (S 294; B 365)

BATTLE OF AZANULBIZAR The final battle of the War of the Dwarves and Orcs, fought in the winter of TA 2799. At first the battle went against the Dwarves, but with the aid of the Dwarves of the Iron Hills, who arrived late, the Orcs were defeated and Azog was killed. Many Dwarves were killed, including a number of members of the royal family of Durin's Folk. The Orcs of the Misty Mountains suffered even greater losses, and were so weakened by the battle that they did not recover their strength for over a century.

Also called the Battle of Nanduhirion and the Battle of Dimrill Dale, by Elves and Men, respectively. (III 442-44)

BATTLE OF BYWATER The last battle of the WR, fought on November 3, TA 3019. In the battle about a hundred of the Chief's Men were defeated by a band of Hobbits led by Merry and Pippin. Seventy ruffians and nineteen Hobbits were killed. (III 364-65)

BATTLE OF DAGORLAD Battle fought in SA 3434 between the forces of the Last Alliance and the armies of Sauron. According to Gollum, the battle lasted for months, but in the end the Last Alliance had the victory, for Gil-galad and Elendil were invincible. Many of the graves of the slain were later engulfed by the Dead Marshes.

The Battle of Dagorlad may actually have been a siege of the Morannon, with a number of sorties made by the defending Orcs. (I 319; II 294, 297)

BATTLE OF DALE Battle of the WR, fought March 15-17, TA 3019, in which the Men of Dale, aided by the Dwarves of Erebor, were defeated by Easterling allies of Sauron. Both King Brand and King Dáin II were slain, and the remnants of their armies were besieged in Erebor. (III 467)

BATTLE OF FIVE ARMIES See: the Battle of the Five Armies. (H 266)

BATTLE OF FORNOST Battle fought in TA 1975 in which Círdan and Eärnur of Gondor, aided by the remnants of the people of Arnor and a force from Rivendell led by Glorfindel, utterly defeated the Witch-king, annihilated his army, and broke the power of Angmar.

It is said that the Shire sent a company of bowmen to the battle. (I 24; III 411-12)

BATTLE OF GREENFIELDS Battle fought in TA 2747 in the Northfarthing between a band of Hobbits, led by Bandobras Took, and a band of marauding Orcs, led by Golfimbul. The Hobbits had the victory.

Also called the Battle of the Green Fields. (III 365; H 30)

BATTLE OF NANDUHIRION The Battle of Azanulbizar (q.v.), as called by the Elves. (III 442-43)

BATTLE OF SUDDEN FLAME Dagor Bragollach (q.v.). (S 151; B 182)

BATTLE OF THE CAMP Battle fought in North Ithilien in TA 1944 between Gondor and the Wainriders, in which Eärnil, leading the Southern Army of Gondor and the remnants of the Northern Army, defeated the unprepared Wainriders as they were celebrating their conquest of Gondor in their camp. Eärnil drove the panic-stricken Wainriders out of Ithilien; some fled eastward over Dagorlad, but many perished in the Dead Marshes. This battle, coupled with Eärnil's earlier victory over the Wainriders and Haradrim in South Ithilien, ended the Wainrider threat to Gondor. (III 409, 458)

BATTLE OF THE CROSSINGS OF ERUI Battle fought in TA 1447 during the Kin-strife (q.v.), in which Eldacar defeated Castamir's army and slew the Usurper. The remnants of the rebel army fled to Pelargir, where they were besieged by Eldacar. (III 406)

BATTLE OF THE CROSSINGS OF ISEN Battle fought in TA 2758 in which the Rohirrim, led by Helm, were defeated by Wulf and his army of Dunlendings. The Rohirrim were thrown back to Edoras, the Hornburg, and their other refuges. (III 432)

BATTLE OF THE CROSSINGS OF POROS Battle fought in Ithilien in TA 1885 in which Steward Túrin, with aid from Folcwine of Rohan, defeated the Haradrim. In the battle the twin sons of Folcwine, Fastred and Folcred, were slain. (III 416)

BATTLE OF THE FIELD OF CELEBRANT Battle fought in TA 2510 in northern Gondor. The Northern Army, led by Steward Cirion, had advanced against the Balchoth, who had overrun Calenardhon, but the latter were reinforced by a horde of Orcs of the Misty Mountains. The Northern Army was surrounded, but as the invaders were preparing to massacre it, the Éothéod, led by Eorl, swept down from the north in answer to a previous request for aid and routed the enemy. For this victory, which ended the Balchoth threat to Gondor, the Éothéod were given Calenardhon. (II 148; III 415, 429)

BATTLE OF THE FIVE ARMIES Battle fought on and around Erebor in TA 2941 between the Men of Esgaroth and Dale, the Elves of Northern Mirkwood, and the Dwarves of Erebor and the Iron Hills on one side and a huge army of Orcs of the Misty Mountains and Wargs on the other. Thanks to timely aid by Beorn and the Eagles of the Misty Mountains, the forces of good had the victory, but Thorin II was slain. The Men were led by Bard, the Elves by Thranduil, and the Dwarves by Thorin II and Dáin Ironfoot; the Orcs were led by Bolg. Other noteworthies in attendance were Gandalf and Bilbo.

Also called the Battle of Five Armies. (III 461; H 266-70, 273-74)

BATTLE OF THE FORDS OF ISEN See: the Battles of the Fords of Isen.

BATTLE OF THE GLADDEN FIELDS Massacre occurring in TA 2, in which Isildur and the Dúnedain of Arnor, marching home after the defeat of Sauron, were ambushed by Orcs of the Misty Mountains. Isildur and his three eldest sons were slain and the Ring was lost in the marshes of the Gladden Fields. Only three men escaped from the massacre, but the shards of Narsil were saved. Arnor never really recovered from this loss of a considerable part of its manpower. (I 83, 320; III 456)

BATTLE OF THE GREEN FIELDS The Battle of Greenfields (q.v.). (H 30)

BATTLE OF THE HORNBURG Battle of the WR, fought March 3-4, TA 3019, between Saruman's army of Dunlendings and Orcs and the Rhirrim, led by Théoden and Éomer. The Rohirrim, including Aragorn, Legolas, and Gimli, were besieged in Helm's Deep and the Hornburg by the invaders, who tried unsuccessfully during the night of the 3rd to breach the defenses; although the gate of the Hornburg was broken, no enemy was able to enter inside.
   At dawn on the 4th, the Riders of Rohan, with Théoden, Éomer, and Aragorn at their head, sallied forth from the Hornburg, and the foot-soldiers in the Hornburg and Helm's Deep also attacked. The invaders were pushed back to the Deeping Coomb, where they were trapped between Théoden's army, Erkenbrand's army (and Gandalf), and the Huorns. The Dunlendings surrendered, while the Orcs passed into the Huorn-forest and were slain. (II 171-87; III 466)

BATTLE OF THE PEAK The final two-day battle between Gandalf and the Balrog, fought on the summit of Zirak-zigil on January 23-25, TA 3019. The battle ended with the casting-down of the Balrog and the passing of Gandalf. In the battle Durin's Tower and the Endless Stair were destroyed. (II 134-35)

BATTLE OF THE PELENNOR FIELDS The greatest battle of the WR and of the Third Age, fought on March 15, TA 3019, between the armies of Sauron, composed of 30,000 Haradrim and a great number of Easterlings, Variags, and Orcs, led by the Lord of the Nazgûl, and the forces of Minas Tirith, aided by 3000 to 4000 men from the southern fiefs, the forces of Osgiliath and Ithilien, and 6000

Riders of Rohan. Before dawn the Lord of the Nazgûl broke the Great Gates of Minas Tirith (see: the Siege of Gondor), but was prevented from entering the city by the unexpected arrival of the Rohirrim, who, led by Théoden, vanquished a Haradrim army early in the morning. Then, however, the Lord of the Nazgûl scattered the Rohirrim and slew Théoden, but was in turn killed by Éowyn and Merry.

Éomer then led the Rohirrim in a furious attack against the Haradrim, but by mid-morning, despite aid from the cavalry of Gondor, led by Imrahil, the southward advance of the Rohirrim had been slowed, for the Oliphaunts of the Haradrim could not be conquered, and the enemy had many more troops than the Rohirrim. Meanwhile, Gothmog, the new enemy commander, had thrown his reserve forces into the battle, and the infantry of Gondor was being driven back to Minas Tirith. About noon the Rohirrim were surrounded about a mile north of the Harlond, but at this point Aragorn, with a great fleet from southern Gondor, where he had defeated the Corsairs, landed at the Harlond. Then the forces of Gondor swept across the Pelennor Fields, and by sunset all the invaders had been killed or driven beyond the Rammas Echor. (III 137-52)

BATTLE OF THE POWERS Battle fought early in the First Age between the Valar and Melkor. Desiring to protect the newly awakened Elves from the evil of Melkor, the Valar decided to free Middle-earth from his domination. After a lengthy struggle, which changed the western shores of Beleriand, Utumno was taken and Morgoth overcome by Tulkas and chained with Angainor.

Also called the War of the Powers. The battle of the Valar mentioned on III 138 is either this battle or the Great Battle. (S 51, 118; B 51-52, 139)

BATTLE OF TUMHALAD The last pitched battle fought between the Exiles and the forces of Morgoth. In the autumn of FA 496 Glaurung led a large army of Orcs through the Pass of Sirion, defiled Eithel Ivrin, and ravaged the northern stretches of Talath Dirnen. The army of

Nargothrond, led by Orodreth and Túrin, marched forth to oppose the Orcs. But they were outnumbered, and only Túrin (wearing his Dragon-helm) could face the fires of Glaurung. The Elves were driven back and trapped in Tumhalad, with the Rivers Narog and Ginglith at their back. There they were slaughtered. Orodreth and Gwindor were slain; Túrin was one of the very few survivors. Glaurung and the Orcs then proceeded to Nargothrond, which they sacked. (S 212, 333; B 261, 415)

BATTLE OF UNNUMBERED TEARS The Nirnaeth Arnoediad (q.v.) (S 238; B 294)

BATTLE PIT A sand-pit near Bywater where the Chief's Men slain in the Battle of Bywater were buried. (III 365)

BATTLE PLAN Dagorlad (q.v.). (II 266)

BATTLES OF THE FORDS OF ISEN Two battles fought during the WR between the Riders of Rohan and Saruman's forces, composed of Dunlendings and Orcs. In the First Battle, fought February 25, TA 3019, Saruman's forces defeated an army led by Prince Théodred. Théodred was killed, but the enemy did not cross the Isen.

In the Second Battle, fought on March 2, Erkenbrand was defeated by the invaders, who this time crossed the river. The casualties in the Second Battle, however, were lighter than originally thought, since the Rohirrim were scattered early in the battle, before they could be destroyed. (II 167-68, 199; III 437, 465, 466)

BAUGLIR (S.: 'constrainer') Epithet applied to Morgoth by the Eldar, probably in Beleriand. (S 104, 319; B 120, 397)

BAY OF BALAR Great bay of Belegaer, south of the Mouths of Sirion. The Bay of Balar was created in the upheavals of the Battle of the Powers. (S 51; B 52)

BAY OF BEL, BAY OF BELFALAS The great bay of

Belegaer lying between Gondor and Umbar. (I 493; TB 8, 36)

BAY OF ELDAMAR, BAY OF ELVENHOME The bay of Belegaer washing the shores of Eldamar. Tol Eressëa was located in the Bay. (S 58, 59, 73; B 61, 80)

BEATER Name given to Glamdring (q.v.) by the Orcs. (H 73)

BEECHBONE (d. TA 3019) Ent, burned to death in the Ents' attack on Isengard during the WR. (II 221)

BEING The material realization of the Vision of Ilúvatar and the Ainulindalë as Eä (q.v.), the World that Is. (S 15, 16, 25; B 4, 17)

BELBA BOLGER (TA 2856-2956) Hobbit of the Shire, eldest daughter of Mungo Baggins and wife of Rudigar Bolger. (III 474)

BELECTHOR I (S.: 'great-eagle') (d. TA 2655) Dúnadan, fifteenth Ruling Steward of Gondor (2628-55). (III 395)

BELECTHOR II (d. TA 2872) Dúnadan, twenty-first Ruling Steward of Gondor (2811-72). At his death the White Tree died and no sapling could be found to replace it. (III 395, 416)

BELEG (S.: 'mighty') (d. FA 487?) Sindarin Elf of Doriath, chief of the marchwardens of that realm, a great woodsman and warrior. Beleg fought on the borders of Doriath and sometimes in other lands; he helped the Haladin to destroy an army of Orcs in Brethil c. 458, and (with Mablung) was the only Elf of Doriath to fight in the Nirnaeth Arnoediad.

Beleg befriended Túrin during the latter's apprenticeship in arms and tried to aid him during his outlawry; together the Two Captains performed great deeds. He succeeded in freeing Túrin from the Orcs who had captured him at Amon Rûdh, but Túrin unknowingly slew him.

Beleg was primarily a bowman, but in the last year of his life he bore the sword Anglachel by which he was slain. His bow, Belthronding, was buried with him.

He was known as Beleg Strongbow, Beleg Cúthalion (the Sindarin equivalent), and the Bow. (S 157, 185, 189, 199, 200-02, 204, 206-08; B 190, 225, 230, 243, 245-47, 250-51, 253-56)

BELEG (d. TA 1029)   Dúnadan, second King of Arthedain (946-1029). (III 394)

BELEGAER (S.: 'great-sea')   The sea separating Middle-earth from Aman, stretching from the Helcaraxë in the north to the uncharted south. The principal islands in Belegaer were Balar, Númenor, the Enchanted Isles, and Tol Eressëa (qq.v.).

See also: the Bays of Balar, Belfalas and Eldamar, the Great Gulf and the Straight Road.

Also called the Western Sea, the Western Seas, the Great Sea of the West, the High Sea, the Great Water, the Sundering Sea and, most often of all, the Sea. (I 452; III 384; S 37, 51; B 32, 51)

BELEGORN (S.: 'great-tree') (d. TA 2204)   Dúnadan, fourth Ruling Steward of Gondor (2148-2204). (III 395)

BELEGOST (S.: 'mighty fortress')   Dwarvish city built under the eastern side of the Ered Luin near Mount Dolmed. The Dwarves of Belegost were relatively friendly with the Noldor of Beleriand, but they had a special friendship with Thingol of Doriath. They fought valiantly in the first battle of the Wars of Beleriand and in the last, the Nirnaeth Arnoediad, during which they fought off the dragons, although their lord Azaghâl was slain by Glaurung. Belegost was ruined in the Great Battle at the end of the First Age, and many of its people went to Khazad-dûm.

Among the great works of the Dwarves of Belegost were the invention of chain mail and the delving of Menegroth.

Part of their payment for the latter was the great pearl Nimphelos.

Called Gabilgathol in Khuzdul and Mickleburg; all three names were probably synonymous. (III 439; S 91, 92, 94, 96, 193, 233, 319)

BELEGUND (S.) (d. FA 460) Adan of the First House, son of Bregolas, father of Rían and one of the twelve outlaw-companions of Barahir. (S 148, 155, 162-63, 307; B 177, 187, 196, 381)

BELEGÛR Sindarin form of Melkor (q.v.), never used. (S 340; B 424)

BELEGURTH (S.: 'great death') A name given Melkor (q.v.), a play on Belegûr. (S 340; B 424)

BELERIAND (S.: 'Balar-land') Area of Middle-earth in the First Age, at first the lands around the Bay of Balar, but later all the lands lying west of the Ered Luin and south of the Ered Wethrin, possibly including Dorthonion and Nevrast. Beleriand was divided into East and West regions by the River Sirion; the populous northern lands were divided from the largely unsettled south by the Andram.

At first, Beleriand was the home of the Sindar of Doriath and the Falas, later joined by the Laiquendi of Ossiriand, the Noldor of Nargothrond, Himlad, East Beleriand and Thargelion, and the Edain. Gradually overrun by the forces of Morgoth, all of Beleriand, save for the portion of Ossiriand later known as Lindon, was ruined in the Great Battle at the end of the First Age.

Also called the Land of the Elves. (I 319; II 421, 422; III 438; S 54, 91, 118-24, 143, 252, 285-86, 318; B 56, 103, 139-48, 172, 313, 354, 396)

BELFALAS (S.: '—coast') Fair coastal area of Gondor, located between the Morthond and the Gilrain. Its main city was **Dol Amroth**.

Belfalas was the fief of the Princes of Dol Amroth. (I 16-17; III 14, 23)

BELL GAMGEE (TA 30th Cent.)   Hobbit of the Shire, wife of Hamfast Gamgee. She bore him six children, including Samwise. Bell was born a Goodchild. (III 477)

BELLADONNA BAGGINS (TA 2852-2934)   Hobbit of the Shire, ninth child of Gerontius Took. She married Bungo Baggins about 2880; Bilbo was their only child. (III 474, 475; H 16)

BELMARIE   A country, in Bilbo's poem *Errantry*. The name is an imitation of Elvish, and Belmarie was probably fictitious. (TB 8, 25)

BELTHIL (S.: 'divine radiance')   Artificial tree with silver flowers, fashioned by Turgon as an image of Telperion and standing in the royal courts in Gondolin. (S 126, 319; B 151, 397)

BELTHRONDING (S.)   The great bow of Beleg, made of black yew-wood. Belthronding was buried with Beleg. (S 208; B 256)

BÉMA   Oromë (q.v.). (III 431; S 363; B 455)

BENT WORLD   Arda (q.v.), so called after it was made spherical at the Change of the World. (S 304; B 378)

BËOR (Ad.?: 'vassal') (fl. FA 4th Cent.)   Adan, first recorded lord of the First House. When he was 48, Bëor led his people into Beleriand and gathered them in Estolad. Later he served Finrod in Nargothrond for 44 years; he died at the age of 93, having passed on willingly.

His birth-name was Balan; he was called Bëor because of his service to Finrod. Also called Bëor the Old. (S 140-42, 148-49, 307; B 167-70, 178, 381)

BEORN (fl. TA 30th Cent.)   Man, chieftain of the

Beornings, a berserker. Beorn violently hated Orcs and was in general distrustful of all strangers, but his heart was good. After Gandalf overcame his initial suspicions in TA 2941, Beorn fed and protected Thorin and Company and was later instrumental in winning the Battle of the Five Armies. In that battle he killed Bolg, the leader of the Orkish forces.

See: Beornings. (H 117-19, 120-36, 274, 278)

BEORNINGS Men of the Vales of Anduin, living on both sides of the river near the Carrock. The Beornings were descended from the Edain or their close kin, and thus spoke a language related to Adûnaic and Rohirric. At the time of the WR the Beornings were not very friendly to any outsiders, but in return for tolls they kept the High Pass and the Ford of Carrock safe for merchants; they greatly hated Orcs. After the WR the Beornings and the Woodmen were given the central portion of Eryn Lasgalen.

The only Beorning encountered in *LotR* is Beorn, who as a skin-changer was probably not representative of his people.

The Beornings were famed for their baking, especially of honeycakes. They did not eat meat, and were very friendly with animals. They may originally have come from the Misty Mountains, whence they were driven by the Orcs. (I 301, 478; II 429, 468, 508)

BEREG (fl. FA 4th Cent.) Adan of the First House, grandson of Baran. Opposed to becoming involved in the Wars of Beleriand, he led a thousand people of his House from Estolad back into Eriador. (S 144-45, 320; B 173, 398)

BEREGOND (S.: '—stone'?) (d. TA 2811) Dúnadan, twentieth Ruling Steward of Gondor (2763-2811) and one of the greatest captains in the history of Gondor. (III 395, 416)

BEREGOND (fl. WR) Man of Gondor, perhaps a Dúnadan, soldier in the Third Company of the Citadel.

During the Siege of Gondor, he left his post and killed men in the Hallows to prevent Denethor II from burning Faramir, to whom Beregond was devoted. After the WR, he was banished from Minas Tirith for this offense, but was made the first Captain of the Guard of Faramir. (III 36, 155-62, 195, 207, 305)

BEREN (S.) (FA) Adan of the First House, a descendant of Bëor. He was the father of Emeldir. (S 328; B 408)

BEREN (c. FA 435-509) Adan, son of Barahir, lord of the First House (FA 460-67?), hero and Elf-friend, fated to achieve the highest success of the Wars of Beleriand. The only survivor of the outlaws of Dorthonion, Beren killed the Orc who slew his father and recovered the ring of Barahir. He remained alone in Doriath for another four years, becoming so deadly to the forces of Morgoth that the price on his head was equal to that on Fingon's. Yet he was so gentle to others that he ate no flesh, and the birds and beasts of Doriath aided him.

Eventually the horrors of Sauron forced Beren to leave Dorthonion, and crossing Ered Gorgoroth and Nan Dungortheb (the only Man or Elf to do so) he came to Doriath. Passing the Girdle of Melian, he saw Lúthien dancing in Neldoreth in the summer of FA 465, and he fell in love with her. She returned his love the following spring, but after a few months they were betrayed to Thingol, who demanded a Silmaril in return for his daughter's hand.

Although Thingol thought he had found a clever way to rid himself of Beren, the hero went to Nargothrond, where Finrod was ready to fulfill his oath to aid the heirs of Barahir. Together with ten companions, Beren and Finrod traveled north. When they were captured by the forces of Tol-in-Gaurhoth, Finrod was defeated by Sauron and at length died saving Beren from the devouring were-wolf of the dungeons.

But Lúthien and Huan overcame Sauron and released Beren, and (after a fight with Curufin and Celegorm) the three entered Angband. Lúthien overcame Carcharoth and Morgoth, and Beren took a Silmaril from the Iron Crown. During their retreat Carcharoth bit off and swallowed Beren's right hand and the Silmaril it held. Rescued by the Eagles, Beren and Lúthien came at last to Doriath, where they were reconciled with Thingol. Slain soon after by Carcharoth, the dying Beren gave the Silmaril to Thingol, thus fulfilling the Quest of the Silmaril.

Lúthien died of grief soon after, but obtained from Mandos the grace that she and Beren might have a second life in Middle-earth. On their return, they lived in isolation on Tol Galen with their son, Dior. Beren left Tol Galen but once, to avenge the murder of Thingol on the Dwarves of Nogrod and recover the Silmaril. He and Lúthien died sometime after this. Their deeds of valor were the noblest of the Children of Ilúvatar and were inspired by their love, the greatest ever known. From their union (the first of Elda and Adan) and their deeds came Eärendil and the salvation of Middle-earth.

Beren was known as Beren One-hand (in Sindarin, Erchamion); he called himself Camlost, the Empty-handed, after his return from Angband. (I 258-61; III 281, 388, 400, 453, 507; S 104-05, 144, 148, 155, 162-88, 234-36, 306, 307; B 121, 172, 177, 187, 195-229, 290-91, 381, 382)

BEREN (d. TA 2763) Dúnadan, nineteenth Ruling Steward of Gondor (2743-63). During his reign, in 2757, Gondor was attacked by three great fleets from Umbar, and the attackers were repulsed with difficulty. Beren gave Isengard to Saruman to dwell in, thinking that the wizard would protect Rohan, which had been weakened by the Long Winter and Wulf's invasion. (III 395, 415-16)

BERGIL (S.: '—star') (b. TA 3008 or 3009) Man of Gondor, son of Beregond. He remained in Minas Tirith during the Siege of Gondor. (III 47 ff.)

BERILAC BRANDYBUCK (b. TA 2980) Hobbit of the Shire, son of Merimac Brandybuck and a guest at the Farewell Party. (III 476)

BERT (d. TA 2941)   A troll of the Trollshaws, one of the three encountered by Thorin and Company and turned to stone as a result of Gandalf's trick. (H 46-52)

BERÚTHIEL (S.: *bereth* 'queen' + *iel* 'female')   Queen whose cats were proverbial for their ability to find their way home. (I 405)

BERYLLA BAGGINS (f. TA 2800)   Hobbit of the Shire, wife of Balbo Baggins. She was born a Boffin. (III 474)

BIFUR (fl. TA 2941-3018)   Dwarf, a member of Thorin and Company. After 2941 he lived in Erebor. (I 302; III 450; H 23, 26)

BIG FOLK, BIG PEOPLE   Men (q.v.), so called by Hobbits. (I 19; H 16)

BILBO BAGGINS (TA 2890-   )   Hobbit of the Shire, adventurer, Elf-friend, Ring-bearer, author, and scholar. Bilbo's involvement in the affairs of Middle-earth began in 2941, when Gandalf coerced him into being the burglar for Thorin and Company. In the course of this adventure he went to Rivendell and other faraway places, stole the One Ring, and played an important part in the death of Smaug and the success of the expedition. He returned home to Bag End with his modest share of the dragon's hoard and the Ring, and lived a comfortable life in the Shire for sixty years. In 2980, on the death of Drogo and Primula Baggins, Bilbo adopted their son Frodo and made him his heir. In 3001, Bilbo gave a huge birthday party, the Farewell Feast, and then disappeared, leaving his goods, including the Ring, to Frodo. Bilbo then went to Imladris and, except for a trip to Dale and Erebor in 3001 or 3002, stayed there for twenty years, writing poetry and studying Elven-lore. In 3021 Bilbo went over Sea with the Last Riding of the Keepers of the Rings.

Bilbo wrote the account of his expedition to Erebor with Thorin and Compar which appears in the Red Book of

Westmarch and, edited by Professor Tolkien, forms *The Hobbit*. He also wrote numerous poems, including walking songs, *Errantry*, and a long poem about Eärendil (I 308-11). Bilbo's chief scholarly contribution was his *Translations from the Elvish;* his primary interest was the First Age.

Bilbo lived for most of his life in Bag End, Hobbiton. He was, unlike most hobbits, a bachelor. Bilbo was the longest-lived hobbit in history, being 131 years and 8 days old when he went over Sea; his longevity was partly due to the influence of the Ring, which otherwise affected him to a surprisingly small degree. Bilbo's Fallohide blood showed in his uncommon love of Elves and adventure and his skill with languages, but apart from this he was very much a normal hobbit.

Bilbo's sword was the famous Elven-knife Sting; he wore a mithril-coat given him by Thorin II. (I 31-32, 303-05; III 381-84, 387, 474, 475; H 9, 15-17, 277; TB 7, 8)

BILBO GAMGEE (b. FO 15) Hobbit of the Shire, tenth child of Samwise Gamgee. (III 477)

BILL (fl. WR) Pony, bought in Bree by Frodo in TA 3018 from Bill Ferny, after whom he was named. When bought, Bill was half-starved, but under the care of Sam Gamgee he became healthy and happy. Bill bore Frodo part of the way to Rivendell, and was later used by the Company of the Ring as a pack animal. Set free outside the West-gate of Khazad-dûm, Bill eventually found his way back to Bree. There he was recovered after the WR by Sam, who dearly loved him. (I 242, 273, 366, 396, 402; III 338, 343-44, 380)

BILL BUTCHER Hobbit of the Shire, the butcher of Michel Delving in the poem *Perry-the-Winkle*. Bill Butcher was perhaps a historical character, but his surname may be more of an epithet than a true family name. (TB 42)

BILL FERNY (fl. WR) Man of Bree, an agent of Saruman. After making trouble in Bree in TA 3019, he went to the Shire and was put in charge of the gate at the Brandywine Bridge. He was expelled from the Shire by Frodo on October 30, 3019.

Called the Chief's Big Man by the Hobbits at the Bridge. (I 224-25, 242, 244; III 335, 343)

BINDBALE WOOD Forest in the Northfarthing. (I 40)

BINGO BAGGINS (TA 2864-2960) Hobbit of the Shire, husband of Chica Grubb. Their son Falco was the first Chubb-Baggins. (III 474)

BIRCHWOODS OF NIMBRETHIL Nimbrethil (q.v.). (S Map)

BITER Name given to Orcrist (q.v.) by the Orcs. (H 72)

BLACK BREATH Name given to the fell influence of the Nazgûl, which resulted in despair, unconsciousness, and bad dreams, and after prolonged exposure in death. Athelas was an effective remedy.

Also called the Black Shadow, by the doctors of Minas Tirith; Black Breath was the name used by Aragorn. (I 235-36; III 171)

BLACK CAPTAIN The Lord of the Nazgûl (q.v.), as commander of the army that attacked Minas Tirith during the WR. (III 110)

BLACK GATE The Morannon (q.v.). (I 319)

BLACK HAND The influence and power of Morgoth. (S 201; B 246)

BLACK HAND The hand of Sauron on which he wore the Ring, so called by Gollum. It was black because of Sauron's inability to assume a fair form after the destruction of his body in the wreck of Númenor, and in the

Third Age had but four fingers, because Isildur had cut one off to get the Ring.

Also used attributively for Sauron. (II 311, 315)

BLACK LAND Mordor (q.v.). (I 203)

BLACK NÚMENÓREANS Those Númenóreans loyal to the King (and thus opposed to the Eldar and Valar) who had settled in Middle-earth, especially those of Umbar. In the course of the Second Age they were corrupted by Sauron and came to hate all good peoples, especially the Faithful; they loved power and domination. After the fall of Sauron in SA 3441, the Black Númenóreans mixed their blood with the Haradrim over whom they ruled, but inherited undiminished their hatred for the Dúnedain of Gondor, the descendants of the Faithful. In the Third Age, operating from Umbar, they frequently attacked the coasts of Gondor, but their power was broken in 933 when King Eärnil I of Gondor took Umbar. They were permanently scattered when Hyarmendacil broke their siege of Umbar in 1050. (III 202, 403; S 293; B 363)

BLACK PIT Khazad-dûm (q.v.). (I 370)

BLACK PITS Something somewhere in Mordor, where Sauron punished his errant servants. The Black Pits were perhaps the dungeons of the Barad-dûr. (III 222)

BLACK RIDER The Lord of the Nazgûl (q.v.), when riding a horse. (III 125)

BLACK RIDERS The Nazgûl (q.v.), when riding horses (I 118)

BLACKROOT The Morthond (q.v.). (III 73)

BLACKROOT VALE The valley of the upper Morthond, in southern Gondor. Erech was in the Blackroot Vale. Also called Morthond Vale. (III 49, 73)

BLACK SHADOW The Lord of the Nazgûl, so called by the Men of Gondor at the beginning of the WR when his presence was felt during the attack on Osgiliath. (I 322, 336)

BLACK SHADOW The Black Breath (q.v.), as called by the doctors of Minas Tirith. (III 165-66)

BLACK SPEECH The language devised by Sauron in the Second Age for use by him and his servants. The Black Speech died out at the end of the Second Age but was re-introduced by Sauron in the Third, when it was used in its pure form only by him, the Nazgûl and other of his close servants, and the Olog-hai. Orcs of Mordor spoke a debased form of the Black Speech, and some of the words of their dialects, such as *ghâsh*, 'fire,' spread throughout all Orcdom.

The Black Speech was probably based to some extent on Quenya, and was perhaps a perversion of that language. It was a very harsh language. The only example given of the pure Black Speech is the Ring-inscription; a number of the Orcs of Mordor have names in their debased form of the Black Speech. (I 333; III 498, 511, 512)

BLACK STONE The Stone of Erech (q.v.). (III 184)

BLACK SWORD (OF NARGOTHROND) Túrin (q.v.). (S 211, 220; B 251, 271)

BLACK WINGS The flying Nazgûl (q.v.). (II 321)

BLACK YEARS The Dark Years (q.v.). (I 81)

BLACK YEARS The Second Age (q.v.). (S 294; B 365)

BLADORTHIN (S.: '—grey') A king, probably an Elf, who ordered spears from the Dwarves of Erebor but died before they were delivered. He died sometime between TA 1999 and 2770. (H 220)

BLANCO (fl. TA 1601) A Fallohide Hobbit of Bree, who with his brother Marcho settled the Shire in 1601. (I 23)

BLESSED REALM Aman, specifically Valinor (q.v.). (III 388; R 62; S 63, 73; B 67, 81)

BLOOTING The name used in Bree for the eleventh month of the year.
See: Blotmath, Shire Reckoning. (III 483)

BLOTMATH The eleventh month of the Shire Reckoning, corresponding to our November. The name was pronounced "Blodmath" or "Blommath" at the time of the WR.
Called Blooting in Bree. (III 478, 483)

BLUE MOUNTAINS The Ered Luin (q.v.). (I 16, 72; S 91; B 103)

BOAR OF EVERHOLT (d. TA 2864) Famous boar of the Firienwood, slain by King Folca of Rohan, who died of the wounds given him by the boar. (III 435)

BOB (fl. WR) Man or Hobbit of Bree, one of the servants at the Prancing Pony. Bob seems to have been in charge of the stables. (I 210, 241-42; III 333)

BODO PROUDFOOT (fl. TA 2900) Hobbit of the Shire, husband of Linda Baggins and father of Odo Proudfoot. (III 474)

BOFFIN A Hobbit family, with members living all over the Shire at the time of the WR. The Boffins, judging by their many marriages with the Tooks and Bagginses, were probably an upper-class and well-to-do family. Since there is no record of any Boffin-Brandybuck marriage, there may have been few Boffins living in the eastern part of the Shire.
Boffin is an Anglicization of the genuine Hobbit surname

Bophîn, of unknown meaning and forgotten origin. (I 30; III 474, 475, 516)

BOFUR (fl. TA 2941-3018)   Dwarf, a member of Thorin and Company. Although descended from Dwarves of Khazad-dûm, he was not of Durin's line.

After 2941, Bofur lived in Erebor. (I 302; III 450; H 23, 26, 208)

BOLG (d. TA 2941)   Large Orc of the Misty Mountains, perhaps an uruk, the son of Azog. Bolg led the Orcs and Wargs at the Battle of the Five Armies, in which he was slain by Beorn.

He was known as Bolg of the North. (III 448; H 265, 274)

BOLGER   An old and aristocratic family of Hobbits of Fallohide origin living in the Shire, principally at Budgeford. The Bolgers frequently gave high-sounding names to their children. (III 474, 475, 476, 516; L 180)

BOMBADIL GOES BOATING   A Buckland poem about Tom Bombadil, probably written after the WR. (TB 8-9, 17-23)

BOMBADIL, TOM   See: Tom Bombadil.

BOMBUR (fl. TA 2941-3018)   Dwarf, a member of Thorin and Company. Bombur was descended from Dwarves of Khazad-dûm, though he was not of Durin's line. After 2941 he lived in Erebor.

Always fat, in later life Bombur was so heavy that he could not move by himself, and it required six Dwarves to lift him. (I 302; III 450; H 23, 26, 144-50, 208)

BONFIRE GLADE   Glade in the Old Forest where the Hobbits of Buckland, sometime before the WR, burned many trees during the attack of the Forest on Buckland. No trees grew there afterward, but there was a profusion of grass, weeds, nettles, and other similar plants. (I 157, 158-59)

BOOK OF MAZARBUL (Kh.: 'records') The chronicle kept by Balin's expedition to Khazad-dûm from TA 2989 to 2994. The Book was found in the Chamber of Mazarbul by the Fellowship of the Ring; Gimli took it and may well have preserved it throughout the WR. (I 417-19)

BOOK OF THE KINGS One of the chronicles of Gondor that has survived to the present day, and has been used by Professor Tolkien in writing *LotR*. (HM I 7)

BOOKS OF LORE Compendia of Elvish wisdom, in Rivendell. Extracts from these Books of Lore were translated by Bilbo Baggins toward the end of the Third Age and, supplemented by oral sources, formed his *Translations from the Elvish*. (III 380)

BOPHÎN (gen. Hobb.) See: Boffin. (III 516)

BÓR (FA 5th Cent.) Man, a chieftain of the Easterlings (q.v.). He probably died before the Nirnaeth Arnoediad. (S 157, 189; B 189, 231)

BORGIL (S.: '—star') A red star, rising before midnight in late September. Perhaps the modern Betelgeuse or Aldebaran. (I 120)

BORIN (TA 2450-2711) Dwarf of Durin's line, second son of Náin II. Borin lived in the Grey Mountains until 2590, when he went to Erebor with Thrór. (III 440, 450)

BORLACH (d. FA 473) Easterling, second son of Bór, a retainer of Maedhros and Maglor. With his brothers, he slew Ulfast and Ulwarth during the Nirnaeth Arnoediad, but was himself slain. (S 157, 193; B 189, 235)

BORLAD (d. FA 473) Easterling, eldest son of Bór,

retainer of Maedhros and Maglor, and brother of Borlach (q.v.). (S 157, 193; B 189, 236)

BOROMIR (S. *boro* + Q. *mir*: 'jewel') (fl. FA 400) Adan, lord of the First House, son of Boron. He was the first lord of Ladros. (III 507; S 148, 320; B 177, 398)

BOROMIR (d. TA 2489) Dúnadan, eleventh Ruling Steward of Gondor (2477-89). In 2475, Boromir defeated the uruks and drove them out of Ithilien, but received a Morgul-wound which shortened his life.

Boromir was one of the greatest Captains of Gondor, noble and strong of body and will. (III 395, 414-15)

BOROMIR (TA 2978-3019) Dúnadan of Gondor, eldest son of Denethor II, named after the preceding. After leading the defense of Osgiliath against Sauron's armies in June, 3018, Boromir went to Imladris to find the answer to a dream he and his brother had had. Arriving there after a long and arduous journey, he took part in the Council of Elrond and became one of the Companions of the Ring. On Amon Hen, the spell of the Ring, which had tempted him at least since Lórien, proved too great for him and he tried to kill Frodo. He immediately repented, but his madness drove Frodo to decide to carry on the Quest alone. This was a good thing, since later that day Amon Hen was raided by Orcs. Boromir died defending Merry and Pippin. Aragorn, Legolas, and Gimli gave him a proper funeral and set his body afloat down Anduin.

Although a strong and handsome man and one of the greatest captains of Gondor, Boromir cared little for anything save arms and battle, and was overly proud. As Denethor's heir, he bore those titles and positions usually possessed by the heir of the Steward. (I 315, 322-23, 365, 463-64, 484, 514-17; II 17-18, 22-24, 337; III 35, 414, 419)

BORON (S.) (FA 4th Cent.) Adan, lord of the First House, grandson of Bëor. He lived in Dorthonion. (S 148; B 177)

BORTHAND (d. FA 473)   Easterling, youngest son of Bór, retainer of Maedhros and Maglor, and brother of Borlach (q.v.). (S 157, 193; B 189, 235)

BOUNDERS   The Shire border-guard, a branch of the Watch. The Bounders turned back undesirable persons and animals at the borders of the Shire. Their numbers varied with need. (I 31, 73-74)

BOW   Epithet referring to Beleg when as one of the Two Captains (q.v.) he harried the forces of Morgoth in Talath Dirnen. (S 205; B 252)

BOWMAN COTTON (b. TA 2986)   Hobbit of the Shire, fourth child and third son of Tolman Cotton.
Bowman was usually called Nick. (III 354, 477)

BRACEGIRDLE   A family of Hobbits of the Shire, probably well-to-do. At least some of the Bracegirdles lived in Hardbottle. (I 52; III 372, 474, 476)

BRALDAGAMBA (gen. Hobb.: 'ale-buck')   See: Brandybuck. (III 520)

BRALDA-HÎM (gen. Hobb.: 'heady-ale')   See: Baranduin. (III 520)

BRAND (d. TA 3019)   Man, third King of Dale (3007-3019), a strong ruler. Brand was slain in the Battle of Dale. (I 301; III 463, 468)

BRANDAGAMBA (gen. Hobb.: 'borderland-buck')   See: Brandybuck. (III 520)

BRANDA-NÎN (gen. Hobb.: 'border-water')   The Baranduin (q.v.). (III 520)

BRANDIR (d. FA 501)   Adan, lord of the Haladin in Brethil (496-501). He built Ethel Brandir and tried to hide from the forces of Morgoth. But late in 496 his people met Túrin. Brandir tended him in his grief at the death of Finduilas, and the next summer he healed Nienor, with whom he fell in love. Brandir was slain by Túrin when he told the hero that his wife Níniel was really his sister Nienor.

Brandir had a club foot. He was a gentle man and a gifted healer. Called Brandir the Lame. (S 216, 220, 221-25, 308; B 266, 271, 272-77, 382)

BRANDYBUCK One of the most important Hobbit families of the Shire, containing a strong Fallohide strain. The family traced its descent from Gorhendad Oldbuck, who about TA 2340 moved to Buckland from the Marish and changed the family name to Brandybuck. Ever after, the head of the family was the Master of Buckland and, with his relatives, lived in Brandy Hall.

The actual name of the family was Brandagamba, which meant 'march-buck' in Hobbitish. Braldagamba, meaning 'ale-buck,' was not used, but Professor Tolkien has translated the name of the family as *Brandybuck* in order to preserve the original similarity between the name of the family and that of the River Brandywine. (I 27; III 476, 516, 520)

BRANDY HALL The chief dwelling of the Brandybucks, a large smial beneath Buck Hill in Buckland. The excavation of Brandy Hall was begun by Gorhendad Oldbuck about TA 2340. (I 40, 45; III 476)

BRANDYWINE The Baranduin (q.v.). (I 24)

BRANDYWINE BRIDGE The most common name for the Bridge of Stonebows (q.v.) at the time of the WR. (III 341)

BREE Town of Men and Hobbits, the principal settlement of the Bree-land. Bree was founded in the Second Age, sometime before the foundation of Arnor in 3320, but its Hobbits did not settle there until about TA 1300. In the days of the glory of Arnor, Bree was an important town, since it was situated at the crossing of the Great East Road and the North Road, but by the time of the WR it had dwindled considerably. However, the Prancing Pony, Bree's ancient and famous inn, was still an important source of news. In the Fourth Age Bree doubtless flourished once more.

Bree was built against Bree Hill. The side not facing the Hill was surrounded by a hedge and a dike. There were two gates in this wall for the entrance and exit of the Great East Road. At the time of the WR Bree contained about a hundred stone houses in which Men lived, and a smaller number of Hobbit dwellings. (I 23, 29, 205-07; III 457, 462, 483, 509)

BREE HILL The big hill in the Bree-land, north of Bree. Also spelled Bree-hill. (I 205, 206; III 332)

BREE-LAND The wooded area at the intersection of the Great East and North Roads, inhabited by Men and Hobbits. The Bree-land contained four villages, Bree, Archet, Staddle, and Combe, and a number of scattered dwellings.

The Bree-land was founded in the Second Age by Men from Dunland, and somehow managed to survive through all the wars of Middle-earth. The Bree-land was part of Arnor and later Arthedain; after the fall of the North-kingdom it was protected by the Rangers of the North. Its economy dwindled when the North-kingdom failed and trade declined, but the Bree-land doubtless revived in the Fourth Age. In any case, its farms provided a comfortable existence for all its inhabitants. (I 205)

BREE RECKONING The calendar system of Bree, similar to the Shire Reckoning (q.v.) except that the first, fourth, sixth, seventh, and ninth through twelfth months were called Frery, Chithing, Lithe, Mede, Harvestmath, Wintring, Blooting, and Yulemath. Also, the Lithes were called the Summerdays. The year 1 of the Bree-reckoning corresponded to TA 1300, the year of the settlement in Bree of Hobbits. (III 482, 483)

BREGALAD (S.: 'swift-tree') (fl. WR)   Ent of Fangorn Forest, physically resembling and caring for rowan trees. Bregalad entertained Merry and Pippin during the Entmoot of TA 3019 because, as a result of Saruman's slaughter of his rowan trees, he had already made up his mind about what course of action should be taken. In general, he thought and acted much more quickly than most Ents, which is how he got his name.

Called in Westron Quickbeam. (II 109-11; L 172)

BREGO (TA 2512-70)   Man, second King of Rohan (2545-70). He drove the last remnants of the Orcs and Balchoth out of the Wold, and built the hall of Meduseld. Brego died of grief over the loss of his son Baldor. (III 84, 85, 434)

BREGOLAS (S.: 'swift-leaf'?) (d. FA 455)   Adan, lord of the First House, son of Bregor. He fell fighting beside Angrod and Aegnor during Dagor Bragollach. (S 148, 151-52, 307; B 177, 182, 381)

BREGOR (S.) (fl. FA 5th Cent.)   Adan, lord of the First House, father of Bregolas and Barahir. He died before Dagor Bragollach. (S 148, 307; B 177, 381)

BREREDON   Village in Buckland, near Haysend. (TB 9, 19)

BRETHIL (S.: 'birch')   Forested area of Beleriand, lying between Sirion and Teiglin. Although outside the Girdle of Melian, Brethil was claimed by Thingol. In the 4th Century FA the Haladin, led by Haleth, settled here and were granted the land in return for guarding the Crossings of Teiglin. For more than a century the Men of Brethil shielded Nargothrond at great cost from the incursions of Orcs, but in 496 Lord Handir and many of his men were slain. After this time, save for the years (496-501) when Túrin lived with them, the Men of Brethil had little might.

Frequently called the Forest of Brethil. (S 120, 147, 155,

157, 195, 212, 216-17, 220, 229; B 142, 176, 187, 190, 238, 260, 266, 271, 282)

BRIDGEFIELDS Area in the Eastfarthing near the Bridge of Stonebows. (I 40)

BRIDGE-HOUSE One of the ugly and uncomfortable Hobbit guardhouses built at the west end of the Brandy-wine Bridge on the site of the Bridge Inn during Lotho's control of the Shire. The Bridge-house had two floors, narrow windows, and inadequate fireplaces. (III 342, 344-45, 348)

BRIDGE INN Inn in the Shire, located on the Great East Road at the west end of the Brandywine Bridge. The inn was torn down during Lotho's control of the Shire. (III 344)

BRIDGE OF ESGALDUIN Iant Iaur (q.v.). (S 132; B 157)

BRIDGE OF MITHEITHEL Three-arched bridge cross-ing the Mitheithel, on the Great East Road.
   The Bridge was called the Last Bridge because it was the easternmost bridge on the Road. (I 268-69, 280)

BRIDGE OF STONEBOWS Bridge across Baranduin, on the Great East Road, built by Arnor.
   Also called the Great Bridge and the Brandywine Bridge; the latter was the most common name, at least among Hobbits, at the time of the WR. (I 23; III 342, 402)

BRILTHOR (S.: 'glittering torrent') River of Os-siriand, a tributary of Gelion. (S 123, 320; B 152, 399)

BRITHIACH (S.: 'gravel-ford') Ford on the upper Sirion, connecting Brethil and Dimbar.
   Also called the Ford of Brithiach. (S 131, 158, 206, 227, 229, 356; B 157, 190-91, 253, 281, 282, 447)

BRITHOMBAR (S.: 'Brithon-dwelling') One of the havens of the Falas, located at the mouth of the River Brithon. Originally built by the Falathrim early in the First Age, Brithombar was later rebuilt and strengthened with the aid of Finrod. In 497 it was taken by siege and destroyed. (S 58, 120, 196, 356; B 60, 142, 239, 447)

BRITHON (S.: 'gravel') River of West Beleriand, flowing south through the Falas and emptying into Belegaer at Brithombar. (S 196; B 239)

BROCKENBORINGS Village in the Eastfarthing near the hills of Scary. During the WR Fredegar Bolger made Brockenborings the headquarters for his band of rebels.
Also called the Brockenbores. (I 40; III 372)

BROCKHOUSE Surname used by Hobbits in Bree and the Shire. (I 52, 212)

BRODDA (d. FA 496) An Easterling. He probably fought for Morgoth in the Nirnaeth Arnoediad and afterward was relocated in Hithlum. There he married Aerin, an Adan of the Third House. Brodda was slain by Túrin in one of his rages. (S 198, 215; B 243, 264)

BROWN A family of working-class Hobbits of the Shire. (III 477)

BROWN LANDS Area between Mirkwood and the Emyn Muil, desolate and treeless. Of old the Entwives made their gardens here, but they were driven away and the land ruined during the war between Sauron and the Last Alliance at the end of the Second Age.
Also called the Noman-lands and the Noman Lands. (I 17, 492; II 100, 302)

BROWNLOCK A family of Hobbits of the Shire, perhaps rather well-to-do. (III 474)

BRUINEN (S.: 'loud-water') River in Eriador, which

joined the Mitheithel at Tharbad to form the Gwathlo. The Bruinen was crossed by the Great East Road at the Ford of Bruinen. The upper reaches of the river were under the control of Elrond, who could cause it to flood whenever an enemy tried to cross it.

Also called the River of Rivendell and, in Westron, Loudwater. (I 16, 268-69, 283-86)

BRYTTA (TA 2752-2842) Man, eleventh King of Rohan (2798-2842). During his reign Rohan was troubled by Orcs driven from the Misty Mountains by the War of the Dwarves and Orcs.

Brytta was called Léofa (tr. Roh.: 'beloved') by his people because of his generosity. (III 435)

BUCCA OF THE MARSH (fl. TA 1979) Hobbit, first Thain of the Shire (1979-?). Bucca was probably the founder of the Oldbuck family. (III 458)

BUCK HILL Hill near Bucklebury in which was delved Brandy Hall. (I 143)

BUCKLAND Area of the Shire, located between the Baranduin and the Old Forest, the folkland of the Brandybucks. Buckland was settled by Gorhendad Oldbuck in TA 2340. Originally outside the Shire, Buckland was officially added to it by the gift of King Elessar in FO 42, and was then known as the East March.

Buckland was ruled by the Master of Buckland, although the rule was of course largely nominal.

Also called "the Buckland." (I 30, 40, 141-42; III 459; TB 8-9)

BUCKLAND GATE Gate in the High Hay, the entrance to Buckland from the Great East Road.

Also called the Hay Gate and the North Gate. (I 239; III 341, 342)

BUCKLEBURY Chief village of Buckland, in central

Buckland about a mile east of the Brandywine. (I 101, 142; L 180)

BUCKLEBURY FERRY   Ferry across the Brandywine between Bucklebury and the Marish. The Ferry was self-operated, and the boat was kept on the east side of the river. (I 40, 138, 141, 142)

BUDGE FORD   Ford across the Water north of Whitfurrows in the Eastfarthing. (I 40)

BUDGEFORD   Village or town in Bridgefields, the Eastfarthing, the main residence of the Bolgers. (I 153; L 180)

BULLROARER   Bandobras Took (q.v.). (H 30)

BUMPKIN (fl. WR)   One of the ponies provided by Merry for Frodo's journey from Buckland to Rivendell in TA 3018. Bumpkin was driven off in Bree, but was later recovered; he spent the rest of his life working for Barliman Butterbur.
Bumpkin was named by Tom Bombadil. (I 155, 198, 199, 242)

BUNCE   A Hobbit family, living in the Shire. At least some Bunces seem to have lived in Michel Delving.
Mrs. Bunce, a character in Sam Gamgee's poem *Perry-the-Winkle,* may have been a historical personage. (III 474; TB 41-42)

BUNDUSHATHÛR (Kh.: 'cloudyhead')   One of the three Mountains of Moria.
Called in Westron Cloudyhead, and by Elves Fanuidhol the Grey. Called Shathûr for short by the Dwarves. (I 370; L 181)

BUNGO BAGGINS (TA 2846-2926)   Hobbit of the Shire, father of Bilbo. Bungo married Belladonna Took about 2880, and built Bag End to be the family residence. (III 474; H 16-17)

BURDEN   The One Ring (q.v.) when borne by Frodo on the Quest of Mount Doom. (I 520)

BURROWS   Hobbit family of the Shire, perhaps well-to-do. Spelled "Burrowes" on H 284. (I 52; III 474; H 284)

BUTCHER   See: Bill Butcher. (TB 42)

BUTTERBUR   A family of Men of Bree, owners of the Prancing Pony. (I 29; L 162)

BYWATER   Village in the Westfarthing, located on the Great East Road about three miles west of the Three-Farthing Stone. In TA 3019 the Battle of Bywater was fought here.
   The chief inn of Bywater was the Green Dragon.
   See: Pool Side, Pool of Bywater. (I 40, 48, 72; III 349 ff.)

BYWATER POOL   The Pool of Bywater (q.v.). (I 40)

BYWATER ROAD   Road leading from the Great East Road through Bywater and then northwest along the Water for about thirty miles. (I 40; III 364, 366)

CABED-EN-ARAS (S.)   Gorge on the River Teiglin, near Dimrost. Túrin slew Glaurung and himself here.
   Cabed-en-Aras was called Cabed Naeramarth after Nienor cast herself into its waters. Also called the Ravines of Teiglin. (S 221-24, 225; B 272-74, 278)

CABED NAERAMARTH (S.: 'leap of dreadful doom')   Later name for Cabed-en-Aras (q.v.). (S 224, 229; B 276, 282, 283)

CAIR ANDROS (S.: 'ship long-foam')   Island in Anduin about fifty miles north of Minas Tirith. Cair Andros was fortified by Gondor about TA 2900 to protect Anórien from attack from the east; the island was captured by an army from the Morannon during the WR but was soon freed.

Cair Andros was shaped like a ship and had a high prow facing upstream against which Anduin broke with much foam. (III 15, 103, 199, 416, 466)

CALACIRIAN (Q.: 'region of Calacirya') That part of Eldamar in and near the entrance to the Calacirya. Here the light from the Two Trees before their poisoning was strongest and the land the most beautiful. Tirion was located here.

The full form of the name was Calaciriande, with the spelling Anglicized from *kalakiryande*. (I 310; R 62)

CALACIRYA (Q.: 'light-cleft') The great ravine in the Pelóri, the only opening in the Mountains, through which the light of the Two Trees flowed eastward into Eldamar. The hill of Túna was set in the Calacirya. After the poisoning of the Two Trees the Valar heavily fortified the pass.

Also called the Pass of Light. (I 489; R 62; S 59, 102, 248; B 62, 117, 307)

CALAQUENDI (Q.: 'light-elves') The Eldar who came to the West early in the First Age and saw the light of the Two Trees. The Calaquendi comprised all of the Vanyar and Noldor, many of the Teleri, and Elwë.

Also called the Elves of the Light. Synonymous with the Amanyar until the end of the First Age. (S 53, 309; B 54, 383)

CALEMBEL (S.) Town in Lamedon, Gondor, near the Ciril. (III 14, 75)

CALENARDHON (S.: 'green region') Area of Gondor between the Anduin and Isen, possibly extending west of the Isen. Largely depopulated by the Great Plague of TA 1636, Calenardhon was overrun by the Balchoth in 2510 and its remaining inhabitants slain or driven away. In that year, Calenardhon was given to the Eothéod by Steward Cirion in return for their services in the Battle of the Field of Celebrant.

For the history of Calenardhon after 2510, see: Rohan. (III 406, 415, 430, 459; S 317; B 394)

CALENDAR OF IMLADRIS   The calendar of the Elves of Rivendell, probably representative of Elvish reckoning in Middle-earth. The yén was divided into 144 loa of six seasons and various extra days. The loa began with yestarë, the first day, which was approximately equivalent to March 29 in the Gregorian calendar. The first three seasons were tuilë, lairë, and yávië, which contained 54, 72, and 54 days, respectively. Then followed three enderi, and then the seasons of quellë (or lasse-lanta), hrívë, and coirë, which also contained 54, 72, and 54 days, respectively. The loa closed with mettarë, the last day.

Every twelfth loa, except the last of every third yén, the enderi were doubled to correct the inaccuracies of this system.

The Calendar of Imladris also contained an astronomical year, the coranar, and a six-day ritual week, the enquië (qq.v.).

Also called the Reckoning of Rivendell. (I 480, 486)

CALENHAD (S.)   The sixth of the northern beacon-tower hills of Gondor. (III 14, 20)

CALIMEHTAR (Q.: 'light—')   (fl. TA 14th Cent.) Dúnadan of Gondor, younger brother of Rómendacil II and grandfather of Castamir. (III 406)

CALIMEHTAR (d. TA 1936)   Dúnadan, thirtieth King of Gondor (1856-1936). In 1899, Calimehtar won a great victory over the Wainriders, who were weakened by a rebellion in Rhovanion. (III 395, 409)

CALIMMACIL (Q.) (fl. TA 19th-20th Cent.)   Dúnadan

of the royal house of Gondor, nephew of King Narmacil II and grandfather of Eärnil II. (III 410)

CALION, TAR- (Q.) The unused Elvish name of Ar-Pharazôn (q.v.). (S 270; B 333)

CALMA (Q.: 'lamp') Name for the tengwa **ᴄ𝑓** (number 3). (III 498, 500)

CALMACIL, TAR- (Q.: 'lamp-bright spark'?) (d. SA 2899) Dúnadan, eighteenth King of Númenor (?-2899). (III 390)

CALMACIL (d. TA 1304) Dúnadan, eighteenth King of Gondor (1294-1304). During his reign Gondor was governed by his son, Minalcar. (III 395, 404)

CALMATÉMA (Q.: 'calma-series') Name given to the velar stops and spirants (*k, g, kh, gh*) by Elvish grammarians. The calmatéma was usually represented by téma III or IV of the Tengwar. The values for the fifth and sixth grades of the calmatéma were optional, but were usually velars. (III 496-7, 500)

CAMELLIA BAGGINS (fl. TA 2900) Hobbit of the Shire. She was born a Sackville, but married Longo Baggins. She bore him one son, Otho Sackville-Baggins. (III 474)

CAMLOST (S.: 'hand-empty') Name given by Beren (q.v.) to himself after he lost the Silmaril and the right hand which held it to Carcharoth. (S 184, 356; B 224, 447)

CAPE BALAR Cape in western Arvernien dividing the Bay of Balar from Belegaer. (S Map)

CAPE OF ANDRAST See: Andrast. (PB)

CAPE OF FOROCHEL Headland shutting off the northwest side of the Ice Bay of Forochel (q.v.), the refuge of the Lossoth. (III 399)

CAPTAIN OF DESPAIR The Lord of the Nazgûl (q.v.). (III 112)

CAPTAIN OF MORGOTH One of the commanders of the armies of Morgoth, specifically the leader of the western forces during the first stage of the Nirnaeth Arnoediad. By butchering Gelmir he induced the forces of Fingon to leave their fortified positions. (S 191; B 234)

CAPTAIN OF SAURON The Lord of the Nazgûl (q.v.) as commander of Sauron's armies during the Siege of Gondor and the Battle of the Pelennor Fields. (S 303; B 377)

CAPTAIN OF SHIPS The title of the head of the fleets of Gondor. (III 406)

CAPTAIN OF THE HAVEN Title of the ruler or of some high person of Umbar, in TA 2980. (III 417)

CAPTAIN OF THE HOSTS Chief military leader of the forces of Gondor. (III 403)

CAPTAIN OF THE SOUTHERN ARMY Title of the commander of the Southern Army of Gondor. The only Captain named in *LotR* is Eärnil, who held the post prior to his election to the throne in TA 1945. (III 409)

CAPTAIN OF THE WHITE TOWER Title of the head of the Guards of the Citadel, a position traditionally held in the time of the Ruling Stewards by the heir of the Steward, and probably in the time of the Kings by the heir to the throne. (III 419)

CAPTAINS OF THE WEST The leaders of the Army of the West. The Captains were King Éomer of Rohan, Aragorn, Prince Imrahil of Dol Amroth, Gandalf, and perhaps Elladan and Elrohir. Aragorn was the chief Captain.

The Captains were also called the Lords of the West,

although this term may have referred only to Aragorn, Éomer, and Imrahil. (III 193, 198 ff.)

CARACH ANGREN (S.: 'jaws of iron') Isenmouthe (q.v.). (III 241; S 357; B 447)

CARADHRAS (S.: 'red-horn') Elvish name for Barazinbar (q.v.). (I 370; III 487)

CARAGDUR (S.: 'fang-dark') Precipice of black rock in Gondolin, located on the north side of Amon Gwareth. Here Eöl and Maeglin were thrown to their deaths. (S 138, 243, 357; B 165, 301, 447)

CARANTHIR (S.: 'red—') (d. FA 6th Cent.) Noldorin Elf, fourth son of Fëanor. With his brothers he took the Oath of Fëanor and suffered the Doom of the Noldor (qq.v.). In Middle-earth Caranthir settled in Thargelion, where he grew rich from trade with the Dwarves of Ered Luin. His dwelling was at Lake Helevorn, and his people fortified the mountains east of Maglor's Gap.

When Thargelion was overrun by Orcs during Dagor Bragollach, Caranthir fled south to join Amrod and Amras. Later he took the treacherous sons of Ulfang into his service. He fought with the eastern forces in the Nirnaeth Arnoediad, was wounded, and later came to Ossiriand. Caranthir was slain by Dior at Menegroth when he and his brothers tried to recover the Silmaril.

Caranthir was haughty, the harshest and most quick to anger of the sons of Fëanor. He hated the sons of Finarphin. His complexion was dark. (S 60, 83, 112-13, 124, 145-46, 153, 157, 192-93, 195, 236, 305; B 64, 93, 131-32, 148, 174-75, 184, 189, 235, 238, 292, 379)

CARAS GALADON (S.: 'city of the trees') Chief city of Lórien, site of the court of Celeborn and Galadriel. Caras Galadon consisted of many large telain in a walled grove of very large mellyrn. The city was deserted at the end of the Third Age with the passing of Galadriel and the removal of Celeborn to East Lórien.

The name of the city was probably of Silvan origin, adapted to Sindarin. Called in Westron the City of the Trees. (I 455-56, 457-80; III 468, 506)

CARC (fl. TA 2770)   Raven of Erebor, friendly with the Dwarves of the Mountain. (H 244)

CARCHAROTH (S.: 'fang—')   (d. FA 468)   Wolf, the mightiest that ever walked in the world. Carcharoth was bred by Morgoth from the line of Draugluin to be the bane of Huan, and he was set to guard the doors of Angband. He was placed under a spell by Lúthien when she and Beren entered Angband, but he barred their exit and bit off Beren's right hand, swallowing it and the Silmaril. Crazed by the burning heat of the jewel, Carcharoth ran wild through Taur-nu-Fuin and Doriath. Finally, in the Hunting of the Wolf Carcharoth slew Beren and Huan but was himself slain by the great hound.

Also called Anfauglir, the Wolf of Angband, and the Red Maw, an alternate translation of Carcharoth. (I 260; S 179-82, 184-86, 357; B 218-21, 223-26, 447)

CARCHOST (S.: 'fang-citadel')   One of the Towers of the Teeth (q.v.). (III 215; S 357; B 447)

CARDOLAN (S.: 'red-hill-land'?)   Kingdom, one of the divisions of Arnor, founded in TA 861. Cardolan included all the land south of the Great East Road between Baranduin and Gwathlo-Mitheithel. The Dúnedain of Cardolan defended their land against Angmar until 1409, when the country was overrun and the surviving Dúnedain were forced to take refuge in the Old Forest or the Barrowdowns. In this war the last prince of Cardolan was killed, but when Angmar was for a time defeated by the Elves, the people of Cardolan returned to their homes. In 1636, the Great Plague killed the last of the Dúnedain of Cardolan, and large portions of the country, especially Minhiriath in the south, were depopulated. After this time Cardolan does not seem to have existed as a nation, although there were doubtless still scattered settlements there at the time of the WR. (III 396, 397, 398; S 291; B 360)

CARL (b. TA 2863) Working-class Hobbit of the Shire, the second son of Cottar. (III 477)

CARL COTTON (b. TA 2989) Hobbit of the Shire, youngest son of Tolman Cotton. He was usually called Nibs. (III 354, 477)

CARN DÛM (S.) Fortress and chief city of Angmar, located at the northern end of the Misty Mountains. (I 198, 201; III 412)

CARNEN (S.: 'red-water') River flowing from its source in the Iron Hills into the River Running. The Carnen was about 250 miles long. The name of the river formed by the confluence of the Carnen and the River Running is not given.
  Called in Westron the Redwater. (III 440)

CARNIL (Q.: 'red—') One of the stars wrought by Varda in preparation for the awakening of the Elves. Carnil was red. (S 48, 321; B 48, 400)

CARNÍMIRIË (Q.: 'red-jeweled') Rowan tree of Fangorn Forest, cut down by Orcs of Isengard near the end of the Third Age. (II 110; S 357; B 447)

CARROCK A great rock in the Anduin about thirty miles north of the Old Ford. Beorn carved steps and a high seat in the Carrock and ofter came there. (H 116-17)

CASTAMIR (Q.: '—jewel') (d. TA 1447) Dúnadan, twenty-second King of Gondor (1437-47). The grandson of a younger brother of Rómendacil II, at the time of the Kin-strife he was Captain of Ships. He aided in the overthrow of King Eldacar, and as the most popular of the rebels (he commanded the loyalty of the entire fleet and of the peoples of the coasts), he was made King. However,

Castamir proved to be a cruel and arrogant ruler. He put Eldacar's captured son Ornendil to death and lavished all his affection on the fleet, ignoring the land and the army. In the tenth year of his reign, therefore, when Eldacar returned, the people of inland Gondor rebelled against Castamir. He attempted to flee, but was caught and slain by Eldacar in the Battle of the Crossings of Erui.

He was known as Castamir the Usurper. (III 395, 406)

CAT   A traditional Shire-poem, reworked by Sam Gamgee. (TB 7, 51)

CATBARION   An error for Oatbarton (q.v.). (I 40)

CAUSEWAY   Road in the Shire, going through Deephallow, Stock, and Rushey. (I 138; TB 9, 20)

CAUSEWAY   Walled road in Gondor, leading from Osgiliath to Minas Tirith. (III 23, 97)

CAUSEWAY FORTS   Fortifications in the Rammas Echor guarding the Causeway at the time of the WR. The Causeway Forts were guarded by Faramir against the army of the Lord of the Nazgûl during the WR, but they were easily captured.

Also called the Guard-towers. (III 23, 97, 110, 467)

CAVERNS OF HELM'S DEEP   The Aglarond (q.v.). (II 193-95)

CAVERNS OF NAROG   Caves under the High Faroth on the west bank of the River Narog. First explored and worked by the Noegyth Nibin, the Caverns were later the site of Nargothrond (q.v.).

Called in Khuzdul Nulukkizdîn. (S 114, 204, 230; B 134, 250, 284)

CAVES OF MENEGROTH   Menegroth (q.v.). (S 121-22)

CAVES OF THE FORGOTTEN Caves in which Ar-Pharazôn and those of his soldiers who landed on Aman were entombed in the upheavals of the Change of the World. (S 279; B 345)

CELANDINE BRANDYBUCK (b. TA 2994) Hobbit of the Shire, youngest child and only daughter of Seredic Brandybuck. She was a guest at the Farewell Party. (III 476)

CELDUIN (S.: 'running-river') The River Running (q.v.). (III 405)

CELEBDIL (S.: 'silvertine') Elvish name for Zirak-zigil (q.v.). Also Celebdil the White. (I 370)

CELEBORN (S.: 'silver-tree') (FA-   ) Sindarin Elf, a prince of Doriath and kinsman of Elwë. He married Galadriel in Doriath and probably fled with her to Arvernien after the fall of Doriath.
   At the end of the First Age, Celeborn decided to remain in Middle-earth, and he dwelt in Lindon for a while. After that, he and Galadriel went to Eregion; they later settled Lórien, where Celeborn was for long Lord of the Galadrim. During the WR Celeborn led the army of Lórien that took Dol Guldur. In the Fourth Age, he was for a while King of East Lórien, but without Galadriel he grew weary of Middle-earth and went to Rivendell. Perhaps after that he went over Sea.
   Although Celeborn was an Elven-lord of great fame and was called Celeborn the Wise, in *LotR* he does not seem especially bright. (I 39, 459-62; III 452, 468; R 60; S 115, 234, 254; B 134-35, 290, 315)

CELEBORN White Tree, a seedling of Galathilion. It grew in Tol Eressëa, and from it sprang Nimloth. (I 321; S 59, 263; B 62, 324)

CELEBRANT (S.: 'silver-course') Fair river flowing from springs in Nanduhirion through Lórien and into

Anduin. Its tributaries included Nimrodel and other mountain streams.

Also called Silverlode in Westron and Kibil-nâla in Khuzdul. (I 370, 434 ff., 449; RHM III 430; L 191)

CELEBRÍAN (S.: 'silver—') (FA-) Eldarin lady, daughter and seemingly only child of Celeborn and Galadriel. In TA 100 she wed Elrond; she bore him three children: Elladan, Elrohir, and Arwen. In 2509, while traveling from Imladris to Lórien, her party was ambushed by Orcs in the Misty Mountains. Celebrían was soon rescued by her sons, but a poisoned wound caused her to go over Sea the next year. (I 300, 486; III 401, 456, 459)

CELEBRIMBOR (S.: 'silver-fist, Hand of Silver') (FA-SA 1697) Noldorin Elf of the House of Fëanor, son of Curufin. After the death of Finrod he repudiated the deeds of his House and remained in Nargothrond.

In the Second Age Celebrimbor remained in Middle-earth and became lord of Eregion and the greatest craftsman of that land. Yet in the end his skill betrayed him, for he joined with the disguised Sauron to make the Rings of Power; Celebrimbor was the sole forger of the Three Rings. When Sauron forged the One Ring, Celebrimbor perceived his treachery, hid the Three Rings, and prepared for war. He was slain when Eregion was overrun during the War of the Elves and Sauron.

The Quenya form of his name was Telperinquar. (I 318, 332, 398; III 453-54; S 176, 286, 288, 321, 357; B 214, 354, 357, 400, 447)

CELEBRINDAL (S.: 'silverfoot') The epithet of Idril (q.v.). (S 126, 357; B 151, 447)

CELEBRINDOR (S.: 'silver—') (d. TA 1272) Dúnadan, fifth King of Arthedain (1191-1272). (III 394)

CELEBROS (S.: 'silver-foam') Stream in Brethil. It fell into Teiglin by the Dimrost. (S 220; B 270)

CELEGORM (S.) (d. FA 6th Cent.) Noldorin Elf, the third son of Fëanor. With his brothers he took the Oath of Fëanor and suffered the Doom of the Noldor (qq.v.). On his return to Middle-earth Celegorm played a major role in the victory of Dagor-nuin-Giliath and later guarded Aglon and Himlad with his brother Curufin. When their forces were overwhelmed during Dagor Bragollach, they fled to Nargothrond.

There the two brothers opposed Finrod in his desire to aid Beren in the Quest of the Silmaril, vowing anew the Oath of Fëanor. They probably had designs on the throne of Finrod. Soon after, the brothers met Lúthien and Celegorm fell in love with her, forced her to come to Nargothrond with him, and sent word to Thingol that he planned to marry her. Celegorm and Curufin were banished from Nargothrond when their plots were exposed. On their way to seek Maedhros the brothers tried to kill Beren but were foiled by the valor of the Adan and the integrity of Huan, who turned on his master Celegorm.

Celegorm was wounded fighting with the eastern forces in the Nirnaeth Arnoediad, and afterward lived in Ossiriand. He was slain by Dior at Menegroth when at his instigation he and his brothers tried to recover the Silmaril.

Like his brothers, Celegorm was overly proud; he acted more by force than by deceit. In Valinor he learned much about animals and hunting from Oromë, who gave him Huan. His complexion was fair. (S 60, 62, 83, 107, 123, 152, 169-70, 172-73, 176-77, 192-93, 195, 236, 305; B 63, 65-66, 93, 124, 147, 183, 205-06, 208-10, 213-15, 235, 238, 292, 379)

CELEPHARN (S.) (d. TA 1191) Dúnadan, fourth King of Arthedain (1110-91). (III 394)

CELON (S.: 'stream flowing down from heights') Small river of Beleriand, rising at Himring and flowing southwest past Nan Elmoth until it emptied into the Aros. (S 96, 124, 135, 322, 360; B 109, 148, 161, 400, 452)

CELOS (S.: 'flowing-snow'?) River in southern Gondor,

flowing from its sources in the Ered Nimrais into the Sirith. The Celos was about 60 miles long.
Also spelled Kelos. (III 14, 185)

CEMENDUR (Q.: 'earth-lord') (d. TA 238)   Dúnadan, fourth King of Gondor (158-238). (III 394)

CEORL (fl. WR)   Man, a Rider of Rohan. He fought under Erkenbrand in the Second Battle of the Fords of Isen. (II 167-68)

CERIN AMROTH (S.)   Hill in Lothlórien where Amroth had his house. By the time of the WR, the house was no longer there, and the hill was covered with grass, elanor, and niphredil. Aragorn and Arwen plighted their troth on Cerin Amroth, and here Arwen came to die. (I 454; III 425, 428)

CERMIË (Q.)   Seventh month of the Kings' and Stewards' Reckonings and the fourth of the New Reckoning, corresponding roughly to our July.
    The Sindarin form of the name, used only by the Dúnedain, was Cerveth. (III 483)

CERTAR (Q.: 'runes')   The Cirth (q.v.). (III 493)

CERTHAS DAERON (S.: 'runes of Daeron')   The original form of the cirth (q.v.) developed during the third age of the Chaining of Morgoth by Daeron of Doriath along the lines of the Tengwar. (III 500; S 95, 226; B 108, 278)

CERVETH (S.)   Cermië (q.v.). (III 483)

CHAINING OF MELKOR   The imprisonment of Melkor after the Battle of the Powers, when he was bound with Angainor and placed in the halls of Mandos for three ages.
    This period coincided roughly with the Noontide of Valinor. (S 51-52, 63, 65, 91-92; B 53, 67, 70, 104)

CHAMBER OF MAZARBUL (Kh.: 'records') The Chamber of Records of Khazad-dûm, the center of Balin's Dwarf-colony. Balin's throne and tomb were here, and here the last members of his colony were slain. During the Quest the Fellowship of the Ring recovered the records of the Dwarf-colony, but they were attacked by Orcs. They retreated through the east door of the Chamber, but when Gandalf attempted to guard the door against the Balrog, it and the roof of the Chamber collapsed.

The Chamber was on the Seventh Level, and was the Twenty-first Hall of the North-end. (I 415-25)

CHAMBERS OF FIRE The Sammath Naur (q.v.). (III 269)

CHANGE OF THE WORLD The removing of Aman from Arda in SA 3319 at the destruction of Númenor, when new seas and continents were formed from Ekkaia and the Empty Lands, and Arda became a globe. (S 48, 101, 102, 279; B 48, 116, 118, 345)

CHETWOOD The forest of the Bree-land. (I 23, 205, 245-46)

CHICA BAGGINS (fl. TA 2900) Hobbit of the Shire, wife of Bingo Baggins and mother of Falco Chubb-Baggins. She was born a Chubb. (III 474)

CHIEF, THE Name by which Lotho Sackville-Baggins was known during his control of the Shire, short for Chief Shirriff. (III 343, 360)

CHIEF'S MEN Those Men who during the WR served Lotho Sackville-Baggins and, when he came to the Shire, Saruman. They were offensive, coarse, ugly, and greedy.

The Chief's Men seem to have been a motly assortment of ruffians, at least some of whom were agents of Saruman's before the WR. They tended to be squint-eyed, sallow-faced, and otherwise esthetically displeasing; they may have been selected from among the more mannish of Saruman's Half-orcs.

Also called Sharkey's Men. (III 347-73 passim)

CHIEFTAINS OF THE DÚNEDAIN OF THE NORTH
The rulers of the Dúnedain of the North after the fall of Arthedain, the heirs of Arvedui, last king of Arthedain. The line of the Chieftains never failed, and most of them lived out their full lifespan despite the fact that they were almost continually involved in the struggle to protect Eriador from Orcs and other evil creatures. The waning of the lifespan of the Chieftains was slower than that of the Dúnedain of Gondor. The sixteenth and last Chieftain was Aragorn II, who became King of the Reunited Kingdom after the WR.

The Chieftains were raised in Imladris, and the heirlooms of their house, the Line of Isildur, were also kept there. (III 394, 400-02)

CHILDREN OF EARTH The Children of Ilúvatar (q.v.). (S 249; B 308)

CHILDREN OF ERU The Children of Ilúvatar (q.v.). (S 26; B 19)

CHILDREN OF HURIN Túrin and Nienor (qq.v.), victims of the curse of Morgoth on their father. (S 226; B 278)

CHILDREN OF ILÚVATAR Elves and Men (qq.v.), conceived by Ilúvatar alone in the third theme of the Ainulindalë. Arda was prepared as their habitation and they were given the dominion over all other created things in Arda.

Elves were the Elder Children, the Firstborn, and Men were the Younger Children, the Followers.

Also called the Híni Ilúvataro, the Eruhíni, and the Erusén; the Children of Eru and of God; the Children of Earth, of the Earth, and of the World; and the Two

Kindreds. (S 15, 18, 20, 41, 45, 48, 322; B 4, 7, 10, 37, 43, 48, 400)

CHILDREN OF THE EARTH The Children of Ilúvatar (q.v.), or perhaps only the Elves. (S 48; B 48)

CHILDREN OF THE SUN Men (q.v.). (S 103; B 119)

CHILDREN OF THE WORLD The Children of Ilúvatar (q.v.). (S 166; B 201)

CHITHING Name given Astron (q.v.) in Bree. (III 483)

CHUBB A family of Hobbits of the Shire, probably rather well-to-do. (I 52; III 474, 475)

CHUBB-BAGGINS A family of Hobbits in the Shire, tracing its descent from Falco, the son of Bingo Baggins and Chica Chubb. (III 474)

CIRCLES OF THE WORLD When capitalized, the confines of Eä, the limit of the Ainulindalë; Ilúvatar is beyond the Circles of the World. The "confines of the world" refers to the same thing. (S 187, 253, 265; B 228, 313, 327)
    When not capitalized, the phrase frequently refers to the limits of the sphere of Arda after the Change of the World; in this sense Aman is beyond the circles of the world. (III 389, 392, 519)
    The dying words of Aragorn are ambiguous; on III 427 he seems to use the phrase "circles of the world" to mean Arda as opposed to Aman, but on III 428 he clearly refers to the uncertain ultimate fate of Men and Elves, which may lead beyond Eä.

CÍRDAN (S.: 'ship-maker') Elf, one of the wisest of the Sindar, in the First Age lord of the Falas, a mariner and shipwright. Círdan long avoided the quarrels of the

Noldor and Sindar and was especially friendly with Elwë, who was probably his overlord, and Finrod.

The Falas, with its havens of Eglarest and Brithombar, prospered until FA 474, when it was overrun. Círdan withdrew to the Isle of Balar, and for the rest of the First Age succored the remnants of the Elves and Edain of Beleriand, notably Gil-galad and Elwing. He built Vingilot for Eärendil.

In the Second and Third Ages Círdan was Lord of the Grey Havens and possessed Narya, one of the Three Rings, from its making until he gave it to Gandalf when the latter came to Middle-earth. Círdan fought against Sauron with the army of the Last Alliance, and in the Third Age frequently aided the Dúnedain of the North. He was also a member of the White Council. It is said that he remained in Middle-earth, serving with his wisdom and his ships, until the sailing of the last white ship sometime in the Fourth Age.

Círdan was very tall; at the end of the Third Age he had a long beard and looked old. (I 315, 320; III 383-84, 396, 397, 411, 456; S 58, 92, 96, 120, 128, 196, 212, 244, 246, 247, 254, 298, 299, 300, 304; B 60, 105, 109, 142, 153, 239, 240, 260, 302, 304, 305, 315, 370, 372, 373, 378)

CIRIL (S.)   River in Lamedon, Gondor, flowing into the Ringló. Also spelled Kiril. (III 14, 75, 184)

CIRION (S.: 'ship—')   (d. TA 2567) Dúnadan, twelfth Ruling Steward of Gondor (2489-2567). During his reign Gondor was greatly troubled by its enemies, chiefly the Corsairs of Umbar and the Balchoth, and although Cirion was an able ruler, Gondor did not have the strength to repel its foes. However, with the unexpected aid of the Rohirrim, in 2510 Cirion won the Battle of the Field of Celebrant, which ended the Balchoth threat. Cirion then granted Calenardhon to the Rohirrim in return for the Oath of Eorl. This alliance greatly aided both kingdoms, and without it Gondor probably would have been overwhelmed in the WR, or even earlier. (III 395, 415)

CIRITH GORGOR (S.: 'pass haunted') Great pass into Mordor at the meeting of the Ered Lithui and the Ephel Dúath. The great gate of the Morannon was built across the pass, which connected Dagorlad and Udûn. Cirith Gorgor was further guarded by the Towers of the Teeth.

Called in Westron the Haunted Pass. (II 308; III 258)

CIRITH NINNIACH (S.: 'rainbow cleft') Gorge in the Ered Lómin at the head of Drengist. (S 238)

CIRITH THORONATH (S.: 'cleft of the eagles') Narrow and dangerous pass in the northern side of the Echoriath. Tuor, Idril, Eärendil, and the survivors of Gondolin escaped over this pass. (S 243; B 294)

CIRITH UNGOL (S.: 'pass of the spider') Pass over the Ephel Dúath just north of Minas Morgul, guarded by the Tower of Cirith Ungol. This pass was used in TA 2000 by the Nazgûl when they issued forth from Mordor to besiege Minas Ithil, and also by Frodo during the Quest to get into Mordor. Although well-guarded, it was an easier route to travel undetected than was the main pass behind Minas Ithil.

Cirith Ungol was actually only the road and cleft east of Shelob's Lair, but in common usage the term referred to the entire path from Imlad Morgul to the Morgai.

Also called the High Pass by Sam Gamgee. Also spelled Kirith Ungol. (II 380-81, 382, 403 ff.; III 15, 212 ff.)

CIRTH (S.: 'runes') Alphabet devised by Daeron of Doriath in the third age of the Chaining of Morgoth, intended for inscriptions. Although little used by the Sindar until near the end of the First Age, the cirth were quickly adopted by the Dwarves, who spread them throughout Middle-earth.

The original cirth formed an unsystematic mode, as did all of its descendants (see: Angerthas Moria) except the Angerthas Daeron (q.v.).

Called certar in Quenya and runes in Westron. (III 493, 495, 500-04; S 95; B 108)

CIRYAHER (Q.: 'ship-lord') See: Hyarmendacil I. (III 395)

CIRYANDIL (Q.: 'ship-lover') (d. TA 1015) Dúnadan, fourteenth King of Gondor (936-1015) and the third Ship-king. Ciryandil continued his father's policy of building ships, but was killed in Haradwaith while fighting the Haradrim. (III 395, 403)

CIRYATAN, TAR- (Q.: 'ship-builder') (d. SA 2251) Dúnadan, twelfth King of Númenor. During his reign the Númenoreans began to speak openly against the Ban of the Valar and to colonize and subjugate the coasts of Middle-earth. (III 390; S 265; B 327)

CIRYON (Q.: 'ship—') (d. TA 2) Dúnadan, third son of Isildur. He was slain in the Battle of the Gladden Fields. (S 295; B 366)

CITADEL The seventh level of Minas Tirith, containing the Place of the Fountain and the White Tower.
Also called the High City. (III 25, 26 ff.)

CITADEL OF THE STARS Osgiliath (q.v.). (I 321)

CITY, THE Minas Tirith (q.v.). (I 330)

CITY OF THE CORSAIRS The city of Umbar (q.v.). (I 17)

CITY OF THE TREES Caras Galadon (q.v.). (I 458)

CLEFT The narrow path, surrounded on either side by sheer cliffs, at the top of Cirith Ungol. (II 435, 436)

CLOSED DOOR Fen Hollen (q.v.). (III 123)

CLOUD OF UNGOLIANT The Unlight (q.v.). (S 76; B 85)

CLOUDYHEAD Westron name for Bundushathûr (q.v.). (I 370)

COIMAS (Q.: 'life-bread') Lembas (q.v.). (S 338; B 421)

COIRË (Q.: 'stirring') The last division of the Eldarin loa (q.v.), corresponding to our February and March. Called in Sindarin echuir. (III 480)

COLD-DRAKE A kind of dragon, found in the Ered Mithrin. In TA 2589 a cold-drake slew King Dáin I and drove Durin's Folk out of the Ered Mithrin. (III 440)

COLDFELLS Wild region north of Rivendell, perhaps the Ettenmoors. (III 420)

COMBE Village in a valley in the eastern Bree-land. (I 205, 245)

COMMON SPEECH Westron (q.v.), so called because it was the *lingua franca* of Middle-earth beginning in the late Second Age. (I 23; III 508)

COMPANIONS OF THE RING The members of the Company of the Ring (q.v.). (III 306)

COMPANY OF THE RING The company of Free Peoples which accompanied Frodo Baggins on the first stage of the Quest of Mount Doom. The Company was composed of Frodo, Sam Gamgee, Peregrin Took, and Merry Brandybuck, representing Hobbits; Aragorn II and Boromir, representing Men; Legolas, representing Elves; Gimli, representing Dwarves, and Gandalf. The Company did not plan to accompany Frodo all the way to Mordor; Boromir was going to Minas Tirith, and the plans of some of the other Companions were uncertain. As the Company was deliberating its course of action on Amon Hen, it was broken by Boromir's attempt to seize the Ring and by an attack of Orcs. Boromir was slain and Merry and Pippin captured by the Orcs. Aragorn, Legolas, and Gimli followed the Orcs, while Frodo and Sam continued the Quest. Gandalf, the leader of the Company, had earlier been lost in Khazad-dûm.

Also called the Companions of the Ring, which referred specifically to the members of the Company, the Fellowship of the Ring, the Nine Walkers (as opposed to the Nine Riders, the Nazgûl), and the Nine Companions. (I 360; III 320)

CORMALLEN See: Field of Cormallen.

CORMARË (Q.: 'ring-day') Feast-day of the New Reckoning, falling on Frodo's birthday, Yavannië 30. In leap years Cormarë was doubled. (III 486)

COROLLAIRË (Q.: 'mound of summer' or 'green mound') Ezellohar (q.v.). (S 38, 357; B 33, 448)

CORANAR (Q.: 'sun-round') A period, corresponding to one astronomical year, observed by the Eldar in Middle-earth.

Also called a Year of the Sun. (III 480; S 103; B 119)

CORSAIRS OF UMBAR Name given to any of the groups of pirates and raiders based at Umbar, among the greatest enemies of Gondor. The first Corsairs were Black Númenoreans and their allies, whose attack on Gondor began before TA 933. After the Kin-strife, Umbar was seized by the defeated followers of Castamir, who soon became Corsairs and raided Gondor's coasts until 1810, when King Telumehtar Umbardacil took Umbar and killed the last descendants of Castamir. Umbar was soon lost to Men of Harad, who again quickly became Corsairs. From this time, Umbar was merely one of the kingdoms of Harad, although because of their sea-power the Corsairs were always an immediate threat to Gondor. The Corsairs were probably destroyed by King Elessar at the beginning of the Fourth Age.

The Corsairs at the time of the WR sailed in ships with

black sails. (III 148-49, 186-87, 403, 406-07, 408, 415, 417; L 162)

COTMAN (b. TA 2860) Working-class Hobbit of the Shire, who gave his name to the Cotton family, his descendants.

Cotman's real name, in Hobbitish, was Hlothram, which meant 'cottager.' (III 477, 520)

COTTAR (b. TA 2820) Working-class Hobbit of the Shire, father of Cotman and Carl. (III 477)

COTTON Working-class family in the Shire, at least some of whose members were farmers. At the time of the WR, Tolman Cotton was one of the most prominent Hobbits in Bywater, and as a result of his role in the Battle of Bywater and the close connection of his family with the Gamgees, the family at this time became quite influential and rather well-to-do.

The real name of the family, in genuine Hobbitish, was Hlothran, which was derived from Hlothram (Cotman), the first member of the family, or from the village of Hlothran (q.v.). (III 365, 477, 520; L 162)

COUNCIL The White Council (q.v.). (I 328)

COUNCIL OF ELROND Council held at Rivendell on November 25, TA 3019, to discuss the Rings of Power, especially the One Ring, and to answer questions of various groups of Free Peoples. Those in attendance included Elrond, who presided; Gandalf; Glorfindel, Erestor, and other counsellors of Elrond's household; Frodo; Bilbo; Sam, who was not invited; Glóin and Gimli, come to seek counsel for the Dwarves of Erebor; Galdor, representing Círdan; Legolas, representing Thranduil; and Boromir, who had come to Rivendell seeking the answer to the dream he and Faramir had had.

The Council learned of the state of the West and Sauron's preparations for war, the treachery of Saruman, the escape of Gollum, and the history of the Rings and Sauron's attempts to recover the One. The outcome of the Council was the decision to destroy the Ring in the Sammath Naur, and Frodo's undertaking of this Quest of Mount Doom. (I 314-55)

COUNCIL OF GONDOR Council of the highest officials of Gondor, both civil and military, serving the Kings and Ruling Stewards in an advisory capacity. (III 108, 409)

COUNCIL OF THE NORTH-KINGDOM Advisory body to the Kings of Arnor and Arthedain. In FO 14 the Thain and Mayor of the Shire and the Master of Buckland were made Counsellors. (III 471)

COUNCIL OF THE WISE Any of the gatherings of the Wise (q.v.), particularly the White Council (q.v.). (I 83; S 300; B 373)

COUNT OF TIME The recording of years, which began with the creation of the Two Trees and the cycles of the Years of the Trees (q.v.). (S 39; B 34)

COURT OF THE FOUNTAIN Plaza in the Citadel of Minas Tirith containing a fountain in the middle of which stood the White Tree, or the Withered Tree.
Also called the Place of the Fountain. (III 25, 26, 27)

CRACK OF DOOM The great volcanic rent in the floor of the Sammath Naur of Orodruin. In the depths of the Crack of Doom burned the Fire of Doom, the flame in which the One Ring was forged and the only flame in which it could be unmade.
Also called the Cracks of Doom. (I 94; III 274-76)

CRAM Traveling food prepared by the Men of Esgaroth, a hard and tasteless but very nutritious biscuit or small cake. (I 478; H 232, 247)

CREBAIN (S.) Black crows of Fangorn and Dunland.

At the time of the WR they were controlled by Saruman and were used by him as spies.

The crebain may not actually have come from Fangorn; at the time Aragorn made this claim he had never been to the Forest.

The singular form of the word is *craban*. (I 372-74; II 48)

CRICKHOLLOW Place in Buckland, north of Bucklebury. The Brandybucks had a house here, in which Frodo stayed after leaving Hobbiton in TA 3018. (I 40, 101, 143-44)

CRISSAEGRIM (S.: 'cleft—') Mountains south of Gondolin, probably part of the Echoriath. Inaccessible to creatures that walk, the Crissaegrim were the home of the Eagles of Manwë. (S 121, 154, 200, 363; B 144, 186, 246, 455)

CROSSINGS OF ERUI Ford across the Erui in Lebennin, site of a major battle during the Kin-strife. (III 15, 406)

CROSSINGS OF ISEN The Fords of Isen (q.v.). (III 432)

CROSSINGS OF POROS Ford across the Poros on the Harad Road, site of a great victory over the Haradrim by Gondor in TA 2885. (III 15, 416)

CROSSINGS OF TEIGLIN Ford in Brethil on the road from Nargothrond to East Beleriand and the Pass of Sirion, apparently the only place where the River Teiglin could be forded. Of great strategic importance for the defense of Nargothrond, the Crossings were guarded by the Haladin and, for a few years, by Túrin. The Crossings were the site of numerous battles between the Haladin and Orcs. (S 147, 205, 216, 217, 219, 223, 229; B 176, 252, 266, 267, 269, 275, 282)

CROSS-ROADS OF THE FALLEN KING The crossing of the Morannon-Harad and Morgul-Osgiliath roads, in central Ithilien. In the early Third Age the Men of Gondor grew tall trees about the Cross-roads and set up a statue of a crowned king. The statue was later despoiled by the servants of Sauron, but it was restored during the WR by the Army of the West. (II 395; III 196-97)

CUIVIÉNEN (Q.: 'awakening-water') Bay on the eastern shore of Helcar (q.v.), lying at the foot of the Orocarni near the Wild Wood. The Elves first awoke by its shores. Cuiviénen was ruined sometimes, perhaps in the Change of the World. (S 48-49, 51, 53; B 48, 51, 54)

CULUMALDA (Q.: 'golden red tree') A type of tree growing in Ithilien at the Field of Cormallen. (S 361; B 453)

CULÚRIEN (Q.: 'golden-red-hot—'?) Laurelin (q.v.). (S 38, 357; B 33, 448)

CURTAIN The Window-curtain (q.v.). (II 370)

CURUFIN (Q.?: 'skill—') (d. FA 6th Cent.) Noldorin Elf, the fifth son of Fëanor and father of Celebrimbor. With his brothers he took the Oath of Fëanor and suffered the Doom of the Noldor (qq.v.).

On his return to Middle-earth Curufin guarded Aglon and Himlad with his brother Celegorm (q.v.), whose fortunes he shared thereafter. He was slain by Dior in Menegroth.

Of the sons of Fëanor, Curufin inherited most his father's skill, but he was also cunning and treacherous. He was a great horseman. Curufin bore the knife Angrist until Beren took it from him. (S 60, 83, 123, 152, 169-70, 172-73, 176-77, 192-93, 195, 236, 305; B 63, 93, 147, 183, 205, 208-09, 235, 238, 292, 379)

CURUFINWË (Q.: 'skill—') The birth-name of Fëanor (q.v.). (S 63; B 67)

CURUNÍR (S.: 'man of skill') Saruman (q.v.). (III 455; S 322; B 401)

CÚTHALION (S.: 'strongbow') Epithet applied to Beleg (q.v.). (S 199; B 244)

❧ ☙

DAERON (S.: 'shadow-one'?) (FA-) Sindarin Elf of Doriath, loremaster and minstrel of Thingol. Daeron loved Lúthien and twice betrayed her and Beren to Thingol. When Lúthien escaped from Hírilorn and disappeared, Daeron wandered off in despair to look for her. In time he came to the East of Middle-earth, where for many ages he lamented his love.

Besides inventing the Cirth, Daeron was the greatest minstrel who ever lived East of the Sea, for his compositions were inspired by the beauty of Lúthien and his love for her. (III 493; S 95, 113, 166, 172, 183, 357; B 108, 133, 200, 208, 222, 448)

DAERON'S RUNES The Cirth (q.v.) or any of its adaptations. In this case, the Angerthas Moria is meant. (I 416)

DAGNIR (S.: 'bane') (d. FA 460) Adan of the First House, one of the last twelve of Barahir's outlaw band in Dorthonion. (S 155, 162-63, 357; B 187, 195-96, 448)

DAGNIR GLAURUNGA (S.: 'Glaurung's bane') Epithet applied to Túrin (q.v.) and carved on his tombstone. (S 226; B 278)

DAGOR AGLAREB (S.: 'battle glorious') The third of the five major battles of the Wars of Beleriand, fought c. FA 60. Morgoth, seeking to take the Noldor unawares, sent forces of Orcs through the Pass of Sirion and Maglor's Gap, while his main army assaulted Dorthonion. But the

Orcs were easily contained, and Fingolfin and Maedhros attacked the main force from west and east. Morgoth's army attempted to retreat across Ard-galen, but it was caught and annihilated within sight of Angband.

Warned by this attack, the Elves began the Siege of Angband. (S 115; B 136)

DAGOR BRAGOLLACH (S.: 'battle quick-flame') The fourth of the great battles of the Wars of Beleriand, fought in the winter of FA 455. The battle began when Morgoth broke the Siege of Angband, sending out rivers of flame that burned Ard-galen and the lower slopes of Dorthonion and Ered Wethrin, killing many Noldor caught on the plain.

Behind the fire came Morgoth's vast armies, composed of Orcs, Balrogs, and Glaurung. In the west, Fingolfin and Fingon were driven back to the Ered Wethrin, and Hador was slain at Eithel Sirion. Finrod, defending the Pass of Sirion, was nearly killed, but he was rescued by Barahir and the Pass was held. In Dorthonion, the Noldor and Edain were overwhelmed; Aegnor, Angrod, and Bregolas were slain, and the First House of the Edain never fully recovered from its losses.

In the east, Aglon was forced after bitter fighting, but Maedhros rallied the forces of his House at Himring and reclosed the pass. But then Glaurung overran Lothlann and forced Maglor's Gap, and Thargelion and East Beleriand north of the Ramdal were ravaged.

Fingolfin, infuriated by this crushing defeat, rode to Angband and challenged Morgoth to single combat. In the end the High King was slain, but he gave Morgoth seven great wounds.

Although Morgoth never ceased his offensive after Dagor Bragollach, the battle itself was considered to end with the coming of spring. The net result was the loss of Ard-galen and Dorthonion and the serious weakening of the March of Maedhros.

Also called the Battle of Sudden Flame and the Fourth Battle. (S 150-54, 361; B 180-85, 452)

DAGORLAD (S.: 'battle-plain') The great, treeless, open plain between the Dead Marshes and Cirith Gorgor. Dagorlad was the site of the great battle between Sauron and the Last Alliance in SA 3434, and in the Third Age was the gateway into Gondor for many groups of Easterling invaders and the site of many battles with them, especially in 1899 and 1944.

Called the Battle Plain in Westron. (I 319; II 294; III 409, 455, 458)

DAGOR-NUIN-GILIATH (S.: 'battle-beneath-stars') The second of the major battles of the Wars of Beleriand, fought for ten days soon before the first rising of the Moon. Morgoth, made aware of the return of Fëanor to Middle-earth by the echoes of Lammath and the fire at Losgar, resolved to destroy the Noldor before they could establish themselves. He attacked the Elves at Mithrim with a numerically superior force, but the Noldor, strengthened by their life in Aman, slaughtered the Orcs and drove them back into Ard-galen. A second Orc-host, which had assailed the Falathrim in the south, attempted to march to the aid of the main army but was slaughtered by Celegorm near Eithel Sirion.

The campaign that followed was disastrous for the Elves, for Fëanor overextended himself in the pursuit and was fatally wounded by Gothmog near Angband. Soon after, Maedhros was captured by Balrogs during a parley and was taken to Angband. The campaign ended when the forces of Morgoth fled into Angband at the first rising of the Sun and Fingolfin marched through Dor Daedeloth.

Also called the Second Battle. (S 106-09; B 124-27)

DÁIN I (TA 2440-2589) Dwarf, King of Durin's Folk (2585-89). He was slain in his palace in the Ered Mithrin by a cold-drake. (III 440, 450)

DÁIN II IRONFOOT (TA 2767-3019) Dwarf, King of Durin's Folk (2941-3019). A great warrior, Dáin first won fame by killing Azog in the Battle of Azanulbizar in 2799. In 2805, Dáin became lord of the Dwarves of the

Iron Hills. In 2941 he led an army to the aid of Thorin II, who was besieged in Erebor, and later was one of the commanders on the good side in the Battle of the Five Armies. After Thorin died in that battle, Dáin, as his rightful heir, became King of Durin's Folk and King under the Mountain. He ruled wisely and justly and brought wealth to Erebor until the WR, when he was killed in the Battle of Dale while defending the body of his friend King Brand. (III 443-44, 448-49, 450, 468; H 246, 275)

DAIRUIN (S.: '—red flame'?) (d. FA 460)   Adan of the First House, one of the last twelve of Barahir's outlaw band in Dorthonion. (S 155, 162-63; B 187, 195-96)

DAISY BOFFIN (b. TA 2950)   Hobbit of the Shire, daughter of Dudo Baggins and wife of Griffo Boffin. She was a guest at the Farewell Party. (III 474)

DAISY GAMGEE (b. TA 2972)   Hobbit of the Shire, third child and eldest daughter of Hamfast Gamgee. (III 477)

DAISY GAMGEE (b. FO 12)   Hobbit of the Shire, eighth child and fourth daughter of Sam Gamgee. (III 477)

DALE   City-kingdom of Men, located on the southern slopes of Erebor. The Men of Dale traced their descent to the Edain, and Dale may have been quite ancient when it was destroyed in TA 2770 by Smaug. The Men of Dale were then scattered, and many went to Esgaroth. After the death of Smaug in 2941, Dale was rebuilt by Bard, a descendant of the old Kings of Dale, who became its first King. With the simultaneous refounding of the Kingdom under the Mountain, the ancient friendship between the two realms was re-established and Dale again became wealthy and famous. During the WR Dale was attacked by Easterlings allied with Sauron, but its inhabitants took refuge in Erebor after an initial defeat; the combined force of Men and Dwarves broke the siege after the downfall of Sauron. In the Fourth Age Dale retained its independence but was allied with and protected by the Reunited Kingdom.

At the time of the WR, Dale extended far to the east and south of the city, and probably included all the land between the Carnen and the River Running. (I 51, 301, 302-03; III 440, 460, 461, 468-69; H 34-36, 195, 234)

DAMROD (S.) (fl. WR) Dúnadan of Gondor, a Ranger of Ithilien. (II 338)

DARK   The Darkness (q.v.) of Melkor. (S 272; B 336)

DARK   The regions of Aman not lighted by the Two Trees, perhaps Araman and Avathar. (S 62; B 65)

DARK   The Unlight (q.v.) of Ungoliant. (S 79; B 87)

DARK DAYS   Probably the Dark Years (q.v.), so called by the Elves of Lórien. (I 445)

DARK DOOR   The north entrance to the Paths of the Dead, at the foot of the Dwimorberg.

Also called The Door, the Forbidden Door, and the Gate of the Dead. (III 69-70, 85, 459)

DARK ELF   Eöl (q.v.). (S 137; B 164-65)

DARK ELVES   The Moriquendi (q.v.) (S 103; B 120)

DARKENING OF VALINOR   The poisoning of the Two Trees. (S 39; B 34)

DARK GATE   The Outer Gate of Gondolin (q.v.). (S 137; B 163)

DARK GUARD   The guard stationed at the entrance to Gondolin. Also called the Guard.

See: the Way of Escape. (S 136-37, 239; B 163, 295)

DARK KING   Melkor (q.v.), so called by Men. (S 144, 145; B 223)

DARK LORD   Melkor (q.v.). (I 182; S 227; B 280)

DARK LORD   The most common epithet of Sauron (q.v.). (I 81; S 289; B 359)

DARKNESS   The nature, influence, and extent of evil, the absence or denial of the Light of Ilúvatar. At times (as in the Darkness Unescapable, III 297) the word refers to the dominion of evil; at others (as in the Ancient Darkness, q.v.) it refers to the Void, the absence of Ilúvatar perceived at the ending of the Vision and later embraced by Melkor as a vehicle of evil. The word most often refers to the general power or influence of Melkor or his servant, Sauron.
　　Also called the Dark and the Shadow (q.v.). See also: the Great Darkness. (I 250, 329; II 97; III 297, 331; S 19, 31, 141, 259, 271; B 9, 25, 169, 335, 451)

DARKNESS   The Unlight (q.v.) of Ungoliant. (S 76, 79; B 84, 87)

DARKNESS   The Great Darkness (q.v.). (II 89, 99)

DARKNESS   An emanation sent by Sauron which covered Mordor, Gondor, and Rohan before and during the Siege of Gondor. The Darkness had a depressing effect. It was blown away by the south wind which carried Aragorn's fleet up Anduin.
　　Also called the Shadow and the Storm of Mordor. (III 52, 75, 88-89, 95, 98, 240, 314)

DARK PLAGUE   Name given to the Great Plague (q.v.) of TA 1636-37 in the Shire. (I 24)

DARK POWER   Sauron (q.v.). (I 79)

DARK POWER OF THE NORTH   Melkor (q.v.). (III 507)

DARK THRONE   The throne of Morgoth in Angband, or, by allusion, Melkor himself. (S 228; B 282)

DARK TOWER   The Barad-dûr (q.v.). (I 81)

DARK YEARS   The years of Sauron's great and almost undisputed domination of Middle-earth, during which many peoples were enslaved or corrupted. The Dark Years lasted from c. SA 1000, when Sauron settled in Mordor, to 3441, when he was overthrown by the Last Alliance. During this period Sauron built the Barad-dûr, forged the Rings of Power, and won the War of the Elves and Sauron.

Also called the Accursed Years, the Black Years, the Days of Flight, and perhaps the Dark Days. (I 81; III 84, 439, 452; S 263, 289, 294; B 324, 359, 365)

DAWNLESS DAY   The first day of the Darkness, March 10, TA 3019. (III 95, 466)

DAY   The Noontide of Valinor (q.v.). (I 321; S 298; B 370)

DAY OF DOOM   See: the End. (S 279; B 345)

DAYS, DAYS OF BLISS   The Noontide of Valinor (q.v.). (I 309; III 519; S 63, 244; B 67, 302)

DAYS OF DEARTH   The Long Winter (q.v.) of TA 2758-59 and the ensuing famine, so called in the annals of the Shire. (I 24)

DAYS OF FLIGHT   The Dark Years (q.v.). (S 289; B 359)

DAYS OF THE BLISS OF VALINOR   The Noontide of Valinor (q.v.). (S 39; B 34)

DAYS OF THE RINGS   The period during which the Rings of Power were influential in the affairs of Middle-earth, extending from SA 1590 to TA 3019. (III 383)

DAYSTAR   The Sun (q.v.). (S 100; B 115)

DEAD MARSHES   Marshes east of the Emyn Muil. The marshes expanded eastward throughout the Third Age, and at some point engulfed the graves of the Men and Elves slain in the Battle of Dagorlad. The graves became the Mere of Dead Faces (q.v.). In TA 1944 many of the Wainriders defeated in the Battle of the Camp were driven into the Dead Marshes, where they perished. (I 332; II 294-98; III 409, 458)

DEAD MEN OF DUNHARROW   Men of the White Mountains, related to the Dunlendings. When Gondor was founded, they swore allegiance to Isildur, but as they had been corrupted by Sauron during the Dark Years they broke their oath when called to battle by the Last Alliance. For this betrayal, they were condemned to remain in and near the White Mountains as spirits, until called to fulfill their oath by the heir of Isildur.

For the entire Third Age the Dead Men haunted the area above Dunharrow, especially the Paths of the Dead. In 3019, during the WR, they were called by Aragorn to fulfill their oath, and repaid their debt by routing the Corsairs of Umbar at Pelargir. They then vanished from Middle-earth.

The Dead Men were also known as the Dead, the Sleepless Dead, the Grey Host, the Shadow Host, the Shadowmen, the Shadows, the Shadows of Men, and the Men of the Mountains. (III 64-65, 71-75, 186, 509)

DEADMEN'S DIKE   Name given to Fornost (q.v.) after its ruin and desertion in TA 1974. (I 321; III 337)

DEAD ONES   The corpses in the Mere of Dead Faces (q.v.). (II 296-98)

DÉAGOL (d. TA 2463)   Stoor of the Gladden Fields. While fishing with his cousin Sméagol, he found the One Ring and was murdered by Sméagol, who coveted it.

The name Déagol is a translation into Old English of

the Northern Mannish name Nahald, meaning "secret." (I 84-85; III 459, 509, 518)

DEATH DOWN Mass grave outside Helm's Dike in which the Huorns buried the Orcs killed in the Battle of the Hornburg.

The Death Down was a large mound of stones built over a deep pit. (II 201; III 58)

DEATHLESS The Valar and Maiar (qq.v.) (S 37, 264, 265, 278; B 32, 326, 327, 344)

DEATHLESS LANDS The Undying Lands (q.v.). (S 278; B 344)

DEEP ELVES The Noldor (q.v.). Also spelled Deep-elves. (H 164; S 53; B 54)

DEEPHALLOW Village in the southern part of the Eastfarthing, near where the Shirebourn flowed into the Brandywine. (I 40; TB 9)

DEEPING COOMB Valley in Rohan in front of Helm's Deep. The side of the Coomb near the Hornrock was fortified and was known as Helm's Dike. The Deeping Stream flowed through the Deeping Coomb, not surprisingly. (II 170; L 181)

DEEPING STREAM Stream in Rohan coming from Helm's Deep. It passed around the Hornrock, over Helm's Dike, and through the Deeping Coomb into Westfold Vale. (II 169-70)

DEEPING WALL The wall across Helm's Gate, guarding the entrance to Helm's Deep. The Deeping Wall was twenty feet high and broad enough for four men to walk abreast on its top; it was unscalable. The only flaw in the Wall was a rather sizable culvert in its base through which the Deeping Stream flowed. During the Battle of the Hornburg soldiers of Saruman twice entered Helm's Deep through this culvert. (II 169, 173 ff.)

DEEPS OF TIME The vast extent of the dimension of Time. Used loosely to mean the distant, unfathomable past, the phrase really refers to Time as a principle within which objects and persons (such as Arda and Varda) are fixed by the laws of Eä, the realization of the Ainulindalë. (II 78; III 438, 519; S 18, 19, 20, 22, 48; B 7, 9, 10, 13, 47)

DEFICIT The millennial errors in the Kings' and Stewards' Reckonings and, by extension, the adjustments made to correct them. The original Deficit corrected the small error caused by the inaccuracy of the leap year system. In the Third Age adjustments had to be made because of the dislocation of the end of the century, since TA 1000 was equivalent to SA 4441. These adjustments eventually led to the Stewards' Reckoning. (III 481)

DELDÚWATH (S.: 'horror-night-shadow') Taur-nu-Fuin (q.v.). (S 155, 323, 357, 358; B 186, 402, 448)

DENETHOR (S.: '—eagle') (FA) Sindarin Elf, a lord of the Nandor, the son of Lenwë. He led a remnant of his people from the Vales of Anduin and Eriador into Beleriand, where they settled in Ossiriand. Denethor was slain on Amon Ereb by Orcs in the first battle of the Wars of Beleriand. (S 54, 94, 96, 122; B 56, 108, 110, 146)

DENETHOR I (d. TA 2477) Dúnadan, tenth Ruling Steward of Gondor. Toward the end of his rule Ithilien was overrun by uruks from Mordor, but they were defeated by Denethor's son Boromir. (III 395, 415)

DENETHOR II (TA c. 2935-3019) Dúnadan, twenty-sixth and last Ruling Steward of Gondor (2984-3019). Denethor was a noble man, valiant, proud and wise, yet in his younger days he was overshadowed by Thorongil. It was later believed that he realized that Thorongil was actually Aragorn II, and feared that Aragorn and Gandalf were plotting to supplant him; Denethor, like his predecessors, was opposed to giving the crown of Gondor to the heir of Isildur.

In 2976, Denethor married Finduilas of Dol Amroth. She bore him two children, Boromir and Faramir, but died in 2988. After her death Denethor became grim and withdrawn. Desiring knowledge of Sauron's plans, for he knew that the great attack against Gondor would come in his time, Denethor began to look into the palantír of Minas Tirith. Although he gained knowledge with which he was able to prepare Gondor as well as possible for the onslaught, Denethor was aged prematurely and became fixed in pride and despair. When his elder and favorite son, Boromir, died in 3019, and Faramir was stricken with the Black Breath, Denethor lost his reason and tried to cremate Faramir. Although prevented in this by Beregond and Gandalf, Denethor succeeded in burning himself. It is likely that the immediate cause of Denethor's fatal depression was a vision in the palantír of the fleet of the Corsairs sailing up the Anduin; since Sauron was able partially to control the image Denethor saw, the Steward was unable to know that the ships were in reality commanded by Aragorn.

Despite his dislike of Gandalf, which hindered the wizard and deprived Gondor of an excellent counsellor, Denethor was an able ruler, worthy of honor despite his ignoble end. (I 330-31; III 27, 28-29 ff., 115, 121-23, 153-62, 395-96, 417-19)

DEÓR (TA 2644-2718)   Man, seventh King of Rohan (2699-2718). During his reign Rohan was troubled by the Dunlendings. (III 435)

DEÓRWINE (d. TA 3019)   Man of Rohan, chief of the knights of Théoden's household. He was killed in the Battle of the Pelennor Fields. (III 146, 152)

DERNDINGLE   Great bowl in Fangorn, site of Entmoots. (II 103, 104-09)

DERNHELM   Name used by Éowyn (q.v.) when she disguised herself as a Rider of Rohan in order to ride with the Rohirrim to the Battle of the Pelennor Fields. (III 93)

DERRILYN   Supposedly a river, in Bilbo Baggins' poem *Errantry*. The name is an imitation of Elvish, and Derrilyn was probably fictitious. (TB 8, 24)

DERUFIN (S.) (d. TA 3019)   Man of Gondor, son of Duinhir of Morthond. He and his brother Duilin were archers. They were slain in the Battle of the Pelennor Fields while attacking the Oliphaunts of the Haradrim. (III 49, 152)

DERVORIN (S.) (fl. WR)   Man of Gondor, son of the lord of Ringló Vale. He led his father's troops to the defense of Minas Tirith during the WR and fought in the Battle of the Pelennor Fields. (III 49)

DESOLATION OF SMAUG   From TA 2770 to 2941, Erebor and the surrounding area, devastated by Smaug's extravagant respiration and general unsociability.
   Also called the Desolation of the Dragon and, probably, the Waste. (I 303; H 13, 195)

DESOLATION OF THE MORANNON   The foul and reeking area between the Morannon and Dagorlad, despoiled by the servants of Sauron. The Desolation was scarred with many pits and slag-mounds. (II 302-03; III 467)

DIAMOND TOOK (fl. FO 7)   Hobbit of the Shire, wife of Peregrin Took. Diamond came from Long Cleeve and was probably a North-took. (III 471, 475)

DIMBAR (S.: 'sad-home')   Area of northern Beleriand, bounded by the Rivers Sirion and Mindeb and the Crissaegrim. Although crossed by the road from the Brithiach through Nan Dungortheb to Himring, Dimbar seems to have been uninhabited. After Orcs from Taur-nu-Fuin built a road through Anach, Dimbar became the scene of fighting between the forces of Morgoth and the border-guard of Doriath. (S 121, 132, 176, 201, 356; B 144, 157, 214, 246, 447)

DIMHOLT Small forest of black trees in Rohan, near the Dark Door. (III 69, 81)

DIMRILL DALE Westron name for Azanulbizar (q.v.). (I 370)

DIMRILL GATE The Great Gates (q.v.). (I 387)

DIMRILL STAIR Path leading from Azanulbizar to the Redhorn Pass. The Dimrill Stair was built along the bank of a swift and many-falled stream. (I 359, 370, 432)

DIMROST (S.: 'rainy stair') The waterfall in Brethil near Cabed-en-Aras by which Celebros fell into the River Teiglin. Dimrost was renamed Nen Girith because of the shuddering (a premonition of her death and Túrin's near that place) which overcame Nienor as she passed it for the first time. (S 220, 221, 224; B 270, 272, 276)

DINGLE The valley of the Withywindle in the Old Forest, the center of the evil in the Forest. Many willow trees, including Old Man Willow, grew in the Dingle. (I 163-70; TB 8-9, 11)

DINODAS BRANDYBUCK (b. TA 2914 to 2919, d. after 3001) Hobbit of the Shire, youngest son of Gorbadoc Brandybuck. He was a guest at the Farewell Party. (III 476)

DIOR (S.) (c. FA 470-509) Son of Beren and Lúthien, born and raised in Tol Galen. He married Nimloth of Doriath and lived with her and their children, Eluréd, Elurín and Elwing, at Lanthir Lamath. Dior fought with Beren in the battle at Sarn Athrad in which the Dwarves of Nogrod who had sacked Menegroth were destroyed.

Afterwards he lived at Menegroth and attempted to restore the kingdom of Doriath; he may have been King of Doriath.

After the second death of Beren and Lúthien, Dior received the Nauglamír. He was soon attacked by the sons of Fëanor, who coveted the Silmaril set in the necklace. Dior and Nimloth were slain in Menegroth, although Dior killed Celegorm, Curufin, and Caranthir before he died.

Dior was very beautiful, for the blood of three races (the Edain, Eldar, and Maiar) flowed in him. He was known as Dior Aranel and Dior Eluchíl, Thingol's Heir. (I 261; S 188, 234, 235-36; B 229, 290, 291-92)

DIOR (d. TA 2435)　Dúnadan, ninth Ruling Steward of Gondor (2412-35). (III 395)

DÍRHAEL (S.) (fl. TA 2930)　Dúnadan of the North, a descendant of Aranarth. Dírhael was the husband of Ivorwen and the father of Gilraen. (III 420)

DÍRHAVEL (S.) (FA 6th Cent.)　Adan of the Havens of Sirion, a poet. He is said to have written the *Narn i Hîn Húrin*. Dírhavel was killed when the Havens were attacked by the sons of Fëanor. (S 342-43; B 427)

DÍS (b. TA 2760)　Dwarf of Durin's Line, third child and only daughter of Thráin II. Dís was the mother of Fíli and Kíli. (III 440, 449, 450)

DISPOSSESSED　The House of Fëanor (q.v.), so called because it lost the overlordship of the Noldor. It also lost the Silmarils, the bliss of Aman, and, in the end, its honor and integrity. (S 88, 111; B 99, 130)

DODERIC BRANDYBUCK (b. TA 2989)　Hobbit of the Shire, eldest son of Seredic Brandybuck. He was a guest at the Farewell Party. (III 476)

DODINAS BRANDYBUCK (b. TA 2908 to 2913, d.

before 3001) Hobbit of the Shire, fourth child of Gorba-doc Brandybuck. (III 476)

DOL AMROTH (S.: 'hill of Amroth') Castle and port, the chief city of Belfalas, Gondor. Until about TA 1981, the white ships of the Elves of Lórien sailed from Dol Amroth, and the Dúnedain of that city were said to have Elven blood in their veins. The emblem of the Princes of Dol Amroth was the Ship and Silver Swan; their banners were blue.

See also: Sea-ward Tower. (III 23, 50, 180, 181, 301; TB 8, 37-38)

DOL BARAN (S.: 'golden-brown hill') The southern-most foothill of the Misty Mountains, rounded and covered with heather. (II 248)

DOL GULDUR (S.: 'hill of sorcery') Fortress in south-western Mirkwood. Dol Guldur was probably built by Sauron about TA 1050; it was first mentioned about 1100, when the Wise discovered that an unknown evil power had settled there. For the next thousand years, the power grew stronger and corrupted the forest. In 2063 Gandalf went to Dol Guldur to learn the identity of its master, but the evil power fled.

The power returned with increased strength in 2460, but in 2850 Gandalf again entered the fortress and dis-covered that its master was Sauron. Sauron continued to rule his many servants from Dol Guldur until 2941, when he was driven out by the White Council. Sauron retreated to Mordor, but ten years later sent three of the Nazgûl to occupy Dol Guldur. During the WR, armies from Dol Guldur attacked Lórien and the Wood-land Realm, but they were defeated. After the fall of Sauron, Celeborn took Dol Guldur and Galadriel threw down its walls and cleansed its pits. (I 328, 336; III 415, 448, 456-59, 460, 461, 462, 467, 468, 469)

DOLMED (S.: 'head-wet') Mountain in the central Ered Luin, known as the home of Dwarves. Belegost and

Nogrod may have been delved beneath its northern and southern faces.

Dolmed was probably destroyed at the breaking of Beleriand.

Also called Mount Dolmed. (S 91, 96, 193, 235; B 104, 110, 236, 290)

DOME OF STARS Building in Osgiliath where the palantír of the city was kept. The Dome of Stars was ruined during the Kin-strife.

Also called the Tower of the Stone of Osgiliath. (II 259; III 406)

DOMINION OF MEN The Fourth Age, in which the Elves and Dwarves dwindled and Men became supreme in Arda. The Dominion began when the Three Rings failed and their Keepers passed over Sea, although the events of the Third Age (see: the Fading Years) prepared the Dominion. (III 308, 452; S 20, 298-99; B 9, 371-72)

DONNAMIRA BOFFIN (TA 2856-2948) Hobbit of the Shire, tenth child of Gerontius Took. She married Hugo Boffin. (III 475)

DOOM OF MANDOS The Doom of the Noldor (q.v.). (S 125-26; B 150)

DOOM OF MEN The Gift of Men (q.v.). (III 390; S 265; B 327)

DOOM OF THE NOLDOR The torment, destruction, and loss of integrity foretold by Mandos for the Exiles, especially the House of Fëanor, and those (the Sindar and the Edain) who became involved in their futile attempt to recover the Silmarils. The curse was provoked by the disobedience of the Noldor to the will of the Valar and by the Kinslaying, which defiled Aman. By this Doom the sons of Fëanor became treacherous, deceitful, and overbearing; the burning of the ships at Losgar, the distrust of Thingol for the House of Fëanor, and the deaths of

Finrod and Dior showed the effect of this stain on the spirits of the Noldor.

Delivered by Mandos as the Exiles reached the northern border of Aman, the Doom was also known as the Prophecy of the North, the Doom of Mandos, and the curse of Mandos. (S 87-88, 90, 109, 128, 129, 139, 141, 148, 167, 169, 170, 171, 176, 240; B 98-99, 102, 127, 153, 154-55, 166, 169, 177-78, 202, 204, 205, 207, 213, 297)

DOOM OF THE WORLD The ordained fate of Eä, which can be altered only by Ilúvatar. (S 264; B 326)

DOOR, THE The Dark Door (q.v.). (III 84)

DOOR OF NIGHT Gate in the Walls of the World (q.v.) between Eä and the Void. At the end of the First Age Morgoth was cast out through the Door. (S 254; B 315)

DOORS OF DURIN The West-gate (q.v.) of Khazad-dûm. (I 398)

DOORS OF FELAGUND The front gate of Nargothrond, looking out over the River Narog. The Doors were broken by Glaurung when Nargothrond was sacked. (S 211, 213; B 259)

DOORS OF NIGHT Gates in the Walls of the Night (q.v.) between Arda and Ilmen. Eärendil passed through the Doors to enter the sky as a star.

Cf.: the Gates of Morning. (S 250; B 262)

DORA BAGGINS (TA 2902-3006) Hobbit of the Shire, eldest child of Fosco Baggins. She was a guest at the Farewell Party, where she was given a waste-paper basket. Dora was noted for her lengthy letters of good advice. (I 64; III 474)

DOR CARANTHIR (S.: 'land of Caranthir') Thargelion (q.v.). (S 124; B 148)

DOR-CÚARTHOL (S.: 'land of bow-helm') Name given to the area around Amon Rûdh (and perhaps all of Talath Dirnen) in FA 487, when it was defended against Orcs by the outlaws of Túrin and Beleg, the Helm and the Bow. (S 205; B 252)

DOR DAEDELOTH (S.: 'land of shadow-horror') Name given to the area around Angband. It does not seem to have been used after Dagor Aglareb and the establishment of the Siege of Angband. (S 107, 109, 111, 324, 357; B 124, 127, 130, 403, 448)

DOR DÍNEN (S.: 'silent land') Deserted area of Beleriand north of Doriath and south of Dorthonion, bounded by the Rivers Esgalduin and Aros. (S 121, 324; B 145, 403)

DOR-EN-ERNIL (S.: 'land of the prince') Area of Gondor west of the Gilrain. (III 14)

DOR FIRN-I-GUINAR (S.: 'land of the dead that are quick') The area in Ossiriand around Tol Galen, so called because Beren and Lúthien lived there after their return from the Houses of the Dead.
Also called the Land of the Dead that Live, a translation of the Sindarin name. (S 188, 235, 357; B 229, 291, 448)

DORI (fl. TA 2941-3018) Dwarf of the House of Durin, a member of Thorin and Company. Dori settled in Erebor after the expedition. (I 302; III 450; H 22, 26, 44)

DORIATH (S. 'land of the fence') The great Sindarin kingdom of Beleriand, established early in the First Age by Thingol and Melian. After the first battle of the Wars of Beleriand, Melian wove the Girdle of Melian (q.v.) to protect Neldoreth, Region, and Nivrim (qq.v.), the inner lands of Doriath. Thingol also claimed wide lands outside the Girdle, such as Brethil and perhaps Dimbar.
Protected by the power of Melian and the discretion of Thingol, Doriath was not involved in the great battles of

the Wars of Beleriand, although its borders were constantly defended by the strength of Beleg and his border-guards. Indeed, Doriath was frequently strengthened by Sindar fleeing the Wars. Although friendly with the house of Finarfin and with the Dwarves, Thingol forbade Men or the House of Fëanor to enter Doriath; and after he learned the true story of the return of the Noldor, he forbade the speaking of Quenya within his realm.

Yet in the end Doriath was caught in the Doom of the Noldor, for Thingol demanded a Silmaril as the wedding-price for his daughter Lúthien, and for the sake of this jewel Thingol was slain by Dwarves of Nogrod. After his death Melian left Middle-earth, the Girdle was broken, and Doriath was invaded by Dwarves. When Dior was slain by the sons of Fëanor, Doriath was deserted and its surviving Elves went to the Mouths of Sirion.

Doriath was called Eglador early in the First Age. Also called Elvenhome, the Hidden Kingdom, and the Land of the Girdle; the latter is a loose translation of the Sindarin name. (I 258-60, 319; III 506; S 56, 96-97, 111-12, 121-22, 127-29, 144, 151, 167-68, 183-85, 189, 205, 218, 231-37, 244; B 58, 110-11, 130-31, 145, 152-54, 172, 182, 202-03, 222-25, 230, 251, 269, 286-92, 302)

DORLAS (S.) (d. FA 601)   Adan of Brethil. He was the leader of a company rescued from Orcs by Túrin, and later incited Túrin to return to battle after his marriage to Nienor. Dorlas volunteered to accompany Túrin against Glaurung but later withdrew in fear and was slain by Brandir. (S 216, 220, 221; B 266, 271, 273)

DOR-LÓMIN (S.)   Land between the Ered Lómin and the Mountains of Mithrim, part of Hithlum. On the return of the Noldor to Middle-earth, Dor-lómin became the lordship of Fingon, but in the 5th Century FA Fingolfin gave it to Hador. Dor-lómin became the home of the Third House of the Edain, which flourished there, strengthened by refugees of the First House from Dorthonion, until the Nirnaeth Arnoediad. Morgoth gave Dor-lómin, together with the rest of Hithlum, to his Easterlings, who absorbed or enslaved the surviving Edain. (S 119, 147, 155, 195, 198, 238; B 140, 177, 187, 239, 242, 294)

DOR-NU-FAUGLITH (S.: 'land under thirst-ash') Anfauglith (q.v.). (S 153, 324; B 184, 403)

DORTHONION (S.: 'land of pines') Highlands south of Ard-galen, created during the upheavals of the Battle of the Powers. Its northern slopes were gentle, but to the south the land fell in the precipices of Ered Gorgoroth. Dorthonion extended sixty leagues from east to west; it was covered with pine-forests, but the land was not fruitful.

When the Noldor returned to Middle-earth, Aegnor and Angrod settled in Dorthonion, and in the 4th Century FA the First House of the Edain established itself there. But the northern slopes of Dorthonion were ruined in Dagor Bragollach, and the land was overrun by Orcs soon after. Dorthonion was deserted by Elves and Men, save for the outlaw band of Barahir, and the land was renamed Taur-nu-Fuin (q.v.) because of the horrors of Morgoth that corrupted the forests. Dorthonion was freed for a short time by the Union of Maedhros, but it was lost again after Nirnaeth Arnoediad.

Also called Orod-na-Thôn. (II 90; S 51, 111, 119-20, 143, 148, 151, 153, 155, 160, 162-63, 189, 324; B 52, 130, 141, 172, 177, 181, 184, 186, 194, 195, 231, 403)

DORWINION (S.) Land on the northwest shores of the Sea of Rhûn. The wines drunk by the Elves of the Woodland Realm were made here. (H 172, 175; PB)

DOWNFALL OF THE LORD OF THE RINGS AND THE RETURN OF THE KING Frodo's memoirs, the basis for the narrative of *LotR*. (I title page; III 380)

DOWNLANDS The area of the Barrow-downs. (I 223)

DRAGON-HELM OF DOR-LÓMIN The greatest heirloom of the House of Hador, a war-helm made by Dwarves. After the Nirnaeth Arnoediad the Dragon-helm was preserved by Morwen until she sent it to Doriath with Túrin. Later Beleg brought it to Túrin during his first outlawry, and Túrin wore it during many of his adventures. It may have been buried with Túrin.

Also called the Helm of Hador. (S 199, 204, 205, 212; B 244, 251, 252, 260)

DRAGONS Evil creatures of northern Middle-earth, huge, powerful, scale-covered, long-lived, greedy for treasure, and full of malice. They could bewilder anyone who looked in their eyes, and their words were cunning and seductive.

Dragons were probably first bred by Morgoth when he returned to Angband with the Silmarils. There appear to have been three strains of dragons: the Urulóki, the winged dragons, and the cold-drakes. The first of the Urulóki, the fire-drakes of the North, was Glaurung (q.v.). They breathed fire but did not fly; they were the most common type of dragon in the First Age. The winged dragons, who also breathed fire, first appeared in the Great Battle, but thereafter are not mentioned until TA 2570, when they reappeared in the Ered Mithrin and harassed the Dwarves and the Éothéod. The greatest winged dragon of the Third Age was Smaug, who took Erebor in 2770 and was slain in 2941. The cold-drakes were found only in the Ered Mithrin; they probably did not breathe fire.

Also called the Great Worms. (III 440, 459; H 35, 207, 212, 214; TB 54; S 116, 192-93, 242, 252; B 137, 235, 300, 312)

DRAUGLUIN (S.: 'wolf-blue'?) (d. FA 466 or 467) Greatest of the werewolves of Morgoth and Sauron, slain at Tol-in-Gaurhoth by Huan when the hound and Lúthien came to free Beren. His pelt was worn by Huan and later by Beren when he went to Angband, where he abandoned it. (S 174, 178-81, 358; B 210, 216-19, 448)

DRENGIST (S.) Firth running from the Sea into Dorlómin, cutting through the Ered Lómin. The Exiles of the

House of Fëanor landed here on their return to Middle-earth.

Often called the Firth of Drengist. (S 89, 106; B 101, 123)

DROGO BAGGINS (TA 2908-80)   Hobbit of the Shire, second child and eldest son of Fosco Baggins. Drogo married Primula Brandybuck; their only child was Frodo Baggins. Drogo and his wife died in a boating accident on the Brandywine.

Until his irregular death, Drogo was considered a proper and unexceptionable Hobbit, very fond of good food. (I 45-46; III 474, 476)

DRUADAN FOREST (S.: 'wild man'?)   Forest in Anórien, thirty miles northwest of Minas Tirith, the home of the Woses (q.v.). After the WR, in return for the aid they gave the Rohirrim, King Elessar gave the forest to the Woses and forbade anyone to enter it without their permission.

Also called the Crey Wood. (III 15, 127, 313)

DRÚWAITH IAUR (S.: 'old wild-folk')   Land bounded by the Ered Nimrais and the Rivers Isen and Adorn, probably at one time the home of a people related to the Woses and the Men of the Mountains.

Also called Old Púkel-land. (PB)

DRY RIVER   River formerly flowing into Sirion from the Echoriath, especially the subterranean riverbed which was the entrance to Gondolin.

See: the Way of Escape. (S 125, 136, 228; B 149, 163, 281)

DUDO BAGGINS (TA 2911-3009)   Hobbit of the Shire, youngest child of Fosco Baggins. He was a guest at the Farewell Party. (III 474)

DUILIN (S.: 'river-song'?)   (d. TA 3019)   Man of Gondor, son of Duinhir, the lord of Morthond. Duilin, like his brother Derufin, was trampled to death by Oliphaunts during the Battle of the Pelennor Fields. (III 49, 152)

DUILWEN (S.) One of the seven rivers of Ossiriand, flowing from the Ered Luin into the Gelion. (S 123; B 147)

DUINHIR (S.: 'river-lord') (fl. WR) Man of Gondor, lord of Morthond at the time of the WR. He fought in the Battle of the Pelennor Fields, in which he lost both his sons. (III 49)

DÚLIN (S.: 'dark-singer') A lómelindë (q.v.). (S 358; B 448)

DUMBLEDORS A probably imaginary race of insects in Bilbo's poem *Errantry*. (TB 27)

DÚNADAN, THE Aragorn (q.v.). (I 304)

DÚNEDAIN (S.: 'edain of the west') Men, those of the Edain (q.v.) who at the beginning of the Second Age sailed to Númenor (q.v.), and their descendants. After the fall of Númenor in SA 3319, the Dúnedain survived only in the Faithful (q.v.) and the Black Númenóreans of Umbar (qq.v.). Two kingdoms were founded by the Faithful, Gondor and Arnor (qq.v.), and after the death of Elendil in SA 3441 the Dúnedain were split into two groups, those of the North and those of Gondor.

The Dúnedain of the North were attacked from TA 1300 onward by Angmar, and slowly they lost territory and their numbers dwindled. The Dúnedain of Rhudaur were few by 1409, and the last Dúnedain of Cardolan perished in the Great Plague of 1636. After the fall of Arthedain in 1974, the Dúnedain of the North became few, and survived only with the aid of Elrond. However, adversity preserved their hardiness, and many or all of the male Dúnedain became Rangers, who protected the innocent Men and Hobbits of Eriador and were implacable foes of

Sauron and his servants. The Dúnedain of the North were ruled by the Line of Isildur, which never failed.

In Gondor, the Dúnedain flourished for many years despite threats from Harad and Rhûn, but many of the Dúnedain became decadent and over-proud. The Line of Anárion, the family of the Kings of Gondor, failed five times because of the childlessness or early death of the king. Also, the Dúnedain of Gondor, like their forebears in Númenor, became concerned with their shortened life-span (which waned more rapidly than that of their northern kinsmen), and even had a disastrous civil war, the Kin-strife, about this. The purity of the Dúnadan blood was lessened by intermarriage with lesser Men, especially the Northmen, and, more importantly, by sloth and love of luxury. However, some of the Dúnedain families, notably the House of Húrin and the house of the Princes of Dol Amroth, retained their nobility; the latter family was enriched by Elvish blood. By the time of the WR, although Gondor was still strong and some of her Dúnedain were still noble and wise, the Dúnedain of Gondor had waned considerably.

The Dúnedain were superior to other Men in nobility of spirit and body, although they were of course capable of evil if corrupted. They were tall, with dark hair and grey eyes. The lifespan of the royal family, originally three times that of lesser Men (210 years), was by the time of the WR still about 150 years or more; lesser Dúnedain lived somewhat shorter lives. The age of adulthood seems to have been about 20 or 30, although most of the Kings did not succeed their fathers until they were much older. The Dúnedain, especially those of high rank, possessed great wisdom and discernment, and occasional foresight. The Faithful and their descendants loved the Elves and were liked by them; there was great hatred between them and Sauron.

The Dúnedain spoke Westron, which they enriched with many Elvish words. Many of the Dúnedain knew Sindarin, and some also knew Quenya. The Dúnedain of Númenor, and probably also those of Umbar, spoke Adûnaic.

The Dúnedain were also known as the Men of Westernesse, the Men of the West, and the Númenóreans. They were also called the Kings of Men, the Men of the Sea (since the Númenóreans were great mariners), the Tall Men (by the Woses), and the High (in the lore of Gondor). The singular of Dúnedain is Dúnadan. (I 29, 326, 330; II 335-38, 362-64; III 394-419, 507-08; S 259-61, 296; B 320-21, 367)

DUNGORTHEB Nan Dungortheb (q.v.). (S 164; B 198)

DÚNHARG See: Dunharrow. (III 492)

DUNHARROW Fortress and refuge above Harrowdale, built in the Dark Years by the Men of the Mountains. It was used by Gondor and later by Rohan, and was one of the chief refuges of the latter country.

Dunharrow was easily defended, since it was reached by a switch-back path that went up a steep cliff; each level was overlooked by the ones above.

Dunharrow is a modernized form of the translated Rohirric *Dúnharg*. "Dunharrow" referred to the area generally, while "the Hold of Dunharrow" referred specifically to the refuge. (II 163; III 14, 65, 76 ff.; L 183)

DÚNHERE (d. TA 3019) Man of Rohan, lord of Harrowdale. He was killed in the Battle of the Pelennor Fields. (III 79, 83, 152)

DUNLAND Area west of the Misty Mountains and south of the Glanduin, at the time of the WR neither prosperous, civilized, nor organized into a state, being a land of backward herdsmen and hillmen.

Dunland was inhabited before the founding of Gondor by the Dunlendings (q.v.). About TA 1150 some Stoors came to Dunland, but they migrated to the Shire in 1630. From approximately TA 2770 to 2800 Dwarves who had escaped from the sack of Erebor, led by Thrór, lived in Dunland. At the time of WR, Dunland, though a fair, fertile land, was sparsely inhabited. (I 16; II 168, 180; III 322, 325, 441, 457, 505)

DUNLENDINGS Men, last remnant of the people that once inhabited the valleys of the Ered Nimrais. Some of these folk were assimilated by Gondor; one group became the Dead Men of Dunharrow. In the Second Age, however, some of these people had moved north; some settled in Dunland, while others moved into Eriador. The Men of Bree were the northernmost surviving branch at the time of the WR.

In Dunland the Dunlendings preserved their ancient language and primitive culture. In the Third Age they hated the Rohirrim, who had driven them out of the northern valleys of the Ered Nimrais and the plains of western Rohan, and so they frequently attacked that country. The two greatest Dunlending attacks on Rohan were in 2758, when they were led by Wulf, and during the WR, when the Dunlendings were aroused by Saruman.

The Dunlendings were tall and somewhat swarthy; they had dark hair. They were primitive, uncultured, and superstitious. (II 180; III 432, 434, 435, 505, 509)

DURIN I (FA) Dwarf, eldest and most renowned of the Seven Fathers of the Dwarves and the ancestor of Durin's Folk, the most important family of the Dwarves in the Third Age. Durin named Azanulbizar and its prominent features and began the building of Khazad-dûm.

Durin lived to a very great age, and for that reason he was called Durin the Deathless. The Dwarves believed that he would one day rise again. (I 411-12; III 438-39; S 44; B 42)

DURIN II (c. SA 750) Dwarf, King of Durin's Folk and of Khazad-dûm. He was probably King at the time of the building of the West-gate. (I 398)

DURIN III (fl. SA 16th Cent.) Dwarf, King of Durin's Folk and of Khazad-dûm at the time of the forging of the

Rings of Power. He was given the chief of the Seven Rings by Celebrimbor. (III 445)

DURIN VI (TA 1731-1980) Dwarf, King of Durin's Folk and of Khazad-dûm. In his time the Balrog was released, and Durin was slain by it. (III 439, 450)

DURIN VII (FO or later) Dwarf, last King of Durin's Folk. (III 450)

DURIN'S AXE The weapon of Durin I, a great heirloom of the Dwarves of Durin's Folk. Durin's Axe remained in Khazad-dûm when it was deserted in TA 1981; Balin's expedition found it in 2989. When Balin's colony was destroyed in 2994, the Axe was lost once again. (I 418)

DURIN'S BANE The Balrog (q.v.) who dwelt in Khazad-dûm, so called by the Dwarves because of his murder of Durin VI in TA 1980. (I 413)

DURIN'S BRIDGE A single fifty-foot arch of stone spanning the great abyss at the eastern end of the Second Hall of Khazad-dûm, built as a last defense against invaders from the east. During the Quest of Mount Doom Gandalf defended the Bridge against the Balrog, and broke it.

Also called the Bridge of Khazad-dûm and the Bridge. (I 419, 427-30; II 134)

DURIN'S CROWN Constellation of seven stars, the modern Plough, first seen by Durin I reflected around his head in Kheled-zâram. Ever after, the reflection of Durin's Crown could be seen in the lake, even in the daytime. Durin's Crown was the emblem of the line of Durin.

See: Valacirca. (I 397, 399, 433-34; RHM III 439-40)

DURIN'S DAY The time of Durin I, early in the First Age. (I 412, 454)

DURIN'S DAY   The first day of the Dwarvish year, so called only if the moon and the sun shone in the sky at the same time. The Dwarves' New Year was the first day of the last new crescent moon of autumn. (H 62-63)

DURIN'S FOLK   The eldest and greatest of the seven folk of the Dwarves, descended from Durin I. The ancestral hall of Durin's Folk was Khazad-dûm, and they were little concerned with the Wars of Beleriand. But they were friendlier with the Elves than most Dwarves, and in the Second Age they prospered from their contact with the Noldor of Eregion. Durin's Folk fought with the forces of the Last Alliance against Sauron.

In the Third Age Durin's Folk flourished in Khazad-dûm for nearly two thousand years, growing rich from the treasures of its mines, especially mithril. Although they had weathered all assaults from without, they were driven from Khazad-dûm by the rising of the Balrog in TA 1980. Durin's Folk then became a fragmented and wandering people, settling at various places in the Ered Mithrin, and in Erebor, until they were driven out by dragons. By TA 2800 only their paltry mines in the Ered Luin and the Iron Hills remained to them. In 2790, Thrór attempted to visit Khazad-dûm, but was slain by the Orcs who dwelt there. His son Thráin, in revenge, began the War of the Dwarves and Orcs (2793-99), in which Durin's Folk played the major role.

In 2941 Thorin II recovered Erebor, and Durin's Folk once more had a home and could become wealthy. Although Balin's colonization of Khazad-dûm in 2989 failed, with the death of the Balrog and the passing of Sauron in the WR Khazad-dûm may have been recovered by Durin's Folk in the Fourth Age.

Durin's Folk were ruled by the Kings of Durin's Folk (q.v.), who were the heirs of Durin. Because the Kings possessed the last and greatest of the Seven Rings, they and their people were the especial targets of Sauron's malice throughout the Third Age.

Durin's Folk were also known as the Longbeards; many

of them had long, frequently plaited and forked beards. (III 439-50; S 44, 294; B 42, 364)

DURIN'S STONE Pillar in Azanulbizar marking the spot where Durin I first looked into Kheled-zâram and saw Durin's Crown. Balin was slain here in TA 2994. (I 418, 433)

DURIN'S TOWER Chamber at the top of the Endless Stair of Khazad-dûm, carved in the rock of the pinnacle of Zirak-zigil. Durin's Tower was ruined in the Battle of the Peak in TA 3019. (II 135)

DURTHANG (S.: 'dark-oppression') Castle built early in the Third Age by Gondor on the ridge on the western side of the Udûn, used to guard that entrance to Mordor. Durthang, together with other similar fortifications, was deserted by Gondor about TA 1640. It was later turned into an orc-hold. (III 15, 251; S 364; B 457)

DWALIN (TA 2772-FO 92) Dwarf of Durin's Folk, second son of Fundin. Dwalin was one of the companions of Thráin during his wanderings from 2841 to 2845, and later was a member of Thorin and Company. After the recovery of Erebor Dwalin settled there. (III 446, 450; H 20, 26)

DWALING Village in the northern Eastfarthing. (I 40)

DWARF RINGS See: the Seven Rings.

DWARF-ROAD The trading-route built by the Dwarves of the Ered Luin. The road began at Mount Dolmed, went down the valley of the Ascar, and crossed Gelion at Sarn Athrad. The road then forked, the northern branch going past Nan Elmoth to the Arossiach and the southern branch going somewhere in East Beleriand.

Besides being a route for commerce, the Dwarf-road was the easiest entrance to Beleriand from Eriador. The Edain entered Beleriand in this way, and so did bands of ravishing Orcs. (S 92, 133, 140, 143, 145; B 104, 158, 167, 171, 174)

DWARROWDELF Khazad-dûm (q.v.). (III 519)

DWARVES One of the speaking races of Middle-earth, and one of the Free Peoples. Created by Aulë because of his impatience to behold the Children of Ilúvatar, they are not counted among the Children, although their life was later confirmed by Ilúvatar. After their making, the Seven Fathers (q.v.) slept until the awakening of the Elves, when they too awoke in widely differing places; ever after, they were divided into seven Folk, each with its own King and ancestral halls.

The final fate of the Dwarves is uncertain. The Elves said that they have no life beyond Arda and the death of their bodies, but the Dwarves themselves claimed that Aulë would bring them to the halls of Mandos, whence they will join the Children of Ilúvatar at the End.

Intended by Aulë to endure the power of Melkor, Dwarves were short (four and a half to five feet tall), stocky, strong, resistant to fire, and hardier than any other race. Unswerving and proud, Dwarves could not be dominated by evil and never forgot a wrong or a debt; they went to war frequently and wielded axes. They were fair but not overly generous, honest but secretive. As the children of Aulë, Dwarves were attracted to substances, to the depths of the earth, and to crafts; they were great miners and craftsmen and worked wonders with stone, metal, and jewels. Although never very friendly with other races, they got on well with the Noldor, with whom they shared a love of crafts and a reverence for Aulë. Their greatest flaws were a tendency toward wrath, possessiveness, and gold-lust.

Dwarves lived about 250 years and married about the age of 100. Although they sometimes flourished, the numbers of the Dwarves waned through the ages. They suffered heavily in their many wars (caused as often by their own pride as by the greed of others for their treasures) and were the especial target of Sauron, who resolved to destroy them when he found he could not dominate them. Also, few Dwarf women were born, and many of them did not marry.

The Dwarves had their own language, Khuzdul (q.v.), but it was a secret tongue. In public the Dwarves used the speech of their neighbors, in the First Age Sindarin and in the Third Age usually Westron or other tongues of Men. The names of the Dwarves in *H* and *LotR* are of northern Mannish form, and are thus Anglicized equivalents of names in the languages of Dale or Esgaroth. The Dwarves wrote with modified versions of the cirth; Durin's Folk used the Angerthas Moria.

The Dwarves called themselves the Khazâd, the name given them by Aulë. The Sindarin equivalent was Hadhod, but the Elves more commonly called them the Naugrim (in the First Age) or the Nogothrim or Noegyth (sing. Nogoth). Also called the Folk of the Mountain and the Gonnhirrim. (I 411; III 304, 396, 430, 438-51, 455, 493-95, 501-04, 512-13, 514, 518-19; H 16, 165, 204, 227, 263; S 43-45, 91-95, 113, 193, 288-89, 362; B 40-42, 103-08, 132, 236, 357-58, 454)

DWARVISH See: Khuzdul. (III 488)

DWIMMERLAIK (tr. Roh.: 'work of necromancy, spectre') Name given to the Lord of the Nazgûl by Eowyn during the Battle of the Pelennor Fields. (III 140-42; RHM III 421)

DWIMORBERG (tr. Roh.: 'haunted-mountain') Mountain in the Ered Nimrais behind Dunharrow, in which was the Dark Door.

Called in Westron the Haunted Mountain. (III 69 ff., 81)

DWIMORDENE (tr. Roh.: 'haunted-valley') Name given Lórien (q.v.) by the Rohirrim. (II 150)

EÄ (Q.: imperative of *to be*)   The Creation, the realization of the Vision and the Ainulindalë by the will of Ilúvatar. Eä comprises Arda and the heavens (Ilmen or menel), is animated by the Secret Fire, and is bound by the principles of matter, space, and Time. Outside Eä are the Timeless Halls and the Void (qq.v.).

Also called the World (q.v.) and the World that Is.

See also: Arda, the Circles of the World, the Deeps of Time, the End. (I 261; III 316, 390; K 59; S 17, 19, 20, 21, 25, 49, 260; B 6, 8, 10, 11, 17, 49, 320)

EAGLES   The greatest and noblest of birds, created by Manwë (and Yavanna) before the awakening of the Children of Ilúvatar, apparently as the lords of the kelvar. Charged to aid Elves and Men against Morgoth, in the First Age the Eagles of the Encircling Mountains, led by their lord Thorondor, nested in the Crissaegrim. Aside from the individual exploits of Thorondor, the great deeds of the Eagles included the protection of Gondolin from the spies of Morgoth; the rescue of Beren and Lúthien outside Angband; the protection of Tuor, Idril, and the survivors of Gondolin as they fled the city; and the defeat (with Eärendil) of the winged dragons in the Great Battle.

In the Second Age many of the Eagles may have gone to Aman. They flew from the west to warn Númenor of its imminent destruction.

In the Third Age the Eagles of the Misty Mountains, led by Gwaihir, aided Gandalf and Radagast. They played key roles in the expedition of Thorin and Company and the Battle of Five Armies, and during the WR freed Gandalf from Orthanc and rescued Frodo and Sam from the burning slopes of Orodruin.

The Eagles were easily large enough to carry a Man (or a Dwarf plus a Hobbit); Thorondor, the largest, had a wingspan of 180 feet. They could speak the tongues of Men and Elves. Eagles lived a very long time, and may have been immortal; Thorondor's deeds spanned nearly 600 years.

Called the Eagles of Manwë, of the King, of the Lords of the West, and of the North. Also called the Great Eagles. The Sindarin for eagle is *thoron*. (I 342-43; III 278; H 108, 110-16, 273; S 46, 110, 182, 228, 241, 243, 277-78; B 45, 129, 221, 281, 297, 301, 343)

EÄRENDIL (Q.: 'sea-lover') (b. FA 504)   Adan of the Third House, son of Tuor and Idril. Born in Gondolin, as a child Eärendil was brought to Arvernien, where he became friendly with Círdan and loved the Sea. In time he became the lord of Arvernien and married Elwing. Their sons were Elrond and Elros. Yet he could not be content on land; in his ship Vingilot he explored all of Belegaer, looking for his parents and for the western shore, but he was confounded by the Shadowy Seas.

When Arvernien was ravaged by the sons of Fëanor, by the power of Ulmo Elwing flew to Eärendil at sea, and with her Silmaril they won through to Aman. There Eärendil gained the mercy of the Valar for the peoples of Beleriand, but he, a mortal who had walked in the Undying Lands, his ship, and the Silmaril were set in the sky as a sign of hope to those oppressed by evil. He slew Ancalagon in the Great Battle, and later guided the Edain to Númenor.

Eärendil possessed the beauty, wisdom, and hardiness of his noble Eldarin and Adanic ancestry. He was known as Bright Eärendil, Eärendil the Mariner, and Eärendil the Blessed.

As a star, Eärendil seems to have corresponded to Venus, and was referred to as the Flammifer of Westernesse, as well as the Morning Star, the Evening Star, and Gil-Estel. He was the star most beloved of the Elves, and his light had great power. (See: the Phial of Galadriel) (I 308-12; III 389; K 58; S 105, 148, 241, 242-44, 246-50, 252, 255, 259, 260, 286, 305, 306, 307; B 122, 177, 298, 300-02, 304-09, 312, 315, 319, 321, 354, 379, 380, 381)

EÄRENDIL (d. TA 324)   Dúnadan, fifth King of Gondor (238-324). (III 394)

EÄRENDUR (Q.: 'sea-friend') (fl. SA 31st Cent.) Dúnadan of Númenor, Lord of Andúnië. (S 268, 362; B 331)

EÄRENDUR (Q.: 'sea—') (d. TA 861) Dúnadan, tenth King of Arnor (777-861). At his death Arnor was divided among his sons. (III 394; S 296; B 454)

EÄRENYA (Q.: 'sea-day')   Sixth day of the Númenórean and subsequent enquier.
    Called in Sindarin (used only by the Dúnedain) Oraearon, and Meresdei by the Hobbits. (III 484)

EÄRNIL I (Q.: 'sea-lover') (d. TA 936) Dúnadan, thirteenth King of Gondor (913-36) and the second Shipking. Eärnil repaired Pelargir, built a great navy, and took Umbar from the Black Númenóreans. He died when his fleet was caught in a great storm off Umbar. (III 395, 403; S 362; B 454)

EÄRNIL II (d. TA 2043)   Dúnadan, thirty-second King of Gondor (1945-2043). A great soldier, Eärnil was Captain of the Southern Army, which in 1944 defeated the Haradrim and the Wainriders in two decisive battles that saved Gondor from being overrun. Since King Ondoher and both his sons had been killed by the Wainriders, after a year of dissension the crown was given to Eärnil, who as a descendant of Umbardacil was a member of the royal family.
    Eärnil was a wise ruler; he strengthened Gondor and in 1974 dispatched a fleet commanded by his son Eärnur (q.v.) to the aid of Arthedain. (III 395, 409-11; S 297; B 368)

EÄRNUR (Q.: 'sea-friend') (d. TA 2050) Dúnadan, thirty-third King of Gondor (2043-50). In 1974, Eärnur, then Captain of Gondor, was sent to Arthedain by his father Eärnil to aid the Dúnedain of the North against Angmar. His army comprised the major part of the Host of the West which defeated Angmar in the Battle of Fornost in 1975. Eärnur, however, was shamed when his horse bolted from the presence of the Lord of the Nazgûl. In 2043, when the Lord of the Nazgûl was in Minas Morgul and Eärnur was King of Gondor, the former challenged the king to personal combat, taunting that Eärnur had fled from him in 1975. Eärnur was restrained by Mardil the Steward, but in 2050 he was challenged again and rode off to Minas Morgul, whence he never returned.

Eärnur was a great captain, but was proud and cared little for anything but arms. He took no wife, and thus produced no heir. At his death the Line of Anárion ended. (III 303, 395, 411-13; S 297, 362; B 369, 454)

EÄRRÁMË (Q.: 'sea-wing') The ship built by Tuor in which he and Idril sailed into the West. (S 245; B 303)

EARTH Arda (q.v.). (S 19; B 8)

EÄRWEN (Q.: 'sea-lady') (FA-) Elda of the Teleri, the daughter of Olwë, wife of Finarfin and mother of Finrod, Orodreth, Angrod, Aegnor, and Galadriel. (S 60, 111, 305, 306; B 63, 130, 379, 380)

EAST BELERIAND That part of Beleriand east of Sirion and west of Gelion, at its widest a hundred leagues in extent. East Beleriand included the realm of Doriath and the regions of Dimbar, Nan Dungortheb, Dor Dínen, Himlad, Estolad, and the deserted forests of Taur-im-Duinath (qq.v.). East Beleriand was ruled by Thingol (Doriath and its northern marches) and the House of Fëanor (the lands east of Aros). (S 121-23, 124; B 144-46, 148)

EAST-ELVES The Silvan Elves (q.v.). (III 505)

EASTEMNET That part of Rohan east of the Entwash. (I 17; II 35)

EASTERLINGS Tribes of Men who entered into Beleriand after Dagor Bragollach, some at the instigation of Morgoth and some out of desire for the rich lands of Beleriand. Many of them entered the service of the House of Fëanor and played a crucial part in the Nirnaeth Arnoediad. The sons of Bór remained faithful to Maedhros in that battle, but the sons of Ulfang betrayed Caranthir and caused the collapse of the eastern army of the Elves. After the battle, the Easterlings who served Morgoth were shut away in Hithlum, where they married some of the surviving women of the Edain and enslaved the rest of the Edain and Elves. They perished in the Great Battle.

The Easterlings were short and broad; they were dark of skin, eye, and hair. Their culture was rather primitive.

Also called the Swarthy Men. (S 157, 189, 193, 195, 198, 238, 251; B 189, 231, 235, 239, 242-43, 294, 311)

EASTERLINGS The Men of Rhûn. Beginning in TA 490, waves of Easterlings of various tribes and races periodically attacked Gondor, usually over Dagorlad. Some of these invasions were clearly military, and were no doubt inspired by Sauron, but others, such as the invasion of the Balchoth in 2510, seem to have involved the migration of entire peoples.

The Easterlings were in general primitive, and were motivated chiefly by hatred of Gondor and greed for her riches. In the Fourth Age, the Easterlings living nearest Gondor were subdued by Elessar.

The Easterlings who fought in the Battle of the Pelennor Fields were bearded and bore great axes, but they seem to have been atypical.

See: Balchoth, Wainriders. (I 322; III 115, 148, 403, 404-05, 438, 468-69; L 163)

EASTFARTHING One of the Four Farthings of the Shire. Its inhabitants had a strong Stoorish strain. (I 26, 40)

EASTFOLD Area of Rohan bounded by the Mering

Stream, the Entwash, the Snowbourn, and the Ered Nimrais. (III 14, 89, 93-94)

EAST LÓRIEN An Elven-realm founded by Celeborn at the beginning of the Fourth Age and peopled with Silvan Elves from Lórien. East Lórien comprised all of Eryn Lasgalen south of the Narrows. (III 468)

EAST MARCH, THE Buckland (q.v.). (I 30)

EAST ROAD The Great East Road (q.v.). (I 207)

EAST WALL The great cliff at the western edge of the Emyn Muil (q.v.), which marked the eastern boundary of Rohan at that point. (II 29-30)

EAST-WEST ROAD The Great East Road (q.v.). (I 72)

ECHOING HILLS, ECHOING MOUNTAINS Ered Lómin (q.v.). (S 106, 119; B 123, 140)

ECHORIATH (S.: 'circle' + collective plural) Mountains between the Pass of Sirion and Dorthonion, in the midst of which was the hidden valley of Tumladen. The Eagles nested in the Crissaegrim, the southern Echoriath.
    Also called the Encircling Mountains. (III 278; S 115, 138, 228; B 135, 166, 282)

ECHUIR (S.) The Sindarin form of coirë (q.v.). (III 480)

ECTHELION OF THE FOUNTAIN (S.) (d. FA 511) Elf, captain of Gondolin and warden of the Gate. In the fall of Gondolin he slew and was slain by Gothmog, Lord of Balrogs. (S 194, 239, 242; B 237, 296, 300)

ECTHELION I (d. TA 2698) Dúnadan, seventeenth Ruling Steward of Gondor (2685-98). (III 395)

ECTHELION II (d. TA 2984) Dúnadan, twenty-fifth Ruling Steward of Gondor (2953-84). During his rule Aragorn, disguised as Thorongil, served Gondor, and in 2980 he led the force which destroyed a large part of the fleet of Umbar. (III 395, 417)

EDAIN (S.: 'the second ones') Men of the Three Houses of the Elf-friends. In the 4th Century FA the Edain, drawn toward the Light of the West, entered Beleriand, where many of them entered the service of the Eldar and fought valiantly in the Wars of Beleriand. Some, however, remained in Estolad or fled south or east from the power of Morgoth, and pass from history until the Third Age. Despite their mighty heroes, the Edain were decimated by the hordes of Morgoth, but one of their number, Eärendil of the House of Hador, sailed to Aman and obtained from the Valar the aid by which Morgoth was defeated in the Last Battle. The remnant of the Edain, increased in body and mind by Eönwë, then sailed to Númenor and became known as the Dúnedain (q.v.).

The Edain were tall and fair and strong; their spirits were noble, they were fierce in war, and they shunned all dealings with evil. In Beleriand the Edain loved the Eldar, from whom they learned much wisdom, and they were further ennobled by the two marriages of Elda and Adan: Beren and Lúthien and Tuor and Idril. The lifespan of the Edain before they entered Beleriand was probably about 70 years; in Beleriand it was lengthened to 90, but few of the Edain lived to old age in peace.

The language of the Edain (at least those of the First and Third Houses) was related to Adûnaic, but in Beleriand most of the Edain spoke Sindarin.

Also called the Elf-friends, the Atanatári, the Fathers of Men, and the Men of the Three Houses. The Quenya form was Atani.

See also: the First House, the Haladin, the Third House, and the Men of the Twilight. (III 388, 390-93, 404, 506-07; 508; S 41, 103-04, 140-49, 156-57, 251, 259, 260, 318; B 37, 120, 168-79, 189, 311, 320, 395)

EDGE OF THE WILD The boundary between the settled lands of Eriador and the dangerous lands of the Wild; roughly speaking, a line drawn north and south through a point slightly west of the Ford of Bruinen. (H 12, 65)

EDHELLOND (S.: 'elf-haven') The harbor, either at Dol Amroth or at the mouth of the Morthond-Ringló, from which the southern white ships of the Eldar sailed to Aman. (PB)

EDHIL (S., sing. *edhel*) The Elves or the Eldar (qq.v.). Cf.: Ost-in-Edhil, Peredhil. (R 62)

EDORAS (tr. Roh.: 'the courts') Capital of Rohan, located on the Snowbourn at the foot of the Ered Nimrais. Edoras was built by Eorl and Brego, and contained the great feast-hall of Meduseld. (I 343; II 141, 144 ff.; III 430, 432, 433)

EDRAHIL (S.) (d. FA 466 or 467) Elf of Nargothrond, the chief of the band of ten Elves who accompanied Beren and Finrod on the Quest of the Silmaril. He died in the dungeons of Minas Tirith. (S 170, 172, 174; B 206, 208, 210)

EGALMOTH (S.) (d. TA 2743) Dúnadan, eighteenth Ruling Steward of Gondor (2698-2743). (III 395)

EGLADIL (S.) The heart of Lórien, the area between Anduin and Celebrant near their confluence.
    Called in Westron the Angle. (I 450)

EGLADOR (S.: 'land of the forsaken'?) Early name for the lands contained within the Girdle of Melian, later called Doriath (q.v.). (S 97, 326; B 111, 405)

EGLANTINE TOOK (fl. TA 3000) Hobbit, wife of Paladin Took and mother of Peregrin Took. She was born a Banks, and was a guest at the Farewell Party. (III 475)

EGLAREST (S.)   One of the Havens of the Falas (q.v.), located at the mouth of the River Nenning. Built early in the First Age and strengthened with the aid of Finrod after the return of the Noldor, Eglarest was besieged and destroyed by the armies of Morgoth in 474. The survivors fled to Balar. (S 58, 120, 196; B 60, 142, 239)

EGLATH (S.: 'forsaken' + collective plural)   Those of the Teleri (q.v.) who remained in Middle-earth for the love of Elwë. When he awoke from his trance, they gathered around him in Doriath. (S 58; B 61)

EILENACH (S.)   The second of the northern beacon-tower hills of Gondor, located in Druadan Forest. (III 14, 20, 127)

EILINEL (S.) (d. FA 455?)   Adan of the First House, wife of Gorlim. She was slain when Dorthonion was over-run after Dagor Bragollach. Sauron used her husband's love for her to trick Gorlim into betraying Barahir. (S 162; B 195-96)

EITHEL IVRIN (S.: 'springs of Ivrin')   The source of the River Narog, springs (and perhaps waterfalls) at the southern foot of the Ered Wethrin. The pools of Ivrin were beautiful and their water pure, being guarded by Ulmo. But Eithel Ivrin was defiled by Glaurung as the Worm moved on Nargothrond.

Also called the Falls of Ivrin and the Pools of Ivrin. (S 113, 120, 209, 210, 212, 215, 358, 360; B 132, 142, 256, 257, 261, 264, 449, 452)

EITHEL SIRION (S.: 'wells of Sirion')   The source of the River Sirion, located at the foot of the eastern Ered Wethrin. The strategic fortress of Barad Eithel (q.v.) was located here. The springs were defiled after the Nirnaeth Arnoediad.

Eithel Sirion refers to both springs and fortress. (S 119, 120, 152, 212; B 140, 141, 183, 260)

EKKAIA (Q.?)   The great Sea of the First and Second Ages encircling the lands of Arda, itself bounded by the Walls of the Night. It met Belegaer at the Helcaraxë. Ekkaia was totally refashioned at the Change of the World.

Also called the Outer Ocean, the Outer Sea, and the Encircling Sea. (S 37, 89, 100; B 32, 100, 116)

ELANOR (S.: 'star-sun')   Yellow winter flower of Lórien, shaped like a star. (I 454)

ELANOR GAMGEE (b. FO 1)   Hobbit of the Shire, eldest child of Sam Gamgee. In her youth she was a maid of honor to Queen Arwen. In FO 31 Elanor married Fastred of Greenholm, and in 35 they moved to the Tower Hills, where they lived at Undertowers. In 62 Elanor was given the Red Book of Westmarch by her father, and the Book was kept by her descendants, the Fairbairns of the Tower.

Elanor was called "the Fair" because of her beauty; she had blonde hair. (III 378-79, 402, 470, 471-72, 477; RHM III 378)

ELBERETH (S.: 'star-queen')   The most common Sindarin name for Varda (q.v.). (I 117; R 61; S 26; B 19)

ELDACAR (Q.: 'high-elf—') (d. TA 339)   Dúnadan, fourth King of Arnor (249-339). (III 394)

ELDACAR (d. TA 1490)   Dúnadan, twenty-first King of Gondor (1432-37, 1447-90). Because his mother was not a Dúnadan, and because he had been born in Rhovanion and called in his youth Vinitharya, Eldacar was believed to be less than a true Dúnadan of Gondor, and so the royal family rebelled against him. This rebellion, the Kin-strife, lasted for five years, for Eldacar was a noble man and a valiant soldier and was not easily defeated. Eventually, however, he was besieged in Osgiliath, but he escaped and fled to Rhovanion. Ten years later, in 1447, Eldacar returned to Gondor with an army of Northmen. Gaining much support from the people of northern Gondor, Eldacar slew his cruel successor, Castamir the Usurper, in the Battle of the Crossings of Erui and recovered his throne. Despite his mixed blood, Eldacar did not age more swiftly than other Dúnedain, and he proved a good ruler. (III 395, 405-07)

ELDALIE (Q.: 'people of the Eldar') The Eldar (q.v.). (S 22, 53, 190; B 12, 54, 55, 232)

ELDAMAR (Q.: 'elvenhome') The lands of the Eldar in the west, including Calacirian, the coastal area east of the Pelóri, and Tol Eressëa. Its chief cities were Tirion in Calacirian, Alqualondë on the coast, and Avallónë on Tol Eressëa, but there were other settlements as well.

Called Faerie in *The Hobbit*. The Westron name was Elvenhome. Also called Elendë and Elvenland. (I 309, 482; III 289, 506; H 164; TB 63; R 62; S 59-62; B 62-65)

ELDAR (Q.: 'people of the stars') The Vanyar, Noldor, and Teleri (qq.v.), the Three Kindreds of Elves (q.v.) of the Great Journey. Summoned to Aman by Oromë early in the First Age, the Eldar made their slow way west from Cuiviénen to Beleriand, save for the Nandor (q.v.), who turned south down the Vales of Anduin. The Vanyar and Noldor were towed to Aman by Ulmo, but the Teleri lingered in Beleriand. At length a part of the Teleri also went over Sea, dwelling first on Tol Eressëa and later at Alqualondë, but many of the Teleri remained in Beleriand and became known as the Sindar (q.v.).

In later years the Vanyar dwelt in Valinor and the Teleri in Eldamar, but Fëanor led most of the Noldor back to Middle-earth in pursuit of the Silmarils stolen by Morgoth. There the Eldar first encountered the Edain, but at length the two races were virtually destroyed by Morgoth. At the end of the First Age most of the Eldar of Middle-earth went to Aman, where they renewed their friendship with the Dúnedain, now in Númenor.

In the Second Age, many of the Eldar who remained in Middle-earth lived in Lindon, where they were ruled by

Gil-galad, last heir of the Noldorin kings in Middle-earth, while others, led by Celebrimbor, founded Eregion. Still others of the Eldar, such as Thranduil, Galadriel, and Celeborn, went farther east and founded Elven-realms, peopled mostly by Silvan Elves. However, the Eldar were troubled by Sauron, and their numbers dwindled and they did little new. With the waning of the Three Rings at the end of the Third Age, many of the mightiest Eldar passed over Sea, and those who remained dwindled in power.

The Eldar were tall, grey-eyed, and fair; save for the blond Vanyar and the House of Finarfin, they were dark-haired. The noblest of the Firstborn of Ilúvatar, the Eldar were further strengthened in wisdom and power by their stay in Aman, and those who had seen the light of the Two Trees had power against the Seen and the Unseen rivaling that of the Maiar who followed Morgoth. When aroused they shone with the strength of their spirits. They had great skill in all things, but especially with words. Within all Eldar burned a desire for Aman, instilled by the summons of Oromë, and for the Sea by which Aman was reached, instilled by the horns of Ulmo; never quieted in the minds of the Exiles, this desire slept in the Sindar, but once awakened could not be ignored. The Eldar had a great reverence for stars, living things, the Sea and the Valar, especially Varda.

The Eldar originally spoke Quenya. The dialect of the Teleri seems to have diverged somewhat from that of the Eldar of Aman during their stay on Tol Eressëa, but in Middle-earth the speech of the Sindar developed into a new language, Sindarin. They wrote with the Tengwar or the Cirth, both of which they devised.

The term Eldar first referred to all the Elves, but later was limited to the Three Kindreds. They were also called the High Kindred, the Three Kindreds, the Eldalië, the People of the Stars, and the People of the Great Journey. The term High Elves refers to all the Eldar sometimes and to the Tareldar (q.v.) at others. Called the Nómin by the early Edain. The Sindarin form was eledh or edhel (pl. edhil). (I 294, 472; III 388, 389, 390, 392, 393, 455, 505-06, 514, 519; H 164; R 60, 62, 65-66; S 49, 52-54, 57-62,

102, 254, 263, 286, 304, 309, 326; B 49, 52-55, 59-65, 117, 315, 324, 354, 378, 383, 406)

ELDARIN General name for the languages spoken by the Eldar. The two of which examples are given in *LotR* are Quenya and Sindarin (qq.v.). (III 506; S 326; B 406)

ELDARION (Q.: 'of the Eldar') (b. FO 1st Cent.) Dúnadan, second King of the Reunited Kingdom (FO 120-?). He was the only son of Elessar and Arwen. (III 427)

ELDER CHILDREN OF ILÚVATAR The Elves (q.v.). (S 49, 210; B 49, 258)

ELDER DAYS The First Age (q.v.). In the Fourth Age all earlier ages were sometimes called the Elder Days. (I 21; III 452)

ELDER KINDRED The Elves (q.v.). (III 308)

ELDER KING Manwë (q.v.). (I 310; III 392; S 249; B 309)

ELDER RACE The Elves (q.v.). (III 101)

ELDEST DAYS The First Age (q.v.). (S 103, 294; B 119, 365)

ELDEST OF TREES Telperion (q.v.). (S 291; B 361)

ELEDHWEN (S.: 'elfsheen') Epithet applied to Morwen (q.v.). (S 155, 229, 358; B 187, 283, 449)

ELEMMÍRE (Q.: 'star-jewel') A star, wrought by Varda in preparation for the awakening of the Elves. (S 48; B 48)

ELEMMÍRE (FA-) Elda of the Vanyar, the author of *Aldudénië*. (S 76; B 84)

ELENDË (Q.: 'elf-middle'?) Eldamar (q.v.). (S 61, 85, 107; B 65, 96, 124)

ELENDIL, TAR- (Q.: 'star-lover' or 'elf-friend') (fl. SA 600) Dúnadan, fourth King of Númenor. During his reign Númenórean ships first returned to Middle-earth. (III 390, 391; RHM III 421; S 268; B 331)

ELENDIL (d. SA 3441) Dúnadan of Númenor, son of Amandil of Andúnië and leader of the Faithful, the noblest of the Dúnedain to survive the fall of Númenor. A great mariner, Elendil gathered his sons Isildur and Anárion and some of the Faithful in ships off the coast of Númenor before the fleet of Ar-Pharazôn sailed to Aman. With four ships he was blown to Middle-earth by the storms of the Change of the World and landed in Lindon. He established the Kingdom of Arnor, which he ruled directly, and was the first High King of Arnor and Gondor. Elendil was one of the leaders of the Last Alliance which overthrew Sauron and, with his friend Gil-galad, its greatest warrior. He was slain, along with Gil-galad, by Sauron on the slopes of Orodruin, but they in turn overthrew their enemy.

Elendil's sword was the famous Narsil.

He was known as Elendil the Tall and Elendil the Fair. (I 83, 319, 320; II 363; III 303, 391, 392-93, 394; S 272, 275-76, 279-80, 290-91, 292, 293-94; B 337, 340-42, 346, 360-61, 362, 364-65)

ELENDILI (Q.: 'elf-friends') The Faithful (q.v.). (S 266; B 328)

ELENDILMIR (Q.: 'Elendil-jewel') The Star of Elendil (q.v.) (III 401)

ELENDUR (Q.) (d. TA 2) Dúnadan, the eldest son of Isildur. He was slain in the Battle of the Gladden Fields. (S 295; B 366)

ELENDUR (Q.) (d. TA 777) Dúnadan, ninth King of Arnor (652-777). (III 394)

ELENNA (Q.: 'starwards,' 'star' + essive case ending) Númenor (q.v.), or the island on which the kingdom was founded. (III 390; S 261; B 321)

ELENTÁRI (Q.: 'star-queen') Epithet of Varda (q.v.). (I 489; R 59, 66; S 48; B 47)

ELENWË (Q.) (FA) Elda of the Vanyar, the wife of Turgon and mother of Idril. One of the Exiles, she died in the crossing of the Helcaraxë. (S 90, 136; B 102, 163)

ELENYA (Q.: 'star's-day') The first day of the enquië in all Elven, Dúnedain, and related calendars.
Called in Sindarin Orgilion, and Sterrendei (later Sterday) by the Hobbits. (III 484)

ELERRÍNA (Q.: 'star-crowned') Taniquetil (q.v.). (S 37; B 32)

ELESSAR (Q.: 'elf-stone') The name under which Aragorn (q.v.) took the throne of the Reunited Kingdom. It was foretold for him by Galadriel, and was given him by the people of Gondor during the WR because of the great emerald brooch, a gift from Arwen, which he wore. (I 486; III 302-10)

ELF-FRIENDS The Three Houses of the Elf-friends, the Edain (q.v.).
"Elf-friend" was also a title or epithet bestowed by Elves upon those of other races who aided them or liked them. Hador, Húrin, Beren, Túrin, Bilbo, and Frodo, for example, were Elf-friends. (I 119, 124, 173, 355; II 364; III 507; H 277; S 143; B 171)

ELF-FRIENDS The Elendili, the Faithful (q.v.) of Númenor. (S 266, 272; B 328, 336)

ELFHELM (fl. WR) Rider of Rohan, marshal of the éored with which Éowyn and Merry rode to the Battle of the Pelennor Fields. Later in the WR, Elfhelm commanded the Rohirrim who defended Anórien while the Host of the West rode to the Morannon. (III 127, 135, 193)

ELFHILD (d. TA 2978)   Woman of Rohan, wife of King Théoden. Elfhild died giving birth to her only child, Théodred. (III 437)

ELFSTAN FAIRBAIRN (b. FO 34)   Hobbit of the Shire, eldest son and heir of Fastred and Elanor, and first of the Fairbairns of the Tower. He was probably Warden of Westmarch.

Elfstan's name means "elfstone" in translated Hobbitish; he was probably named after King Elessar. (III 471)

ELFSTONE   Aragorn II (q.v.). (III 302)

ELFWINE (early FO)   Man, nineteenth King of Rohan (63-?). He was known as Elfwine the Fair. (III 438)

ELLADAN (S.: 'elf-man') (TA 139-FO?)   Elda, son of Elrond and Celebrían and identical twin brother of Elrohir. With his brother he rescued Celebrían from an Orc-hold in TA 2509, and ever after the brothers rode against the Orcs with the Rangers to avenge their mother's torment. During the WR Elladan and Elrohir rode south with Halbarad, and accompanied Aragorn from Rohan to the Morannon. Because of their Elven-wisdom and the counsel they had received from their father before setting forth, Elladan and Elrohir were present at the councils of the Lords of the West, and may themselves have been numbered among the Lords.

Elladan and Elrohir remained in Imladris well into the Fourth Age, and since they did not accompany Elrond over Sea they seem to have chosen to become mortal. (I 39, 300; III 60, 389, 456, 468)

ELOSTIRION (S.: 'star-watch')   The tallest and westernmost of the White Towers (q.v.). The palantír which looked to the Undying Lands was kept here. (I 27; S 292; B 362)

ELROHIR (S.: 'elf-horse-master') (TA 139-FA?) Elda, son of Elrond and Celebrían and identical twin brother of Elladan (q.v.). (I 39, 300; III 60, 389, 456, 468)

ELROND (S.: 'star-dome') (FA-) One of the Peredhil, the son of Eärendil and Elwing and brother of Elros. Born in Arvernien, Elrond was captured by the sons of Fëanor when they attacked Arvernien to recover the Silmaril. He was befriended by Maglor and may have fought in the Great Battle. At the end of the First Age the Valar allowed Elrond to choose his race; he decided to join the Elven-kind, and was made an Eldarin lord of great power and penetrating wisdom.

Elrond dwelt in Lindon with Gil-galad until SA 1695, when he was sent by the latter to Eregion to aid in the defense of that realm against Sauron. When Eregion was overrun in 1697, Elrond fled with the surviving Noldor and founded Imladris (Rivendell), which became, especially after the fall of Gil-galad, one of the greatest Elven refuges in Middle-earth. During the war of the Last Alliance, Elrond was Gil-galad's herald and stood by him when he fell.

In TA 100 Elrond married Celebrían, the daughter of Galadriel and Celeborn; their children were Elladan, Elrohir, and Arwen. Throughout the Third Age Elrond gave aid and counsel to the Dúnedain of the North, first military aid for the protection of Arnor and Arthedain and later shelter for the Dúnedain, especially the Line of Isildur, his distant nephews. At the end of the Third Age Elrond departed over Sea with the Last Riding of the Keepers of the Rings.

Elrond bore the greatest of the Three Rings, Vilya, which he was given by Gil-galad. He was known as Elrond Half-elven and Master Elrond. (I 258, 292, 296, 299, 319; III 381-84, 389, 454, 456; H 60-61; S 246, 247, 249, 254, 286, 288, 297-98, 300, 305, 306, 307, 327, 363; B 304, 305, 308, 315, 354, 357, 369-70, 372, 373, 379, 380, 381, 407, 456)

ELROS (S.: 'star-foam') (FA-SA 422) One of the

Peredhil, son of Eärendil and Elwing and brother of El-rond, born 58 years before the end of the First Age. Like his brother, he was born in Arvernien, captured by the sons of Fëanor, and befriended by Maglor. At the end of the First Age he chose the Gift of Men, but was granted a life-span of 500 years.

Elros led the remnant of the Edain to Númenor and was appointed first King of the Dúnedain (32-442) by the Valar. His heirs were the Kings of Númenor, Arnor, and Gondor.

Elros took Tar-Minyatur as his regnal name; he built the royal tower and citadel at Armenelos. (III 389-90, 453; S 246, 247, 249, 254, 261, 305, 306, 307, 327; B 304, 305, 308, 315, 322, 379, 380, 381, 407)

ELU The Sindarin form of Elwë (q.v.). (S 56, 327; B 58, 407)

ELUCHÍL (S.: 'Elu's heir') Epithet applied to Dior (q.v.). (S 188; B 229)

ELURÉD (S.: 'Elu's heir') (FA) Eldarin Elf, son of Dior and Nimloth. During the assault of the sons of Fëanor on Menegroth, Eluréd and his brother Elurín were abandoned in the forest by the servants of Celegorm. The two children were never heard from again. (S 234, 236-37; B 290, 291-92)

ELURÍN (S.: 'Elu-remembrance') (FA) Eldarin Elf, son of Dior and Nimloth and brother of Eluréd (q.v.). (S 234, 236-37; B 289, 292)

ELVEN DOOR The West-gate (q.v.) of Khazad-dûm. (I 393)

ELVENESSE The land of Elves, possibly Nargothrond or Eldamar but seemingly the collective realms of all Elves. (S 171; B 207)

ELVENHOME Eldamar (q.v.). (I 309; III 289; TB 63; S 58; B 61)

ELVENHOME Doriath (q.v.), in the song of Beren and Lúthien. (I 258)

ELVENHOME An Elven-realm, perhaps Nargothrond, probably somewhere in Beleriand. (TB 8, 53)

ELVENKING, THE Thranduil (q.v.). (H 168)

ELVENLAND Eldamar (q.v.). (S 171; B 207)

ELVEN-RINGS The Rings of Power, especially the Three Rings (qq.v.). (S 287; B 356)

ELVEN-RIVER Esgalduin (q.v.). (I 258)

ELVEN-SMITHS The Gwaith-i-Mírdain (q.v.). (I 318; S 288; B 357)

ELVES The Firstborn, the Elder Children of Ilúvatar, conceived by Eru alone in the third theme of Ainulindalë, the eldest and noblest of the speaking races of Middle-earth. They awoke by Cuiviénen in the starlight of the Sleep of Yavanna, and there they were visited by Oromë, who loved them, and by Melkor, who captured some of them and bred them into Orcs.

Early in the First Age the Elves were divided into two groups—the Eldar (q.v.), who accepted the summons of the Valar, undertook the Great Journey, and were ennobled by their life in Aman; and the Avari, who refused the summons and became the lesser Silvan Elves. The Elves flourished in the First Age, but the Eldarin realms of Beleriand were destroyed by Morgoth, and in later ages their power waned. In the Second and Third Ages some Elves still lived in Wandering Companies, traveling through the broad lands they loved, but many were gathered in Elven-realms and refuges such as Lindon, Imladris, the Woodland Realm, and Lórien, where Eldarin lords ruled over Silvan populations. But by the end of the Third Age the Dominion of Men was at hand, and the Elves who remained in Middle-earth dwindled and became a secret people. Yet in Eldamar the Eldar live nigh to the Valar until the End of the World.

Elves were the fairest of all earthly creatures and resembled the Ainur in spirit. They were about six feet tall and somewhat slender, graceful but strong and resistant to the extremes of nature. Their senses, especially of hearing and sight, were much keener than those of Men. Elves apparently did not sleep, but rested their minds in waking dreams or by looking at beautiful things. The Eldar, and perhaps all Elves, could talk directly from mind to mind without words.

Elves loved all beautiful things, but especially the wonders of nature, above all the waters of Ulmo and the stars of Elbereth that shone on them at their awakening. Their curiosity and desire for knowledge was insatiable; one of their great achievements was to teach the Ents to talk. As their own name for themselves (Quendi, 'the speakers') implies, they valued communication highly. They were by nature good and abhorred all works of evil, although they could be seduced by evil that seemed fair.

At first the Elves of Middle-earth welcomed Men, but after the treachery of the Nirnaeth Arnoediad the two races were estranged, except for the Edain and their descendants. There were three marriages between the Edain and the Eldar, and apparently others between the Edain (especially the Dúnedain of Dol Amroth) and lesser Elves. The Elves (except for the Noldor) never had much to do with the Dwarves; the hunting of the Noegyth Nibin by Elves of Beleriand and the murder of Thingol and sack of Doriath by Dwarves of Nogrod were perhaps the earliest of the many events that alienated the two races.

Although they could be slain or die of grief, Elves were not subject to age or disease. An Elf who lost his life went to the halls of Mandos, whence he could go elsewhere in Valinor but not return to Middle-earth. In this *Guide* death-dates for Elves indicate the death of their bodies in Middle-earth. The fate of Elves is bound to Eä, and they cannot leave the Circles of the World until the End, when they will join with the Ainur (and perhaps Men) in the Second Music before the throne of Ilúvatar.

The Elves had three Rings of Power, which were given to the three greatest of the Eldar.

They called themselves Quendi, the Speakers. Also called the Elder Children of Ilúvatar, the Firstborn of Ilúvatar, the Firstborn, the Elder Kindred, the Elder Race, the Elder People, the Fair Folk, the Merry People, and the Folk of the Wood. The name Eldar originally referred to all Elves. (I 17, 123-24, 472, 503; II 37, 55, 84, 90; III 181-82, 289, 325-26, 421, 519; H 57-60, 150-53, 164-65; TB 53; S 18, 41-42, 48-50, 52-54, 56, 88, 104-05, 195, 264-65, 304; B 7-8, 37-39, 47-50, 53-56, 58, 99, 121-22, 238, 326, 378)

ELVES OF THE FALAS The Falathrim (q.v.). (S 190; B 232)

ELVES OF THE LIGHT The Calaquendi (q.v.). (S 53, 56; B 54, 58)

ELVES OF THE TWILIGHT The Sindar (q.v.). (S 56; B 58)

ELVET-ISLE Island in the lower Withywindle; in Hobbit-lore the home of the Old Swan. (TB 19, 23)

ELVISH The language of the Elves. Although of one origin (the language spoken by the Quendi at Cuiviénen, represented most closely by Quenya), Elvish split into a number of different dialects and languages, of which the only three named are Quenya, Sindarin, and Silvan (qq.v.).

Elvish influenced the languages of the Edain a number of times, especially in Beleriand (when many Edain spoke Sindarin as their birth tongue) and in the Dúnadan kingdoms (where Westron was enriched with many Elvish words). (III 505-06, 508; S 141, 147-48, 346; B 169, 177, 432)

ELWË (Q.) (d. c. FA 505) Elf of the Teleri, one of

the greatest of Elven-lords. He awakened at Cuiviénen and was one of the ambassadors sent by Oromë to Valinor to see its beauty. Elwë returned to his people and persuaded many of them to undertake the Great Journey; with his brother Olwë he led the Teleri on the Journey. But after the Teleri came to Ossiriand Elwë encountered Melian the Maia; stricken with love for her, he fell into a trance for many years, and during that time most of the Teleri followed Olwë over Sea.

When Elwë recovered from his trance he married Melian, and gathering many of the remaining Teleri about him, founded the realm of Doriath. As King of Doriath and overlord of the Sindar, Elwë was known as Elu Thingol, King Greymantle. In the long years of the Peace of Arda, Thingol, guided by his own wisdom and the foresight of Melian, hired the Dwarves of Belegost to help build his beautiful mansions of Menegroth and fill its armories. During these happy years was born Lúthien, the only child of Thingol and Melian, the fairest of all the Children of Ilúvatar.

On the return of Morgoth and the pursuing Exiles to Middle-earth, Thingol enclosed Doriath in the Girdle of Melian; after learning of the Kinslaying he refused to have any dealings with the House of Fëanor and forbade the use of Quenya within his realm. Later, he refused to allow any Edain to enter Doriath.

Thus Thingol prospered for many hundreds of years. But at last, desiring to keep his beloved Lúthien from Beren, he demanded a Silmaril as her bride-price, and thus was drawn into the Doom of the Noldor. After this time Thingol was more involved in the Wars of Beleriand. He was reconciled with Beren, who later saved his life during the Hunting of the Wolf, refused the demands of the sons of Fëanor for the Silmaril, succored homeless Edain, notably Túrin, Morwen, and Nienor, and won the hatred and fear of Morgoth. After the fall of Nargothrond, Húrin gave Thingol the Nauglamír in gratitude for his kindness to his family, but when Thingol decided to set the Silmaril in the Necklace he was slain by the workmen, Dwarves of Nogrod who coveted the treasures of their people and of Fëanor.

Thingol was the only Sinda to have seen the Two Trees, and thus was numbered among the Calaquendi. His inborn nobility was greatly enhanced by his journey to Valinor and his marriage to Melian; he had silver hair and was the tallest of the Children of Ilúvatar. Usually cautious and discerning, he was quick to anger and pride when he encountered injustice. He bore the sword Aranrúth.

Elwë was surnamed Greycloak, in Quenya Elwë Sinda-collo or Singollo, in Sindarin Elu Thingol, whence his most common name, Thingol, in later histories. Also called King Greymantle, Thingol Greycloak, and the Hidden King. (I 260, 261; III 388, 506; S 52-53, 55-56, 58, 91-97, 111, 121, 127-29, 143-44, 157, 166-68, 172, 183-86, 188, 189, 190, 199, 201-02, 227, 231-33; B 53-54, 58, 60, 103-11, 130, 145, 152-55, 172, 200-03, 208, 223-27, 229, 230, 243-44, 246-47, 280, 285-88)

ELWING (S.: 'star-spray') (FA)   Princess of Doriath, daughter of Dior and Nimloth. While very young she escaped from the Noldorin attack on Menegroth in which her parents were slain, and grew up in Arvernien. There she married Eärendil and bore him two sons, Elrond and Elros. When the sons of Fëanor descended on Arvernien, she cast herself and the Silmaril into the Sea. Ulmo saved her and turned her into a bird, in which form she flew to Eärendil at sea. Together with three crewmen they sailed Vingilot to Aman, winning through the Shadowy Seas because of the Silmaril. While Eärendil went before the Valar, Elwing spoke with the Teleri of Alqualondë, the kin of her great-grandfather Elwë; she later persuaded them to sail the ships of the Host of Valinor.

Elwing was the first to make the choice of the Half-elven, and decided to be of the Firstborn. When the Silmaril and Eärendil were set in the sky, Elwing settled in a tower on the northern shores of Aman, whence she flew to meet her husband when he drew near to Arda.

She was known as Elwing the White. It was said that she could speak with birds. (I 261, 309; S 105, 148, 234-

37, 246-47, 248, 250, 251, 305, 306, 307; B 122, 177, 290-93, 304-06, 307, 309-10, 379, 380, 381)

EMBLEMS   Identifying insignia used on banners, shields, and sometimes also used attributively.
The emblems described in *LotR* are:
Anárion—the (setting) sun. (I 362)
Dol Amroth—a white swan-ship on a blue field, or a swan and a white ship. (III 180)
Dúnedain of the North—a many-pointed silver star. (II 60)
Durin and his heirs—an anvil and hammer surmounted by a crown set with seven eight-rayed stars. (I 397, 399; RHM III 439-40)
Eldar—Galathilion, bearing a crescent moon. (I 397)
Elendil and his heirs—in Gondor, the White Tree, surmounted by a silver crown and surrounded by Seven Stars (q.v.). In the North, the emblem was just the Seven Stars. (III 26, 150)
Eregion—holly. (I 395)
Gondor—the White Tree and seven stars on a black field. (III 150)
House of Fëanor—an eight-rayed silver star. (I 397; RHM III 439)
House of Fingolfin—blue and silver. (S 108, 194; B 126, 237)
Isildur—a (rising) moon. (I 362)
Minas Morgul—a moon (for Minas Ithil) disfigured by a death's-head. (III 219)
Morgoth—sable unblazoned. (S 153; B 185)
North-kingdom—the Star of Elendil (q.v.). (RHM III 439)
Rohan—a white horse on a green field. (III 138, 438)
Saruman—a white hand on a black field, sometimes with an *s*-rune. (II 20)
Sauron—The Red Eye or the Lidless Eye. (II 21; III 117)
Stewards of Gondor—a white field with no device. (III 414)
Vanyar—white banners. (S 254; B 315)

EMELDIR (S.) (FA 5th Cent.)   Adan of the First House, daughter of Beren, wife of Barahir, and mother of Beren One-hand. When Dorthonion became infested with evil after Dagor Bragollach, Emeldir led the women and children of the First House to Brethil, although she would rather have remained to fight.

She was known as Emeldir the Manhearted. (S 155, 328; B 187, 408)

EMPTY LANDS   Area east of Middle-earth, refashioned in the Change of the World. (S 279; B 345)

EMYN ARNEN (S.: 'hills of the royal water'?)   Hills in South Ithilien, across Anduin from Minas Tirith. After the WR Emyn Arnen was the dwelling-place of the Princes of Ithilien. (I 23, 305)

EMYN BERAID (S.: 'hills of the towers')   The Tower Hills (q.v.). (III 471; S 291; B 360)

EMYN MUIL (S.: 'hills—')   Rough hill-country on either side of Anduin above Rauros, mostly composed of sharp ridges and deep valleys running north and south. (I 492, 498; II 27 ff., 265 ff.)

ENCHANTED ISLES   Islands in the Shadowy Seas, created by the Valar after the poisoning of the Two Trees and the revolt of the Noldor as part of the guard of Valinor. Any mariner who set foot on the Enchanted Isles slept until the Change of the World. (S 102, 248; B 118, 306)

ENCHANTED RIVER   River in Mirkwood, flowing north from its source in the Mountains of Mirkwood until it joined the Forest River. Anyone who drank of its waters or bathed in it fell into a deep sleep and dreamed of Elven-feasts in Mirkwood. (H 13, 133, 142-45, 149)

ENCIRCLING MOUNTAINS   The Echoriath (q.v.). (III 278; S 115; B 135)

ENCIRCLING SEA Ekkaia (q.v.). (S 89; B 100)

END The culmination of Eä. Although the phrase "until the end of days" is often used to mean "while the world exists," the true End will be not a termination but a triumph. Evil will be defeated in the Last Battle, the Day of Doom will occur, Arda will be healed of its wounds, and Eä will display the perfect realization of the Ainulindalë. Presumably the halls of Mandos will be emptied, although the place of Men and Dwarves in the End is unclear, as is the role of Eä, the World of the first Music, in the Second Music. (I 487; III 316, 321, 423; K 64-65; S 15, 20, 42, 44, 48, 67, 98, 279; B 4, 10, 38, 42, 72, 112, 345)

ENDERI (Q.: 'middle-days') Days added to the calendar in the middle of the year to make the year of the proper length without ruining the equal lengths of the months.

In the Calendar of Imladris there were three enderi between yávië and quellë, and six in leap years. In the Kings' and Stewards' Reckoning, the two enderi replaced loëndë in leap years, while in the New Reckoning there were three Enderi between Yavannië and Narquelië, the second of which was called Loëndë. The Lithe was in the Shire Reckoning equivalent to the enderi. (III 480-82, 486)

ENDLESS STAIR Spiral stair in Khazad-dûm going from the lowest dungeon to Durin's Tower. The Endless Stair was built early in the First Age and was ruined in TA 3019, during the Battle of the Peak. (II 134)

ENDOR (Q.: 'middle-land') Middle-earth (q.v.). (S 89, 357; B 101, 448)

ENDÓRE (Q.: 'middle-land') Middle-earth (q.v.). (III 490)

ENEDWAITH (S.: 'middle-folk') Land south of the Gwathlo, perhaps including Dunland. Once part of Gondor, Enedwaith was devastated by great floods in TA 2912, and whatever people still lived there at that time left or died.

Also spelled Enedhwaith. (I 16; III 461; PB; S 359; B 451)

ENEMIES The Valar (q.v.), so called by the Orcs of Angband. (S 208; B 255)

ENEMY Morgoth (q.v.). (S 107; B 124)

ENEMY Sauron (q.v.). (I 72; S 289; B 359)

ENGWAR (Q.: 'sickly') Men (q.v.). (S 103; B 119)

ENNOR (S.: 'middle-land') Middle-earth (q.v.). (III 490)

ENQUIË (Q.: 'week') The six-day ritual week of the Eldar, and the seven-day week of the Númenóreans, the Dúnedain, and the Westron area. The Quenya names for the days of the Eldarin enquië were Elenya, Anarya, Isilya, Aldúya, Menelya, and Valanya or Tárion. The Dúnedain names were the same except that Aldëa was the fourth day, Valanya was the seventh day, and Eärenya was the sixth.

The enquië was adopted throughout Middle-earth by Men and Hobbits. For Hobbits, and probably also for others, Highdei (Valanya) was the chief day. (III 479, 484)

ENT-DRAUGHTS The drinks given to Merry and Pippin by Fangorn, which seem to have comprised, with water, the sole nourishment of the Ents. Two kinds of Ent-draughts are described, one primarily refreshing and the other primarily nourishing. The Ent-draughts made the Hobbits uncommonly large. (II 93, 103)

ENTISH The language of the Ents, a "slow, sonorous, agglomerated, repetitive" language with very fine distinctions of tone and length. No one not an Ent ever managed to learn Entish, as the language was exceedingly difficult and unlike all others. (III 510)

ENTMOOT A formal council of Ents, traditionally held in the Derndingle in Fangorn Forest. The Entmoot held in TA 3019 which decided to attack Isengard lasted only three days, which seems to have been rather short. (II 103, 105-09)

ENTS Tree-herds, evidently trees inhabited by spirits summoned by the thought of Yavanna to be the guardians of the olvar until the Dominion of Men. The nature of the Ents was closely connected with that of the trees they protected and the tree-spirits (cf. Huorns) they guarded. The Ents awoke at the same time as the Elves; the Eldar gave them the desire to speak and taught them Quenya and Sindarin. In the First Age the Ents roamed through Beleriand and the eastern lands, although they enter into history only once, when they helped destroy the Dwarves of Nogrod who had sacked Menegroth.

Sometime in the First or Second Age the male and female Ents became estranged; the Entwives crossed Anduin and tended their favorite plants—small trees, grasses, fruit trees, flowers, and vegetables—in what was later called the Brown Lands, while the male Ents tended their larger trees, especially in the great forest that stretched from the Old Forest to Fangorn. The Entwives were greatly honored by Men, to whom they taught the skills of agriculture, but sometime before the end of the Second Age their gardens were destroyed and they vanished.

The Ents in the Third Age remained in the Forest of Fangorn, growing old without hope of having children. Some of the Ents grew "treeish" and ceased moving or speaking, but some, like Fangorn, remained active and alert. About TA 2950 Saruman began harassing the Ents and cutting down their trees; in 3019, spurred by the appearance of Merry and Pippin, Fangorn realized that something had to be done. He aroused the remaining active Ents, and they attacked and destroyed Isengard. In the

Fourth Age the Ents remained in Fangorn Forest and dwindled.

An Ent looked like a fourteen-foot-tall cross between a tree and a Man; a full description of an Ent is given on II 83, although Fangorn's beard may have been exceptional. Ents resembled different trees; individual Ents cared for and honored the kind of tree they looked like and to a certain extent possessed the personality one might expect of that tree. Ents did not die naturally; their skin was extremely tough, but they could be burned. Ents thought slowly and were slow to act, but once aroused they possessed the strength of the age-long action of trees compressed in a few seconds; they could crack rocks and move large quantities of earth easily and quickly. Ents were nourished by Ent-draughts.

The Ents spoke Entish. They also knew many other languages but preferred Quenya, which they spoke after the same fashion as they did Entish.

The name "Ent" was given them by the Rohirrim, and means "giant" in Old English. They were called Onodrim or Enyd in Sindarin by the Elves; the singular was *Onod*.

Also called the Shepherds of the Trees and the Shadow of the Wood. (I 73; II 83, 84, 88-89, 99-100, 105-16, 131, 189, 196-97, 216-22; III 320-21, 510; S 45-46, 235; B 44, 290)

ENTWADE Fords on the Entwash northeast of Edoras. (II 45; III 14)

ENTWASH River coming out of Fangorn and flowing through Rohan to Anduin, which it joined in a large marshy delta, the Mouths of Entwash. (I 17; II 38; III 14. 93, 94)

ENTWASH VALE The valley of the lower Entwash, including the Mouths of Entwash. Entwash Vale was a green, fenny area. (II 30)

ENTWOOD Fangorn Forest, so called in Rohan. (II 197)

ENYD (S.) The Ents (q.v.). (III 510)

EÖL (S.) (d. FA 4th Cent.) Elf of the Teleri, of the kin of Elwë. Early in the First Age Eöl dwelt in Region, but he was ill at ease in Doriath; when the Girdle of Melian was set he moved outside it, to Nan Elmoth, receiving permission from Thingol to dwell there in return for the sword Anglachel. In Nan Elmoth Eöl became a smith, and friendship grew between him and the Dwarves. About FA 300 he encountered Aredhel, brought her to him, and married her. They had one child, Maeglin. When Maeglin and Aredhel fled to Gondolin, Eöl followed them there. Given by Turgon the choice of life in Gondolin or death, he chose the latter and tried also to slay Maeglin with a poisoned dart. But Aredhel stepped into its path and died; Eöl was cast over the Caragdûr, cursing Maeglin with his last words.

Eöl was a noble Elf, tall and skilled in learning, but he was grim and aloof, wherefore he was called the Dark Elf. His greatest invention was the metal galvorn. (S 92, 132-38, 201-02; B 104, 158-65, 247)

ÉOMER (TA 2991-FO 63) Man, eighteenth King of Rohan (TA 3019-FO 63), son of Théodwyn and Éomund and nephew of King Théoden. Before the WR, Éomer was the Third Marshal of Riddermark, in charge of the Eastmark. He was a valiant warrior and a discerning man, friendly to Gandalf and hating Gríma. Although he fell into Théoden's disfavor as a result of Gríma's plots, his loyalty was proven, and during the WR he fought nobly at the Hornburg, the Pelennor Fields, and the Morannon, and became friendly with Aragorn. Théoden, at his death during the Battle of the Pelennor Fields, named Éomer as his heir. After the WR Éomer became King of Rohan and renewed the Oath of Eorl with King Elessar. During his long reign he ruled Rohan well and often fought beside Elessar in foreign lands.

In 3020 Éomer married Lothíriel of Dol Amroth; she bore him at least one child, Elfwine the Fair. (II 42-51; III 135, 144-52, 437-38)

ÉOMUND (d. TA 3002) Man of Rohan, husband of Théodwyn and father of Éomer and Éowyn. Éomund was the chief marshal of the Mark, and was in charge of the east marches. He was noted for his hot and unwary pursuit of raiding Orcs; during one of these pursuits he was ambushed and slain.

Éomund came from Eastfold. (II 42; III 437)

EÖNWË (Q.) Maia, the herald and standard-bearer of Manwë. He was frequently the messenger of Manwë, and after the Great Battle he was the judge of the Eldar and the instructor of the Dúnedain.

Eönwë was the mightiest in arms of any in Arda. (S 30, 248-49, 251, 252-53, 260, 285; B 24, 308, 311, 313-14, 321, 353)

ÉORED A fighting-force of Rohan, composed of the men of a lord's household. Éomer's, which was perhaps typical, had 104 men. All the éoreds were probably cavalry units. (II 39, 45, 48; III 127)

EORL (TA 2485-2545) Man, Lord of Éothéod (2501-10) and first King of Rohan (2510-45). In 2510, answering a summons for aid from Cirion of Gondor, Eorl and his Riders defeated an army of Balchoth and Orcs in the Battle of the Field of Celebrant. As a reward, the Riders were given Calenardhon, and Eorl swore the Oath of Eorl. He was slain in battle with Easterlings in the Wold.

Eorl was a great warrior and horse-master. His horse, Felaróf, was the first of the mearas (qq.v.). Eorl was known as "the Young" because he succeeded his father Léod in his youth and kept his yellow hair throughout his life. (II 143, 148; III 415, 428-31, 434)

EORLINGAS The Rohirrim (q.v.), so called because they considered themselves the descendants of Eorl. (II 155; III 430)

ÉOTHAIN (fl. WR) Man of Rohan, a member of Éomer's éored. (II 45)

ÉOTHÉOD Land near the sources of Anduin, named after the Éothéod (q.v.), who founded it in TA 1977 after the fall of Angmar, which had previously controlled the area. In 2510 Eorl Lord of Éothéod led an army to Gondor to fight in the Battle of the Field of Celebrant, and he and his people then settled in Rohan. (III 428-29, 458)

ÉOTHÉOD, THE Men of the Vales of Anduin, related to the Third House of the Edain. They originally lived between the Carrock and the Gladden, but in TA 1977, being crowded and hearing of the fall of Angmar, they moved to an area near the sources of Anduin. They drove out the Orcs living there and named the land Éothéod.

In 2510, under their lord Eorl, the Éothéod rode to Gondor to aid Cirion against the Balchoth. After winning the Battle of the Field of Celebrant, the Riders of Éothéod were granted Calenardhon to live in. From this time on they called themselves the Eorlingas and were called the Rohirrim (q.v.) by the men of Gondor.

Éothéod is translated Rohirric; it is Old English for 'horse-folk.' (III 428-29, 458)

ÉOWYN (TA 2995-FO?) Woman of Rohan, daughter of Éomund and Théodwyn and sister of Eomer. During the WR she met and fell in love with Aragorn; when he rode the Paths of the Dead she despaired greatly, thinking him lost. Being of a martial spirit, in her desperation she disguised herself as a man and, calling herself Dernhelm, rode to Gondor with Elfhelm's éored. In the Battle of the Pelennor Fields, with the aid of Merry she won great renown by slaying the Lord of the Nazgûl and his steed. The evil coming from contact with the Nazgûl-lord, amplified by the years of waiting on Théoden in his dotage and by her hopeless love for Aragorn, caused her to succumb to a severe case of the Black Breath.

Aragorn released her from the illness with athelas, and while recovering she realized her true heart. Giving up her desire to be a free, independent shield-maiden, she married Faramir and became Lady of Ithilien.

Éowyn was very beautiful; she was tall, slim, and graceful, with golden hair. Faramir called her the White Lady of Rohan. (II 152, 162, 163; III 91, 93, 141-45, 174-77, 291-300, 315-16, 437)

EPHEL BRANDIR (S.: 'outer fences of Brandir') Stockade of the Haladin, built late in the 6th Century FA atop Amon Obel. (S 216, 362; B 266, 454)

EPHEL DÚATH (S.: 'outer-fences dark-shadow') The mountains forming the west and south borders of Mordor, a great chain perhaps 800 miles long. In the north the Ephel Dúath met the Ered Lithui at Isenmouthe and Cirith Gorgor.

Called in Westron the Mountains of Shadow or the Shadowy Mountains. (I 17; II 308, 402-47 passim.; III 236; S 359; B 450)

ERADAN (S.) (d. TA 2116) Dúnadan, second Ruling Steward of Gondor (2080-2116). (III 395)

ERCHAMION (S.: 'one-handed') Epithet of Beren (q.v.). (S 183, 356; B 222, 447)

EREBOR (S.: 'single-mountain') Mountain east of Mirkwood and west of the Iron Hills. Erebor was first settled by Thráin I, who came there with a large part of Durin's Folk after fleeing from Moria, and founded the Kingdom under the Mountain in TA 1999. The Kingdom was for a while (from about 2190 to 2590) lessened in numbers and glory while the Kings of Durin's Folk dwelt in the Ered Mithrin, but dragons caused Thrór to return to Erebor in 2590. The fame and richness of Erebor grew for nearly two hundred years, until in 2770 Smaug plundered the Dwarf-kingdom. Smaug dwelt in Erebor with his hoard until 2941, when he was disturbed by Thorin and Company and slain by Bard. Dáin II re-established the Kingdom under the Mountain, and its halls became once more fair and its people wealthy. During the WR Erebor was besieged by an army of Easterlings, but after the downfall of Sauron the Dwarves and the Men of Dale routed the besiegers. In the Fourth Age Erebor was independent, but it was allied with and protected by the Reunited Kingdom.

Called in Westron the Lonely Mountain and the Mountain.

See: Great Hall of Thráin, the Lower Halls, the Front Gate, Ravenhill. (I 302-03; III 439, 459-61, 468-69; H 27-28, 196-271 passim)

ERECH Hill in Lamedon upon which stood the Stone of Erech (q.v.). Here the King of the Mountains swore allegiance to Isildur, and throughout the Third Age Erech was haunted by the Dead Men of Dunharrow.

Erech is of pre-Númenórean origin, and thus comes from some Mannish tongue of the Second Age. Also called the Hill of Erech. (III 14, 64-65, 73-74, 508; S 291; B 361)

ERED ENGRIN (S.: 'mountains iron') Mountains raised by Melkor in the north of Middle-earth, covered with snow and ice. The Ered Engrin formed a great curve open to the north, and Angband and Thangorodrim (q.v.) were located at their southwest extreme.

Also called the Iron Mountains and the Mountains of Iron. (S 36, 109, 116, 120, 151; B 31, 128, 136, 142, 181)

ERED GORGOROTH (S.: 'mountains of terror') The mountains and precipices at the southern edge of Dorthonion, named because Ungoliant and her brood lived in Nan Dungortheb at their base. Beren was the only person to survive a crossing of the Ered Gorgoroth.

Also called Gorgoroth and the Mountains of Terror. (I 260; II 422; S 81, 95, 121, 164; B 90, 109, 144, 198)

ERED LINDON (S.: 'mountains of Lindon') The Ered Luin (q.v.). (S 123; B 148)

ERED LITHUI (S.: 'ashy mountains') The mountain chain forming the northern border of Mordor, stretching east about 400 miles from the Morannon.

Called in Westron the Ash Mountains or the Ashen Mountains. (I 17; II 308)

ERED LÓMIN (S.: 'echoing mountains') Mountain chain of Middle-earth in the First Age, running northwest from Eithel Ivrin and forming the western border of Hithlum. The Ered Lómin was split by the Firth of Drengist.

Also called the Echoing Hills and the Echoing Mountains. The name was given because the Ered Lómin amplified any loud cry made in Lammath (q.v.). (S 80, 106, 118, 119; B 88, 123, 140)

ERED LUIN (S.: 'blue mountains') Mountain chain forming the boundary between Beleriand and Eriador in the First Age, and later between Lindon and Eriador. In the First Age the great Dwarf cities of Belegost and Nogrod were located here, near Mount Dolmed, but they were destroyed when the Ered Luin was cloven in the Great Battle and the Gulf of Lhûn was formed in the gap. In later ages Dwarves (including the Kings of Durin's Folk from TA 2810 to 2941) continued to live here. In TA 1974 Arvedui hid in deserted Dwarf-mines in the northern Ered Luin.

Called by the Noldor the Ered Lindon. The Westron names were the Blue Mountains and the Mountains of Lune. (I 16, 72; II 90; III 396, 398, 439, 445; S 9, 123, 124, 285; B xiii, 146-47, 354)

ERED MITHRIN (S.: 'grey mountains') Mountains north of Mirkwood, home of the dragons. About TA 2200, most of Durin's Folk gathered in the Ered Mithrin, but they were forced to leave by 2589 because of the rise of dragons and cold-drakes; the mountains were also infested with Orcs. (I 17; III 430, 440, 459; H 12-13, 138)

ERED NIMRAIS (S.: 'white horn mountains') Snow-covered mountain chain of Gondor, running westward from Minas Tirith almost to the Sea. Originally home of a race of Men related to the Dunlendings (q.v.), in the Third Age the Ered Nimrais was chiefly the site of refuges of the Rohirrim and Men of Gondor such as Dunharrow and Helm's Deep. The Paths of the Dead went through the Ered Nimrais.

Important peaks of the Ered Nimrais included Mindolluin, Dwimorberg, Starkhorn, the Thrihyrne, and the peaks of the northern beacon-towers of Gondor.

Called in Westron the White Mountains. (I 338; II 167, 371; III 416; S 94, 329; B 107, 409)

ERED WETHRIN (S.: 'mountains of shadow') Mountains of northern Middle-earth in the First Age, the eastern and southern border of Hithlum. The Ered Wethrin were heavily fortified by Fingolfin against Morgoth.

Also called the Mountains of Shadow and the Shadowy Mountains. (S 106, 113, 118-19, 143, 151, 152; B 124, 133, 140, 172, 181, 183)

EREGION (S.: 'holly-region') Land in Eriador between the Rivers Glanduin and Bruinen, settled about SA 750 by the Gwaith-i-Mírdain (q.v.). Its chief city was Ost-in-Edhil. Eregion was laid waste in 1697 during the War of the Elves and Sauron.

Called in Westron Hollin. The land had many holly trees. (I 76, 318, 369 ff.; III 396, 453-54; L 187; S 286, 287-88; B 354, 356)

EREINION (S.: 'scion of kings') The birth-name of Gil-galad (q.v.). (S 154, 356; B 186, 446)

ERELAS (S.: 'single-leaf'?) The fourth of the northern beacon-tower hills of Gondor. (III 20)

ERELLONT (S.) (fl. FA 600) Mariner, companion of Eärendil on his voyages. (S 248, 250; B 307, 309)

ERESSËA Tol Eressëa (q.v.). (I 321)

ERESTOR (S.) (fl. WR) Elf of Rivendell, Elrond's chief counsellor. (I 315)

ERIADOR (S.: '—land') Area between the Misty Mountains and the Ered Luin, bounded on the south by the Rivers Gwathlo and Glanduin and on the north by the Forodwaith. In the First Age Eriador was little known to the Eldar, but Men dwelt there and Morgoth had some power there. In the Second Age Eriador was long under the shadow of Sauron, but toward the end of the age Arnor was founded there.

During the Third Age Eriador was at first prosperous and well-populated, but with the waning of Gondor, the Great Plague, and the wars with Angmar, Eriador was decimated. By the end of the Third Age only a few people lived in Rivendell, the Bree-land, the Shire (qq.v.), and other scattered habitations.

See also: Minhiriath, Eregion, Cardolan, Rhudaur, Arthedain, the Ettendales, etc. (I 16; III 396, 398, 454, 457; S 54, 124, 145, 290, 357; B 55, 148, 174, 360, 488)

ERKENBRAND (fl. WR) Man of Rohan, master of Westfold and the Hornburg, a noted warrior. Erkenbrand commanded the forces of Rohan at the Second Battle of the Fords of Isen. He regrouped his forces after the battle and returned to Helm's Deep in time to complete the rout of Saruman's forces at the Battle of the Hornburg. (II 168, 170, 172, 186, 191)

ERLING (b. TA 2854) Hobbit of the Shire, of the working class. Erling was the third child of Holman the green-handed. (III 477)

ERRANTRY A cyclical narrative poem contained in the Red Book of Westmarch, probably written by Bilbo Baggins soon after 2941. Although most of the names in the poem are borrowed from Elvish verse, the poem is not serious and the names are not real.

Errantry does, however, contain some possible references to the history of Eärendil or of the Dúnedain of Númenor, and it is not inconceivable that on his trip to Erebor with Thorin and Company Bilbo heard scraps of tales of the First and Second Ages and used them, somewhat fancifully, in the poem. (TB 7-8, 24-27)

ERUHÍNI (Q.: 'children of Eru') The Children of Ilúvatar (q.v.). (S 322; B 400)

ERUI (S.) River of Gondor, flowing from Lossarnach into Anduin. Erui was the southern boundary of Ithilien. See: Crossings of Erui. (III 15, 185; L 192)

ERUSËN (Q.? S.?) The Children of Ilúvatar (q.v.). (R 66)

ERYN LASGALEN (S.: 'wood of green leaves') Name given to Mirkwood after its cleansing in TA 3019. The southern part, ruled at the beginning of the Fourth Age by Celeborn, was called East Lórien, while the part north of the Mountains was the Woodland Realm. The land in between was inhabited by the Beornings and the Woodmen. (III 468)

ERYN VORN (S.: 'black woods') Forest on the coast of Minhiriath south of the outlet of the River Baranduin. (PB)

ESGALDUIN (S.: 'screen-river') River of Beleriand, flowing south from Dorthonion to Menegroth and then west into Sirion. It had at least one waterfall, above Menegroth. The Esgalduin was somehow enchanted.
   Also called the Elven-river. (I 258, 260; S 93, 121, 184, 185, 218, 329, 359; B 105, 144, 223, 225, 269, 410, 450)

ESGAROTH City of Men, located on the Long Lake. Its location was good for commerce, and Esgaroth supplied food and drink to Erebor and the Woodland Realm from the south and east, while the products of Erebor and Dale were funneled through Esgaroth. Esgaroth was destroyed by Smaug in TA 2941, but was rebuilt using gold from his hoard.
   Esgaroth was governed by a Master, chosen by the people, or perhaps by the important local merchants.
   Esgaroth was built of wood on stilts driven into the

bottom of the Long Lake. (I 55; H 172, 185-93, 234-38, 239, 286)

ESMERALDA BRANDYBUCK (b. TA 2936) Hobbit of the Shire, wife of Saradoc Brandybuck and mother of Merry. Esmeralda was the fifth and youngest child of Adalgrim Took. She was a guest at the Farewell Party. (I 56; III 475, 476)

ESSE (Q.: 'name') Alternate name for the tengwa $\mathcal{E}$ (number 31, used when this sign represented *ss* after Quenya *z* (as in *áze*) had changed to *r*. (III 500)

ESTË (Q.: 'rest') Ainu, one of the Valier, the wife of Lórien. She is concerned with healing and rest and with the fountains and pools of the gardens of Lórien. She wears grey. (S 25, 28, 30, 99, 100; B 18, 21, 24, 114, 115)

ESTEL (S.: 'hope') The name by which Aragorn II (q.v.) was known in his youth, to keep Sauron from learning that he was the heir of Isildur. (III 420)

ESTELLA TOOK (b. TA 2985) Hobbit of the Shire, daughter of Odovacar Bolger and younger sister of Fredegar. Estella married Merry Brandybuck sometime after the WR. (III 475, 476)

ESTOLAD (S.: 'encampment') Land in East Beleriand south of Nan Elmoth and east of the River Celon. The First and Third Houses of the Edain made Estolad their first home in Beleriand, and the Haladin came there from Dor Caranthir. Although most of the Edain later moved elsewhere, some remained in Estolad until East Beleriand was overrun during Dagor Bragollach. (S 142, 143, 144, 146; B 170, 171, 172, 175)

ETHIR ANDUIN (S.) The delta of Anduin, in southern Gondor. Called in Westron the Mouths of Anduin. (I 518)

ETHRING (S.)   Fords or town on the Ringló, on the road from Erech to Pelargir. (III 15)

ETHUIL (S.)   The Sindarin form of tuilë (q.v.). (III 480)

ETTENDALES, ETTENMOORS   Troll-fells north of Rivendell. The source of the Mitheithel was in the Ettenmoors.

   The Ettenmoors and the Coldfells may have been the same place. (I 268, 271; III 458)

EVENDIM   Name given to undómë (q.v.) in the Shire. (III 485)

EVE OF MIDSUMMER   Midsummer's Eve (q.v.). (III 309)

EVERARD TOOK (b. TA 2980)   Hobbit of the Shire, youngest child of Adelard Took. He was a guest at the Farewell Party. (I 54; III 475)

EVER-EVE, EVEREVEN   Valinor (q.v.). (I 310, 482)

EVERHOLT   A place in the Firien Wood. (III 435)

EVERLASTING DARK, EVERLASTING DARKNESS   The Void (q.v.). (S 83, 253; B 93, 312)

EVERMIND   Simbelmynë (q.v.). (II 142)

EVERNIGHT   The Shadowy Seas (q.v.). (I 309)

EVIL OF THE NORTH   Melkor (q.v.). (S 212; B 260)

EXILES   Those of the Noldor (q.v.) who returned to Middle-earth to recover the Silmarils from Melkor. The banishment of those who survived was lifted at the end of the First Age, save for Galadriel. (III 506; S 85, 106; B 95, 123)

EXILES The Dúnedain who survived the fall of Númenor and came to Middle-earth. (III 393; S 281; B 348)

EYE The Eye of Sauron, the form in which he appeared in the Third Age and his emblem. The Eye was rimmed with fire but glazed like a cat's; its pupil was a slit. As an emblem, the Eye was usually all red.

Also used attributively for Sauron.

Also called the Evil Eye, the Great Eye, the Lidless Eye, the Red Eye, the Eye of Barad-dûr, and the Eye of Mordor. (I 471, 519; II 21, 61, 101, 131, 248, 267; III 117, 202; S 280-81, 293; B 347, 363)

EZELLOHAR (Q.) Green mound before the western gate of Valimar. The Two Trees grew upon it. Ezellohar was blackened when the Trees were poisoned.

Also called Corollairë and the Green Mound. (S 38, 42, 72, 74, 75; B 33, 38, 79, 82)

~~§~~ ~~§~~

FADING YEARS The Third Age (q.v.), from the perspective of the Elves. (III 455; S 299; B 371)

FAELIVRIN (S.) Name given to Finduilas (q.v.) by Gwindor. It suggests the gleam of the Sun on Eithel Ivrin. (S 210; B 257)

FAERIE Eldamar (q.v.). (H 164)

FAERIE An Elven-realm, in Bilbo's poem *Errantry*. Any relationship to real places of any Age is probably accidental. (TB 25)

FAIRBAIRN OF THE TOWER A Hobbit family, descended from Elfstan Fairbairn, son of Fastred of Green-holm and Elanor Gamgee. The Fairbairns were Wardens of Westmarch; they also kept, added to, and made copies of the Red Book of Westmarch. The Fairbairns lived at Undertowers. They were noted for their "elvish" beauty, inherited from Elanor. (I 37; III 471, 477; L 165)

FAIR ELVES   The Vanyar (q.v.). (S 53; B 54)

FAIR FOLK   The Elves (q.v.). (I 74)

FAITHFUL   The minority of the Númenóreans who re-mained friendly with the Eldar and obedient to the Valar, despite their fear of death and the Doom of Men. The Faithful arose about SA 2300 and founded Pelargir in 2350 as their chief haven in Middle-earth. They continued to sail to the northern coasts of Middle-earth and to aid Gil-galad against Sauron. Beginning with the accession of Ar-Gimilzôr c. 3100, the Faithful were actively persecuted, being punished for speaking Eldarin or meeting with the Eldar of Tol Eressëa. The Faithful were forced to move from western Númenor to the east, where Rómenna became their chief city; many emigrated to Lindon. During the captivity of Sauron in Númenor (3262-3319) the Faith-ful, now led by Amandil, Lord of Andúnië, were bitterly oppressed, and some were burned as sacrifices to Melkor in the Temple built by Sauron. Yet in the end a remnant of the Faithful survived the downfall of Númenor and, led by Elendil, Isildur, and Anárion, founded the kingdoms of Arnor and Gondor in Middle-earth.

Also called the Elendili or Elf-friends. (III 391-93; S 266-76 passim, 280, 291; B 329-42 passim, 347, 361)

FALAS (S.: 'coast')   The coasts of Beleriand south of Nevrast, especially near the mouths of Brithon and Nen-ning, home of the Falathrim ruled by Círdan (qq.v.). The chief ports of the Falas were Brithombar and Eglarest. (S 58, 120; B 60, 142)

FALASTUR (Q.: 'coast-lord') (d. TA 913)   Dúnadan,

twelfth King of Gondor (830-913) and the first Ship-king. His birth-name was Tarannon; he took the crown as Falastur to commemorate his victories as Captain of the Hosts. Falastur began the policy, kept until after 1200, of building great fleets and extending Gondor's power along the coasts of the Bay of Belfalas, and even farther to the south. The first childless king, Falastur was succeeded by his nephew Eärnil. (III 394, 403)

FALATHAR (S.: 'coast—') (fl. FA 600)   Mariner, companion of Eärendil on his voyages. (S 248, 250; B 307, 309)

FALATHRIM (S.: 'coast-people')   Sindarin Elves living in the Falas of Beleriand in the First Age. In origin they were Teleri persuaded to stay in Middle-earth by Ossë, but in the course of the Wars of Beleriand their ranks were swelled by Sindar and Noldor fleeing the armies of Morgoth. They were the first mariners and shipwrights of Middle-earth. Under their lord, Círdan, they prospered for many years, although the Falas was invaded by Orcs of Morgoth between the first and second battles of the Wars of Beleriand, and the Falathrim were forced to withdraw to their walled Havens. Throughout the First Age the Falathrim built all the ships sailed by Men or Elves of Beleriand. They sent a force to fight with the Union of Maedhros.

When the Falas was overrun in 474, the surviving Falathrim removed to the Isle of Balar, where they continued to build ships and aid the Elves and Men of Arvernien.

Also called the Elves of the Falas and the Elves of the Havens. (S 58, 90, 96, 97, 120, 190, 196, 246; B 60, 101-02, 109, 111, 142, 232, 239, 304)

FALCO CHUBB-BAGGINS (TA 2903-2999)   Hobbit of the Shire, son of Bingo Baggins and Chica Chubb. Falco was the first Chubb-Baggins. (III 474)

FALL OF GIL-GALAD, THE   Elven-song, translated

175

into Westron by Bilbo. The song dealt with the death of Gil-galad during the Siege of the Barad-dûr. (I 250, 251)

FALL OF GONDOLIN, THE The account of the invasion and destruction of Gondolin and of the heroic deeds of the defenders. (S 242; B 300)

FALLOHIDES The least numerous of the three strains of Hobbits. About TA 1150 the Fallohides left their ancestral home on the upper Anduin, crossed the Misty Mountains north of Rivendell, and entered Eriador, where they mingled with other Hobbits. Because of their adventurous spirit, Fallohides were frequently found as leaders of tribes of other kinds of Hobbits. Marcho and Blanco, the founders of the Shire, were Fallohides, as were the Tooks, Brandybucks, and Bolgers. Bilbo and Frodo Baggins also had Fallohide blood.

The Fallohides were taller and slimmer than other Hobbits and had fairer skin and hair. They liked trees and forests and had more skill in the arts than in handicrafts. They were friendlier with Elves than were other Hobbits. (I 22; III 457, 516)

FALLS OF IVRIN See: Eithel Ivrin. (S 170; B 206)

FALLS OF RAUROS Rauros (q.v.). (S 297; B 369)

FALLS OF SIRION Great waterfall by which the River Sirion plunged over the edge of the Andram, located at the south end of the Meres of Twilight. (S 122, 168; B 146, 203)

FALMARI (Q.: 'those of the waves') The Teleri (q.v.). (S 53; B 54)

FANG (fl. WR) One of Farmer Maggot's wolf-like dogs. (I 133, 134)

FANGORN (S.: 'beard-tree') (FA-) Ent, the guardian

of Fangorn Forest. At the time of the WR Fangorn was the oldest surviving Ent, and thus the oldest living being in Middle-earth. Fangorn was responsible for arousing the Ents against Saruman during the WR; he probably also sent the Huorns to the Hornburg.

Fangorn was bearded, and seems to have resembled an evergreen tree.

Called in Westron Treebeard; he was called Eldest by Celeborn. (II 83 ff., 131; III 317-21, 510)

FANGORN FOREST Wood of great age east of the southern end of the Misty Mountains, watered by the Entwash and Limlight. Fangorn was the eastern remnant of the great forest that once covered all of Eriador and extended into Beleriand. The Ents lived in Fangorn Forest at the time of the WR. During the last century of the Third Age Orcs of Isengard did great damage to Fangorn, but this stopped with the destruction of Isengard by the Ents during the WR.

Fangorn was a wild, visibly old forest. There were places in it where the shadow of the Great Darkness had never been lifted.

Fangorn was named after Fangorn the Ent, the oldest Ent living there at the time of the WR and the guardian of the Forest. Called the Entwood by the Rohirrim; also called Fangorn and the Forest of Fangorn. Ambarona, Tauremorna, Aldalómë, and Tauremornalómë were epithets applied to the Forest by Fangorn the Ent. (I 17, 484; II 55, 80 ff., esp. 89, 90, 91)

FANTASIE A probably imaginary land in Bilbo's poem *Errantry*. (TB 25)

FANUIDHOL (S.: 'cloudy-head') Elvish name for Bundushathûr. (q.v.).

Also called Fanuidhol the Grey. (I 370)

FANUILOS (S.: *'fana*-ever-white') Varda (q.v.). (I 312; R 66)

FARAMIR (Q.?: '—jewel') (d. TA 1944) Dúnadan of Gondor, son of King Ondoher. He was slain in battle with the Wainriders. (III 409)

FARAMIR (TA 2983-FO 82) Dúnadan of Gondor, second son of Denethor II. Faramir was a gentle, discerning man, a lover of lore and music and a reader of men's minds. Unlike his brother Boromir, he did not care for battle for its own sake, but nonetheless he was a brave warrior, much loved by his soldiers. Because of his gentle nature and his love of Gandalf, he displeased his father.

Before the WR, Faramir was Captain of the Rangers of Ithilien. During the WR Faramir led the retreat from Osgiliath to Minas Tirith before the Siege of Gondor. He fell under the Black Breath and was nearly cremated by Denethor in his madness. After being rescued by Beregond and Gandalf, he was healed by Aragorn. While recovering, he met and fell in love with Éowyn, whom he married after the WR. With the return of the King to Gondor, Faramir was made Steward of Gondor, Prince of Ithilien, and Lord of Emyn Arnen. (II 336 ff.; III 101, 114-15, 153-62, 171-73, 292-303, 315, 396, 419, 462)

FARAMIR TOOK (FO 10-?) Hobbit of the Shire, son of Peregrin Took and thirty-third Thain of the Shire, from FO 64 to his death. Faramir married Goldilocks Gamgee in 43. (III 471, 475)

FARAWAY Hills in Eriador near the western border of the Shire, home of the Lonely Troll in the Shire-poem of the same name. Faraway may have been fictitious. (TB 41, 43)

FAR DOWNS Down marking the western boundary of the Shire until its expansion in FO 32.

On I 24, Fox Downs is a misprint. (I 16, 24; III 383, 471)

FAREWELL PARTY Birthday party held in the Party Field on September 22, TA 3001, to celebrate the eleventyfirst birthday of Bilbo and the coming of age of Frodo. The Party was quite spectacular, with 144 guests, huge amounts of food, fireworks by Gandalf, and presents made as far away as Erebor. Toward the end of the Party, Bilbo put on the One Ring and disappeared from the Shire. (I 50-56; III 473)

FAR HARAD The southern part of Harad. The Men of Far Harad were allied with Sauron in the WR, and some of them fought in the Battle of the Pelennor Fields. (III 148)

FARIN (TA 2560-2803) Dwarf of Durin's line, son of Borin and father of Fundin and Gróin. (III 450)

FARMER COTTON Tolman Cotton (q.v.). (III 365)

FARMER MAGGOT See: Maggot. (I 132)

FAR WEST The Undying Lands (q.v.). (III 452)

FASTOLPH BOLGER (TA 29th Cent.) Hobbit of the Shire. He married Pansy Baggins. (III 474)

FASTITOCALON A giant, perhaps mythical, beast, the last of the Turtle-fish, in the Hobbitish poem of the same name. Fastitocalon was mistaken for an island by sailors, who were drowned when he submerged. (TB 48-49)

FASTITOCALON A Hobbit-poem found in a margin of the Red Book of Westmarch. The poem may be a nonsense-rhyme. (TB 48-49)

FASTRED (TA 2858-85) Man of Rohan, son of King Folcwine and twin brother of Folcred. He and his brother led an army to aid Rohan against the Haradrim. The enemy was defeated in the Battle of the Crossings of Poros, but both Fastred and his brother were slain. (III 436)

FASTRED (d. TA 3019) Man of Rohan, slain in the Battle of the Pelennor Fields. (III 152)

FASTRED OF GREENHOLM (FO 1st Cent.) Hobbit of the Shire. In FO 31 he married Elanor Gamgee; their son Elfstan Fairbairn was born three years later. In 35 Fastred was made first Warden of Westmarch, and the family moved to Undertowers. (III 471, 477; RHM III 378)

FATHERS OF MEN The Edain (q.v.). (III 506; S 260; B 320-21)

FATTY LUMPKIN (fl. WR) Tom Bombadil's pony. (I 199)

FËANÁRO (Q.: 'spirit-fire') The name given to her only son by Míriel Serindë. The Sindarin form, by which he was known to history, was Fëanor (q.v.). (S 330, 362; B 410, 454)

FËANOR (S.: 'spirit of fire') (d. FA 1) Noldorin prince, only son of Finwë by his first wife Míriel. The mightiest of the Noldor and in many ways the greatest of the Children of Ilúvatar, especially in skill of mind and hands, Fëanor was unfortunately as quick to pride, jealousy, and anger as to invention. In Eldamar he married Nerdanel, who bore him seven sons and restrained the excesses of his passion. During this time, the Noontide of Valinor, Fëanor, instructed by his father-in-law Mahtan and by Aulë, made his great inventions: the Tengwar, and the art of fabricating gems and crystals, especially the Silmarilli and perhaps also the Palantíri.

But Melkor, coveting the Silmarils, sowed dissension between Fëanor and his half-brother Fingolfin, until at last Fëanor spoke against the Valar and drew a sword on Fingolfin. For this he was banished from Tirion for twelve years, although he was reconciled with Fingolfin. Even though he saw through the plots of Melkor, Fëanor remained distrustful of the Valar and grew excessively fond of the Silmarils; when the Two Trees were poisoned he refused to give up the Silmarils which preserved their light.

But when he heard the further tragedy of Melkor's murder of Finwë and theft of the Silmarils, Fëanor resolved to return to Middle-earth in pursuit of Melkor, defying the Valar and swearing the terrible Oath of Fëanor (q.v.), by which he, his sons, and Beleriand were later doomed. Undeterred by the banishment of Manwë and the Doom of Mandos, the fey Fëanor led the Noldor forth, in his haste and pride instigating the Kinslaying at Alqualondë and the desertion of Fingolfin in Araman.

In Middle-earth Fëanor immediately won Dagor-nuin-Giliath, but in his wrath he recklessly pursued the fleeing Orcs into Dor Daedeloth, where he was overwhelmed by Balrogs and fatally wounded. Although rescued by his sons, he died near Eithel Sirion, he who brought to the Noldor "their greatest renown and their most grievous woe."

His birth-name was Curufinwë; he was called Fëanor (from the Quenya Fëanáro, the name given him by Míriel) because of the burning spirit evident within him. (II 258, 260; III 388, 493; S 60-72 passim, 75, 78-79, 82-90, 98, 106-07, 305, 335; B 64-79 passim, 83, 86-88, 91-102, 112, 123-25, 410, 417)

FËANTURI (Q.: 'spirit-masters') The Valar Mandos and Lórien (qq.v.). (S 28; B 21)

FELAGUND (Kh.: *felak* 'cave' + *gundu* 'hewer') Epithet applied to Finrod (q.v.) by the Dwarves because of his excavation of Nargothrond. (S 61, 114, 330; B 64, 134, 410)

FELARÓF (b. before TA 2500, d. 2545) Horse, the mount of King Eorl and the first of the mearas. Originally a wild horse in Éothéod, Felaróf slew Léod, Eorl's father and a great horse-tamer, when Léod tried to mount him. As a wergild for this, Felaróf submitted himself to Eorl.

Felaróf was called Mansbane because he had slain Léod, and "father of horses" because he was the ancestor of the mearas. (II 143; III 430-31, 434)

FELLOWSHIP OF THE RING The Company of the Ring (q.v.). (III 320)

FELL RIDERS Name given to the Nazgûl (q.v.) in Gondor. (III 41)

FELL WINTER The winter of FA 496, marked by early snow and a late spring. (S 215, 239; B 264, 295)

FELL WINTER The winter of TA 2911, as called in the annals of the Shire. Many rivers in Eriador, including the Baranduin, froze over, and much of the land, including the Shire, was invaded by White Wolves. (I 239, 377; III 461)

FENGEL (TA 2870-2953) Man, fifteenth King of Rohan (2903-53). Quarrelsome, greedy, and gluttonous, Fengel was very unpopular. (III 436)

FEN HOLLEN (S.: 'the closed door') Door in the western side of the sixth level of Minas Tirith, through which one went to reach the Hallows. Fen Hollen was so called because it was kept closed and guarded by a porter, being opened only for funerals.
     Called in Westron the Closed Door. Also called the Steward's Door. (III 121, 123, 160)

FENMARCH Area in Rohan, the marshy land along the Mering Stream. (III 14, 93-94; L 184)

FEN OF SERECH Marshes above the Pass of Sirion on the east side of the river, the site of a number of battles in the Wars of Beleriand, particularly the heroic rearguard defense of the army of Gondolin by Huor, Húrin, and the Edain of Hithlum during the Nirnaeth Arnoediad. (S 107, 152, 163, 191, 194; B 124, 182, 197, 233, 237)

FENS OF SIRION The marshes around Aelin-uial (q.v.). (S 168; B 203)

FERDIBRAND TOOK (b. TA 2983) Hobbit of the Shire, son of Ferdinand Took. He was a guest at the Farewell Party. (III 475)

FERDINAND TOOK (b. TA 2940) Hobbit of the Shire, son of Sigismond Took. He was a guest at the Farewell Party. (III 475)

FERNY Family of Men of Bree. (I 212)

FERUMBRAS TOOK (TA 2701-2801) Hobbit of the Shire, son of Isumbras Took. As Ferumbras II he was the twenty-fourth Thain of the Shire (2759-2801). (III 475)

FERUMBRAS TOOK (TA 2916-3015) Hobbit of the Shire, son of Fortinbras Took. As Ferumbras III he was the thirtieth Thain of the Shire (2980-3015). Ferumbras was unmarried. He was a guest at the Farewell Party. (III 475)

FIELD OF CELEBRANT Meadow-lands between the Limlight and Silverlode, site in TA 2510 of the Battle of the Field of Celebrant. (I 17)

FIELD OF CORMALLEN (Q.: 'circle-golden') Place in northern Ithilien near Henneth Annûn. The celebration of the downfall of Sauron in the WR was held here.

Cormallen was named because of the culumalda trees that grew there; the name was also quite appropriate to the celebration, made possible by the destruction of the One (golden) Ring. (III 284-90; S 361; B 453)

FIELDS OF PELENNOR See: the Pelennor. (III 426)

FIERY MOUNTAIN Orodruin (q.v.). (I 94)

FÍLI (TA 2859-2941) Dwarf of Durin's Line, son of Dís and nephew of Thorin II. Fíli was a member of Thorin and Company and was slain, with his brother Kíli, defending Thorin's body in the Battle of Five Armies. (III 450; H 22, 26, 275)

FILIBERT BOLGER (fl. TA 3000)   Hobbit of the Shire. He married Poppy Baggins, and was a guest at the Farewell Party. (III 474)

FIMBRETHIL (S.: 'thin-birch')   An Entwife, loved by Fangorn.
Called in Westron Wandlimb. (II 99, 100; III 510; RHM III 423; L 175)

FINARFIN (Q.)   Noldorin prince, third son of Finwë, his mother was Indis. Finarfin married Eärwen of the Teleri; among their five children were Finrod and Galadriel. Finarfin tried to remain apart from the disputes of the Noldor in Eldamar, but he reluctantly joined in the pursuit of Melkor. Deterred by Fëanor's conduct in the Kinslaying and by the Doom of Mandos, Finarfin returned to Tirion, where he was forgiven and given the rule of the Noldor remaining in the West. He led his people to Middle-earth in the Great Battle.
Finarfin was the fairest and wisest of the sons of Finwë. Called Finarphir on III 506.
See also: House of Finrod. (S 60, 83, 84, 85, 88, 176, 251, 305, 306; B 63, 93, 95, 100, 213, 310, 379, 380)

FINARPHIR   Finarfin (q.v.). (III 506)

FINDARÁTO (Q.: 'hair-eminent man')   The Quenya form of Finrod (q.v.). (S 356; B 446)

FINDEGIL (S.: '—star') (fl. FO 172)   Man of Gondor, a King's Writer. Findegil made a copy of the Red Book of Westmarch for the Thain of the Shire. (I 38)

FINDUILAS (S.: 'hair—') (d. FA 496)   Noldorin princess, daughter of Orodreth. She and Gwindor loved each other, but when Túrin came to Nargothrond Finduilas fell in love with him. Although Túrin loved her not,

Gwindor at his death laid on him the duty to protect her, prophesying that she alone could save the Adan from his fate. Finduilas was captured by Orcs during the Sack of Nargothrond, but Túrin, deceived by Glaurung, went to Dor-lómin after Morwen and Nienor. Finduilas was slain by her captors when they were ambushed by the Haladin of Brethil at the Crossings of Teiglin. The Haladin buried her in Haudh-en-Elleth.

She was given the epithet Faelivrin by Gwindor. (S 209, 210-11, 213, 214, 216, 225, 305; B 257, 258-59, 261, 263, 266, 277, 379)

FINDUILAS (TA 2950-2988) Dúnadan of Gondor, daughter of Adrahil of Dol Amroth, wife of Denethor II and mother of Boromir and Faramir. A beautiful and gentle woman, Finduilas after her marriage missed the Sea and the freedom of the south and dreaded the Shadow of Mordor; she faded and died twelve years after marrying Denethor in 2976. (III 296, 418, 461, 462)

FINGLAS (S.: 'hair-leaf'?) (FA-) Ent, one of the three eldest Ents still living at the time of the WR. By the end of the Third Age Finglas had grown quite sleepy and "tree-ish," and moved very little. He was covered with leaf-like hair.

Called in Westron Leaflock. (II 97-98)

FINGOLFIN (S.) (d. FA 455) Noldorin prince, second son of Finwë; his mother was Indis. His children were Fingon, Turgon, and Aredhel. Although insulted and attacked by Fëanor in Eldamar, Fingolfin remained temperate and forgiving. He joined the revolt of the Noldor at the urging of his sons and to protect his people from the rashness of Fëanor; he also led the people of Finarfin.

Deserted by Fëanor in Araman, Fingolfin led the dangerous crossing of the Helcaraxë. As he marched into Middle-earth the Moon rose, flowers sprang up at his feet, and the forces of Morgoth retreated. But Fingolfin prudently established himself in Hithlum, preparing for a long war. After the death of Fëanor he was named High King of the

Noldor (1-455), and for hundreds of years he coordinated the Siege of Angband. When the Edain entered Beleriand, Fingolfin established ties with the Third House, which he allowed to settle in Dor-lómin.

During Dagor Bragollach Fingolfin and his forces were forced to retreat from Ard-galen to Eithel Sirion and the Ered Wethrin. At last, perceiving the defeat of the Noldor on all fronts, Fingolfin was overwhelmed by the rage of despair. He charged alone across Ard-galen to the Gate of Angband and challenged Morgoth to single combat. Fingolfin gave Morgoth seven wounds, but finally he was overborne and slain. His body was recovered by Thorondor and buried in the northern Echoriath.

Fingolfin was the strongest and most valiant of the mighty sons of Finwë. His banners were blue and silver, and he bore the sword Ringil. He was called the King of the North. (S 60, 69-71, 75, 83-90, 100, 108-09, 111, 113, 115, 119, 121, 143, 147, 150, 152-54, 305; B 63, 74-77, 83, 93-102, 115, 126-27, 129, 133, 135, 140, 143, 171, 177, 181, 183-86, 379)

FINGON (S.) (d. FA 473)   Noldorin Elf, son of Fingolfin, father of Gil-galad, and High King of the Noldor in Middle-earth (455-73). In Eldamar he was friendly with Maedhros, Angrod, and Aegnor, and was one of the group of young Noldorin princes who favored the pursuit of Melkor and the Silmarils, although he loved Fëanor little. Fingon led the vanguard of the host of Fingolfin during the return and fought in the Kinslaying.

On the return to Middle-earth Fingon resolved to heal the breach between the House of Fëanor and the rest of the Noldor, and, aided by Thorondor, he heroically freed Maedhros from his chains on the face of Thangorodrim. He then settled in Dor-lómin (until the coming of the Edain) and fought valiantly in the Wars of Beleriand; about 260 he defeated Glaurung.

Fingon became High King on the death of his father during Dagor Bragollach, but he himself was slain by Balrogs in the Nirnaeth Arnoediad.

The original (Quenya) form of his name was probably

Findakáno. (S 60, 84, 85, 87, 109-11, 116, 119, 121, 152, 154, 160, 164, 189, 191, 192, 193-94, 305, 358, 360; B 63, 94, 96, 98, 128-29, 137, 140, 143, 183, 186, 194, 198, 231, 234, 236, 379, 449, 452)

FINROD (S.: 'hair-eminent one') (d. FA 466) Noldorin Elf, eldest son of Finarfin. In Eldamar Finrod was friendly with Turgon and joined the revolt of the Noldor reluctantly; his beloved, Amarië of the Vanyar, did not go into Exile with him.

Finrod was one of the leaders of the host of Fingolfin on its long march to Middle-earth. In Beleriand he first settled in Tol Sirion and built Minas Tirith, but, guided by Ulmo, he found the Caverns of Narog and began the building of Nargothrond, capital of the largest Noldorin realm in Beleriand; he was its king.

Finrod was the first of the Eldar to encounter the Edain, whom he instructed in Ossiriand. He fought in the Wars of Beleriand; during Dagor Bragollach he was surrounded by Orcs in the Fen of Serech but was rescued by Barahir, to whom he gave the ring of Barahir as a pledge of aid to his house. When Beren later came to Nargothrond for that aid, Finrod gallantly went forth to his doom in the Quest of the Silmaril. Overcome by Sauron in a duel of songs of power, Finrod was imprisoned with Beren in what had been his own dungeons of Minas Tirith. Finrod was slain by a wolf defending Beren and was buried on Tol Sirion.

Finrod was very powerful, but also wise and just. He was a great traveler.

He was called Felagund and Master of Caves by the Dwarves for his labors at Nargothrond, Nóm by the Edain whom he instructed, and the Faithful and Friend-of-Men for giving his life for Beren. The original (Quenya) form of his name was Findaráto. (III 453, 506, 519; S 61, 73, 85, 90, 109, 114, 120-21, 124, 128-30, 140-43, 151-52, 169-72, 174, 175-76, 305, 306, 356, 358; B 64, 80, 96, 102, 127, 134, 142-44, 148, 154-55, 167-71, 182, 204-07, 210-11, 213, 379, 380, 446, 449)

FINWË (Q.) Noldorin Elf, one of the ambassadors

chosen by Oromë to visit Aman and later the leader of the Noldor on the Great Journey. Finwë had two wives: Fëanor was his son by the first, Míriel; Indis bore him two sons, Fingolfin and Finarfin. During the Noontide of Valinor Finwë was king in Tirion. He loved Fëanor dearly and shared his twelve-year exile in Formenos, where he was slain by Melkor defending the treasure-house of his family. (S 52-53, 60, 62, 63-65, 69-72, 75, 79, 305; B 53, 63, 65, 67-69, 75-78, 83, 87, 379)

FIRE   The Flame Imperishable (q.v.). (S 16; B 4)

FIREFOOT (fl. WR)   A horse of Rohan, mount of Eomer during the WR. (II 164)

FIRE OF DOOM   The flames of the heart of Orodruin, found in the depths of the Crack of Doom. (III 272)

FÍRIEL (Q.: 'mortal-woman') (fl. TA 1940)   Dúnadan of Gondor, daughter of King Ondoher. In 1940 she married Arvedui of Arthedain. (III 409; TB 8)

FÍRIEL (fl. FA 100)   Hobbit of the Shire, daughter of Elanor and Fastred. (TB 8)

FÍRIEL   Woman of Gondor, chief character in a Hobbit poem originally derived from Gondor. Fíriel was very beautiful, and for this reason Elves departing over Sea offered to take her with them. Fíriel, however, was unable to accompany them because of her mortality. (TB 61-64)

FIRIENFELD (Tr. Roh.: 'mountain-field')   The meadow of Dunharrow. (III 80-81)

FIRIEN WOOD, FIRIENWOOD   Oak-wood at the foot of the Ered Nimrais, on the border between Rohan and Gondor. The boar of Everholt dwelt in the Firienwood until it was slain by Folca in TA 2864. The last of Gondor's beacon-tower hills, Halifirien, was in the Firienwood. (III 14, 92, 94, 435)

FÍRIMAR (Q.: 'mortal-people') Men (q.v.), so called by the Eldar. (S 103; B 119)

FIRITH (S.) Sindarin name for quellë (q.v.). (III 480)

FIRMAMENT The heights of the Timeless Halls, the opposite of the Abyss. (S 17; B 6)

FIRST AGE The first of the recorded ages of Middle-earth. The First Age may have begun with the completion of Arda or with the awakening of the Elves. Its early history, save for the Battle of the Powers and the Great Journey, is obscure, for most of the Eldar were in the West, and other races kept few records. Moreover, until the rising of the Moon and Sun there seems to have been no count of years in Middle-earth.

This was the Age of the Eldar and of Morgoth. It ended with the Wars of Beleriand and the Great Battle, in which Morgoth was cast out of Eä.

Also called the Elder Days and the Eldest Days.

For an attempt to establish a chronology of the First Age, see the Appendix to this *Guide*. (III 452, 519; S 7, 294; B 365)

FIRST BATTLE OF THE FORDS OF ISEN See: Battles of the Fords of Isen. (III 465)

FIRST-BORN, FIRSTBORN OF ILUVATAR The Elves (q.v.), especially the Eldar. (I 294; S 18, 48; B 7, 48)

FIRST DAY The period of the first blooming and waning of the Two Trees. (S 39; B 34)

FIRST DEEP Level of Khazad-dûm just below the Great Gates. (I 426)

FIRST EASTFARTHING TROOP See: the Watch. (III 347)

FIRST HOUSE OF THE EDAIN The kindred of Bëor, the first group of Edain to enter Beleriand. They dwelt for a time in Ossiriand and then in Estolad, but finally they allied themselves with the house of Finarfin and settled in Dorthonion, especially in Ladros. Some, though, led by Bereg, refused to enter the Wars and moved south out of Beleriand.

The First House was shattered during Dagor Bragollach and its aftermath. Most of the few survivors of the first onslaught and of Barahir's defense of Finrod fled to Hithlum, where they were absorbed into the Third House. A few warriors, led by Barahir, became outlaws in Dorthonion; Beren was the only warrior of the First House to survive there. A remnant of the women and children of the House, led by Emeldir, fled Dorthonion and were absorbed into the other Houses.

The people of the First House were dark-haired and grey-eyed. In spirit they were like the Noldor, skilled of hand and eager and thoughtful of mind. Also called the House of Bëor. (III 388; S 140-43, 148, 151-52, 155, 157, 307; B 168-72, 177, 182, 187, 189, 381)

FIRST LINE The first nine Kings of Rohan. The First Line began with Eorl, and the Kings of the First Line were descended from father to son. The last king of the First Line was Helm, who was succeeded by his nephew, his sons having fallen in the war against Wulf. (III 434-35)

FIRST SHIRRIFF An office and title of the Mayor of Michel Delving in his capacity of head of the Watch. (I 31)

FIRST WAR The initial conflict in Eä between the Valar and Melkor, in which Melkor hindered the completion of Arda until he fled at the coming of Tulkas. At length Arda was made firm, although its plan was altered. (S 21-22, 35; B 12, 29)

FIRTH OF DRENGIST Drengist (q.v.). (S 80; B 89)

FISHER BLUE A kingfisher of the Withywindle, in the Shire-poem *Bombadil Goes Boating.* (TB 18, 23)

FLADRIF (S.: 'skin-bark') (FA-)   Ent, one of the three eldest surviving Ents at the time of the WR. Fladrif lived west of Isengard, and when Saruman became evil he was wounded by Orcs and many of his trees killed. After this, Fladrif retreated to the higher slopes of Fangorn and refused to come down from there.
   Fladrif probably resembled a birch tree.
   Called in Westron Skinbark. (II 97-98)

FLAMBARD TOOK (TA 2887-2989)   Hobbit of the Shire, son of Isembard Took. (III 475)

FLAME IMPERISHABLE The creating spirit of Ilúvatar, by which the Ainur and Eä were made, possessed by Ilúvatar alone.
   Also called the Imperishable Flame, the Fire, and perhaps the Flame of Anor.
   See also: the Secret Fire. (S 15, 16, 20; B 3, 4, 12)

FLAME OF ANOR The power wielded by Gandalf, possibly an allusion to the white light of the Sun as a symbol of the Secret Fire. (I 429)

FLAME OF UDÛN The fire of the Balrog.
   See: Udûn. (I 429)

FLAMMIFER OF WESTERNESSE Eärendil (q.v.), as a star, so called because it guided the Edain to Númenor. (I 311)

FLET Talan (q.v.). (I 444)

FLOATING LOG, THE A good inn in Frogmorton, closed during the WR by Sharkey's Men. (III 345-46)

FLÓI (d. TA 2989)   Dwarf. Flói went to Khazad-dûm with Balin in 2989 and was slain by an orc-arrow in a battle outside the Great Gates. It seems that before he was slain Flói killed an important enemy fighter, perhaps a troll or an uruk. He was buried near the Mirrormere. (I 418)

FLOWER OF SILVER The Moon (q.v.), so called because it was the last flower of Telperion. (S 100; B 115)

FOAMRIDERS The Teleri (q.v.) of Eldamar. (S 171; B 207)

FOE OF THE VALAR Melkor (q.v.). (S 85; B 95)

FOLCA (TA 2804-64) Man, thirteenth King of Rohan (2851-64). A great hunter. Folca killed the last of the Orcs remaining in Rohan from the invasion of 2799, and also slew the boar of Everholt. He died of the tusk-wounds given him by the boar. (III 435)

FOLCO BOFFIN (fl. WR) Hobbit of the Shire, a good friend of Frodo Baggins. Folco was most probably a guest at the Farewell Party. (I 71, 102)

FOLCRED (TA 2858-85) Man of Rohan, son of King Folcwine and twin brother of Fastred (q.v.). (III 436)

FOLCWINE (TA 2830-2903) Man, fourteenth King of Rohan (2864-2903). Folcwine recovered the area between the Adorn and Isen from the Dunlendings, and in 2885 he sent an army commanded by his twin sons Fastred and Folcred to the aid of Gondor in the Battle of the Crossings of Poros. (III 435-36)

FOLDE Area of Rohan near Edoras, the homeland of the royal family. (III 14, 92, 93; L 185)

FOLK OF THE MOUNTAIN The Dwarves (q.v.). (III 304)

FOLK OF THE WOOD The Elves (q.v.). (III 304)

FOLLOWERS Men (q.v.). (S 18; B 7)

FORBIDDEN DOOR The Dark Door (q.v.). (III 459)

FORD OF BRITHIACH Brithiach (q.v.). (S 131; B 157)

FORD OF BRUINEN Ford across the Bruinen, on the Great East Road. On their way to Rivendell in TA 3018, Frodo and his companions were attacked here by the Nazgûl, but the Black Riders were defeated by Aragorn and Glorfindel and a flood created by Elrond.

Also called the Ford of Rivendell. (I 16, 269; H 12, 55)

FORD OF CARROCK Ford across Anduin, kept open at the time of the WR by the Beornings.

In *H*, the Ford of Carrock only connects the Carrock and the east bank of the Anduin; perhaps the reference on I 301 should be to the Old Ford. (I 301; H 116-18, 131)

FORD OF RIVENDELL The Ford of Bruinen (q.v.). (I 283)

FORDS OF ISEN Fords across the Isen in western Rohan, the chief entrance into Rohan from the west. In TA 2758 the Fords were the site of a battle between King Helm and Wulf, and during the WR two battles were fought here between the Rohirrim and Saruman's forces.

Also called the Crossings of Isen. (II 168, 198-99; III 432)

FORELITHE The sixth month of the Shire Reckoning (q.v.), coming before the Lithe, and thus roughly corresponding to our June.

Called Lithe in Bree. (III 478, 483)

FOREST GATE Western entrance to an elf-path crossing northern Mirkwood. Thorin and Company were shown this gate by Beorn in TA 2941, and entered Mirkwood through it. (H 13, 140)

FOREST OF BRETHIL   Brethil (q.v.). (S 120; B 142)

FOREST OF NELDORETH   Neldoreth (q.v.). (S 121; B 145)

FOREST OF REGION   Region (q.v.). (S 132; B 158)

FOREST RIVER   River flowing from the Ered Mithrin through northern Mirkwood and into the Long Lake. (H 13, 172, 180)

FOREYULE   The last month of the Shire Reckoning (q.v.), roughly corresponding to our December.
Called Yulemath in Bree and the Eastfarthing. (III 478, 483)

FORGOIL   (Dunlendings: 'strawhead')   Name given the Rohirrim by the Dunlendings. (II 180; III 509)

FORLINDON   (S.: 'north Lindon')   That portion of Lindon north of the Gulf of Lhûn. In the Second Age Gil-galad lived in Forlindon. (I 16; III 452)

FORLOND   (S.: 'north-haven')   Harbor on the northern side of the Gulf of Lhûn.
Misspelled *Forland* on I 16. (I 16; III 411)

FORLONG   (d. TA 3019)   Man of Gondor, Lord of Lossarnach. Although old, he fought valiantly in the Battle of the Pelennor Fields, where he was slain by Easterlings after becoming separated from his men.
He was called Forlong the Fat because he was. *Forlong* is of pre-Númenórean (early Second Age) Mannish origin. (III 49, 148, 152, 508)

FORMEN   (Q.: 'north')   Name for the tengwa ᚻ (number 10). This tengwa was commonly used to indicate the compass-point "north," even in languages in which the word for "north" did not begin with this sign. (III 500)

FORMENOS (Q.: 'north-citadel') The fortress and treasury of the house of Finwë, built in northern Valinor during Fëanor's exile from Tirion. Melkor stole the Silmarils from Formenos and slew Finwë there. (S 71, 75, 76; B 78, 83, 84)

FORN Name given Tom Bombadil (q.v.) by the Dwarves. (I 347)

FORNOST ERAIN (S.: 'north fortress of the kings') City on the North Downs, second capital of Arnor and its chief city in the Third Age. Fornost was also the capital and chief city of Arthedain, but it was captured by Angmar in TA 1974. Although freed the next year in the Battle of Fornost, Fornost was deserted, since the North-kingdom ended.

A palantír (q.v.) was kept at Fornost until 1974.

Called Norbury, or Norbury of the Kings, in Westron. After its abandonment, Fornost was known as Deadman's Dike. (I 16, 320-21; III 337, 398, 411; S 291; B 360)

FOROCHEL (S.: 'north—') Cold, barren area in northern Middle-earth, about 300 miles north of the Shire. Its climate was imposed by Morgoth. In the Third Age the Lossoth were its sole inhabitants.

See also: Cape of Forochel. (I 16; III 398-400)

FORODWAITH (S.: 'north-people') Men of the First Age, the inhabitants of Forochel and other areas in the extreme north of Middle-earth. (III 399)

FORSAKEN ELVES The Úmanyar (q.v.). (S 233; B 288)

FORSAKEN INN, THE Inn one day's journey east of Bree, the easternmost inn on the Great East Road. (I 253)

FORTINBRAS TOOK (TA 2745-2848) Hobbit of the Shire, son of Ferumbras Took and, as Fortinbras I, twenty-fifth Thain of the Shire (2801-48). (III 475)

FORTINBRAS TOOK (TA 2878-2980)   Hobbit of the Shire, son of Isumbras II and, as Fortinbras II, twenty-ninth Thain of the Shire (2939-80). (III 475)

FOSCO BAGGINS (TA 2864-2960) Hobbit of the Shire, paternal grandfather of Frodo Baggins. He married Ruby Bolger. (III 474)

FOUR FARTHINGS   The Shire (q.v.). (I 306)

FOURTH AGE   The age of the Dominion of Men. The Fourth Age began with the passing of the Three Rings and various heroes of the Third Age after the defeat of Sauron (September, TA 3021), but the first day of the Fourth Age was March 25, TA 3021.

In the Fourth Age most of the Elves, especially the Eldar, passed over Sea, and those of the non-Mannish races that remained in Middle-earth dwindled and hid, for their time was past and Men no longer understood them.

Also called the New Age and the Younger Days. (III 308, 387, 470, 486; S 304; B 378)

FOX DOWNS   Misprint for the Far Downs (q.v.). (I 24)

FRAM (fl. TA 21st Cent.)   Man, Lord of Éothéod, son of Frumgar. Fram slew the dragon Scatha and won his hoard. He later quarreled with the Dwarves, who claimed the treasure, and may have been slain by them. (III 430)

FRAMSBURG   Town or fortress on the extreme northern Anduin, probably a stronghold of the Éothéod. (PB)

FRÁR (d. TA 2994)   Dwarf. Frár went to Khazad-dûm with Balin, and was slain in the defense of Durin's Bridge and the Second Hall. (I 419)

FRÉA (TA 2570-2659)   Man, fourth King of Rohan (2645-59). (III 434)

FRÉALÁF (TA 2726-98) Man, tenth King of Rohan (2759-98) and the first of the Second Line, son of Hild, King Helm's sister. During the Dunlending invasion of 2758, Fréaláf took refuge in Dunharrow with many of the Rohirrim, and early the next spring he took Meduseld and Edoras in a surprise attack in which Wulf was slain. In the course of 2759, Fréaláf, with aid from Gondor, drove the Dunlendings out of all of Rohan. Since King Helm and his sons had died in the invasion, Fréaláf was made king.

During Fréaláf's reign Saruman came to Isengard, and the wizard aided the Rohirrim, who had been greatly weakened by the war with Wulf and the Long Winter. (III 433, 435)

FRÉAWINE (TA 2594-2680) Man, fifth King of Rohan (2659-80). (III 435)

FRECA (d. TA 2754) Man of mixed Rohirric and Dunlending blood, father of Wulf. Freca was very rich and powerful and had much land near the Adorn. King Helm distrusted him, and after Freca insulted the king for refusing an offer to marry his daughter to Wulf, Helm slew him. (III 431-32)

FREDEGAR BOLGER (fl. WR) Hobbit of the Shire, son of Odovacar Bolger, a guest at the Farewell Party, and a good friend of Frodo Baggins. He came from Budgeford. In 3018 Fredegar helped cover Frodo's departure from Crickhollow and was nearly slain by the Nazgûl. During Lotho's and Saruman's control of the Shire, Fredegar led a band of rebels in the Brockenbores, but was captured and imprisoned in the Lockholes.

Fredegar was called Fatty before he was imprisoned and half-starved. He was a typical Hobbit in that, despite his friendship with Frodo, he had no desire to leave the Shire with him in 3018 to seek adventure, but became a partisan when it was necessary. (I 71, 153, 238-39; III 372, 475)

FREE FAIR Fair held once every seven years on the Lithe. The Fair was held on the White Downs and was attended by Hobbits. The Mayor of the Shire was elected at the Free Fair. (I 31; III 377)

FREE FOLK See: the Free Peoples. (I 368)

FREE LORDS OF THE FREE A general term used by Boromir to refer to the mighty lords of the Free Peoples such as the Steward of Gondor and Elrond. (I 350)

FREE PEOPLES The "good" races of Middle-earth: Men (especially the Dúnedain), Elves, Dwarves, and Hobbits. The term was used specifically to refer to those races which were in opposition to Sauron.
  The Free Folk were those individuals who comprised the Free Peoples.
  Also called the Free. (I 361, 368)

FRERIN (TA 2751-2799) Dwarf of Durin's line, second son of Thráin II and younger brother of Thorin II. Frerin escaped with his family from Erebor when Smaug attacked the Dwarf-kingdom in 2770, and wandered with Durin's Folk until he was slain in the Battle of Azanulbizar. (III 440, 443, 450)

FRERY In Bree and the Eastfarthing, the name given Afteryule (q.v.). (III 483)

FRIEND OF THE NOLDOR Aulë (q.v.), so called because he instructed the Noldor, who shared his interest in substances and crafts. (S 39; B 35)

FRODO BAGGINS (TA 2968-) Hobbit of the Shire, Ring-bearer, Elf-friend, and hero, the only son of Drogo Baggins and Primula Brandybuck. In 2980, on the death of his parents, he was adopted by his cousin Bilbo and went to live with him in Bag End. In 3001, when Bilbo left the Shire, Frodo inherited all his goods, including Bag End and the One Ring.
  In 3018, on Gandalf's advice, Frodo, under the name of Mr. Underhill, went to Rivendell to escape the Nazgûl.

Along the way, he met Aragorn and was nearly slain by the Lord of the Nazgûl. In Rivendell, he volunteered to undertake the Quest of Mount Doom. After great adventures and heroic deeds with the Fellowship of the Ring, Frodo reached the Sammath Naur, but at the last moment he claimed the Ring for himself. However, Gollum bit off Frodo's ring-finger and then fell into the Sammath Naur, thus fulfilling the Quest.

After the WR, Frodo was for a while (November 3019-Midyear's Day, 3020) Mayor of Michel Delving. However, discontented in mind and wounded in body (from his stabbing by the Nazgûl-lord and his poisoning by Shelob), he passed over Sea with the Last Riding of the Keepers of the Rings, leaving his goods to his beloved servant and friend, Sam Gamgee.

Frodo wrote the account of the War of the Ring and the Quest of Mount Doom contained in the Red Book of Westmarch; he also composed a few songs.

Even before the WR, Frodo was more thoughtful and moody than Hobbits were wont to be, and eagerly sought out news of far lands. Although this was in part because of Frodo's responsibility as Ring-bearer, he was also uncommonly perceptive of the hearts of those he met. The Ring influenced Frodo surprisingly little; although it caused him to age very slowly and he was greatly troubled by the burden and eventually succumbed to it, his resistance was very great. Frodo knew Sindarin and a little Quenya, and was said to show uncommon skill in pronouncing foreign languages. He seems to have had few friends of his own age, although he was close to Bilbo and a number of Hobbits younger than himself. He was unmarried.

Called the Ring-bearer, Frodo of the Nine Fingers, and Nine-fingered Frodo. (I 32, 43-44, 45, 154; III 271-77, 281, 303-04, 312, 331, 373, 380-84, 474, 475, 476, 490; TB 9; S 299-300; B 372)

FRODO GARDNER (b. FO 3) Hobbit of the Shire, second child and eldest son of Samwise Gamgee. Frodo was founder of the family of Gardner of the Hill. He probably lived in Bag End. (III 382, 477)

FRODOS DREME   See: *The Sea-Bell.* (TB 9)

FROGMORTON   Village in the Eastfarthing on the Great East Road. The Floating Log, a good inn, was located in Frogmorton, and during Lotho's control of the Shire the village was the headquarters of the First Eastfarthing Troop of the Watch. (I 40; III 345-46)

FRONT GATE   The main gate of Erebor, out of which flowed the River Running. The Front Gate was the only obvious gate to Erebor not blocked up by Smaug, who used it as his entrance.
   Also called the Gate of Erebor and the Gate. (III 449, 468; H 33, 196, 230, 246-48)

FRONT PORCH   Name given by a group of Orcs of the Misty Mountains to the cave forming the main entrance to their tunnels. The Front Porch opened onto the High Pass, and was built sometime in the years immediately preceding TA 2941. (H 66-67, 71)

FRÓR   (TA 2552-89)   Dwarf of Durin's Folk, second son of Dáin I. He was slain with his father in the Ered Mithrin by a dragon. (III 440, 450)

FRUMGAR (fl. TA 1977)   Man, Chieftain of the Éothéod. In TA 1977 he led the Éothéod north from their previous home between the Gladden and the Carrock to the land called Eothéod.
   Misspelled "Frungor" on III 458. (III 430, 458; RHM III 368)

FUINUR (S.: 'darkness—') (fl. SA 3300)   Black Númenórean. In Middle-earth he became a powerful lord of the Haradrim. (S 293, 358; B 363, 449)

FUNDIN (TA 2662-2799)   Dwarf of Durin's line, son of Farin and father of Balin and Dwalin. He was slain in the Battle of Azanulbizar. (III 443, 450)

GABILGATHOL (Kh.) Belegost (q.v.). (S 91; B 104)

GAERYS (S.: 'sea—') Sindarin name for Ossë (q.v.). (S 359; B 450)

GALABAS (gen. Hob.) See: Gamwich. (III 520)

GALADHRIEL (S.: 'tree-lady') A variant form of Galadriel (q.v.), referring to her rule of the forest of Lórien. (S 360; B 451)

GALADRIEL (S.: 'lady of light') (FA-) Noldorin princess, the daughter of Finarfin. Galadriel was the only woman to play a prominent role in the debate of the Noldor following the theft of the Silmarils, and, eager to return to Middle-earth, she was one of the leaders of the host of Fingolfin.

In Middle-earth she dwelt with Finrod on Tol Sirion, but when her brother moved to Nargothrond she went to Doriath, where she married Celeborn and was instructed in wisdom by Melian. She had one child, Celebrían. At the fall of Doriath she probably fled to Arvernien or the Mouths of Sirion. Galadriel was the only leader of the revolting Noldor to survive the Wars of Beleriand, and at the end of the First Age a ban was set on her return to Valinor.

In the Second Age Galadriel dwelt for a time in Lindon and Eregion, and then founded and became Queen of Lórien, which she made on the model of Doriath and the Girdle of Melian and sustained with the aid of her own power and that of Nenya, one of the Three Rings, which was given to her at its making. Thoughout the Second and Third Ages Lórien remained safe from Sauron, for Galadriel's power was such that she knew his mind but hers was closed to him, and she could protect Lórien from assault by any power less than Sauron himself.

During the WR, Galadriel gave shelter and great gifts to the Companions of the Ring, and she refused the One Ring when it was offered to her by Frodo. Because of this, and because of her endless opposition to Sauron, at the end of the Third Age the Valar permitted her to return to Valinor. Galadriel fulfilled her age-old desire in TA 3021, when she went over Sea with the Last Riding of the Keepers of the Rings.

Galadriel was very tall and the greatest beauty of the house of Finwë; she had the golden hair of her mother's kindred.

The Quenya form of her name was Altariel. She was known as the Lady of Lórien, Galadhriel, the Lady of the Wood, the Lady of the Galadrim, the Sorceress of the Golden Wood (by Gríma), the Mistress of Magic (by Faramir), the White Lady, and Queen Galadriel. (I 456, 459 ff., esp. 462, 472, 503; II 150; III 57, 381-84, 451, 453, 506; R 60; S 61, 83-84, 90, 114, 115, 126-27, 254, 298, 300, 305, 306, 360; B 64, 93-94, 102, 134-35, 151-52, 315, 370, 373, 379, 380, 451-52)

GALADRIM (S.: 'tree-people') The Elves (mostly Silvan) of Lórien, ruled by Celeborn and Galadriel. The Galadrim flourished undisturbed from the founding of Lórien in the Second Age until TA 1980, when with the freeing of the Balrog in Khazad-dûm many of the Galadrim fled south to Dol Amroth. Many of the Galadrim at this time sailed over Sea. Although forced to become more martial, the Galadrim lived happily in Lórien until the end of the Third Age, when with the departure over Sea of Galadriel Lórien was deserted. Most of the Galadrim went with Celeborn to East Lórien.

The Galadrim lived in telain (see: talan) built in the trees of Lórien. They spoke a dialect of Sindarin.

Called in Westron the Tree-people. (I 442; III 458, 468, 506)

GALATHILION (S.: 'tree-moon white') The White

Tree of the Eldar, made for them by Yavanna and planted before the Mindon in Tirion. Galathilion was a model of Telperion, but it did not shine. Celeborn was one of its many seedlings.

Called the White Tree, the Tree of Silver, the Tree of the High Elves, the Tree of Túna, and the Tree of Tirion. (I 397; III 308; RHM III 440; S 59, 263, 364; B 62, 324, 456)

GALBASI (gen. Hob.)   See: Gamgee. (III 520)

GALDOR (S.) (d. FA 462)   Adan of the Third House, elder son of Hador. He married Hareth about 440; their sons were Húrin and Huor. Galdor became Lord of the Third House and captain of Eithel Sirion on the death of his father in 455, but was slain by an arrow when Eithel Sirion was besieged by Morgoth.

He was called Galdor the Tall. (S 148, 152, 158, 160, 308; B 177, 183, 190, 191, 194, 382)

GALDOR (S.) (fl. WR)   Elf of the Grey Havens, messenger of Círdan and his representative at the Council of Elrond in TA 3018. (I 315, 327-28)

GALENAS (S.)   See: pipe-weed. (I 29; RHM III 438)

GALION (S.) (fl. TA 2941)   Elf of the Woodland Realm, butler of Thranduil. (H 173-76)

GÁLMÓD (fl. TA 30th Cent.)   Man of Rohan, the father of Gríma. (II 151)

GALPSI (gen. Hob.)   See: Gamgee. (III 520)

GALVORN (S.: 'shining-black')   Black, shining metal invented by Eöl. Malleable but as hard as steel even when thin, galvorn was an ideal substance for armor. Since galvorn is not mentioned apart from Eöl, the secret of its manufacture may have died with him. (S 133, 359, 360; B 159, 450, 451)

GAMGEE   A Hobbit family of the Shire, originally of the working class. The Gamgees took their name from the village of Gamwich, their first home; at the time of the WR one branch of the family lived at Number 3, Bagshot Row, Hobbiton. The most illustrious member of the family was Samwise, who as the heir of Frodo and the son-in-law of Tolman Cotton was both well-to-do and influential; he was elected Mayor of the Shire seven times. Samwise's children included the founders of the families of Fairbairn of the Tower and Gardner of the Hill.

The name Gamgee evolved through such forms as Gammidge and Gammidgy, from the original Gamwich. The genuine Hobbitish forms were Galpsi, from Galbasi, from Galabas. (I 44; III 477, 520)

GAMLING (fl. WR)   Man of Rohan, leader of the men who guarded Helm's Dike before the Battle of the Hornburg. Gamling was probably Erkenbrand's lieutenant.

He was known as Gamling the Old, because at the time of the WR he was. (II 172, 178-79, 180)

GAMMIDGE   See: Gamgee. (III 477)

GAMMIDGY   See: Gamgee. (III 520)

GAMWICH   A village in the Shire, home of Hamfast of Gamwich, the founder of the Gamgee family.

Gamwich is the translated Hobbitish form of the genuine Hobbitish *Galabas*, a common Shire village-name meaning 'game-village.' (III 477, 520)

GAMWICH   Hobbit surname, used by a working-class family in the Shire c. TA 2800. The name was derived from the village of Gamwich.

The genuine Hobbitish form was Galbasi.

See: Gamgee. (III 477, 520)

GANDALF   One of the Istari (q.v.), as Gandalf the Grey the second most powerful of the Order. Gandalf can be said to have been the person most responsible for the victory of the West and the downfall of Sauron in the Third Age; he labored ceaselessly and ever faithfully for two thousand years toward that goal, and by his foresight he built up many powers to oppose Sauron in the final struggle.

On his arrival in Middle-earth about TA 1000, Círdan gave him Narya, one of the Three Rings. Gandalf had many adventures and trials during the Third Age, only the chief of which can be mentioned here. In 2063, at the request of the White Council, he went to Dol Guldur as a spy but was unable to determine the identity of its lord. In 2850 he again entered Dol Guldur, discovered that its lord was Sauron, received the key to Erebor from Thráin, and managed to escape. Later, in 2941, Gandalf interested Thorin in the recovery of Erebor, his goal being the establishment of a strong realm in the north to oppose an attack by Easterlings allied with Sauron. Gandalf's further action of persuading Thorin to hire Bilbo Baggins as burglar for the expedition, perhaps because he wished to use the latent strength of the Shire-folk at a later date, had even more important consequences, since Bilbo obtained the One Ring. Gandalf suspected that Bilbo's treasure was indeed the One, and from 2941 to 3001, with the aid of the Rangers he put a close watch over Bilbo and the Shire.

In 3001 Gandalf persuaded Bilbo to give the Ring to Frodo (an unparalleled action which confirmed Gandalf's high opinion of Hobbits), and in 3018 set into motion the Quest of Mount Doom. Gandalf was an important influence at the Council of Elrond, since he alone knew the full history of the Ring and of Saruman's treachery; later he was one of the Companions of the Ring. Although he was slain defending the Company from the Balrog in Khazad-dûm, he was sent back to Middle-earth as Gandalf the White to complete his task. During the WR he released King Théoden from Gríma's spells, cast Saruman out of the order of the Istari, and gave invaluable counsel to Gondor and Rohan. During the Battle of the Pelennor Fields Gandalf contested the gates of Minas Tirith with the Lord of the Nazgûl for the few crucial minutes between their breaking and the arrival of the Rohirrim.

After the successful completion of the WR, his task being completed, Gandalf went over Sea with the Last Riding of the Keepers of the Rings.

Gandalf looked like a grey-cloaked, grey-haired (after his resurrection, his hair and cloak were white) bent old man, and passed easily for a meddlesome old conjuror; at times, however, he revealed his true majesty and power. Prior to his fight with the Balrog, his body was apparently mortal, vulnerable both to weapons and "magical" force; but as Gandalf the White, no weapon could harm him, and his power over the Unseen was greatly increased.

Gandalf traveled mostly in the West and had no permanent home. Of all the Istari, he was the closest to the Eldar and was the only Wizard who truly cared about things of seemingly small value like Hobbits and trees. He was a great master of lore and (perhaps due to Narya) of fire. Gandalf was a friend and teacher to Aragorn seemingly above all other Men, and the two helped each other greatly. After 2941, in addition to his staff Gandalf bore the great sword Glamdring. In 3018, after escaping from Isengard, he tamed Shadowfax, the greatest of the mearas of Rohan, and rode him for the rest of the WR.

"Gandalf" was the name given him by the Men of the North. He was called Mithrandir by the Elves; the Westron forms Grey Wanderer and Grey Pilgrim were also used. He was called Tharkûn by the Dwarves, Incánus by the Haradrim, Gandalf Greyhame by the Rohirrim, and at various times Stormcrow (by Théoden and himself), Láthspell (by Gríma), and the Grey Fool (by Denethor II, who disliked him because of his friendship with Thorongil, the rival of his youth). He was also known as the Enemy of Sauron and (during the WR) the White Rider. His real name, given him in Valinor in his youth, was Olórin (q.v.); he may have been a Maia. (I 57-63, 299, 336-47, 366, 380, 387, 519; II 46, 86, 134-35, 149, 353; III 22, 100, 125-26, 303-04, 308, 383, 418, 447-48, 455-56, 459, 460; H 17-20, 26, 29, 100, 184; S 300-04; B 372-77)

GAP OF ROHAN Area in Rohan between the White and Misty Mountains. (I 338)

GARDNER OF THE HILL Famous and influential family of Hobbits of the Shire, whose first member was Frodo, eldest son of Samwise Gamgee. The Gardners, who took their name from Sam's trade, most probably lived in Bag End. (III 473, 477)

GÁRULF (d. TA 3019) Man of Rohan, a Rider of Éomer's éored. He was killed in the battle between the éored and Uglúk's Orcs. (II 51)

GATE The great arched entrance to Angband, set at the foot of the Ered Engrin beneath Thangorodrim. (S 118, 179-80, 192; B 139, 217-18, 234)

GATE OF EREBOR The Front Gate (q.v.). (III 449)

GATE OF KINGS The Argonath (q.v.). (II 24)

GATE OF THE DEAD The Dark Door (q.v.). (III 69-70)

GATES OF ARGONATH The Argonath (q.v.). (S 297; B 369)

GATES OF GONDOR The Argonath (q.v.). (I 351)

GATES OF MORNING A place in the uttermost East of Arda in the Second Age, probably the gates in the Wall of the Night (q.v.) through which the Sun passed in the morning.
Cf.: the Doors of Night. (S 263; B 324)

GATES OF SIRION Caverns in the base of the Andram out of which the River Sirion flowed from its subterranean channel. (S 122; B 145)

GATES OF SUMMER Festival of Gondolin, probably held on Midsummer's Day. During the festival the Elves sang as the Sun rose. (S 242; B 300)

GELION (S.) River of Beleriand, flowing southward from sources in Lake Helevorn and Mount Rerir (Greater Gelion) and Himring (Little Gelion). The Gelion formed the western boundary of Ossiriand. The river was twice as long as the Sirion, although less wide and deep. (S 122, 123, 124; B 145, 146-47, 148)

GELMIR (S.) (d. FA 473) Noble Elf of Nargothrond, son of Guilin and brother of Gwindor. Captured by Morgoth during Dagor Bragollach and blinded, Gelmir was later mutilated and slain before the walls of Barad Eithel. (S 188, 191; B 230, 233)

GELMIR (fl. FA 496) Noldorin Elf, companion of Arminas (q.v.) (S 212; B 260)

GELYDH (S.) Plural of Golodh.
See: Golodhrim. (S 238; B 294)

GERONTIUS TOOK (TA 2790-2920) Hobbit of the Shire, son of Fortinbras Took and twenty-sixth Thain of the Shire (2848-2920). He married Adamanta Chubb; they had twelve children.
Gerontius reached the second greatest age of any Hobbit in history, being surpassed only by Bilbo. He was known as the Old Took. (II 80-81; III 475; H 17)

GHÂN-BURI-GHÂN (fl. WR) Man, chieftain of the Woses. During the WR Ghân-buri-Ghân guided the Rohirrim through Druadan Forest, thus enabling them to avoid the superior force of Orcs and Easterlings guarding the Great West Road.
Also called Ghân. (III 129-33, 313)

GIANTS See: stone-giants. (H 99-100, 118)

GIFT OF MEN The special fate of Men, placed upon them at their making by Ilúvatar, that the desires and fates of Men should extend beyond the preordained pattern of the Ainulindalë. At their deaths in Arda Men go to the halls of Mandos, but then pass to an unknown destiny beyond the Circles of the World. Thus, unlike the Elves, Men age and die utterly with respect to Eä, but this death is the means to a greater freedom.

In the Second and Third Ages this blessing was frequently seen as a curse by those Men, especially the Númenóreans, who did not look beyond the end of their lives in Arda. Therefore it was frequently called the Doom of Men. Also called the gift of Ilúvatar. (III 390, 425, 427-28; S 41-42, 149, 187, 265; B 38, 178, 227, 327)

GILDOR (S.: 'star—') (d. FA 460) Adan of the First House, one of the last twelve outlaw-followers of Barahir in Dorthonion. (S 155, 162-63; B 187, 195-96)

GILDOR INGLORION (fl. WR) Elda of the House of Finrod. At the time of the WR he lived at Rivendell. He sailed over Sea with the Last Riding of the Keepers of the Rings. (I 118-24; III 381; R 65-66)

GIL-ESTEL (S.: 'star of hope') Name given to the star Eärendil (q.v.) on his first rising by the people of Middle-earth. (S 250; B 310) ˙

GIL-GALAD (S.: 'star of radiance') (FA-SA 3441) Noldorin Elf, son of Fingon, last High King of the Noldor in Middle-earth. Born in Hithlum, Gil-galad was sent to safety in the Falas after the death of Fingolfin during Dagor Bragollach. When the Havens were overrun he escaped to Balar; he was named High King after the death of Turgon in the fall of Gondolin.

In the Second Age Gil-galad remained in Middle-earth as lord of Lindon, fighting off Sauron during the Dark Years with aid from Númenor. When Sauron arose again after the fall of Númenor and attacked Gondor, Gil-galad formed the Last Alliance of Men and Elves with Elendil, and with Elendil he led the army that in 3434 defeated Sauron in the Battle of Dagorlad and besieged the Barad-dûr. In 3441 Gil-galad and Elendil overthrew Sauron but were themselves slain; Gil-galad was burned to death by Sauron's heat.

Gil-galad's weapon was the famous spear Aeglos. He was the first bearer of Vilya, the greatest of the Three Rings.

His birth-name was Ereinion. He was later called Ereinion Gil-galad, but as High King he was called Gil-galad alone. (I 83, 250, 257, 319-20, 332; III 389, 452, 453-55; R 65; S 154, 196, 244, 247, 254, 267, 286, 287, 290, 292, 293-94, 305; B 186, 239, 302, 305, 315, 329, 330, 354, 355, 356, 360, 362, 364-65, 379)

GILLY BAGGINS (d. after TA 3001)   Hobbit of the Shire, wife of Posco Baggins and a guest at the Farewell Party. She was born a Brownlock. (III 474)

GILRAEN (S.: 'wandering star') (TA 2907-3007) Dúnadan of the North, daughter of Dírhael. In 2929 she married Arathorn II, and in 2931 their only child, Aragorn, was born. Gilraen lived in Rivendell from the death of her husband in 2933 until 2954, when she returned to her family home somewhere in Eriador.

She was called Gilraen the Fair. (III 420, 422, 426, 461, 463)

GILRAIN (S.)   River in Lebennin, Gondor, flowing southward from its source in the Ered Nimrais until it entered the Bay of Belfalas just west of the Ethir Anduin. Its principal tributary was the Serni. (III 14, 185)

GILTHONIEL (S.: 'star-kindler')   Epithet of Varda (q.v.). (R 65; S 48; B 48)

GIMILKHÂD (Ad.) (fl. SA 3175)   Dúnadan of Númenor, younger son of Ar-Gimilzôr and father of Ar-Pharazôn. A strong, harsh man, he led the King's Men during the reign of his brother, Tar-Palantir. Gimilkhâd died at the age of 198. (S 269; B 332)

GIMILZÔR, AR- (Ad.) (fl. SA 3125)   Dúnadan,

twenty-second King of Númenor. He married Inzilbêth of Andúnië despite her wishes; the two sons of their unhappy marriage were Tar-Palantir and Gimilkhâd. Gimilzôr neglected the White Tree and the Hallow of Eru. (III 390; S 268-69; B 331-32)

GIMLI (TA 2879-) Dwarf of Durin's line, son of Glóin. He probably spent his youth in the Ered Luin and moved to Erebor with his father in 2941. In 3018 Gimli accompanied Glóin to Imladris. There he was chosen to represent the Dwarves in the Company of the Ring, and guided the Companions through Khazad-dûm. He was the first Dwarf to enter Lórien since Durin's Day, and in that land became devoted to Galadriel and a close friend of Legolas. After the breaking of the Fellowship, Gimli traveled with Legolas and Aragorn to Rohan, where he fought valiantly in the Aglarond during the Battle of the Hornburg. He then traveled the Paths of the Dead and came to Minas Tirith with Aragorn, fighting in the Battle of the Pelennor Fields and the battle outside the Morannon.

After the WR, Gimli brought a group of Dwarves from Erebor to Rohan, where he became Lord of the Glittering Caves. He remained friendly with Legolas and the other members of the Fellowship of the Ring, and forged new gates of mithril and steel for Minas Tirith. In FO 120, after the passing of Elessar, Gimli sailed over Sea with Legolas. This action was unprecedented; it was no doubt prompted by Gimli's love for Legolas and Galadriel.

Gimli was called Elf-friend. He was known as Lockbearer because of the lock of her hair given him by Galadriel. (I 315, 361, 365-66, 453-54, 461-62, 464-65, 481, 486-87; II 193-95; III 317, 387, 449-51)

GINGLITH (S.) Small river of West Beleriand, a tributary of the Narog. Ginglith formed the western boundary of the plain of Tumhalad. (S 169, 209; B 204, 356)

GIRDLE OF MELIAN The enchanted barrier raised by Melian to protect Doriath, enclosing Region, Neldoreth, Nivrim, and part of Aelin-uial. Created soon after the return of Morgoth to Middle-earth with the Silmarils, the Girdle hid Doriath until Melian went over Sea after the death of Thingol. In all those hundreds of years only twice was the maze of shadow and bewilderment breached: by Beren, whose doom was greater than the power of Melian, and by Carcharoth, whose rage was fed by the power of the Silmaril.

Besides barring intruders, the Girdle sheltered Doriath from the dark influence of Morgoth. (S 97, 122, 144, 164-65, 184, 216, 231, 234; B 110, 145, 172, 198, 223, 265, 286, 289)

GIRDLEY ISLAND   Island in the Brandywine just above the Bridge of Stonebows, perhaps a part of the Shire. (I 40)

GIRION (S.?) (d. TA 2770)   Man, last King of Dale of the old line. He was killed by Smaug, but his wife and children escaped to continue the royal line. (H 215, 220, 237, 239)

GIRITHRON (S.: 'shivering'?)   Name for Ringarë (q.v.), used only by the Dúnedain. (III 483)

GLADDEN   River flowing east from its source in the central Misty Mountains. It emptied into the Anduin in a marsh. An important pass over the Misty Mountains was located at the source of the Gladden. (I 17, 359)

GLADDEN FIELDS   Marshy fields at the meeting of the Gladden and Anduin. In TA 2 the Battle of the Gladden Fields was fought here, and the One Ring remained hidden here from that time until TA 2463, when it was found by Déagol. A band of Stoors lived in or near the Gladden Fields from about TA 1410 until after 2460, and this may have been the original home of the Stoors.

Many irises grew in the Gladden Fields.

Called in Sindarin Loeg Ningloron. (I 17, 83, 320; III 456; L 185; S 295; B 366)

GLAMDRING (S.: 'foe-hammer') The sword of Gandalf. Originally made by the Elves of Gondolin for the Wars of Beleriand, Glamdring was worn by Turgon. After the fall of Gondolin, Glamdring eventually found its way into a troll-hoard, where it was found by Gandalf in TA 2941. Gandalf used Glamdring from then until the end of the WR. It is not said if he took the sword over Sea with him.

As with all such weapons, Glamdring shone with a blue light in the presence of Orcs. It was the mate of Orcrist (q.v.).

Called by the Orcs Beater. (I 366, 429; II 147; III 336; H 53, 61, 73)

GLAMHOTH (S.: 'din-horde') The Orcs (q.v.). (S 360; B 451)

GLANDUIN (S.) River flowing west from its source in the Misty Mountains and joining the Mitheithel above Tharbad.

Called Swanfleet in Westron because of the many swans that lived on the lower reaches of the river. (III 325, 396)

GLAURUNG (S.) (d. FA 501) Dragon, first and greatest of the Urulóki. Bred by Morgoth in Angband, Glaurung first appeared c. FA 260 and ravaged Ard-galen. Being still half-grown, he was driven off by mounted archers led by Fingon.

Glaurung did not emerge again until Dagor Bragollach, when he was full-grown and the greatest terror of Morgoth's armies. In that campaign Glaurung ravaged Lothlann and forced Maglor's Gap. In the Nirnaeth Arnoediad Glaurung's presence turned the tide of battle; he separated the eastern and western armies of the Noldor and then, aided by the treachery of the Easterlings, proceeded to destroy the eastern army. He was stopped only by the fire-hardy Dwarves of Belegost; although Glaurung slew their lord Azaghâl, he was wounded by Azaghâl and forced to withdraw.

In 496 Glaurung led the campaign against Nargothrond.

He defiled Eithel Ivrin, burned the Talath Dirnen, broke the army of Nargothrond at Tumhalad with his heat, destroyed the Doors of Felagund and the bridge before them, gathered the treasures of Nargothrond, and lay down on this hoard. During this time Glaurung bewitched Túrin and Nienor, preventing the former from rescuing Finduilas and taking away the memory of the latter. He thus prepared their incestuous marriage and suicides; but at the last Túrin was revenged, for at Cabed-en-Aras the hero gave Glaurung a mortal wound in the belly.

Although the words of dragons are little to be trusted, Glaurung's conversations with Túrin suggest that his malice toward the Children of Húrin was as much a product of the will of Morgoth as of his own draconian evil.

Glaurung the golden, father of dragons, was also known as the Great Worm and the Worm of Morgoth. (S 116, 151, 153, 192, 193, 212-15, 217-18, 220-23; B 137, 181, 184, 235, 236, 261-65, 267-68, 271-75)

GLÉOWINE (fl. WR) Man of Rohan, Théoden's minstrel. After the WR he made a song about Théoden and his death, and composed no song after that. (III 314)

GLINGAL (S.: 'hanging flame' or 'gleaming light') Artificial tree of gold fashioned by Turgon as an image of Laurelin and standing in the royal courts in Gondolin. (S 126, 332; B 151, 413)

GLIRHUIN (S.) (FA 6th Cent.) Man of Brethil, a seer and minstrel. He prophesied that the Stone of the Hapless would survive the ruin of Beleriand. (S 230; B 283-84)

GLITTERING CAVES The Aglarond (q.v.). (II 195)

GLÓIN (TA 2136-2385) Dwarf, King of Durin's Folk (2283-2385) in the Ered Mithrin. (III 450)

GLÓIN (TA 2783-FO 15) Dwarf of Durin's line, son of Gróin and father of Gimli. He was a companion of Thráin and Thorin in their wanderings after the Battle of

Azanulbizar and was a member of Thorin and Company, as a result of which expedition he became rich and important in Erebor. In 3018, with Gimli, Glóin went to Rivendell to obtain advice from Elrond on behalf of the Dwarves of Erebor, and he took part in the Council of Elrond. (I 300, 316-17; III 445, 450; H 22, 26)

GLÓREDHEL (S.: 'golden-elda') (fl. FA 440) Adan of the Third House, daughter of Hador. She married Haldir of Brethil; their son was Handir. (S 158, 308, 361; B 190, 382, 452)

GLORFINDEL (S.: 'golden-hair') (d. FA 511) Eldarin lord of Gondolin, one of the captains of Turgon. Glorfindel commanded the left flank of the retreat of the Gondolindrim during the Nirnaeth Arnoediad. When Gondolin fell, Glorfindel accompanied Tuor, Idril, and the other survivors in their escape, but when the company was ambushed in Cirith Thoronath he fought with the Balrog who led the enemy. Both fell to their deaths.

Since Glorfindel was golden-haired, he was probably of the house of Finarfin. He was chief of the House of the Golden Flower. (S 194, 243, 358, 361; B 237, 301, 449, 452)

GLORFINDEL (fl. TA 1975-   ) Eldarin lord of great power, probably of the House of Finarfin. At the time of the WR Glorfindel seems to have been the second most important Elf, after Elrond, in Rivendell. Glorfindel led the Elvish force that helped rout Angmar in the Battle of Fornost in TA 1975. In 3018 he met and protected Frodo and his companions on their way to Rivendell, and he fought the Nazgûl at the Ford of Bruinen.

Glorfindel's horse was the great white steed Asfaloth. (I 279-81, 294, 299; III 412)

GOATLEAF Family of Men of Bree. (I 212)

GOBLIN-GATE An entrance to the Orc-tunnels of the Misty Mountains, probably the back-door (q.v.). (H 12)

GOBLINS The Orcs (q.v.). (H 30, 138)

GOBLIN-WARS The Wars of Beleriand (q.v.). (H 61, 72)

GOD Ilúvatar (q.v.). (R 66)

GODS The Valar (q.v.), so called by the Edain. (S 144; B 173)

GOLASGIL (S.: 'leaf-star') (fl. WR) Man of Gondor, probably a Dúnadan, lord of Anfalas. (III 50)

GOLDBERRY (fl. WR) Woman, wife of Tom Bombadil (q.v.). She was the daughter of the River-woman of the Withywindle.

Goldberry was fair and golden-haired, gracious and calm, with a beauty like to that of Elves yet more easily encompassed by Hobbitish hearts.

Also called River-daughter. (I 168, 169, 171, 172 ff., 187-88; TB 11-12, 15-16)

GOLDEN HONEYCOMB Trophy or prize of war won by the messenger of *Errantry,* probably fictitious. (TB 27)

GOLDEN PERCH Inn in Stock, reputed at the time of the WR to have the best beer in the Eastfarthing. (I 128; L 186)

GOLDEN TREE Laurelin (q.v.). (I 482)

GOLDEN WOOD Lórien (q.v.). (I 439)

GOLDILOCKS TOOK (b. FO 10) Hobbit of the Shire, daughter of Sam Gamgee and wife of Faramir Took. She was most probably golden-haired. (III 382, 477)

GOLDWINE (TA 2619-99) Man, sixth King of Rohan (2680-99). (III 435)

GOLDWORTHY   Family of Hobbits of the Shire, perhaps well-to-do. (III 476)

GOLFIMBUL (d. TA 2747)   Orc, called by Hobbits of the Shire King of the Orcs of Mount Gram, leader of the Orc-band that was defeated in the Battle of Greenfields. In that battle, Golfimbul was slain by Bandobras Took, who knocked his head off with a club.

The name *Golfimbul* is either facetious and fictitious or else translated Westron, since Professor Tolkien derives the source of the game and name of golf from it. Also, since the Orc-band was probably not very large, Golfimbul, if a historical personage, was probably somewhat less than a king. (H 30)

GOLLUM (TA c. 2430-3019)   Hobbit of the Stoor strain, born in the Stoor settlement near the Gladden Fields. About 2463 his cousin Déagol found the One Ring while fishing, and Gollum murdered him for it. Soon he became odious to his family and was driven out of the Stoor community. Gollum hid in the Misty Mountains, falling more and more under the control of the Ring, until 2941, when he lost it. Bilbo Baggins found the Ring and took it with him to the Shire. Gollum, suspecting that Bilbo had the Ring, came out of the Misty Mountains to search for Bilbo, his need for the Ring overcoming his hatred and fear of the Sun, the Moon, and other living things.

A few years before the WR, Gollum was captured by Sauron, who thus discovered about "Baggins." Sauron released Gollum in 3017 and he was captured by Aragorn, who turned him over to Gandalf. The wizard learned that part of the story of the Ring which he had not previously known, and then gave Gollum over to the Elves of the Woodland Realm. In June, 3018, Gollum escaped during an Orc-raid and immediately went off in search of the Ring. He caught up with Frodo and the Company of the Ring outside the West-gate of Khazad-dûm, and followed the Company through Moria and Lórien. Gollum was captured by Frodo and Sam in the Emyn Muil. Partly out of fear of the Ring-bearer and partly to ensure that Sauron

did not recover the Ring, Gollum led the Hobbits faithfully to Cirith Ungol, the least guarded route into Mordor.
However, there he betrayed Frodo and Sam to Shelob,
hoping to recover the Ring when Shelob discarded their
clothing. His plan failed, and so he followed the Hobbits
to Orodruin. There his last ambush of Frodo failed, but
when the latter claimed the Ring as his own, Gollum attacked him once more. In the struggle which followed,
Gollum bit off Frodo's ring-finger and thus got the Ring.
This betrayal of his oath to serve Frodo doomed Gollum;
the other part of the oath—to prevent Sauron from recovering the Ring—was fulfilled at once, for Gollum fell
into the Crack of Doom, destroying both himself and the
Ring.

Gollum originally looked like a normal Hobbit, but his
long years in dark and damp under the influence of the
Ring drastically affected his appearance. The descriptions
of him vary somewhat, but he seems by the time of Bilbo
and Frodo to have been extremely thin and wiry, with
black skin, flat feet, long thin hands, and large pale eyes.
Although his sight was poor, his hearing was acute, and he
could move silently and climb like an insect. Because of
his long domination by the Ring, Gollum pathologically
feared all things Elven; Elven ropes burned his flesh and
lembas tasted like dust. He hated all creatures and was,
because of the influence of the Ring on his naturally somewhat nasty character, generally despicable.

Gollum's real name was Trahald, a northern Mannish
name meaning 'burrowing, worming in'; the Anglicized
Mannish equivalent was Sméagol. He was called Gollum
because of the disgusting noise he made in his throat; the
name was originally given to him by his family after he
found the Ring. The Orcs of Cirith Ungol called him Her
Sneak for his service to Shelob. He called himself "my
preciouss," perhaps confusing himself and the Ring. Sam
devised two names, Slinker and Stinker, for the two aspects
of Gollum's nature while he was serving Frodo. The
former referred to his fawning behavior toward Frodo as
Ring-bearer and his sworn master, which was in part a
sincere desire to be a good person and escape the control

of the Ring, while the latter referred to Gollum's spiteful, treacherous, hating behavior toward all else, which sometimes carried over to Frodo. (I 32-34, 85-91, 329-36 ff., 497; II 278-80 ff., 285, 442; III 279-86 ff., 459, 462, 463; H 79-93)

GOLODHRIM (S.: 'Noldo-people')   The Sindarin form of Noldor (q.v.).
The plural of *Golodh* is *Gelydh*. (S 134, 238, 332; B 160, 294, 413)

GONDOLIN (S.: 'rock-hidden')   Elven city and kingdom in the hidden valley of Tumladen, built in secret by Turgon between FA 52 and 104. Surrounded by the Echoriath, the only easy entrance to Gondolin was the Way of Escape, difficult to find and heavily guarded by the Gondolindrim (q.v.). The city of Gondolin, built of white stone on Amon Gwareth, was modeled on Tirion, whose beauty it came to rival.

Blessed by Ulmo and protected by the unceasing vigilance of the Eagles, who drove off all spies of Morgoth in the Echoriath, Gondolin remained securely hidden for centuries, with few passing outward and only four people— Maeglin, Eöl, Húrin and Huor—passing inward who had not entered with Turgon at the realm's founding. During these long years Gondolin prospered and ignored the affairs of the outside world, and Morgoth could not spy it out.

Although the forces of Gondolin did not fight in Dagor Bragollach, Turgon marched forth to the Nirnaeth Arnoediad with ten thousand men. Yet the secret of Gondolin was kept, for Turgon managed to withdraw unseen behind the defense of Húrin and Huor. In the years that followed, Tuor came to Gondolin and Eärendil was born. However, on his release from Angband Húrin had inadvertently revealed to Morgoth the approximate location of Gondolin, and later Maeglin betrayed the secrets of its passes. Gondolin was overwhelmed in 511 by a horde of Orcs, Balrogs, wolves, and dragons, the last of the Elven realms of Beleriand to suffer the Doom of the Noldor.

The city of Gondolin was the fairest and most famous

Elven city in Middle-earth; it was said to have had seven names. The original name of city and realm was Ondolindë. Also called the Hidden Kingdom. The battles near Gondolin mentioned on H 72 are inconsistent with the history given in the *Quenta Silmarillion*. (I 319, 412; III 389; H 61, 72; S 115, 125-26, 136-39, 154, 158-59, 190, 194, 228, 239-43, 359; B 135, 150-51, 163-66, 186, 191-92, 232, 237, 282, 295-301, 450)

GONDOLINDRIM (S.: 'Gondolin-people') The Elves of Gondolin, comprising a third of the Noldor of Fingolfin's host and many Sindar. Prosperous and eager, they were very active in crafts and constructions, but when their doom came they proved themselves also mighty in war. After the fall of Gondolin the remnant of the Gondolindrim, led by Tuor and Idril, dwelt in Arvernien and the Mouths of Sirion. (H 61, 72; S 126, 138, 192, 244; B 151, 166, 234, 302)

GONDOR (S.: 'stone-land') One of the Dúnedain kingdoms in Middle-earth, founded by Elendil in SA 3320 and committed by him to the joint rule of his sons Isildur and Anárion. At the height of its power (c. TA 1100), Gondor extended north to Celebrant, east to the Sea of Rhûn, south to the River Harnen inland and Umbar on the coast, and west to Gwathlo. In addition, various realms to the east and south were tributary states. The chief cities of Gondor were Osgiliath, Minas Anor, Minas Ithil, Dol Amroth, and Pelargir.

From its founding, Gondor was always under attack by Sauron or his allies in Rhûn, Harad, or Umbar. Ithilien was invaded a number of times, beginning in SA 3429, until in TA 2002 Minas Ithil was taken by the Nazgûl and held until the end of the WR. In the Third Age, Gondor suffered three great evils: the Kin-strife of 1432-48, the Great Plague of 1636, and the invasions of the Wainriders between 1851 and 1954. These difficulties, combined with the degeneration of the Dúnedain, sapped Gondor's strength, decreased her population, and dulled her vigilance.

After the death of Elendil in SA 3441, Gondor was ruled by the Line of Anárion (q.v.) until it failed in TA 2050. From that time until the restoration of the kingdom by Elessar in 3019, Gondor was governed by the Ruling Stewards.

Gondor was a feudal kingdom. Originally the two greatest fiefs, the royal fiefs of Ithilien (Isildur) and Anórien (Anárion and his heirs), were of equal rank, but after the removal of Isildur to Arnor and the moving of the capital from Osgiliath to Minas Anor, Anórien became more important than Ithilien.

Also called the South-kingdom, in opposition to Arnor. Called Stonelending and Stoningland by the Rohirrim.

See: Calenardhon, Lebennin, Belfalas, Enedwaith, etc. (I 319, 321; II 363; III 394-96, 402-19, 454-62 passim; S 290, 296; B 360, 367)

GONNHIRRIM (S.: 'stone-lord-people') The Dwarves, so called by the Elves in the First Age. (S 91; B 103)

GOODBODY Family of Hobbits of the Shire, perhaps of the upper class. (I 52; III 474)

GOODCHILD Family of Hobbits of the Shire, perhaps of the working class. (III 477)

GOOD PEOPLE The Elves, or perhaps more generally the Free Peoples. (H 60, 165)

GOOLD Family of Hobbits of the Shire, perhaps of the upper class. (III 476)

GORBADOC BRANDYBUCK (TA 2860-2963) Hobbit of the Shire· Master of Buckland (2910-63). He married Mirabella Took; they had seven children, including Frodo's mother Primula.

Gorbadoc was noted for his generous table and matching waistline; he was called "Broadbelt." (I 45; III 475, 476)

GORBAG (d. TA 3019) Uruk of Minas Morgul, captain of a company of Orcs. He was killed in the fight between his company and Shagrat's over Frodo's mithril coat. (II 437; III 223-24)

GORBULAS BRANDYBUCK (b. TA 2908, d. before 3001) Hobbit of the Shire, son of Orgulas Brandybuck. (III 476)

GORGOROTH Ered Gorgoroth (q.v.) (S 164; B 198)

GORGOROTH (S.: 'haunted—') The great plateau of northwestern Mordor, a desolate area scarred with countless Orc-dug pits. Points of interest in Gorgoroth included Orodruin and the Barad-dûr. (I 519; II 308; III 245-67; S 292, 294; B 363, 365)

GORGÛN Orcs (q.v.), as called by Ghân-buri-Ghân. (III 133)

GORHENDAD OLDBUCK (fl. TA 2340) Hobbit of the Shire. He originally lived in the Marish, but in 2340 he crossed the Brandywine, settled Buckland, and built Brandy Hall. He changed the family name to Brandybuck; his heirs were the Masters of Buckland. (I 141; III 476, 520)

GORLIM (S.) (d. FA 460) Adan of the First House, son of Angrim. Gorlim was one of the last twelve members of Barahir's outlaw band in Dorthonion. Captured by Sauron, Gorlim was tricked into betraying Barahir in return for being reunited with his beloved wife Eilinel. But the image of her which Gorlim saw was a phantom of Sauron's, and the reunion was in death. (S 155, 162-63; B 187, 195-96)

GORMADOC BRANDYBUCK (TA 2734-2836) Hobbit of the Shire, Master of Buckland (?-2836). He married Malva Headstrong; they had many children.

Gormadoc was called "Deepdelver"; perhaps he enlarged Brandy Hall. (III 476)

GORTHAUR THE CRUEL (S.: 'abominable dread') Name given to Sauron (q.v.) by the Sindar in Beleriand. (S 32, 155, 285; B 26, 187, 353)

GORTHOL (S.: 'terror-helm') Pseudonym used by Túrin (q.v.) as one of the Two Captains in Talath Dirnen. (S 205; B 252)

GOTHMOG (d. FA 511) Balrog, Lord of Balrogs and high-captain of Angband, one of the mightiest warriors of Morgoth. Gothmog slew Fëanor in the aftermath of Dagornuin-Giliath, slew Fingon and captured Húrin during the Nirnaeth Arnoediad, and slew Ecthelion during the destruction of Gondolin, but he was in turn slain by Ecthelion.

Gothmog had a personal guard of trolls. (S 107, 193, 195, 242; B 125, 236, 238)

GOTHMOG (fl. WR) The lieutenant of Minas Morgul and commander of Sauron's army during the Battle of the Pelennor Fields after the fall of the Lord of the Nazgûl.

Gothmog may have been a Nazgûl. (III 148)

GRAM (TA 2668-2741) Man, eighth King of Rohan (2718-41). (III 435)

GREAT ARMAMENT The vast armada built by Ar-Pharazôn between SA 3310 and 3319 for the Númenórean assault on Valinor. The flagship was Alcarondas. (III 454; S 277-78; B 343-44)

GREAT BARROWS The graves on the Barrow-downs (q.v.), in which were buried chieftains of the Edain, and also Dúnedain of Cardolan. The Barrows were taken over by Barrow-wights in the middle of the Third Age. (I 181)

GREAT BATTLE The massive conflict which ended the First Age, fought between the Host of Valinor (q.v.)

and the forces of Morgoth, composed of Orcs, Balrogs, winged dragons, other monsters, and Easterlings. Virtually all of Morgoth's forces were destroyed, Thangorodrim was ruined and Angband laid bare, and Morgoth was overcome, but Beleriand and other northwestern regions of Middle-earth were broken and sank beneath the waves of Belegaer.

Also called the War of Wrath and (probably) the battle of the Valar. (III 138, 452; S 251, 285; B 348, 354)

GREAT BRIDGE   The Bridge of Stonebows. (III 402)

GREAT DANGER   Term used by Frodo to describe the period of the WR, when the Shire (and the rest of Middle-earth) was nearly enslaved by Sauron. (III 382)

GREAT DARKNESS   The period of the dominion of Morgoth in Middle-earth, or his influence and its extent. The term is used only by Fangorn.

See also: the Darkness. (II 89, 90, 96, 99, 113)

GREAT EAGLES   The Eagles (q.v.). (I 343)

GREAT EAST ROAD   The road running from the Grey Havens to Rivendell, passing through the Shire and the Bree-land.

Also called the Great Road, the East-West Road, the East Road, the Road, and the Old Road. (I 16, 72, 189, 202 ff.)

GREAT ENEMY   Morgoth (q.v.). (I 260)

GREATER GELION   Larger of the two branches of the River Gelion, flowing southwest from sources at Mount Rerir and Lake Helevorn. (S 123; B 146)

GREAT GATE OF MINAS TIRITH   The gate in the first level of Minas Tirith, the chief entrance to the city. The Gate was broken by the Lord of the Nazgûl during the Siege of Gondor, but after the WR it was rebuilt of mithril and steel by the Dwarves of Aglarond.

Also called the Gate of the City and the Gate. (III 24, 25, 125, 301, 451)

GREAT GATES   The eastern gate of Khazad-dûm, facing the Dimrill Dale. The Gates were broken when Balin's Dwarf-colony was attacked in TA 2994; they had not been repaired by the time of the WR.
Also called the Dimrill Gate and the Gate. (I 430; III 441, 443-44)

GREAT GOBLIN (d. TA 2941)   Orc, perhaps leader of all the Orcs of the Misty Mountains, or at least of those near the High Pass. The Great Goblin was slain by Gandalf after he had captured Thorin and Company. (H 70-72)

GREAT GULF   Gulf of Belegaer in the First Age, located in the extreme south of Arda. (S 51; B 51)

GREAT HALL   The first royal hall (either room or building) of Gondor, located in Osgiliath. The thrones of Isildur and Anárion were set here, and the Kings of Gondor sat in judgment here until Osgiliath was depopulated after the Great Plague. (III 408; S 291; B 361)

GREAT HALL OF THRÁIN   The main hall of Erebor.
Also called the Great Hall. (III 440)

GREAT HORN   Heirloom of the House of the Stewards of Gondor from the time of Vorondil (c. TA 2000) until the WR. Made from the horn of one of the Kine of Araw, the Horn was borne by the heir of the Steward. It was believed that if the Horn were blown anywhere within the ancient boundaries of Gondor, help would come. In TA 3019, Boromir blew it when attacked by Orcs near Rauros. Although Denethor and Faramir heard the call hundreds of miles away, no help arrived and Boromir was slain and the Horn cloven in two. The Horn was set on Boromir's funeral barge, but the shards were recovered by Denethor. (I 315; II 17, 18, 22, 347, 364; III 29)

GREAT HOUSE The dwelling of the Master of Esgaroth. (H 189-91, 236)

GREAT JEWEL The Silmaril (q.v.) recaptured from Morgoth by Beren. (I 362; III 281)

GREAT JEWELS The Silmarilli (q.v.). (I 362)

GREAT JOURNEY The migration of the Eldar from Cuiviénen to Eldamar early in the First Age. The Journey took many years, for the Eldar, loving the beauty of Middle-earth, tarried frequently, despite the urging of Oromë and their chieftains, Ingwë, Finwë, Elwë, and Olwë. The Vanyar marched first, followed by the Noldor; the more numerous Teleri straggled behind.

After passing around the northern end of the Sea of Helcar the Eldar turned west, and some abandoned the Journey. But most reached the Vales of Anduin after many years, and Oromë led the Vanyar and Noldor across the Misty Mountains. The Teleri hesitated, and many of them, known as the Nandor, went south down Anduin.

Finally the remaining Eldar gathered in Beleriand, the Teleri as usual farthest east. The Vanyar and Noldor were floated to Eldamar by Ulmo on the island which later became Tol Eressëa. Later many of the Teleri, led by Olwë, also crossed on this island, which was then anchored in the Bay of Eldamar. But many Teleri remained in Beleriand, where they became known as the Sindar. (III 506, 519; R 66; S 52-54, 57-59, 309; B 53-55, 59-62, 383)

GREAT LAKE Lake in the middle of Arda during the Spring of Arda, probably changed beyond recognition by the upheavals caused by Morgoth's destruction of the Two Lamps. The dwelling of the Valar, the Isle of Almaren, was located in the Great Lake. (S 35; B 30)

GREAT LANDS Middle-earth (q.v.). (II 362; S 263; B 324)

GREAT MUSIC Ainulindalë (q.v.). (S 15; B 3)

GREAT ONES   The Ainur, especially the Valar (qq.v.). (S 21, 26; B 11-12, 19)

GREAT ORCS   The Uruk-hai (q.v.). (II 48)

GREAT PLACE OF THE TOOKS   Room in the Great Smials. Gerontius Took spent the last part of his life here, and the room was left untouched after his death. (II 80)

GREAT PLAGUE   The plague that swept across Middle-earth from the southeast in TA 1636-37. Harad, and perhaps also Rhûn, suffered greatly. Gondor, which was struck next, was devastated. King Telemnar, all his children, and the White Tree died. Osgiliath was especially hard hit, and those of its inhabitants who survived by fleeing to the country did not return. The guard on Mordor was discontinued as a result of the Plague.

In Eriador, especially in the north, the Plague was somewhat less severe, but most of the inhabitants of Cardolan, including all the Dúnedain, perished.

Called in the Shire the Dark Plague. (I 24; III 398, 407-08)

GREAT RIDER   Oromë (q.v.) as he first appeared to the Elves in Cuiviénen. (S 50; B 50)

GREAT RING   The One Ring (q.v.). (I 331)

GREAT RINGS   The Rings of Power (q.v.). (I 333)

GREAT RIVER   Anduin (q.v.). (I 17)

GREAT ROAD   The Great East Road (q.v.). (III 396)

GREAT SEA, GREAT SEA OF THE WEST, GREAT SEAS   Belegaer (q.v.). (I 452; S 37, 279; B 32, 345)

GREAT SHELF   The dwelling place of the King of the Eagles in the Third Age, located in the Misty Mountains near the Old Forest Road. (H 112-13)

GREAT SHIPS The vessels of the Númenóreans. (II 95)

GREAT SIGNAL The signal from the Barad-dûr or Orodruin during the WR that sent the army of Minas Morgul against Gondor on March 10, TA 3019. This signal may also have served to unleash Sauron's other armies. (II 399, 441)

GREAT SMIALS Chief dwelling of the Tooks, a vast (for Hobbits) series of tunnels at Tuckborough. The excavation of the Great Smials was begun by Isengrim II in TA 2683.
Also called the Smials. (I 27; II 80; III 357, 459)

GREAT SPIDERS Large and evil creatures found in Nan Dungortheb at least as early as the end of the Spring of Arda; they were probably among the monsters with which Melkor blighted the Spring. When Ungoliant came to Nan Dungortheb she bred with the spiders, and no doubt they were increased in power and malice.
When Beleriand was destroyed at the end of the First Age, most of the spiders were slain, but at least one, Shelob, survived. She fled to the Ephel Dúath, and her incestuous offspring spread through the mountains of Mordor. In the Third Age, great spiders of Mordor moved to Mirkwood when Sauron established himself there, and for the rest of the Age they plagued the Woodmen and the Elves of the Woodland Realm. The spiders of Mirkwood were probably destroyed early in the Fourth Age, and Shelob may have died of wounds given her by Sam Gamgee, but the lesser spiders of Mordor may well have survived well into the Fourth Age.
Shelob stood at least five feet tall, for Sam was able to stand underneath her belly, and the great spiders of Beleriand were probably this size. The spiders of Mirkwood and Mordor were smaller than this, but were still quite large. (II 422-23; H 153-62; S 36, 81, 164; B 31, 90, 198)

GREAT TOWER   The Barad-dûr (q.v.) (III 204)

GREAT WARS   The struggles of Men and Elves against Morgoth and Sauron, so called by Fangorn. (II 95)

GREAT WATER   Belegaer (q.v.). (S 260; B 321)

GREAT WEST ROAD   The West Road (q.v.). (III 14)

GREAT WOOD   Mirkwood, in particular the Woodland Realm. (III 188)

GREAT WORM   Glaurung (q.v.). (S 192; B 235)

GREAT WORMS   The Dragons (q.v.). (H 10)

GREEN DRAGON   Inn in Bywater, located on the Hobbiton side of the village, frequented by Hobbits from both villages. (I 72; III 350)

GREEN-ELVES   The Laiquendi (q.v.). (S 96, 113, 309; B 110, 133, 383)

GREENFIELDS   Village or area in the Shire, probably in the Northfarthing. In TA 2747 the Battle of Greenfields was fought here.
 Also spelled Green Fields. (III 365)

GREENHAND   Family of working-class Hobbits of the Shire, descended from Halfred, the eldest son of Holman the greenhanded. The Greenhands lived in Hobbiton and were gardeners; the name was no doubt derived from the epithet applied to Holman because of his skill in his trade. (III 477)

GREEN HILL COUNTRY   Wooded area in the Eastfarthing and Southfarthing. (I 40, 107 ff.)

GREEN HILLS   Hills in the Southfarthing and Westfarthing, the center of Tookland. (I 40; III 357)

GREEN HILLS   The Pinnath Gelin (q.v.). (III 50)

GREENHOLM   Town in the Shire, located on the Far Downs, the home of Fastred of Greenholm. (III 471)

GREEN MOUND   Ezellohar (q.v.). (S 78; B 86)

GREENWAY   Name given to the North Road (q.v.) in the latter part of the Third Age, when it was not frequently used. (I 29, 210)

GREENWOOD THE GREAT   The vast forest east of Anduin. About TA 1050 the shadow of Dol Guldur fell on the forest, and it became known as Mirkwood (q.v.). After its cleansing at the end of the Third Age, it was renamed Eryn Lasgalen (q.v.). (III 404, 408, 456; S 299; B 371)

GREY COMPANY   Those who rode the Paths of the Dead with Aragorn during the WR. The Grey Company was composed of Legolas, Gimli, Elladan, Elrohir, and a company of thirty Rangers of the North. (III 55, 73)

GREY-ELVES   The Sindar (q.v.). (S 56, 113, 309; B 58, 133, 383)

GREYFLOOD   Gwathlo (q.v.). (I 268)

GREY HAVENS   Town and harbor of Círdan, located at the head of the Gulf of Lhûn. The Grey Havens were founded in SA 1, and it is said that Círdan dwelt there until the last white ship sailed over Sea sometime in the Fourth Age.
  Called in Sindarin Mithlond. Also called the Havens. (I 72, 74, 315; III 383, 453, 456; S 286; B 354)

GREY MOUNTAINS   The Ered Mithrin (q.v.). (III 440)

GREY WOOD, GREYWOOD   Thickets east of Amon

Dîn, in Anórien. The Grey Wood may have been part of Druadan Forest. (III 15, 132, 313)

GRIFFO BOFFIN (fl. TA 3000)   Hobbit of the Shire, husband of Daisy Baggins. He was a guest at the Farewell Party. (III 474)

GRÍMA (d. TA 3019)   Man of Rohan, chief counsellor to King Théoden. An agent of Saruman, Gríma gave his master information about Rohan at the same time that he enfeebled Théoden with his lying counsel; his reward was to have been Éowyn. After Gandalf renewed Théoden, Gríma fled to Isengard, where he kept Saruman company during his imprisonment by Fangorn. Gríma accompanied Saruman to the Shire, where, after great mistreatment by his master, he killed him in front of Frodo and was himself slain by Hobbits.

Gríma was called Wormtongue in Rohan because of his evil counsel; Saruman shortened this to Worm. (II 148-51; 158-60; III 323-24, 369-70)

GRIMBEORN (fl. WR)   Man, son of Beorn and chieftain of the Beornings. He was perhaps a shape-shifter like his father. During his rule, the High Pass and the Ford of Carrock were kept open, and no Orc or wolf dared enter the land of the Beornings.

He was known as Grimbeorn the Old. (I 301)

GRIMBOLD (d. TA 3019)   Man and Marshal of Rohan, from Grimslade. He was distinguished in the Battles of the Fords of Isen, and later commanded the third éored in the Battle of the Pelennor Fields. He was slain in the latter battle. (III 135, 152; RHM III 424)

GRIMSLADE   Place in Rohan, home of Grimbold. (III 152)

GRINDING ICE   The ice floes of the Helcaraxë (q.v.). Also called the Ice, the Ice of the North, and the Narrow

Ice. (I 308; S 57, 73, 89-90, 108, 109, 116; B 80, 126, 127, 136)

GRINDWALL   Village in the southern part of Buckland, outside the High Hay. (TB 9, 19)

GRIP (fl. WR)   One of Farmer Maggot's wolf-like dogs. (I 133, 134)

GRIP   Bill Butcher's dog, in the poem *Perry-the-Winkle*. Grip may have been modeled on a historical personage. (TB 42)

GRISHNÁKH (d. TA 3019)   Orc of the Barad-dûr, captain of the Mordor-orcs in the band that slew Boromir and captured Merry and Pippin. Somehow, Grishnákh knew of the Ring. Desiring it for himself and presuming that Merry or Pippin had it, he stole the two Hobbits away from their guard of Isengard Orcs while the Orc-camp was surrounded by the Rohirrim. Although slain by the Rohirrim, he carried Merry and Pippin far enough to enable them to escape the slaughter. (II 60-75 passim; III 511)

GRÓIN (TA 2671-2923)   Dwarf of Durin's line, second son of Farin and father of Oin and Glóin. (III 450)

GROND   The Hammer of the Underworld, the great mace which was Morgoth's chief weapon in battle. (III 124; RHM III 438; S 154; B 185)

GROND   The great, hundred-foot-long battering ram prepared in Mordor to break the Great Gate of Minas Tirith during the WR. Grond's head was made of black steel and was formed in the shape of a wolf's-head.

Grond was named after the mace of Morgoth. (III 124-25)

GRÓR (TA 2563-2805)   Dwarf of Durin's line, youngest son of Dáin I and father of Náin. He founded the Dwarvish realm in the Iron Hills. (III 440, 450)

GRUBB   A family of Hobbits of the Shire, perhaps of the upper class. (I 52; III 474)

GUARD   The Dark Guard (q.v.). (S 136, 137; B 163)

GUARDED PLAIN   Talath Dirnen (q.v.). (S 172; B 208)

GUARDED REALM   Valinor (q.v.). (S 74, 87; B 82, 98)

GUARD OF FARAMIR   The White Company (q.v.). (III 305)

GUARD OF THE TOWER OF GONDOR   The Guards of the Citadel (q.v.). (III 45)

GUARDS OF THE CITADEL   An elite military unit of Gondor which guarded the Citadel of Minas Tirith and the White Tree and participated in official functions. There were at least three companies of the Guards, each of which had its own storehouse. Beregond belonged to the Third Company; Pippin's Company is not named.

The Guards wore Númenórean sea-helms (see: the Silver Crown) made of mithril and black surcoats bearing the livery of Elendil. The Guards were the only ones in Gondor to bear this livery in the time of the Stewards.

The traditional Captain-general of the Guards was the heir of the Steward, and in the time of the Kings the Captain was probably the heir to the throne.

Also called the Guard of the Tower of Gondor. (III 26, 37-39, 45, 96-97, 123, 162)

GUESTS   Men (q.v.), so called because of their mortality and because their ultimate fate lies outside Arda. (S 42; B 38)

GUILIN (S.) (FA)   Noble Elf of Nargothrond, father of Gelmir and Gwindor. (S 188; B 230)

GÛL (B.S.: 'wraith')   Any of the major invisible servants of Sauron, given life and dominated entirely by his will. Obviously the Nazgûl were gûl (the word seems to be both singular and plural), and perhaps also the werewolves of Tol-in-Gaurhoth. (L 172)

GULF OF LHÛN   Great gulf of Belegaer cutting through the Ered Luin to the mouth of the River Lhûn, created in the breaking of Beleriand at the end of the First Age. It's harbors were the Harlond, the Forlond, and the Grey Havens.
Also called the Gulf of Lune. (I 16; III 396; S 285, 286; B 354)

GULF OF LUNE   The Gulf of Lhûn (q.v.). (III 396)

GUNDABAD   Mountain in the northern Misty Mountains, at the time of the War of the Dwarves and Orcs the site of the northernmost Orc-hold in the Mountains captured by the Dwarves. (I 17; III 442)

GUNDABALD BOLGER (fl. TA 29th Cent.)   Hobbit of the Shire. He married Salvia Brandybuck. (III 476)

GUNDOR (S.) (d. FA 455)   Adan of the Third House, younger son of Hador. He was slain by Orc-arrows while fighting beside his father at Eithel Sirion during Dagor Bragollach. (S 148, 152, 308; B 177, 183, 382)

GURTHANG (S.: 'death-iron')   Name given to the reforged Anglachel (q.v.) by Túrin. (S 210; B 258)

GUTHLÁF (tr. Roh.: 'survivor of the battle')   Man of Rohan, banner-bearer of Théoden in the Battle of the Pelennor Fields. He was slain in the battle. (III 137, 145)

GÚTHWINË (tr. Roh.: 'battle-friend')   The sword of Éomer. (II 176)

GWAERON (S.: 'wind—') Sindarin form of Súlimë, used only by the Dúnedain. (III 483)

GWAIHIR (S.: 'wind-lord') (fl. TA 2941-3019) Lord of the Eagles of the Misty Mountains. Gwaihir befriended Gandalf when the wizard healed him of a poisoned wound. In 2941 he and his eagles rescued Gandalf and Thorin and Company from Orcs. Gwaihir later brought his Eagles to the Battle of the Five Armies, in which they played a crucial role. In the time of the WR he aided Gandalf three times, first freeing him from Isengard, then rescuing him from the peak of Zirak-zigil after his fight with the Balrog, and finally rescuing Frodo and Sam from the slopes of Orodruin. Gwaihir and his people also served Gandalf and Radagast as messengers and spies.

Sometime after 2941 Gwaihir became the King of All Birds. (I 343; II 126, 135; III 278, 280-82; H 107-08, 112-13, 116, 270, 273)

GWAITH-I-MÍRDAIN (S.: 'people-of-the-jewel-smiths') The Noldor of Eregion, the greatest craftsmen of all times, save for Fëanor. Eregion was settled about SA 750 by Noldor from Lindon, led by Celebrimbor of the House of Finwë, because of its proximity to the mithril-mine in Khazad-dûm. For nearly a thousand years the Gwaith-i-Mírdain and Durin's Folk worked together in prosperity and friendship, the greatest that ever arose between Elves and Dwarves.

Yet the yearning of the Jewel-smiths for skill and beauty led to their downfall, for about 1200 Sauron, disguised as Annatar, approached them, and they accepted his instruction and gifts. About 1500 the Gwaith-i-Mírdain began to forge the Rings of Power under Sauron's direction, although Celebrimbor alone forged the Three Rings. After the Rings were completed about 1590, Sauron betrayed the Noldor and forged the One Ring. Celebrimbor discovered Sauron's plot and the Three Rings were hidden, but Sauron turned to open war. In 1697 Eregion was overrun and Celebrimbor and most of the Gwaith-i-Mírdain slain. Elrond led the survivors to Rivendell. Possibly these smiths forged Andúril for Aragorn in TA 3018.

Also called the Elven-smiths. (I 318; III 453-54; S 286-88; B 354-56)

GWATHLO (S.: 'shadow—') Name given by some people to the large river formed by the junction of the Mitheithel and Glanduin. Gwathlo flowed southwest from Tharbad and marked the boundary between Minhiriath and Enedwaith.

Called in Westron the Greyflood. Also spelled Gwathló. (I 268; S 359; B 450)

GWINDOR (S.) (d. FA 496) Elf, a lord of Nargothrond, son of Guilin and brother of Gelmir. Gwindor led a small company of Elves of Nargothrond to the Nirnaeth Arnoediad, wishing to avenge the loss of his brother; they followed Fingon.

Stationed at Barad Eithel, Gwindor began the battle by madly charging the host of Morgoth when he saw Gelmir mutilated and slain. Gwindor won through to the Stairs of Angband, but there he was trapped and captured; all his followers were slain.

After fourteen years in Morgoth's mines Gwindor escaped and was found in Taur-nu-Fuin by Beleg. The two Elves freed Túrin from the Orcs who had captured him, and Gwindor guarded Túrin in his despair at his slaying of Beleg. Gwindor gained admittance into Nargothrond for Túrin, but there his beloved Finduilas fell in love with the Adan. Gwindor accepted this nobly, but seeing the doom of Nargothrond approach, he counselled against Túrin's policy of open resistance to Morgoth. However, the strength and beauty of his body had been ruined in the mines, and his advice was ignored. Gwindor was slain in the disastrous Battle of Tumhalad. (S 188, 190, 191-92, 204-11, 212-13; B 230, 232, 233-34, 350-59)

GWIRITH (S.) Sindarin form of Víressë, used only by the Dúnedain. (III 483)

HADHODROND (S.: 'Khazâd-delving') The first Elvish name for Khazad-dûm (q.v.). (S 91, 359; B 104, 451)

HADOR (tr. Ad.: 'bright'?) (FA 389-455) Adan of the Third House, Elf-friend and hero, son of Hathol and father of Galdor and Gundor. In his youth Hador served Fingolfin, who loved him and gave him the lordship of Dor-lómin, where Hador gathered the Third House and became the greatest chieftain of the Edain. During Dagor Bragollach Hador commanded the rearguard of Fingolfin and was slain in the defense of Eithel Sirion.

Hador's nobility was such that he was considered the peer of Elven-lords, and in the years of his rule in Dor-lómin the Edain reached their greatest glory in Beleriand. He was known as Hador Lórindol, Goldenhead, and the Golden-haired. (I 355; II 364; S 147, 148, 152, 308; B 177, 178, 183, 382)

HADOR (d. TA 2395) Dúnadan, seventh Ruling Steward of Gondor (2278-2395). In 2360 he made the last millennial adjustment in the Stewards' Reckoning. (III 395, 481)

HAERAST (S.: 'far shore') The shores of Aman, in opposition to Nevrast, the Hither Shore of Middle-earth. (S 343; B 428)

HALADIN The Second House of the Edain. Entering into Beleriand about a year after Finrod encountered the First House, the Haladin settled first in Thargelion, where they were ignored by the Noldor of Caranthir. In Thargelion the Haladin lived in isolated homesteads until they were attacked by Orcs. The survivors, led by Haldad, retreated to the angle of land between Ascar and Gelion, where they built a stockade and were besieged, until at last they were rescued by Caranthir.

Many of the survivors, led by Haleth, moved first to Estolad and then, taking the dangerous road that skirted Nan Dungortheb, to Talath Dirnen and Brethil. Haleth was granted Brethil by Thingol of Doriath on condition that she defend the Crossings of Teiglin; for many years the woodsmen of Brethil guarded the northern flank of Nargothrond, their numbers swelled by refugees of their own people and (after the loss of Dorthonion) of the First House.

After the fall of Tol Sirion (FA 457) there were frequent Orc-raids at the Crossings and in the Forest of Brethil, but the Haladin kept their strength until the Nirnaeth Arnoediad, when they suffered heavy losses on Anfauglith while covering the retreat of Fingon. In 496, the Haladin were defeated in Brethil, thus opening the way for the sack of Nargothrond. After that disaster the Haladin remained in their woods, ambushing Orcs at the Crossings when they could. For a few years they rallied under the leadership of Túrin, who used the *noms de guerre* Wildman of the Woods and Turambar, but in general they dwindled and passed out of history.

The Haladin differed from the other Edain in a number of ways. Their language was apparently unrelated, and they were smaller and less interested in learning and speech, loving instead solitude and the forest. They bore axes in battle.

Also called the People of Haleth. (S 142-43, 145-47, 148, 155, 157, 158, 189, 190, 192, 195, 212, 216 ff., 308; B 171, 174-76, 178, 187, 190, 231, 232, 234, 238, 261, 266 ff., 382)

HALBARAD (S.: 'tall-tower'?) (d. TA 3019) Dúnadan, Ranger of the North. Halbarad led the company of Rangers that met Aragorn in Rohan during the WR, and accompanied his Chieftain through the Paths of the Dead. He was Aragorn's standard-bearer during the Battle of the Pelennor Fields, in which he was slain. (III 55, 152)

HALDAD (d. FA 4th Cent.) Adan of the Haladin, father of Haleth and Haldar. When the Haladin were attacked by Orcs in Thargelion, Haldad gathered the survivors, organized a defense, and built the stockade at the angle of Ascar and Gelion. He was slain in a sortie during the siege of the stockade. (S 145-46; B 174-75)

HALDAN (FA 4th Cent.)   Adan of the Haladin, son of Haldar and lord of the Haladin after the death of his aunt Haleth. He probably dwelt in Brethil. (S 146; B 175)

HALDAR (d. FA 4th Cent.)   Adan of the Haladin, son of Haldad and father of Haldan. He was slain by Orcs during the siege of the Haladin stockade in Thargelion when he rushed out to defend his father's body. (S 146; B 175)

HALDIR (d. FA 473)   Adan, Lord of the Haladin (473), son of Halmir, husband of Glóredhel, father of Handir and foster father of Húrin and Huor. Haldir led the Haladin force of the Union of Maedhros, and was slain with most of his men guarding the retreat of Fingon across Anfauglith during the Nirnaeth Arnoediad. (S 158, 189, 190, 192, 308; B 190, 231, 232, 234, 382)

HALDIR (fl. WR)   Elf of Lórien, one of the three brothers who intercepted the Company of the Ring and escorted its members to Caras Galadon.
Haldir had traveled outside Lórien and knew Westron. (I 445-60, 464; II 273)

HALETH (FA 4th Cent.)   Adan, first chief of the Haladin. She led her people westward from Thargelion, taking the dangerous road near Nan Dungortheb. Haleth settled in Brethil, which she held in return for guarding the Crossings of Teiglin. She was buried in Tûr Haretha. (S 146-47, 308; B 175-76, 382)

HALETH (d. TA 2758)   Man of Rohan, eldest son of King Helm. He was slain while defending the doors of Meduseld against Wulf. (III 432)

HALFAST OF OVERHILL (b. TA 2972) Hobbit of the Shire, son of Halfred of Overhill. He lived in Overhill and worked there for a Mr. Boffin. Halfast enjoyed hunting in the Northfarthing, and once saw an Ent there. (I 73; III 477)

HALF-ELVEN The Peredhil (q.v.). (S 246; B 304)

HALFLINGS The name given to Hobbits (q.v.) by Men. (III 510)

HALF-ORCS Servants of Saruman, used by him as spies and soldiers. They were seemingly the product of a cross between Men and Orcs. Although tall as Men, they were sallow-faced and squint-eyed. The Chief's Men were half-orcs.
  The half-orcs (the term is not used in *LotR*) were definitely not Uruk-hai. (II 96, 218; III 350, 364)

HALFRED GAMGEE (b. TA 2969) Hobbit of the Shire, second son of Hamfast Gamgee. He moved to the Northfarthing. (III 477)

HALFRED GREENHAND (b. TA 2851) Hobbit of the Shire, eldest son of Holman the greenhanded and the first Greenhand. He lived in Hobbiton, where he was a gardener. (III 477)

HALFRED OF OVERHILL (b. TA 2932) Hobbit of the Shire, youngest son of Hobson Gamgee and brother of Hamfast Gamgee. He lived in Overhill. (III 477)

HALIFIRIEN The seventh and last of the northern beacon-tower hills of Gondor, located in the Firien Wood on the border of Rohan. (III 20)

HALIMATH The ninth month of the Shire Reckoning (q.v.), corresponding roughly to our September.
  Called Harvestmath in Bree. (III 478)

HALLA (Q.: 'tall') Tehta originally used in Quenya for *h*, written Ⅰ , also used to make a following consonant voiceless. (III 500)

HALLAS (S.: 'tall-leaf'?) (d. TA 2605) Dúnadan, thirteenth Ruling Steward of Gondor (2567-2605). (III 395)

HALL OF FIRE Great hall in the house of Elrond. Although the Hall was used only on high days, a fire was kept lit here at all times. (I 303; II 430)

HALL OF THE KINGS The Tower Hall (q.v.). (III 304)

HALLOW OF ERU The only temple in Númenor before the coming of Sauron, an unroofed shrine located atop Meneltarma. As the Shadow fell on Númenor, worship at the Hallow was neglected and was finally forbidden by Ar-Pharazôn, but no one dared to defile it. It was said that the Hallow rose again above the waves after the sinking of Númenor. (S 261, 266, 272, 281; B 322, 329, 336, 348)

HALLOWS The area behind Minas Tirith where the Kings and Stewards of Gondor, and other great men of the realm, were buried. The Hallows were reached by a path from the sixth level of the city which went through Fen Hollen.
    Also called the Tombs.
    See: the House of the Kings, the House of the Stewards. (III 121-22, 153-60, 305, 313)

HALLS OF AWAITING The Houses of the Dead (q.v.). (S 67; B 72)

HALLS OF EREBOR The halls of the Kingdom under the Mountain (q.v.). (III 440)

HALMIR (d. FA 473?) Adan of the Haladin, Lord of

Brethil, father of Haldir and Hareth. With Beleg he led the force that defeated the Orc-legion ravaging West Beleriand after the fall of Tol Sirion. Halmir joined the Union of Maedhros but died before the war came. (S 157, 189, 308; B 190, 231, 382)

HÁMA (d. TA 2759)   Man of Rohan, younger son of King Helm. He was lost in the snow during the Long Winter while on a foraying mission from the Hornburg. (III 432)

HÁMA (d. TA 3019)   Man of Rohan, doorward of King Théoden and captain of the King's guard. He was slain defending the Gate in the Battle of the Hornburg. (II 146-47, 191, 237)

HAMFAST GAMGEE (TA 2926-FO 8)   Hobbit of the Shire, son of Hobson Gamgee. He married Bell Goodchild; they had six children, including Samwise Gamgee. While young, Hamfast moved to Hobbiton and worked with his cousin Holman Greenhand as a gardener. About 2960 he became the gardener at Bag End.

Hamfast was noted for his loquacity and his knowledge of plants, especially potatoes.

Hamfast was known as the Gaffer and Old Gamgee at the time of the WR. Hamfast, or Ham for short, is the translated Hobbitish equivalent of the genuine Hobbitish forename Ranugad (shortened to Ran), which meant 'stay-at-home.' (I 44, 105; III 359, 362-63, 477, 517)

HAMFAST GAMGEE (b. FO 12)   Hobbit of the Shire, fourth son and seventh child of Sam Gamgee. (III 477)

HAMFAST OF GAMWICH (b. TA 2760)   Hobbit of the Shire, founder of the family of Gamwich, later Gamgee. (III 477)

HAMSON GAMGEE (b. TA 2965)   Hobbit of the Shire, eldest son of Hamfast Gamgee. He moved to Tighfield and worked with his uncle Andwise Roper as a roper. (III 477)

HANDIR (d. FA 496) Adan of the Haladin, Lord of Brethil (473-96), son of Haldir and father of Brandir. Handir fell in battle with Orcs in Brethil. (S 195, 212, 308; B 238, 260, 382)

HANNA BRANDYBUCK (fl. TA 2800) Hobbit of the Shire, wife of Madoc Brandybuck. She was born a Goldworthy. (III 476)

HARAD (S.: 'south') The lands south of the River Harnen. Except that Oliphaunts lived there, nothing much is said of the land, except for Umbar. Harad was most probably hot, and perhaps had deserts.
Harad was divided into Near Harad and Far Harad. Politically, it was divided into the many kingdoms of the Haradrim. Called by the Hobbits of the Shire the Sunlands. Also called Sutherland and Haradwaith. (I 17, 325, 518; II 322, 338-39; III 456)

HARADRIM (S.: 'south-people') The primitive and savage Men of Harad. In the Second Age some of the Haradrim paid tribute to Númenor, but in the Third they were influenced by Sauron and were a constant threat to Gondor's southern borders. Some Haradrim were ruled by Black Númenóreans. The most serious attacks of the Haradrim on Gondor took place in TA 1014-50, over Umbar; in 1944, when the Haradrim were allied with the Wainriders; in 2885, when they were defeated in the Battle of the Crossings of Poros; and during the WR, when Haradrim fought in the Battle of the Pelennor Fields and elsewhere. In addition, from the 19th Century TA onward, the Corsairs of Umbar were Haradrim.
The Haradrim were tall and dark-skinned, with black hair and eyes. They loved bright clothing and ornaments, and some tribes of Haradrim painted their bodies. In battle they used all weapons, but were noted for their use of Oliphaunts.

Called in Westron Southerns and Southrons. Also called the Swarthy Men (by Hobbits) and the Swertings. (I 322; II 321, 322, 340-41; III 139-40, 148, 403-04, 409, 416; S 293; B 363)

HARAD ROAD   Road running from Ithilien into Harad, passing over fords on the Poros and Harnen. At the time of the WR the southern part of the Road had fallen into disuse and had disappeared.

The Harad Road was probably built by Gondor in the early Third Age, when her power extended into Harad. (I 17)

HARADWAITH (S.: 'south-folk')   The Haradrim and the land where they lived. (I 17; III 403)

HARANYË (Q.)   The last year of a century in the King's Reckoning, and probably in the Stewards' and New Reckonings as well. (III 481)

HARDBOTTLE   Village in the Northfarthing, the home of the Bracegirdles. The dwellings of Hardbottle were excavated in or built of stone. (III 372; L 186)

HARDBOTTLE   Village in the Shire, home of a family member. (III 372)

HARDING (d. TA 3019)   Man of Rohan, killed in the Battle of the Pelennor Fields. (III 152)

HARDING OF THE HILL (b. FO 81)   Hobbit of the Shire, son of Holfast Gardner. He probably lived in Bag End.

Harding's full name may have been Harding Gardner of the Hill. (III 477)

HARETH (Q.: 'lady') (FA 5th Cent.)   Adan of the Haladin, daughter of Halmir. About 440 she married Galdor, later Lord of the First House, and bore him two sons, Húrin and Huor. (S 158; B 190)

HARFOOTS   The most common of the three branches of Hobbits. The Harfoots were the first Hobbits to cross the Misty Mountains into Eriador, doing so about TA 1050.

The Harfoots were the most typical Hobbits. They were browner than the Stoors and Fallohides, and also smaller and shorter. They liked highlands and hillsides best, and kept the habit of living underground longer than the other strains. The Harfoots were friendlier with Dwarves than other Hobbits. (I 22; III 456; L 167-68)

HARLINDON (S.: 'south Lindon')   That portion of Lindon south of the Gulf of Lhûn. Celeborn and Galadriel lived in Harlindon at the beginning of the Second Age. See: Lindon. (I 16; III 452)

HARLOND (S.: 'south-haven')   Harbor on the southern side of the Gulf of Lhûn. (I 16; III 411)

HARLOND   Harbor and quays on the west side of Anduin, three or four miles south of Minas Tirith, the port of the city. The Harlond was within the Rammas Echor. (III 23, 150)

HARMA (Q.: 'treasure')   Original name for the tengwa 𐂏 (number 11), having the value *ch*. Later, this *ch* became *h* at the beginning of words, and the name was changed to aha. (III 500)

HARNEN (S.: 'south-water')   River flowing from the southern Ephel Dúath westward to the Bay of Belfalas, in the early Third Age the boundary between Gondor and the kingdoms of Harad. (I 17; III 403)

HARONDOR (S.: 'south Gondor')   The land between the Poros and the Harnen, part of Gondor early in the Third Age and thereafter a land debated between Gondor and the Haradrim.

Called in Westron South Gondor. (I 17; III 407)

HARROWDALE   Valley in Rohan above Edoras. During the WR, the Muster of Rohan was held here. (III 66, 76 ff.)

HARRY GOATLEAF (fl. WR)   Man of Bree, keeper of the western gate of Bree. He joined Bill Ferny and his ruffians as a bandit outside Bree during the WR. (I 207-08, 236; III 332, 335)

HARVESTMATH   Name given Halimath (q.v.) in Bree. (III 483)

HASUFEL (tr. Roh.: 'dark skin'?) (fl. WR)   Large grey horse of Rohan, lent by Éomer to Aragorn. (II 51)

HATHALDIR (S.) (d. FA 460)   Adan of the First House, one of the last twelve survivors of Barahir's outlaw band in Dorthonion. (S 155, 162-63; B 187, 196)

HATHOL (fl. FA 400)   Adan, Lord of the Third House, son of Magor and father of Hador. (S 147; B 177)

HAUDH-EN-ARWEN (S.: 'mound of the royal maiden') Tûr Haretha (q.v.). (S 147; B 176)

HAUDH-EN-ELLETH (S.: 'mound of the Elfmaid') Burial mound of Finduilas, located in Brethil near the Crossings of Teiglin. The mound was kept free of Orcs by Túrin while he lived, and here he met (but did not recognize) his sister Nienor for the first time. (S 216-17, 219, 223; B 267, 270, 275)

HAUDH-EN-NDENGIN (S.: 'mound of the slain')   The great mound in the middle of Anfauglith in which were buried the Elves and Men who fell on the plain during the Nirnaeth Arnoediad. Grass grew long and green on the mound, even though the rest of Anfauglith was a barren waste.
    Also called Haudh-en-Nirnaeth. (S 197, 198, 357; B 241, 242, 448)

HAUDH-EN-NIRNAETH (S.: 'mound of tears') Haudh-en-Ndengin (q.v.). S 197; B 241)

HAUDH IN GWANÛR (S.: 'mound of the—') Mound in which Princess Folcred and Fastred of Rohan were buried, located near the Crossings of Poros, where they fell in battle with the Haradrim. (III 416)

HAUNTED MOUNTAIN The Dwimorberg (q.v.). (III 81)

HAUNTED PASS Cirith Gorgor (q.v.). (II 308)

HAVEN Alqualondë (q.v.). (S 87; B 97)

HAVEN OF THE ELDAR Avallónë (q.v.). (III 390)

HAVEN OF THE SWANS Alqualondë (q.v.). (S 87; B 97)

HAVENS OF MITHLOND The Grey Havens (q.v.). (S 8; B xiii)

HAVENS OF SIRION The port and refuge at the Mouths of Sirion, maintained by the mariners of Círdan to succor Elves and Men fleeing from the armies of Morgoth. First mentioned after the fall of the Falas, the Havens in time became a substantial community, seemingly tolerated by Morgoth. In the 6th Century Eärendil was lord of the Havens, and his people were mostly Elves of Gondolin and Doriath. Near the end of the First Age the Havens were attacked and destroyed by the sons of Fëanor, who sought the Silmaril of Elwig. (S 196, 237-38, 244, 246-47; B 239, 293-94, 302, 305)

HAVENS OF THE FALAS Brithombar and Eglarest (qq.v.), the ports of the Falathrim.
Frequently called the Havens. (S 107, 120, 196; B 124, 142, 239)

HAY   The High Hay (q.v.). (TB 9)

HAY GATE   The Buckland Gate (q.v.). (III 342)

HAYSEND, HAYS-END   Village in Buckland at the mouth of the Withywindle, so called because it was located at the southern end of the High Hay. (I 40, 142; TB 18, 19)

HAYWARD   Family of Hobbits of the Eastfarthing. Probably an early member of the family was a hayward. (III 342)

HEADSTRONG   Family of Hobbits of the Shire, perhaps well-to-do. (III 476)

HEATHERTOES   Family of Men of Bree. (I 212)

HEAVY-HANDED   Epithet applied to Men (q.v.) by the Eldar. (S 103)

HEDGE   The High Hay (q.v.). (I 40, 155-57)

HEIR OF EÄRENDIL   Title claimed by Ar-Pharazôn as head of the House of Elros, ignoring of course the line of Elrond. (S 270; B 334)

HEIR OF ISILDUR   Aragorn (q.v.). (S 303; B 377)

HEIRS OF ANÁRION   The Kings of Gondor (q.v.). (III 394)

HEIRS OF ISILDUR   The eldest sons of the Line of Isildur, unbroken throughout the Third Age. Isildur's son, Valandil, was King of Arnor, and his heirs were Kings of Arnor (to TA 861) or of Arthedain (861-1974), or Chieftains of the Dúnedain of the North (1974-3019). After the WR the heirs of Isildur, the Telcontari (q.v.), were the Kings of the Reunited Kingdom.
The Heirs of Isildur survived after the fall of Arthedain

only because of the aid of Elrond, but most of them lived their full lifespan, which waned less rapidly than that of the Kings of Gondor.

The heirlooms of Isildur's heirs were the ring of Barahir, the shards of Narsil, the Elendilmir, and the sceptre of Annúminas.

Also called the Northern Line. (III 394, 401, 402, 422; S 298; B 369)

HELCAR (Q.: 'icy-cold') Inland sea in the far east of Middle-earth in the First Age, occupying the site of the pillar of Illuin. Cuiviénen was a bay of Helcar.

Also called the Sea of Helcar and the Inland Sea of Helcar. (S 49, 53, 360; B 49, 54, 452)

HELCARAXË (Q.: 'ice-fangs') (Q.) Strait in the north of Arda in the First Age between Araman and Middle-earth. Here the waters of Belegaer and Ekkaia came together with great turbulence and mist. Helcaraxë was filled with the Grinding Ice, ice floes by which the strait could be crossed on foot, although with great danger. The Ice may have extended onto the land as well. (I 308; S 51, 57, 73, 80, 89-90, 109, 357, 360; B 51-52, 59, 80, 88, 101, 127, 447, 452)

HELEVORN (S.: 'glass-black') Deep, dark lake located in Thargelion south of Mount Rerir. Caranthir dwelt near the lake. (S 112, 124, 153, 335, 360; B 132, 148, 184, 417, 452)

HELLUIN (S.: 'ice-blue') Blue star, identified with Sirius. (S 48, 64, 335; B 48, 69, 417)

HELM Name given to Túrin (q.v.) as one of the Two Captains in Talath Dirnen, when he wore the Dragon-helm to battle. (S 205; B 252)

HELM (TA 2691-2759) Man, ninth King of Rohan (2741-59) and last of the First Line. His reign was remembered chiefly for its end, for in 2758 Rohan was in-

vaded by a horde of Dunlendings led by Wulf, son of
Helm's enemy Freca (qq.v.). Helm, after losing a battle
at the Crossings of Isen, retreated to the Hornburg, which
he held during the Long Winter. Toward the end of the
winter, Helm froze to death during a night sortie.

Helm was known as Hammerhand because of his great
strength; he killed Freca with one blow of his fist. (III
431-33, 435)

HELMINGAS Name given by the Rohirrim to the men
of Westfold, or perhaps of Rohan. (II 179)

HELM OF HADOR The Dragon-helm of Dor-lómin
(q.v.). (S 205; B 205)

HELM'S DEEP Gorge winding into the Ered Nimrais
below the Thrihyrne. Helm's Deep was the defensive center of the Westfold of Rohan; it and Dunharrow were
the major fortresses and refuges of the realm. Helm's
Deep was defended by Helm in TA 2758-59, and this
defense gave it and everything in the area its name. During
the WR it was defended by Théoden.

The Deeping Stream flowed out of Helm's Deep, and
the Aglarond was found in it. The Deeping Wall was built
across the entrance to the Deep.

"Helm's Deep" was the most common name used to
refer to the entire system of fortifications in the area, including the actual fortress, the Hornburg. (II 169 ff.; III
432; L 185)

HELM'S DIKE Trench and rampart built along the side
of the Deeping Coomb nearest the Hornburg. (II 169 ff.,
esp. 171)

HELM'S GATE The entrance to Helm's Deep, across
which the Deeping Wall was built. (II 169 ff.)

HENDING (b. TA 2859) Hobbit of the Shire, third son
and fourth child of Holman the greenhanded. (III 477)

HENNETH ANNÛN (S.: 'sunset window,' 'west window') Hidden refuge of the Rangers of Ithilien, built behind a waterfall in North Ithilien by Túrin of Gondor in TA 2901. It was manned continuously until Faramir's retreat to Minas Tirith before the Siege of Gondor during the WR.

Called in Westron the Window of the Sunset and the Window on the West. (II 357 ff.; III 103, 416)

HENSDAY Hevenesdei (q.v.). (III 484)

HERBLORE OF THE SHIRE A book written by Merry Brandybuck, describing among other things the history of pipe-weed. (I 28-29)

HEREFARA (d. TA 3019) Man of Rohan, slain in the Battle of the Pelennor Fields. (III 152)

HERION (d. TA 2148) Dúnadan, third Ruling Steward of Gondor (2116-48). (III 395)

HERUBRAND (d. TA 3019) Man of Rohan, killed in the Battle of the Pelennor Fields. (III 152)

HERUGRIM The sword of Théoden. (II 157)

HERUMOR (Q.: 'lord-black') (fl. SA 3300) Black Númenórean. He became a great lord among the Haradrim. (S 293; B 363)

HERUNÚMEN (Q.: 'lord-west') The Eldarin name of Ar-Adûnakhor (q.v.), inscribed in the Scroll of Kings. (S 267; B 330)

HEVENESDEI Early form of the name of the fifth day of the week in the Shire Reckoning, a translation of the Quenya Menelya. At the time of the WR, the form of the name was Hevensday or Hensday.

Called in *LotR* Wednesday. (III 484)

HEVENSDAY   See: Hevenesdei. (III 484)

HIDDEN KINGDOM   Doriath (q.v.). (S 115; B 135)

HIDDEN KINGDOM   Gondolin (q.v.). (S 131; B 156)

HIDDEN LAND   Lórien (q.v.). (II 349)

HIDDEN WAY   See: The Way of Escape. (S 137; B 164)

HIDING OF VALINOR   The Nurtalë Valinóreva (q.v.). (S 102; B 118)

HIGH CITY   The Citadel (q.v.) of Minas Tirith. (III 310; RHM III 430)

HIGH COURT   A court in the seventh level of Minas Tirith, not the Court of the Fountain. (III 25)

HIGHDAY   See: Highdei. (III 484)

HIGHDEI   Early form of the name of the seventh and chief day of the week in the Shire Reckoning, equivalent to the Eldarin and Westron Valanya. At the time of the WR, the form of the name was Highday.
    Called in *LotR* Friday. (III 484, 485)

HIGH ELDARIN   Quenya (q.v.). (S 262)

HIGH-ELVEN   Quenya (q.v.). S 267; B 329)

HIGH ELVES   The Eldar (q.v.). (III 452, 506)

HIGH FAROTH   Taur-en-Faroth (q.v.). (S 114, 122; B 134, 146)

HIGH HAY   A twenty-mile-long hedge separating Buckland from the Old Forest. The High Hay was built by the

Brandybucks as a defense against the Forest; it extended from the Great East Road in the north to the Withywindle in the south.

Also called the Hay and the Hedge. (I 40, 142, 155-56)

HIGH KING OF ARNOR Elendil, so called because he was King over both the Dúnedain realms of Arnor and Gondor, ruling Arnor directly and Gondor through his sons. After his death, however, the two kingdoms were separated and there were no further High Kings, although it is possible that some Kings of the Northern Line considered themselves High Kings. In the Fourth Age, Elessar and the later rulers of the Telcontar family may have been High Kings, although they ruled both kingdoms directly. (III 394)

HIGH KING OF THE NOLDOR Title of the head of the House of Finwë in Middle-earth in his role of overlord of the Noldorin realms. The first overlord might have been Fëanor, but his early death prevented him from claiming that authority. Fingolfin was recognized as High King from FA 1 until his death in 455, and his son Fingon after him. At Fingon's death in 473 the title passed to his brother Turgon of Gondolin, who of course did not exercise any authority outside his Hidden Kingdom. When Turgon died in 511 the Kingship passed to Fingon's son, Gil-galad, who remained High King until his death in SA 3441, at which time no heirs of the Houses of Fëanor or Fingolfin remained in Middle-earth. Had she desired it, Galadriel of the House of Finarfin might have been able to claim the Kingship.

Also called King of the Noldor. (S 111, 113, 160, 240, 244; B 130, 132, 193, 297, 302)

HIGH NAZGÛL The Lord of the Nazgûl (q.v.), as called by the Orcs of Minas Morgul. (II 442)

HIGH PASS Pass over the Misty Mountains east of Rivendell. Toward the end of the Third Age the High Pass became one of the most important passes over the

Mountains because it was believed safe from Orcs. However, about 2940 the Orcs opened an entrance to their tunnels on the Pass, and Thorin and Company were captured here in 2941. After that time, though, the Pass was kept open by the Beornings; it was an important trade route at the time of the WR. (I 301; H 64-67, 122)

HIGH PASS The Cirith Ungol (q.v.). (II 438)

HIGH SEA Belegaer (q.v.). (III 384)

HIGH SPEECH OF THE WEST Quenya (q.v.). (S 129; B 155)

HILD (fl. TA 2726) Woman of Rohan, daughter of Gram and mother of Fréaláf. (III 433)

HILDA BRANDYBUCK (fl. TA 3000) Hobbit of the Shire, wife of Seredic Brandybuck. She was born a Bracegirdle. Hilda was a guest at the Farewell Party. (III 476)

HILDIBRAND TOOK (TA 2849-2934) Hobbit of the Shire, eighth son of Gerontius Took. (III 475)

HILDIFONS TOOK (b. TA 2844) Hobbit of the Shire, sixth son of Gerontius Took. He went on a journey and never returned. (III 475)

HILDIGARD TOOK (b. TA 2833 to 2837) Hobbit of the Shire, second son of Gerontius Took. He died young. (III 475)

HILDIGRIM TOOK (TA 2840-2941) Hobbit of the Shire, fourth son of Gerontius Took. He married Rosa Baggins; they had one son, Adalgrim. (III 474, 475)

HILDOR (Q.: 'followers, aftercomers') Name given to Men (q.v.) by the Eldar.
The word is related to Quenya *hildinyar* 'heirs.' (S 99, 103; B 114, 119)

HILDÓRIEN (Q.: 'land of the Hildor') Area in eastern Middle-earth, the place where Men awoke. (S 103; B 120)

HILL One of the westernmost hills of the Barrow-downs. Tom Bombadil's house was built on its western side. (I 168, 171; TB 11)

HILL, THE Hobbiton Hill (q.v.). (III 486; H 15)

HILL-MEN An evil people, living perhaps in the Etten-moors or the western Misty Mountains near the Angle, allied with Angmar. The Hill-men seized control of Rhudaur about TA 1350 and fought with Angmar against Arthedain and Cardolan until the fall of Angmar in 1975, when they were probably annihilated or scattered. (III 397)

HILL OF ERECH See: Erech. (III 73)

HILL OF GUARD The easternmost spur of Mindolluin, upon which Minas Tirith was built. The massive Hill was joined to the main part of the mountain by a narrow ridge. (III 25)

HILL OF HEARING Amon Lhaw (q.v.). (I 510)

HILL OF HIMRING Himring (q.v.). (S 112; B 131)

HILL OF ILMARIN Taniquetil (q.v.). (I 309)

HILL OF SIGHT Amon Hen (q.v.). (I 510)

HILL OF SPIES Amon Ethir (q.v.). (S 217; B 267)

HILL OF THE EYE Amon Hen (q.v.). (I 517)

HILLS OF EVENDIM Hills north and south of Lake Evendim. Probably called in Sindarin Emyn Nenuial. (I 16; III 411)

HILLS OF SCARY Hills in the Shire north of Scary. (I 40; III 372)

HIMLAD (S.: 'cool-plain') Plain in East Beleriand south of Himlad, bounded by the Rivers Celon and Aros. During the Siege of Angband, Curufin and Celegorm guarded Himlad and the Pass of Aglon at its northern end, but the pass and plain were overrun during Dagor Bragollach. (S 123-24, 132, 335, 359; B 147, 158, 417, 451)

HIMRING (S.: 'cool-cold'?) The greatest of the hills located between Aglon and Maglor's Gap on the northern border of East Beleriand. Fortified by Maedhros, Himring anchored the defense of East Beleriand. When the passes were overrun by Morgoth's forces during Dagor Bragollach, the sons of Fëanor regrouped at Himring and apparently held the hill until the disaster of the Nirnaeth Arnoediad, when their power was broken.

Himring was treeless, broad, and not especially high; its summit was flat. Usually called the Hill of Himring. Evercold is either a descriptive epithet or a translation. (S 112, 123, 152, 153; B 131, 147-48, 183, 184)

HÍNI ILÚVATARO (Q.: 'children of Ilúvatar') The Children of Ilúvatar (q.v.). (S 322; B 400)

HIRGON (S.: 'lord-stone') (d. TA 3019) Man of Gondor, messenger of Denethor II. During the WR he brought the Red Arrow to Théoden, but was slain by Orcs while returning to Minas Tirith. (III 86, 134)

HÍRILORN (S.: 'lady-tree') (FA) The greatest tree of Neldoreth, a three-trunked beech standing near Menegroth. A house was built in its heights, and here Lúthien was kept by Thingol to prevent her from following Beren.

Perhaps also called Neldor. (S 172, 335, 362; B 208, 417, 454)

HIRLUIN (S.: 'lord-blue') (d. TA 3019) Man of Gondor, Lord of Pinnath Gelin. He was slain in the Battle of the Pelennor Fields.

He was known as Hirluin the Fair. (III 50, 148, 152)

HÍSILÓMË (Q.: 'mist-shadow') Hithlum (q.v.). (S 118; B 140)

HISIME (Q.: 'mist—') Eleventh month of the Kings' and Stewards' Reckonings, and the eighth of the New Reckoning, corresponding roughly to our November.
The Sindarin form, used only by the Dúnedain, was Hithui. (III 483)

HITHAEGLIR (S.: 'mist-peak-line') The Misty Mountains (q.v.). (S 54, 335; B 55, 417)

HITHAIGLIN An error for Hithaeglir (q.v.). (I 16-17)

HITHER LANDS, HITHER SHORES Eldarin names for Middle-earth (q.v.). (I 311; S 55; B 57)

HITHLAIN (S.: 'mist-thread') Substance used by the Elves of Lórien in their ropes, a tough, light, soft-feeling grey substance. (I 481; II 273; RHM III 438)

HITHLUM (S.: 'mist-shadow') Area north of Beleriand, bounded on the west by the Ered Lómin and on the east and south by the Ered Wethrin. Its southern lands were divided into two parts—Dor-lómin in the west and Mithrim in the east—by the Mountains of Mithrim. A cold but fair plateau, Hithlum was shaped by the upheavals of the Battle of the Powers. At first inhabited only by a few Sindar, Hithlum was settled by Fingolfin and Fingon when the Noldor returned to Middle-earth, and later the House of Hador lived there as well. After Dagor Bragollach the population was swelled by Elves and Edain of the First House fleeing the wars, for Morgoth's forces never breached the Ered Wethrin, defended by great fortresses such as Barad Eithel, and Morgoth's two attempts to attack Hithlum from the west or north (c. 160 and 462) failed, perhaps because a large enough army could not be sent through the northern wastes.
But the armies of Hithlum did not return from the

Nirnaeth Arnoediad, and Morgoth granted the land to his Easterlings. The remaining Eldar and Edain were enslaved, killed, or absorbed, although a few (notably Tuor) became outlaws and did great damage to the Easterlings.

The Quenya form was Hísilómë; the name was given because at the first coming of the Noldor the land was covered by mists and vapors sent from Thangorodrim by Morgoth. Also called the Land of Mist. (S 51, 106, 109, 111, 116, 118-19, 152, 160, 190, 195, 227, 238, 359; B 52, 123, 128, 130, 137, 140-41, 183, 194, 232, 239, 280, 294, 451)

HITHUI (S.: 'misty') Hísimë (q.v.). (III 483)

HLOTHRAM (gen. Hobb.: 'cottager') A Hobbit forename.
See: Cotman. (III 520)

HLOTHRAN (gen. Hobb.: *hloth* 'two-room dwelling' + *ranu* 'collection of these on a hillside') Fairly common village-name in the Shire. (III 520)

HLOTHRAN A Shire surname, derived from the preceding.
See: Cotton. (III 520)

HOARD, THE Poem written by a Hobbit of the Shire in the Fourth Age, containing scraps of legends from the First Age. The Dwarf and the King in the poem may have been modeled on Mîm and Túrin, and the dragon on Glaurung. (TB 8, 53-56)

HOARWELL The Mitheithel (q.v.). (I 268)

HOBBITISH The language used in the Shire at the time of the WR, a provincial dialect of Westron with some vocabulary taken from the Mannish languages of Dunland and the Vales of Anduin. The Hobbits seem to have freely adopted whatever Mannish language was used around them and to have used these tongues carelessly and without great regard for form. These tendencies may be seen by comparing Rohirric *kûd-dûkan* with Hobbitish *kuduk,* both forms meaning 'hole-dweller, hobbit.'

Since Hobbitish was so closely related to Westron, Professor Tolkien has translated it in *LotR* into real or likely (but invented) English forms of various periods related to the Old English forms he uses for Westron. There are, however, a few "genuine Hobbitish" words recorded on III 519-20, and various Hobbit personal names have been left untranslated. (III 509-10)

HOBBITON   Village in the Shire, located in the West-farthing north of the Great East Road.
See: Bagshot Row, the Mill, the Old Grange, etc. (I 40, 43; III 365 ff.)

HOBBITON HILL   Hill in the Westfarthing, located between Hobbiton and Overhill.
Usually called the Hill. (I 40, 44; III 486; H 15)

HOBBITON ROAD   Road running from Bywater over the Water and thence to Hobbiton and Overhill. (I 40; III 349)

HOBBITRY-IN-ARMS   General mobilization of the Shire, held only in times of emergency and led by the Thain. As times of emergency did not occur frequently in the Shire, this mobilization was not common.
The Hobbitry-in-arms was probably the same as or similar to the Shire-muster. (I 30)

HOBBITS   One of the speaking races of Middle-earth, originally closely related to Men. Although created in the First Age, Hobbits were unobtrusive and lived in the Vales of Anduin largely unnoticed by other races until well into the Third Age. About TA 1050 the Hobbits, who by this time had become divided into three distinct groups, the Fallohides, the Harfoots, and the Stoors (qq.v.), fled westward because of the evil in Mirkwood. The wanderings of each strain are described in their individual entries. In 1600 the Shire was founded, and soon almost all Hobbits came to live there or in Bree, although in 2463 there was a colony of Stoors in the Gladden Fields, and at the time of the WR there were wandering Hobbits.

Except for the Great Plague of 1636 and the Long Winter of 2758, the Hobbits of Eriador lived for the most part peacefully and comfortably in the Shire and Bree, thanks to the protection of Gandalf and the Rangers. Their population grew, and twice the boundaries of the Shire were extended; in 2340 the Oldbucks settled Buckland, and in FO 32 the Westmarch was added to the Shire by gift of King Elessar. Except for Gandalf and the Rangers, before the WR nobody was concerned with Hobbits; after the War, however, because of the heroic deeds of Frodo and his companions, Hobbits were included in the songs and chronicles of other peoples, a courtesy which in general the Hobbits did not return.

A thorough description of Hobbits is given on I 19-36 and H 16, and there is no purpose in repeating those passages. It may be mentioned that the Stoors of the Gladden Fields in TA 2463 were matriarchal, and all Hobbits may at one time have been organized into matriarchal clans. It is also worth stressing that Hobbits, although comfort-loving, provincial, and distrustful of the outside world, were in times of danger courageous, skillful, and relatively undaunted by great terrors. Toward the end of the Third Age, the Hobbits alone in Middle-earth (with the Men of Bree) used surnames. They lived for about one hundred years; thirty-three was considered the age of adulthood.

Hobbits at the time of the WR spoke Hobbitish (q.v.), a provincial dialect of Westron. They wrote mostly with a mode of the cirth, although some of the better-educated Hobbits knew the Tengwar.

Hobbit is an anglicization of *kuduk,* the name they called themselves; it is related to the translated Rohirric *holbytla* (pl. *holbytlan*), a translation of the genuine Rohirric *kûd-dûkan,* 'hole-dweller.' They were called the Periain or Periannath in Sindarin and banakil (sing.) in genuine Westron; the translated Westron equivalent is 'Halfling.' They were also known as the Little Folk and the Little

People. (I 19-36, 79, 89, 146, 206; III 456-57, 509-10, 514, 515-16, 519-20; H 15-16, 77-78; TB 9; L 168)

HOB GAMMIDGE (b. TA 2846)   Hobbit of the Shire, son of Wiseman Gamwich. He married Rowan, eldest daughter of Holman the greenhanded; they had at least one child, Hobson Gamgee.

Hob was known as Hob Gammidge the Roper, and also as Old Gammidgy. (III 477)

HOBGOBLINS   Evil creatures of the Ered Mithrim. Mentioned only in a passage in which Gandalf is trying to frighten Bilbo, hobgoblins were probably Orcs, perhaps Uruk-hai. (H 138)

HOB HAYWARD (fl. WR)   Hobbit of the Eastfarthing. Before the WR he guarded the Hay Gate, but during Saruman's domination of the Shire he was a guard at the Brandywine Gate.

At the time of the WR he seems to have been fairly old. (III 342)

HOBSON GAMGEE (TA 2885-2984)   Hobbit of the Shire, son of Hob Gammidge. Like his father, he was a roper in Tighfield.

Hobson was also called Roper Gamgee. (II 276; III 477)

HOGG   Perhaps a family of Hobbits of the Shire. Old Farmer Hogg appears in the poem *Perry-the-Winkle* and may well have been a historical personage. (TB 42)

HOLBYTLA, HOLBYTLAN   See: Hobbits. (II 207; III 510)

HOLD OF DUNHARROW   See: Dunharrow. (III 80 ff.)

HOLDWINE   Name given Meriadoc Brandybuck (q.v.) in Rohan. (III 438)

HOLFAST GARDNER (b. FO 42) Hobbit of the Shire, son of Frodo Gardner. Holfast probably lived in Bag End. (III 477)

HOLLIN Eregion (q.v.). (I 369; S 286; B 354)

HOLMAN (b. TA 2810) Hobbit of the Shire, an excellent gardener and founder of the family of Greenhand. Holman lived in Hobbiton.
Holman was known as Holman the greenhanded. (III 477)

HOLMAN COTTON (b. TA 2902) Hobbit of the Shire, son of Cotman. He lived in Bywater.
Holman was known as Long Hom. (III 477)

HOLMAN GREENHAND (b. TA 2892, d. c. 2961) Hobbit of the Shire, son of Halfred Greenhand. He lived at Number 3, Bagshot Row, Hobbiton, and was gardener to Bilbo Baggins. Holman taught the craft of gardening to Hamfast Gamgee. (I 44; III 477)

HOLY MOUNTAIN Taniquetil (q.v.). (S 76; B 84)

HOLY ONES The Ainur (q.v.). (S 15; B 3)

HONEYBEES A race of creatures battled by the messenger in Bilbo Baggins' poem *Errantry*. Their existence in this context is probably fictitious. (TB 27)

HONEYCAKES OF BEORN Tasty traveling food prepared by Beorn. Like cram, they were very nourishing and could be preserved for long periods of time. (H 133)

HORN (d. TA 3019) Man of Rohan, killed in the Battle of the Pelennor Fields. (III 152)

HORNBLOWER Family of Hobbits of the Shire, all or most of whom dwelt in the Southfarthing. (I 28, 52; III 474)

HORNBURG Fortress in western Rohan, built by Gondor in the days of its power on the Hornrock near the Thrihyrne. It was said that no enemy could take the Hornburg if it were defended. Helm took refuge there against the Dunlendings in TA 2758-59, and during the WR Théoden fought the Battle of the Hornburg (q.v.) against the forces of Saruman.

The Hornburg was so named because a horn sounded in its tower echoed loudly in the winding depths of Helm's Deep. In times of peace it was the dwelling of the master of Westfold. (II 169 ff.; III 432)

HORN-CALL OF BUCKLAND The alarm of Buckland, not used very often.

Also called the Horn-cry. (I 239; III 354)

HORN OF THE MARK Small silver horn made by the Dwarves in ancient times, taken by the Éothéod from the hoard of Scatha. After the WR, Éowyn gave the horn to Merry as a keepsake, and he used it to hearten the Hobbits during the scouring of the Shire. Afterwards, it was blown each year on the anniversary of its first use in the Shire. (III 316, 353-54, 486)

HORNROCK Rock upon which the Hornburg (q.v.) was built, a black spur jutting out from the northern cliff of Helm's Deep. (II 169 ff.)

HORSE-COUNTRY Rohan (q.v.), so called by Orcs. (II 61)

HORSE-MEN The Wild Men's name for the Rohirrim (q.v.). (III 130)

HOST OF THE WEST The Host of Valinor (q.v.). (III 439)

HOST OF THE WEST The army that defeated the Witch-king and destroyed Angmar in TA 1975 in the Battle of Fornost. The Army was composed of Elves of

Lindon and Men of Arthedain and Gondor, and was led by Círdan and Eärnur. (III 411)

HOST OF THE WEST   The Army of the West (q.v.). (III 467)

HOST OF VALINOR   The army of the Valar that came to the aid of the Eldar and the Edain of Beleriand at the end of the First Age. The Host was apparently led by Eönwë, but it may have included other Valar and Maiar, especially Oromë. The Vanyar and the Noldor of Finarfin marched with the Host, and the Teleri of Alqualondë sailed its ships. In Middle-earth the Host was swelled by the Eagles and Eärendil, and it destroyed the power of Morgoth in the Great Battle.

Also called the Host of the West. (I 319; III 138, 439, 452; S 251-54; B 311-14)

HOUSE OF ANÁRION   The line of the Kings of Gondor (q.v.). (III 158)

HOUSE OF BËOR   The First House of the Edain (q.v.). (S 144, 307; B 173, 381)

HOUSE OF DURIN   The royal family of Durin's Folk, descended from Durin I. (III 450)

HOUSE OF ELENDIL   The royal line of the Dúnedain established in Middle-earth by Elendil, represented in the North by the Line of Isildur and in the South by the Kings of Gondor (qq.v.). Under King Elessar the House of Elendil returned to Gondor. (I 324)

HOUSE OF ELROND   The Last Homely House (q.v.). (I 359)

HOUSE OF ELROS   The Dúnadan line of the Kings of Númenor, which began with Elros Tar-Minyatur in SA 32 and ended with the death of Ar-Pharazôn in 3441. (III 390; S 266; B 328)

HOUSE OF EORL The Kings of the Mark (q.v.). (II 158)

HOUSE OF FËANOR Noble Noldorin family, comprising Fëanor, his seven sons, and their descendants, notably Celebrimbor. Although famed for its skill in crafts—especially the working of jewels and metals, but also language and music—the House of Fëanor suffered from its arrogance and willful pride. Fëanor quarreled with his half-brothers even during the Noontide of Valinor, and he and his sons brought about the disastrous revolt of the Noldor. As a result of Fëanor's harshness, his House was alienated from the rest of the Noldor and lost the overlordship of that kindred.

In Middle-earth the House of Fëanor, led by Maedhros, often tried to act with moderation, but the fateful pressure of the Oath of Fëanor subverted their intentions, and time after time the sons of Fëanor, impelled by their desire for the Silmaril, became enmeshed in treachery and violence, until at last their power was broken and they died shamefully. In the Second Age the House of Fëanor survived for a time among the Gwaith-i-Mírdain, but Celebrimbor, apparently its last member, died in the fall of Eregion.

The emblem of the House of Fëanor was an eight-rayed silver star. Also called the Dispossessed. (I 397; RHM III 439; S 60, 88, 109, 111, 189, 192-93, 195, 236, 246, 305; B 63, 99, 127, 129, 230, 235, 238, 292, 305, 379)

HOUSE OF FINARFIN See: the House of Finrod.

HOUSE OF FINGOLFIN The line of the High Kings of the Noldor in Middle-earth and of their heirs, from whom came in time Eärendil and the Peredhil. Wise but eager, the lords of the House of Fingolfin joined the revolt of the Noldor out of desire for the adventure of Middle-earth, but in Beleriand their discretion and the friendship of Ulmo protected them. At last, however, Hithlum and Gondolin fell, and the House of Fingolfin survived only in the person of Gil-galad, High King of the Noldor in the Second Age.

The banners of the House of Fingolfin were blue and silver. (S 60, 108, 134, 189, 195, 196, 305; B 64, 126, 160, 230, 238, 240, 379)

HOUSE OF FINROD   The third branch of the House of Finwë, properly the House of Finarfin. But Finarfin withdrew from the revolt of the Noldor, and among the Exiles the leader of the House was Finrod, King of Nargothrond. Wise and peaceful, the leaders of the House of Finrod were less involved in the Wars of Beleriand than the other Houses. They also seem to have remained in Middle-earth after the First Age in surprisingly large numbers; Galadriel, Gildor, and probably Glorfindel were members of the House.

The House of Finrod was golden-haired, since the mother of Finarfin was Indis of the Vanyar. (I 118; III 519; S 61, 305; B 64, 379)

HOUSE OF FINWË   Royal house of the Noldor. From its members were chosen the High Kings of the Noldor in Eldamar and Middle-earth.

See: the Houses of Fëanor, Fingolfin, and Finrod. (S 60-61, 305; B 64, 379)

HOUSE OF HADOR   Name given to the descendants of Hador Lórindol.

See: the Third House of the Edain. (III 389; S 148, 308; B 178, 382)

HOUSE OF HÚRIN   The House of the Stewards (q.v.). (III 395-96, 414)

HOUSE OF THE GOLDEN FLOWER   Noble family of Gondolin. The chief of the House was Glorfindel. (S 243; B 301)

HOUSE OF THE KINGS   Building in the Hallows (q.v.) of Minas Tirith where the Kings of Gondor were laid to rest. (III 427, 472)

HOUSE OF THE STEWARDS Noble Dúnadan family from which the Stewards of Gondor were chosen after TA 1621. The first Steward of the House was Húrin of Emyn Arnen, Steward to King Minardil. After Húrin all the Stewards were chosen from among his descendants, and after Pelendur (d. 1998) the Stewardship became hereditary.

The Stewards seem to have had hereditary lands in Emyn Arnen; Húrin came from there, and Faramir was made Lord of Emyn Arnen after the WR.

The chief heirloom of the House was the Great Horn originally used by Vorondil; after his time it was carried by the heir of the House.

Also called the House of Húrin. (III 118, 414)

HOUSE OF THE STEWARDS Building in the Hallows of Minas Tirith where the Stewards of Gondor were laid to rest. During the WR, Denethor II burned himself in the House, which was destroyed by the fire. (III 122, 155-61)

HOUSES OF HEALING The hospital of Minas Tirith, built against the southern wall of the sixth level of the city. The House had a fair, tree-girt garden. (III 161, 165-80, 291-300)

HOUSES OF THE DEAD The halls of Mandos, located in far western Valinor on the shores of Ekkaia and decorated with the tapestries of Vairë. Here come the spirits of Men and Elves (and perhaps Dwarves) after their deaths, and in the dim silence they sit and think. The spirits of Elves are released from the Houses after a time and are free to live in Aman, but after their time of awaiting, the spirits of Men pass west out of Arda. If the Dwarves do indeed come to the Houses, they remain there until the End.

Also called the Halls of Awaiting. (S 28, 42, 44, 52, 67, 186; B 21, 38, 42, 52, 72, 226)

HRÍVË (Q.: 'winter') The next-to-last division of the Eldarin loa (q.v.), corresponding to our December and

January. Called in Sindarin rhîw. Also used by Men as the name for the season winter. (III 480, 485)

HUAN (S.?: 'great dog') (d. FA 468) Great hound born in Valinor, one of the hunting dogs of Oromë, who gave him to Celegorm. Huan followed his new master to Beleriand and thus fell under the Doom of the Noldor. It was decreed that Huan would die, but only at the jaws of the mightiest wolf ever seen in Arda.

Huan's integrity and love for Lúthien led him to put her interests above those of the treacherous Celegorm. The hound performed great deeds in the Quest of the Silmaril; he slew the werewolves of Sauron, including their sire Draugluin, defeated Wolf-Sauron, and slew Carcharoth, the great wolf bred by Morgoth to be his bane. In the last fight Huan met his doom.

Huan had much of the nature of the Eldar or Valar; he was tireless and ageless, was impervious to wizardry, and did not need to sleep. He spoke with words three times in his life: once each to advise Lúthien and Beren, and once to bid Beren farewell.

Also called the Hound of Valinor. (S 172-79, 182-83, 185-86; B 209-17, 222, 225)

HUGGINS Surname of William, one of the trolls turned to stone during the expedition of Thorin and Company in TA 2941. (H 48)

HUGO BOFFIN (fl. TA 2900) Hobbit of the Shire. He married Donnamira Took. (III 475)

HUGO BRACEGIRDLE (fl. TA 3000) Hobbit of the Shire, a guest at the Farewell Party. He was noted for borrowing books and not returning them. (I 64)

HUMMERHORNS A probably fictitious insect race fought by the messenger in Bilbo Baggins' poem *Errantry*. (TB 27)

HUNTER The Rider (q.v.). (S 49; B 49)

HUNTER'S MOON   The name given by the Hobbits of the Shire to the bright full moon of mid-November. (I 358-59)

HUNTHOR (S.) (d. FA 501)   Adan of the Haladin of Brethil, a kinsman of Brandir. Hunthor was the only person to dare to accompany Túrin when he went to kill Glaurung. As the two Edain crouched beneath the brink of Cabed-en-Aras, Hunthor was struck by a stone dislodged by Glaurung and fell to his death. (S 221-22; B 272-73)

HUNTING OF THE WOLF   The final adventure of the Quest of the Silmaril, in which a party led by Thingol, Beren, Mablung, Beleg, and Huan sought to slay Carcharoth, who was ravaging the valley of the Esgalduin. In the hunt Beren, Huan, and Carcharoth were slain, but the Silmaril was recovered from the wolf's belly. (S 185-86; B 224-26)

HUOR (S.?) (FA 444-475)   Adan of the Third House, Elf-friend and hero, son of Galdor and Hareth and younger brother of Húrin. Fostered in Brethil, when Huor was thirteen he and Húrin went to war against the Orcs. Separated from their comrades, the brothers were rescued by Ulmo and finally came to Gondolin, where they stayed for a year. They then returned to Dor-lómin, where Huor married Rían of the First House; their child was Tuor.

Huor and Húrin commanded the right wing of the army of Hithlum in the Union of Maedhros and anchored the defense of the Pass of Sirion during the Nirnaeth Arnoediad. After prophesying the salvation of Elves and Men by Eärendil and thus persuading Turgon to retreat to Gondolin, Huor fought valiantly in the rearguard until he was struck in the eye by a poisoned arrow. (III 389; S 126, 148, 158-59, 190, 194, 307, 308; B 151, 177, 190-92, 232, 237, 238, 381, 382)

HUORNS (S.?)   Creatures of Fangorn, probably Ents (or trees) that had become wild and dangerous in the

Great Darkness. Huorns moved little, but when they desired they could travel quickly and wrap themselves in shadow. Huorns could still speak, and were controlled by the true Ents. Although wild, they were not really evil, and they hated Orcs. (II 186-87, 192-93, 200-01, 217)

HÚRIN (S.?) (c. FA 440-503)   Adan, Lord of the First House (462-73), Elf-friend and hero, elder son of Galdor and Hareth and brother of Huor (q.v.). Húrin spent a year in Gondolin with Huor; after returning to Dor-lómin he married Morwen of the First House sometime before 465; their children were Túrin, Lalaith, and Nienor.

In 462 Húrin broke the siege of Barad Eithel in which his father was slain, and with Huor he led the Edain in the Union of Maedhros and the Nirnaeth Arnoediad. The only survivor of the rearguard which covered the retreat of Turgon to Gondolin, Húrin slew seventy trolls before he was captured and brought to Angband. There Húrin refused to reveal the location of Gondolin or to beg for mercy, and Morgoth cursed him, Morwen, and their children, and set Húrin in a high place of Thangorodrim, where for twenty-eight years he saw the affairs of the world through the deceiving senses of Morgoth.

Freed by Morgoth a year after the death of his son Túrin, Húrin wandered through Beleriand, embittered by the lies of Morgoth. In Dimbar he called to Turgon to come to him, thus revealing to Morgoth the approximate location of Gondolin. At Cabed Naeramarth he came upon Morwen on the day of her death, and he buried her with Túrin. In Nargothrond he slew Mîm and recovered the Nauglamír, which he brought to Thingol in Menegroth. There Melian freed him from Morgoth's deceptions, and Húrin went away to die.

Húrin was short but strong both in mind and body, a great warrior but also cautious and wise in strategy. He was called Húrin Thalion and Húrin the Steadfast, for his sacrifice to save Gondolin, his refusal to retreat from his homeland, and his fortitude in bearing the torment of Morgoth and his doom, the greatest of undeserved ruins suffered by any among the Edain. (I 355; S 126, 148, 158-

59, 160, 190-99 passim, 209, 227-32, 307, 308; B 150, 177, 191-92, 193-94, 232-43 passim, 256, 257, 280-86, 381, 382)

HÚRIN (fl. TA 1634)   Dúnadan of Gondor, Steward of King Minardil and founder of the House of the Stewards. He was known as Húrin of Emyn Arnen. (III 414)

HÚRIN I (d. TA 2244)   Dúnadan, fifth Ruling Steward of Gondor (2204-44). (III 395)

HÚRIN II (d. TA 2628)   Dúnadan, fourteenth Ruling Steward of Gondor (2605-28). (III 395)

HÚRIN (fl. WR)   Dúnadan of Gondor of high rank, Warden of the Keys of Minas Tirith. Húrin fought in the Battle of the Pelennor Fields and later was given charge of Minas Tirith when the Army of the West rode to the Morannon.
     He was called Húrin the Tall and Húrin of the Keys. (III 148, 292, 301-02)

HWESTA (Q.: 'breeze')   Name of the tengwa 𝐝 (number 12), used in Quenya to represent voiceless *w* and in Sindarin to represent *chw*. (III 500)

HWESTA SINDARINWA (Q.: 'grey-Elven *hw*')   Name for the tengwa 𝐝 (number 34), which seems to have been a modified form of hwesta. It was used only in Sindarin, in which it represented voiceless *w*. (III 500)

HYARMEN (Q.: 'south')   Name for the tengwa 𝝀 (number 33). This tengwa was commonly used to indicate the compass-point "south" even in languages in which the word for "south" did not begin with this sign. (III 500)

HYARMENDACIL I (Q.: 'south-victor')   (d. TA 1149) Dúnadan, fifteenth King of Gondor (1015-1149) and the last Ship-king. He took the crown under the name Ciryaher, but changed his royal name to Hyarmendacil in

1050, after crushing the Haradrim and forcing them to acknowledge the overlordship of Gondor. During his reign Gondor reached the height of its power. (III 394, 403-04)

HYARMENDACIL II (d. TA 1621) Dúnadan, twenty-fourth King of Gondor (1540-1621). He was originally named Vinyarion, but took the name Hyarmendacil in commemoration of a great victory he won over the Haradrim in 1551. (III 395, 457)

HYARMENTIR (Q.: 'south-watch'?) Mountain of the Pelóri, the highest peak in southern Aman. (S 74; B 81)

∽ᘔ ᘔ∾

IANT IAUR (S.: 'bridge old') Stone bridge in Beleriand, crossing Esgalduin on the road from Brithiach to Arossiach. The bridge was built, probably by Dwarves, in the years before the return of the Noldor.
    Also called the Bridge of Esgalduin. (S 121, 132, 360; B 144-45, 157, 451)

IARWAIN BEN-ADAR (S.: 'old— without-father') Elvish name for Tom Bombadil (q.v.). (I 347)

IAVAS (S.) The Sindarin form of yávië (q.v.). (III 480)

IBUN (fl. FA 5th Cent.) Dwarf of the Noegyth Nibin, son of Mîm. Ibun was captured with his father by Túrin and later by Orcs. (S 203, 206; B 249, 252)

ICE The Grinding Ice (q.v.). (S 73; B 80)

ICE BAY OF FOROCHEL Bay in the far north of Middle-earth in the Third Age. The Ice Bay was the southern inlet of the vast unnamed bay opening onto the

Sea. The Bay froze over in winter. (I 16; III 399, 400; PB)

ICE OF THE NORTH The Grinding Ice (q.v.). (S 109; B 127)

IDRIL (S.: 'sparkle-brilliance') (FA) Noldorin Elf, daughter of Turgon and Elenwë. She returned to Middle-earth with Turgon and dwelt with him in Nevrast and Gondolin. Idril was loved by Maeglin, her first cousin, but she disliked him. In 503 she married Tuor; this was the second wedding of the Eldar and the Edain. The next spring their son Eärendil was born.

Fearing the fall of Gondolin and foreseeing the treachery of Maeglin, Idril secretly built a tunnel leading out of the city, and when Gondolin was invaded she escaped by that road with Tuor, Eärendil, and a small following. Idril and the survivors fled down Sirion to Nan Tathren and later to Arvernien. When Tuor grew old, he and Idril sailed into the West; it is not known if they were admitted to Aman.

Idril was very beautiful and had the golden hair of the Vanyar. She was known as Celebrindal, Silver-foot. The Quenya form of her name was Itarillë or Itarildë. (III 388-89; S 126, 136, 139, 240, 241, 242-43, 245, 305, 307, 308, 363; B 151, 163, 166, 296, 300, 303, 379, 381, 382, 455)

ILBERIC BRANDYBUCK (b. TA 2991) Hobbit of the Shire, second son of Seredic Brandybuck. He was a guest at the Farewell Party. (III 476)

ILLUIN (Q.?: '—blue') The northern of the Lamps of the Valar (q.v.), said to have stood in the place later occupied by the Inland Sea of Helcar. (S 35, 36, 49; B 29, 31, 48)

ILMARË (Q.) One of the greatest of the Maiar, the handmaid of Varda. (S 30; B 24)

ILMARIN (Q.: 'mansion of the high airs') The mansion of Manwë and Varda atop Taniquetil. Ilmarin has domed halls, and from it Manwë and Varda can look out to survey Arda. (I 309, 310, 482; R 61; S 360; B 451)

ILMEN (Q.: *il* 'up'? + *men* 'direction') The heavens of Eä, where the stars are; "space."
See also: Tarmenel. (S 99, 282, 336; B 113, 349, 419)

ILÚVATAR (Q.: 'all-father') God. Dwelling alone in the Timeless Halls, Ilúvatar created the Ainur with the Flame Imperishable of his spirit, and he revealed to each of them a part of his mind. Desiring to make their comprehension more complete, he revealed to the Ainur the three great themes of the Ainulindalë. When Melkor created discord within that Music, but others of the Ainur were drawn to the Vision which came from it, Ilúvatar gave it Being, and Eä was created.

Within Eä, the Valar independently tried to fulfill the Music, but some things—the creation of Men and Elves, the destiny of Men, and the End, for example—remained known only to Ilúvatar. He intervened directly in the affairs of Eä only twice: to sanctify Aulë's creation of the Dwarves, and to change Arda at the request of the Valar, when the Númenóreans landed on Aman.

Ilúvatar is the name given him in Arda; he is also called Eru, Eru Ilúvatar, the One, and (once) God. (III 392; R 66; S 15-22, 25, 43-44, 90, 187, 264-65, 278-79, 336, 360; B 3-13, 17, 41, 102, 227-28, 326-27, 334-35, 419, 451)

IMLACH (FA 4th Cent.) Adan of the Third House, son of Marach and father of Amlach. (S 144; B 173)

IMLAD MORGUL (S.: 'valley of black magic') Valley in the western side of the Ephel Dúath, through which the Morgulduin flowed. Minas Morgul was located at the head of the valley. During the WR the Captains of the West set fire to the evil meadows of Imlad Morgul and broke the bridge across the Morgulduin, but even after the War the terror of the valley was too great for it to be resettled. Also called Morgul Vale, Morgulvale, the Valley of the Wraiths, and the valley of Living Death. (II 388, 397 ff.: III 197-98, 305; S 361; B 452)

IMLADRIS (S.: 'deep-dale-cleft') Rivendell (q.v.). (I 323; L 156, 190)

IMLOTH MELUI (S.: 'deep-blossom —') Valley in Gondor, perhaps in Lossarnach, noted for its roses. (III 173)

IMPERISHABLE FLAME The Flame Imperishable (q.v.). (S 16; B 4)

IMRAHIL (of Númenórean origin) (fl. WR) Dúnadan of Gondor, Prince of Dol Amroth. During the WR Imrahil fought in the Battle of the Pelennor Fields, and he ruled Minas Tirith after the death of Denethor II while Faramir was ill. He was one of the Captains of the West, and fought in the battle outside the Morannon.

Imrahil was a great warrior, and was known as Imrahil the fair because he bore the signs of his Dúnadan and Elvish ancestry. (III 23, 50, 119, 148-52, 181, 487)

INCÁNUS Name given to Gandalf (q.v.) in the south of Middle-earth. (II 353)

INDIS (Q.) Elda of the Vanyar, closely related to Ingwë. In Eldamar she married Finwë as his second wife and bore him two children, Fingolfin and Finarfin.

Indis was tall and blonde, and was known as Indis the Fair. (S 60, 64; B 63, 68)

INGOLD (S.?) (fl. WR) Man of Gondor, leader of the soldiers at the northern gate of the Rammas Echor before the Siege of Gondor. (III 21, 115)

INGWË (Q.) Elda of the Vanyar. One of the ambassadors chosen by Oromë to visit Valinor and encourage the Eldar to undertake the Great Journey, Ingwë became King of the Vanyar and led his people quickly to the West. In Aman he dwelt first in Tirion and later at the feet of Manwë upon Taniquetil, and was named High King of the Elves. Revered by all Elves, he never returned to Middle-earth. (S 52-53, 62; B 53-54, 65)

INLAND SEA The sea of Rhûn (q.v.). (III 43)

INLAND SEA OF HELCAR Helcar (q.v.). (S 49; B 49)

INNER SEAS Belegaer and the inland seas and coastal waters of Middle-earth, in contrast to Ekkaia. (S 40; B 36)

INSCRUTABLE One of the epithets applied to Men (q.v.) by the Elves. (S 103; B 119)

INZILADÛN, AR- (Ad.: 'flower of the west') See: Tar-Palantir. (III 390; S 269; B 332)

INZILBÊTH (Ad.: 'flower—') (fl. SA 3125) Dúnadan of Númenor of the house of Andúnië, one of the Faithful. Desired for her beauty, she was forced to marry Ar-Gimilzôr. Their unhappy marriage produced two children, Palantir and Gimilkhâd. (S 268; B 331)

IORETH (S.) (fl. WR) Woman of Gondor, originally from Lossarnach. At the time of the WR she was the eldest of the women who served in the Houses of Healing in Minas Tirith. Her folk wisdom was exceeded only by her loquacity. (III 166, 170-71, 302-03)

IORLAS (S.: '—leaf') (fl. WR) Man of Gondor, uncle of Bergil. He probably lived in Minas Tirith. (III 47)

IRENSAGA Saw-toothed mountain of the Ered Nimrais. Irensaga formed the north wall of Dunharrow. (III 81)

IRMO (Q.: 'desirer, master of desire') The true name of Lórien the Vala (q.v.). (S 28, 336; B 21, 419)

IRON CROWN The great crown of Morgoth, forged by him in Angband on his return to Middle-earth, symbol of his claim to be King of the World. The Silmarils were set in the Crown, fastened by iron claws.

Beren pried one Silmaril loose from the Iron Crown, and after the Great Battle the other two jewels were removed and the Crown beaten into a collar for Morgoth's neck. (I 260; II 408; S 81, 167, 181, 252; B 90-91, 202, 219, 312)

IRON HILLS Hills east of Erebor settled about TA 2590 by Grór and Dwarves of Durin's Folk after the desertion of the Ered Mithrin. The Dwarves of the Iron Hills under Náin, coming late to the field, turned the tide of the Battle of Azanulbizar in 2799. In 2941, five hundred Dwarves of the Iron Hills, led by Dáin, came to Erebor to support Thorin II, and fought valiantly in the Battle of the Five Armies. Dáin then became King of Erebor; the Iron Hills pass out of records after this, but they may not have been deserted.

The Dwarves of the Iron Hills seem to have been prosperous, but not wealthy. It is likely that the Hills had much iron, but no gold. (I 17; III 440, 443-44, 448; H 246, 256-57, 263-65)

IRON MOUNTAINS The Ered Engrin (q.v.). (S 109; B 127)

ISEMBARD TOOK (TA 2847-2946) Hobbit of the Shire, seventh son of Gerontius Took. (III 475)

ISEMBOLD TOOK (TA 2842-2946) Hobbit of the Shire, fifth son of Gerontius Took. (III 475)

ISEN (tr. Roh.: 'iron') River flowing from Nan Curunír south through the Gap of Rohan and then west to the Sea. During the WR, the Ents temporarily diverted its waters in order to flood Isengard.

The Isen was the western boundary of Rohan, and was defended against the Dunlendings. The Isen seems not to have been bridged, but it was crossed by the Fords of Isen about thirty miles south of Isengard. (I 16; II 198-202; III 431)

ISENGAR TOOK (TA 2862-2960) Hobbit of the Shire, youngest son of Gerontius Took. He was said to have gone to sea in his youth. (III 475)

ISENGARD (tr. Roh.: 'iron-enclosure') Fortress built by Gondor in the days of its power in Nan Curunír. Isengard consisted of a natural circular stone wall surrounding a broad plain, in the center of which was the tower of Orthanc (q.v.). Isengard had only one gate, which faced south.

When Calenardhon was given to the Rohirrim in TA 2510, Isengard was kept by Gondor, but it was deserted. About 2700 it was taken by the Dunlendings, but they were driven out in 2759 by Fréaláf. In that year, with the permission of Beren of Gondor, Saruman began to live in Isengard, and in 2963 he took it as his own and began to fortify it, replacing its grass and trees with stone and machinery. There he housed Orcs, Men, and wolves until Isengard was attacked and demolished by the Ents during the WR. The Ents planted the Watchwood (q.v.) there, and renamed Isengard the Tree-garth of Orthanc.

Called in Sindarin Angrenost. Also called the Ring of Isengard, which referred specifically to the physical arrangement of wall and plain. (I 338; II 203-04 ff.; III 317, 416, 417, 432, 433-34, 460, 462; L 187-88; S 291; B 361)

ISENGRIM TOOK (TA 2620-2722) Hobbit of the Shire, as Isengrim II the twenty-second Thain of the Shire (2653-2722). He began the excavation of the Great Smials. (III 459, 474, 482)

ISENGRIM TOOK (TA 2832-2930) Hobbit of the Shire, eldest son of Gerontius Took and, as Isengrim III, twenty-seventh Thain of the Shire (2920-30). He had no children. (III 475)

ISENMOUTHE Pass in Mordor between Gorgoroth and Udûn, at the meeting of the Ered Lithui and Ephel Dúath. The Isenmouthe was fortified, and across it was built a fence of pointed iron posts.

Called in Sindarin Carach Angren. (III 15, 241, 251, 258; L 187-88)

ISIL (Q.: 'silver-sheen'?) The Moon (q.v.). (S 99; B 114)

ISILDUR (Q.: 'moon—') (d. TA 2) Dúnadan of Númenor, elder son of Elendil. In his youth Isildur stole a fruit of Nimloth from the guarded courts of Armenelos; although he was seriously wounded, he managed to preserve the line of the White Tree in mortal lands. At the downfall of Númenor Isildur escaped with three ships to Pelargir, where he founded the kingdom of Gondor with his brother Anárion; he was Lord of Ithilien and joint King of Gondor. Isildur founded Minas Ithil, where he lived until SA 3429, when Sauron took the city. He escaped to Arnor, leaving Anárion to defend Osgiliath and Minas Anor, and returned to Gondor with the army of the Last Alliance. In 3441 Isildur stood by his father in the final battle against Sauron and, cutting off the Enemy's finger, claimed the One Ring.

After the defeat of Sauron Isildur ruled Gondor for two years (SA 3441-TA 2), planting a seedling of the White Tree in Minas Anor in memory of Anárion and instructing his young nephew Meneldil in the art of kingship. He then traveled north to assume the rule of Arnor, of which he had become King on his father's death in 3441. On the way, however, his party was ambushed in the Gladden Fields by a host of Orcs. Isildur tried to escape by putting on the Ring and swimming in the Anduin, but the Ring slipped off and he was slain. (I 83, 319, 320, 331-32; III 394; S 272-73, 280, 291, 293, 294, 295; B 337, 346, 360-61, 364, 365, 366)

ISILDUR'S BANE The One Ring (q.v.). (I 323, 324)

ISILYA (Q.: 'moon-day') The third day of the enquië, dedicated to the Moon.

Called in Sindarin Orithil and by the Hobbits Monendei, later Monday. The last name is used for Isilya in *LotR*. (III 484)

ISLE OF ALMAREN Almaren (q.v.). (S 35; B 30)

ISLE OF BALAR Balar (q.v.). (S 57; B 60)

ISLE OF ERESSËA Tol Eressëa (q.v.). (S 260; B 320)

ISLE OF MENELTARMA The summit of Meneltarma, in the Third Age believed to have risen above the waves again after the sinking of Númenor because of the sacred Hallow of Eru. But mariners never found the Isle. (S 281; B 348)

ISLES OF THE WEST General reference to Aman, perhaps with the single island of Tol Eressëa most in mind. (III 424)

ISTARI (Q.) Five (or more) beings sent to Middle-earth by the Valar about TA 1000 to unite and counsel the Free Peoples in their struggles against Sauron. They were forbidden to dominate the peoples of Middle-earth or to match Sauron's power with power. When Saruman, the greatest of the Wizards, disobeyed this injunction, he was cast from the order and banished from Valinor. At the end of the Third Age the Istari passed from sight, for with the fall of Sauron their work was done. Gandalf passed over Sea with the Last Riding of the Keepers of the Rings, and the other surviving Istari may also have returned to the West.

The Istari bore the forms of old Men, although they were vigorous and aged very slowly. They possessed great skill of body and mind; their powers were focused through their staffs. Each of the Istari had his own color and grade within the Order. Saruman the White was the eldest and Gandalf the Grey second. The other Istari were Radagast the Brown and several, unnamed, who dwelt far in the east.

The origins of the Istari are veiled. Professor Tolkien said that they were Valar "of a sort." If Olórin the Maia can be equated with the name Olórin borne by Gandalf "in his youth in the West," then the Istari were Maiar, a conclusion made plausible by the equality of the power wielded by Gandalf and the Balrog of Moria.

Called Wizards in Westron. (I 429; II 241; III 33-34, 308, 325-26, 455; RP oral, summer 1965; S 299-300; B 372)

ISUMBRAS TOOK (fl. TA 2340)   Hobbit of the Shire, as Isumbras I the thirteenth Thain of the Shire (2340-?) and the first of the Took line. (III 459)

ISUMBRAS TOOK (TA 2666-2759)   Hobbit of the Shire, son of Isengrim Took and, as Isumbras III, twenty-third Thain of the Shire (2722-59). (III 475)

ISUMBRAS TOOK (TA 2838-2939)   Hobbit of the Shire, third son of Gerontius Took and, as Isumbras IV, twenty-eighth Thain of the Shire (2930-39). (III 475)

ITARILDË, ITARILLË (Q.: 'sparkle-brilliance')   The original form of the name of Idril (q.v.). (S 363; B 455)

ITHIL (S.: 'silver-sheen'?)   The Moon (q.v.). (S 90; B 102)

ITHILDIN (S.: 'star-moon')   Substance fashioned by the Noldor of Eregion from mithril, and used by them for gateways and such. Ithildin was visible only by starlight or moonlight, and only after it was touched by one who spoke certain words of lore. (I 397, 413; S 365; B 457)

ITHILIEN (S.: 'moon-land')   Area of Gondor between Anduin and the Ephel Dúath, bounded on the south by the Poros, divided into North and South Ithilien. Ithilien was originally the fief of Isildur. It bore the brunt of the attacks on Gondor from the east and south, beginning with

Sauron's capture of its chief city, Minas Ithil, in SA 3429. The city was freed, but its capture by the Nazgûl in TA 2002 caused many of the remaining inhabitants of Ithilien to flee, and more fled when Mordor-orcs began to ravage the land in 2901. The desertion was not complete, however, until 2954, when Mount Doom burst into flame and Sauron openly declared himself. Before this time, secret refuges like Henneth Annûn had been built, and the Rangers of Ithilien harried Sauron's force in Ithilien until the WR.

Since Sauron had not controlled Ithilien for long, during the WR it was still a fair, pollen-perfumed land. In 3019, with the return of the King, Faramir became Prince of Ithilien. Legolas and other Elves of the Woodland Realm lived in Ithilien, and it became once more the fairest land in the Westlands.

Originally called Ithiliend. (I 322; II 325 ff.; III 14-15, 413, 414 ff., 451, 461, 462, 490)

ITHIL-STONE The palantír of Minas Ithil, placed there soon after the founding of the city. The fate of the Stone when Minas Ithil was captured by Sauron in SA 3429 is uncertain, but in the Third Age it remained in Minas Ithil until the city fell to the Nazgûl in TA 2002. After then it was used by Sauron, notably to ensnare Saruman and deceive Denethor. The Ithil-stone was probably destroyed in the fall of the Barad-dûr. (II 259, 315)

IVANNETH Name used by the Dúnedain for Yavannië (q.v.). (III 483)

IVORWEN (S.) (fl. TA 2907-29) Dúnadan of the North, wife of Dírhael and mother of Gilraen. (III 420)

IVRIN Eithel Ivrin (q.v.). (S 113; B 132)

IVY BUSH, THE Tavern on the Bywater Road, frequented by Hobbits from Bywater and Hobbiton. (I 44)

JEWELS OF FËANOR The Silmarils (q.v.). (S 181; B 219)

JOLLY COTTON Wilcome Cotton (q.v.). (III 354)

KALI See: Kalimac. (III 517)

KALIMAC (gen. Mannish) Buckland personal name, originally derived from the language used by the Stoors before coming to the Shire. It was almost always shortened to Kali, which meant 'jolly, gay' in Westron.
See: Meriadoc Brandybuck. (III 517)

KARNINGUL (gen. West.: 'cut valley') Rivendell (q.v.). (III 515)

KEEPERS OF THE THREE RINGS The Eldar who wielded the Rings of Power of the Elves. At first Gil-galad held Vilya, Círdan Narya, and Galadriel Nenya. Sometime before his death Gil-galad gave his Ring to Elrond, and at the coming of the Istari to Middle-earth Círdan gave Narya to Gandalf. At the end of the Third Age the Last Riding of the Keepers (q.v.) carried the Rings over Sea.
  Also called the Keepers of the Rings and the Three Keepers. (III 456, 471; S 304; B 378)

KELOS See: Celos. (III 14)

KELVAR (Q.: 'quick ones') Animate living things under the care of Yavanna—that is, all animate beings except the Children of Ilúvatar, the Ents, and the Dwarves.

283

Apparently the Eagles of Manwë are the highest of the kelvar, just as the Ents are of the olvar. (S 45-46, 337; B 43-44, 419)

KEMENTÁRI (Q.: 'earth-queen') The surname of Yavanna (q.v.) (S 28, 360; B 21, 452)

KEY OF ORTHANC Actually, two black keys of intricate shape, used to lock the door of Orthanc. (III 240, 245)

KEYS OF BARAD-DÛR The keys to the Dark Tower, a symbol of Sauron's power. (II 240)

KHAND Realm southeast of Mordor, home of the Variags (q.v.). Because of its location, Khand was probably always strongly influenced by Sauron. (I 17; III 148, 409)

KHAZÂD (Kh.) The name given to the Dwarves (q.v.) by Aulë at their making, their own name for themselves.

The Sindarin form is Hadhod. (III 519; S 91; B 104)

KHAZAD-DÛM (Kh.: 'dwarf-mansion') Greatest of the Dwarf-halls, the mansion and folk-home of Durin's Folk, carved by Durin I early in the First Age in the caves overlooking Azanulbizar. Here was located the tomb of Durin, and here dwelt the heart of his people. Expanded many times, Khazad-dûm ultimately took up much of the area beneath Barazinbar, Zirak-zigil, and Bundushathûr, and in the Second Age a tunnel was built to Eregion. Khazad-dûm consisted of many large halls on a number of levels, as well as mines, etc.

At the end of the First Age, the population of Khazad-dûm was increased, as many skilled Dwarves from the Ered Luin came there after the ruin of Nogrod and Belegost. Early in the Second Age, mithril was discovered in Khazad-dûm, and the friendship between Durin's Folk and the Noldor of Eregion began. The gates of Khazad-dûm were closed during the War of Elves and Sauron, and thus the Dwarves survived through the Second Age.

In TA 1980, the Dwarves, while extending their mithril-mine, released the Balrog hidden beneath Barazinbar. The next year, after two Kings of Khazad-dûm had been slain by the Balrog, the Dwarves fled. About 2480 Sauron began to keep Orcs in Khazad-dûm, and these Orcs murdered Thrór in 2790. This led to the War of the Dwarves and Orcs, which ended in 2799 with the Battle of Azanulbizar. Despite the Dwarves' victory, Dáin Ironfoot refused to re-enter Khazad-dûm because of the presence of the Balrog. In 2989, however, a large group of Dwarves of Erebor, led by Balin, established a Dwarf-kingdom in Khazad-dûm. However, they were trapped by the Watcher in the Water at the West-gate and a large army of Orcs at the East-gate, and they perished in 2994. In January, 3019, the Company of the Ring (and Gollum) passed through Khazad-dûm, and Gandalf slew the Balrog in a series of battles which ruined the Chamber of Mazarbul, Durin's Bridge, the Endless Stair, and Durin's Tower (qq.v.). There is no mention of a recolonization of Khazad-dûm by the Dwarves in the Fourth Age, despite the death of the Balrog.

The Dwarvish kingdom of Khazad-dûm included Azanul-bizar as well as the halls within the mountains. Except for Balin, all the Kings of Khazad-dûm were also Kings of Durin's Folk.

Khazad-dûm was called the Dwarrowdelf in Westron and Hadhodrond in Sindarin, although the more usual Elvish name, especially after the freeing of the Balrog, was Moria. From the latter name came the Westron Black Pit, Black Chasm, and Mines of Moria. (I 316, 370, 402-31; II 134-35; III 438-39, 442, 444, 458, 459, 462, 519; H 61, 65; S 44, 91, 286, 337; B 42, 104, 354, 420)

KHELED-ZÂRAM (Kh.: 'glass-lake') Lake in Azanul-bizar. Here, early in the First Age, Durin I beheld the reflection of Durin's Crown. Ever after, these stars could be seen reflected in the water of Kheled-zâram at any time of the day or night, and the lake was always smooth.

However, the faces of those who looked into the waters could not be seen.

The Westron name was the Mirrormere. Also spelled Kheledzâram. (I 370, 411, 412, 432-34; L 190)

KHÎM (d. FA 486) Dwarf of the Noegyth Nibin, son of Mîm. He was slain by an arrow shot by one of Túrin's outlaws. (S 202, 203; B 249)

KHUZDUL (Kh.: 'Dwarvish') The language of the Dwarves, invented by Aulë, who taught it to them at their first awakening. It was a secret tongue of lore, and few who were not Dwarves ever learned it. Khuzdul seems to have been a rather harsh tongue, with an emphasis on aspirated stops and voiced spirants, but it no doubt assumed some grace when properly spoken.

The only examples of Khuzdul given are a few personal and place-names, the Dwarves' battle-cry, and the inscription on the tomb of Balin. (III 488, 504, 512-13; S 43; B 40)

KIBIL-NÂLA (Kh.) Either the Silverlode or the springs that were its source. The springs were located in Azanulbizar and were icy cold. (I 370-71, 461)

KÍLI (TA 2864-2941) Dwarf of Durin's line, son of Dís and nephew of Thorin, a member of Thorin and Company. Kíli, with his brother Fíli, was slain in the Battle of the Five Armies while defending Thorin's body. (III 450; H 22, 26, 275)

KINE OF ARAW A kind of large white ox found near the Sea of Rhûn. The Kine were often hunted; the most famous hunters were Oromë in the First Age and Vorondil of Gondor in the Third. The Great Horn worn by the heirs of the Stewards was made from a horn of one of the Kine killed by Vorondil. (III 29, 395)

KINGDOM OF ARDA, KINGDOM OF EARTH Arda (q.v.), the realm of Manwë. (S 25, 35, 62; B 17, 29, 66)

KINGDOM OF MANWË   Arda (q.v.). (S 73; B 80)

KINGDOM UNDER THE MOUNTAIN   The Dwarf-realm in Erebor (q.v.), ruled by the King of Durin's Folk. (III 448)

KING OF ARDA   The title of Manwë (q.v.). (S 45; B 43)

KING OF MEN   Apparently a traditional title of the greatest of the Dúnedain, the Kings of Men. When Sauron claimed this title because of his dominions in Middle-earth, the pride of Ar-Pharazôn of Númenor was aroused; he sailed to Middle-earth, humbled Sauron, and secured the title. (S 270; B 333)

KING OF NARGOTHROND   Finrod (q.v.). His only successor was Orodreth. (S 142; B 170)

KING OF THE DEAD (fl. SA 3429-TA 3019)   Man, chief of the Men of the Mountains at the time of the founding of Gondor. On behalf of his people, he swore allegiance to Isildur at Erech, but broke the Oath when called to fight with the army of the Last Alliance. For this, he and his people were doomed to dwell in the Ered Nimrais until they repaid their debt, which they did during the WR.

While a normal Man, he was known as the King of the Mountains. (III 64, 187)

KING OF THE MOUNTAINS   The King of the Dead (q.v.). (III 64)

KING OF THE NINE RIDERS   The Lord of the Nazgûl (q.v.). (II 401)

KING OF THE WORLD   Title claimed by Melkor (q.v.) on his return to Angband with the Silmarils. (S 81; B 90)

KING'S COURT Court in the royal palace of Armenelos in Númenor. Nimloth grew here.
Also called the courts of the King. (III 484; S 263, 273; B 324, 337)

KINGSFOIL Athelas (q.v.). (III 170)

KING'S HOUSE The royal palace of Gondor, originally in Osgiliath but moved to Minas Anor by King Tarondor in TA 1640.
See: the White Tower, the Tower Hall. (III 28, 457)

KING'S MEN The majority party of Númenor, arising in the reign of Tar-Ancalimon, that opposed the Ban of the Valar and became estranged from the Eldar. In Middle-earth the King's Men established dominions in the south; their greatest stronghold was at Umbar. Easily corrupted by Sauron in Middle-earth and Númenor, they turned to tyranny and Darkness. Their descendants were known as the Black Númenóreans. (III 403; S 266, 267, 269; B 328, 329, 332)

KINGS OF ARNOR The Kings of Arnor were Dúnedain, Elendil, Isildur, and the Line of Isildur (qq.v.) from SA 3320 to TA 861, TA 1349 to 1974, and from TA 3019 into the Fourth Age. From 861 to 1349, Arnor was divided into three realms, but after 1349, since the royal line had died out in two of the kingdoms, the Kings of Arthedain claimed lordship over all of Arnor. From TA 1974 to 3019 the Dúnedain of the North were scattered, and although the royal line survived, it did not claim kingship.
The Kings of Arnor at first dwelt in Annúminas, but before 861 the royal court was moved to Fornost. At the beginning of the Fourth Age Annúminas was rebuilt and once more became the site of the court.
The symbols of the authority of the Kings of Arnor were the sceptre of Annúminas, the Elendilmir, and the ring of Barahir; they wore no crown. (III 394, 401)

KINGS OF ARTHEDAIN The Kings of Arthedain were Dúnedain of the Line of Isildur, Amlaith and his descendants from TA 861 until 1974. Amlaith was the eldest son of Eärendur of Arnor, and thus the Kings of Arthedain were the heirs of Isildur. Beginning with Argeleb I in 1349, the Kings of Arthedain claimed lordship over all of Arnor, but this claim was contested by Rhudaur. The last King of Arthedain was Arvedui; with his death in 1974 and the conquest of Arthedain by Angmar the kingdom ended. (III 394)

KINGS OF DURIN'S FOLK The Kings of Durin's Folk were the heirs of Durin I, whether in Khazad-dûm or in exile. From its making in the Second Age, when it was given to Durin III, until TA 2845, when Sauron recovered it from Thráin II, the Kings of Durin's Folk bore the greatest of the Seven Rings.

It was believed by the Dwarves that six times the King of Durin's Folk would so resemble Durin the Deathless as to be named Durin, and that the line would end with Durin VII.

The Kings of Durin's Folk were also known at certain times as the Kings of Khazad-dûm (First Age-TA 1981) and the Kings under the Mountain (TA 1999-2190, 2590-2770, 2941-FO ?). (III 439, 450)

KINGS OF GONDOR The Kings of Gondor were Dúnedain, Elendil, Isildur, and Anárion, the Line of Anárion and the Telcontari. Elendil was the first King, but he committed the rule of Gondor to his sons, Isildur and Anárion. On Elendil's death, Isildur became King of Arnor, and Meneldil, the son of Anárion, King of Gondor; the two lines were separated. In the Third Age the line of the Kings was broken five times, until in 2050 King Eärnur, who was unmarried, disappeared, and the kingdom was ruled by the Stewards. The line of the Kings was restored by Elessar Telcontar, the heir of Isildur, after the WR.

The Kings wore the Silver Crown and bore a sceptre. Their banner was black, with a blossoming white tree under seven stars.

The titles of the Kings are not given in *LotR,* but they were probably similar to those of the Ruling Stewards. The Kings, or their heirs, when capable led in person the armies and fleets of Gondor.

Also known as the Lords of the White Tree, the Line of Anárion, and the House of Anárion. (III 394-95)

KINGS OF KHAZAD-DÛM Those of the Kings of Durin's Folk (q.v.) who lived in Khazad-dûm. There was such a king from the time of Durin I to TA 1981, when Khazad-dûm was deserted by the Dwarves because of the Balrog. Balin, who was not King of Durin's Folk, was King of Khazad-dûm from TA 2989-94. (III 445)

KINGS OF MEN The Dúnedain (q.v.), especially the Kings of Númenor and Gondor.
See: King of Men. (I 318; III 405, 428; S 294; B 365)

KINGS OF NÚMENOR The House of Elros, ruling Númenor by authority of the Valar from its founding until its downfall. At first the descent passed from father to eldest son; after the death of Tar-Aldarion the sceptre passed to the eldest child, and there were three Ruling Queens.

The first eighteen rulers took the throne with Quenya regnal names; the last six (except Tar-Palantir) used Adûnaic names, although many or all of them recorded Quenya forms in the Scroll of Kings. The symbol of the Kings was the Sceptre. Their sword was Aranrúth. (III 390-91; S 148, 261, 266, 267-68; B 177, 322, 328, 329-31)

KINGS OF THE MARK Men, the Kings of Rohan, of the House of Eorl. The King was the First Marshal of the Mark, and had his court (after its building in TA 2569) in Meduseld.

The line of the Kings was broken twice, and so the line was divided into the First, Second, and Third Lines (qq.v.). (II 158; III 434-37)

KINGS OF THE WEST The Telcontari (q.v.). (III 469)

KINGS' RECKONING The calendar system used in Númenor and in the Westron area of Middle-earth until about TA 2100, a synthesis of the systems of the Eldar and the Edain. The enquië (q.v.) had seven days, and the asta (q.v.) thirty or thirty-one. The loa (q.v.) contained twelve astar and a number of extra days, forming a total of 365 days. The calendar for one loa was as follows:

yestarë: first day	Çermië: 31 days
Narvinyë: 30 days	Úrimë: 30 days
Nénimë: 30 days	Yavannië: 30 days
Súlimë: 30 days	Narquelië: 30 days
Víressë: 30 days	Hísimë: 30 days
Lótessë: 30 days	Ringarë: 30 days
Nárië: 31 days	mettarë: last day
loëndë: Midsummer's Day	

The year began at the winter solstice. In leap years (every fourth year except the last of a century) loëndë was replaced by two enderi. Further adjustments were made as a result of the Deficit (q.v.).

About TA 2100 the Kings' Reckoning was replaced by the Stewards' Reckoning everywhere in the Westron area except the Shire. (See: the Shire Reckoning) The Quenya names given above were the names most commonly used, but the Dúnedain used Sindarin names and the Hobbits used Mannish ones. (III 480-81)

KINGS UNDER THE MOUNTAIN Dwarves, those Kings of Durin's Folk who ruled in Erebor. There was such a King during the years TA 1999-2190, 2590-2770, and 2941-FO ?. (III 439; H 190)

KING'S WRITERS The royal scribes of Gondor. (I 38)

KINSLAYING AT ALQUALONDË The first great tragedy of the revolt of the Noldor and the first slaying of Elf by Elf. The battle began when the Teleri of Alqualondë refused to give ships to the Nolder, and Fëanor in his haste and pride resolved to take them by force. The Teleri resisted with arms until the host of Fëanor was reinforced by the vanguard of the host of Fingolfin, led by Fingon. A large part of the lightly armed Teleri was slain. The consequences of the Kinslaying were serious. The storm raised by the grief of Uinen killed many Noldor sailing the stolen ships, and the shedding of blood in Aman directly caused the Doom of the Noldor (q.v.). In Middle-earth the Kinslaying caused Thingol (brother of Olwë, Lord of Alqualondë) to divorce himself and the power of Doriath from the House of Fëanor. Despite the atonement of the House of Fingolfin on the Grinding Ice, the shadow of the Kinslaying lay on the spirits of all the Noldor. It incited the incestuous love of Maeglin for Idril, and was the weakness by which Sauron overcame Finrod. (S 87, 88, 127, 128-29, 139, 141, 171; B 98, 100, 152, 153-54, 166, 169, 207)

KIN-STRIFE The great civil war of Gondor, lasting from TA 1432 to 1448. The war resulted from the belief of some of the Dúnedain that Eldacar was unfit to rule because he was not of pure Dúnadan blood, and stemmed ultimately from the discontent of various members of the royal family over the favor shown to the Northmen by Eldacar's father Valacar. Before Valacar's death in 1432 there was rebellion in southern Gondor, and on Eldacar's accession there was widespread warfare. The rebels, the most powerful of whom was Castamir, the Captain of Ships, besieged Eldacar in Osgiliath. In 1437, the king was forced to flee to his mother's kin in Rhovanion, but Osgiliath was burned and its palantír lost. Eldacar's son Ornendil was captured and put to death by Castamir, who was made king.

The new king was cruel and thought only of the navy, and was soon disliked in the inland areas of Gondor. After ten years of exile, in 1447 Eldacar returned to Gondor with an army of Northmen. He received much support from the folk of Calenardhon, Ithilien, and Anórien, and slew Castamir in the Battle of the Crossings of Erui. The remaining rebels were besieged in Pelargir, and in 1448 they took the entire fleet of Gondor and sailed to Umbar. There they rapidly degenerated into Corsairs who troubled Gondor's coasts for many generations. (III 405-07)

KIRIL   See: Ciril. (III 14)

KIRITH UNGOL   See: Cirith Ungol. (III 15)

KÛD-DÛKAN   (gen. Roh.: 'hole-dweller')   Rohirric name for the Hobbits (q.v.) (III 520)

KUDUK (gen. Hob.: 'hobbit')   Name by which the Hobbits of the Shire and Bree called themselves at the time of the WR, related to the Rohirric *kûd-dûkan*. (III 519-20)

❁ ❀

LADROS (S.)   Area in northeastern Dorthonion, the home of the Lords of the First House of the Edain. (S 148; B 177)

LADY OF THE WOOD   Galadriel (q.v.). (II 49)

LAER (S.)   The Sindarin form of lairë (q.v.). (III 480)

LAER CÚ BELEG (S.: 'song of the great bow')   Túrin's lament for Beleg, composed soon after his death. (S 209; B 256)

LAGDUF (d. TA 3019)   Orc of the Tower of Cirith Ungol, killed in the fight over Frodo's mithril-mail between Lagduf's company and Orcs of Minas Morgul. (III 217, 222)

LAIQUENDI (Q.: 'green-elves')   Teleri, the remnant of the Nandor who remained in Ossiriand, lordless and hidden, after the death of Denethor in the first battle of the Wars of Beleriand. The Laiquendi were excellent woodsmen and enjoyed the protection of Ulmo, who loved the River Gelion, and so they lived in secret through the First Age. The closest they came to fighting an open battle was when they helped Beren and Dior ambush the Dwarves of Nogrod who had sacked Menegroth.

The Laiquendi wore green, especially in spring and summer, and they were very fond of singing. Their favorite weapon was the bow.

Also called the Green-elves. (S 96, 113, 123, 235, 309; B 110, 133, 147, 290, 383)

LAIRË (Q.) The second season of the Calendar of Imladris, equivalent to summer. Lairë contained 72 days.

Called in Sindarin laer. (III 480, 485)

LAKE HELEVORN Helevorn (q.v.). (S 124; B 148)

LAKE MITHRIM The great long lake in Mithrim. On its northern shore was the first encampment of the host of Fëanor on its return to Middle-earth, and here was fought Dagor-nuin-Giliath. Later the host of Fingolfin settled along the northern shore, while the sons of Fëanor moved to the southern shore before taking up their permanent abodes in East Beleriand. (S 106, 109, 119; B 123, 127, 128, 140)

LAKE NENUIAL Nenuial (q.v.). (S 290; B 360)

LAKE NÚRNEN Núrnen (q.v.). (III 246)

LAKE-TOWN Esgaroth (q.v.). (H 172)

LALAITH (S.: 'laughter') (b. and d. between FA 466 and 472) Adan of the Third House, elder daughter of Húrin and Morwen and sister of Túrin. She died of plague when she was three years old. (S 198; B 242)

LAMBE (Q.: 'tongue') Name for the tengwa ⲧ (number 27), which seems to have had the value *1* in almost all systems. (III 500)

LAMEDON (S.)   Area in Gondor around the headwaters of the Ciril. The chief town of Lamedon seems to have been Calembel. Lamedon was probably a fief. (III 14, 50, 75)

LAMMOTH (S.: 'tongue-host'?)   Wasteland north of Drengist between Ered Lómin and the Sea. Ungoliant and Morgoth fought over the Silmarils here, and in his distress Morgoth let out a great cry, summoning the Balrogs to his aid. Ever after the echoes of his voice remained there, and any loud noise aroused them. The host of Fëanor landed here on its return to Middle-earth.
Also called the Great Echo. (S 80-81, 106; B 89-90, 123)

LAMPS OF THE VALAR   The two great globes, Illuin and Ormal (qq.v.), made by the Valar to light the Earth in the Spring of Arda. The Lamps were wrought by Aulë, filled with light by Varda and hallowed by Manwë, and were set atop great pillars of stone. The Lamps were destroyed by Melkor, an act which marked the end of the Spring. (S 35-37; B 30-31)

LAMPWRIGHTS' STREET   Rath Celerdain (q.v.). (III 46)

LAND OF AMAN   Aman (q.v.). (S 37; B 32)

LAND OF SHADOW   Mordor (q.v.). (I 526)

LAND OF THE DEAD THAT LIVE   Dor Firn-i-Guinar (q.v.) (S 188, 235; B 229, 291)

LAND OF THE ELVES   Beleriand (q.v.). (II 422)

LAND OF THE STAR   Númenor (q.v.). (III 407)

LANDROVAL (S.) (fl. WR) Eagle of the Misty Mountains, brother of Gwaihir. He was one of the Eagles that rescued Frodo and Sam from the slopes of Orodruin. (III 278, 280-82)

LANGSTRAND Anfalas (q.v.). (I 16)

LANTHIR LAMATH (S.: 'fall of echoing voices') Waterfall in Ossiriand, located beside the house of Dior, perhaps in Dor Firn-i-Guinar.
For the name, cf. lasselanta and Lammoth. (S 235, 337; B 290, 291, 420)

LARGO BAGGINS (TA 2820-2912) Hobbit of the Shire, third son and fourth child of Balbo Baggins. Largo married Tanta Hornblower; they had one child, Fosco. (III 474)

LASSELANTA (Q.: 'leaf-fall') Another name for quellë (q.v.).
Also spelled lasse-lanta. (III 480, 485)

LASSEMISTA (Q.: 'leaf—') Rowan-tree of Fangorn, cut down by Orcs of Isengard. (II 110)

LAST ALLIANCE OF ELVES AND MEN Alliance made between Elendil and Gil-galad in SA 3430 to defeat Sauron. In 3434 the army of the Last Alliance, after the Host of Valinor the largest and most splendid army ever seen in Middle-earth, marched south, won the Battle of Dagorlad, and besieged the Barad-dûr. In 3441, in a battle on the slopes of Orodruin, Sauron was overthrown, but both Gil-galad and Elendil were slain. (I 319; III 454-55; S 293-94; B 364-65)

LAST BATTLE The conflict which is to take place at the End of days, probably the ultimate and complete defeat of Darkness in Eä. (S 44, 48, 279; B 42, 47, 345)

LAST BRIDGE The Bridge of Mitheithel (q.v.). (I 268, 269)

LAST DESERT A probably imaginary place mentioned by Bilbo. According to him, it was very far in the east and contained wild Were-worms. (H 31)

LAST HOMELY HOUSE EAST OF THE SEA The house of Elrond in Rivendell, so called because it was the easternmost true house of the Eldar in Middle-earth.

Called for short the Last Homely House. Also called the house of Elrond. (I 296-97 ff.; H 60)

LAST MOUNTAIN Methedras (q.v.). (II 92)

LAST RIDING OF THE KEEPERS OF THE RINGS Procession from Rivendell to the Grey Havens in September, TA 3021. The company was composed of Galadriel, Elrond, Bilbo, and many Elves, including Gildor. Frodo and Sam joined the Last Riding in the Green Hills, and Gandalf at the Havens. All the riders, except Sam, then sailed over Sea. (III 381-84, 470; S 304; B 378)

LAST SHIP, THE A Shire-poem of the Fourth Age, ultimately derived from Gondor. (TB 8, 61-64)

LAST SHORE The shore of Eldamar; a general term for the Undying Lands. (III 289; TB 63)

LATER AGES The ages of Middle-earth after the Third Age. (S 20; B 9)

LAURA BAGGINS (fl. TA 29th Cent.) Hobbit of the Shire, wife of Mungo Baggins. She was born a Grubb. (III 474)

LAURELIN (Q.: 'gold-song') The younger of the Two Trees of Valinor (q.v.). Her leaves were light green and edged with gold, her horn-shaped flowers bright yellow, and her dew a golden rain.

Also called Culúrien, Malinalda, the Golden Tree, the Tree of Gold, and other names. (III 388; S 38-39, 99, 338, 361; B 33-34, 114, 420, 452)

LAURELINDÓRINAN (Q.: 'gold-song-land-valley') The Land of the Valley of Singing Gold, the original name of Galadriel's Lórien (q.v.). (II 88)

LAY OF EÄRENDIL The song of the life and voyages of Eärendil, of which Bilbo's version was no doubt a pale shadow. (S 246; B 304)

LAY OF LEITHIAN The account of the love and adventures of Beren and Lúthien, the second longest of the songs recounting the history of Beleriand. The song of Aragorn on I 258-60 is probably not a part of the Lay.

Also called Release from Bondage, which may be a translation of Leithian, and perhaps the Lay of Lúthien. (S 162, 186, 358; B 195, 226, 449)

LAY OF LÚTHIEN Perhaps the Lay of Leithian, perhaps the song translated by Aragorn on I 258-60. (III 421)

LAY OF NIMRODEL One of many Silvan Elvish and Mannish songs about Nimrodel and Amroth, and of Lórien in its early days. (I 440-42; III 119)

LEAF Pipe-weed (q.v.). (I 24)

LEAFLOCK Finglas (q.v.). (II 98)

LEAP OF BEREN One of the great feats of the First Age. When Beren and Lúthien were assailed by Celegorm and Curufin on horseback, Curufin seized Lúthien and rode ahead of Beren, while Celegorm tried to ride Beren down. Beren leaped out of the way and forward onto Curufin's galloping horse, where he seized Curufin and threw him to the ground. (S 177; B 214)

LEBENNIN (S.) Area of Gondor, roughly those lands watered by the Gilrain, Serni, Celos, Sirith, and Erui. The inhabitants of Lebennin were of mixed Dúnadan and lesser blood. (III 14-15, 23)

LEBETHRON (S.) Tree of Gondor, growing probably in the Ered Nimrais, much liked by the woodwrights of Gondor. Its wood, or at least the wood of one variety of lebethron, was black. The staffs Faramir gave to Frodo and Sam were made of lebethron, as was the casket in which the Silver Crown was kept. (II 384-85; III 302)

LEFNUI (S.) River in western Gondor, flowing from its source in the western Ered Nimrais south and west into the Sea. (I 16)

LEGOLAS (S.: 'green-leaf') (fl. TA) Sindarin Elf of the Woodland Realm, son of Thranduil. In TA 3019 Legolas went to Rivendell as a messenger and took part in the Council of Elrond. He then became one of the Companions of the Ring, representing the Elves. In Lórien Legolas became very friendly with Gimli, a friendship which was maintained for the rest of their lives. After the breaking of the Fellowship, Legolas went with Aragorn and Gimli in search of Merry and Pippin, and fought in the Battle of the Hornburg. He was one of the Grey Company, and fought in the Battle of the Pelennor Fields. While in southern Gondor Legolas for the first time saw the Sea, and the Eldarin yearning for Eldamar was awakened in him.

After the WR Legolas led a number of Elves of the Woodland Realm to Ithilien, where they beautified the war-ravaged land. In FO 120, after the death of Elessar, Legolas finally sailed over Sea, taking Gimli with him. (I 315, 361, 366, 381-82, 462, 464-65, 481, 501; II 136; III 183, 185, 451)

LEGOLIN (S.) One of the seven rivers of Ossiriand, flowing from the Ered Luin westward into Gelion. (S 123; B 147)

LEMBAS (S.: 'way-bread') The waybread of the Elves, formed into thin cakes, each of which was enough for a day's journey. Lembas remained fresh for many days if kept unbroken in its leaf wrapping. Unlike cram, lembas was tasty.

The name derives from early Elvish *lenn* 'journey' and *mbass* 'bread.' Called in Quenya coimas. (I 478, 502; II 35, 117, 289-90; III 233; RHM III 438; S 202, 338; B 247, 421)

LENWË (Q.) (FA)   Elda of the Teleri. During the Great Journey he marched with the host of Olwë, but when he reached the Anduin he led part of the host, the Nandor, downstream. Lenwë's son Denethor later led the Nandor to Ossiriand; perhaps Lenwë died in the Vales of Anduin or in Eriador. (S 54, 94; B 55-56, 107-08)

LÉOD (TA 2459-2501)   Man, Lord of Eothéod, father of Eorl. A great horse-tamer, Léod was killed when he tried to master Felaróf. (III 429, 430)

LÉOFA   Brytta (q.v.). (III 435)

LHÛN (S.)   River in western Middle-earth, in the Second and Third Ages flowing south from the northern Ered Luin into the Gulf of Lhûn, and forming the boundary between Arnor and the Elvish and Dwarvish lands to the west. The Lhûn drained all the land between the Ered Luin and the Hills of Evendim.
Called in Westron the Lune. (I 16; III 396, 515; S 281; B 348)

LIDLESS EYE   The Eye (q.v.). (III 117)

LIGHT   The opposite of Darkness or Shadow (qq.v.), the presence of Ilúvatar, the acceptance of his will or the beauty of his creation, especially the Two Trees. (III 284; S 31, 76, 78, 83, 141; B 25, 84, 86, 92-93, 169)

LIGHT-ELVES   One of the Three Kindreds of the Eldar, almost certainly the Vanyar (q.v.), who dwelt in Valinor in the Light of Aman. (H 164)

LIGHTFOOT (fl. TA 3000)   Meara of Rohan, sire of Snowmane. (III 146)

LIGHT OF AMAN   The light of the Two Trees, the closest semblance of the Light (q.v.) of Ilúvatar which the Eldar could see.

Also called the Light of Valinor. (S 79, 127, 149; B 88, 152, 179)

LIGHT OF VALINOR   The Light of Aman (q.v.). (S 79; B 88)

LILY COTTON   (fl. WR)   Hobbit of the Shire, wife of Tolman Cotton and mother of five children. She was born a Brown. (III 355, 477)

LILY GOODBODY   (TA 2822-2912)   Hobbit of the Shire, youngest child of Balbo Baggins. She married Togo Goodbody. (III 474)

LIMLIGHT   River flowing from its source in Fangorn Forest into Anduin. At the time of the WR it marked the northern boundary of Rohan. (I 17, 493)

LINAEWEN   (S.: 'lake of birds')   Lake in the middle of the Marshes of Nevrast, the home of many waterfowl. (S 119, 361; B 141, 452)

LINDA PROUDFOOT   (TA 2862-2963)   Hobbit of the Shire, fourth child and second daughter of Mungo Baggins. She married Bodo Proudfoot and bore him at least one child. (III 474)

LINDAR   (Q.: 'singers')   The name of the Teleri (q.v.) for themselves. (S 350; B 437)

LINDIR   (S.: 'song—')   (fl. WR)   Elf of Rivendell. (I 311)

LINDON   (Q.?: 'song—')   In the First Age, the name given to Ossiriand (q.v.) by the Noldor because of the singing of the Laiquendi who dwelt there.

After the Great Battle Lindon (including parts of Ossiriand and Thargelion) comprised the only surviving portion of Beleriand, and thus included all the lands west of the Ered Luin. As a remnant of Beleriand it was dear to the Eldar; in the Second Age the realm of Gil-galad was here, as well as the Grey Havens of Círdan.

In SA 1700 Gil-galad, fearing attack from Sauron during the War of the Elves and Sauron, appealed to Númenor for aid, and Tar-Minastir sent a fleet to Lindon, which enabled Gil-galad to drive Sauron out of Eriador. At the end of the Second Age, Gil-galad led the forces of Lindon in the army of the Last Alliance. During the Third Age Círdan aided the Dúnedain of Arnor as best he could in the wars against Angmar, especially in the Battle of Fornost. Lindon, or at least the Grey Havens, was probably the last dwelling of the Eldar in Middle-earth.

Lindon was divided by the Gulf of Lhûn into Forlindon and Harlindon (qq.v.). (III 383-84, 396, 452, 453, 454; S 123, 285-86, 289; B 147, 354, 359)

LINDÓRIË (Q.) (fl. SA 31st Cent.) Dúnadan of Númenor, sister of Eärendur, Lord of Andúnië, and mother of Inzilbêth. (S 268; B 331)

LINE OF ANÁRION The line of the Kings of Gondor (q.v.). (III 404)

LINE OF ISILDUR The royal family of the North-kingdom, whose heirs were the Kings of Arnor, Arthedain, and the Reunited Kingdom, as well as Chieftains of the Dúnedain of the North. Cadet branches of the family were the Kings of Cardolan and Rhudaur. (III 396)

LINHIR (S.) Town in Lebennin, Gondor, above the mouth of the Gilrain. During the WR, a battle was fought here between the men of Lamedon and the Corsairs; the battle ended when both sides fled at the approach of the Dead Men of Dunharrow. (III 184-85)

LINNOD (S.: 'song') Elvish literary form, a dualistically balanced type of aphorism with some playing on words. The line was composed of two parts, each of which was composed of a dactyl and two trochees.

It is possible that linnod referred only to the meter of the line, and not to the use to which it was put. (III 426)

LITHE The name used in Bree for Forelithe (q.v.). (III 483)

LITHE, THE or **THE LITHEDAYS** The name used in the Shire to refer to the three days between Forelithe and Afterlithe, which were 1 Lithe, Midyear's Day, and 2 Lithe. In leap years, there were four Lithedays, including Overlithe.

Called in Bree the Summerdays. (III 478, 481-82; L 199)

LITHLAD (S.: 'ash-plain') One of the great plains of Mordor, located either in the southwest or in the east. (II 308)

LITTLE DELVING Village in the northwest part of the Westfarthing of the Shire. (I 40)

LITTLE GELION The smaller of the two branches of the River Gelion, rising near Himring and meandering southeast. (S 123; B 146)

LITTLE KINGDOM Arda (q.v.). (S 35; B 29)

LITTLE PEOPLE Hobbits (q.v.) (III 380; S 303; B 376)

LOA (Q.: 'growth') The nature-year of the Eldar in Middle-earth, divided into six seasons. The method of division varied, but the only one recorded in *LotR* is that of the Calendar of Imladris (q.v.).

Loa was probably also the name used for the year of the various Dúnadan calendar systems. (III 480)

LOBELIA SACKVILLE-BAGGINS (b. before TA 2920,

d. TA 3020) Hobbit of the Shire, wife of Otho Sackville-Baggins and mother of Lotho. She was born in Hardbottle and was a Bracegirdle. Known for her shrewish temper and grasping ways, Lobelia tried for most of her life to gain possession of Bag End from Bilbo and Frodo by one means or another, until finally in TA 3018 Frodo sold it to her when he left the Shire. During Saruman's control of the Shire, Lobelia was imprisoned in the Lockhole for arguing with some of the Chief's Men. On her release she was popular for the first time in her life, but being crushed by her son's death, she returned to her family in Hardbottle and gave Bag End back to Frodo. When she died, she left her money to Frodo to be used to aid Hobbits made homeless by her son and Saruman. (I 52, 64, 66-67, 101, 103-04; III 361-62, 372, 474)

LOCKHOLES The Shire's prison, located in Michel Delving. During Saruman's control of the Shire many dissident Hobbits were kept here, but in more normal times the Lockholes seems to have been used more to store goods than people. (III 348, 356, 372; TB 42; L 189)

LOEG NINGLORON (S.: 'pools of golden water-flowers') The Gladden Fields (q.v.). (S 295, 338; B 366, 421)

LOËNDË (Q.: 'year-middle-day') Midyear's Day, in the Kings' and Stewards' Reckonings coming between Nárië and Cermië and thus corresponding roughly to Midsummer's Day. In the New Reckoning Loëndë was the second of the three enderi coming between Yavannië and Narquelië, since the loa began in the spring. (III 481, 486)

LÓMELINDI (Q.: 'dusk-singers,' sing, *lómelindë*) Nightingales, which always accompany Melian.
Also called dúlin and tinúviel in Sindarin and tindómerel in Quenya (all singular). (S 55, 165, 338, 358, 365; B 57, 199, 421, 449, 457)

LÓMION (Q.: 'of the twilight') The secret name given to Maeglin by his mother, Aredhel. (S 133; B 159)

LOND DAER (S.: 'shadow haven'?) Harbor in Eriador at the mouth of the River Gwathlo, deserted and in ruins at the time of the WR. (PB)

LONE-LANDS Name given to the lands between Bree (or perhaps the Forsaken Inn) and Rivendell. (H 43)

LONELY ISLE Tol Eressëa (q.v.). (S 59; B 62)

LONELY MOUNTAIN Erebor (q.v.). (I 366)

LONELY TROLL A troll, a chief character in the poem *Perry-the-Winkle*. He was well-behaved but friendless, and was an excellent baker. He was probably fictitious. (TB 41-44)

LONGBEARDS Durin's Folk (q.v.). (III 438; H 62)

LONGBOTTOM Village in the Southfarthing, home of a family of Hornblowers. About TA 2670, Tobold Hornblower grew pipe-weed for the first time in the Shire in Longbottom. (I 28)

LONGBOTTOM LEAF A variety of pipe-weed (q.v.). (I 28; II 213)

LONG CLEEVE Village in the Shire, home of the North-tooks. Long Cleeve was probably in the Northfarthing. (III 471, 475)

LONGHOLES Surname used by Hobbits of Bree, and perhaps also of the Shire. (I 212)

LONG LAKE An oval-shaped lake east of Mirkwood near Erebor, fed by the Forest River and the River Running. The latter flowed out of the Long Lake over a waterfall at its southern end.
Esgaroth was built on the Long Lake. (H 184-85, 194)

LONG LIST OF THE ENTS A lore-song of the Ents in

which was listed every variety of living creature. Since the Ents probably would not have made the descriptions quite so brief, the Long List may originally have been Elvish. (II 84-85, 244)

LONG MARSHES Marshes along the Forest River east of Mirkwood. At the time of the expedition of Thorin and Company (TA 2941) the marshes were spreading. (H 138, 183, 184)

LONG NIGHT The period between the poisoning of the Two Trees and the first rising of the Moon and Sun, when Valinor was in darkness. (S 101; B 116)

LONGO BAGGINS (TA 2860-2950) Hobbit of the Shire, second son and third child of Mungo Baggins. He married Camellia Sackville and was the father of Otho Sackville-Baggins. (III 474)

LONG PEACE The golden age of the Noldor in Beleriand, when Morgoth did not try to break the Siege of Angband and the Eldar enjoyed nearly two hundred years of peace. The Long Peace began with the defeat of the immature Glaurung c. FA 260 and ended with the fires of Dagor Bragollach in 455. During this time the Edain came to Beleriand and the Eldar prospered, but they made no attempt to overcome Morgoth or prevent him from building his armies. (S 117, 140; B 137, 167)

LONG WINTER The winter of TA 2758-59, during which Eriador and Rohan were snowbound for as much as five months. In Rohan, Helm was besieged in Helm's Deep by the Dunlendings, and both sides suffered greatly. In the Shire, great losses were averted through the aid of Gandalf, but famine was elsewhere widespread.

In the Shire this winter and its aftermath were referred to as the Days of Dearth. (I 24; III 432-33, 460)

LÓNI (d. TA 2994) Dwarf of Erebor. He went to Khazad-dûm with Balin in 2989, and was slain by Orcs while defending Durin's Bridge and the Second Hall. (I 419)

LORD OF BALROGS Gothmog (q.v.). (S 193; B 236)

LORD OF BELERIAND The title claimed by Elwë (q.v.) as overlord of the Sindar. (S 111, 233; B 130, 288)

LORD OF MORGUL The Lord of the Nazgûl (q.v.). (S 303; B 377)

LORD OF THE DARK Melkor (q.v.). (S 144; B 173)

LORD OF THE EAGLES Gwaihir (q.v.). (H 107)

LORD OF THE EARTH Title claimed by Sauron (q.v.) during the Dark Years, the time of his greatest power. (S 289; B 358)

LORD OF THE GLITTERING CAVES Title of Gimli and the succeeding lords of Aglarond in the Fourth Age. (III 451)

LORD OF THE NAZGÛL (SA c. 1600-TA 3019) The chief Nazgûl (q.v.), the mightiest of Sauron's servants. Originally a king and sorcerer, he was enslaved by Sauron when he received the greatest of the Nine Rings. His fortunes rose and fell with Sauron's through the Second Age. With the other Nazgûl, he arose again about TA 1300. Disguising himself, he formed the evil realm of Angmar and became its Witch-king, seeking to destroy the already weakened Dúnedain of Arnor. As the Witch-king of Angmar, he directed the wars against the North-kingdom until 1975, when, after finally crushing Arthedain, his forces were routed by armies led by Círdan, Glorfindel, and Eärnur of Gondor in the Battle of Fornost.

After the battle, the Lord of the Nazgûl disappeared from the North, but soon after, in 2000, he and other Nazgûl attacked Minas Ithil and took it after a two-year siege. The Nazgûl-lord renamed the city Minas Morgul and became its lord. In 2043 and 2050 he challenged Eärnur, now King of Gondor, to single combat because the latter, owing to the terror of his horse, had not faced him during the Battle of Fornost. In 2050 Eärnur accepted the challenge and was slain, probably treacherously.

During the WR the Nazgûl-lord led the search for Frodo during the latter's journey to Rivendell, and seriously wounded him at Weathertop. He led the army that attacked Minas Tirith in the Siege of Gondor, and broke the gates of the city. He was prevented from entering the city by the arrival of the Rohirrim. Although he killed King Théoden in the Battle of the Pelennor Fields, he was in turn slain by Eowyn and Merry Brandybuck, fulfilling Glorfindel's prophecy at the Battle of Fornost that he was not to fall by the hand of Man.

The Lord of the Nazgûl was taller than the other Nazgûl and wore a crown; his fear and power were also greater than theirs. All blades that touched him perished, and only blades with special spells could harm him.

He was called the Lord of the Nine Riders and the King of the Nine Riders; the Wraith-lord and the Wraith-king; the Morgul-lord, the Morgul-king, the King of Minas Morgul, and the Lord of Morgul; the Black Captain, the Captain of Despair, and the Captain of Sauron (as head of the army of Minas Morgul during the WR); the Black Rider, the Black Shadow, the Dwimmerlaik (by Eowyn), and the High Nazgûl (by Orcs of Minas Morgul). His real name is not given. (I 263, 337; II 400-01; III 112, 124-26, 139-43, 146, 397, 412, 413, 437; S 303; B 377)

LORD OF THE NINE RIDERS The Lord of the Nazgûl (q.v.). (II 40)

LORD OF THE RING, LORD OF THE RINGS Sauron (q.v.). (I title page, 298)

LORD OF THE WESTERN LANDS A title of the Kings of the Reunited Kingdom, who were kings of Arnor and Gondor and overlords of such realms as Erebor and Dale. (III 284)

LORD OF THE WHITE TREE Title of the Kings of Gondor (q.v.). (III 188)

LORD OF WATERS Ulmo (q.v.). (S 26, 240; B 19, 296-97)

LORDS The Valar (q.v.). (S 74; B 81)

LORDS OF ANDÚNIË Dúnedain, chief counsellors of the Kings of Númenor and (toward the end of the kingdom) leaders of the Faithful. The Lords of Andúnië were the heirs of Silmariën, eldest child of Tar-Elendil. The last Lord of Andúnië was Amandil, father of Elendil the Tall.

The heirlooms of the Lords of Andúnië were the ring of Barahir and the palantíri. The symbol of their authority was a silver sceptre, which later became known as the sceptre of Annúminas. (III 391, 393, 401; S 268; B 331)

LORDS OF NÚMENOR The Kings of Númenor, or perhaps the major nobility of the realm. (S 266; B 328)

LORDS OF THE CITY The Ruling Stewards (q.v.) of Gondor. (S 297; B 369)

LORDS OF THE SEA The beings who taught shipbuilding to the Teleri of Alqualondë: Ossë (who apparently taught the craft to the Falathrim) and perhaps Ulmo and Uinen. (S 86; B 97)

LORDS OF THE SEA The Dúnedain of Númenor in the days of its power. (S 267; B 330)

LORDS OF THE VALAR The seven male Valar (q.v.). (S 25; B 18)

LORDS OF THE WEST The Valar (q.v.). (III 392; S 248; B 307)

LORDS OF VALINOR The Valar (q.v.). (S 262; B 323)

LÓRELLIN (Q.: 'dream—') Lake in Valinor, in which lies the island where Estë sleeps. Lórellin is probably located in Lórien. (S 28; B 21)

LORGAN (fl. FA 489) Man, chief of the Easterlings of Hithlum. Lorgan enslaved Tuor and later put a price on his head. (S 238; B 294)

LÓRIEN (Q.: 'dream-land') The more common name of Irmo, one of the Lords of the Valar. Lórien is one of the Fëanturi, brother of Mandos and Nienna; his spouse is Estë. He is the master of visions and dreams, and with Estë he provides rest and recovery to the Valar and Eldar. His dwelling is in the gardens of Lórien (q.v.), whence his name. (S 25, 28, 63, 100; B 18, 21, 68, 115)

LÓRIEN The dwelling of Irmo and Estë in Valinor, the place of repose for the Valar and Eldar. The gardens of Lórien are the most beautiful in Arda, and the waters of its fountains refresh the inhabitants of Valinor. Lórien contains lakes, many flowers, and silver willows; it is a place of soft beauty, and its dominant color seems to be silver. (S 28, 30, 64, 99, 234; B 21, 24, 68, 114, 289)

LÓRIEN (S., from Silvan) Elven realm west of Anduin, at the meeting of Celebrant and Anduin, ruled by Celeborn and Galadriel (qq.v.). The mellyrn woods of Lórien were protected from Sauron by the power of Galadriel, and here alone in Middle-earth was the true beauty and timelessness of Eldamar preserved.

Lórien was made and founded in the Second Age by Galadriel on the model of Doriath. Although most of its people were Silvan Elves, Sindarin was spoken in Lórien. In the Second and Third Ages, Lórien aided Elrond at need, especially in TA 1409, but otherwise Lórien remained isolated from the outside world. In 1981, as a result of the appearance of the Balrog in Khazad-dûm, many of the Elves of Lórien fled south, among them Amroth and Nimrodel. During the Quest of Mount Doom the Companions of the Ring rested in Lórien for a month; this was the first time a Dwarf had entered Lórien for many years. In the WR, Lórien was assaulted three times from Dol Guldur, but the attackers were defeated; after the downfall of Sauron the forces of Lórien, led by Celeborn, took Dol Guldur, and Galadriel destroyed its pits. With the passing of Galadriel over Sea at the end of the Third Age and Celeborn's removal to East Lórien, Lórien was largely deserted.

The capital and chief city of Lórien was Caras Galadon. The Elves of Lórien were known as the Galadrim.

The original name of Lórien was Laurelindórinan, which was later changed to Lothlórien. Also called the Golden Wood and the Hidden Land in Westron, and Dwimordene by the Rohirrim.

See also: Cerin Amroth, Egladil, the Naith, the Tongue. (I 434 ff.; II 88; III 428, 468-69, 506; S 298, 338; B 370, 421)

LÓRINDOL (S.: 'golden-head') Epithet applied to Hador for his golden hair. (S 147, 357; B 177, 448)

LOSGAR (S.) Place in Lammoth at the mouth of Drengist. The host of Fëanor landed at Losgar on its return to Middle-earth, and here the infamous burning of the ships occurred. (S 90; B 101)

LOSSARNACH (S.: 'snow' + *arnach*) Area of Gondor, comprising probably the mountain-valleys just southwest of Minas Tirith.

Also called Arnach. *Arnach* was a name of pre-Númenórean origin. (III 23, 152, 508)

LOSSOTH (S.: 'snow-people') Men dwelling in Forochel in the Third Age. Primitive and poor, they were the descendants of the Forodwaith of the First Age. In TA 1974 the Lossoth sheltered Arvedui and his men after the fall of Arthedain.

Called in Westron the Snowmen. (III 398-99; R 62)

LOST ISLE   Tol Eressëa (q.v.). (III 289)

LÓTESSE (Q.: 'blossom-month') The fifth month of the Kings' and Stewards' Reckonings, and the second of the New Reckoning, corresponding roughly to our May.

The Sindarin name, used only by the Dúnedain, was Lothron. Called Thrimidge in the Shire. (III 483)

LOTHÍRIEL (S.: 'blossom—female') (fl. WR) Dúnadan of Gondor, daughter of Imrahil. In TA 3020 she married King Eomer of Rohan. (III 438)

LOTHLANN (S.) A great plain of the First Age, bordered on the west by Ard-galen, on the south by the March of Maedhros, and on the north by the Ered Engrin. Bleak and uninhabited, Lothlann was patrolled by the cavalry of the House of Fëanor during the Siege of Angband. During Dagor Bragollach Lothlann was overrun by the forces of Morgoth, led by Glaurung. After this time the plain may have been considered part of Anfauglith. (S 123, 153; B 147, 184)

LOTHLÓRIEN (S.: 'blossom-dream-land') Lórien (q.v.).

The Westron equivalent was Dreamflower. (I 434)

LOTHO SACKVILLE-BAGGINS (TA 2964-3019) Hobbit of the Shire, son of Otho and Lobelia Sackville-Baggins, probably unmarried. In September, 3018, Lotho and his mother moved into Bag End after buying it from Frodo. Shortly afterward, using money obtained from Isengard and elsewhere from the sale of pipe-weed grown on his lands in the Southfarthing, he began buying up property and supporting outside Men, known as ruffians or the Chief's Men. Lotho then imprisoned Will Whitfoot, the Mayor, and naming himself Chief Shirriff, he took over the Shire, industrializing and regimenting its life. In September, 3019, with the arrival of Saruman, his power collapsed. Sometime in September or October he was slain, perhaps by Gríma, who may have eaten him.

Lotho was frequently called, at his own insistence, the Chief, which was short for Chief Shirriff. The Hobbits of the Shire called him Pimple or Little Pimple; he seems to have had a number of facial blemishes. (I 103; III 343, 360-61, 370, 474)

LOTHRON (S.: 'blossom—') Sindarin form of Lótessë, used only by the Dúnedain. (III 483)

LOUDWATER Bruinen (q.v.). (I 268)

LOWER HALLS The lower level of Erebor (q.v.), where Smaug collected his hoard. The Side-door led to the Lower Halls. (H 32, 205-06, 224-29)

LOWLAND OF THE YALE See: the Yale. (I 114)

LUGBÚRZ (B.S.: 'tower-dark') The Barad-dûr (q.v.). (II 61)

LUGDUSH (Orkish: 'tower—') (d. TA 3019) Uruk-hai of Isengard, a member of Uglúk's band. He was slain by Éomer's éored near Fangorn. (II 64)

LUINIL (Q.: 'blue—') A blue star, wrought by Varda from the dews of Telperion in preparation for the awakening of the Elves. (S 48; B 48)

LUMBAR (Q.) A star, wrought from the dews of Telperion by Varda in preparation for the awakening of the Elves. (S 48; B 48)

LUNE See: Lhûn, Gulf of Lhûn. (II 259; III 396)

LÚTHIEN (S.) (FA) Eldarin princess, daughter of Thingol and Melian, the most beautiful of the Children of

Ilúvatar. Born in Doriath at the end of the first age of the Chaining of Melkor, Lúthien spent long years dancing to the songs Daeron composed for her beauty, but she also learned, probably from Melian, the wisdom and power of her heritage.

In FA 465 Lúthien was seen by Beren in Neldoreth, and the next spring she gave her love to him and received his mortality and the anguish of his fate. Torn between love for Beren and obedience to her father, Lúthien decided on the former, and she aided Beren during his Quest of the Silmaril. Despite being betrayed to Thingol by Daeron and kidnapped by Curufin, Lúthien, accompanied by Huan, at length came to Tol-in-Gaurhoth, defeated Sauron, and freed Beren. Later she insisted on accompanying Beren to Angband, where her spells overcame Carcharoth and Morgoth. Lúthien healed Beren of the envenomed wound he received from Carcharoth and returned with him to Doriath.

When Beren was slain in the Hunting of the Wolf, Lúthien's spirit broke, and she came to Mandos in the Houses of the Dead. There she sang to him and moved him to pity, and Manwë offered her a new life. She chose a mortal life with Beren, and for about forty years the two lovers lived in Tol Galen. There Lúthien bore her only child, Dior, and there, wearing the Nauglamír containing the Silmaril, she was the greatest vision of beauty ever seen outside Valinor.

Lúthien's beauty was so great that it impelled many beings to love or lust, and in that impulse the integrity of Beren and Huan may be distinguished from the baseness of Daeron, Curufin, and Morgoth. Yet her beauty was not merely of form, for her singing could charm even Morgoth and Mandos, great among the Ainur, and the nobility of her spirit and of her lineage strengthened her spells so that she could enchant Sauron and even Morgoth.

Lúthien was called Tinúviel for the beauty of her singing; the name was first used by Beren. (I 258-61; III 388; S 91, 123, 148, 165-88, 198, 234-36, 306, 307; B 103, 147, 177, 199-229, 242, 289-92, 380, 381)

LÚVA (Q.: 'bow') One of the components of the primary letters of the Tengwar. The lúva could be open, as in tinco, or closed, as in parma, and could also be doubled and reversed. (III 495-96)

MABLUNG (S.: 'heavy hand') (d. c. FA 505) Sindarin Elf of Doriath, chief captain of Thingol. Mablung participated in many of the great deeds of Beleriand. He joined in the Hunting of the Wolf; he fought with the host of Fingon in the Union of Maedhros and the Nirnaeth Arnoediad; he was present at the tragic end of the lives of Nienor and Túrin. Mablung died defending the Nauglamír during the Dwarves' sack of Menegroth.

He was known as Mablung of the Heavy Hand. (S 113, 184, 185, 189, 200, 217-19, 225-26, 234, 339; B 133, 223, 225, 230, 244, 267-69, 277-78, 290, 422)

MABLUNG (fl. WR) Man of Gondor, a Ranger of Ithilien. He led the scouts of the Army of the West. (II 338; III 198)

MADOC BRANDYBUCK (TA 2775-2877) Hobbit of the Shire, son of Gormadoc Brandybuck, Master of Buckland (2836-77). Madoc married Hanna Goldworthy. He was known as "Proudneck." (III 476)

MAEDHROS (S.) (FA) Noldorin Elf, eldest son of Fëanor and the leader of the House in Middle-earth. Maedhros eagerly swore the Oath of Fëanor and returned to Middle-earth, but he was more temperate than his father and opposed the burning of the ships at Losgar. Soon after, Maedhros was captured by treachery and hung by his right wrist from the face of Thangorodrim. He was rescued by Thorondor and his old friend Fingon, but he lost his hand. In gratitude for this deed and in atonement for the burning of the ships, Maedhros gave the overlordship of the Noldor to the House of Fingolfin.

For many years Maedhros dwelt at Himring, guarding the March of Maedhros and curbing the arrogant pride of his brothers. A patient ruler and strong warrior, Maedhros led the eastern forces in the Wars of Beleriand, winning a great victory in Dagor Aglareb and regrouping the eastern Noldor at Himring after Dagor Bragollach. About 472 Maedhros, strengthened by the Easterlings of Bór and heartened by the triumphs of Beren and Lúthien, formed the Union of Maedhros to assault Angband. But the Union was betrayed by the Easterlings of Ulfang, and after the Nirnaeth Arnoediad Maedhros fled to Ossiriand or Amon Ereb.

After the death of Beren and Lúthien, the Oath of Fëanor overcame Maedhros, and he participated in the sacks of Doriath and the Havens of Sirion. Although he repented of his cruelties, he remained driven by the Oath. Finally, after the Great Battle, Maedhros persuaded Maglor to join him in stealing the Silmarils, and claimed one jewel as his own. Tormented by the pain of the jewel, which burned his hand, and by the knowledge of his moral decay, which had deprived him of his right to the Silmaril, Maedhros cast himself and the Silmaril into a fiery chasm.

Maedhros was tall and, after Maglor, the most temperate of the sons of Fëanor. But his spirit was fierce, especially after his torment on Thangorodrim, and the sword he wielded with his left hand, deadly. (S 60, 83, 90, 108, 110-11, 112, 115, 116, 119, 122, 124, 152-53, 157, 188-90, 192-93, 195, 236-37, 246-47, 250, 252-54, 305; B 63, 93, 101, 126, 129, 130, 131, 135, 136, 140, 146, 148, 183-84, 189, 229-31, 235, 239, 292, 305, 310, 313, 379)

MAEGLIN (S.: 'sharp-gleam') (d. FA 511) Elda of Beleriand, son of Eöl and Aredhel. Maeglin learned mining and forging from Eöl and the Dwarves, but his mother's tales of the Noldor awoke his pride and ambition. Realizing that he was the heir of Turgon, he persuaded Aredhel to leave Eöl and go with him to Gondolin.

In Gondolin Maeglin won great favor for his knowledge of metals, and he prospered there, save for his dark and incestuous desire for Idril. Captured by Orcs while on a secret prospecting trip outside Gondolin, Maeglin agreed to betray the realm, for his integrity was weakened by his unreturned love for Idril and his jealous hatred of Tuor. During the attack on Gondolin Maeglin seized Idril and Eärendil, but Tuor threw him from the Caragdûr.

Although learned and valiant, perceptive and persuasive, Maeglin was taciturn and moody. Maeglin was the name given him by Eöl; Aredhel secretly called him Lómion. He bore the sword Anguirel, which he stole from Eöl. (S 92, 133-39, 159, 194, 202, 240, 241, 242-43, 305, 359, 361; B 104, 159-66, 192, 237, 247, 297, 298, 299-300, 379, 450, 453)

MAGGOT Family of Hobbits of the Shire, living in the Marish. At the time of the WR, Farmer Maggot, his wife, and their three daughters and two or more sons lived on a prosperous farm, Bamfurlong, famous for its mushrooms. Farmer Maggot was an important Hobbit in the area, and he and Tom Bombadil exchanged visits.

Farmer Maggot was called Muddy-feet in jest by Tom Bombadil. (I 132-40, 147, 184; TB 20-21)

MAGGOT'S LANE Road in the Marish going from Rushey to Bamfurlong. (TB 21)

MAGLOR (S.) (FA—?) Noldorin Elf, second son of Fëanor. He swore the Oath of Fëanor and joined the revolt of the Noldor. In Middle-earth he settled in Maglor's Gap, between Himring and the Ered Luin. When the Gap was overrun during Dagor Bragollach, Maglor fled to Maedhros on Himring. For the rest of the First Age Maglor accompanied his brother in war and peace; during the Nirnaeth Arnoediad he slew Uldor the Easterling, and after the sack of the Havens of Sirion he fostered Elrond and Elros. After the Great Battle Maglor tried to repudiate the Oath of Fëanor, but Maedhros persuaded him to steal the Silmarils. Burned by his jewel, he threw it into the Sea and wandered off, singing in pain and regret.

Maglor was apparently the most temperate of the sons of Fëanor; he was the only one to try to relinquish his claim to the Silmarils. He was (after Daeron) the greatest singer of the Eldar in Middle-earth; one of his compositions was the *Noldolantë*. (S 60, 83, 87, 115, 117, 124, 153, 157, 183, 193, 195, 236, 247, 250, 252-54, 305; B 63, 93, 98, 135, 138, 148, 184, 189, 223, 235, 238, 292, 305, 310, 313-14, 379)

MAGLOR'S GAP   Plain lying between Himring and the Ered Luin, the most difficult to defend of the northern entrances into Beleriand. Guarded by Maglor, the Gap was overrun twice, by Orcs during Dagor Aglareb and by Glaurung during Dagor Bragollach. (S 115, 124, 153; B 135, 148, 184)

MAGOR (FA 4th Cent.)   Adan of the Third House, son of Aradan and father of Hathol. (S 147; B 177)

MAHAL (Kh.?)   The name given Aulë (q.v.) by the Dwarves. (S 44; B 42)

MÁHANAXAR (Q.)   The place of council and judgment of the Valar, located near the gates of Valimar. The thrones of the Valar were set in a circle in Máhanaxar, which was either a hall or a court.
Also called the Ring of Doom. (S 38, 50, 70, 98; B 33, 50, 77, 112)

MAHTAN (Q.) (FA-   )   Noldorin Elf, father of Nerdanel. Mahtan was a great smith, a beloved pupil of Aulë. He taught his knowledge of crafting metal and stone to Fëanor, his daughter's husband. Mahtan probably did not join the revolt of the Noldor. (S 64, 69; B 69, 75)

MAIAR (Q.)   Those of the lesser Ainur (q.v.) who chose to enter Eä. The Maiar tended Arda under the direction of the Valar (q.v.), although some, notably Sauron and the Balrogs, were seduced from their allegiance by Melkor.
Although far more numerous than the Valar, only eight of the loyal Maiar are named: Ilmarë, Eönwë, Ossë, Uinen,

Melian, Olórin, Arien, and Tilion. The Istari may have been Maiar.

Also called the people of the Valar. The singular is *Maia*. (III 388; S 30-32, 55, 99, 234; B 24-26, 57, 114, 289)

MALACH The birth-name of Aradan (q.v.). (S 143; B 172)

MALBETH (S.: 'gold—') (fl. TA 20th Cent.) Dúnadan of Arthedain, seer and royal counsellor. Malbeth foretold the events of Arvedui's life and gave him his name. He also prophesied concerning the Paths of the Dead and the role of Isildur's Heir in the final battle with Sauron.

He was generally called Malbeth the Seer. (III 63-64, 410)

MALDUIN (S.: 'yellow or golden river') River in northern Beleriand, a tributary of the Teiglin. Malduin arose in the Ered Wethrin and flowed south, joining the Teiglin above the Crossings. (S 205; B 251)

MALINALDA (Q.: 'golden-tree') Laurelin (q.v.). (S 38; B 33)

MALLOR (S.: 'gold—') (d. TA 1110) Dúnadan, third King of Arthedain (1029-1110). (III 394)

MALLORN (S.: 'gold-tree,' plural *mellyrn*) The tree of Lórien, having grey or silver bark and golden blossoms. Its leaves turned to gold in the autumn and did not fall until the beginning of the spring. The trunk of the mallorn divided near the top into a crown, and here the Galadrim built their telain.

The second Party Tree was a mallorn; there were also mellyrn in Aman. (I 434, 443, 444, 448; II 117; III 375; S 62; B 64)

MALLOS (S.: 'gold-snow') Yellow flower growing in Lebennin. (III 185)

MALTA (Q.: 'gold') Name for the tengwa 𝕸 (number 18), which usually had the value *m*. (III 500)

MALVA BRANDYBUCK (fl. TA 2800) Hobbit of the Shire, wife of Gormadoc Brandybuck. She was born a Headstrong. (III 476)

MALVEGIL (S.: 'gold—') (d. TA 1349) Dúnadan, sixth King of Arthedain (1272-1349). (III 394)

MANDOS (Q.: 'prison-fortress') Ainu, one of the Fëanturi and of the Aratar, brother of Lórien and Nienna and spouse of Vairë. As a Vala, Mandos is the Doomsman of the Valar, keeping the Houses of the Dead, knowing all fates within the Great Music, and revealing those fates and judgments when Manwë wills it. Because his dooms are the awareness of the will of Ilúvatar as contained in the Great Music, Mandos is inflexible and dispassionate. Only once, when Lúthien sang to him, has he been moved to pity.
His real name is Námo. He dwells in Mandos, whence his more common name. (S 25, 28, 29, 65, 67, 70, 87-88, 98, 186-87, 249, 356, 362; B 18, 21, 22, 70, 73, 77, 98-99, 112, 227, 308, 446, 454)

MANDOS The dwelling of Námo, in western Valinor. Mandos contains the Houses of the Dead. (S 28, 52; B 21, 22, 52)

MAN IN THE MOON A character in the folk tales of the Shire and Gondor, perhaps reflecting some (but not much) knowledge of Tilion. (I 216-18; TB 8, 31-38)

MAN IN THE MOON CAME DOWN TOO SOON, THE A Shire-poem written in the Red Book of Westmarch in the Fourth Age, ultimately derived from Gondor. (TB 8, 34-38)

MAN IN THE MOON STAYED UP TOO LATE, THE

A poem written by Bilbo Baggins and recorded in the Red Book of Westmarch. (I 216-18; TB 7, 31-33)

MANKIND Men (q.v.). (S 148; B 178)

MANNISH General term referring to the languages of Men, especially the Men of the Vales of Anduin and others related to the Edain. Mannish tongues were the basis for the original language of the Hobbits, and of the outer names of the Dwarves of Erebor. Rohirric was a Mannish tongue.

In the First Age four Mannish languages are mentioned. Adûnaic derived from the speech of the Third House of the Edain, which was strongly influenced by Eldarin; the language of the First House was closely related. The Haladin and the Easterlings spoke distantly related languages. Since the first Men awoke in one place at the same time, all Mannish tongues are probably ultimately derived from one language.

In *LotR,* most Mannish forms have been translated into their Germanic, Old English, or Norse equivalents. (III 506, 509, 513, 517-18; S 142; B 170)

MANWË (Q.: 'good, pure') The noblest of the Ainur and the mightiest of the Aratar, the brother of Melkor and spouse of Varda. Manwë is the dearest of the Ainur to Ilúvatar and understands his will and thought best. During the Ainulindalë Manwë gave most attention to the ideas of air, wind, and clouds, and in Arda he is most concerned with these things, and with the birds that fly in the air.

Within Eä Manwë is the King of Arda and the lord of the Valar, ruling their councils, confirming their deeds, and hallowing their artifacts. His throne is set in Ilmarin atop Taniquetil, whence he looks out over the world.

Compassionate and wise, Manwë interceded to prevent the sundering of Elda-Adan lovers and attempted to avert the revolt of the Noldor and the downfall of Númenor. But he does not understand evil, and so he was deceived into unchaining Melkor, thus allowing the tragedy and glory of the wars of Elves and Men against the Darkness.

Manwë loves the Vanyar best among the Eldar, and he delights in poetry. The clothing and eyes of his fana are blue, and his sceptre is made of sapphire. His surname is Súlimo, Lord of the Breath of Arda. Also called the King of Arda, the Elder King, and the Lord of the West. (I 310; III 392; R 60, 61, 66; S 19, 20, 25, 26, 30, 31, 35, 37, 40, 65-66, 75, 76, 85, 98, 99, 110, 187, 244, 249, 260, 264, 361; B 9, 10, 18-19, 24, 25, 29, 32, 35, 70, 82, 83, 85, 95, 112, 113, 129, 227, 302-03, 308, 320, 326, 453)

MARACH (fl. FA 310)   Adan, first recorded chieftain of the Third House. He led his people into Beleriand and settled in Estolad. (S 142, 143, 308; B 170, 171, 382)

MARCHO (fl. TA 1601)   Fallohide Hobbit of Bree. In 1601, with his brother Blanco, he settled the Shire. (I 23)

MARCH OF MAEDHROS   The hills and plains between Dorthonion and the Ered Luin, separating East Beleriand from Lothlann. The March was settled and defended by Maedhros and the other sons of Fëanor; its chief fortress was at Himring. Frequently assaulted by the forces of Morgoth, the March was finally overrun after the Nirnaeth Arnoediad. (S 112, 123; B 131, 147)

MARDIL (Q.: 'friend of the house')   (d. TA 2080) Dúnadan, first Ruling Steward of Gondor (2050-80). He was Steward to King Eärnil and King Eärnur from 2029 to 2050, and in 2043 dissuaded Eärnur from accepting the challenge of the Lord of the Nazgûl. In 2050, however, he was unable to restrain the King, and on Eärnur's disappearance he was made ruler "until the return of the King" to prevent a civil war among the members of the royal family. A wise ruler, Mardil could claim among his accomplishments the institution of the Stewards' Reckoning.

Mardil was called Mardil Voronwë, the Steadfast, because of his faithfulness. (III 395, 413, 481; S 297, 356; B 369, 447)

MARIGOLD COTTON (b. TA 2983) Hobbit of the Shire, youngest child of Hamfast Gamgee. She married Tolman Cotton. (III 477)

MARISH Fertile, boggy area in the Eastfarthing between Stock and Rushey, home of the Oldbucks before the founding of Buckland. The people of the Marish, who were largely of Stoor blood, acknowledged the authority of the Master of Buckland. (I 26, 40, 128 ff., 142, 146)

MARK, THE Rohan (q.v.). (II 43)

MARMADAS BRANDYBUCK (b. TA 2943) Hobbit of the Shire, son of Gorbulas Brandybuck. He was a guest at the Farewell Party. (III 476)

MARMADOC BRANDYBUCK (TA 2817-2910) Hobbit of the Shire, son of Madoc Brandybuck, Master of Buckland (2877-2910). He married Adaldrida Bolger; they had four children.

Marmadoc was known as "Masterful." (III 476)

MAR-NU-FALMAR (Q.: 'home-beneath-waves') Name given to Númenor (q.v.) after its destruction. (S 281; B 347)

MARRING OF ARDA The ruin of the order and beauty of Arda as conceived in the Great Music by the malice of Melkor. (S 79, 255; B 87, 316)

MARROC BRANDYBUCK (b. c. TA 2780) Hobbit of the Shire, youngest son of Gormadoc Brandybuck. (III 476)

MARSHES OF NEVRAST Broad marshes around the shores of Linaewen in central Nevrast. (S 115, Map; B 135, map xiv-xv)

MASTER Sauron (q.v.). (H 87)

MASTER OF BUCKLAND   The head of the Brandy-buck family. The authority of the Master was acknowledged in the Marish as well as in Buckland, but his rule was largely nominal. In FO 12 the Master of Buckland, who at that time was Meriadoc Brandybuck, was made a Counsellor of the North-kingdom.

The Masters of Buckland had attributive titles added to their names, probably by the chroniclers.

Also called the Master of the Hall, since the Master of Buckland lived in Brandy Hall. (I 142; III 471, 476)

MASTER OF ESGAROTH   The ruler of Esgaroth, seemingly elected by the merchants of the town. The office was not hereditary. At the time of the expedition of Thorin and Company (TA 2941), the Master was greedy and selfish, and was not much good in an emergency. After the fall of Smaug, he absconded with the money given him by Bard for the repair of Esgaroth, and later died in the Waste. The Master who followed him was wiser, and in his day, thanks to the refounding of Dale and Erebor, Esgaroth was very prosperous. (H 180-90, 193, 236, 238-40, 286)

MASTER OF LIES   Epithet of Melkor (q.v.), given him by Amlach the Adan. (S 145; B 174)

MASTER OF THE HALL   The Master of Buckland (q.v.). (I 142)

MASTER-STONE   The chief palantír (q.v.), not given to Amandil with the Seven Stones. The Master-stone was kept in the Tower of Avallónë. (S 292; B 362)

MAT HEATHERTOES (d. TA 3019)   Man of Bree, killed in a fight between Bree-landers and Bill Ferny and his friends. (III 335, 517)

MATHOM-HOUSE   The museum in Michel Delving, a repository of arms and other mathoms. Bilbo lent his mithril-mail to the Mathom-house, but reclaimed it before leaving the Shire in TA 3001. (I 25; H 285)

MATTA Genuine Hobbitish personal name, usually shortened to Mat. (III 517)

MAUHÚR (B. S.) (d. TA 3019) Orc of Isengard, probably an Uruk. During the WR he led a band of Orcs which unsuccessfully tried to break the ring of Rohirrim surrounding Uglúk's Orc-band. (II 72, 75-76)

MAY GAMGEE (b. TA 2928) Hobbit of the Shire, third child and first daughter of Hobson Gamgee. (III 477)

MAY GAMGEE (b. TA 2976) Hobbit of the Shire, fourth child and second daughter of Hamfast Gamgee. (III 477)

MAYOR OF MICHEL DELVING The only real official in the Shire at the time of the WR, elected every seven years at the Free Fair. The Mayor seems to have been chosen from among popular and responsible members of the working class. As First Shirriff and Postmaster, he was in charge of the Watch and the Messenger Service. However, his most important duty was to preside at banquets. In FO 14 the Mayor, who at that time was Sam Gamgee, was made a Counsellor of the North-kingdom.

The only Mayors mentioned in *LotR* are Will Whitfoot (TA 3013 or earlier-FO 7) and Sam Gamgee (FO 7-56). Frodo Baggins was Deputy Mayor in 3019-20.

Also called the Mayor of the Shire. (I 31; III 372-73, 471)

MEARAS (tr. Roh.) Horses of Rohan, Felaróf and his descendants. Except for Shadowfax, the mearas would allow none but the King of the Mark or his sons to ride them. It was believed that Oromë brought the first meara to Middle-earth from Valinor, such was their beauty and strength.

The mearas were the greatest horses of Rohan, and thus of the world, being extremely strong, swift, and intelligent. They were white or grey and lived about eighty years. (II 46, 137; III 431)

MEDE Name given Afterlithe (q.v.) in Bree. (III 483)

MEDUSELD The palace of the Kings of the Mark, in Edoras, built by King Brego in TA 2569. Its roof was made of gold. Also called the Golden Hall. (II 50, 141, 145 ff.; III 84, 314, 432, 459)

MEE A young Elven-princess in the Hobbit nonsense-poem *Princess Mee*. Any resemblance to historical personages is probably coincidental. (TB 28-30)

MELIAN (Q.: 'love-gift') Maia. In Valinor she served Vána and Estë, and tended the flowering trees of Lórien. Early in the First Age she encountered Elwë in Beleriand and for his love took on a human form. Together with him she founded the kingdom of Doriath, which she enhanced by her power and beauty and protected with her wisdom and the Girdle of Melian (q.v.). She bore Elwë one child, Lúthien.

For many years Melian remained in the enchanted forests of Doriath, counseling Elwë to caution and security and instructing Lúthien and, after the return of the Noldor, Galadriel. But finally, as she had foreseen, the doom of Doriath approached. Melian was separated from Lúthien until the End, and when Elwë was slain in Menegroth Melian withdrew her power from Doriath, abandoned her body, and returned to Lórien.

Melian was both beautiful and wise. Her singing was exquisite, and she was always accompanied by nightingales, whom she taught to sing. Skilled in enchantment, she had the power to foil the searching thought of Morgoth. She was also compassionate and aided the Edain, especially Túrin.

The full Quenya form of her name was Melyanna. (III 388; S 30, 55-56, 58, 91-97 passim, 122, 126-28, 144, 162, 167-68, 183, 188, 189, 202, 205, 227, 233-34, 306, 356, 361; B 24, 57-58, 61, 103-11 passim, 145, 151-53, 172, 195, 202-03, 223, 229, 230, 247, 251, 280, 288-89, 380, 446, 453)

MELILOT BRANDYBUCK (b. TA 2985) Hobbit of the Shire, younger daughter of Marmadas Brandybuck. She was a guest at the Farewell Party. (I 54; III 476)

MELKOR (Q.: 'He who arises in Might') Ainu, given by Ilúvatar greater power and knowledge than any other of his kindred. Wise in all things, Melkor was, like Aulë, especially gifted in the knowledge of substances and of crafts. Impatient with the slow designs of Ilúvatar, Melkor desired to bring things into Being himself, and he searched in the Void for the Flame Imperishable. On these solitary journeys he began to have thoughts different from those of his fellows. These thoughts caused the discord of the Ainulindalë, and Ilúvatar wrought the Vision and Eä to show Melkor and the other Ainur the ultimate source of all thoughts and all power.

Melkor was one of the Ainur who entered into Eä, but there his eagerness turned to jealousy and he was excluded from the numbers of the Valar. Desiring to dominate created things and the wills of others, Melkor in his envy and malice claimed Arda as his own and, foiled in this by Manwë, hindered its completion and corrupted many of the Maiar into serving him. In these struggles, the First War, Melkor assumed a fana of majesty and terror, dark and huge. At last Melkor was defeated by Tulkas, but Arda was Marred.

Soon after the Valar created the two Lamps, Melkor returned to Arda and secretly built the stronghold of Utumno in the far North. By now his desire had turned from Light to Darkness, and his ability to imagine and create new things had been reduced to deception and distortion, imitation and destruction. His chief weapons were cold and darkness. The Valar became aware of him by the blight that came over the Spring of Arda, but he forestalled their attack by destroying the Lamps. Melkor then retreated to Utumno, and while the Valar dwelt in the light of the Two Trees, he built Angband as a first defense against the Valar, forged weapons, bred monsters, and extended his dominion. When the Elves awoke he appeared among them as a dark Rider (seeking to make them fear Oromë and the Valar), and probably captured Elves and from them bred Orcs.

At last the Valar became concerned for the safety of the Elves, and in the Battle of the Powers Melkor was defeated and carried back to Valinor in chains. There he was imprisoned for three ages, but in Middle-earth his servants continued to labor.

At the end of the third age of his Chaining, Melkor put on a fair countenance and deceived Manwë into freeing him. Forced to remain in Valimar, Melkor grew covetous of the Silmarils and the light of the Two Trees. Fiercely jealous of the Elder Children of Ilúvatar, he kindled dissension within the House of Finwë, but he could not seduce Fëanor, although his lies did make the Noldo distrust the Valar. When Fëanor perceived his purposes Melkor fled from Valinor. Assuming permanently his old fana of the Dark Lord, Melkor came to Avathar, where he enlisted the aid of Ungoliant to obtain the Silmarils and deprive all others of their light. Melkor and Ungoliant poisoned the Two Trees, stole the Silmarils, and slew Finwë. They fled to Middle-earth, where their quarrel over the spoils led to violence; Melkor's cry gave rise to the echo of Lammoth, but it summoned his Balrogs, with whose aid he escaped Ungoliant and came to Angband.

Now known as Morgoth (a name given him by Fëanor), Melkor defended the Silmarils against the Noldorin Exiles, although he also found time to corrupt the newly awakened Men. At first, dismayed by the light of the Moon (which he unsuccessfully assaulted) and the Sun, as well as by the fierceness of the Noldor, Melkor was defeated, and for nearly four hundred years he was besieged in Angband. He spent this time strengthening his forces, and he renewed the Wars of Beleriand with the assault of Dagor Bragollach, which marked the beginning of his conquest of Beleriand.

Although not courageous in person, and although he was severely wounded by Fingolfin and Thorondor in 455 and lost a Silmaril to Beren and Lúthien c. 467, at last Melkor produced in Angband enough fires, vapors, pestilences, and monsters (dragons, trolls, Orcs, wolves, and bats) to wear down his foes, and the lies and treachery he fomented pre-

vented the Eldar from fighting effectively or wisely. Even
the loss of the Silmaril aided him, for the Oath of Maedhros
and the Doom of the Noldor caused his enemies to slay
each other. But when all seemed won, the Valar, moved by
Eärendil and the Silmaril, interceded once more, and in the
Great Battle Melkor's forces were destroyed. He was captured in the depths of Angband and cast out of Eä into the
Void. Yet the Shadow of his malice and his lies remains
on the hearts of Elves and Men and is mirrored in the
broken patterns of Arda Marred. In later ages Melkor was
worshipped by the Númenóreans and other Men deceived
by Sauron.

Melkor's fana was a tall, dark figure of great majesty and
terror. By the end of the First Age it had burned hands
(from the heat of the Silmarils) and eight great wounds
(from the blows of Fingolfin and Thorondor); he was in
constant pain. The symbol of his power in Middle-earth
was the Iron Crown in which he had set the Silmarils. His
weapon was the mace Grond. He dressed in black; his
emblem was a field of sable, unblazoned.

The Sindarin form of his name, Belegûr, was not used
except in the punning variant Belegurth. In Middle-earth he
was most commonly named Morgoth or Morgoth Bauglir.
Also called the Foe of the Valar, the Enemy, the Great
Enemy, the Dark King, the Dark Lord, the Lord of the
Dark, the Dark Power of the North, the Evil of the North,
the Black Hand, the Master of Lies, the Hunter and the
Rider (by the Elves in Cuiviénen), and (by Sauron in
Númenor) the Lord of the Darkness, the Lord of All, and
Giver of Freedom. He called himself the King of the
World. (I 260; III 388, 389, 452, 507, 511; S 16-22, 25-
27, 30, 31-32, 35, 36-40, 47, 49-52, 65-66, 67-77, 80-82,
100, 101, 115-17, 141-42, 150-60 passim, 180-81, 195-97,
205, 227-28, 244, 250-52, 254-55, 260, 264, 272, 273,
340; B 4-13, 18-20, 24, 25-26, 29, 30-36, 46-47, 49-
52, 70-71, 73-85, 89-91, 114, 116, 135-37, 169, 180-93
passim, 218-20, 239-41, 251, 252, 280-81, 302, 310-12,
315, 320, 325, 336, 338, 424)

MELLYRN See: mallorn. (I 443)

MELYANNA (Q.: 'dear gift') The original form of Melian (q.v.). (S 361; B 453)

MEN The Younger Children of Ilúvatar, one of the speaking races of Middle-earth. Men awoke in Hildórien at the first rising of the Sun. Early in their history Men were befriended by Dark Elves but were also approached by Melkor, whose Shadow fell on them. Men prospered and divided into many races, of which the only two mentioned in the First Age are the Edain and the Easterlings (qq.v.). Aside from the Edain, most Men lived in Darkness, either fearing or worshipping Melkor without any knowledge of Ilúvatar or the Valar.

In later ages some Men—the Dúnedain, the Rohirrim, the Men of Dale and the Vales of Anduin, for example—rose above the Shadow, but the vast hordes of Rhûn and Harad and many of the peoples of the West-lands remained caught in their ignorance and barbarity. Yet the history of Arda is one of the rise of Men, for they are outside the fate of the Great Music, and by the Fourth Age, the Dominion of Men, they were the dominant race of Middle-earth.

In most ways Men were inferior to the Elves. They were subject to aging and disease, less resistant to the extremes of nature, less perceptive of the minds of others and the messages of the Valar, blind to the future, and less skilled in lore and crafts. Yet Men have unquenchable ambition, and they have the ultimate freedom of the Gift of Men (q.v.). In the End, they may approach Ilúvatar and dwell with him.

Men were too diverse physically and culturally to be described in one entry. The Dúnedain of Gondor divided Men into three groups: the Men of the West, the Dúnedain; the Men of the Twilight, peoples such as the Rohirrim; and the Men of Darkness, or the Wild, men of lesser stature and nature, unrelated to the Edain.

Called by the Eldar the Atani (Quenya) or the Edain (Sindarin); Hildor, the Followers, and the Aftercomers; Apanónar, Engwar, Fírimar, the Usurpers, the Strangers, the Guests, the Inscrutable, the Self-cursed, the Heavy-handed, the Night-fearers, and the Children of the Sun.

Hobbits called them the Big Folk or the Big People. Also called Mortal Men and Mankind.

See: Beornings, Dúnedain, Dunlendings, Easterlings, Haradrim, Northmen, Númenóreans, Rohirrim, Variags and the various entries under "Men of . . . ." (II 364; III 182, 506-09; S 18, 25, 41-42, 99, 103-05, 141-42, 251, 263, 289-90; B 8, 18, 37-38, 114, 119-22, 168-70, 311, 324, 325, 358-59)

MENEGILDA BRANDYBUCK (fl. TA 30th Cent.) Hobbit of the Shire, wife of Rorimac Brandybuck and mother of Saradoc and Merimac. She was born a Goold. (III 476)

MENEGROTH (S.) The underground halls of Thingol, built for him by the Dwarves of Belegost during the third age of the captivity of Melkor at the urging of Melian. Menegroth was built in a rocky hill on the south bank of the Esgalduin at the point where it began to flow westward. Its only entrance was by a bridge of stone over the river.

Menegroth prospered until the death of Thingol, when it was sacked by the Dwarves of Nogrod. Dior later settled here, but the city was deserted after his murder by the sons of Fëanor.

Also called the Caves of Menegroth and the Thousand Caves. (S 56, 92-93, 121-22, 232-36; B 58, 105-06, 145, 286-91)

MENEL (Q. and S.) The heavens of Arda.
See: Tar-menel. (R 64; L 190)

MENELDIL (Q.: 'heaven-lover') (d. TA 158) Dúnadan, son of Anárion and third King of Gondor (2-158). (I 331; III 394; S 295; B 366)

MENELDOR (S.: 'heaven—') (fl. WR) Eagle of the Misty Mountains, one of the Eagles that rescued Frodo and Sam from the slopes of Orodruin. (III 280-82)

MENELDUR, TAR– (Q.: 'heaven—') (b. c. SA 550) Dúnadan, fifth King of Númenor. (III 390, 410)

MENELMACAR (Q.: 'heaven-swordsman') The constellation Orion, formed by Varda in preparation for the awakening of the Elves. Menelmacar forebodes the Last Battle.

The Sindarin form was Menelvagor. Also called Telumehtar. (I 120; III 488; S 48; B 48)

MENELTARMA (Q.: 'heaven-pillar') The great mountain in central Númenor. From its peak, where was the Hallow of Eru, the farsighted could see the Tower of Avallónë, while the Tombs of the Kings were located at its foot.

After the fall of Númenor, the tip of Meneltarma may have risen above the Sea again to form the Isle of Meneltarma. (III 390; S 261, 270, 279, 281; B 322, 333, 345, 348)

MENELVAGOR (S.: 'heaven-swordsman') Menelmacar (q.v.). (I 120)

MENELYA (Q.: 'heaven's day') Quenya name for the fifth day of the Eldarin and Dúnadan enquier, named for the heavens.

The Sindarin form was Ormenel, and the Hobbitish Hevenesdei, later Hevensday or Hensday. Called in *LotR* Wednesday. (III 484)

MEN OF BREE Men, related to the Dunlendings and other Men of the Ered Nimrais. In the Second Age some of these Men moved northward, and in the Third they became subject to Arnor, learned Westron, and forgot their origin.

The Men of Bree were cheerful, provincial, short, and brown-haired. They got on extremely well with people of all races and were the only Men anywhere to live with Hobbits. (I 205; III 509, 516)

MEN OF BRETHIL See: the Haladin. (S 192; B 234)

MEN OF DALE Men, at the time of the WR living in Dale, closely related to the Men of the Long Lake. The Men of Dale were related to the Edain, and in the Third Age they still spoke a language akin to Adûnaic. After the destruction of Dale by Smaug in TA 2770, many of the Men of Dale lived in Esgaroth, but after the dragon's death in 2941 they returned to their home. After this time they were known as the Bardings, because they were ruled by King Bard and his descendants.

The Men of Dale were very friendly with the thrushes of Dale and could speak with them. They wrote with a mode of the cirth. (I 301; III 493, 508; H 218, 237)

MEN OF DARKNESS In the lore of Gondor, those Men, such as the Easterlings and the Haradrim, not related to the Dúnedain.

Also called the Wild. (II 364)

MEN OF DOR-LÓMIN See: the Third House of the Edain. (S 194; B 237)

MEN OF DORTHONION The outlaw band of Barahir (q.v.). (S 163; B 197)

MEN OF ÉOTHÉOD The Éothéod (q.v.). (III 428)

MEN OF HADOR The Third House of the Edain (q.v.). (S 194; B 238)

MEN OF THE LONG LAKE Men, closely related to the Men of Dale and more distantly to the Edain, dwelling in and near Esgaroth at the time of the WR. Like the Men of Dale, they could speak with thrushes.

Also known as the Lake-men. (III 508; H 218, 239)

MEN OF THE MOUNTAINS See: the Dead Men of Dunharrow. (III 64)

MEN OF THE NORTH-WEST The Edain (q.v.)

This term implies that Middle-earth extended beyond Rhûn and Harad. (III 480)

MEN OF THE RIDDERMARK   The Rohirrim (q.v.). (III 508)

MEN OF THE SEA   The Dúnedain (q.v.). (II 100)

MEN OF THE THREE HOUSES   The Edain (q.v.). (S 148; B 178)

MEN OF THE TWILIGHT   In the lore of Gondor, those of the Edain and their close kin who did not go to Númenor, and their descendants. The Men of the Twilight included the Rohirrim and the Northmen, and probably also the Beornings, the Men of Dale and of the Long Lake, the Woodmen, and the other Men of the Vales of Anduin.
Also known as the Middle Peoples. (II 364)

MEN OF THE VALES OF ANDUIN   Various kindreds of Men living between Mirkwood and the Misty Mountains, many of them related to the Edain. Although at the time of the WR only the Beornings and the Woodmen are mentioned as living there, the Rohirrim, the Men of Dale and of the Long Lake, and the Northmen originally dwelt there.
The Men of the Vales of Anduin spoke various languages related to Adûnaic. They were for the most part good, aiding Gondor and fighting Orcs to the best of their ability, but being located between Mirkwood and the Mountains they were frequently hard put to it to survive. (III 404, 483, 508)

MEN OF THE WEST   Translated Westron of Dúnedain (q.v.) (I 266, 291, 307)

MEN OF THE WEST   The soldiers of the Army of the West (q.v.). (III 279)

MEN OF WESTERNESSE   The Dúnedain (q.v.). (III 215; S 293; B 363)

MENTHA BRANDYBUCK (b. TA 2983) Hobbit of the Shire, second child of Marmadas Brandybuck. She was a guest at the Farewell Party. (III 476)

MERE OF DEAD FACES Dark pool in the Dead Marshes containing the graves of Men and Elves killed in the Battle of Dagorlad. The faces of the dead and lit candles showed beneath the surface of the water, but they could not be reached. (II 296-97, 302)

MERESDEI Early form of the name of the sixth day of the Hobbit week, a translation of the Quenya Eärenya. By the time of the WR, the name was Mersday.

Meresdei, the day before Highdei, corresponds to our Saturday, but in *LotR* it is called Thursday. (III 484, 485)

MERES OF TWILIGHT Aelin-uial (q.v.). (S 114; B 133)

MERETH ADERTHAD (S.: 'feast of reuniting') Great celebration held at Eithel Ivrin by Fingolfin in FA 21. Attended by Sindar and Noldor from every part of Beleriand except Doriath, Mereth Aderthad was an occasion of unity and fellowship. (S 113; B 133)

MERETHROND (S.: 'feast-hall') The Great Hall of Feasts in Minas Tirith. (III 312)

MERIADOC BRANDYBUCK (TA 2982-FO c. 65) Hobbit of the Shire, son of Saradoc Brandybuck, adventurer and Master of Buckland (FO 12-64). In his youth Merry was a close friend of Frodo Baggins, and therefore accompanied him to Rivendell in 3018. There he became one of the Companions of the Ring; he traveled with the Company until Parth Galen, where he and Peregrin Took were captured by Orcs. While taking the Hobbits to Isengard the Orc-band was attacked by the Rohirrim, and Merry and Pippin escaped into Fangorn. There they were befriended by Fangorn the Ent and were instrumental in launching the Ents' attack on Isengard. Merry later took service with King Théoden of Rohan and, as his esquire, returned with him to Edoras. Although ordered to remain in Rohan when the Rohirrim rode to Gondor, Merry rode to Minas Tirith with Éowyn, and together they slew the Lord of the Nazgûl during the Battle of the Pelennor Fields. Merry nearly died of the Black Breath, but was healed by Aragorn.

After the WR, Merry was made a knight of Rohan and was rewarded for his valor. He then returned to the Shire, where he was one of the leaders of the Hobbit forces in the Battle of Bywater. On his father's death, Merry became Master of Buckland, and in FO 14 he was made a Counsellor of the North-kingdom. Merry married Estella Bolger, the sister of his friend Fredegar. Throughout his life he maintained contact with the friends he had made during the war, and in 64 he and Pippin resigned their offices and rode to Rohan and Gondor. They died a few years later in the latter realm, and were buried in the House of the Kings.

Merry wrote *Herblore of the Shire, The Reckoning of Years, Old Words and Names in the Shire,* and other scholarly works.

Because he drank Ent-draughts while in Fangorn, Merry was, with Pippin, the largest Hobbit in history, at least four and a half feet tall.

Meriadoc was always called Merry. He was also known as Master Holbytla and Holdwine of the Shire in Rohan, and as Master Perian in Gondor. As Master of Buckland, he was known as Meriadoc the Magnificent. Merry's real name, in genuine Hobbitish, was Kalimac, which was usually abbreviated to Kali, which meant 'jolly, gay' in genuine Westron. (I 28, 71; III 58-59, 89-90, 141-47, 177-78, 316, 363-64, 377, 471, 472, 476, 517)

MERIMAC BRANDYBUCK (TA 2942-FO 10)   Hobbit of the Shire, second son of Rorimac Brandybuck. He was a guest at the Farewell Party. (III 476)

MERIMAS BRANDYBUCK (b. TA 2981)   Hobbit of the Shire, son of Marmadas Brandybuck. He was a guest at the Farewell Party. (III 476)

MERING STREAM Stream flowing from the Ered Nimrais through the Firien Wood and into the Mouths of Entwash. The Mering Stream marked the boundary between Gondor and Rohan. (III 14)

MERLOCK MOUNTAINS Probably, the mountains where the Merlocks lived. The Merlock Mountains were probably fictitious, since they are only mentioned in a traditional Shire-poem, *The Mewlips,* but they were possibly based on what little the Hobbits knew about the Misty Mountains. (TB 45, 46)

MERRY BRANDYBUCK See: Meriadoc Brandybuck. (III 517)

MERRY GAMGEE (b. FO 7) Hobbit of the Shire, fourth child and second son of Sam Gamgee. (III 382, 477)

MERRY PEOPLE The Elves (q.v.). (H 282)

MERSDAY See: Meresdei. (III 484)

MESSENGER SERVICE The mail system of the Shire, run by the Mayor in his capacity of Postmaster. The Messenger Service probably included the Quick Post. (I 31)

MESSRS. GRUBB, GRUBB, AND BURROWES A Shire firm, either of lawyers or of auctioneers. (H 284)

METHEDRAS (S.: 'last-peak') The southernmost peak of the Misty Mountains east of Nan Curunír. Its eastern slopes were part of Fangorn Forest.
Called in Westron the Last Mountain. (II 38, 91, 92)

METTARË (Q.: 'last-day') The last day of the loa in the Eldarin and Dúnadan calendars. In the former, mettarë was not part of any season, and in the latter, it was not part of any month. In the Stewards' Reckoning, and perhaps in the other Dúnadan systems as well, mettarë was a holiday. (III 480, 481, 486)

MEWLIPS In the Shire-poem of the same name, a probably fictional evil race, perhaps modeled on Orcs. (TB 45-46)

MEWLIPS, THE A poem written by a Hobbit of the Shire. Although perhaps totally fictitious, there may be echoes in the poem of the Misty ("Merlock") Mountains, Mirkwood ("spider-shadows" and "wood of hanging trees and the gallows-weed"), and the Long Marshes. The Mewlips themselves may be patterned on vague rumors of Orcs. (TB 45-46)

MICHEL DELVING Town in the Westfarthing, located on the White Downs, chief township and more or less the capital of the Shire. Michel Delving contained the dwelling of the Mayor, the Lockholes, and the Mathom-house.

Also called Delving. (I 25; III 356; TB 41)

MIDDLE DAYS The Second and Third Ages, the years between the Elder Days, the First Age of the Elves, and the Younger Days, the Fourth Age of Men. (I 339)

MIDDLE-EARTH The lands of Arda lying east of Belegaer, extending at least as far south and east as Harad and Rhûn. In Volume II, Number 2, page 1 of the Tolkien Journal, Henry Resnick quotes Professor Tolkien as saying that "Middle-earth is Europe." However, this seems to mean only that Europe and the setting of the events of *LotR* are related.

Middle-earth in the First and Second Ages included Cuiviénen and Hildórien, and probably all of the lands north of Beleriand and Eriador as far as Ekkaia. But in the very far east in the Elder Days there were inner seas separating Middle-earth from something else, perhaps the Empty Lands. In the south there may have been lands which, if they were part of Middle-earth, were ignored by geographers and mariners. The Change of the World at the downfall of Númenor damaged the coasts of Middle-earth but apparently did not alter its boundaries.

Called Endórë in Quenya and Ennor in Sindarin; Endor is an Anglicization of the former form (cf. Númenor). Also called the Great Lands, the Hither Lands, the Hither Shores, the Wide World, and the Outer Lands. (II 362; III 303; H 164; S 49, 103, 263, 280; B 48, 119, 324-25, 347)

MIDDLE PEOPLES The Men of the Twilight (q.v.). (II 364)

MIDGEWATER MARSHES Marshes north of the Great East Road between Bree and Weathertop, infested with midges and other insects. (I 245, 246-47)

MIDSUMMER'S EVE The day before Midyear's Day in the Kings' (31 Nárië), Stewards' (30 Nárië), and Shire (1 Lithe) Reckonings. Midsummer's Eve was a holiday in the Shire.
Also called the Eve of Midsummer. (III 309, 425; H 19)

MIDYEAR'S DAY 2 Lithe, the middle day of the year in the Shire Reckoning, corresponding roughly with the day of the summer solstice.
Cf.: the enderi, Loëndë. (III 478)

MIGHTY The Valar (q.v.). (S 65; B 70)

MILL The mill of Hobbiton, located on the Water, run toward the end of the Third Age by the Sandymans. During Lotho's control of the Shire, the Mill was torn down and replaced by a brick building that polluted both air and stream. This in turn was torn down after the death of Saruman. (III 360, 361, 365-66; H 48)

MILO BROCKHOUSE A misprint for Milo Burrows. (RHM III 420)

MILO BURROWS (b. TA 2947)   Hobbit of the Shire, son of Rufus Burrows and Peony Baggins. He was a guest at the Farewell Party. (I 64; III 474, 476)

MÎM (d. FA 502)   Dwarf, one of the last of the Noegyth Nibin. Captured by Túrin's outlaws in 486, Mîm purchased his life by leading them to his halls under Amon Rûdh. He and his son Ibun remained there with the outlaws for a year, and Mîm became friendly with Túrin. In the winter of 487 Mîm was captured by Orcs and again betrayed Bar-en-Danwedh in return for his life.

In 501, after the departure of Glaurung, Mîm settled in the ruined halls of Nargothrond, which had first been delved by his people. There he was slain by Húrin, who thus avenged the betrayal of his son Túrin. (TB 8; S 202-06, 230; B 248-53, 284)

MIMOSA BAGGINS (f. TA 29th Cent.)   Hobbit of the Shire, wife of Ponto Baggins. She was born a Bunce. (III 474)

MINALCAR (Q.: 'tower-glorious')   Rómendacil II (q.v.). (III 395, 404)

MINARDIL (Q.: 'tower-lover') (d. TA 1634)   Dúnadan, twenty-fifth King of Gondor (1621-34). He was slain in a battle at Pelargir with the Corsairs of Umbar. (III 395, 407)

MINAS ANOR (S.: 'tower of the sun')   The fortress-city of Anárion, built in Anórien on the eastern slopes of Mindolluin in SA 3320. As Osgiliath and Minas Ithil decreased in importance in the first part of the Third Age, Minas Anor became the chief city of Gondor. In 420 the city was rebuilt, and in 1640 the King's House was moved there from Osgiliath. In 1900 the White Tower (q.v.) was built. Soon after the fall of Minas Ithil in 2002, Minas Anor was renamed Minas Tirith, and it was under this name that it was known ever after.

A palantír was kept in Minas Anor.

Also called the Tower of the Rising Sun. (I 321; II 259; III 403, 408, 413, 456-58; S 291; B 361)

MINAS ITHIL (S.: 'tower of the moon')　Fortress-city of Isildur, built high on a western spur of the Ephel Dúath in SA 3320. Taken by Sauron in SA 3429, it was reinhabited at the beginning of the Third Age, but it never regained its equality with Minas Anor, for the heirs of Isildur did not dwell there. In TA 2000 Minas Ithil was besieged by the Nazgûl and fell after two years. The city was then called in Gondor Minas Morgul (q.v.). After the WR it was again called Minas Ithil, but was not inhabited because of the dread remaining there.

A palantír was kept there, but it was captured by the Nazgûl and taken to the Barad-dûr. Minas Ithil was lit at night by moonlight welling through its marble halls.

Also called the Tower of the Rising Moon and the Tower of the Moon. (I 321; II 259, 396; III 305, 412, 454; S 291; B 361)

MINAS MORGUL (S.: 'tower of black-magic')　Name given Minas Ithil in TA 2002 after its capture by the Nazgûl, who made it their home. Terror and war were directed against Gondor from Minas Morgul until Ithilien was deserted. During the WR, the army that attacked Osgiliath and undertook the Siege of Gondor came from Minas Morgul.

In fashion Minas Morgul seems to have been much like Minas Ithil, except for the replacement of beauty by terror. The topmost course of the tower revolved slowly, and the walls of Morgul shone with a pale, frightening light.

Also called the Tower of Sorcery and the Dead City. (I 321; II 396 ff.; III 305, 412-13)

MINASTAN (Q.: 'tower-*adan*') (fl. TA 1600)　Dúnadan of Gondor, second son of King Minardil and father of King Tarondor. He probably died in the Great Plague of 1636, or perhaps earlier. (III 395)

MINASTIR, TAR- (Q.: 'tower-watch') (fl. SA 1700)

Dúnadan, eleventh King of Númenor. In 1700 he sent a great fleet to aid Gil-galad in the War of the Elves and Sauron, and with this aid Sauron was defeated.

Tar-Minastir built the tower on Oromet. (III 390, 391, 454; S 267, 269; B 330, 332)

MINAS TIRITH (S.: 'tower of guard') Fortress built on Tol Sirion by Finrod soon after his return to Middle-earth. When Finrod moved to Nargothrond he gave Tol Sirion to his brother Orodreth.

Minas Tirith was the key to the defense of the Pass of Sirion, and thus of West Beleriand. After Dagor Bragollach the fortress was held by the Noldor for a time, but in 457 Sauron assaulted it, and the defenders, including Orodreth, fled. As the fortress of Sauron, Minas Tirith effectively closed the Pass of Sirion to Elves and Men. Even small groups disguised as Orcs could be detected, and thus Finrod and his companions died in the dungeons of Minas Tirith during Beren's Quest of the Silmaril. But soon after, Lúthien and Huan overcame Sauron, and Lúthien leveled the fortress and laid bare its dungeons. (S 120, 155-56, 170-75; B 142, 187-88, 206-11)

MINAS TIRITH The name given to Minas Anor after the fall of Minas Ithil in TA 2002. Minas Tirith was built in seven levels on the Hill of Guard (q.v.) in such a manner that the gate of each of the levels faced a different direction from the one beneath it, with the Great Gate facing eastward. Behind the Great Gate a cliff rose seven hundred feet to the wall of the seventh level, the Citadel (q.v.). So strong was the city that no enemy was able to enter it until the WR.

As the chief city of Gondor, Minas Tirith was the focal point of the struggle to contain Sauron in the Third Age. However, as Gondor slowly declined over the centuries, Minas Tirith became underpopulated. The city was not attacked until TA 3019, when the forces of Mordor, led by the Lord of the Nazgûl, undertook the Siege of Gondor and broke the Great Gate. However, the enemy was prevented from entering beyond the courtyard of the Great

Gate by the arrival of the Rohirrim and the subsequent victory of the West in the Battle of the Pelennor Fields. After the WR the Great Gate was rebuilt by the Dwarves of Aglarond, the White Tree was replanted, and Minas Tirith remained the capital and chief city of Gondor.

Called in Westron the Tower of Guard and the Guarded City, and in translated Rohirric Mundburg. Also called the Tower of Anor and the City of the Kings. Ghân-buri-Ghân called it Stone-city and Stone-houses, referring to its position as the chief city of Gondor and to its construction.

See: the White Tower, the Houses of Healing, the Hallows, Merethrond, etc. (I 321; III 25 ff., 116, 413)

MINDEB (S.)   River of East Beleriand, a tributary of Sirion. Mindeb flowed south from the Crissaegrim and formed the boundary between Dimbar to the west and Nan Dungortheb and Neldoreth to the east. (S 121, 201; B 144, 246)

MINDOLLUIN (S.: 'towering-head-blue')   The easternmost mountain of the Ered Nimrais, located just west of Minas Tirith, which was built on the Hill of Guard, an eastern spur of the mountain. The Hallows were located on an eastern flank of Mindolluin. (II 371; III 25-26, 307-08; S 341; B 425)

MINDON ELDALIÉVA (Q.: 'lofty tower of the Eldalië')   The highest tower of Tirion. A great silver lamp was set in the Mindon.

Also called the Mindon and the Tower of Ingwë; it may have been his residence before he went to dwell on Taniquetil. (S 59, 70, 85, 341; B 62, 76, 96, 425)

MINES OF MORIA   Khazad-dûm (q.v.). (I 386)

MINHIRIATH (S.: 'between the rivers')   Region of Arnor (later Cardolan) between the Gwathlo and the Baranduin. Minhiriath was the area of Eriador most severely affected by the Great Plague of TA 1636 and was largely deserted after that time. In 2912 great floods devastated the remnant of its people. (I 16; III 398, 461; S 364; B 456)

MIN-RIMMON (S.) The fifth of the northern beacon-towers of Gondor, built on Rimmon. (III 14, 20)

MINTO BURROWS (b. TA 2996) Hobbit of the Shire, youngest son of Milo Burrows. (III 474)

MINUIAL (S.) See: tindómë. (III 485)

MINYATUR, TAR- (Q.: 'first-lord') Elros (q.v.) (III 390; S 361; B 453)

MIRABELLA BRANDYBUCK (TA 2860-2960) Hobbit of the Shire, youngest daughter of Gerontius Took. She married Gorbadoc Brandybuck and had seven children by him. (III 475, 476)

MÍRIEL (Q.: 'jewel-woman') (FA) Elda, perhaps of the Noldor, first wife of Finwë. The love of Míriel and Finwë was great, but the bearing of her only child, Fëanor, tired her so much that she went to Lórien, where her spirit left her body.

She was known as Míriel Serindë because of her embroidery. (S 60, 63-64, 305, 341; B 63, 67-68, 379, 425)

MÍRIEL, TAR- (d. SA 3319) Dúnadan of Númenor, only child of Tar-Palantir. After the death of her father she was forced to marry her first cousin Pharazôn, who then usurped the sceptre and changed her name to Ar-Zimraphel.

When Númenor was destroyed, Tar-Míriel, who was of the Faithful, tried to find sanctuary at the Hallow of Eru, but the waves overtook her before she reached the summit of Meneltarma. (III 390; S 269, 279; B 332, 345)

MIRKWOOD Name given Greenwood the Great (q.v.) when the shadow of Dol Guldur fell on it about TA 1050. With the growth of the power of Sauron in Dol Guldur, black squirrels, Orcs, and great spiders spread through the forest, but the Woodmen and the Elves of the Woodland

Realm of northern Mirkwood remained in Mirkwood. In the course of the Third Age the Old Forest Road fell into disuse.

In TA 2941 Thorin and Company passed through Mirkwood on an old elf-path and encountered an enchanted stream, queer eyes and insects at night, the great spiders, and a feeling of oppression and darkness.

After the WR, Mirkwood was cleansed and renamed Eryn Lasgalen (q.v.).

Called in Sindarin Taur e-Ndaedelos. Also called the Wood and the Great Wood.

See also: the Forest River, the Enchanted River, the Mountains of Mirkwood, and the Narrows. (I 17, 81; III 456, 515; H 12-13, 136, 140 ff.)

MIRRORMERE Kheled-zâram (q.v.). (I 370)

MIRROR OF GALADRIEL Basin in Caras Galadon. When filled with water, it gave glimpses of scenes far away in time or space. The Phial of Galadriel (q.v.) contained water from the Mirror. (I 468-72, 488)

MIRUVOR (Q.? S.?) The cordial of Rivendell. Elrond gave a flask of miruvor to Gandalf at the beginning of the Quest of Mount Doom, and this saved the lives of the Hobbits in the snows of Caradhras.

Its name is clearly related to miruvóre (q.v.), but miruvor was probably a different substance. (I 379, 385)

MIRUVÓRE The nectar of the Valar, made from the flowers of the gardens of Yavanna and served at the festivals of the Valar.

The form *miruvórë* is probably Quenya; the Eldar believed this word to be derived from the language of the Valar. (See: Valinorean) (R 61)

MISTRESS OF MAGIC Epithet applied to Galadriel (q.v.) by Faramir. (II 349)

MISTY MOUNTAINS Great mountain chain of

Middle-earth, running nine hundred miles from the Northern Waste to the Gap of Rohan. Originally raised by Melkor sometime before the awakening of the Elves to hinder the riding of Oromë, during the Great Journey the Misty Mountains delayed the Eldar and caused the Nandor to turn aside. Throughout the Third Age the Mountains were infested with Orcs.

Individual peaks of the Misty Mountains included Gundabad, Zirak-zigil, Barazinbar, Bundushathûr, and Methedras, while the High Pass and the Redhorn Pass were two of the important passes over the Mountains.

In addition to its habitation by Orcs, the great Dwarf-palace of Khazad-dûm was delved beneath the Misty Mountains. Carn Dûm may also originally have been a dwelling-place of the Dwarves. The Eagles lived in the central Misty Mountains in the Third Age, and perhaps in the Second as well.

Called in Sindarin the Hithaeglir. Also called the Towers of Mist. (I 16-17, 252; II 124; H 65-66; S 54; B 56)

MITHE The outflow of the Shirebourn into the Baranduin. A landing-stage was built here from which a road led to Deephallow. (TB 9, 17)

MITHEITHEL (S.: 'grey-spring') River flowing southwest from the Ettenmoors, crossed by the Great East Road on the Bridge of Mitheithel. At Tharbad the Mitheithel was joined by the Glanduin, and was then often called the Gwathlo. Its principal tributary was the Bruinen.

Called in Westron the Hoarwell. (I 16, 268, 269)

MITHE STEPS The landing-stage at the Mithe. (TB 20)

MITHLOND (S.: 'grey-haven') The Grey Havens (q.v.). (II 259)

MITHRANDIR (S.: 'grey pilgrim') Gandalf (q.v.). (I 465)

MITHRIL (S.: 'grey-gleam') Metal, found only in

Khazad-dûm. Mithril was loved by the Dwarves above all things, and was also treasured greatly by the Elves, the Dúnedain, and Sauron. Mithril could be beaten and polished without being weakened, and it was both light and hard. Its silver color did not tarnish.

The Noldor of Eregion made ithildin from mithril. Bilbo's mail, Nenya, and the helms of the Guards of the Citadel were made of mithril.

The mithril-vein of Khazad-dûm was what made Durin's Folk wealthy, and what drew them to their ancestral home despite all danger. This vein also caused the Noldor, led by Celebrimbor, to settle Eregion in the Second Age. However, the vein led north, under Barazinbar, and by TA 1980 the Dwarves had delved so deeply that they released the Balrog imprisoned there. Such was his terror that even the Orcs refused to mine there, and so no more mithril was produced after TA 1980. By the end of the Third Age, therefore, mithril had become priceless.

Also called silver-steel, Moria-silver, and true silver. (I 413-14, 418; III 439; H 228)

MITHRIL-MAIL A corselet and helmet of mithril made in Erebor for a young Elf-prince and incorporated into Smaug's hoard. During the expedition of Thorin and Company, Thorin gave it to Bilbo Baggins, who in turn gave it to Frodo. Frodo wore the corselet during the Quest of Mount Doom, and it saved his life in Khazad-dûm. The mithril corselet was captured with Frodo in Cirith Ungol, and when two Orc-bands quarreled over its possession Frodo was able to escape. Gandalf reclaimed the corselet from the Mouth of Sauron, and Frodo wore it on his return to the Shire, where it foiled Saruman's attempt on his life. (I 363, 413-14; II 203, 205; H 228, 285)

MITHRIM (S.: 'grey-folk') The Sindar who dwelt around Lake Mithrim before the return of the Noldor to Middle-earth. (S 341; B 425)

MITHRIM Southeastern Hithlum, the area around Lake Mithrim (q.v.) between the Mountains of Mithrim and

Ered Wethrin. The host of Fëanor camped in Mithrim on its return to Middle-earth, and here was fought Dagor-nuin-Giliath. Later the Noldor of Fingolfin settled here, and Mithrim became the center of Eldarin Hithlum. (S 106, 108, 119, 341; B 123, 125, 126, 140, 425)

MODE OF BELERIAND A system of the Tengwar in which vowels were represented by full letters. Diphthongs were made by using the vowel-sign plus the tengwa for *w* or *y*, or by placing the "following *y*" tehta or a modified *u*-curl (**ʾ**) over the vowel. The West-gate inscription exemplifies a typical adaptation of the mode of Beleriand. (I 399; III 498-99)

MODE OF EREBOR A variation of the Angerthas Moria. It was fundamentally the same, but had perhaps a dozen differences, some of which represented a return to the Angerthas Daeron. This mode was developed by the Dwarves of Erebor and was used in the Book of Mazarbul. (III 504)

MODE OF FËANOR The most common system of the Tengwar (q.v.). (III 491, 493)

MONDAY See: Monendei. (III 484)

MONENDEI Early form of the name of the third day of the Hobbit week. The name was a translation of the Quenya Isilya. By the time of the WR the name had changed to Monday.
Called Monday in *LotR*. (III 484)

MONEY Contrary to the claims of some, there are references to money in *LotR*, chiefly in connection with Bree. There, a pony was worth about four silver pennies, the loss of thirty silver pennies was a hard blow to the well-off Barliman Butterbur, and a gold piece was a truly extravagant reward for good news. Nár was given "a few coins of little worth" by Azog as an insult. Bilbo's gold and silver from Erebor were probably minted. In all probability there were many different kinds of currency, and these currencies were no doubt mutually exchangeable, as in medieval Europe. (I 242, 345; III 442)

MOON The elder of the two lamps of heaven created by the Valar after the poisoning of the Two Trees to aid the Elves and hinder Melkor. The light of the Moon was the last flower of Telperion, placed in a vessel made by Aulë and guided through the heavens by Tilion.

The Moon first rose as Fingolfin entered Middle-earth, and completed seven cycles before the Sun rose. After this the courses of Tilion became erratic, for he desired to approach the Sun but was scorched and blackened by her heat. Early in its career the Moon was assaulted by Melkor, who hated its light, but Tilion beat off the attack.

Like the Sun, the Moon at first traveled from west to east; it may have changed direction during the reform which returned night to Arda.

Called in Quenya Isil, the Sheen (the name was invented by the Vanyar), and in Sindarin Ithil. Also called Rána, the Wayward (by the Noldor), and the Flower of Silver. (I 411; S 90, 99-101; B 102, 114-16)

MOON-LETTERS Runes that could only be seen when they were exposed to a moon of the same phase and on the same day of the year as when they were written. Moon-letters were invented by the Dwarves and were written with silver pens. (H 62)

MORANNON (S.: 'black-gate') The rampart across Cirith Gorgor, the exit from Mordor best suited to large armies. The Morannon had one iron gate, with three vast doors. It was ruined when the One Ring was unmade during the WR.

Called in Westron the Black Gate. (II 308; III 200-06, 279)

MORDOR (S.: 'black-land') Realm east of the lower Anduin, bounded and protected on the north by the Ered Lithui and on the south and west by the Ephel Dúath.

First settled by Sauron about SA 1000, Mordor was ever after a stronghold of evil. From Mordor Sauron directed the War of the Elves and Sauron, and he remained there until he submitted to Ar-Pharazôn in 3262. After the fall of Númenor Sauron returned to Mordor, and in 3429 he attacked Gondor. Mordor was invaded by the army of the Last Alliance in 3434, and with Sauron's defeat in 3441 Mordor was cleansed of his servants.

In the Third Age Gondor built fortresses such as Durthang, the Towers of the Teeth, and the Tower of Cirith Ungol to prevent any evil thing from re-entering Mordor. After the Great Plague of 1636 these fortresses were abandoned, and the Nazgûl entered Mordor and began the slow preparation of the land for the return of Sauron, who was then dwelling in disguise in Dol Guldur. In 2942 Sauron returned to his home and in 2951 openly declared himself and began the rebuilding of the Barad-dûr. During the WR the armies gathered in Mordor were unleashed against Gondor, but with the unmaking of the One Ring many of Sauron's works were destroyed and Mordor was devastated by earthquakes.

Points of interest in Mordor included Gorgoroth, Lithlad and Núrn, three of its chief plains, the Sea of Nurnen, Udûn, Orodruin, Cirith Gorgor, the Isenmouthe, Cirith Ungol, Morgul Pass, the Morgai, etc.

Called in Westron the Black Land, the Land of Shadow, or the Dark Country. Also called the Nameless Land. (I 17; III 15, 213 ff., 404, 408, 412, 417, 453-68)

MORGAI (S.: 'black—') Mountain-ridge east of, and lower than, the Ephel Dúath, the inner fence of western Mordor. Although dreary, the Morgai was not altogether desolate, since hardy shrubs and thorn bushes grew there. (III 214, 243-45)

MORGOTH (S.: 'dark enemy') The name given Melkor (q.v.) by Fëanor when he learned of the theft of the Silmarils and the murder of Finwë. Thereafter, Morgoth was the only name by which he was known among the Eldar.

The fullest sense of the name is 'Dark Enemy of the World' or 'Black Foe of the World.' (S 31, 79; B 25, 88)

MORGULDUIN (S.: 'black-magic-river') Stream flowing into Anduin from Imlad Morgul. Morgulduin glowed with a pale, evil light and smelled noisome. (II 388, 397 ff.)

MORGUL-KNIFE An enchanted knife with which the Lord of the Nazgûl stabbed Frodo on Weathertop. A fragment of the knife-blade remained in the wound and slowly worked its way toward Frodo's heart, but it was extricated by Elrond. The knife-blade vaporized when it was exposed to the sun. (I 263, 265-66, 281, 292)

MORGUL PASS Pass leading from Minas Morgul over the Ephel Dúath into Mordor.
Also called the Nameless Pass. (II 405; III 215)

MORGUL-RATS The Orcs of Minas Morgul, so called by an Orc of the Tower of Cirith Ungol. (III 222)

MORGUL VALE Imlad Morgul (q.v.). (I 332)

MORIA (S.: 'black pit') Khazad-dûm (q.v.). (I 316; H 37; S 360; B 451)

MORIA-SILVER Mithril (q.v.). (I 413)

MORIQUENDI (Q.: 'dark elves') Name given by the Eldar of Eldamar, who called themselves the Calaquendi, to those Elves who never saw the Light of the Two Trees. The Moriquendi comprised the Avari and the Úmanyar or, in a different system of reckoning, the Silvan Elves, the Nandor and Laiquendi, and all the Sindar except Elwë. Sometimes the term refers to all non-Eldarin Elves. It was frequently a term of opprobrium. (S 53, 309, 323; B 54, 383, 402)

MORMEGIL (S.: 'black-sword') Name given to Túrin

(q.v.) by the Elves of Nargothrond while he lived there. The name was inspired by his black sword, Anglachel or Gurthang. (S 210, 216; B 258, 266)

MORO BURROWS (b. TA 2991)   Hobbit of the Shire, second son of Milo Burrows. He was a guest at the Farewell Party. (III 474)

MORROWDIM   Tindómë (q.v.). (III 485)

MORTAL MEN   Men (q.v.). (S 68; B 74)

MORTHOND (S.: 'black-root')   River in Gondor, flowing from its source in the Paths of the Dead (whence its name) past Erech and south to the Sea, which it entered near Dol Amroth.
    Called in Westron the Blackroot. (III 49, 72-3; TB 8; L 179)

MORTHOND VALE   The Blackroot Vale (q.v.). (III 73)

MORWEN (S.: 'dark-lady') (d. FA 502)   Adan of the First House, daughter of Baragund. After Dagor Bragollach Morwen fled Dorthonion with Emeldir and came to Dorlómin, where she married Húrin sometime before 465. They had three children, Túrin, Lalaith, and Nienor.
    Morwen remained in Dor-lómin after the Nirnaeth Arnoediad, succored by her kinswoman Aerin and protected from the Easterlings by the majesty of her bearing, but she sent Túrin to Doriath. Twenty years later she and Nienor followed him there, but they found him gone, and for a few years Morwen dwelt in Doriath. After the fall of Nargothrond Morwen unwisely insisted on going there to find news of Túrin. Her party was scattered by Glaurung. Morwen wandered distraught for six years, until she was reunited with Húrin at the Stone of the Hapless on the day of her death. Húrin laid her in a grave beside their son.
    Morwen's beauty earned her the epithet Eledhwen, Elfsheen. Also called (as wife of Lord Húrin) the Lady of

Dor-lómin. (S 148, 155, 160-61, 198-99, 211, 217-18, 227, 229, 307, 308; B 177, 187, 194, 243, 260, 267-68, 280, 283, 381, 382)

MORWEN (b. TA 2922) Dúnadan of Gondor, born in Lossarnach. In 2943 she married King Thengel of Rohan; she bore him five children, including Théoden and Théodwyn.

Morwen was called Steelsheen by the Rohirrim. (III 436, 437)

MOSCO BURROWS (b. TA 2987) Hobbit of the Shire, eldest son of Milo Burrows. He was a guest at the Farewell Party. (III 474)

MOUNDS OF MUNDBURG The burial-mounds of those slain in the Battle of the Pelennor Fields, so called by the Rohirrim. (III 152)

MOUNTAIN, THE Taniquetil (q.v.). (I 309, 310; S 278)

MOUNTAIN, THE Erebor (q.v.). (I 51; S 278; B 344)

MOUNTAIN OF FIRE Orodruin (q.v.). (I 318; S 288; B 356)

MOUNTAIN OF SHADOW Probably a misprint for the Mountains of Shadow, the Ephel Dúath. (I 321)

MOUNTAINS OF AMAN The Pelóri (q.v.). (S 37; B 32)

MOUNTAINS OF DEFENCE The Pelóri (q.v.). (S 101; B 116)

MOUNTAINS OF ERED LUIN The Ered Luin (q.v.). (S 289; B 359)

MOUNTAINS OF IRON The Ered Engrin (q.v.). (S 151; B 181)

MOUNTAINS OF LUNE The Ered Luin (q.v.). (II 90)

MOUNTAINS OF MIRKWOOD The mountains of northern Mirkwood, the source of the Enchanted River. After the WR the Mountains became the southern boundary of the Woodland Realm. (I 17; III 468; H 13)

MOUNTAINS OF MITHRIM Mountains in Hithlum running northwest from the Ered Engrin. The Mountains of Mithrim formed the boundary between Mithrim and Dor-lómin.

The caves of Androth were probably located on the eastern slopes of the Mountains. (S 119, 238; B 140, 294)

MOUNTAINS OF MORIA Bundushathûr, Zirak-zigil, and Barazinbar, the three mountains under which Khazad-dûm was delved. (I 432)

MOUNTAINS OF SHADOW The Ered Wethrin (q.v.). (S 106; B 123)

MOUNTAINS OF SHADOW The Ephel Dúath (q.v.). (I 17, 330)

MOUNTAINS OF TERROR The Ered Gorgoroth (q.v.). (I 260; II 422; S 176; B 214)

MOUNTAINS OF THE EAST The Orocarni (q.v.). (S 49; B 49)

MOUNTAINS OF THE MOON The home of the Man in the Moon, in a Hobbit poem originally derived from Gondor. Although the Mountains were probably imaginary, it is possible that some sort of jesting reference to the Ered Luin, which were in the Shire called the Mountains of Lune, was being made. (TB 38)

MOUNTAINS OF VALINOR The Pelóri (q.v.). (R 61)

MOUNTAIN WALL Probably the Pelóri, but quite possibly the Walls of the Night (qq.v.). (I 310)

MOUNT DOLMED Dolmed (q.v.). (S 87; B 98)

MOUNT DOOM Orodruin (q.v.). (III 393)

MOUNT EVERWHITE Oiolossë (q.v.). (I 489)

MOUNT FANG Orthanc (q.v.). (II 204)

MOUNT GRAM One of the Misty Mountains, home of the Orcs that attacked the Shire in TA 2747 and were defeated in the Battle of Greenfields. (H 30)

MOUNT MINDOLLUIN Mindolluin (q.v.). (S 291; B 361)

MOUNT RERIR (S.) Mountain in Beleriand, part of a northern spur of the Ered Luin. Mount Rerir was fortified and held by the Noldor of Caranthir, but the fortress was taken in the aftermath of Dagor Bragollach. (S 112, 123, 124, 153; B 132, 146, 148, 184)

MOUNT TARAS Mountain in Beleriand on the shore of Belegaer at the southern boundary of Nevrast. The city of Vinyamar (q.v.) was built either beneath Mount Taras or on its northern slopes. (S 119, 238; B 141, 295)

MOUTH OF SAURON (SA ?-TA 3019) Black Númenórean. In the Third Age (and perhaps in the Second as well) he served Sauron, rising in his service because of his cunning and evil. He became a great sorcerer, which is how he preserved his life for thousands of years. By the time of the WR he had become the Lieutenant of the Tower of Barad-dûr and had forgotten his real name. He was doubtless killed when Sauron fell, or in the battle with the Army of the West which followed.

Also called the Messenger of Mordor. (III 202-06)

MOUTHS OF ANDUIN   Ethir Anduin (q.v.). (III 14)

MOUTHS OF ENTWASH   Marshy area in Gondor on the border with Rohan, where the Entwash flowed into Anduin.

For more information, see Entwash Vale, of which the Mouths of Entwash were a part. (III 14-15, 94)

MOUTHS OF SIRION   The delta of the Sirion, consisting of marshes and islands of reeds or sand. During the Great Journey many of the Teleri, led by Olwë, dwelt here for a long time and were befriended by Ossë and Uinen. After these Teleri departed, either to the West or the Falas, the Mouths of Sirion seem to have been uninhabited for many years.

After the fall of the Falas Círdan maintained a refuge and port, the Havens of Sirion (q.v.), somewhere in the delta. (S 57, 120, 196; B 60, 142, 239)

MUGWORT   Family of Hobbits of Bree. (I 212)

MÛMAKIL   Oliphaunts (q.v.). (II 341)

MUNDBURG   Name by which Minas Tirith was called by the Rohirrim. (II 143)

MUNGO BAGGINS (TA 2807-2900)   Hobbit of the Shire, eldest son of Balbo Baggins. He married Laura Grubb; they had five children. (III 474)

MUSIC, MUSIC OF THE AINUR   The Ainulindalë (q.v.). (S 17, 19; B 6, 8)

MUSIC OF THE AINUR Ainulindalë (q.v.). (S 15; B 3)

MUZGASH (Orkish?) (d. TA 3019)   Orc of Cirith Ungol, killed in the battle between his company and one from Minas Morgul over Frodo's mithril-mail. (III 217, 222)

MYRTLE BURROWS (b. TA 2993) Hobbit of the Shire, third child and only daughter of Milo Burrows. She was a guest at the Farewell Party. (III 474)

⁀⁀ ⁀⁀

NAHALD (gen. Mannish: 'secret') See: Déagol. (III 518)

NAHAR (Q.?) The white horse of Oromë, perhaps the ancestor of the horses of the Noldor and the mearas.

Nahar was so named for his voice. (S 41, 49, 95, 342; B 37, 49, 108, 426)

NÁIN I (TA 1832-1981) Dwarf, King of Durin's Folk and King of Khazad-dûm (1980-81). He was slain by the Balrog. (III 439, 450)

NÁIN II (TA 2338-2585) Dwarf, King of Durin's Folk (2488-2585) in the Ered Mithrin. (III 450)

NÁIN (TA 2665-2799) Dwarf of the House of Durin, son of Grór and father of Dáin Ironfoot. Náin was slain by Azog in the Battle of Azanulbizar. (III 443, 450)

NAITH (S.) That part of Lórien between Celebrant and Anduin. The Naith included Egladil but was of greater extent.

Called in Westron the Gore. (I 450)

NÁLI (d. TA 2994) Dwarf of Erebor. Náli went to Khazad-dûm with Balin in 2989. He was slain by Orcs while defending Durin's Bridge and the Second Hall. (I 419)

NAMÁRIË (Q.: 'farewell') A Quenya chant sung (and doubtless composed) by Galadriel as the Fellowship of the Ring left Lórien. The song expresses Galadriel's yearning for Valinor and her hope that Frodo might be allowed to attain that bliss. (I 489; R 57-63)

NAMELESS, NAMELESS ENEMY, NAMELESS ONE
With "the Unnamed," the most common epithets used by the Men of Gondor to refer to Sauron (q.v.). (I 322; II 350, 363)

NAMELESS LAND Mordor (q.v.). (II 384)

NAMELESS PASS Morgul Pass (q.v.). (II 405)

NÁMO (Q.: 'ordainer, judge') The personal name of Mandos (q.v.). (S 28, 342; B 21, 426)

NAN CURUNÍR (S.: 'valley of Saruman') Great valley in the southern Misty Mountains, opening into the Gap of Rohan. Isengard was located in Nan Curunír. Nan Curunír was at one time a fertile and fruitfully tilled valley watered by the Isen, but at the time of the WR only a few acres near Isengard were cultivated by the slaves of Saruman; the rest of the valley had become a bramble-infested waste.
Called in Westron the Wizard's Vale. (II 115, 202 ff.)

NANDOR (Q.?: 'those who turn back') The group of Teleri who, led by Lenwë, gave up the Great Journey out of fear of the Misty Mountains. At first they seem to have wandered down Anduin, but later they spread throughout the Vales of Anduin, the coasts west of Ethir Anduin, and Eriador.
The Nandor were a woodland people, loving running water and having greater understanding of living things than any other Elves, but in the wilds of Eriador they suffered greatly from the evil servants of Morgoth.
Some of the Nandor, later called the Laiquendi (q.v.), came to Beleriand under the leadership of Denethor, settled in Ossiriand, and fought in the first battle of the Wars of Beleriand; lightly armed, they suffered heavy casualties. (S 54, 94, 96, 199, 309, 342; B 55, 107, 110, 244, 383, 426)

NANDUHIRION (S.: *nan* + *dur* + *sirion* 'valley of the dark streams') Azanulbizar (q.v.)
Also spelled Nan Duhirion. (I 370; L 182)

NAN DUNGORTHEB (S.: 'valley of dreadful death')
The valley at the feet of the Ered Gorgoroth, bounded on the south by Doriath and on the east and west by the Rivers Esgalduin and Mindeb. Nan Dungortheb had been haunted by evil spider-like creatures even before the Chaining of Melkor, but its horror was increased when Ungoliant fled there after the poisoning of the Two Trees. The valley became filled with terrifying creatures and all sorts of webs, traps, and shadows; its waters were defiled. Throughout the First Age the perils of Nan Dungortheb increased with the power of Melkor. As late as the fourth century the ancient road that passed through Nan Dungortheb along the borders of Doriath was used fairly frequently, although even then it was no route for untrained and mortal Men. The horrors became overwhelming when Sauron spread his sorcery through Dorthonion; by the late fifth century, Nan Dungortheb had become so perilous that its crossing was accounted one of the great deeds of Beren.
Also called Dungortheb. (S 81, 121, 132, 146-47; B 90, 144, 157, 176)

NAN ELMOTH (S.: 'valley of star-dusk') Forest in East Beleriand, on the eastern bank of the Celon above Estolad. Elwë first saw Melian in Nan Elmoth, and her enchantment lay on the forest in later years. Left outside the Girdle of Melian, Nan Elmoth became the home of Eöl, who dwelt in the shadows formed by its trees, the tallest and darkest in Beleriand. (S 55, 132, 362; B 58, 158, 453)

NAN-TASARION (Q.: 'valley of the willows') Nan-tathren (q.v.). (II 90)

NAN-TATHREN (S.: 'valley-willowy') Land in Beleriand around the confluence of Narog and Sirion. Many willows grew here. Nan-tathren seems to have been at most sparsely populated. In FA 511 the survivors of Gondolin, led by Tuor and Idril, rested here a while and held a feast in memory of their slain.

Also called Tasarinan and Nan-tasarion (in Quenya) and the Land of Willows. Also spelled Nan Tathren. (II 90; III 321; S 120, 195, 243-44, 364; B 142, 239, 301-02, 457)

NÁR (fl. TA 28th Cent.) Dwarf, companion of Thrór in his wanderings. Nár was used by the Orcs of Khazad-dûm as a messenger to tell the Dwarves of the murder of Thrór. (III 441-42)

NARBELETH (S.: 'sun-waning') Another name for firith (q.v.). (III 480)

NARBELETH The Sindarin form of Narquelië, used only by the Dúnedain. (III 483)

NARCHOST (S.: 'fire-tooth') One of the Towers of the Teeth (q.v.) (III 215)

NARDOL (S.: 'fire-hill') The third of the northern beacon-tower hills of Gondor, located west of Druadan Forest. (III 20, 132)

NARGOTHROND (S.: 'Narog-fortress-vaulted hall') The Noldorin kingdom of Finrod in West Beleriand and the underground halls which were its chief fortress and palace. The Caverns of Narog (q.v.) on the west bank of Narog under the High Faroth were first delved by the Noegyth Nibin, who named their halls Nulukkizdîn. In the first century of the return of the Noldor Finrod was advised by Ulmo to make a refuge, and he, desiring to delve halls on the model of Menegroth, was told of the Caverns by Thingol.

Built by the Noldor of Finrod and the Dwarves of the Ered Luin, Nargothrond was both fair and impregnable, and from its halls Finrod ruled the largest of the Noldorin realms, extending from Sirion and Teiglin in the east to

Nenning in the west. Guarded by the wisdom of Finrod (and later Orodreth) and the valor of the Haladin in Brethil, Nargothrond long remained secure. After Dagor Bragollach and the Nirnaeth Arnoediad (to which Orodreth sent a very small company) the realm was strengthened by Elves fleeing from the North, although the fall of Tol Sirion (457) and the decimation of the Haladin opened Talath Dirnen to the Orcs. In 466-67 Curufin and Celegorm tried to usurp the crown, but they were driven out when their malice toward Finrod and Lúthien became known.

The defensive policy of Nargothrond—to harass Morgoth from secret forts hidden in Talath Dirnen—seemed somewhat shameful to the Noldor, and in the late fifth century Túrin persuaded the people of Nargothrond to oppose Morgoth more actively. A bridge was built across the Narog to the front gates of the city, and for a few years armies issued forth to free all the lands of the realm from the forces of Angband. In 496 Morgoth responded by sending a great army, led by Glaurung, against Nargothrond. Orodreth and Túrin unwisely met it in open battle, and their army was destroyed at Tumhalad. Glaurung then sped to Nargothrond and entered it before the great stone bridge could be destroyed. The city was sacked and its inhabitants killed or enslaved.

Glaurung sat on his horde for nearly five years until he went to Brethil and was slain. Mîm then returned to the ancient halls of his people and dwelt there until he was slain by Húrin. After that, Nargothrond seems to have been utterly deserted. (I 412; III 453, 506; TB 53; S 114, 120, 122, 151, 157, 168, 170, 173, 176, 188, 211-15, 230, 362, 363; B 134, 141, 146, 182, 190, 203, 205, 210, 213, 214, 230, 259-64, 285, 454, 456)

NÁRIË (Q.) The sixth month of the Kings' and Stewards' Reckonings and the third of the New Reckoning, corresponding roughly to our June.

The Sindarin form, used only by the Dúnedain, was Nórui. (III 483)

NARN (S.) A literary form, a long verse tale designed to be spoken, not sung. (S 343; B 427)

NARN I HÎN HÚRIN (S.: 'tale of the children of Húrin') Lay, longest of the tales of Beleriand, ascribed to Dírhavel. The narn recounted the twisted fates of Túrin and Nienor.

Also called the Tale of Grief. (S 198-99, 342-43; B 243, 427)

NAROG (S.?) One of the great rivers of Beleriand, flowing southward from its source in Eithel Ivrin until it joined the Sirion in Nan-tathren. The Narog crossed the Andram (there called the Taur-en-Faroth) in a great gorge; Nargothrond was built there.

The principal tributaries of the Narog were Ginglith and Ringwil. (S 114, 122; B 134, 145-46)

NARQUELIË (Q.: 'sun-waning') The tenth month of the Kings' and Stewards' Reckonings and the seventh of the New Reckoning, corresponding roughly to our October.

The Sindarin form, used only by the Dúnedain, was Narbeleth. (III 483, 486)

NARMACIL I (Q.: 'sun-sword'?) (d. TA 1294) Dúnadan, seventeenth King of Gondor (1226-94). Narmacil was both lazy and childless, and in 1240 he entrusted the rule of Gondor to his nephew and heir Minalcar. (III 395, 404)

NARMACIL II (d. TA 1856) Dúnadan, twenty-ninth King of Gondor (1850-56). He was slain fighting the Wainriders. (III 395, 408)

NARROW ICE The Grinding Ice (q.v.). (I 308)

NARROWS Area in southern Mirkwood where the western and eastern borders of the wood drew together to form a narrow waist. In the Fourth Age the Narrows formed the northern boundary of East Lórien. (III 468)

NARSIL (Q.: 'sun-moon') The mighty sword of Elendil, forged by Telchar of Nogrod in the First Age. Narsil broke and its light was extinguished when Elendil fell in SA 3441 while fighting Sauron; Isildur used the hilt to cut the One Ring from Sauron's finger.

Brought back to Arnor by Ohtar, the shards of Narsil were one of the heirlooms of the Line of Isildur; Elrond foretold that the sword would not be reforged until Sauron rose again and the One Ring was found. After the fall of the North-kingdom the shards of Narsil were kept in Imladris.

Elrond presented Narsil to Aragorn II when he came of age, and on the eve of the WR the sword was reforged and named Andúril (q.v.).

Called the Sword of Elendil and the Sword or Blade that was Broken. The Elvish name carried a connotation of 'red and white flame.' (I 231, 233, 319, 320, 323-25; II 147; III 401, 421; RHM III 438; S 294, 295-96, 298, 303; B 364, 367, 370, 377)

NARSILION (Q.: 'of the Sun and Moon') The song of lore recounting the creation of the Sun and Moon by the Valar.

Also called the Song of the Sun and Moon. (S 99; B 113)

NARVI (fl. SA 750) Dwarf of Khazad-dûm, maker of the West-gate. (I 398)

NARVINYË (Q.: 'new sun'?) The first month of the Kings' and Stewards' Reckonings and the tenth of the New Reckoning, corresponding roughly to our January.

The Sindarin form, used only by the Dúnedain, was Narwain. (III 483)

NARWAIN (S.) The Sindarin form of Narvinyë (q.v.), used only by the Dúnedain. (III 483)

NARYA (Q.: 'fire—') The third of the Three Rings of the Elves (q.v.), originally worn by Círdan, but given by him to Gandalf when the latter came to Middle-earth. Narya was the Ring of Fire and had a red stone. It had the power to strengthen hearts.

Called Narya the Great, the Ring of Fire, and the Red Ring of Fire. (III 383-84, 456; S 288, 298, 304; B 357, 370, 378)

NAUGLAMÍR (S.: 'dwarf-necklace') Gold necklace made for Finrod by Dwarves of the Ered Luin (probably of Nogrod) in the 1st Century FA, the most renowned of their works in that age. Set with many gems brought by Finrod from Valinor, the Nauglamír sat lightly on the neck despite its great weight and gave grace and beauty to its wearer.

The Nauglamír remained in Nargothrond until Húrin took it from the hoard of Glaurung and gave it to Thingol. The King of Doriath hired Dwarves of Nogrod to re-fashion the necklace and set the Silmaril in it. The Dwarves slew Thingol to obtain the wonderful jewels, above all the Silmaril, but the Nauglamír was recovered and returned to Menegroth. Soon after, it was retaken by the Dwarves in the sack of Menegroth but again recovered, by Beren at Sarn Athrad. For some years Lúthien wore the Nauglamír and achieved the greatest beauty ever seen outside Valinor. At her death it passed to Dior; when the Noldor killed him, Elwing saved the necklace. The Nauglamír, with its Silmaril, remained intact until the voyage of Eärendil and Elwing to Aman. When Eärendil was set in the sky as a star, he may have worn the other jewels of the Nauglamír about his neck, but the Silmaril was bound to his brow.

Also called the Necklace of the Dwarves. (I 309; S 114, 230-33, 235-37, 247; B 134, 284-88, 291-93, 305)

NAUGRIM (S.: 'stunted people') The most common Elven name for the Dwarves (q.v.), especially in the First Age. (III 518; S 91)

NAZGÛL (B.S.: *nazg* 'ring' + *gûl* 'wraith') Nine beings, slaves of the Nine Rings and the chief servants of Sauron. Originally Men, three of them Black Númenóreans,

the Nazgûl were each given one of the Nine Rings by
Sauron in the Second Age, and, being desirous of power,
were easily corrupted. About SA 2250 they first appeared as
the Nazgûl, beings utterly dependent on Sauron, or, more
accurately, on his power acting through the One Ring.
When Sauron fell at the end of the Second Age, the
Nazgûl were overthrown or went into hiding. They reappeared about TA 1300, at which time their chief, the
Lord of the Nazgûl (q.v.), became the Witch-king of
Angmar. The other eight stayed in the East until about
1640, when they secretly entered Mordor and began to
prepare that realm for Sauron, who was in Dol Guldur.
In 2000, joined by their Lord, the Nazgûl besieged Minas
Ithil, capturing the city and its palantír in 2002. From this
time, the Nazgûl were closely associated with Minas
Morgul, as Minas Ithil was then called. In 2951, ten years
after its desertion by Sauron, three Nazgûl went to Dol
Guldur and stayed there until the WR.

In 3018 Sauron sent the Nazgûl, who at this time were
known as the Black Riders because they rode swift black
horses, to the Shire to search for Frodo and the Ring. Although the Lord of the Nazgûl wounded Frodo on Weathertop, he escaped from them, and their steeds were later destroyed in the Ford of Bruinen. A few months later, in 3019,
they reappeared, mounted on flying beasts. The winged Messenger was a Nazgûl. The Nazgûl were active in the Siege
of Gondor and the Battle of the Pelennor Fields, in which
their Lord was slain, but the remaining Nazgûl were
destroyed, with their Rings, when the One Ring was unmade in Orodruin.

The Nazgûl were the principal tools through which
Sauron worked; they wielded a great power and terror, and
were used as messengers and scouts, and to lead Sauron's
armies and cow his enemies. Their power together at night
was nearly as great as Gandalf's. They could be wounded
only by weapons with special spells on them, and any blade
which touched them melted. The Nazgûl were strongest at
night and in deserted places, and were afraid of fire and
the name Elbereth. Because of their evil power, people who
were near them for long developed the Black Breath (q.v.).

As with others corrupted by the Rings, they were invisible to normal eyes, and could be seen only by their black clothing. The Nazgûl had a keen sense of smell, but they were seemingly blind by normal standards. They could emit extremely loud, piercing, frightening cries. The Nazgûl used the Black Speech.

None of the names of the Nazgûl are given, although Gothmog was possibly the name of the second highest Nazgûl.

Called in Elvish the Úlairi and in Westron the Ringwraiths. Also called the Black Riders, the Fell Riders, the Nine Riders, and the Black Wings when appropriate, and the Shadows, the Nine, the Nine Servants of the Lord of the Rings, and, by Orcs of the Tower of Cirith Ungol, the Shriekers. (I 82, 111-13, 135, 236, 263, 284-86, 337, 345-46, 357, 501; II 256; III 98-100, 276, 409, 412-13, 414, 454, 457, 462, 511; S 267, 289, 296-97; B 330, 358, 368-69)

NEAR HARAD   That portion of Harad (q.v.) west of Khand, so called because it was near Gondor. (III 409)

NECKLACE OF THE DWARVES   The Nauglamír (q.v.). (S 114, 231; B 134, 286)

NECROMANCER   Sauron (q.v.). (I 328; H 37)

NEEDLEHOLE   Village in the Westfarthing, located on the Water north of Rushock Bog. (I 40)

NEEKERBREEKERS   Sam Gamgee's name for a kind of noisy insect found in the Midgewater Marshes. (I 247; L 170)

NEITHAN (S.: 'one who is deprived, wronged')   The first of the pseudonyms of Túrin, adopted by him after the death of Saeros, when he was an outlaw near Amon Rûdh. (S 200, 343; B 245, 427)

NELDORETH (S.: 'beech—' or 'three-tree—')   Forest

of Beleriand, bounded by Esgalduin, Sirion, and Nan Dungortheb. During the Great Journey a number of Noldor tarried in Neldoreth. Enclosed within the Girdle of Melian, Neldoreth formed part of Doriath. Here Lúthien was born, and here she met Beren.

The trees of Neldoreth were mostly hemlocks and beeches.

Also called Taur-na-Neldor and the Forest of Neldoreth. (I 258, 260; II 90; S 55, 91, 97, 121, 165, 172, 362; B 57, 103, 110, 145, 199, 208, 454)

NÉNAR (Q.)   One of the stars wrought by Varda in preparation for the awakening of the Elves. (S 48; B 48)

NEN GIRITH (S.: 'water shuddering')   Name given to Dimrost after Nienor's premonitory shuddering. (S 220; B 270)

NEN HITHOEL (S.: 'water misty')   A long, pale lake on Anduin. The northern entrance to Nen Hithoel was the Argonath, and at its southern end stood Tol Brandir, Amon Lhaw, and Amon Hen, and beyond them the falls of Rauros. (I 17, 509)

NÉNIMË (Q.: 'water—')   The second month of the Kings' and Stewards' Reckonings and the eleventh of the New Reckoning, corresponding roughly to our February.

The Sindarin form, used only by the Dúnedain, was Nínui. (III 483)

NENNING (S.)   River of West Beleriand, flowing south to Belegaer, which it entered at Eglarest. Nenning (or its upper reaches) formed the western boundary of Nargothrond. (S 120, 196; B 142, 239)

NENUIAL (S.: 'lake of twilight')   Lake in Arnor north of the Shire. On its shores was built Annúminas.

Called in Westron Lake Evendim. Also called Lake Nenuial. (I 16, 320; III 411; S 286; B 354)

NENYA (Q.: 'water—') The second of the Three Rings of the Elves (q.v.), worn by Galadriel. Nenya was made of mithril and had a white stone with a soft, flickering light.

Also called the Ring of Water and Ring of Adamant. (I 472-73; III 381, 456; S 288, 298; B 357, 370)

NERDANEL (Q.) Noldo, daughter of Mahtan. In Eldamar she married Fëanor and bore him seven sons. Firm of will but patient and discerning, for a while she curbed the passion of Fëanor's temper, but finally they were estranged. Nerdanel did not join the revolt of the Noldor. (S 64, 66; B 69, 71)

NESSA (Q.?) Ainu, the least of the Queens of the Valar. The sister of Oromë, Nessa is lithe and swift of foot; she loves deer and dancing. Nessa married Tulkas in Almaren, during the Spring of Arda. (S 25, 29, 36; B 18, 22, 31)

NETHER DARKNESS In the First and Second Ages, the area of far southern Arda not lit by the Sun and Moon. Although accessible by sea, the Nether Darkness was probably (if it was land at all) an uninhabited waste. (S 263; B 324)

NEVRAST (S.: 'hither shore') The coastlands of Beleriand, at first including the Falas but later referring only to the land west of the Ered Lómin between Drengist and Mount Taras. Nevrast was a mild, sheltered land, surrounded on all sides by mountains or headlands and warmed by sea breezes; it was considered by some a part of Beleriand. The rivers of Nevrast did not flow to the sea, but rather emptied into Linaewen and the Marshes of Nevrast.

When the Noldor returned to Middle-earth, Nevrast was settled by Turgon, who built Vinyamar. After Turgon departed for Gondolin, Nevrast was deserted. (S 114, 115, 119, 126, 238, 343; B 133, 135, 141, 150, 294, 428)

NEW AGE The Fourth Age, so called by Gandalf at the end of the Third. (III 318)

NEWBURY   Village in Buckland north of Crickhollow.
(I 40)

NEW RECKONING   The calendar adopted by the Reunited Kingdom under King Elessar in TA 3021. The New Reckoning was basically the same as the Kings' Reckoning, but it began in the spring, like the Eldarin loa, and contained various holidays commemorating the WR and its heroes. All of the months had thirty days.

The calendar for one year was:

yestarë—first day; old Súlimë 25, the day of the downfall of Sauron.
Víressë
Lótessë
Nárië
Cermië
Úrimë
Yavannië
enderi—three days, the second called Loëndë.
Narquelië
Hísimë
Ringarë
Narvinyë
Nénimë
Súlimë
mettarë—last day.

The leap year was provided for by doubling Yavannië 30, Frodo's birthday, which was called Cormarë. The week and the millennial adjustments seem to have been the same as those of the Kings' Reckoning. (III 486)

NEW ROW   Name given the street in Hobbiton that had been Bagshot Row (q.v.), after it was completely rebuilt following its ruin by the Chief's Men in TA 3018-19.

New Row was jokingly called Sharkey's End in Bywater, since Saruman had been killed here. (III 373-74)

NEW YEAR OF THE ELVES   The first day of the Eldarin loa. In the Calendar of Imladris the New Year corresponded to Shire 4 Astron, about 5 days after the vernal equinox. (III 468, 486)

NGOLDO (Q.)   Older form of noldo (q.v.). (III 500; RHM III 401)

NGWALME (Q.)   Older form of nwalme (q.v.). (III 500; RHM III 401)

NIBS COTTON   Carl Cotton (q.v.). (III 354-55)

NICK COTTON   Bowman Cotton (q.v.). (III 354)

NIENNA (Q.?)   Ainu, one of the Queens of the Valar and one of the Aratar. She is the sister of Mandos and Lórien and has no spouse. Nienna is concerned with mourning, and she pities the suffering of others, especially the Marring of Arda by Melkor. Her tears bring healing; they flowed to quicken the Two Trees and to bring forth their last flower and fruit after their poisoning. Yet the lesson of Nienna is not of endless grief, but rather of pity, hope, and the endurance of the spirit. Olórin was her greatest pupil, but she comforts all who dwell in the Halls of Awaiting.

Nienna dwells in far western Valinor near Mandos, and she seldom comes to Valimar. Her windows look out beyond the Walls of the Night. (S 25, 28, 29, 31, 38, 65, 98; B 18, 21-22, 25, 33, 70, 113)

NIENOR (S.: 'mourning') (FA 474-501)   Adan of the Third House, daughter of Húrin and Morwen. Born after her father was captured in the Nirnaeth Arnoediad and her brother Túrin sent to Doriath, Nienor lived in Dor-lómin for twenty years and then went to Doriath with her mother. When Morwen went to Nargothrond after its fall to seek tidings of Túrin, Nienor, thinking to dissuade her mother, accompanied her in disguise, and thus furthered the doom of the Children of Húrin. Glaurung cast a spell of forgetfulness on her, and she wandered in the wild until she was found by Túrin (calling himself Turambar) at Haudh-en-

Elleth. He named her Níniel and took her toward Ephel Brandir. As they passed Dimrost near Cabed-en-Aras Nienor shuddered, for her fate lay at that place, which was then renamed Nen Girith. Nienor fell sick for a long time, and during her recovery she relearned language and the ways of society.

Loved by Brandir and Túrin, she married the latter in 500 and conceived a child the next spring. Soon after, Túrin went to hunt Glaurung. Following him to Cabed-en-Aras, Nienor arrived in time to bind his wounds and hear the last words of Glaurung, which restored her memory. Realizing that she had married her brother and now carried his child, Nienor leaped to her death from Cabed-en-Aras. Her body was never recovered.

Nienor possessed the courage and beauty of her line, but her life was blighted by the curse of Melkor on her family. (S 199, 211, 217-21, 226; B 243, 260, 267-72, 279)

NIGHT-FEARERS Epithet applied to Men (q.v.) by the Eldar. (S 103; B 119)

NIGHT OF NAUGHT The darkness of the Shadowy Seas (q.v.). (I 308)

NIGHT OF THE VOID The blackness of the Void (q.v.), the total absence of the Flame Imperishable. (S 36; B 31)

NIMBRETHIL (S.: 'white-birch') Birchwoods in Arvernien. Círdan and Eärendil built Vingilot of timbers felled in Nimbrethil. (I 308; S 246; B 304)

NIMLOTH (S.: 'white blossom') (d. c. FA 509) Sindarin Elf of Doriath, kinswoman of Celeborn. Nimloth married Dior and bore him three children, Eluréd, Elurín and Elwing. She was slain by the Noldor who sacked Menegroth. (S 234, 235-36, 344; B 290, 291, 428)

NIMLOTH (d. c. SA 3300) The White Tree of Númenor, a seedling of Celeborn, given by the Eldar of Tol

Eressëa to Elros. Nimloth grew in the King's Court. Starting in the reign of Ar-Gimilzôr, the tree was untended and began to decline, until finally it was cut down by Ar-Pharazôn, at the instigation of Sauron, and burned by Sauron on the altar of his Temple. But a little while earlier Isildur had stolen a fruit of Nimloth, and so the line was preserved in the White Tree of Gondor.

Called Nimloth the Fair. (III 308, 393, 484; S 59, 263, 268, 272-73; B 62, 324, 331, 336-37)

NIMPHELOS (S.: 'white—') A great pearl, the size of a dove's egg, found by the Falathrim off the Isle of Balar. Círdan gave Nimphelos to Thingol, who in turn gave it to the Lord of the Dwarves of Belegost as part of the payment for the delving of Menegroth. (S 92; B 105)

NIMRODEL (S.: 'white-cave-lady') Shallow stream flowing from the Misty Mountains into the Silverlode, which it met at the boundary of Lórien. Its water was refreshing and cold.

Nimrodel was of Silvan origin adapted to Sindarin. (I 16-17, 439; III 506; S 359; B 450)

NIMRODEL (fl. TA 1980) Elf of Lórien, the lover of Amroth. She lived near the River Nimrodel. Nimrodel was one of the Elves who fled from Lórien when the Balrog arose in Khazad-dûm, but on her way to Dol Amroth she was lost in the Ered Nimrais. (I 440-42; III 181)

NINDALF (S.) Marshes east of Anduin and south of the Emyn Muil, caused by the merging of Anduin and Ent-wash and the division of Anduin into many channels.

Called in Westron the Wetwang. (I 17, 483-84)

NINE COMPANIONS The Companions of the Ring (q.v.). (III 182)

NINE RIDERS The Nazgûl (q.v.). (I 360)

NINE RINGS The Rings of Power (q.v.) given to Men.

The bearers of the Nine, the Nazgûl, were easily corrupted by Sauron and showed themselves in their new form about SA 2250. The Nine Rings preserved them, but they became invisible and totally dependent on Sauron and the One Ring. The Nine Rings were destroyed in Orodruin when the One was destroyed during the WR, although the greatest of the Nine, worn by the Lord of the Nazgûl, may have been preserved, although it was powerless.

As with the other lesser Rings of Power, the Nine were each set with a gem. (I 82, 330; III 276; S 267, 288, 289; B 330, 357, 358)

NINE WALKERS The Companions of the Ring (q.v.). (I 360)

NÍNIEL (S.: 'tear-female') Name given to Nienor (q.v.) by Túrin when he found her, dumb and witless, at Haudh-en-Elleth. (S 219; B 270)

NINQUELÓTË (Q.: 'silver-blossom') Telperion (q.v.). (S 38; B 33)

NÍNUI (S.: 'watery, wet') The Sindarin form of Nénimë (q.v.), used only by the Dúnedain. (III 483)

NIPHREDIL (S.) A small flower with a slender stem, found in Neldoreth and Lórien. In Neldoreth the niphredil was white; in Lórien white and pale green varieties grew on Cerin Amroth. (I 454; III 428; S 91; B 103)

NIRNAETH ARNOEDIAD (S.: 'tears unnumbered') The fifth and most disastrous of the battles of the Wars of Beleriand, fought on Anfauglith in the summer of FA 473 between the forces of Morgoth, led by Gothmog and Glaurung, and the Union of Maedhros (q.v.). The campaign began when Morgoth marched against the western army of the Union, commanded by Fingon. Gwindor of Nargothrond, enraged by the mutilation and murder of his brother, broke the defensive alignment of Fingon at Eithel Sirion and, followed by most of the western army, drove the host of Morgoth back to the Gate of Angband in three days.

At this point, on the fourth day of the war, the Nirnaeth Arnoediad began. Morgoth released a huge army from hidden doors in Thangorodrim, and for two days Fingon was forced back with heavy losses. The rearguard, composed of Haladin led by Haldir, was decimated, and by the second evening Fingon was surrounded by Orcs. After a night of bitter fighting, Fingon was reinforced by Turgon and ten thousand Gondolindrim, who advanced from the Pass of Sirion.

Meanwhile, the eastern army of the Union, led by Maedhros, had been delayed by reports of treachery, but at last they arrived to attack the Orcs from the rear. However, Morgoth unleashed his Balrogs, wolves, and dragons on the right flank of Maedhros, and the two armies of the Union could not link up. The battle hung in the balance until the Easterlings of Ulfang, marching with Maedhros, went over to Morgoth and attacked the eastern Union force from the rear. Attacked from three sides and unable to withstand the dragons, Maedhros' forces broke, but the Dwarves of Belegost, led by Lord Azaghâl, stood firm against Glaurung and enabled an orderly retreat.

The combined forces of Morgoth, commanded by Gothmog, then fell on the western Union army. The host of Fingon was surrounded again and annihilated, but the Gondolindrim and the Men of the Third House, led by Húrin and Huor, fell back to the Fen of Serech. In order to allow Turgon and the Gondolindrim to escape without pursuit, the Edain withdrew behind Rivil, where they stood firm. Húrin, who was taken prisoner by Gothmog, was the only survivor.

The result of the Nirnaeth Arnoediad was that effective opposition to Morgoth's entry into Beleriand was destroyed. In the west, the annihilation of the Edain and Noldor of Hithlum secured Morgoth's flank for an attack on the Pass of Sirion; there was no organized opposition to Morgoth in West Beleriand north of the city of Nargothrond. In the east, the scattering of the sons of Fëanor opened Aglon and Maglor's Gap permanently and enabled

Morgoth to overrun Thargelion and all of East Beleriand north of Ramdal.

Also called the Fifth Battle and Unnumbered Tears. (S 192 ff.; B 234 ff.)

NIVRIM (S.: 'westmarch') The narrow strip of woodland west of Sirion included within the Girdle of Melian. Nivrim extended from Teiglin to Aelin-uial. Nivrim was connected to the rest of Doriath by a bridge which crossed Sirion near the inflowing of Esgalduin.

The trees of Nivrim were mostly oaks. (S 122, 218; B 145, 268)

NOAKES Family of working-class Hobbits of the Shire. At the time of the WR Old Noakes lived in Bywater and frequented the Ivy Bush. (I 45)

NOB (fl. WR) Hobbit of Bree, servant at the Prancing Pony. (I 210, 211, 241; III 333)

NOBOTTLE Village in the Westfarthing. (I 40)

NOEGYTH NIBIN (S.: 'petty Dwarves') A group of Dwarves of Beleriand. Exiled from their homes during the Peace of Arda, they were the first Dwarves to enter Beleriand, where they were hunted by the unknowing Sindar. They delved dwellings at Amon Rûdh and Nulukkizdîn, but they dwindled before the Noldor returned to Middle-earth. By the 5th Century FA the only Noegyth Nibin left alive were Mîm and his two sons. (S 204, 230; B 250, 284)

NOGROD (S.: 'dwarf dwelling') Dwarf city of the First Age, located in the Ered Luin south of Mount Dolmed. The Dwarves of Nogrod traded throughout Beleriand and were employed by the Elves for various delvings, probably including Nargothrond. The craftsmen of Nogrod, above all Telchar, were renowned for the forging of weapons, but they also made the Nauglamír.

Thingol asked craftsmen of Nogrod staying in Menegroth to set the Silmaril in the Nauglamír, but they coveted the jewel, killed Thingol, and stole the necklace. They in turn were caught and killed, but in retaliation an army from Nogrod sacked Menegroth. While returning to Nogrod they were ambushed and slain at Sarn Athrad by Beren, Dior, the Laiquendi, and the Ents.

The Dwarves of Nogrod probably fought in the same battles of the Wars of Beleriand as their kin of Belegost, but in general they were less friendly with the Elves.

The Khuzdul name was Tumunzahar. Nogrod was altered from an earlier Sindarin Novrod, the Hollowbold. (III 439; S 91, 92, 94, 189, 232-33, 235, 335, 359; B 104, 107, 231, 287-88, 291, 418, 422)

NOLDO (Q.: 'one of the Noldor') Later form of the name for the tengwa **CCJ** (number 19). The original name, ngoldo, was given because the letter usually had the value *ng* (as in *sing*), but this sound later changed to *n* at the beginning of words. (III 500)

NOLDOLANTË (Q.: 'Noldo-fall') Lament describing the revolt of the Noldor and their fate in Middle-earth, written by Maglor. (S 87; B 98)

NOLDOR (Q.: 'knowledgeable') One of the Three Kindreds of the Eldar. On the Great Journey, led by Finwë, the Noldor followed the Vanyar but preceded the Teleri; they sailed to Eldamar with the Vanyar on the first voyage of Tol Eressëa. In Eldamar the Noldor, ruled by Finwë, dwelt in Tirion, but their thirst for knowledge impelled them to travel throughout Aman.

Stirred by their pride in their craftsmanship and by the lies of Melkor (who was jealous of their creations), the Noldor grew restive and rebellious. The two elder sons of Finwë, Fëanor and his half-brother Fingolfin, distrusted each other, and many Noldor felt restricted by the Valar. After Melkor stole their greatest creation, the Silmarils of Fëanor, and slew the High King Finwë, fully nine-tenths of the Noldor resolved to pursue Melkor to Middle-earth, although some, among them Finwë's third son Finarfin, repented.

Exiled by the Valar for disobeying their will and for shedding blood in the Kinslaying at Alqualondë, the Noldor returned to Middle-earth to suffer their Doom. Although their nobility, courage, and skill preserved them for many years, in the end the Noldor were overwhelmed by treachery, superior odds, and the stain of their Doom. The Houses of Fingolfin and Finrod fought with dignity and heroism, but the House of Fëanor fell victim to its arrogance and the overweening Oath of Fëanor; the eucatastrophe of Beleriand—the recovery of the Silmaril and the mission of Eärendil—was more the work of the Sindar and the Edain than of the Noldor.

After the First Age a few Noldor remained in Middle-earth, especially in Eregion and Lindon; by the end of the Third Age Galadriel was the most prominent Noldo left on the Hither Shores.

Finwë was the first overlord of the Noldor, and his eldest son Fëanor after him. When Fëanor rebelled, the High Kingship in Eldamar passed to Finarfin. In Middle-earth, the High Kings after Fëanor came from the House of Fingolfin: Fingolfin, Fingon, Turgon, and Gil-galad.

The Noldor were the most eager for learning of the Eldar. Especially attracted to crafts, they were beloved by Aulë, who taught them much. As the craftsmen of the Eldar, they excelled in learning and inventing languages and scripts, sewing and embroidering, drawing, carving stone and gems, working metal, and making gems. The greatest of their craftsmen was Fëanor, and the Silmarils, his greatest work, rivaled the creations of the Valar.

Except for the golden-haired House of Finarfin, the Noldor had dark hair and grey eyes.

Called in Sindarin the Golodhrim or Gelydh and in Westron the Deep-elves. (III 452, 453, 493; H 164; R 60; S 27, 39, 53-54, 57-71 passim, 75, 82-90, 103, 106-30 passim, 156, 251, 309, 344, 359; B 20, 35, 55-56, 59-78 passim, 82-83, 91-102, 119, 123-55 passim, 188, 310, 383, 429, 450)

NÓM (S. or Mannish: 'wisdom') Name given to Finrod (q.v.) by the Edain whom he instructed on their first arrival in Beleriand. (S 141, 344; B 168, 429)

NOMAN-LANDS, NOMAN LANDS The Brown Lands (q.v.). (I 484; II 302)

NÓMIN (S. or Mannish: 'wise') Name given the Eldar (q.v.) by the Edain after their first contact. (S 141; B 168)

NOONTIDE OF THE BLESSED REALM The Noontide of Valinor (q.v.). (S 63; B 67)

NOONTIDE OF VALINOR The period of the greatest bliss of Valinor. The Noontide began with the Chaining of Melkor and the arrival in Eldamar of the Three Kindreds, and ended with the poisoning of the Two Trees and the revolt of the Noldor. The Noontide lasted for three ages.

Also called the Noontide of the Blessed Realm, the Days of the Bliss of Valinor, the Days of Bliss, the Days. and the Day. (S 65, 69, 99; B 70, 75, 114)

NORI (fl. TA 2941) Dwarf of the House of Durin, one of the members of Thorin and Company. (III 450; H 22. 26, 44)

NORLAND A northern land of Middle-earth in the First Age. (I 310)

NORTH DOWNS High hills in Arnor about one hundred and fifty miles northeast of the Shire. Fornost was located on the North Downs. (I 16, 320; III 411)

NORTHERLAND For Boromir, Eriador, and perhaps all lands north of Rohan. (I 484; L 190)

NORTHERN ARMY OF GONDOR One of the two armies of Gondor in the days of its greatest power. The

Northern Army engaged in battles north and east of Minas Tirith, mostly against Easterlings.

Cf.: the Southern Army of Gondor. (III 409, 429)

NORTHERN FENCES The northern border of Lórien (q.v.). (I 480)

NORTHERN KINGDOM Arnor (q.v.). (S 291; B 361)

NORTHERN LINE The Line of Isildur (q.v.). (III 402)

NORTHERN MIRKWOOD The Woodland Realm (q.v.). (I 315)

NORTHERN WASTE The lands north of the Misty Mountains and the Ered Mithrin.

See: Forodwaith. (I 17)

NORTHERN WORLD A term loosely referring to the known areas of Middle-earth. (II 193)

NORTHFARTHING One of the Four Farthings of the Shire, where the barley for the Shire's beer was grown. Only in the Northfarthing was snow common in the Shire. The Northfarthing was also the site of hunting. Its soil tended to be rocky.

Also spelled North Farthing. (I 40, 377; II 325; III 375; L 186)

NORTH GATE The Buckland Gate (q.v.). (I 239)

NORTH ITHILIEN That portion of Ithilien north of the Morgulduin. (III 15)

NORTH KINGDOM or **NORTH-KINGDOM** The northern Dúnadan realm, either Arnor or Arthedain. (I 23)

NORTHLANDS   A vague term for the lands north of Beleriand, including Ard-galen, the Ered Engrin, and probably Hithlum. (S 109, 154; B 128, 185)

NORTH MARCH   The area around Rauros, the northern boraer of Gondor at the time of the WR. (III 350)

NORTHMEN   Men related to the Rohirrim and the Edain. The Northmen originally came from northern Rhovanion, but because of their distant relation to the Dúnedain and Gondor's need for aid against the Easterlings, they were given much land east and south of Mirkwood about TA 1000. Rómendacil II ensured their doubtful loyalty by crushing the Easterlings in TA 1248 and by taking many Northmen into the army of Gondor. The Northmen remained loyal to Gondor thereafter as long as Gondor had any power in the East, and Northmen formed a considerable part of the army that restored Eldacar in 1447.

In 1856 the Northmen were enslaved by the Easterlings, but in 1899 they revolted and, thanks to an attack by King Calimehtar of Gondor at the same time, freed themselves. After this, however, Gondor could not aid the Northmen, and they fought off the Easterlings for the next thousand years with varying success. During this time various tribes of Northmen allied themselves with Gondor, and Northmen warriors comprised part of the army of Eärnur at the Battle of Fornost in 1975.

In the 27th and 28th Centuries the Northmen between Celduin and Carnen were allied with the Dwarves of Erebor and, using Dwarvish weapons, drove their enemies back into Rhûn. By the time of the WR, however, they were again weak, and the Easterlings reached the gates of Erebor in 3019. In the Fourth Age those Northmen who survived this invasion were probably allied with the Reunited Kingdom. (III 404 ff., 408-09, 411, 440)

NORTH MOORS   Moors in the Northfarthing. In TA 3001 Halfast of Overhill saw an Ent there. (I 73)

NORTH ROAD Road running from below Tharbad to Fornost, crossing the Great East Road at Bree. After the fall of the North-kingdom and the desolation of Eriador, the North Road became known as the Greenway because of its disuse.

Also called the Old South Road south of Tharbad. (I 210, 359)

NORTH STAIR Portage-way leading from the southern end of Nen Hithoel to the foot of Rauros, made by Gondor early in the Third Age. (I 504)

NORTH-TOOKS A branch of the Took family, living in Long Cleeve. The North-tooks were descended from Bandobras Took. (III 475)

NORTH-WAY This, of course, is another name for the West Road. It all depended where one was standing. (III 306)

NORÚI (S.) Sindarin form of Nárië (q.v.), used only by the Dúnedain. (III 483)

NOVROD (S.: 'hollow-delving') The original Elvish name for Nogrod (q.v.). (S 359; B 450)

NULUKKIZDIN (Kh.) The name given by the Noegyth Nibin to the Caverns of Narog (q.v.). (S 230; B 284)

NUMBER 3 BAGSHOT ROW Hole in Bagshot Row where the Gamgees lived at the time of the WR. It was ruined by the Chief's Men during Lotho's control of the Shire, but was later rebuilt and lined with brick. (I 44; III 373)

NUMEN (Q.: 'west') Name for the tengwa ⚹ (number 17), which usually had the value *n*. This tengwa was commonly used to indicate the compass-direction "west" even in languages in which the word for "west" did not begin with *n*. (III 500)

NÚMENDOR (Q.: 'west-land') An early name for Númenor (q.v.). (S 357; B 448)

NÚMENOR The rich and powerful kingdom of the Dúnedain in the Second Age, founded in SA 32 on a great island raised by the Valar in the western waters of Belegaer. The westernmost of mortal lands, Númenor was granted to the Edain as a reward for their valor and faithfulness in the War of the Great Jewels. The Kings of Númenor were Elros Tar-Minyatur and his descendants; after 1075 the sceptre passed to the eldest child of the King, whether male or female.

Enriched by gifts from the Eldar, the Númenóreans became great mariners, powerful and wise, but they were forbidden to set foot on the Undying Lands or to become immortal. About 600 ships of Númenor first returned to Middle-earth, and the Dúnedain instructed the primitive Men they found there and helped them free themselves from the Shadow. About 1200 Númenor began to establish permanent havens in Middle-earth, of which Umbar and Pelargir were the greatest. In 1700 Tar-Minastir sent a great fleet to the aid of Gil-galad in Lindon, and with this aid Sauron, who had overrun all of Eriador in the War of the Elves and Sauron, was defeated.

However, the Dúnedain began to grow proud and discontented. Situated between Middle-earth and the Undying Lands, the Númenóreans lost sight of the significance of the Gift of Men, and their later history shows a failure to understand both mortality and immortality. About 1800 they started to establish dominions on the shores of Middle-earth, exacting tribute and domination. This desire for power was partly a result of irritation at the Ban of the Valar, which barred the Dúnedain from the fair towers of Eldamar which they could see from their ships, but all these discontents ultimately stemmed from the growing fear of death. Viewing the Gift of Men as their Doom, the Dúnedain tried to find immortality in lordship and ornate tombs, and satisfaction in riches and revelry.

By the 23rd Century, in the reign of Tar-Atanamir, the Dúnedain began to speak openly against the Valar. Soon the Eldar were estranged and the Hallow of Eru neglected. Only the Faithful (q.v.) remained loyal to the Valar and friendly with the Eldar. In succeeding generations the majority of Númenóreans, known as the King's Men (q.v.), abandoned the use of the Elven tongues, persecuted the Faithful, and lost the joy of life through the fear of death. The Kings in 2899 began to take their royal names in Adûnaic, and the dwindling of their life-spans increased. In 3175 Tar-Palantir tried to return to the old ways, but his reign was marked by civil war, and on his death in 3255 his nephew usurped the crown and became Ar-Pharazôn.

Resolving to gain the kingship of the world, Ar-Pharazôn humbled Sauron in 3262 and took him to Númenor as a prisoner. Sauron quickly corrupted Númenor. Within fifty years he had built a Temple to Melkor in which human sacrifices were held, persuaded Ar-Pharazôn to destroy Nimloth, and induced the King to assault Valinor and seize the right to immortality by force. Amid civil anarchy, frenzied sacrifices to Melkor, the enslavement of Men in Middle-earth, and portents from the West, Ar-Pharazôn prepared the Great Armament. When he landed on Aman in 3319, the Valar laid aside their Guardianship and called upon Eru, and Númenor was destroyed in the Change of the World. Elendil, son of the Lord of Andúnië, escaped from the ruin with his sons and a small following of the Faithful and came to Middle-earth. The only other Dúnedain to survive were those living in Middle-earth, the Faithful of Lindon and Pelargir and the Black Númenóreans of Umbar and Harad. Sauron also escaped, but his body was destroyed.

At first, Andúnië on the west coast was the major city of Númenor, but later Armenelos, the site of the King's Court at the foot of Meneltarma in central Númenor, eclipsed Andúnië. Rómenna was the major port of the east coast.

Númenor is a slightly Anglicized (or Westronized) form of the Quenya Númenórë; the Adûnaic form was Anadûnê

and the Westron Westernesse. More properly called Númendor. Andor, Elenna, and the Land of the Star tended to
refer to the island as opposed to the kingdom. After its fall
Númenor was called Akallabêth in Westron and Mar-nu-
Falmar or Atalantë in Quenya; the last form gives the
modern Atlantis. (I 489; III 297, 390-93, 407, 453-54,
507; S 260-82; B 321-49)

NÚMEN(N)ÓRË (Q.: 'west—') The full Quenya form
for Númenor (q.v.). (S 261, 357; B 321, 448)

NÚMENÓREAN Adûnaic (q.v.). (III 488)

NÚMENÓREANS The Dúnedain of Númenor (qq.v.).
Also called the Men of the Sea, the Lords of the Sea,
and the Sea-kings. (III 390; S 261; B 321)

NURN (S.?) Area in southwestern Mordor around
Nûrnen. At the time of the WR the slave-tilled fields of
Nurn provided food for the armies of Mordor. After the
War the slaves were freed and King Elessar gave the fields
to them for their own. (I 17; III 246, 305)

NÛRNEN (So: 'Nurn water') Bitter inland sea in south-
ern Mordor. Into Nûrnen flowed rivers draining all of
Mordor except for Gorgoroth and Udûn; it had no outlet.
Also called Lake Núrnen and the Sea of Nurnen. (I 17;
III 308; III 246, 305)

NURTALË VALINÓREVA (Q.: 'hiding of Valinor')
The time soon after the revolt of the Noldor, when the
Valar raised the height of the Pelóri, fortified the Calacirya,
and established the Enchanted Isles and Shadowy Seas as a
barrier to Morgoth and to the Exiles.
  Nurtalë Valinóreva was probably also the title of the
song of lore describing these events. (S 102; B 118)

NWALME (Q.: 'torment') Later form of the name of
the tengwa ᴄ (number 20), originally called ngwalme.

The change in name was due to a phonological change in Quenya as it was spoken in Middle-earth. (III 500)

ᘿᘿ ᘿᘿ

OATBARTON Village in the Northfarthing. Spelled in error "Catbarion" on I 40. (RHM I 26)

OATH OF EORL Oath sworn by Eorl the Young to Cirion, the Steward of Gondor, in TA 2510. The Oath stated that Eorl and his heirs would aid the Stewards of Gondor at need, in return for the gift of Calenardhon. The token of this call for aid seems to have been the Red Arrow (q.v.). Rohan fulfilled the Oath a number of times in the Third Age, especially in the time of King Folcwine and Steward Túrin II (2885), and during the WR. After the WR Eomer of Rohan renewed the Oath with King Elessar. (III 415, 416, 438)

OATH OF FËANOR The great and terrible oath taken by Fëanor and his sons at the beginning of the revolt of the Noldor. They swore by Ilúvatar, Manwë, Varda, and Taniquetil that they wished the Everlasting Darkness on themselves if they should ever fail to pursue anyone who stole or kept a Silmaril from them. This oath bound the House of Fëanor to hatred and revenge at all costs and caused anyone's desire for the Silmarils to have an evil end; the Doom of the Noldor was merely the working-out of this Oath.

The rashness and pride of Fëanor and his sons were immediately affected by the Oath. Their Exile, the Kinslaying, and probably the burning of the ships at Losgar can be attributed to the Oath, as can the failure of the Union of Maedhros and the murders of Dior, Nimloth, the Elves of the Havens of Sirion, and the guards of Eönwë after the Great Battle.

Yet the effects of the Oath were broader than this. Thingol's desire for the Silmaril caused the death of Finrod at the hands of Sauron and ultimately his own murder by the Dwarves of Nogrod. Indeed, it may be that the Valar, despite their pity for the suffering of Beleriand, were unable to help the Noldor before the Oath was fulfilled. (S 83, 85, 86, 169, 188, 189, 236, 244, 246-47, 253, 254; B 93, 95, 97, 204, 230, 292, 303, 305, 314)

ODO PROUDFOOT (TA 2904-3005) Hobbit of the Shire, son of Bodo Proudfoot and Linda Baggins. He was a guest at the Farewell Party. (I 53-54, 56; III 474)

ODOVACAR BOLGER (fl. TA 30th Cent.) Hobbit of the Shire, father of Fredegar Bolger. He was a guest at the Farewell Party. (III 475)

OF THE RINGS OF POWER AND THE THIRD AGE
Book of lore, describing the history of the Rings of Power. The book was clearly written in the Fourth Age, probably after the death or departure of all participants in the WR. Its tone is comfortable with the Dúnedain, profoundly respectful to the Eldar and Gandalf, and distant toward Hobbits; the author was no doubt a Dúnadan scholar. *Of the Rings of Power* may have been one of the manuscripts copied for the Tooks and preserved at Great Smials. (I 39; S 8, 285-304; B xiii, 353-78)

OHTAR (S.?: 'warrior') (fl. TA 1st Cent.) Dúnadan of Arnor, the esquire of Isildur. He was one of the three survivors of the Battle of Gladden Fields, and brought the shards of Narsil to Arnor. (I 320; S 295; B 367)

ÓIN (TA 2238-2488) Dwarf, King of Durin's Folk (2385-2488) in the Ered Mithrin. (III 450)

ÓIN (TA 2774-2994) Dwarf of the House of Durin, elder son of Gróin. He was a member of Thorin and Company, and lived in Erebor after its recovery. In 2989 Oin went with Balin to Khazad-dûm, and in 2994 he was taken by the Watcher in the Water. (I 302, 418, 419; III 450; H 22, 26)

OIOLOSSË (Q.: 'ever snow-white') The most common name used by the Eldar for Taniquetil (q.v.), perhaps referring only to its summit. (I 489; R 61; S 37, 345; B 32, 430)

OIOMÚRË (Q.: 'ever—') Region of northern Araman near Helcaraxë, covered with dense mists. The mists may have been caused by contact between the Grinding Ice and warmer sea water. (I 308; S 80, 89; B 88, 101)

OLDBUCK A Hobbit family, originally living in the Marish, where they were quite influential. It seems that the family was descended from Bucca of the Marish, the first Thain of the Shire. His heirs were also Thains until TA 2340, when Gorhendad Oldbuck moved to Buckland and changed the family name to Brandybuck (q.v.).

The genuine Hobbitish form of the name was Zaragamba. (III 459, 476, 520)

OLD FARMER HOGG See: Hogg. (TB 42)

OLD FORD Ford across Anduin, for ponies or horses, on the Old Forest Road. (H 13, 134)

OLD FOREST Forest between Buckland and the Barrow-downs, remnant of the great forest that once covered most of Eriador. The trees of the Old Forest, especially Old Man Willow (q.v.) and others by the Withywindle (q.v.), were malevolent and mobile. In appearance the trees were much like those of Fangorn Forest, and may have been as old. Tom Bombadil, who lived just outside the eastern end of the Forest, had great power over all the inhabitants of the Old Forest.

In TA 1409 some of the Dúnedain of Cardolan took refuge in the Old Forest when their land was overrun by Angmar. At some time later in the Third Age, the trees of the Forest attacked Buckland and tried to get over the Hay, but they were driven off when the Hobbits set a fire in the area later known as the Bonfire Glade. (I 16, 40, 156-71, 347; II 89)

OLD FOREST ROAD   Road leading east from the High Pass and, crossing Anduin at the Old Ford, going through Mirkwood south of the Mountains. By TA 2941 the eastern end of the Road had become marshy and impassable, and the Road had been deserted because of the danger from Orcs. (I 17; H 12-13, 134)

OLD GRANGE   Granary on the west side of the Hobbiton Road north of the Water. The Old Grange was torn down by the Chief's Men during Lotho's control of the Shire. (III 366)

OLD GUESTHOUSE   Large building in Minas Tirith, in Rath Celerdain. During the Siege of Gondor the few boys remaining in the city stayed here. (III 46, 47)

OLD MAN WILLOW   See: Willow, Old Man.

OLD SOUTH ROAD   A name for that part of the North Road south of Tharbad. (I 16)

OLD SWAN   Swan, one of the denizens of the Withywindle in a Shire-poem about Tom Bombadil. (TB 19, 23)

OLD TOBY   A variety of pipe-weed (q.v.), named after Tobold Hornblower. (I 28)

OLD TOOK   Gerontius Took (q.v.). (II 80)

OLD WINYARDS   A strong red Hobbit wine, made in the Southfarthing. (I 65, 103)

OLD WORDS AND NAMES IN THE SHIRE   A book by Merry Brandybuck discussing the relationship between Rohirric and Hobbitish. (I 39)

OLIPHAUNT   A Shire-poem traditional at the time of the WR. (II 322; TB 47)

OLIPHAUNTS Elephants, used by the Haradrim as beasts of war. They carried war-towers, and also frightened horses; being virtually invulnerable, they formed centers of Haradrim defense in battle. They could be killed only by being shot in the eye, although they did have a tendency to run amok. Oliphaunts were similar to modern elephants, except that they were much larger.

The Rangers of Ithilien called Oliphaunts mûmakil (sing. mûmak), which may have been their name in Westron, Sindarin, or the language of the Haradrim. Oliphaunts was the name given them by the Hobbits. (II 322, 341-42; III 141, 147-48; TB 7, 47)

OLOG-HAI (B.S.: 'troll-people') A race of trolls of southern Mirkwood and northern Mordor, bred by Sauron toward the end of the Third Age. Unlike other trolls, the Olog-hai were cunning, and could endure the sun when controlled by Sauron. The Olog-hai probably perished when Sauron was overthrown.

The Olog-hai used the Black Speech; they knew no other language. (III 512)

OLO PROUDFOOT (TA 2946-FO 15) Hobbit of the Shire, son of Odo Proudfoot. He was a guest at the Farewell Party. (III 474)

OLÓRIN (Q.?) Ainu, the wisest of the Maiar. Olórin dwelt in Lórien, but he learned pity and patience from Nienna.

Olórin was also the name of Gandalf in his "youth in the West that is forgotten." It is very tempting to equate the two characters, for Gandalf's compassion was great, and his seeming impatience usually designed to quell pompous Men or irrepressible Hobbits. (II 353; S 30-31, 345; B 24-25, 430)

OLVAR (Q.: 'growing things with roots in the ground') Inanimate living things, as opposed to the kelvar. Trees are the highest of the olvar, and the Ents are their guardians, defenders, and representatives. (S 45-46, 345; B 43-44, 430)

OLWË (Q.) Elda of the Teleri, brother of Elwë and with him leader of their Kindred on the Great Journey. After Elwë disappeared in Beleriand, Olwë gathered many of the Teleri at the Mouths of Sirion. As King of the Teleri Olwë led them to Tol Eressëa and Alqualondë, and during the revolt of the Noldor he refused to give his swan-ships to Fëanor.

Olwë's daughter was Eärwen; his wife is not named. (S 53, 55, 58, 61, 62, 86; B 54, 58, 61, 65, 97)

ONDOHER (Q.: 'stone-lord') (d. TA 1944) Dúnadan, thirty-first King of Gondor (1936-1944). During his reign, Gondor was attacked from the east and south by the Wainriders and Haradrim allied with them, and Ondoher and both his sons were slain in the battle with the invaders on Dagorlad. (III 395, 409)

ONDOLINDË (Q.: 'rock-song') The original name of Gondolin (q.v.), meaning 'the Rock of the Music of Water.' (S 125, 359; B 149, 450)

ONE, THE Eru.
See: Ilúvatar. (III 392; S 15; B 3)

ONE, THE The One Ring (q.v.). (I 321)

ONE RING The greatest of the Rings of Power (q.v.). After the forging of the other Rings, Sauron secretly forged the One Ring by himself in Orodruin, intending thereby to control the other Rings and their bearers. However, Celebrimbor perceived his designs and kept the Three Rings free from Sauron's domination. Sauron did, however, control the Nine Rings through the One Ring. He let much of his power pass into the Ring, and many of his works, including the Barad-dûr, were linked to its power. The Ring was completely evil.

At the first downfall of Sauron in SA 3441, Isildur took

the Ring, but it slipped off his finger during the Battle of the Gladden Fields and was lost in Anduin. About TA 2463 Déagol the Stoor found the Ring, and Gollum immediately murdered him to get it. Gollum then hid in the Misty Mountains with the Ring until 2941, when he lost it and Bilbo Baggins found it. Bilbo gave the Ring to Frodo in 3001. In the meantime Gandalf, suspecting that the Ring was indeed the One Ring, did research in Gondor, confirmed his suspicions, and decided that something had to be done. Frodo, despite the efforts of Sauron to recover the Ring and of the Ring to corrupt him, eventually destroyed the One Ring in Orodruin in 3019, thus permanently (we hope) crippling Sauron and preventing him from ever taking shape again.

In appearance the Ring was a plain gold band. The Ring-inscription (q.v.) was finely engraved on it, but could only be read when the Ring was heated. The Ring could only be melted in the Fire of Doom in which it was forged.

Because of its great evil power, the Ring had curious properties. It possessed a certain measure of self-determination; Gandalf, who had wisdom in such matters, claimed that Bilbo found the Ring because it wanted to be found in order to be reunited with Sauron. The Ring also used and devoured its bearers unless, like Sauron, they were of very great power. Their lives were extended, but they became enslaved to it and were physically changed (see: Gollum) as their bodies and souls were consumed by the Ring's hunger. The Ring also incited greed on the part of others to possess it, and jealous hate and fear on the part of its bearer. Isildur seized the Ring instead of destroying it, Gollum killed his friend and cousin Déagol to get it, Saruman was corrupted by his desire for it, Bilbo lied about how he got it (thus warning Gandalf of the Ring's power for evil), Bilbo and Frodo became distrustful of each other and of Gandalf while under its influence, and Boromir tried to kill Frodo to obtain it. Only the very wise, such as Gandalf, Galadriel, and Aragorn, or the very simple, such as Sam and Tom Bombadil, could resist the lure of the Ring. Those of little power who wore the Ring became invisible, but their sight and hearing were increased, and this sensory acuteness remained to an extent even when they did not wear the Ring. The awareness of Sauron and of the other Rings of Power was especially heightened. The Ring was a constant weight and torment to Frodo's mind and body because he bore it at a time when Sauron's power was very great, and because he bore it in Mordor.

Called also the Great Ring, the One, the Ring, the Ring of Rings, the Ring of Doom, the Ring of Power, the Ruling Ring, the Master-ring, Isildur's Bane (for its treachery at the Gladden Fields), the Burden (in connection with Frodo), and Preciouss (by Gollum). (I vii, 55, 80-88, 94, 184-85, 188-89, 263, 276, 319-21, 330, 331-32, 352, 406, 472-74; II 300-01; III 189-90, 216, 276, 453; H 77, 87, 89, 94; S 287-88, 294, 295-96, 300-04; B 356-57, 365, 366-67, 373-77)

ONODRIM (S.: 'ent-people') The Ents (q.v.). (II 55; III 510)

OPENING HOUR The first hour of the Two Trees, during which Telperion began to bloom for the first time before Laurelin shone. The Opening Hour was not counted in the tale of hours of the Valar, but was the time from which their reckoning, the Years of the Trees (q.v.), began. (S 38; B 34)

ORAEARON (S.: 'day-sea') Eärenya (q.v.). (III 484)

ORALD Mannish name for Tom Bombadil (q.v.).
The name is actually translated Mannish; it means 'very old' in Old English. (I 347)

ORANOR (S.: 'day-sun') Anarya (q.v.). (III 484)

ORBELAIN (S.: 'day-Valar') Valanya (q.v.). (III 484)

ORCH (S.) See: Orcs. (III 511)

ORCRIST (S.: 'goblin cleaver') The sword of Thorin

Oakenshield, the mate of Glamdring (q.v.). Although taken from Thorin in the halls of Thranduil, Orcrist was later placed on his tomb, where it warned the Dwarves of Erebor of the approach of any enemy.

Called Biter by the Orcs. (I 366; H 53, 61, 72, 189, 275)

ORCS Evil race of Middle-earth. Orcs were apparently bred by Melkor in Utumno early in the First Age (after the awakening of the Elves but before the Battle of the Powers), using Elves whom he had captured near Cuiviénen and corrupted in his dungeons. The Orcs increased their numbers during the Chaining of Melkor. First seen in Beleriand toward the end of the third age of the Chaining, Orcs appeared in force during the first battle of the Wars of Beleriand. Ever after they were the most numerous of Melkor's servants and soldiers. After the overthrow of Morgoth, tribes of Orcs survived in the Misty Mountains and elsewhere, and in the Second and Third Ages they were Sauron's chief servants, although they were also used by Saruman and seem to have acted independently on occasion.

In the Third Age, Orcs began to multiply in the Misty Mountains about 1300, and by the time of the WR they were found there and in Mordor, Minas Morgul, Mirkwood, and other areas controlled by Sauron. Orcs took part in all the vast enterprises of Sauron, from the realm of Angmar in the north to the assaults on Gondor in the south. They occupied Khazad-dûm after it was deserted by the Dwarves and destroyed Balin's colony there in 2994, waylaid travelers in the passes of the Misty Mountains, raided in eastern Eriador and even attacked the Shire in 2747, invaded Rohan in 2800, and constantly troubled the Elves of Lórien and Mirkwood. After 2950 Saruman used Orcs in his attacks on Rohan. Although all the many conflicts between the Free Peoples and the Orcs cannot be mentioned here, two especially should be noted: the War of the Dwarves and Orcs, which destroyed a large part of the Orcs of the Misty Mountains in TA 2793-99, and the

Battle of the Five Armies, which did the same thing in 2941.

Orcs were bred in mockery of Elves, and, like Elves, they were fierce warriors and did not die naturally. However, in all else they were different. Although Orcs varied from tribe to tribe, they tended to be short, squat, and bow-legged, with long arms, dark faces, squinty eyes, and long fangs. Most Orcs, except for the Uruk-hai, were weakened by the Sun, and all preferred the dark. They were skilled in tunneling, in making weapons, and in other practical skills; their medicines were harsh but extremely effective. Orcs wore foul, coarse clothing and heavy shoes. They hated all things of beauty and loved to kill and destroy. Orcs used many weapons, including bows, spears, stabbing swords, and long knives, but they seem to have preferred scimitar-like swords. Orcs liked blood and raw flesh and ate, among other things, Men, ponies, and their own kind.

There were many different tribes of Orcs, and although there was cooperation within the tribe, between tribes Orcs hated each other as much as they did everything else. However, there was some organization among tribes, and the Orcs of the Misty Mountains had a capital, Gundabad. Cooperation was, not surprisingly, greater in wartime, when large numbers of Orcs, often under the control of Sauron, were able to work together to fight the Free Peoples. Nothing is said about Orkish tribal structures or female Orcs; Orcs were said to be spawned. Physical variation between tribes was not very great, although some tribes of Orcs (such as the tracking Orcs of III 246-49) may have been specially bred for certain functions. The Uruk-hai (q.v.), however, were a different strain and were quite different physically, being larger and more warlike. (See also: Half-Orcs) Orc tribes mentioned in *LotR* are those of Minas Morgul, the Tower of Cirith Ungol, the Barad-dûr, Isengard, and various tribes of the Misty Mountains and Mirkwood. Some of these places may have had more than one tribe of Orcs, and in most of them there were probably Uruk-hai commanding lesser Orcs.

The Orkish tribes invented exceedingly crude languages for intra-tribal communication, and most of these languages included a few words of the Black Speech. For communication between tribes, Orcs used a debased form of Westron. (See: Orkish) Those Orcs who could write used a form of the Cirth.

The names for the Orcs were similar in most languages: *orch* in Sindarin (pl. *yrch*), *uruk* in the Black Speech, *orc* in translated (and perhaps genuine) Rohirric (*orc* in Old English means 'demon'), and *gorgûn* in the language of the Woses. The Hobbits, however, called them goblins, and the Eldar also called them the Glamhoth. (I 83, 387, 422-23; II 20, 30, 60-75, 96, 113; III 133, 233, 246-49, 493, 511, 514; H 65, 68-72, 88, 95; L 171; S 50, 93, 96, 260; B 50, 106, 110, 320)

ORE (Q.: 'heart' or 'inner mind')   Name for the tengwa **ᚱ** (number 21), which had the value of weak (untrilled) *r* in most systems. (III 500)

ORFALCH ECHOR (S.: '—circle')   The last barrier on the main entrance to Gondolin, a deep ravine in southwestern Tumladen leading up from the tunnel from the Dry River. Orfalch Echor was barred by seven gates.
See: the Way of Escape. (S 239; B 296)

ORGALADH (S.: 'day-tree')   Aldëa (q.v.). (III 484)

ORGALADHAD (S.: 'day-trees')   Aldúya (q.v.). (III 484)

ORGILION (S.: 'day-stars')   Elenya (q.v.). (III 484)

ORGULAS BRANDYBUCK (b. TA 2868)   Hobbit of the Shire, youngest child of Marmadoc Brandybuck and father of Gorbulas Brandybuck. (III 476)

ORI (d. TA 2994)   Dwarf of the House of Durin, a member of Thorin and Company. In 2989 Ori left Erebor and went to Khazad-dûm with Balin, where he died in the last defense of the Dwarves in the Chamber of Mazarbul. (I 302, 418; III 450; H 22, 26)

ORITHIL (S.: 'day-moon')   Isilya (q.v.). (III 484)

ORKISH   The languages, such as they were, of the Orcs. They were mostly composed of snatches of other languages put together coarsely. For communication between tribes, a debased form of Westron was used, and Westron was the base of some of the tribal tongues. Some common inter-tribe words were derived from the Black Speech, and a few tribes had made a debased Black Speech their tribal tongue in the Third Age. The Orkish tongues were rich in curses but weak in grammar. (III 511)

ORMAL (Q.: 'lofty gold'?)   The southern of the two Lamps of the Valar (q.v.). (S 35, 36; B 29, 31)

ORMENEL (S.: 'day-heaven')   Menelya (q.v.). (III 484)

ORNENDIL (Q.) (d. TA 1437)   Dúnadan of Gondor, son of King Eldacar. He was captured and slain by Castamir during the Kin-strife. (III 406, 457)

OROCARNI (Q.: 'red mountains')   Mountains of the First Age, located in eastern Middle-earth east of Helcar.
Also called the Mountains of the East. (S 49; B 49)

OROD-NA-THÔN (S.: 'mountain-of-pine')   Dorthonion (q.v.). (II 90)

ORODRETH (S.) (d. FA 496)   Noldo, second son of Finarfin and father of Finduilas, second and last King of Nargothrond (467-96). In Eldamar Orodreth was very friendly with the sons of Fingolfin. During the council which led to the revolt of the Noldor, Orodreth alone of the grandchildren of Fëanor spoke for moderation and reflection, but he joined his brothers in the revolt.
    In Middle-earth Orodreth held Minas Tirith under the overlordship of his brother Finrod. He defended the fortress and the Pass of Sirion during Dagor Bragollach, but in 457 he was driven out by Sauron and fled to Nargothrond. Orodreth was regent of Nargothrond while Finrod

went with Beren on the Quest of the Silmaril. His power was undermined by Curufin and Celegorm, but when they were driven out Orodreth was named King.

At first Orodreth maintained Finrod's policy of secrecy and isolation in Nargothrond. Because of this (and his hatred of Celegorm and Curufin), Orodreth refused to join the Union of Maedhros, and later he refused to meet in open battle the forces of Morgoth raiding Talath Dirnen. But in the early 490's he was persuaded by Túrin to change his policy, and for a while his realm was cleansed of Orcs. Morgoth retaliated by sending a huge army, led by Glaurung, against Nargothrond. Orodreth marched to meet the enemy, and the army of Nargothrond was slaughtered at Tumhalad; Orodreth died fighting in the front line.

In general, Orodreth appears to have been cautious but somewhat weak of will. (S 61, 83, 120, 151, 155-56, 170, 173, 176, 188, 211, 212; B 64, 93, 142, 182, 187, 206, 209, 213, 230, 259, 260)

ORODRETH (S.) (d. TA 2685) Dúnadan, sixteenth Ruling Steward of Gondor (2655-85). (III 395)

ORODRUIN (S.: 'mountain of red flame') Volcanic mountain in Mordor, on the plain of Gorgoroth. In its fires about SA 1600 Sauron forged the One Ring, and always at his rising Orodruin erupted. Orodruin burst into flame in SA 3429, and erupted intermittently from TA 2954 until the end of the WR. When Gollum fell into the Fire of Doom with the One Ring in 3019, there was a major eruption.

Orodruin was only about 4500 feet high, but standing alone on a great plain it appeared higher. It had a great base about 3000 feet high, and on top of that there rose a tall cone ending in a wide crater. The Sammath Naur (q.v.) were located in this cone, and entering these chambers one came to the Crack of Doom, a great fissure in the mountain, in the depths of which burned the Fire of Doom (q.v.).

Also called Mount Doom (Sindarin: Amon Amarth), which was a name given the mountain by the people of

Gondor when it erupted at the end of the Second Age. Called in Westron the Fire-mountain, the Fiery Mountain, or the Mountain of Fire. (I 94; III 214, 269-72, 393, 453, 462; L 182; S 292, 345; B 363, 430)

OROFARNË (Q.) Rowan tree of Fangorn, cut down by Orcs of Isengard toward the end of the Third Age. (II 110)

OROMË (Q.: 'horn-blowing') Ainu, one of the Lords of the Valar and of the Aratar, the spouse of Vána. A great hunter, Oromë loved Middle-earth, where he rode frequently on his great steed Nahar, hunting the monsters of Melkor. On one of these journeys Oromë discovered the Elves, whom he led on the Great Journey.

With Tulkas, Oromë is the Vala who performs their deeds of prowess. He is stern and dreadful in anger. Oromë may have brought the mearas and the Kine of Araw (qq.v.) to Middle-earth; he also loved trees. His horn was the Valaróma. In Aman his wooded lands lie in southern Valinor.

Called Araw in Sindarin and Béma by Men. Also called Aldaron and Tauron for his love of trees, Oromë the Great, and the Great Rider. (III 29, 138, 395, 431; S 25, 29, 41, 47, 49-50, 52-54, 60, 72-73, 74, 76, 95, 345; B 18, 22, 37, 47, 49-51, 53-56, 63, 79-81, 82, 85, 108, 430)

OROMET (Q.: 'last mountain') Hill in western Númenor near Andúnië. Tar-Minastir built a tower here. (S 269; B 332)

OROPHIN (S.? Silvan?) (fl. WR) Silvan Elf of Lórien, brother of Haldir. He was a guard on the northern border of Lórien. (I 445, 448)

ORTHANC (S.: 'forked height') The tower of Isengard, built from four pillars of unbreakable black rock by the Dúnedain of Gondor. The top of Orthanc, a flat floor inscribed with astronomical figures, stood 500 feet above the plain of Isengard.

Abandoned by the Dúnedain sometime in the Third Age, Orthanc stood deserted until 2759, when Saruman came to dwell there. During the WR Orthanc defied the Ents, who could break other stone with ease, and so the tower passed unharmed through the War. It was again controlled by Gondor in the Fourth Age.

In translated Rohirric *Orthanc* meant 'the cunning mind.' Called Mount Fang in Westron. Also called the Pinnacle of Orthanc. (I 338, 341-43; II 204, 232 ff.; III 319; S 291, 345; B 361, 430)

OSGILIATH (S.: 'citadel of the stars') City and first capital of Gondor, built on both sides of the Anduin between Minas Anor and Minas Ithil. Osgiliath was burned during the Kin-strife and its greatest building, the Dome of Stars, was ruined. Many of its inhabitants died during the Great Plague of TA 1636; most of its inhabitants who survived by fleeing refused to return, and in 1640 the royal court removed to Minas Anor.

In 2475 Osgiliath was taken by Uruks of Mordor; although soon liberated by Boromir, the city was completely deserted and became an outpost guarded against attack from the East. During the WR, Osgiliath was attacked in June, 3018; its last bridge was broken and the eastern half of the city was taken by Sauron's forces. Later, in March, 3019, the western half of the city was defended by the Rangers of Ithilien, but was easily captured. There is no record of its rebuilding in the Fourth Age.

The chief palantír was kept in Osgiliath until its loss during the Kin-strife. (I 321, 322; III 15, 41, 406, 408, 414, 457, 459, 465; S 291; B 361)

OSSË (Q.) Ainu, one of the Maiar of Ulmo. With his spouse Uinen, Ossë was given the lordship of the Inner Seas. He loves storms and the roaring of waves and is unpredictable.

Ossë was seduced by Melkor early in the history of Arda, but Uinen persuaded him to return to his allegiance to Ulmo. Ossë befriended the Teleri on the shores of Beleriand and taught them to build ships; he persuaded the Falathrim to remain in Middle-earth, and also induced Ulmo to anchor Tol Eressëa off the shore of Aman as a dwelling accessible to him for the Teleri in Eldamar. At the beginning of the Second Age he raised the island of Númenor out of the Sea.

Called Gaerys in Sindarin. (S 30, 40, 57-59, 196, 260; B 24, 36, 60-61, 240, 321)

OSSIRIAND (S.: 'seven-rivers-land') Area of Beleriand, bounded by the Ered Luin and the Rivers Ascar, Gelion, and Adurant, named because of the seven rivers (Gelion and its tributaries) that flowed through it. Heavily wooded (at least some of its trees were elms), Ossiriand was the home of the Laiquendi, and it suffered little during the Wars of Beleriand. Part of Ossiriand survived the Great Battle.

Also known as Lindon, the only name used in later Ages. (II 90; S 94, 123, 151, 153, 285; B 108, 147, 182, 184, 354)

OST-IN-EDHIL (S.: 'city-of-the-Elves') The city of the Gwaith-i-Mírdain in Eregion, destroyed in SA 1697 during the War of the Elves and Sauron. (S 286, 287; B 354, 356)

OSTOHER (Q.: 'fortress-lord') (d. TA 492) Dúnadan, seventh King of Gondor (411-92). Ostoher rebuilt Minas Anor and began the custom of dwelling there in summer. (III 394, 403)

OTHO SACKVILLE-BAGGINS (TA 2910-3012) Hobbit of the Shire, son of Longo Baggins and Camellia Sackville, and founder of the family of Sackville-Baggins. Otho married Lobelia Bracegirdle; their only child was Lotho. He was a guest at the Farewell Party.

Like the rest of his family, Otho was offensive and greedy. (I 52, 66; III 474)

OUTER GATE OF GONDOLIN One of the gates on the Way of Escape (q.v.).

Also called the Dark Gate. (S 136, 137; B 163, 164)

OUTER LANDS The areas of Arda outside Aman,

roughly synonymous with Middle-earth. (S 39, 41, 80, 249; B 35, 36, 88, 308)

OUTER OCEAN   Ekkaia (q.v.), in opposition to the Inner Seas. (S 40, 326; B 36, 405)

OUTER SEA   Ekkaia (q.v.). (S 37, 100, 101; B 32, 116)

OUTER VOID   The Void (q.v.). (S 181; B 219)

OUTLANDS   The fiefs of Gondor, at the time of the WR coastal lands lying along the Bay of Belfalas south and west of Anórien. (III 48, 49; L 193)

OUTSIDE   According to Tom Bombadil, whence Morgoth came to disturb the Peace of Arda. Outside is either the Void or the empty places of Eä. (I 182)

OUTSIDERS   Hobbits who did not live in the Shire, so called by the Hobbits of the Shire. (I 206)

OVERBOURN MARSHES   Marshes in the Southfarthing south of the lower Shirebourn. (I 40)

OVER-HEAVEN   Tarmenel (q.v.). (II 260; L 190)

OVERHILL   Village in the Westfarthing north of Hobbiton Hill. (I 40)

OVERLITHE   The leap-day in the Shire Reckoning, coming after Midyear's Day every fourth year except the last of a century. Overlithe was a special holiday. (III 478, 482)

ᘐ   ᘑ

PALADIN TOOK (TA 2933-FO 14)   Hobbit of the Shire, son of Adalgrim and father of Peregrin Took. Paladin was, as Paladin II, the thirty-first Thain of the Shire. When Lotho took over the Shire during the WR, Paladin refused to give up control of the Tookland or let the Chief's Men enter it, and organized an armed defense of the area. (III 356-57, 475)

PALANTIR, TAR- (Q.: 'far-sighted') (d. SA 3255) Dúnadan, twenty-third King of Númenor (3175-3255). Inziladûn, as he was named at birth, was trained in the ways of the Faithful by his mother, Inzilbêth. Perceptive and foreknowing, he took the sceptre in an Eldarin name and tried to stem the corruption of Númenor. But the King's Men, led by his younger brother Gimilkhâd and his nephew Pharazôn, secretly opposed Tar-Palantir, who eventually died of weariness and grief, leaving the sceptre to his only child, Míriel. (III 390, 392, 454; S 269, 292, 362; B 332, 362, 454)

PALANTÍRI (Q.: 'far-seer'; sing. *palantír*) Crystal globes wrought by the Noldor in Eldamar. The Masterstone was kept in the Tower of Avallónë, but the Eldar gave seven palantíri to Amandil of Andúnië. The palantíri showed scenes far away in time and space, especially things near to another palantír; two Stones thus could be used for communication. A person of strong will could learn to control the palantír and with it see where and whenever he wished.

At the fall of Númenor, Elendil brought the palantíri to Middle-earth and placed them throughout his realm. The chief palantír he placed in the Dome of Stars in Osgiliath; this stone alone could view all the others at one time. The others were placed in Minas Ithil, Minas Anor, Orthanc, Annúminas, Elostirion in the Tower Hills, and the Tower of Amon Sûl. After the fall of Elendil the Eldar took back into their care the palantír of the Tower Hills, which only looked to the Undying Lands, and from time to time the Eldar made pilgrimages to the Tower Hills to look at Eldamar and Valinor. This palantír was put aboard the white ship of the Last Riding of the Keepers of the Rings in TA 3021. The palantír of Amon Sûl was long coveted by Rhudaur and Cardolan, for it was the chief stone of the North-kingdom and the other two were possessed by Arthedain and the Eldar. In TA 1409 the Tower of Amon Sûl was destroyed by Angmar, but Arthedain recovered the palantír and carried it to Fornost. The palantíri of Amon Sûl and Annúminas were kept at Fornost until the fall of Arthedain, when they were lost in the shipwreck that killed Arvedui.

In Gondor, the palantír of Osgiliath was lost when the city was burned during the Kin-strife. The palantír of Minas Ithil was captured by the Nazgûl when they took the city in TA 2002, and Sauron gained control of it. This made the other palantíri dangerous to use, especially the stone of Minas Anor, to which the Ithil-stone was most closely aligned. The Ithil-stone was probably destroyed when Sauron fell in the WR. The Kings and Stewards of Gondor did not use the palantír of Minas Anor after the fall of Minas Ithil until the time of the WR, when Denethor II, grown grim after the death of his wife, felt that he needed the knowledge that the palantír could give him in order to counter Sauron. However, Sauron so manipulated Denethor's visions and assaulted his mind that the Steward went mad during the Battle of the Pelennor Fields and burned himself with the palantír in his hands. After this time, the only picture that could be seen in the palantír, except by one of very strong will, was of two burning hands.

The seventh palantír, that of Orthanc, was unused for most of the Third Age. In 2759, Saruman came to Orthanc in order to find the stone, but in using it he ensnared by Sauron. During the WR, Gríma threw the Orthanc-stone out of the tower and it was recovered by Aragorn, who as its rightful user wrested it to his own will. With the palantír of Orthanc Aragorn discovered many things, including the fleet of the Corsairs that was approaching Gondor, and with this knowledge he planned the course of action that resulted in the victory of the West in the Battle of the Pelennor Fields. After the WR, Aragorn used this palantír to show him the state of his kingdom.

Also called the Seeing-stones, the Seven Stones, and the Seven Seeing-stones. The palantír of the Tower Hills was called the Stone of Elendil. (II 241-42, 250-53, 254, 258-

60, 283; III 62-63, 159, 161-62, 321, 393, 397, 400, 406, 412, 418-19; R 65; S 292, 362; B 362, 454)

PANSY BOLGER (b. TA 2812)   Hobbit of the Shire, second child of Balbo Baggins. She married Fastolph Bolger. (III 474)

PARADISE   A land with dragon-flies, in Bilbo's poem *Errantry*. Any resemblance to places real, East or West, is probably coincidental. (TB 27)

PARMA (Q.: 'book')   Name for the tengwa **ᴘ** (number 2), which had the value *p* in most systems. (III 500)

PARMATÉMA (Q.: '*p*-series')   The second series of the Tengwar. In the Third Age the parmatéma was usually applied to the labials and bilabials. Number 22, in the sixth grade, was generally not rigidly incorporated into the series, although its commonest value, *w*, was a bilabial. (III 496-97, 500)

PARTH GALEN (S.)   Fair lawn running from Nen Hithoel to the slopes of Amon Hen. (I 511, 524)

PARTY FIELD   Field behind Bagshot Row in Hobbiton, site of Bilbo's Farewell Party in TA 3001. The Party Tree (q.v.) grew in the middle of the Field. (III 375)

PARTY TREE   Tree in the Party Field, under which Bilbo made his speech at the Farewell Party. The Party Tree was cut down by the Chief's Men during the WR, but after the War Sam Gamgee planted the seed given him by Galadriel on the spot where it had grown. The new Party Tree was the only mallorn in Eriador. (I 53; III 366)

PASS OF AGLON   Aglon (q.v.). (S 123; B 147)

PASS OF ANACH   Anach (q.v.). (S 200; B 245)

PASS OF CIRITH UNGOL   Cirith Ungol (q.v.). (III 412)

PASS OF SIRION The narrow valley through which the River Sirion flowed between the Ered Wethrin and the Echoriath. The principal entrance into West Beleriand from Ard-galen, the Pass was guarded by the tower of Minas Tirith on Tol Sirion; farther north, the Fens of Serech were also a good defensive position. Frequently assaulted by Morgoth, the Pass of Sirion was held by the Noldor of Nargothrond until FA 457, when Sauron took Minas Tirith. After he was driven out by Lúthien and Huan in 466 or 467, the Pass was not permanently defended.

The sheer walls of the Pass were covered with pines, but its floor was very fertile. (S 115, 120, 152, 155-56, 194; B 135, 142, 182, 187-88, 237)

PATHS OF THE DEAD Road under the Ered Nimrais leading from the Dead Door above Dunharrow to the source of the Northond near Erech. The Paths of the Dead were closed to all save the Dead, who lived there, and the heir of Isildur. (II 136; III 63-64, 69-72)

PEACE OF ARDA The three ages of the Chaining of Melkor, beginning with the capture of Melkor in the Battle of the Powers and ending with his poisoning of the Two Trees. The Peace of Arda corresponds closely with the Noontide of Valinor and the Sleep of Yavanna (qq.v.). (S 51, 92; B 51, 104)

PEARL TOOK (b. TA 2975) Hobbit of the Shire, eldest child of Paladin Took. She was a guest at the Farewell Party. (III 475)

PEEPING JACK Hobbit of Michel Delving, in the poem *Perry-the-Winkle*. He may have been a historical character. (TB 43)

PELARGIR (S.: 'enclosure of royal ships') City, the chief port of Gondor, built on Anduin at the mouth of the Sirith. Built in SA 2350, Pelargir became the greatest haven of the Faithful in Middle-earth, and Elendil landed here after the downfall of Númenor. Rebuilt by Eärnil I of Gondor about TA 920, Pelargir was used by the Ship-kings as the base for Gondor's many assaults in the Umbar area. During the Kin-strife Pelargir was seized by the rebels after the Battle of the Crossings of Erui and held for one year against Eldacar's siege. During the WR Pelargir was taken by the Corsairs, but they were in turn defeated by the Dead. (III 14, 186-87, 403, 406, 454; S 267, 291, 346; B 329, 361, 431)

PELENDUR (Q.) (d. TA 1998) Dúnadan of the House of Húrin, Steward of Gondor from before 1944 until his death. Pelendur governed Gondor for one year, after King Ondoher's death in 1944, and was instrumental in the rejection of Arvedui's claim to the crown. (III 395, 409-10)

PELENNOR (S.: 'fenced land') The area of Gondor surrounding Minas Tirith, a fair and fertile land. The Pelennor was enclosed by the Rammas Echor (q.v.). During the WR, the Battle of the Pelennor Fields was fought here.

Also called the Pelennor Fields and the Fields of Pelennor. (III 23, 151; RHM III 435; S 362; B 454)

PELÓRI (Q.: 'fenced heights') The great mountain chain of Aman, running in a long crescent eastward from Ekkaia and forming the boundary of Valinor on the north, east, and south.

First raised by the Valar as a defense against Melkor when they settled in Aman, the Pelóri were made sheer and higher during the hiding of Valinor. They were the tallest mountains in Arda. The only pass through the Pelóri was the Calacirya. The only peaks named are Taniquetil, in the central Pelóri near the Calacirya, and Hyarmentir, in the far south.

Also called the Mountains of Aman, of Valinor, and of Defence, and probably the Mountain Wall. (R 62; K 65; S 37, 59, 73, 74, 102, 346; B 32, 62, 80, 81, 117, 431)

PEONY BURROWS (b. TA 2950) Hobbit of the Shire, youngest child of Posco Baggins. She married Milo

Burrows and bore him four children. She was a guest at the Farewell Party. (III 474, 476)

PEOPLE OF HALETH The Haladin (q.v.). (S 146; B 175)

PEOPLE OF THE GREAT JOURNEY The Eldar (q.v.). (III 519)

PEOPLE OF THE STARS The Eldar (q.v.). (III 519)

PEREDHIL (S.: 'half-elven') Elros and Elrond, the two children of Eärendil and Elwing. They were called the Peredhil because of their extremely mixed Adan and Eldarin blood. At the end of the First Age, the Peredhil were given the choice of which race they wished to belong to. Elros chose to remain with the Edain, and he was given by the Valar a life-span many times that of lesser Men. Elrond became an Elven-lord of great power and wisdom. Elrond's children were also given the choice of which kindred they wished to belong to; the choice was to be made when Elrond left Middle-earth. All three of his children chose mortality.

Also called the Half-elven, a name which also refers to Eärendil and Elwing. (I 323; III 389; S 246, 261; B 304, 322)

PEREGRIN TOOK (TA 2990-FO c. 65) Hobbit of the Shire, the thirty-second Thain of the Shire (14-64) and a Counsellor of the North-kingdom (14-64). In his youth Pippin was a close friend of Frodo Baggins, whom he accompanied to Rivendell in 3018. There he became one of the Companions of the Ring. At Parth Galen he and Merry were captured by Orcs and taken toward Isengard. Escaping when the Orc-band was attacked by the Rohirrim, they fled into Fangorn Forest, where they were befriended by Fangorn the Ent, with whom they went to Isengard. There Pippin recovered the palantír which Gríma threw out of Orthanc, and being extremely curious by nature he looked in it and was questioned by Sauron. Gandalf later took him to Gondor, where he entered into the service of Denethor II and was made a Guard of the Citadel. During the Siege of Gondor, Pippin warned Beregond and Gandalf of Denethor's madness and thus helped to save Faramir's life. Later, Pippin marched with the Army of the West to the Morannon and in the final battle slew a great troll.

After the WR Pippin was rewarded by King Elessar and was made a knight of Gondor and a King's messenger. He then returned to the Shire and helped mobilize the Hobbits against the Chief's Men. Throughout his life Pippin maintained contact with the outside world, and in FO 64 he and Merry resigned their offices and rode to Rohan and Gondor. They died in Gondor a few years later and were buried in Minas Tirith with great honor.

Peregrin was universally known as Pippin. In Gondor during the WR he was erroneously called Ernil i Pheriannath, Prince of the Halflings. (I 38, 71; II 241-42, 249-54; III 29-31, 195, 207-08, 289, 321, 363, 471-72, 475, 514)

PERIANNATH (S.: 'halflings') Hobbits (q.v.). (III 510; R 67)

PERRY-THE-WINKLE Young Hobbit of Michel Delving, in the poem of the same name.

Also called the Winkle. The character of Perry-the-Winkle may have been based on a real Hobbit. (TB 42-44)

PERRY-THE-WINKLE Humorous poem written by Sam Gamgee and recorded in the Red Book of Westmarch. Although the Lonely Troll, one of the main characters, is probably fictitious, the Hobbits mentioned in the poem may have been modeled on real people. (TB 7, 41-44)

PERVINCA TOOK (b. TA 2985) Hobbit of the Shire, third daughter of Paladin Took. She was a guest at the Farewell Party. (III 475)

PETTY-DWARVES The Noegyth Nibin (q.v.). (S 204; B 250)

PHARAZÔN, AR- (Ad.: 'golden') (d. SA 3319) Dúnadan, twenty-fourth and last King of Númenor (3255-3319). The son of Gimilkhâd and nephew of Tar-Palantir, he led the rebellious Númenoreans during his uncle's reign after his father died. On the death of Tar-Palantir he forced the heiress, Tar-Míriel, to marry him despite their consanguinity; he then usurped the sceptre.

An ambitious man and a great warrior, Ar-Pharazôn was a popular king. The high point of his reign occurred in 3261, when he assembled a mighty army, sailed to Middle-earth, and humbled Sauron, then at the height of his power. But in his pride Ar-Pharazôn carried Sauron back to Númenor as a prisoner. He and his court quickly fell under the Shadow, and the next fifty years of Ar-Pharazôn's reign saw civil chaos and increased persecution of the Faithful. Finally, after Ar-Pharazôn had cut down Nimloth and worshipped Melkor with human sacrifices, Sauron induced him to attack Valinor and obtain immortality by force. For nine years, beginning in 3310, the King built the Great Armament, and in 3319 he landed on the forbidden shore of Aman the Blessed. Ar-Pharazôn and his landing party were entombed in the Caves of the Forgotten by the Change of the World, and Númenor was destroyed.

Ar-Pharazôn was known as "the Golden." The unused Quenya form of his name was Tar-Calion. (III 390, 392, 454; S 269-79, 290; B 333-45, 359)

PHIAL OF GALADRIEL Jar of crystal, containing the light of Eärendil caught in the water of the fountain that filled the Mirror of Galadriel. The Phial was given by Galadriel to Frodo as a parting gift when he left Lórien during the Quest. The Phial had the virtue of shining in dark places and of bringing strength and courage, and its light was in turn increased by the hope and bravery of its bearer. With the Phial Frodo was able to overcome his desire for the Ring, and Sam used the Phial to cow and blind Shelob. It also aided the breaking of the spell of the gate of the Tower of Cirith Ungol. After the WR, Frodo bore the Phial with him to the West. (I 487-88; II 401, 408, 417-20, 430; III 218, 234-35, 384)

PHURUNARGIAN (gen. West.: 'dwarf-delving') Kha-zad-dûm (q.v.). (III 519)

PICKTHORN Family of Men of Bree. (III 335)

PILLARS OF THE KING The Argonath (q.v.). (I 508)

PIMPERNEL TOOK (b. TA 2979) Hobbit of the Shire, second daughter of Paladin Took. She was a guest at the Farewell Party. (III 475)

PINCUP Village in the Southfarthing, in the Green Hill Country. (I 40)

PINNACLE OF ORTHANC Orthanc (q.v.). (S 291; B 361)

PINNATH GELIN (S.: 'slopes green') Hills in south-western Gondor, north of Anfalas.
Called in Westron the Green Hills. (I 17; III 50, 152)

PIPE-WEED The tobacco of Middle-earth. Originally brought to Middle-earth from Númenor, pipe-weed grew abundantly in Gondor but only with great care in the North, in places like Longbottom and Bree. In Gondor pipe-weed was esteemed for the fragrance of its flowers, but Hobbits, probably in Bree, were the first to smoke it. Dwarves, Rangers, Gandalf, and other wanderers picked up the habit at the Prancing Pony, and about TA 2670 Tobold Hornblower grew pipe-weed for the first time in the Shire. Of the Companions of the Ring, Gandalf, Aragorn, Merry, Pippin, and Gimli were avid smokers, but Legolas, perhaps in common with all Elves, disapproved of the habit.
Famous strains of pipe-weed from the Southfarthing included Longbottom Leaf, Old Toby, and Southern Star. Southlinch was a strain grown in Bree.
Called also in the Shire leaf. Called in Gondor (in Sindarin) galenas or sweet galenas, and in Westron west-mansweed. (I 28-29; II 208, 213-14; III 178, 334, 459)

PIPPIN Peregrin Took (q.v.). (I 71)

PIPPIN GAMGEE (b. FO 9) Hobbit of the Shire, fifth child of Sam Gamgee. His real name may have been Peregrin. (III 382, 477)

PLACE OF THE FOUNTAIN The Court of the Fountain (q.v.). (III 25, 27)

POLO BAGGINS (b. c. TA 2860) Hobbit of the Shire, son of Ponto Baggins. (III 474)

PONTO BAGGINS (TA 2816-2911) Hobbit of the Shire, third child of Balbo Baggins. He married Mimosa Bunce; they had two children. (III 474)

PONTO BAGGINS (b. TA 2946) Hobbit of the Shire, first child of Posco Baggins. He was a guest at the Farewell Party. (III 474)

POOL OF BYWATER Wide pool in Bywater, part of the Water. Another stream, flowing from the north, joined the Water in the Pool.
Also called the Bywater Pool and the Pool. (I 40; III 265, 349)

POOL SIDE The portion of the Hobbiton Road next to the Pool of Bywater. A row of ugly brick houses was built there during Lotho's control of the Shire. (III 349)

POOLS OF IVRIN Eithel Ivrin (q.v.). (S 239; B 296)

POPPY BOLGER (b. TA 2944) Hobbit of the Shire, daughter of Falco Chubb-Baggins. She married Filibert Bolger and was a guest at the Farewell Party. (III 474)

POROS (S.) River flowing from the southern Ephel Dúath into Anduin just above its delta. The Poros formed the southern boundary of Ithilien. It was crossed by the Harad Road at the Crossings of Poros (q.v.), the site of an important battle with the Haradrim in TA 2885. (III 14-15, 409)

PORTO BAGGINS (b. TA 2948) Hobbit of the Shire, second son of Posco Baggins. He was a guest at the Farewell Party. (III 474)

POSCO BAGGINS (b. TA 2902, d. before 3001) Hobbit of the Shire, son of Polo Baggins. He married Lily Brownlock; they had three children. (III 474)

POSTMASTER An office and title of the Mayor of Michel Delving in his capacity of head of the Messenger Service. (I 31)

POTT A Hobbit surname, in Sam Gamgee's poem *Perry-the-Winkle*. Old Pott was Mayor of Michel Delving in the poem. (TB 42)

POWERS The Valar (q.v.). (S 268; B 330)

POWERS OF ARDA, POWERS OF THE WORLD The Valar (q.v.). (S 20, 24; B 10)

PRANCING PONY, THE The inn at Bree, owned and operated for many generations by the Butterbur family. At the time of the WR the proprietor was Barliman Butterbur. The Prancing Pony was the home and center of the art of smoking pipe-weed, and in prosperous times was one of the great centers of news in Eriador.

Called for short the Pony. (I 29, 209-41; III 332-39)

PRIMARY LETTERS The first twenty-four letters of the Tengwar, divided into series (témar) and grades (tyeller) and given values according to consistent phonetic principles. (III 495-96)

PRIMROSE GAMGEE (b. FO 15) Hobbit of the Shire, ninth child of Samwise Gamgee. (III 477)

PRIMULA BAGGINS (TA 2920-80) Hobbit of the Shire, youngest child of Gorbadoc Brandybuck. She married Drogo Baggins and bore him one child, Frodo. She and her husband were drowned in a boating accident on the Brandywine. (I 45; III 474, 476)

PRINCESS MEE A nonsense-poem written by an unknown Hobbit in a margin of the Red Book of Westmarch. (TB 7, 28-30)

PRISCA BOLGER (b. TA 2906, d. before 3001) Hobbit of the Shire, second child of Polo Baggins. She married Wilibald Bolger. (III 474)

PROPHECY OF THE NORTH The Doom of the Noldor (q.v.). (S 87; B 98)

PROUDFOOT Family of Hobbits of the Shire, perhaps of the upper class. (I 52, 53; III 474)

PUDDIFOOT Family of Hobbits, at least one branch of which lived in Stock at the time of the WR. (I 133)

PÚKEL-MEN Name given by the Rohirrim to the grotesque statues on the road leading from Edoras to Dunharrow, carved early in the Second Age by the Men of the Mountains. (III 80, 81, 129)

❧   ☙

QUARRY Village in the Eastfarthing, near Scary. (I 40)

QUEENS OF THE VALAR The seven Valier (q.v.). (S 25; B 18)

QUELLË (Q.: 'fading') The fourth season of the Eldarin loa (q.v.), very roughly equivalent to our October and November. The Sindarin form of the name was firith.

Other names for this season were lasselanta and narbeleth. Quellë or lasselanta was the name given by Men to the end of yávië and the beginning of hrívë. (III 480, 485)

QUENDI (Q.: 'the speakers') The Elves (q.v.). (III 519; S 41, 49, 309; B 38, 49, 383)

QUENTA SILMARILLION (Q.: 'history of the Silmarils') A compendious history of the early days of Arda, beginning with the creation of the Lamps of the Valar and ending with the Great Battle and the casting-out of Melkor at the end of the First Age of Middle-earth. Composed from accounts by the Eldar of Beleriand, *Quenta Silmarillion* focuses on the revolt of the Noldor and the War of the Great Jewels. Great emphasis is placed on the deeds of the Edain, but the main theme of the history, as its title in part implies, is the tragedy that resulted when the evil of Melkor defiled the Two Trees and the Silmarils, the greatest constructions of the Valar and the Children of Ilúvatar.

Quenta Silmarillion was no doubt one of Bilbo's *Translations from the Elvish,* preserved in the Red Book of Westmarch. The *Ainulindalë* and *Valaquenta* were closely associated with it.

Also called *The Silmarillion.* (III 389; S 7-9, 31, 35-255, esp. 247, 362; B ix-xiv, 25, 29-316 esp. 305-06, 454)

QUENYA (Q.: 'speech') The language of the Eldar of Valinor, presumably the closest language to that spoken in Cuiviénen by the first Quendi. In the course of its slow change in the Undying Lands and Middle-earth, Quenya underwent some substantial phonological changes, including the simplification of pre-stress *mb* and *nd* to *m* and *n,* and the change of *th, z,* and initial *ch, w, ng,* and *ngw* to *s, r, h, v, n,* and *nw,* respectively. The vocabulary was enhanced by borrowings from the language of the Valar.

In the West, the Quenya of the Teleri on Tol Eressëa developed into a different dialect from that of the Noldor and Vanyar on the mainland of Aman. In mortal lands, Quenya was spoken by the Noldorin exiles and underwent several minor changes. But its change was slowed when, as the language of the Kinslayers, it was banned by Thingol, and Quenya became a language of lore, loved by the Noldor, the Edain who knew it, and the Ents, but not used in public. It remained a language of lore among the Dúnedain, and in later ages its use was a sign of respect and friendship for the Eldar.

Quenya was a beautiful language, its liquid syllables suited to songs and poetry. Examples of Quenya include *Namárië,* the names of the Tengwar (which was devised to represent Quenya) and of calendar divisions, the royal names of Númenor (before the Shadow fell), Arnor and Gondor, some of Fangorn's rumblings, and many of the names of the Ainur and the Eldar.

Also called the Ancient Speech, the Ancient Tongue, the High Speech of the West Eldarin, High-elven, High Eldarin, and (on III 172) Valinorean. (III 119, 487-501 passim, 506, 507, 510; S 59, 108, 129, 262, 267-68, 326, 346; B 62, 125, 155, 323, 330, 406, 432)

QUESSE (Q.: 'feather') Name for the tengwa ꛃ (number 4), originally having the value *kw.* (III 500)

QUESSETÉMA (Q.: '*kw*-series') A labialized series of the Tengwar, applied in Quenya to Series IV. The first four letters of the quessetéma had the theoretical values *kw, gw, khw,* or *hw* and *ghw* or *w.* The actual Quenya values of the first four tyeller of this series, however, were *kw, ngw, gw,* and *nw.* (III 496-97, 500)

QUESTIONER One of Sauron's servants (the torturer of the Barad-dûr) or Sauron himself. (II 74)

QUEST OF MOUNT DOOM Frodo Baggins's mission to destroy the One Ring in the Sammath Naur of Orodruin. Frodo resolved to undertake the Quest at the Council of Elrond, November 25, TA 3018, and he achieved it on March 25, 3019. (I 367)

QUEST OF THE SILMARIL The mission of Beren to obtain a Silmaril from the Iron Crown of Morgoth, laid on him by Thingol as a bride-price for Lúthien. Beren began the Quest in FA 466 and—aided by Finrod, Lúthien, and Huan—achieved its final goal in 468, when he gave the Silmaril to Thingol at the end of the Hunting of the Wolf. Although the Quest was a glorious success, killing Draugluin and Carcharoth, destroying Sauron's power for the rest of the First Age, and recovering one Silmaril, the price was high. Finrod and Huan were slain, Beren lost one hand and later died for the first time, and the Silmaril, tainted by the Oath of Fëanor, was to cause the death of Thingol and the ruin of Doriath. Yet in time this Silmaril, recovered at great cost by Beren the Adan, brought about the intervention of the Valar and the casting-out of Morgoth. (S 167-86; B 202-26)

QUICKBEAM Bregalad (q.v.). (II 109)

QUICK POST Some sort of fast-delivery mail and message system in the Shire, probably a part of the Messenger Service. During his control of the Shire, Lotho Sackville-Baggins used the Quick Post system for his own purposes. (III 348)

⤦ ⤣

RADAGAST (tr. Mannish) (fl. TA 1000-3018)   One of the Istari. Radagast dwelt at Rhosgobel and was a master of herb- and beast-lore. He was especially friendly with birds. Aside from unwittingly causing Gandalf to be captured by Saruman and equally unwittingly arranging for his escape, Radagast does not seem to have done very much during the WR.

Radagast was, in the order of the Istari, Radagast the Brown. (I 336-37, 342, 359; H 121; S 300, 302; B 372, 375)

RADBUG (d. TA 3019)   Orc of the Tower of Cirith Ungol. Shagrat squeezed his eyes out when he refused to obey an order after the fight between the Orcs of the Tower of Cirith Ungol and Gorbag's company from Minas Morgul. (III 222)

RADHRUIN (S.: '—flame'?) (d. FA 460)   Adan of the First House, one of the last twelve outlaw-companions of Barahir in Dorthonion. (S 155, 162-63; B 187, 196)

RAGNOR (S.) (d. FA 460)   Adan of the First House, one of the last twelve outlaw-companions of Barahir. (S 155, 162-63; B 187, 196)

RAMDAL (S.: 'wall-end')   Hill or hills in East Beleriand, the eastern end of the Andram. (S 122, 363, 364; B 146, 455, 456)

RAMMAS ECHOR (S.: 'great-wall circle')   The wall built around the Pelennor by Steward Ecthelion II after the desertion of Ithilien in TA 2954. The Rammas was repaired at the time of the WR but was easily breached by the army of the Lord of the Nazgûl on March 13, 3019.
    See also: the Causeway Forts. (III 23, 136; S 358; B 449)

RÁNA (Q.: 'wanderer')   A Noldorin name for the Moon (q.v.).
    Also called the Wayward. (S 99, 347; B 114, 432)

RANGERS OF ITHILIEN   Soldiers of Gondor, Dúnedain descended from the inhabitants of Ithilien. After Ithilien was overrun by Orcs in 2901 the Rangers crossed the Anduin from time to time to harry Sauron's forces in Ithilien. They used various secret retreats, of which the most important was Henneth Annûn. At the time of the WR, Faramir was the Captain of the Rangers.
    After the WR, the Rangers may have formed the bulk of the White Company.
    The Rangers wore brown and green camouflage uniforms, with green gloves and masks. They carried spears or great bows as well as swords. (II 335, 338; III 198, 416)

RANGERS OF THE NORTH   Those of the Dúnedain of the North who guarded Eriador from Orcs, wild animals, and other evil things after the fall of Arthedain. The Rangers gave special protection to the Shire, especially during the period just before the WR. It seems that most of the male Dúnedain were Rangers, and that they were led by the Chieftain of the Dúnedain, who was the heir of Isildur.

The Rangers were grim in life, appearance, and dress. They wore grey or dark green cloaks, with no ornament save for a cloak-clasp shaped like a six-pointed star. The Rangers rode rough-haired, sturdy horses and carried spears, bows, and swords.

The Hobbits of the Shire called them the Watchers or the Watchers at Sarn Ford; they were generally considered rather disreputable in the Shire and Bree. (I 205, 214, 291, 325-26; III 59-60, 61-62, 463, 464; TB 21)

RANUGAD (gen. Hobb.: 'stay-at-home')   Hamfast (q.v.). (III 517)

RATH CELERDAIN (S.: 'street of the lampwrights')   Broad street in the first level of Minas Tirith, leading to the Great Gate. The Old Guesthouse was located on Rath Celerdain.

Called in Westron the Lampwrights' Street. (III 46, 47)

RATH DÍNEN (S.: 'silent street')   The main street of the Hallows (q.v.) of Minas Tirith. (III 121-22, 427, 472)

RATHLÓRIEL (S.: 'way-golden' or 'goldenbed')   Name given the River Ascar (q.v.) after the treasure taken from Doriath by the Dwarves of Nogrod was drowned in its depths. (S 123, 235; B 146, 291)

RAUROS (S.: 'roaring-foam')   Waterfalls on Anduin south of Nen Hithoel, where Anduin fell from the height of the Emyn Muil. Rauros was bypassed by the North Stair, a portage-way built by the Kings of Gondor.

Also called the Falls of Rauros. (I 483, 518; S 297, 347; B 369, 432)

RAVENHILL Hill near Erebor at the end of the great southern spur of that mountain. The Dwarves of Erebor built a guardhouse on Ravenhill and gave the hill its name because ravens, wise and famous Dwarf-friends, lived in a nest on top of the guardhouse.

During the expedition of Thorin and Company, the Dwarves stayed here one night, during which they met Roäc and learned of the death of Smaug. During the Battle of the Five Armies the Elves of Mirkwood, and also Gandalf and Bilbo, made their stand on Ravenhill. (H 195, 231-33, 244, 269-70)

RAVENS Birds of Middle-earth. The ravens of Erebor were friendly with the Dwarves and spoke Westron. They were very large and lived to a great age; Roäc was 153 years old in TA 2941. (H 243-44)

RAVINES OF TEIGLIN Cabed-en-Aras (q.v.). (S Map; B Map)

RÉ (Q.: 'day') The solar day of the Eldar, measured from sunset to sunset. The ré may also have been the day of the Dúnedain calendars. (III 479)

REALM OF NARGOTHROND Nargothrond (q.v.). (S Map; B Map)

RECKONING OF RIVENDELL The Calendar of Imladris (q.v.), so called by the Hobbits of the Shire. (III 480)

RECKONING OF YEARS, THE A book by Merry Brandybuck discussing the relationship between the calendars of the Shire, Bree, Rivendell, Gondor, and Rohan. (I 38)

RED ARROW A black-feathered arrow barbed with steel; its tip was painted red. The Red Arrow was sent from Gondor to Rohan when the former needed aid, and may have been associated with the Oath of Eorl. (III 86)

RED BOOK OF WESTMARCH Large book with red leather covers, written by Bilbo, Frodo, and Sam, and containing additions and notes by other hands. The Red Book contained the story of Bilbo's adventures with Thorin in TA 2941, and an account of the WR and the events of the end of the Third Age as seen by Hobbits. Attached to the Red Book were the three volumes of Bilbo's *Translations from the Elvish* and a volume of genealogies and other Shire matters compiled by one of Sam's descendants.

The Red Book was given by Sam to his daughter Elanor, and was kept by the Fairbairns in Westmarch, whence its name. Although the original of the Red Book was lost, many copies of it were made. The first, and most important, was the Thain's Book (q.v.). An exact copy of this copy, made by Findegil in FO 172, was kept at the Great Smials. This copy, the only extant one to contain all of Bilbo's *Translations,* also contains annotations and corrections made by the scholars of Gondor, as well as various marginalia written by many generations of Hobbits. This copy seems to be the one used by Professor Tolkien.

Also known as the Red Book and (in Gondor) the Red Book of the Periannath. (I 19, 37; III 365, 379-80; TB 7)

REDHORN Barazinbar (q.v.). (I 370)

REDHORN GATE One of the most important passes over the Misty Mountains, located on the southern side of Barazinbar, and connecting Eregion and Azanulbizar. The eastern approach to the Redhorn Gate was known as the Dimrill Stair.

Also called the Redhorn Pass. (I 370, 376 ff.; III 401)

REDHORN PASS The Redhorn Gate (q.v.). (III 401)

RED RING, RED RING OF FIRE Narya (q.v.). (S 298, 304; B 370, 378)

REDWATER Carnen (q.v.). (III 440)

REGINARD TOOK (b. TA 2969) Hobbit of the Shire,

eldest son of Adelard Took. He was a guest at the Farewell Party. (III 475)

REGION (S.: 'thorn, holly'?) Dense forest of East Beleriand, lying between the Rivers Esgalduin and Aros south of Dor Dínen. Some of the Noldor rested in Region during the Great Journey. Later in the First Age it was the home of many Sindar and was included within the Girdle of Melian as part of the Kingdom of Doriath.

Also called the Forest of Region. (S 55, 93, 96, 97, 121, 358; B 57, 105, 110, 145, 449)

REMMIRATH (S.: 'net-jewel-collective plural') The Pleiades.

Called in Westron the Netted Stars. (I 120; III 490)

RERIR Mount Rerir (q.v.). (S 124; B 148)

RETHE The third month of the Shire Reckoning and the calendar of Bree, corresponding roughly to our March. (III 478, 483)

REUNITED KINGDOM The realm ruled by Elessar and the Telcontari who succeeded him, so called because it included all the lands, both Gondor and Arnor, claimed by Elendil and divided after his death. The capitals of the Reunited Kingdom were Annúminas and Minas Tirith. At the beginning of the Fourth Age the Reunited Kingdom included all those lands which were part of Arnor and Gondor at their greatest extent, except for Rohan. In addition, the King of the Reunited Kingdom was overlord of Dale and Erebor, and probably received tribute from much of Harad and Rhûn. (I 37)

RHÎW (S.: 'winter') The Sindarin form of hrívë (q.v.). (III 480)

RHOSGOBEL (S.) The dwelling-place of Radagast, near the southern border of Mirkwood. Rhosgobel was probably located in the Vales of Anduin. (I 336, 359; H 121)

RHOVANION (S.) General name given to the lands between the Misty Mountains and the River Running.
  Called in Westron Wilderland. (I 17; III 405, 406; H 13; L 196; S 291, 347; B 360, 432)

RHUDAUR (S.: 'east—') Region of Eriador and name of the kingdom founded in TA 861 by one of the sons of King Eärendur of Arnor. The kingdom included all the lands between the Weather Hills, the Ettenmoors, and the Misty Mountains, and also included the Angle. The Dúnedain were few in Rhudaur, and by 1350 the kingdom was controlled by Hill-men and was in league with Angmar. With the defeat of the Witch-king of Angmar in 1975 Rhudaur fell and all its people were scattered or destroyed. (I 269 ff.; III 396, 397; S 291; B 360)

RHÛN (S.: 'east') Name given by the Dúnedain of Gondor to the area east of the Sea of Rhûn (q.v.). In the First Age Oromë came here to hunt, and at the height of its power Gondor ruled the western part of Rhûn. After the fifth century of the Third Age, however, the Easterlings (q.v.), Men of various races living in the many countries of Rhûn, made war on Gondor, often at the instigation of Sauron.
  Called in Westron the East or the Eastlands. (I 17, 325, 518; III 29, 403, 404 ff.)

RHYMES OF LORE Poems designed to aid the retention of various ancient facts. Men, Elves, Hobbits, and probably other races had Rhymes of Lore. The Long List of the Ents may be an example of one. (II 258, 259)

RÍAN (S.) (d. FA 473 or 474) Adan of the First House, daughter of Belegund. After Dagor Aglareb Rían fled from Dorthonion to Dor-lómin with Emeldir, and there she married Huor in the spring of 473, two months before his death in the Nirnaeth Arnoediad. That winter Rían gave birth to their son, Tuor, whom she gave for fostering to the Sindar of Mithrim. Rían then went to Haudh-en-

Ndengin, lay down on it, and died. (S 148, 155, 198, 238, 307, 308; B 177, 187, 242, 294, 381, 382)

RIDDERMARK OF ROHAN   Rohan (q.v.). (I 343)

RIDER   The dark, mysterious mounted figure who captured Elves who strayed from Cuiviénen. The Rider was probably Melkor, who needed to capture Elves so that he could breed them into Orcs; he probably appeared in this form to resemble Oromë and thus alienate the Elves from the Valar.
Also called the Hunter. (S 49, 50; B 49, 50)

RIDERS OF ROHAN   The knights of Rohan. Those riders who were grouped in éoreds served one particular lord, as for example Théoden's knights, who were called the Riders of the King's House. However, in addition to the knights of the noble households there also seem to have been many Riders who were soldiers at need only.
The Riders were excellent horsemen and rode together with great skill. They were armed with sword, shield, and lance.
The cavalry of this people was known as the Riders even in Eothéod, and from them derived the Rohirrim's name for their new land, the Riddermark. Also called the Riders of the Mark. (II 40-41; III 79-80, 139-40, 314, 429-30)

RIDDLE-GAME   A game of set and sacred rules, in which two people asked each other riddles, and the first one unable to answer lost the predetermined stakes. The Riddle-game seems to have been played throughout Middle-earth, and was included in the guardianship of the Valar. (I 33, 89; H 80-87, esp. 86)

RIMMON   Mountain in the northern Ered Nimrais upon which was built the beacon-tower of Min-Rimmon.
The name *Rimmon* was of forgotten origin, having originated in the Second Age before the settlement of Gondor. (III 14, 130, 508)

RING   The One Ring (q.v.). (I 32, etc.)

RINGARË (Q.: 'cold—') The twelfth month of the Kings' and Stewards' Reckonings, and the ninth of the New Reckoning, corresponding roughly to our December.

The Sindarin form of the name, used only by the Dúnedain, was Girithron. (III 483)

RINGIL (S.: 'cold-star' or 'cold-spark') The sword of Fingolfin. (S 153-54, 363; B 185, 455)

RING-INSCRIPTION The inscription on the One Ring, written by Sauron in a special Tengwar mode in the Black Speech. The inscription read:

Ash nazg durbatulûk, ash nazg gimbatul,
Ash nazg thrakatulûk agh burzum ishi krimpatul,

the words spoken by Sauron when he forged the One. They meant:

One Ring to rule them all, One Ring to find them,
One Ring to bring them all and in the darkness bind them.

The Ring-inscription, which was visible only when the Ring was heated, was designed to ensnare the other Rings of Power. (I 80-81, 333)

RINGLÓ (S.: 'cold-flood') River in Lamedon, Gondor, the largest tributary of the Morthond, which it joined just above its mouth. The Ciril flowed into the Ringló. (III 14, 184; S 363; B 455)

RINGLÓ VALE The valley of the Ringló, in Lamedon. (III 49)

RING OF ADAMANT Nenya (q.v.). (S 298; B 370)

RING OF BARAHIR An Elven-ring, made by the Noldor in Valinor and given by Finrod to Barahir during Dagor Bragollach as a pledge of his aid to Barahir and his kin. When Barahir was slain in Dorthonion, his hand, bearing the ring, was cut off for proof of his death, but

Beren recovered both hand and ring, at great peril to himself. He brought the ring to Nargothrond during the Quest of the Silmarils, and Finrod fulfilled his pledge, giving his life to save Beren in the dungeons of Minas Tirith.

The ring was somehow preserved through the rest of the First Age (probably by Dior and Elwing), and apparently passed into the hands of the Faithful of Númenor in the Second. In the Third Age it was one of the heirlooms of the North-kingdom; at the fall of Arthedain Arvedui gave it to the chief of the Lossoth, from whom it was afterwards ransomed. Thereafter it was kept at Rivendell.

The ring was in the fashion of two serpents with emerald eyes, one devouring and the other supporting a crown of golden flowers. Also called the ring of Felagund. (III 399-400, 401, 421; S 152, 164, 167, 168-69; B 183, 198, 202, 204)

RING OF DOOM Máhanaxar (q.v.). (S 50; B 51)

RING OF FIRE Narya (q.v.). (S 304; B 378)

RING OF ISENGARD See: Isengard. (II 203)

RING OF SAPPHIRE Vilya (q.v.). (S 298; B 370)

RINGS OF POWER The greatest rings of Middle-earth, forged by the Noldorin smiths of Eregion and by Sauron between SA 1500 and 1590. There were Nine Rings for Men, Seven Rings for Dwarves, and Three Rings for the Elves (qq.v.). Ten years after the forging of these Rings, Sauron treacherously forged the One Ring (q.v.) to rule the others, but his designs were perceived by Celebrimbor. Although the Elves managed to escape from this trap, and the Dwarves proved untamable through the Rings, the Nine Rings ensnared the Nazgûl (q.v.). After the unmaking of the One Ring during the WR, however, all the Rings of Power lost their power.

Any mortal possessing one of the Rings would not die,

but would continue living in great weariness; the Dwarves, however, were unaffected by this.

All the Rings except for the One consisted of a metal band set with a gem.

Also called the Great Rings and the Rings. (I 76, 321, 330, 333, 352, 472-73; III 445-46, 453; S 283-85; B 353)

RINGWIL (S.: 'cold—') River of West Beleriand, flowing eastward through the Taur-en-Faroth and plunging into the Narog at Nargothrond. (S 122, 363; B 146, 455)

RINGWRAITHS, RING-WRAITHS The Nazgûl (q.v.). (I 82; S 267; B 330)

RIVENDELL Elven-refuge in a steep and hidden valley in the Angle, founded in SA 1697 by Elrond, who was fleeing from the destruction of Eregion with the remnant of the Gwaith-i-Mírdain; most of the Elves of Rivendell were Eldar, including the great lords Gildor and Glorfindel.

From Rivendell Elrond succoured the Dúnedain at need in the Third Age. Valandil, the son of Isildur, was raised here, as were, later, all the Chieftains of the Dúnedain. Rivendell survived the War of the Elves and Sauron and the wars against Angmar because of the great Elven-power there; in more peaceful times Rivendell was a center of lore and counsel.

After the WR, Elrond and many of the Elves of Rivendell went over Sea, but Elladan and Elrohir remained there, and they were joined by Celeborn. There is no record of when Rivendell was finally deserted.

Called in Sindarin Imladris and in genuine Westron Karningul. (I 17, 39, 289-368; III 397, 401, 421, 454, 468; H 57-63; R 64; S 288, 297; B 357, 369)

RIVER-DAUGHTER Goldberry (q.v.). (I 171, 176)

RIVER RUNNING River flowing from the Front Gate of Erebor to the Sea of Rhûn, about 600 miles long. The

River Running passed through the Long Lake, which it left by a waterfall. Its principal tributaries were the Forest River and the Carnen.

The River Running was an important trade route.

Called in Sindarin the Celduin. Also called the Running River. (I 17; III 405; H 185, 194-95, 230)

RIVER-WOMAN Denizen of the Old Forest, living in a deep pool of the Withywindle. She was the mother of Goldberry. (TB 11, 15)

RIVIL (S.) Stream flowing northwest from western Dorthonion into Sirion, which it joined in the Fen of Serech. (S 191, 194; B 233, 237)

RIVIL'S WELL Springs in western Dorthonion, the source of the Rivil. Here Beren killed the Orc-chief who had slain his father and recovered the ring of Barahir. (S 163; B 197)

ROÄC (b. TA 2788) Chief of the great ravens of Erebor, son of Carc, friendly to the Dwarves. In 2941 Roäc acted as counsellor and messenger to Thorin, telling him of the death of Smaug and sending ravens to bring Dwarves of Durin's Folk of Erebor. (H 244-46)

ROBIN GAMGEE (b. FO 20) Hobbit of the Shire, twelfth child of Samwise Gamgee. (III 477)

ROBIN SMALLBURROW (fl. WR) Hobbit of the Shire, living in Hobbiton. Robin became a Shirriff before the WR because it was an easy job, but with the expansion of the Shirriffs under Lotho Sackville-Baggins he became, unwillingly, part of the First Eastfarthing Troop.

Also called Cock-robin. (III 346-49)

ROCHALLOR (S.: 'horse—') The steed of Fingolfin, presumably of the breed of Valinor brought to Middle-earth by Fëanor and the Exiles. (S 153; B 184)

RODYN (S.)   See: Valanya. (III 484)

ROHAN (S.: 'horse-land')   Kingdom of the Rohirrim, bounded by the Ered Nimrais, the Isen, the Misty Mountains, Fangorn, the Limlight, Anduin, the Mouths of Entwash, and the Mering Stream. Once a province of Gondor, Calenardhon, the land was given to the Men of Éothéod by Cirion of Gondor in TA 2510 in return for their aid in the Battle of the Fields of Celebrant and their swearing to the Oath of Eorl. Rohan, as the country was then called in Gondor, was ruled by King Eorl and his descendants.

The Rohirrim farmed and raised horses on the green plains of their country and restored ancient fortresses and refuges in the Ered Nimrais, the most important of which were Dunharrow and Helm's Deep. The first kings built the capital of Edoras below Dunharrow, but most of the Rohirrim dwelt in small villages or on farms. Their greatest concern was for their horses, which were the best in the world.

In 2758 Rohan was overrun by Dunlendings led by Wulf, but the invaders were defeated the next spring by Fréaláf. After 2799, Orcs fleeing from the Battle of Nanduhirion troubled Rohan, and they were not entirely driven out of the Ered Nimrais until 2864. About 2960 Saruman began to trouble Rohan, and his harassments increased until the WR, when Rohan was invaded by an enormous army of Orcs and Dunlendings. Although the Rohirrim were defeated in the two Battles of the Fords of Isen, the invaders were crushed, with the aid of Gandalf and the Huorns, in the Battle of the Hornburg.

Throughout its history, Rohan was closely allied with Gondor. Rohan performed its greatest service to the Dúnadan realm during the WR, when the Riders of Rohan played a crucial role in the Battle of the Pelennor Fields.

Rohan was the name given the land in Gondor; the Rohirrim called their land the Riddermark, the Mark of the Riders, or the Mark. The Orcs called it Horse-country.

See also: entries for individual kings of Rohan, Eastfold, Westfold, etc. (I 343; II 30 ff.; III 428-38, 459-72)

ROHERYN (S.: 'horse of the lady') (fl. WR) The horse of Aragorn, shaggy, proud, and strong. During the WR Halbarad brought Roheryn to Aragorn in Rohan, and he rode him for the remainder of the War.

Roheryn was so named because Aragorn received him from Arwen. (III 59, 70; S 363; B 455)

ROHIRRIC The language of the Rohirrim, related to the languages of the Men of the Vales of Anduin. Rohirric was probably descended from Adûnaic or a related language and was thus distantly related to Westron, than which it was more archaic. Rohirric was closely related to the former language of the northern Hobbits, and even by the time of the WR many words in Rohirric and Hobbitish were clearly related.

The Rohirrim continued to speak their ancestral tongue into the Fourth Age, even though their neighbors spoke Westron. (III 508, 510, 517)

ROHIRRIM (S.: 'horse-lord people') Men, the inhabitants of Rohan, descended from the Éothéod (q.v.). Because of the Oath of Eorl and their natural nobility, the Rohirrim were friendly to Gondor and deadly foes of her enemies.

The Rohirrim were tall and blond, with fair faces; they lived to be about eighty and retained their strength even in old age. The Rohirrim loved their horses above all else; they raised the noblest horses and were the best horsemen in all of Middle-earth. The Rohirrim were culturally conservative, keeping even into the Fourth Age their ancient customs and language. They wrote with a primitive mode of the Cirth.

The Rohirrim called themselves the Eorlingas (tr. Roh.: 'sons of Eorl'); Rohirrim was the name given them in Gondor. Also called the Sons of Eorl, the Horse-lords, the Horse-men (by Ghân-buri-Ghân), the Horsemen of the North, Forgoil (by the Dunlendings), the Whiteskins (by Orcs), the Riders (by synecdoche), and the North-men (in opposition to the Haradrim). (I 343; II 39-41, 363-64; III 415, 428-30, 493, 508)

RÓMEN (Q.: 'east') Name for the tengwa Ρ (number 25), which was usually used for full *r*. This tengwa was commonly used to indicate the compass-direction "east" even in languages in which the word for "east" did not begin with this sound. (III 500)

RÓMENDACIL I (Q.: 'east-victor') (d. TA 541) Dúnadan, eighth King of Gondor (492-541). He took his royal name to commemorate his victories over the Easterlings, but he was later slain in battle with them.
His birth-name was Tarostar. (III 394, 403)

RÓMENDACIL II (d. TA 1366) Dúnadan, nineteenth King of Gondor (1304-66), originally called Minalcar. The nephew of King Narmacil, he was a man of great vigor and talent, and so Narmacil, and later his own father Calmacil, made him Regent (1240-1304). In 1248 he won a great victory over the Easterlings and extended Gondor's power to the Sea of Rhûn. After this victory he took the name Rómendacil, with which he was later crowned. Among his other accomplishments, Rómendacil fortified the Anduin frontier and built the Argonath.
Realizing that Gondor was weak in manpower, Rómendacil showed great favor to the Northmen, and in 1250 sent his son Valacar to the court of Vidugavia. This action, although in itself wise, later led to the Kin-strife. (III 395, 404-05)

RÓMENNA (Q.: 'eastwards') Harbor and port in eastern Númenor, after about SA 3100 the main center of the Faithful in Númenor, and in the days of Amandil the main dwelling-place of the Lords of Andúnië. (S 268, 272, 279; B 331, 336, 346)

ROPER Family of Hobbits of the Shire, descended from Andwise Roper, the eldest son of Hobson "Roper" Gamgee. For at least two generations the Ropers kept a rope-walk in Tighfield. (III 477)

ROPER GAMGEE Hobson Gamgee (q.v.). (III 477)

RORIMAC BRANDYBUCK (TA 2902-3008) Hobbit of the Shire, Master of Buckland (2963-3008). He married Menegilda Goold, by whom he had two children. He was a guest at the Farewell Party.

Rorimac was known as Goldfather and, in later life, as Old Rory. (I 56; III 476)

ROSA TOOK (b. TA 2856) Hobbit of the Shire, daughter of Ponto Baggins. She married Hildigrim Took and bore him one child, Adalgrim. (III 474, 475)

ROSAMUNDA BOLGER (b. TA 2938, d. after 3001) Hobbit of the Shire, daughter of Sigismund Took. She married Odovacar Bolger and bore him two children, Fredegar and Estella. She was a guest at the Farewell Party. (III 475)

ROSE (b. TA 2862) Hobbit of the Shire, youngest child of Holman the greenhanded. She married Cotman and bore him one child, Holman Cotton. (III 477)

ROSE GAMGEE (TA 2984-FO 62) Hobbit of the Shire, second daughter of Tolman Cotton. In 3020 she married Samwise Gamgee; she bore him thirteen children.

Also known as Rosie. (III 354-55, 376-77, 472, 477)

ROSE GAMGEE (b. FO 5) Hobbit of the Shire, third child of Sam Gamgee. (III 382, 477)

ROTHINZIL (Ad.: 'foam-flower') Vingilot (q.v.). (S 259, 347; B 319, 433)

ROWAN (b. TA 2849) Hobbit of the Shire, eldest child of Holman the greenhanded. She married Hob Gammidge and bore him one child, Hobson Gamgee. (III 477)

ROWLIE APPLEDORE (d. TA 3019) Man of Bree, killed in the fight between people of the Bree-land and Bill Ferny and his friends. (III 335)

RUBY BAGGINS (fl. TA 2900)   Hobbit of the Shire, wife of Fosco Baggins. She was born a Bolger. (III 474)

RUBY GAMGEE (b. FO 18)   Hobbit of the Shire, eleventh child of Samwise Gamgee. (III 477)

RUDIGAR BOLGER (fl. TA 2900)   Hobbit of the Shire. He married Belba Baggins. (III 474)

RUFUS BURROWS (fl. TA 3000)   Hobbit of the Shire, a guest at the Farewell Party. He married Asphodel Brandybuck. (III 476)

RULERS OF ARDA   The Valar (q.v.). (S 75; B 83)

RULES, THE   The laws of the Shire, originally set down by the Kings of Arthedain. They were kept voluntarily because of their heritage and their justness. During Lotho's and Saruman's control of the Shire in TA 3018-19, the Rules were greatly increased and became a system of oppression. (I 30; III 344 ff.)

RULING RING   The One Ring (q.v.). (S 288; B 357)

RULING STEWARDS OF GONDOR   Those of the Stewards of Gondor (q.v.) who held their office when there was no King. Pelendur ruled in TA 1944-45 during the interregnum following the death of King Ondoher, and all the Stewards from Mardil to Denethor (TA 2050-3019) were Ruling Stewards.

Although the Stewards held their office awaiting the return of the King, few believed in such a return, and the Ruling Stewards did not look with favor on the idea of giving the crown to any heir of Isildur. Still, none of the Ruling Stewards sat on the throne of Gondor or wore the crown; they bore a white rod of office and used a plain white banner. In all other ways, however, their power and position were the same as that of the Kings in whose place they ruled.

Titles of the Ruling Stewards included the Lord and

Steward of Minas Tirith, Lord of the City, and Lord of the White Tower. The heir of the Steward was usually the Captain and High Warden of the White Tower and bore the Great Horn. (III 29, 395-96, 414)

RUMBLE Family of Hobbits of the Shire of the working class, at least one branch of which lived in Hobbiton. At the beginning of the Fourth Age, Widow Rumble looked after Hamfast Gamgee after Sam was married. (III 376)

RÚMIL (Q.?) (FA-) Noldorin Elf of Tirion, a scholar and sage. Rúmil composed the *Ainulindalë* and invented the first writing system, applicable both to inscriptions and writing on paper. Rúmil does not appear to have joined the Exiles. (III 493; S 63, 64, 314, 347; B 67, 68, 390, 433)

RÚMIL (fl. WR) Silvan Elf of Lórien, brother of Haldir. He was a guard on the northern border of Lórien. (I 445)

RUNES The Cirth (q.v.). (III 493; S 95; B 108)

RUSHEY Hobbit village in the Marish, on the Causeway. Spelled "Rushy" on the Shire-map. (I 40, 142; TB 9, 21; L 190)

RUSHLIGHT Family of Men of Bree. (I 212)

RUSHOCK BOG Bog in the Westfarthing on the Water, south of Needlehole. (I 40)

RUSHY Rushey (q.v.). (I 40)

SACKVILLE   Family of Hobbits of the Shire, probably of the upper class. (III 474)

SACKVILLE-BAGGINS   Family of Hobbits of the Shire, founded by Otho, the son of Longo Baggins and Camellia Sackville. The family was extremely obnoxious, but died out after two generations. (I 43, 46; III 474; H 284-85)

SADOC BRANDYBUCK (b. TA 2779)   Hobbit of the Shire, second son of Gormadoc Brandybuck. (III 476)

SAEROS (S.) (d. FA 485)   Nandorin Elf living in Doriath, one of the chief counsellors of Thingol. Jealous of Túrin, Saeros taunted him at table and was injured when Túrin threw a goblet at him. The next day Saeros attacked Túrin, was overcome, and fell over a cliff while fleeing. Túrin, fearing the wrath of Thingol, departed on his first outlawry. (S 199; B 244)

SAKALTHÔR, AR- (Ad.) (fl. SA 31st Cent.)   Dúnadan, twenty-first King of Númenor. (III 390; S 268; B 331)

SALMAR (Q.?)   Ainu, a Maia of the following of Ulmo. Salmar made the Ulumúri. (S 40; B 36)

SALVIA BOLGER (b. TA 2826)   Hobbit of the Shire, third child of Sadoc Brandybuck. She married Gundabald Bolger. (III 476)

SAM (gen. Hobb.)   Shortened version of an actual Hobbit forename, probably Samba. (III 517)

SAM GAMGEE   See: Samwise Gamgee.

SAMMATH NAUR (S.: 'chambers of fire') Chambers high in the core of Orodruin (q.v.), containing the Crack of Doom. The Sammath Naur was reached by Sauron's Road.

Called in Westron the Chambers of Fire. (III 265, 273-76)

SAMWISE GAMGEE (TA 2980-) Hobbit of the Shire, youngest son of Hamfast Gamgee. Like his father, Sam was a gardener; he took care of Bag End when Hamfast grew old. In this way he came to know Bilbo Baggins, who told him stories of his adventures and taught him to read; from this education Sam probably derived his love of Elves and lore.

Because of his curiosity about such things Sam was selected (after being caught eavesdropping) by Gandalf to accompany Frodo, as his servant, to Rivendell in 3018. There, under similar circumstances, he became one of the Companions of the Ring. When the Company was split at Parth Galen, Sam alone accompanied Frodo. On the journey to Mordor Sam many times proved his loyalty and devotion to Frodo. After Frodo was paralyzed by Shelob, Sam, thinking him dead, took the One Ring and vowed to continue the Quest, thus preventing the Ring from falling into the hands of the Orcs. Although tempted, he rejected the lure of the Ring because of his great practicality and honesty. With the aid of the Phial of Galadriel, Sam blinded Shelob and rescued Frodo from the Tower of Cirith Ungol. He then aided his master to reach Orodruin.

After the WR, Sam returned to the Shire and married Rose Cotton. They had thirteen children, including Elanor the Fair and Frodo Gardner, and lived in Bag End, which was given to Sam by Frodo when the latter went over Sea in 3021. Because of the fame he had acquired as a result of his adventures, his friendship with the Thain and the Master of Buckland, his connection with the Cottons, and, as the heir of Frodo, his financial independence, Sam was elected Mayor of the Shire seven times (FO 7-56). In FO 82, after the death of his wife, Sam sailed over Sea, which he was permitted to do because he had been a Ring-bearer.

Sam was somewhat of an author. He contributed to the Red Book of Westmarch and also wrote numerous poems.

Sam's name in genuine Hobbitish was Banazîr, usually shortened to Ban. (I 44, 47, 73-74, 250, 355, 525-26; III 216, 382-85, 471-72, 477, 517; TB 7)

SANCHO PROUDFOOT (b. TA 2990)   Hobbit of the Shire, son of Olo Proudfoot. He was a guest at the Farewell Party, and was discovered after the Party searching for Bilbo's treasure in Bag End. (I 67; III 474)

SANDHEAVER   Family of Hobbits of Bree. There may also have been Sandheavers in the Shire. (I 212)

SANDYMAN   Family of working-class Hobbits of the Shire, one branch of which owned and operated the Hobbiton mill before the WR. (I 46)

SANGAHYANDO (Q.: 'throng-cleaver')   (fl. TA 1634) Dúnadan, great-grandson of Castamir the Usurper. With his brother Angamaitë he led the Corsairs of Umbar on a raid on Pelargir in which King Minardil of Gondor was slain. (III 407; S 364; B 457)

SARADAS BRANDYBUCK (TA 2908-3007)   Hobbit of the Shire, third child of Gorbadoc Brandybuck. He was a guest at the Farewell Party. (III 476)

SARADOC BRANDYBUCK (TA 2940-FO 12)   Hobbit of the Shire, son of Rorimac Brandybuck and Master of Buckland (TA 3008-FO 12). He married Esmeralda Took; they had one child, Meriadoc. Saradoc was a guest at the Farewell Party.

As Master of Buckland he was known as "Scattergold." (III 475, 476)

SARN ATHRAD (S.: 'stone ford')   Ford on the Dwarf-road in East Beleriand, crossing Gelion just above the inflow of Ascar. Sarn Athrad was the site of the ambush by Beren, Dior, and the Laiquendi of the Dwarves of Nogrod who had sacked Doriath. (S 92, 235, 364; B 104, 291, 456)

SARN-ATHRAD The original name of Sarn Ford (q.v.). (L 190)

SARN FORD Ford on the Brandywine south of the Shire. Sarn Ford was guarded by the Rangers as part of their protection of the Shire, since the road leading to the Shire from the south crossed the Brandywine here.

The name was a partial translation of the original Sarn-athrad. (I 16, 234; III 464; L 190; S 364; B 456)

SARN GEBIR (S.: 'stone spikes') Unnavigable rapids on the Anduin above the Argonath. A portage-way was built on the western bank of the river to bypass the rapids.

Also called the Rapids. (I 499-500, 505-06)

SARUMAN (d. TA 3019) One of the Istari, as Saruman the White the greatest of the Order. Saruman had great power over Men's minds and great skill in his hands, and was especially learned in the lore of the Elven-rings and the devices of Sauron. In TA 2463 he was made head of the White Council. Saruman had traveled much in the East, but in 2759, with the consent of Steward Beren of Gondor, he settled in Isengard. At first, Saruman was a true friend to Rohan, but it slowly became apparent that he wished to become a power, and eventually it was learned that he coveted the One Ring. It is for this reason that he settled in Isengard, for he thought to use its palantír. Also for this reason he persuaded the White Council not to drive the Necromancer out of Dol Guldur, since he hoped that the Ring, seeking its master, would reveal itself if Sauron was not disturbed. His duplicity toward the White Council, which trusted him as its Ring-expert, delayed many actions and lulled many justified fears.

In 2953 Saruman took Isengard for his own and fortified it. There he gathered Orcs and Dunlendings, who at his orders began harassing Rohan and Fangorn; he also began spying on Gandalf and keeping agents in Bree and the Shire. About 3000 he used his palantír and was trapped by

Sauron; after this time, although he thought himself free, he was actually controlled by Sauron. His pride grew even more rapidly than his power at this time, and by the time of the WR he called himself Saruman the Many-Coloured. About 3010, through his agent Gríma, he caused Théoden of Rohan to decline into old age, but the King was revived by Gandalf in 3019.

During the WR Saruman brought on his own destruction by sending an Orc-band against the Fellowship of the Ring. The Orcs captured only Merry and Pippin; they later escaped into Fangorn Forest, where their presence aroused the Ents, who attacked Isengard and imprisoned Saruman in Orthanc. Gandalf then cast him out of the order of the Wizards. Later released by Fangorn, Saruman and Gríma went to the Shire, where he had financed Lotho Sackville-Baggins' rise to power. Frodo cast Saruman out of the Shire after he returned from Gondor, and he was slain by Gríma.

Saruman, or Saruman the Wise, was the name given him by Men in the north of Middle-earth; he was called Curunír by the Elves. His emblem, which was also used attributively to refer to him, was the White Hand. He was called Sharkey by the Orcs of Isengard and his Men in the Shire. (I 78, 328-44; II 48, 55-56, 95-96, 219, 234-41; III 318-19, 322-25, 361, 367-71, 416, 417, 433-34, 455, 460-63; S 300-04; B 373-77)

SATURDAY The name used to translate Sterrendei or Elenya (as the day before Sonnendei), but also Meresdei or Eärenya (as the day before Highdei). (III 478, 485)

SAURON (Q.: 'abominable') Ainu, one of the Maiar of Aulë. Seduced by Melkor early in the First Age, Sauron became the chief of his servants and anchored the front line of his defense against the Valar and Eldar. While Melkor dwelt in Utumno, Sauron held Angband; he escaped capture during the Battle of the Powers.

When Melkor returned to Middle-earth with the Silmarils, Sauron joined him in Angband and even directed the War during Melkor's attempt to corrupt Men soon after their awakening. After the breaking of the Siege of Ang-band, Sauron again ventured forth to secure Melkor's south-western front. In 457 he took Minas Tirith on Tol Sirion, filling it with his werewolves and opening West Beleriand to the ravages of Orcs. A few years later Sauron secured Dorthonion by capturing Gorlim and using a sorcerous trick to make him betray Barahir's outlaws. In 466 Sauron cap-tured Finrod and Beren, overcame Finrod in a wizard's duel, and killed Finrod and his Elves one by one in his dungeons. But retribution came soon after, when Lúthien and Huan came to rescue Beren. After Huan slew his were-wolves, Sauron assumed wolf form and fought the hound. Overcome by Huan's strength and Lúthien's magic, Sauron surrendered the tower and fled in vampire form to Taur-nu-Fuin, where he remained, dreadful but passive, for the rest of the First Age.

After the Great Battle Sauron submitted to Eönwë, but was told that he would have to return to Aman to be judged by the Valar. Although his repentance may have been sin-cere, his pride would not allow him to endure such humilia-tion, and he fled and hid himself somewhere in Middle-earth. About SA 500 he began to reveal himself again, and by 1000 he had gathered enough power to establish a stronghold in Mordor and begin building the Barad-dûr. In the long millennia of the Dark Years, Sauron corrupted many races of Men. Under the name Annatar and wearing a fair body, he seduced many groups of Elves, notably the Gwaith-i-Mírdain of Eregion. The combination of Sauron's skill and Noldorin creativity enriched both parties, until about 1500 they began forging the Rings of Power, by which Sauron hoped to ensnare the Free Peoples. Sauron placed much of his power in the One Ring, with which he completed the Barad-dûr. When Celebrimbor of Eregion discovered Sauron's treachery with the Rings, Sauron re-sorted to force and began the War of the Elves and Sauron (1693-1700), in which he destroyed Eregion and overran Eriador, but was defeated by Gil-galad and a fleet sent to Middle-earth by Tar-Minastir of Númenor.

After this Sauron revealed himself openly, gathering in his service Orcs and other monsters of Morgoth, ruling great areas (especially in the east) by force and terror, and apparently converting his vassals to the worship of Melkor, for Sauron remained ever true in his allegiance. In his pride Sauron claimed the title King of Men, thus arousing the equal pride of the Kings of Númenor. In 3262 Ar-Pharazôn landed at Umbar with a vast force. Deserted by his armies, Sauron was forced to submit to Ar-Pharazôn, who took him back to Númenor. In fifty years Sauron played on the Númenoreans' fear of death so effectively that the majority utterly repudiated the Valar and worshipped Melkor at Sauron's Temple. Finally he persuaded Ar-Pharazôn to seize immortality by invading Aman. To his surprise, the Valar reacted by calling on Ilúvatar; Sauron's body was caught in the terrible catastrophe of the destruction of Númenor, and thereafter he was unable to assume a fair-seeming form.

Sauron returned to Mordor and marshaled his forces. In 3429 he attacked Gondor, taking Minas Ithil and destroying the White Tree, a hated symbol of the Light of Aman. In 3434, however, he was defeated in the Battle of Dagorlad by the army of the Last Alliance and was besieged in the Barad-dûr. In 3441, in a final battle on the slopes of Orodruin, Sauron was overthrown by Gil-galad and Elendil, but killed both his foes. Isildur cut off his finger and took the Ring.

In the Third Age, without the One Ring which formed the base of his power, Sauron was extremely cautious. His policy was twofold: to weaken the Dúnedain kingdoms without provoking massive retaliation, and to recover the Ring. The latter policy was clouded by Sauron's uncertainty about the fate of the Ring, which should have been destroyed by Isildur. After Sauron rose again about TA 1000, he hid his identity and was known as the Necromancer or the Sorcerer of Dol Guldur. Since Mordor was guarded by Gondor, he dwelt in Dol Guldur. About 1300 he began to attack the Free Peoples especially the Dúnedain. He sent the Lord of the Nazgûl to the North, where he founded Angmar. In the South, Sauron stirred up the Haradrim and the Easterlings against Gondor.

440

After the Great Plague of 1636, which may have been sent by Sauron, Gondor's watch on Mordor was relaxed, and the Nazgûl re-entered that realm and prepared it for Sauron. In 2002 the Nazgûl took Minas Ithil, thus obtaining a palantír for Sauron, which he later used to ensnare Saruman and trick Denethor II. In 2063, Gandalf went to Dol Guldur to learn the identity of the Necromancer, but Sauron fled to the East. He returned to Dol Guldur in 2460 with increased strength and renewed his plots until 2941, when he was driven out of Dol Guldur by the White Council. Sauron willingly retreated to Mordor, where he openly proclaimed himself, rebuilt the Barad-dûr, and prepared to defeat the West by overwhelming Gondor and the smaller realms of the North with his vast armies of Orcs, trolls, Haradrim, Easterlings, and creatures more foul.

Even though Sauron did not have the Ring, its very existence gave him enough strength to crush the West. Gandalf and Elrond, realizing this, saw that the only way to defeat Sauron was to destroy the Ring. Frodo Baggins volunteered to undertake the Quest of Mount Doom and, escaping Sauron's servants searching for him and the Ring, destroyed the Ring in the Fire of Doom. The Nazgûl were destroyed and Sauron so weakened that he was unable ever to take shape again.

It is almost impossible to describe all the plots of Sauron, the master of deceit and treachery, and so only an outline of his policies is presented here. Among Sauron's other accomplishments stand the invention of the Black Speech; the creation of the Nazgûl, his most powerful servants, ensnared by the Nine Rings of Men; and the breeding of the Olog-hai and, perhaps, the Uruk-hai.

After the ruin of his body in the destruction of Númenor, Sauron had the form of a Man; his skin was black and burning hot. In the Third Age he most frequently appeared as a fearsome, ever-searching Eye.

Sauron comes from the earlier Quenya form *Thauron*; the Sindarin name was Gorthaur the Cruel. Also called Sauron the Deceiver, the Lord of the Earth (in the Second Age), the Enemy, the Master, the Dark Power, the Dark Lord, the Lord of Mordor, the Dark Lord of Mordor, the

Power of the Black Land, the Black Master, the Black One, the Lord of Barad-dûr, the Lord of the Dark Tower, and the Shadow. He was also called, attributively, the Great Eye, the Red Eye, the Eye of Barad-dûr, the Lidless Eye, and the Evil Eye. Also called the Unnamed, the Nameless, the Nameless One, the Nameless Eye, and He or Him. Also the Lord of the Rings, the Lord of the Ring, and the Ring-maker. Also, by Gollum, the Black Hand. (I 81, 82, 83, 260, 318, 328-29, 377, 471-72, 519; II 21, 43, 300-01; III 190-91, 275, 278-79, 391-93, 408, 415, 416, 417, 453-55, 456 ff., 511, 512, 515; H 37; S 32, 47, 51, 141, 155-56, 162-63, 170-72, 174-75, 267, 270-77, 280-81, 285, 286-90, 292-94, 297, 299-304, 348, 364; B 26, 47, 52, 169, 187-88, 196, 206-08, 211-12, 329-30, 333-43, 353, 355-60, 363-65, 369, 372-77, 433, 457)

SAURON'S ROAD   Road leading from the Barad-dûr to the Sammath Naur. Leaving the Dark Tower by a great iron bridge, Sauron's Road went across Gorgoroth and then rose up to Orodruin on a causeway. It then wound counter-clockwise up the mountain and entered an eastern opening of the Sammath Naur. The Road was frequently obstructed by eruptions of Orodruin, but was always repaired. (III 269-74)

SCARY   Village in the Eastfarthing, the site of quarries. (I 40; L 191)

SCATHA (d. c. TA 2000)   Great dragon of the Ered Mithrin, possessor of a large Dwarf-hoard. He was slain by Fram of Éothéod. (III 316, 430)

SCEPTRE OF ANNÚMINAS   Silver rod, once the sceptre of the Lords of Andúnië. Brought to Middle-earth by Elendil, it became the chief mark of royalty of Arnor. After the end of the North-kingdom the sceptre was kept at Rivendell. Elrond gave it to Elessar at his wedding, and it then became once more the mark of royalty of Arnor. (III 310, 401, 421)

SCEPTRE OF THE SEA-KINGS The symbol of royalty of Númenor, presumably destroyed in the Downfall. (S 270; B 333)

SCROLL OF KINGS A document bearing the regnal names of the Kings and Queens of Númenor. The Scroll was inscribed with Eldarin names even after the Kings used only Adûnaic names. (S 267; B 330)

SEA Belegaer (q.v.). (I 452)

SEA-BELL, THE Hobbit poem of the Fourth Age reflecting the Shire distrust of the Sea and of things outside the Shire.

The poem was subtitled *Frodos Dreme,* and was no doubt associated in the Shire with Frodo's unquiet dreams after the WR. (TB 9, 57-60)

SEA-ELVES The Teleri (q.v.), so called for their love of ships and the shores of Belegaer. (H 164; S 53; B 54)

SEA-KINGS The Númenóreans (q.v.). (S 263; B 325)

SEA OF HELCAR Helcar (q.v.). (S 53; B 54)

SEA OF NURNEN Núrnen (q.v.). (I 17)

SEA OF RHÛN Great inland sea northeast of Mordor. According to the maps, the Sea of Rhûn was fed only by the Celduin-Carnen and had no outlet.

Also called the Inland Sea. (I 17; III 395, 404, 405, 438)

SEAT OF SEEING The throne on Amon Hen (q.v.), built by the Kings of Gondor. One who sat in the Seat of Seeing could see all the lands for hundreds of miles around.

Also called the Seat of Amon Hen. (I 518)

SEA-WARD TOWER The tower of Dol Amroth (q.v.), looking toward the Sea.

Called in Sindarin Tirith Aear. (TB 8, 37)

SECOND AGE   The age of Middle-earth beginning after the Great Battle, the casting-out of Morgoth, the destruction of Beleriand, and the departure of many Eldar, and ending with the overthrow of Sauron by the Last Alliance. For much of the Age, Sauron controlled large parts of Middle-earth; Men were killed or enslaved, and the Elves and Dwarves hid. The seeds of later evil were sown with the forging of the Rings of Power; the World was Changed at the destruction of Númenor, and Aman was removed from Arda; and the Dúnedain returned to Middle-earth and founded the realms of Arnor and Gondor.

Also called the Black Years. (III 393, 452-55; S 286-94; B 355-65)

SECOND BATTLE   Dagor-nuin-Giliath (q.v.). (S 106; B 124)

SECOND BATTLE OF THE FORDS OF ISEN   See: the Battles of the Fords of Isen. (III 466)

SECONDBORN   Men (q.v.) (S 46; B 44)

SECOND HALL   Hall in the First Deep of Khazad-dûm, containing Durin's Bridge. (I 426 ff.)

SECOND LINE   The second series of Kings of Rohan, beginning with Fréaláf, Helm's nephew, in TA 2759, and ending with the death of King Théoden and his only son Théodred during the WR. The Second Line contained eight Kings. (III 435-36)

SECOND MUSIC OF THE AINUR   The theme of Ilúvatar which is to be sung by the Ainur and by Men after the End (q.v.). It is said that the Second Music will be greater than the first, although not even the Valar know what the Music will be or what the role of Elves (and Dwarves) will be. (S 15, 42; B 3, 39)

SECOND SPRING OF ARDA   The awakening of growing and mortal things, including Men, from the Sleep of

Yavanna at the first rising of the Moon and Sun. (S 103; B 119)

SECRET FIRE The Holy Spirit, the power giving substance and life to the Creation of Ilúvatar. It was this light, also called the flame of Anor (perhaps loosely), that Gandalf served and the evil followers of Melkor and Sauron envied and feared.

The Secret Fire is most probably the same as the Flame Imperishable (q.v.). (I 429; K 59; S 16, 25; B 4, 17)

SEEING-STONES The palantíri (q.v.). (II 383; S 292; B 362)

SEEN Things visible to normal mortal vision, as opposed to the Unseen, the world of the spirit or of "magic." (I 294)

SELF-CURSED A name given to Men (q.v.) by the Eldar. (S 103; B 119)

SEREDIC BRANDYBUCK (b. TA 2948) Hobbit of the Shire, son of Saradas Brandybuck. Seredic married Hilda Bracegirdle, and he was a guest at the Farewell Party. (III 476)

SEREGON (S.: 'blood-stone' or 'stone's blood') A plant with red flowers growing on the rocky summit of Amon Rûdh. (S 203, 348, 364; B 248, 434, 456)

SERINDË (Q.: 'broideress') Name given to Míriel, the wife of Finwë. (S 63, 348)

SERNI (S.: 'stony') River in Lebennin, Gondor, flowing into the Gilrain above Linhir.

Also spelled Sernui. (III 15; TB 8; S 364; B 434)

SEVEN FATHERS OF THE DWARVES The first seven Dwarves, created by Aulë and blessed by Ilúvatar. After their making and awakening, Ilúvatar commanded that they sleep until the awakening of the Elves, the First-born. Aulë laid the Seven Fathers in widely separated caves; Durin awoke in Khazad-dûm. The Seven Fathers founded the seven houses of the Khazâd, of which only the House of Durin is named, and probably amassed the Seven Hoards. (III 438; S 43-44; B 40-42)

SEVEN GATES The gates in the Orfalch Echor (q.v.). (S 136; B 163)

SEVEN GATES The entrances to the Levels of Minas Tirith. (III 21, 25)

SEVEN HOARDS The treasures of the Dwarf-kings of old, probably amassed by the Seven Fathers of the Dwarves, although possibly gathered around each of the Seven Rings in the Second Age. (S 289; B 358)

SEVEN RINGS The Rings of Power (q.v.) of the Dwarves. They were probably given to the Kings of each of the seven houses of the Dwarves. Despite Sauron's plans, the Seven could not dominate the Dwarves either by making them evil or by lengthening their lives. They did, however, cause their bearers to lust after gold and other precious materials. This failure caused Sauron to hate the Dwarves more than he did already, and he tried to recover the Seven.

Sauron was successful in recovering three of the Rings, and dragons consumed the other four. The only Ring about which much is said is the Ring of Durin's Folk. It was said to have been given to Durin III by the Elves and not by Sauron, and was probably the greatest of the Seven. It was long kept hidden, but the Dwarves believed that Sauron at last discovered its location and for this reason especially persecuted the Kings of Durin's Folk. The ring was taken from Thráin in Dol Guldur about TA 2845.

The Seven had metal bands and were set with single gems. (I 82, 330, 351; III 445-47; S 288-89, 302; B 357-58, 375)

SEVEN RIVERS The major rivers of southern Gondor,

the Lefnui, Morthond-Ciril-Ringló, Gilrain-Serni, and Anduin. (TB 8, 64)

SEVEN RIVERS OF OSSIR   The rivers of Ossiriand. (II 90)

SEVEN STARS   The Valacirca (q.v.). (S 174; B 211)

SEVEN STARS   The six-pointed stars that served as the emblem of Elendil and his heirs. They represented the single stars on the banners of each of the ships of the Faithful that bore a palantír. (II 258; III 150; RHM III 439-40)

SEVEN STONES   The Palantíri (q.v.). (II 258; III 161; S 276; B 342)

SEVENTH LEVEL   One of the levels of Khazad-dûm, the sixth above the Great Gates. The Seventh Level contained many halls, including the Chamber of Mazarbul. (I 420)

SHADOW   The Darkness (q.v.) of Morgoth, his presence and the influence and extent of his evil.
   Also called the Shadow of Morgoth. (S 113, 259, 265; B 132, 133, 319, 327)

SHADOW   The Unlight (q.v.) of Ungoliant. (S 76; B 84)

SHADOW   The Darkness (q.v.) of Sauron, his presence and the extent of his evil, ultimately the evil of Melkor.
   Also called the Shadow in the Forest (when Sauron was at Dol Guldur) and the Shadow in the East (when he was in Mordor). (I 82, 229, 451; II 266, 385; III 43, 233, 244, 283, 300, 408, 425, 439, 468; S 263; B 324)

SHADOW   The evil which fell over Númenor, the rejection of the Eldar, the Valar, and, ultimately, the will of Ilúvatar, who established the Gift of Men. This Shadow was a recurrence of the Shadow of Melkor which fell on all

Men in Hildórien. (III 454; S 141, 265, 267, 268; B 169, 327, 330, 331)

SHADOW The influence or presence of the Nazgûl, the Black Breath (q.v.). Ultimately, of course, this is the Darkness of Sauron, their master, and of Melkor. (I 82; III 171, 294)

SHADOW According to Gandalf, where the Balrog should return, either the Darkness or the Void (qq.v.). (I 429)

SHADOW The Storm of Mordor, the Darkness (q.v.) covering Mordor, Gondor, and Rohan in the days before the Siege of Gondor. (III 314)

SHADOW-BRIDE A Hobbit poem recorded on a margin of the Red Book of Westmarch. The poem seems to have some significance, and may refer to a tale not told in *LotR*. (TB 7, 52)

SHADOWFAX (fl. WR) Meara, the greatest horse of Rohan at the time of the WR. In 3018 King Théoden gave Gandalf any horse of his choosing, and the Wizard chose Shadowfax. The horse bore him faithfully without bridle or saddle throughout the WR.

Shadowfax was extremely strong and swift; he could run twelve hours at a stretch and could outrun the steeds of the Nazgûl. Shadowfax got his name because his coat was silver-grey. (I 343, 344; II 46, 137-38; III 125, 518)

SHADOW HOST The Dead Men of Dunharrow (q.v.) as they went to battle with Aragorn. (III 75)

SHADOW-LAND A land in Bilbo's poem *Errantry*, a dreary place near the Derrilyn. Although possibly an imaginary place, Shadow-land is an acceptable Westron translation of Mordor. If this was intentional, then the Derrilyn could be Anduin. (TB 24)

SHADOW-MEN The Dead Men of Dunharrow (q.v.). (III 74)

SHADOWMERE Lake in Eldamar in which were reflected the lamps of Tirion. (I 309)

SHADOW OF THE WOOD The Ents and Huorns of Fangorn, so called by Saruman. (II 236)

SHADOWS In *LotR* and *R*, it is said that after the poisoning of the Two Trees, Varda, at the command of Manwë, drowned Aman and part of the Sea in twilight, as a sign of mourning for the Light of the Trees and the refusal of the Valar to make war on Morgoth to recover the Silmarils.

But in *S* Aman was darkened by the Unlight, which lasted only until the rising of the Moon and Sun at the end of the Long Night. From then until the Change of the World, only for someone (like Galadriel) looking toward Aman from Middle-earth was Aman in Shadow, for the Shadowy Seas (q.v.) lay between the two continents.

See also: the Twilight. (I 308-11, 489; R 60; S 76-77, 102; B 84-85, 118)

SHADOWS The mists and darkness of the Shadowy Seas (q.v.). (I 308-11, 489; III 389)

SHADOWS The Dead Men of Dunharrow (q.v.). (III 74)

SHADOWS The Nazgûl (q.v.). (III 171)

SHADOWY MOUNTAINS The Ered Wethrin (q.v.). (S 152; B 183)

SHADOWY MOUNTAINS The Ephel Dúath (q.v.), as called by Gollum. (II 316)

SHADOWY SEAS An area of Belegaer extending north and south off the coast (perhaps far off) of Aman. At first the Shadowy Seas may have been a natural phenomenon, the area where the Light of the Two Trees did not penetrate. But after the poisoning of the Trees and the revolt of the Noldor, the Shadowy Seas were increased with bewildering mists and depressing darkness as part of the Hiding of Valinor, and the Enchanted Isles were set in the Seas.

The Shadowy Seas were removed at the Change of the World, although on I 489 Galadriel speaks as if they still existed in the Third Age.

Also called the Shadows, Evernight, and the Night of Nought. (I 308-10, 489; S 59, 102, 244; B 62, 118, 302)

SHAGRAT (fl. WR)   Uruk, Captain of the Tower of Cirith Ungol. He was one of the few survivors of the battle between his band and Gorbag's over Frodo's mithril-mail, and kept the mail for Sauron despite the fact that he was seriously wounded in the arm during the battle. (II 437, 439-46; III 222-25)

SHARKEY (from Orkish *sharkū* 'old man')   Name given Saruman by the Men and Orcs of Isengard, and the name by which he was known in the Shire. (III 367-68)

SHARKEY'S END   See: New Row. (III 374)

SHARP-EARS (fl. WR)   One of the ponies provided by Merry for the journey from Buckland to Imladris in 3018. He was driven off in Bree, but was later recovered and spent the rest of his life working for Barliman Butterbur.

Sharp-ears was named by Tom Bombadil. (I 155, 198, 199)

SHATHÛR   Bundushathûr (q.v.). (I 370)

SHEE   The reflection of Princess Mee, in the Shire-poem. (TB 29-30)

SHELOB (S.) (First Age-Fourth Age)   Great spider,

akin to those of Nan Dungortheb. Somehow Shelob escaped the ruin of Beleriand, and she and her offspring dwelt in the Ephel Dúath and in Mirkwood. Shelob herself had a vast den in Cirith Ungol, and for two ages of Middle-earth she lived on Men, Elves, and Orcs and served as a sure guard to prevent anyone from entering Mordor by that route. About TA 3000 she trapped Gollum, but released him on the condition that he bring her food. In 3019, during the Quest of Mount Doom, Gollum guided Frodo and Sam to Shelob's Lair. Shelob paralyzed Frodo but was herself blinded and stabbed by Sam, who used the Phial of Galadriel and Sting. Shelob may have eventually died of her wounds, or of starvation caused by her inability to hunt while blind.

Shelob was called Her Ladyship by the Orcs of the Tower of Cirith Ungol. She was also known as Shelob the Great. (II 418 ff., esp. 422-24, 425)

SHELOB'S LAIR The dwelling-place of Shelob, a foul and many-tunneled lair under the Ephel Dúath near Cirith Ungol. It was necessary to pass through the Lair in order to get over the Ephel Dúath by that route. Shelob built tunnels from her Lair that intersected every Orc-path built to avoid her. (II 414)

SHEPHERDS OF THE TREES The Ents (q.v.), so called in the First Age as the guardians of the olvar. (S 46, 235; B 45, 290)

SHIP-KINGS Tarannon Falastur, Eärnil I, Ciryandil, and Hyarmendacil I, the Kings of Gondor from TA 830 to 1149 under whom Gondor reached the height of its power. They were so named because the most important element of their policy was the expansion southward and westward of the borders of Gondor through the efforts of her fleets. (III 394, 403-04)

SHIRE, THE Area of about 18,000 square miles in Eriador between the Baranduin and the Far Downs, originally a fertile and well-tilled part of Arnor. In the course of the waning of the North-kingdom the area was deserted, and in TA 1601 it was ceded by King Argeleb II of Arthedain to the Hobbits, led by Marcho and Blanco. By 1630 most of the Hobbits in Middle-earth lived in the Shire, which they divided into four Farthings, subdivided into a number of folklands. The Hobbits lived comfortably in their new land; the only adversities they faced in the Third Age were the Great Plague of 1636, the Battle of Greenfields (2747), the Long Winter and the Days of Dearth (2758-60), the Fell Winter of 2911, and the domination of the Shire by Lotho Sackville-Baggins, Saruman, and evil Men during the WR. Indeed, the Hobbits of the Shire managed to ignore the outside world for so long that they almost forgot it existed, even though the Great East Road went through the middle of the Shire. In part, this safety was due to the ceaseless protection of the Rangers.

Because of overpopulation, the Oldbucks of the Marish crossed the Brandywine in 2340 and settled Buckland. In FO 32 King Elessar formally added Buckland to the Shire and also gave the Hobbits the Westmarch, extending from the Far Downs to the Tower Hills. Earlier, in 17, he had issued a decree making the Shire a Free Land under his protection and forbidding any Men to enter the Shire.

Before the death of Arvedui, the Shire had acknowl-edged the rule of the King, but was so divorced from outside affairs that this rule was only nominal. After the end of the North-Kingdom the Hobbits chose a Thain to rule until the return of the King; the Thain's duties were mostly ceremonial. The only official with active duties was the Mayor of Michel Delving, who had charge of the Watch and the Messenger Service.

The social structure of the Shire seems to have been rather simple. There were a few members of the landed gentry, who were well enough off not to have to work, but most Hobbits were farmers, tradesmen, or laborers. There were some poor, but their plight was not extreme. The Shire was primarily agricultural.

Also called the Four Farthings. The genuine Hobbitish name was Sûza. (I 17, 23-25, 29-31, 40, 43 ff.; III 457-71; L 184, 191)

SHIREBOURN River in the Shire, flowing from its source in the Green Hills south and then east to the Brandywine, which it entered south of Deephallow. The Mithe was at its outflow. The lower Shirebourn formed part of the boundary between the Eastfarthing and Southfarthing. (I 40; TB 9)

SHIRE-MOOT A gathering of Hobbits of the Shire held in times of emergency to take counsel, presided over by the Thain. (I 31)

SHIRE-MUSTER See: Hobbitry-in-arms. (I 31)

SHIRE-RECKONING or **SHIRE RECKONING** The calendar system of the Shire and (under a different name) of Bree, an adaptation of the Kings' Reckoning. The year 1 was equal to TA 1601 in the Shire and 1300 in Bree. The week had seven days, which were Sterrendei, Sunnendei, Monendei, Trewesdei, Hevenesdei, Meresdei, and the chief day, Highdei. (In *LotR* the days are called by modern names, with Sunnendei equal to Sunday.) The year had twelve months and a number of extra days, with leap years being formed by the addition of Overlithe. The yearly calendar for the Shire is shown on III 478; there was some difference in the names used in Bree and the Eastfarthing.

All these names were in use before Hobbits settled in the Shire, and so the Shire Reckoning was rather ancient.

The only major difference between the Shire-reckoning and the Kings' Reckoning was the Shire-reform (q.v.). (III 478, 479, 481-82, 483-85, 486; L 199)

SHIRE-REFORM Calendar reform invented and adopted in the Shire about TA 2700, and adopted in Bree somewhat later. The Shire-reform removed the week-day names from Midyear's Day and Overlithe, thus giving the year exactly 52 weeks and providing each day of the year with an unchanging week-day name. (III 482)

SHIRRIFF-HOUSE Any of the buildings built for the expanded Watch during Lotho's control of the Shire, especially the barracks of the First Eastfarthing Troop. Located at the west end of Frogmorton, this Shirriff-house was a poorly constructed one-story brick building with narrow windows.

All the Shirriff-houses were torn down before the end of 3019. (III 346, 347, 348, 373)

SHIRRIFFS The Watch (q.v.). (I 31; L 173)

SICKLE Ursa Major, as called by the Hobbits. Also called the Wain. See: Valacirca. (I 237; H 185)

SICKLE OF THE VALAR Valacirca (q.v.). (S 174; B 211)

SIDE-DOOR A secret entrance to the halls of Erebor, located on the western side of the mountain. The keyhole was operable only when the setting sun of Durin's Day shone on it, and the door, five feet high and three feet wide, was visible only when open.

Thrór and Thráin escaped from Smaug through the Side-door. In 2850 Gandalf received the key from Thráin in Dol Guldur, and later used it to persuade Thorin (and Bilbo) to burgle Smaug's hoard. Fortuitously arriving at Erebor near Durin's Day, Thorin and Company entered Erebor through the Side-door, which soon after was destroyed by Smaug in his wrath. (III 440, 460; H 10, 32-34, 36, 62-63, 197-202, 209, 221)

SIEGE The Siege of the Barad-dûr (q.v.). (S 294; B 365)

SIEGE OF ANGBAND A phase of the Wars of Beleriand, the period of nearly four hundred years during which Morgoth remained in Angband, closely watched by the Noldor. The Siege began after Dagor Aglareb and ended with the devastating attack of Dagor Bragollach. During the Siege the Eldar did no harm to Morgoth, but the Enemy patiently increased his strength. (S 115-16, 151, 159; B 136-37, 182, 192)

SIEGE OF GONDOR   The siege of Minas Tirith during the WR, lasting from the night of March 13, TA 3019, until the dawn of March 15. The Siege began when the army of the Lord of the Nazgûl broke through the Rammas Echor and swept across the Pelennor, driving the forces of Gondor into Minas Tirith. On March 14, catapults set the first level of the city on fire, and the Nazgûl demoralized the defenders. The next day, before dawn, the Great Gate was broken by the Lord of the Nazgûl, but before he could enter the city the Rohirrim arrived at the Pelennor, and in the Battle of the Pelennor Fields which followed, the Siege was lifted. (III 115-26)

SIEGE OF THE BARAD-DÛR   The final phase of the war between Sauron and the Last Alliance, in which Sauron, after his defeat in the Battle of Dagorlad in SA 3434, was besieged in the Barad-dûr for seven years. In 3440 Anárion was slain by a stone-cast from the Dark Tower, but in the following year Sauron was forced to fight, and he was overthrown in a final battle on the slopes of Orodruin. (I 319; III 401, 455; S 294; B 365)

SIGISMOND TOOK (TA 2890-2991)   Hobbit of the Shire, son of Hildibrand Took. (III 475)

SILENT WATCHERS   The Two Watchers (q.v.). (II 316, 441)

SILIMA (Q.: 'shining substance made by craft')   The substance of unknown composition invented by Fëanor and used by him to fashion the Silmarilli (q.v.). Silima was apparently crystalline, but it was unbreakable. (R 65; S 67, 364; B 72, 456)

SILMARIËN (Q.) (b. SA 548)   Dúnadan of Númenor, eldest child of Tar-Elendil. Her son Valandil was the first Lord of Andúnië. (III 391, 453; S 268; B 331)

SILMARILLI (Q.: 'brilliance or jewels of silima,' sing. *silmaril*)   The three jewels shining with the light of the

Two Trees, made by Fëanor in the years following the unchaining of Melkor. The Silmarilli were the greatest works of craft ever produced by the Children of Ilúvatar, and, like the Two Trees, their creation could not be duplicated. The shell of the jewels was composed of silima, but at their heart was the ever radiant light of the Trees, and the Silmarilli shone by themselves. They were hallowed by Varda so that any impure hand touching them would be burned and withered.

The inhabitants of Aman loved the jewels, but Fëanor gave his heart to them and Melkor lusted after their light. At first Fëanor wore them at festivals, but as the lies of Melkor influenced him, he began to keep them locked away, and his love for them grew arrogant and greedy. When Melkor and Ungoliant poisoned the Trees, Fëanor refused to give up the Silmarilli to restore the Trees, and at that moment they were stolen by Melkor from the Noldorin treasury at Formenos, even though his hands were burned and ceaselessly tormented him.

The lust of Melkor and the arrogance of Fëanor (expressed in his Oath and the revolt of the Noldor) tainted the jewels, so that thereafter all desire for them came to an evil end. Melkor and Ungoliant quarreled over them; after the Dark Lord overcame his former ally, he set the jewels in his Iron Crown. There they remained, luring the Noldorin Exiles to their doom, until Beren, impelled by his love for Lúthien and the demand of Thingol, cut one out. This Silmaril was soon swallowed by Carcharoth, who bit off Beren's hand in the process, and was not recovered for some time, until Carcharoth was slain in the Hunting of the Wolf. The dying Beren gave the Silmaril to Thingol, thus fulfilling his Quest.

At this point the Silmaril began to work the Doom of the Noldor. Thingol refused to give it to the sons of Fëanor; soon after he hired Dwarves of Nogrod to set it into the Nauglamír, but he was killed by the Dwarves, who coveted the jewel. Although the Silmaril was recovered, Doriath was ruined, for after the death of her husband Melian left Doriath, the Girdle of Melian was broken, and Menegroth was sacked by a Dwarf army. The Nauglamír was recovered by Beren, and Lúthien wore it in Tol Galen until her second death, becoming the fairest vision of beauty of all the Children of Ilúvatar.

After that, the sons of Fëanor, driven by their Oath, pursued the Silmaril, sacking Menegroth and the Havens of Sirion and slaying Dior, Nimloth, and their sons. At last Elwing, Dior's heiress, and Eärendil sailed with the Nauglamír to Aman, for the light of the Silmaril enabled them to pass through the Shadowy Seas and obtain the mercy of the Valar. The Silmaril was removed from the Nauglamír and bound to Eärendil's brow, and he was set in the sky as a star signaling hope to the Eldar and Edain in Middle-earth. From this light ultimately came that of the Phial of Galadriel.

The other two Silmarils were recovered after the Last Battle and removed from the Iron Crown, but Maedhros and Maglor stole them from Eönwë. Burned by the jewels (for their Oath had corrupted them), the brothers fled in torment. Maedhros cast himself and his jewel into a fiery abyss, and Maglor threw his into the Sea. It may be that the Silmarilli will be recovered and reunited at the End.

Also called the Great Jewels, the Three Jewels, and the Jewels of Fëanor. The Westronized plural is *Silmarils*. (I 260, 309, 310; III 281, 388, 389; R 65; K 65; S 67-69, 78, 80, 101, 127, 167, 169, 181-82, 184, 186, 189, 232-33, 234-37, 246-48, 250, 252-54, 363, 364; B 72-74, 86, 89, 116, 152, 202, 204, 205, 219-21, 223, 226, 230, 287, 289-93, 305-06, 309, 311-15, 455, 456)

SILMARILLION *Quenta Silmarillion* (q.v.). (III 389; S 7-8; B xii-xiii)

SILMARILS The Silmarilli (q.v.). (S 67; B 72-73)

SILME (Q.: 'starlight') Name for the tengwa ⟨ (number 29), which was almost universally used for *s*. (III 500)

SILME NUQUERNA (Q.: 'reversed *s*') Name for the tengwa ⟨ (number 30), usually a variant of silme used with diacritics. (III 500)

SILPION (Q.: 'shine—') One of the names of Telperion (q.v.). (S 38, 364; B 33, 456)

SILVAN ELVES Those tribes of Elves who were not of the Eldar, than whom they were far more numerous. Although less noble and wise in spirit and body than the Eldar, they were still good. The Silvan Elves dwelt in forests or mountains, and in the Third Age most of them lived in various kingdoms such as Lórien and the Woodland Realm which were ruled by Eldar, although some wandered in the wilderness of eastern Middle-earth.

The Silvan Elves spoke their own languages, which were distantly related to Eldarin.

The Silvan Elves are probably to be identified with the Avari, although it is not said how they came from Cuiviénen to the Vales of Anduin. They may also have included the surviving Nandor who did not enter Beleriand.

Also called the Wood-elves, the woodland Elves, and, in opposition to the Eldar, the East-elves. (III 452, 468, 505-06; H 150-53, 164-65; S 288, 298, 348; B 357, 370, 434)

SILVER CROWN The chief mark of royalty of Gondor. Originally a plain Númenórean war-helm, said to be Isildur's, in the time of Atanatar Alcarin it was replaced by a jeweled helm. The new helm was silver and had wings like those of a sea-bird wrought of pearl and silver. The Crown had seven gems in it to represent Elendil, and also a single gem to represent Anárion.

Also called the White Crown and the Winged Crown. (II 355; III 303, 401; S 296; B 367)

SILVERLODE Celebrant (q.v.). (I 370)

SILVERTINE Zirak-zigil (q.v.). (I 370)

SIMBELMYNË (tr. Roh.: 'evermind') Small white flower that grew on the burial mounds of the Kings of Rohan. Simbelmynë bloomed in all seasons.

Also called Evermind. (II 142; III 433; L 198)

SINDACOLLO (Q.: 'grey-mantle') See: Singollo. (S 350; B 437)

SINDAR (Q.: 'grey ones'; sing. *sinda*) The name given by the Noldorin Exiles to those of the Teleri who lived in Beleriand and did not complete the Great Journey. The original Sindar were the friends of Elwë, who remained waiting for him while he was lost in Nan Elmoth, and the Falathrim, persuaded to remain on the Hither Shores by Ossë. Later the Laiquendi and the other Nandor who entered Beleriand were often counted among the Sindar.

Although they were only Moriquendi, the Sindar achieved great wisdom during the Sleep of Yavanna, for they were guided by Círdan (instructed no doubt by Ossë), Melian the Maia, and Elwë, who as Elu Thingol was their overlord. Many Sindar lived in Mithrim (which was named after them) and the Falas, and some wandered in the forests, but the center of Sindarin power and culture was Thingol and Melian's kingdom of Doriath.

Somewhat scorned by the Noldor, the Sindar did not play a very active offensive role in the Wars of Beleriand, although of course they suffered heavily from the forces of Morgoth. At the end of the First Age many Sindar went over Sea, and throughout succeeding ages there was a steady migration of Sindar to the West. Those of the Sindar who remained in Middle-earth dwelt in Lindon or in Elven-realms such as the Woodland Realm. In later ages the Sindar were counted fully among the Eldar.

The Sindar were happy in Middle-earth, but once the desire for the Sea was aroused in them, they could not be content until they sailed to Eldamar. The Sindar spoke Sindarin (q.v.); they invented the Cirth. Although less learned and powerful than the Calaquendi and less interested in crafts than the Noldor, they were extremely gifted in music, and their voices were very fair.

Also called the Grey-elves or Grey Elves and the Elves of the Twilight. (II 136, 185, 289; III 452, 493, 506, 519; S 56, 91-95, 104, 108, 117, 119, 128, 309, 352; B 58, 103-08, 121, 125, 137-38, 140, 153, 383, 439)

SINDARIN (Q.: 'grey-elven') The language of the Sindar. Sindarin developed in Beleriand after the rest of the Eldar went to Eldamar, but because of the mutability of mortal lands it changed more swiftly than Quenya. Although less lyrical than Quenya, Sindarin was still a gentle, beautiful tongue. In Beleriand it was adopted for everyday use by the Exiles, especially after Thingol forbade the Sindar to use Quenya, the language of the Kinslayers. Sindarin was also adopted by the Edain (especially the Third House) and the Dúnedain; among these Men it was both a language of lore and a secondary common tongue. Its use was forbidden in Númenor during the days of its Shadow, but Sindarin survived to lend many words to Westron.

The most striking differences between Sindarin and Quenya are the former's retention of original Elvish *th* (which in Quenya became *s*) and its use of voiced stops at the beginning of words and after vowels. In part, the latter was due to a different development of consonant clusters; original *mb*, *nd*, and *ng* became *m*, *n*, and *n* in Quenya (*Mar-nu-falmar, numen, Noldo*) but frequently *b*, *d,* and *g* in Sindarin (*Bar-en-Danwedh, adûn, Golodh*).

Between the First and Third Ages Sindarin underwent further phonological changes; the most prominent of these were the reduction of intervocalic *ch* to *h* and of final *nd* to *nn* and then *n* (*Beleriand* and *Rochallor* vs. *Rohan*).

Also called Grey-elven. (III 487-504, 506, 507, 508; S 108, 113, 129, 147, 262, 267-68, 348-49; B 125, 133, 155, 177, 323, 330, 434-35)

SINGOLLO (Q.: 'grey-mantle') The Quenya form of Thingol, the name given Elwë (q.v.) in Beleriand.

The full Quenya form was Sindacollo. (S 53, 350; B 54, 437)

SIRANNON (S.: 'stream-gate') Stream flowing from its source near the West-gate of Khazad-dûm. The Sirannon was dammed by the Watcher in the Water. The ancient road from Ost-in-Edhil to Khazad-dûm ran along the Sirannon.

Called in Westron the Gate-stream.
See also: the Stair Falls. (I 392-403)

SIRION (S.: 'river') The great river of Beleriand, flowing more than 130 leagues from Eithel Sirion in the Ered Wethrin to the Mouths of Sirion at the Bay of Balar. Sirion was created in the Battle of the Powers and destroyed in the Last Battle. Its major tributaries were the Teiglin, Esgalduin, Aros, and Narog; it was also fed by the Rivil and Mindeb. It was crossed by the Brithiach north of Brethil, a bridge within Doriath north of the inflow of Esgalduin, ferries of Doriath near Aelin-uial, and by anyone in the three leagues between the Falls and the Gates of Sirion where the river ran underground.

See also (from north to south): the Fen of Serech, the Vale of Sirion, Tol Sirion, the Dry River, and the Fens of Sirion. (S 51, 120-23, 252; B 52, 142-46, 312)

SIRIONDIL (Q.: 'stream-lover') (d. TA 830) Dúnadan, eleventh King of Gondor (748-830). (III 394)

SIRIONDIL (fl. TA 19th Cent.) Dúnadan of Gondor, father of King Eärnil II. (III 410)

SIRITH (S.: 'flowing') River in Lebennin, Gondor, flowing from its sources in the Ered Nimrais south to Pelargir, where it flowed into Anduin. Its principal tributary was the Celos. (III 15; S 364; B 456)

SKINBARK Fladrif (q.v.). (II 98)

SLAG-HILLS The mounds of wasted metal, stone, and earth left by Orcs in the Desolation of the Morannon, especially those two hills near the Morannon on which the Army of the West was grouped in the battle fought on March 25, TA 3019. (III 200, 201, 206, 467)

SLEEPLESS DEAD The Dead Men of Dunharrow (q.v.). (III 65)

SLEEP OF YAVANNA   The period of Middle-earth between the destruction of the Lamps of the Valar and the rising of the Moon and Sun, when Middle-earth was lit only by the stars and most living things slept, waiting for the return of light. Only in such places of power as Doriath (guided by Melian) and the North (where the monsters of Morgoth multiplied) was there much life, although the Elves and Dwarves walked abroad.

Roughly coterminous with the Peace of Arda. (I 182; S 91-92, 100; B 104, 115)

SLINKER   Sam's name for the more decent, politer "Sméagol" aspect of Gollum (q.v.). (II 311)

SMALLBURROW   Family of working-class Hobbits of the Shire. At the time of the WR, at least one branch of the family lived in Hobbiton. (III 281)

SMAUG (d. TA 2941)   Dragon of the Ered Mithrin, the greatest dragon of his time. In 2770, hearing of the wealth of Erebor, Smaug destroyed Dale and drove the Dwarves away from the Kingdom under the Mountain. For nearly two hundred years he gloried in his treasure, until in 2941, disturbed and angered by Thorin and Company, he attacked Esgaroth and was slain by Bard the Bowman.

In addition to the various honorifics bestowed on him by the frightened Bilbo, Smaug was known as Smaug the Golden. (III 440; H 35-36, 206, 207-38, 248)

SMÉAGOL   See: Gollum. (I 84-85; III 518)

SMIALS   The large tunnels inhabited by well-to-do Hobbits of the Shire. Smials had rounded walls and many branches. Bag End was a smial. Some smials, like the Great Smials or Brandy Hall, were very large and had room for a hundred or more Hobbits. (I 26, 27)

SMIALS, THE   The Great Smials (q.v.). (II 80)

SNAGA (B.S.: 'slave')   Name given lesser Orcs, especially by the Uruk-hai. (III 511)

SNAGA (d. TA 3019) Orc of Isengard, one of Uglúk's band. He was slain by Éomer's éored.

The name may have been just an epithet. (II 67)

SNAGA (d. TA 3019) Orc of the Tower of Cirith Ungol, one of the few survivors of the battle between his company and Gorbag's. He was Frodo's guard, and died when he broke his neck trying to escape from Sam.

The name may have been just an epithet. (III 222-23, 226-27)

SNOWBOURN River in Rohan, flowing from Dunharrow to Edoras, and then east until it joined the Entwash. (III 76, 78, 91, 93)

SNOWMANE (d. TA 3019) Meara, the mount of King Théoden. He was slain by the Lord of the Nazgûl in the Battle of the Pelennor Fields, and in his fall killed Théoden. (II 168-69; III 140, 146)

SNOWMANE'S HOWE The grave of Snowmane, in the Pelennor. Long green grass grew on the Howe, and a carved stone was set over it. (III 146)

SNOW-WHITE Varda (q.v.), a translation of the epithet Fanuilos. (I 117)

SOLMATH The second month of the Shire Reckoning, corresponding roughly to our February. It was pronounced, and often written, "Somath." (III 478, 483)

SOMATH Solmath (q.v.). (III 483)

SONG, THE Ainulindalë (q.v.). (S 45, 46; B 43, 44)

SONG OF PARTING The song, of which part is translated in rhymed octosyllabic couplets, composed by Beren as he went toward Angband during the Quest of the Silmaril. He thought he was leaving Lúthien and approaching his death, but Lúthien and Huan heard him singing and came to him. (S 178; B 216)

SORCERER OF DOL GULDUR   Sauron (q.v.), in his guise of Necromancer. (S 299; B 372)

SORONTAR (Q.: 'lofty or noble eagle')   Thorondor (q.v.). (S 365; B 457)

SORONÚMË (Q.: 'eagle—')   One of the constellations fashioned by Varda in preparation for the awakening of the Elves, perhaps equivalent to the modern Aquila. (S 48; B 48)

SOUTH DOWNS   Dreary, partly wooded downs south of the Great East Road between Bree and the Mitheithel. (I 16, 252, 255, 267-68)

SOUTHERN ARMY OF GONDOR   One of the two armies of Gondor in the days of its might. The Southern Army fought in Harad, but at least once, in TA 1944, it reinforced the Northern Army. (III 409)

SOUTHERN STAR   A variety of pipe-weed (q.v.) grown in the Southfarthing. (I 28)

SOUTHFARTHING   One of the Four Farthings of the Shire, the warmest and the farthest south. Pipe-weed was grown here. The Southfarthing was the first area of the Shire to fall under the control of Lotho Sackville-Baggins, and Saruman kept agents here as early as TA 2953. (I 28, 40; III 360, 462)

SOUTH ITHILIEN   That portion of Ithilien south of the Morgulduin. (III 15)

SOUTH KINGDOM   Gondor (q.v.), in contrast to Arnor. (S 295; B 366)

SOUTH LANE   Road in the Shire leading south from

Bywater. At the time of the WR, the Cottons lived on South Lane. (III 353)

SOUTHLINCH   A variety of pipe-weed (q.v.) grown in Bree. (III 334)

SOUTH ROAD   One of the main roads of Gondor, running from Minas Tirith to Pelargir, crossing the Erui at the Crossings of Erui. (III 48)

SPIES OF THE VALAR   Name given to the Eldar of Tol Eressëa by the King's Men of Númenor in the days of their depravity. (S 268; B 331)

SPRINGLE-RING (tr. Hobb.: 'war-horse ring')   A vigorous Hobbit dance. The dancers gathered in a circle and did a lot of leaping about. (I 54; TB 21; L 200)

SPRING OF ARDA   The period of the Lamps of the Valar when the Valar lived at Almaren and green things flourished in their first growth. Melkor blighted and perverted some of this growth, and when he destroyed the Lamps all growth ceased in the Sleep of Yavanna.
  Cf.: the Second Spring of Arda. (S 35-37, 43; B 29-32, 40)

STADDLE   Village of Men and Hobbits in the Bree-land, on the southeastern side of Bree Hill. (I 205, 245)

STAIR FALLS   Waterfalls in the Sirannon (q.v.) near the West-gate, next to a flight of steps in the road from Eregion to Khazad-dûm. (I 393)

STAIR OF THE HOLD   Steep switchback road in Rohan, leading from Edoras to Dunharrow, built by a forgotten race. As each section overlooked the ones below, it was impossible for any enemy to take the Stair (and Dunharrow) save by siege or by aerial attack.
  The Púkel-men (q.v.) were carved at each turn of the Stair. (III 80, 85)

STAIRS The two flights of steps, the Straight Stair and the Winding Stair (qq.v.), leading from Imlad Morgul to Cirith Ungol. (II 441)

STANDELF Village in southern Buckland. (I 40)

STANDING SILENCE Moment of silence observed in Gondor before meals. The diners stood and looked toward the West, toward Mar-nu-Falmar and Aman. (II 361; III 287)

STARKHORN Mountain in the Ered Nimrais overlooking the southern end of Dunharrow. (III 76, 81)

STAR OF EÄRENDIL The Silmaril, worn by Eärendil and borne aloft in Vingilot.
Also the Star. (S 260, 277; B 321, 342)

STAR OF ELENDIL A diamond, one of the heirlooms of the North-kingdom. It represented Eärendil, which had served as a guide to the Edain when they sailed to Númenor. The Star was worn on the brow of the Kings of the North-kingdom until Elessar gave it to Sam Gamgee in FO 16.
Also called the Star of the Dúnedain, the Star of the North, and the Elendilmir. (III 150, 401, 471; RHM III 439)

STAR OF THE DÚNEDAIN The Star of Elendil (q.v.). (III 471)

STAR OF THE HOUSE OF FËANOR The emblem of Fëanor and his heirs, an eight-rayed star made of silver. (I 397; RHM III 439)

STAR OF THE NORTH The Star of Elendil (q.v.). (III 302)

STEELSHEEN Morwen (q.v.) of Lossarnach. (III 437)

STERDAY   See: Sterrendei. (III 484)

STERRENDEI   Early form of the name of the first day of the Hobbit week, a translation of Elenya. By the time of the WR, the form of the name was Sterday.
Called in *LotR* Saturday. (III 484)

STEWARD'S DOOR   Fen Hollen (q.v.). (III 160)

STEWARDS OF THE HOUSE OF ANÁRION   The chief officials of Gondor, head of the King's Council. Every King had a Steward, but after the time of King Minardil all the Stewards were chosen from the House of Húrin (q.v.), and after Steward Pelendur (d. TA 1998) the office was made hereditary. When the line of the Kings failed, the Stewards became the rulers of Gondor. (See: the Ruling Stewards) When the kingdom was restored by Elessar at the end of the Third Age, Faramir, the heir of the last Ruling Steward, was made Steward to the King. (III 158, 395-96, 409, 414 ff.; S 297; B 369)

STEWARDS' RECKONING   A revision of the Kings' Reckoning made by Steward Mardil about TA 2100 and eventually adopted throughout the Westron area, except in the Shire and Bree. All the months had thirty days, and the five days outside the months were holidays. The calendar was the same as that of the Kings' Reckoning except that tuilérë came after Súlimë 30, Nárië and Cermië had thirty days each, and yáviérë came after Yavannië 30.
   The Stewards' Reckoning was replaced by the New Reckoning at the beginning of the Fourth Age. (III 481)

STING   A well-forged long knife made in Beleriand in the First Age, named by Bilbo Baggins. Sting shone with a blue light when Orcs were near. Bilbo found Sting in a troll-cave during the expedition of Thorin and Company, and he and Frodo used it as a sword throughout their adventures. Frodo gave Sting to Sam in the Tower of Cirith Ungol, after Sam had seriously wounded Shelob with it. (I 363, 421-22; II 428-29; III 250, 287; H 53, 77, 80, 154)

STINKER Sam's name for the nastier, more vicious "Gollumish" aspect of Gollum (q.v.). (II 311)

STOCK Village in the northern Marish, south of the Brandywine Bridge. (I 40, 142; TB 9)

STOCKBROOK Stream in the Eastfarthing, flowing from its source in the Woody End through Stock and then into the Brandywine. (I 40)

STOCK ROAD Road in the Shire, leaving the Great East Road west of Bywater and running through the Green Hills and the Woody End to Stock. Frodo and Sam met the Last Riding of the Keepers of the Rings in Woody End on the Stock Road. (I 40; III 380)

STONE-GIANTS Creatures of great size and strength living in the high passes of the northern Misty Mountains.
The stone-giants are mentioned only in *The Hobbit,* and may be no more serious than Golfimbul. (H 65, 99-100)

STONE-HOUSES The Woses' name for Minas Tirith (q.v.). (III 129)

STONE OF ELENDIL The Palantír (q.v.) of the Tower Hills. (R 65)

STONE OF ERECH Black stone brought to Middle-earth from Númenor by Isildur and set on the hill of Erech at the time of the founding of Gondor. The King of the Mountains swore allegiance to Isildur on the Stone, and during the WR he was called to the Stone by Aragorn to fulfill his oath.
The Stone was round and black and was perhaps six feet in diameter. Also called the Black Stone. (III 64, 74-75)

STONE OF THE HAPLESS The large grey stone raised over Túrin's burial mound at Cabed Naeramarth and inscribed with his name and that of Nienor. Soon after Húrin met Morwen here, and when she died he buried her on the west side of the Stone and carved her name on it.

Glirhuin of Brethil foretold that the Stone would never be defiled or thrown down, and after the ruin of Beleriand it became the center of the island of Tol Morwen. (S 226, 229-30; B 278-79)

STONES The Palantíri (q.v.). (S 292; B 362)

STONE TROLL, THE A humorous poem composed by Sam Gamgee in TA 3018.
    See: Tom. (I 276-78; TB 7, 39-40)

STONE-TROLLS A kind of troll (q.v.) found in Eriador. Bert, Tom, and William Huggins were probably Stone-trolls, since they spoke Westron, which Stone-trolls alone of their kind did. (III 512)

STONEWAIN VALLEY Long, narrow valley running through Druadan Forest from near the Rammas Echor to stone-quarries in the Ered Nimrais. The Men of Gondor had built a great road through the Stonewain Valley which, although overgrown at the time of the WR, was used by the Rohirrim on their ride to Minas Tirith before the Battle of the Pelennor Fields. (III 15, 131-32; L 192)

STONINGLAND Gondor (q.v.), so called in Rohan. (III 152)

STOORS The southernmost of the three strains of Hobbits. The Stoors stayed in the Vales of Anduin longest of any of the three groups, but about TA 1300 they went over the Redhorn Pass and settled in Dunland or the Angle. The Stoors of the Angle fled to Dunland or Rhovanion about a hundred years later because of the threat of Angmar. The Stoor settlement in Rhovanion was in the Gladden Fields; it survived until well after 2460. The Stoors of Dunland emigrated to the Shire about 1630 and settled mostly in the Eastfarthing and Southfarthing. At the time of the WR, Stoors were common in the Marish and Buckland.

Stoors were broader and heavier than other Hobbits and were the only Hobbits to grow beards. Some Stoors wore boots in muddy weather. The Stoors were friendlier with Men than the other strains, and they preferred flat lands and riversides. Stoors were almost the only Hobbits to know anything of boating, swimming, and fishing.

The Stoors of Dunland learned there a language related to Dunlending, and even at the end of the Third Age they retained many strange words and names. (I 22, 84; III 398, 457, 509)

STORM OF MORDOR   The Darkness (q.v.) preceding the Siege of Gondor. (III 75)

STRAIGHT ROAD   The way by which the Eldar sailed to Aman after it was removed from the Circles of the World. In some manner chosen ships left the bent Sea but remained on water until they came to Tol Eressëa and the shores of Eldamar. It was said that sometimes mortal mariners stumbled onto the Straight Road.

Also called the Straight Way. (III 381, 384; S 281-82, 286; B 348-49, 354)

STRAIGHT STAIR   The first stair in the ascent to Cirith Ungol from Imlad Morgul. The Straight stair was a long, steep flight of aged steps, many broken or cracked, and had a wall on both sides. (II 403-04)

STRAIGHT WAY   The Straight Road (q.v.). (S 282; B 349)

STRANGERS   A name given Men (q.v.) by the Eldar because of their mortality. (S 103; B 119)

STRIDER   See: Aragorn, Telcontar. (I 222; III 169)

STRIDER (fl. WR)   The pony that bore Frodo from Minas Tirith to the Shire after the WR. Frodo rode Strider on the Last Riding of the Keepers of the Rings, but the pony probably did not go over Sea. (III 313, 380)

STYBBA (fl. WR) Pony of Rohan, given to Merry by Théoden. Merry rode him from the Hornburg to Dunharrow before the Muster of Rohan. (III 60)

SÚLE See: thúle. (III 500)

SÚLIMË (Q.: 'wind—') The third month of the Kings' and Stewards' Reckonings, and the twelfth of the New Reckoning, corresponding roughly to our March.

The Sindarin name, used only by the Dúnedain, was Gwaeron, and the Shire equivalent was Rethe. (III 483)

SÚLIMO (Q.: 'breather, one of wind') The surname of Manwë (q.v.). (S 26, 349, 364; B 18, 435, 456)

SUMMERDAYS The Lithe (q.v.). (III 481-82)

SUN The younger, brighter, and hotter of the two lamps of heaven created by the Valar after the poisoning of the Two Trees. The light of the Sun was the last fruit of Laurelin, placed in a vessel made by Aulë and guided through the heavens by Arien.

The Sun first rose in the West when the Moon had completed seven cycles, at the moment when Fingolfin marched into Mithrim. This, even more than the rising of the Moon, dismayed Morgoth and his creatures of darkness. The Sun probably changed the direction of her rotation during the reform of her travel which returned night to Arda.

Called Anar in Quenya and Anor in Sindarin. Also called the Daystar and (by Gollum) Yellowface. (S 99-101, 103; B 114-16, 119-20)

SUNDAY See: Sunnendei. (III 484)

SUNDERING SEAS Belegaer. Most of the instances of the term refer to the First Age, when Aman and Middle-earth were sundered by the Shadowy Seas and Enchanted Isles. Pippin's use may be ignorant, and Galadriel's may reflect her continuing Exile (but cf. I 489, where she speaks

471

of the Shadowy Seas in the present). (I 260, 261, 482; II 260; S 250; B 309)

SUNLANDS A Shire-term for the far southern lands of Middle-earth, roughly equivalent to Harad (itself a vague term). (II 322)

SUNLENDING Rohirric name for Anórien (q.v.). (III 92; L 192)

SUNLESS YEAR Probably the Long Night, the time when the Undying Lands were darkened by the Shadows. (I 117)

SUNNENDEI Early form of the name of the second day of the Hobbit week. The form at the time of the WR, and that used in *LotR,* was Sunday. The name was a translation of the Quenya Anarya. (III 484)

SÚRION, TAR- (Q.: 'wind—') (fl. c. SA 1400) Dúnadan, ninth King of Númenor. (III 390)

SUTHERLAND Harad (q.v.). (I 17)

SÛZA (gen. Hobb.: 'shire') The Shire (q.v.). (III 515; L 191)

SWANFLEET Glanduin (q.v.). (III 325)

SWARTHY MEN The Easterlings (q.v.). (S 153, 185; B 189, 225)

SWEET GALENAS Pipe-weed (q.v.). (I 29)

SWERTINGS Shire-name for the Haradrim (q.v.). (II 322)

SWISH-TAIL (fl. WR) One of the ponies provided by Merry for Frodo's journey from Buckland to Rivendell in

TA 3018. He was driven off in Bree, but was later recovered and claimed by Barliman Butterbur.

He was named by Tom Bombadil. (I 155, 198, 199, 242)

SWORD OF ELENDIL Narsil (q.v.). (I 319)

SWORD REFORGED Andúril (q.v.). (III 302)

SWORD THAT WAS BROKEN Narsil or Andúril (qq.v.). (I 231-32, 323, 324)

TALAN (S.: 'flat') The open platform built in a mallorn of Lórien as a living-place for the Elves. The talan was reached by a ladder through a hole in its center. A light screen could be fixed to any side of the platform to keep out the wind.

Called in Westron a flet. The Sindarin plural was probably *telain*. (I 444, 446)

TALATH DIRNEN (S.: 'guarded plain') The forested plain of the realm of Nargothrond, lying between the Rivers Narog and Teiglin. Talath Dirnen was guarded by rangers and hidden towers, but after the fall of Tol Sirion to Sauron in FA 457 the plain was open to Morgoth's forces. For thirty years Talath Dirnen was protected by the Haladin of Brethil, the vigilance of its own defenders, and (in 487) by Túrin and Beleg (see: Dor-Cúarthol). After the capture of Túrin at Amon Rûdh, Orcs began raiding Talath Dirnen. Orodreth of Nargothrond, fearing to draw Morgoth's attention to his city, only countered these raids with ambushes and skirmishes, but in the early 490's Túrin (now known as Mormegil) persuaded the king to fight openly. For a while Talath Dirnen was freed of Orcs, but the plain was lost after the army of Nargothrond was destroyed at Tumhalad in 496.

The exact extent of Talath Dirnen is unclear. In the north it seems to have included all the land at least as far as the Crossings of Teiglin; to the south it may have stretched to the Andram; to the east it probably included the area around Amon Rûdh between Nivrim and Teiglin, but there is no record of Túrin's outlaws there encountering the guards of Nargothrond.

Also called the Guarded Plain. (S 147, 168, 205, 210, 211, 212, 364; B 176, 203, 252, 258, 259, 261, 457)

TALATH RHÚNEN (S.: 'eastern plain') The early name, used by the Sindar, for the area later called Thargelion (q.v.). (S 124; B 148)

TALE OF ARAGORN AND ARWEN, THE Chronicle of Gondor, said to have been written by Barahir in the second century of the Fourth Age. Parts of the *Tale* were added to the Gondor copy of the Thain's Book (q.v.). The excerpts given in Appendix A of *LotR* show evidence of having been edited by a Hobbit. (38; III 420-28)

TALE OF GRIEF Another name for the *Narn i Hîn Húrin* (q.v.). (S 199; B 243)

TALE OF YEARS, THE A chronology of the Second, Third, and early Fourth Ages, compiled by the Tooks in the early years of the Fourth Age and kept at the Great Smials. Material gathered by Merry Brandybuck in Rivendell was incorporated into the *Tale,* which was thus quite accurate. Appendix B of *LotR* is a shortened version of this book.

The subtitle of the *Tale* was *Chronology of the Westlands.* (I 39; III 452-72)

TALES OF THE ELDAR A general term referring to the history and presence of the Eldar. In Middle-earth, the Tales ended with the Last Riding of the Keepers of the Rings at the end of the Third Age. (S 299; B 371)

TANIQUETIL (Q.: *tar* 'high' + *ninque* 'white' + *til* 'point, peak') The highest peak of the Pelóri, and thus the highest mountain of Arda. Located in eastern Aman on the borders of the Sea, Taniquetil is the abode of Manwë and Varda, whose halls, Ilmarin, are built on its summit. The Vanyar dwell on its slopes. Taniquetil is snow-covered, and its white sides gleam afar.

Oiolossë was the name most commonly used by the Eldar. Also called Amon Uilos, Uilos, Mount Everwhite, the White Mountain, the Holy Mountain, Elerrína, the Hill of Ilmarin, and the Mountain. (I 309, 310, 489; R 60, 61; S 26, 37, 40, 61, 278, 349, 362, 365; B 19, 32, 35, 65, 344, 435, 454, 457)

TANTA BAGGINS (fl. TA 29th Cent.) Hobbit of the Shire, wife of Largo Baggins. She was born a Hornblower. (III 474)

TAR- (Q.: 'high, noble') Royal prefix attached to the names of those Kings and Ruling Queens of Númenor who took their names in Quenya. The rulers are entered in this Glossary under the main part of their names. (III 390; S 364; B 457)

TARANNON (Q.: 'royal-gate') See: Falastur. (III 403)

TARCIL (Q.: 'royal—') (d. TA 515) Dúnadan, sixth King of Arnor (435-515). (III 394)

TARCIRYAN (Q.: 'lord-ship—') (fl. TA 900) Dúnadan of Gondor, brother of King Falastur and father of Eärnil I. (III 394)

TARELDAR (Q.: 'high Eldar') Those of the Eldar who ever dwelt in Aman; before the poisoning of the Two Trees equivalent to the Calaquendi.

Also called the High Elves. (S 326; B 406)

TARGON (Q.: 'royal-stone'?) (fl. WR) Man of Gondor, a cook for the Third Company of the Guards of the Citadel. (III 39)

TÁRION (Q.: 'powers') See: Valanya. (III 484)

TARLANG'S NECK A long ridge in Lamedon, crossed by the road between Erech and Calembel about sixty miles north of Calembel. The Neck was a southern spur of the Ered Nimrais.

The ridge was originally called Tarlang, but this was later construed as a personal name. (III 75; L 193)

TARMENEL (Q.: 'high-heaven') The source of the wind of power that blew Eärendil to Aman. Although *menel* generally refers to the firmament, the winds of Manwë are of course found in a lower region of the sky, and Tarmenel seems to be the region below Ilmen.

Also called Over-heaven. (I 309; L 190)

TARN AELUIN Aeluin (q.v.). (S 158; B 191)

TARONDOR (Q.: 'royal rock?') (d. TA 602) Dúnadan, seventh King of Arnor (515-602). (III 394)

TARONDOR (d. TA 1798) Dúnadan, twenty-seventh King of Gondor (1656-1798). He ruled after the Great Plague, and throughout his reign, the longest of any King of Gondor, he was occupied with recovering Gondor's strength. He planted a sapling of the White Tree and permanently moved the King's residence to Minas Anor. (III 395, 408)

TAROSTAR (Q.: 'royal-fortress') Rómendacil I (q.v.). (III 394, 403)

TASARINAN (Q.: 'willow-valley') Nan-tathren (q.v.). (II 90)

TAUREMORNA (Q.: 'forest-black') Epithet applied by Fangorn the Ent to Fangorn Forest (q.v.), perhaps part of the Forest's long name. (II 91)

TAUREMORNALÓMË (Q.: 'forest-black-shadowed')

Epithet applied by Fangorn the Ent to Fangorn Forest (q.v.), perhaps part of the Forest's long name. (II 91)

TAUR E-NDAEDELOS (S.: 'forest of the great fear') Mirkwood (q.v.). (III 515)

TAUR-EN-FAROTH (S.: 'forest of the hunters') The wooded highlands lying west of the River Narog at Nargothrond, the western extension of the Andram. The Ringwil ran through the forest.

Also called the High Faroth and the Hills of the Hunters. (S 114, 122, 168, 358; B 134, 145, 203, 449)

TAUR-IM-DUINATH (S.: 'forest-between-rivers') The dense forests bounded on the east by the River Gelion and on the west by the lower Sirion and the Bay of Balar. Only a few Sindar dwelt here, but the forest seems to have been unmolested by Orcs throughout the First Age. (S 123, 153; B 146, 184)

TAUR-NA-NELDOR (S.) Neldoreth (q.v.). (II 90)

TAUR-NU-FUIN (S.: 'forest-beneath-night') The name given to Dorthonion after Dagor Bragollach, when Morgoth placed terror and dark enchantments on it. For a few years a remnant of the First House of the Edain braved these horrors, but at last the women were forced to flee and Barahir's outlaw followers dwindled until the last twelve were betrayed by Sauron. Finally even Beren, the last survivor, was forced to flee.

After this, Taur-nu-Fuin remained deserted until Sauron fled there in vampire form after being driven out of Tol Sirion. Except for him, no one lived there, although Orcs passed through it on their way to Anach, and Túrin, Beleg, and Gwindor traveled there as well.

Also called Deldúwath. (S 155, 175, 184, 200, 207, 362; B 186, 212, 223, 245, 254, 454)

TAURON (S.: 'lord of forests' or 'forester') An epithet of Oromë (q.v.). (S 29, 350; B 22, 436)

TED SANDYMAN (fl. WR) Hobbit of the Shire, from Hobbiton. He was associated with Lotho Sackville-Baggins during the latter's control of the Shire. (I 73; III 361, 366-67)

TEETH OF MORDOR See: the Towers of the Teeth. (II 308)

TEHTAR (Q.: 'signs'; sing. *tehta*) The additional signs of the Tengwar, principally used to represent vowels, vowel length (see: andaith), diphthongs, various consonantal abbreviations such as following *s* and preceding nasal, and abbreviations for short, very common words. (III 495, 498)

TEIGLIN (S.: '—pool') River of West Beleriand, flowing from sources in the Ered Wethrin south and then east into Sirion, which it joined just above the inflow of Esgalduin. Its principal tributary was the Malduin. Teiglin formed the boundary between Brethil and Talath Dirnen. It could be forded at the Crossings of Teiglin. South of the Crossings the Teiglin went through a deep gorge, Cabeden-Aras. (S 120, 122, 221-22, 361; B 142, 145, 272-73, 452)

TELCHAR (S.) (FA) Dwarf, the most renowned smith of Nogrod. He forged Narsil and Angrist. (II 147; S 94, 177; B 107, 215)

TELCO (Q.: 'stem') One of the basic components of a tengwa. The tyeller of the Tengwar were differentiated by differences in the telco and by the doubling of the lúva in even-numbered tyeller. In Grades 1 and 2 the telco was normal, while it was raised in 3 and 4 and reduced in 5 and 6. An extended stem, which extended both above and below the line, was used in the original Fëanorian system. (III 495-96)

TELCONTAR (Q.) The name of the house of Elessar, the Kings of the Reunited Kingdom and of the West.
The name Telcontar was the Quenya form of Strider, the

name given Aragorn the Ranger, founder of the house, by the Men of Bree. Plural *Telcontari.* (III 169)

TELEMMAITË, TAR- (Q.) (fl. SA 26th Cent.) Dúnadan, fifteenth King of Númenor. (III 390)

TELEMNAR (Q.) (d. TA 1636) Dúnadan, twenty-sixth King of Gondor. He and both his sons died in the Great Plague. (III 395, 407-08; S 296; B 368)

TELERI (Q.: 'last, hindmost') The third and largest of the Three Kindreds of the Eldar. They lagged behind during the Great Journey, whence their name, and were reluctant to leave Middle-earth. They were led by Elwë and Olwë, but in the Vales of Anduin a group of Teleri led by Lenwë left the Journey and moved south; they were called the Nandor.

In Beleriand the Teleri lived in the east, and thus missed the first journey of Tol Eressëa to Aman. When they realized that the Vanyar and Noldor were gone, many Teleri, led by Olwë, moved to the Mouths of Sirion, where they were instructed by Ossë and Uinen. During this time the Teleri developed their love of the Sea. When Ulmo returned to take them to Aman, some of the Teleri, at the request of Ossë, remained in the Falas; together with the Teleri who still wandered inland in search of Elwë, these became the Sindar.

The majority of the Teleri, though, went West on the second voyage of Tol Eressëa, but at the request of Ossë, Ulmo anchored the island in the Bay of Eldamar. There, surrounded by the beloved Sea but within sight of Aman and the Light of the Two Trees, the Teleri lived for a long time.

Finally, their desire for the Light of Aman grew so great that Ossë taught the Teleri the art of shipbuilding. Their white ships, drawn by swans, carried them to the coast of Eldamar, where they built the beautiful city of Alqualondë.

In Alqualondë the Teleri lived somewhat apart from the Valar and the rest of the Eldar, since their hearts still turned toward the Sea. Yet during the revolt of the Noldor they were forced to heed the affairs of Valinor, for Fëanor demanded their swan-ships to sail to Middle-earth. When Olwë refused, Fëanor took the ships by force in the Kinslaying at Alqualondë, many of the lightly armed Teleri were slain.

At the end of the First Age the Teleri befriended Elwing when she and Eärendil came to Aman, and for her sake and that of the Sindar they sailed the Host of Valinor to the Great Battle, although their hate of the Noldor prevented them from actually fighting. In later ages the Teleri lived in Alqualondë.

The Teleri were the fairest singers of the Eldar; they were instructed in music by Ulmo, who was the dearest of the Valar to them. They called themselves Lindar, the Singers. Also called the Falmari, the Foamriders, and the Sea-elves. (S 40, 53-54, 57-59, 61, 75, 86-87, 94, 248, 249, 251, 286, 309, 350, 364; B 36, 54-56, 60-62, 64, 83, 96-98, 107, 306-07, 309, 310, 354, 383, 437, 457)

TELPERIËN, TAR- (Q.) (fl. SA 1600) Dúnadan, tenth Ruler of Númenor and the second Ruling Queen. (III 390)

TELPERINQUAR (Q.: 'silver-fist') The original name of Celebrimbor (q.v.). (S 357; B 447)

TELPERION (Q.: 'silver—') The elder of the Two Trees of Valinor (q.v.). Telperion had leaves dark green above and shining silver below, and a dew of silver light dripped from his leaves.

The stars of Varda were made from the dews of Telperion, and the Moon from his last silver flower. Galathilion and the line of the White Trees were images of Telperion, as was Turgon's Belthil. It is said that at the End Telperion will reappear.

Also called White Telperion, the White Tree, Ninquelótë, Silpion and other names, and Eldest of Trees. (I 260; III 308-09; K 64; S 38-39, 48, 99, 263, 357; B 34, 47, 114, 324, 447)

TELUMEHTAR (Q.: 'vault—') Menelmacar (q.v.). (III 488)

TELUMEHTAR UMBARDACIL (Q.: 'Orion Umbar-victor') (d. TA 1850) Dúnadan, twenty-eighth King of Gondor (1798-1850). In 1810, troubled by Corsair raids, Telumehtar took Umbar. After this victory, Telumehtar added the title "Umbardacil" to his name. (III 395, 408)

TELUMENDIL (Q.: 'lover of the heavens'?) One of the constellations shaped by Varda in preparation for the awakening of the Elves. (S 48; B 48)

TÉMAR (Q.: 'series'; sing. *téma*) The vertical groupings of the Tengwar, representing points of articulation. The four témar were differentiated by variations in the lúva. (III 495)

TEMPLE The temple built by Sauron in Armenelos for the worship of Melkor. A massive dome, the Temple was five hundred feet across and five hundred feet high; its walls were fifty feet thick at their base. The dome was covered with silver, but this was soon blackened by the smoke of the human sacrifices (and the burning of Nimloth) held in the Temple.

The dome of the Temple was cracked by the lightnings preceding the sailing of the Great Armament, but the Temple itself was not destroyed until the downfall of Númenor, when Sauron's body was caught in its ruin. (S 273, 277, 280; B 337-38, 343, 347)

TENGWAR (Q.: 'letters') The writing system first developed in Eldamar by Rúmil and later reworked by Fëanor. The Tengwar later spread to Númenor and large portions of the Elvish and Westron areas of Middle-earth. The Tengwar was a phonemic system written with brush or pen, in which the consonantal letters (tengwar) were arranged into grades (tyeller) representing modes of articulation and series (témar) representing points of articulation. Individual values could be assigned on the basis of the needs of the language in question.

Some of the adaptations of the Fëanorian system, such as the mode of Beleriand, were alphabetic and had full vocalic signs, while in other modes diacritic marks were used to represent vowels. Vowels, abbreviations, and other values required by various systems were represented by additional signs (tehtar).

The Tengwar, which were generally thirty-six in number (although two more tyeller were theoretically available), each had a universal Quenya "full name," which was a Quenya word beginning with the sound that the tengwa represented in an early Quenya mode. The Tengwar were also given unique names based on their values in different languages. (III 493-500; S 63, 64; B 67, 68)

THAIN The ruler of the Shire after the end of the North-kingdom, who ruled until the return of the King. The Thain was master of the Shire-moot and captain of the Hobbitry-in-arms. Since these met only in emergencies, which rarely occurred in the Shire, and since the laws were voluntarily kept, the Thainship was a nominal position.

Bucca of the Marish, the first Thain, was chosen by the chieftains of the Shire in TA 1979, and the Thainship remained in the Oldbuck family until 2340, when, with the removal of the Oldbucks to Buckland, Isumbras Took became Isumbras I, the thirteenth Thain. The Thainship remained hereditary in the Took family into the Fourth Age. In FO 14, on the accession of Peregrin I, the Thain was made a Counsellor of the North-kingdom. (I 24, 30)

THAIN'S BOOK A copy of the original Red Book of Westmarch, made at the request of King Elessar and brought to Gondor by Peregrin Took in FO 64. *The Thain's Book* was heavily annotated and expanded in Gondor, and a century later a copy of it was made in Gondor and kept at the Great Smials. This copy is the most important surviving version of the Red Book. (I 38; III 506)

THALION (S.: 'steadfast, strong') Epithet applied to Húrin (q.v.). (S 211, 336; B 259, 418)

THALOS (S.) River of Ossiriand, the second most northerly of the tributaries of Gelion. Thalos flowed from springs in the Ered Luin. (S 123, 140; B 147, 167)

THANGORODRIM (S.: 'oppression-mountain-group') The three-peaked mountain raised above Angband by Melkor on his return to Middle-earth with the Silmarils. Thangorodrim was made out of the slag and refuse of the delving of Angband, but it was volcanic and emitted foul vapors, smoke, and lava. Thangorodrim was broken when Ancalagon fell on it during the Great Battle, and the ensuing tumult was one of the major causes of the ruin of Beleriand. (I 319; III 388, 452; S 81, 107, 118, 252, 285, 350; B 90, 125, 139, 312, 353, 354, 437)

THARBAD (S.: *thara* 'across' + *pata* 'way') City in southern Eriador at the meeting of the Glanduin and Mitheithel. The Old South Road crossed the Mitheithel at a ford here. In TA 2912 Tharbad was ruined by great floods and deserted. (I 359; III 461; S 364; B 457)

THARGELION (S.: 'across Gelion') Flat wooded area of East Beleriand between the River Gelion and the Ered Luin, bounded on the south by Ossiriand at the River Ascar and on the north by Mount Rerir.

Thargelion was settled by the Noldor of Caranthir, who thus controlled the trade with the Dwarves of the Ered Luin. In the 4th Century FA the Haladin settled for a while in southern Thargelion, where they were attacked by Orcs. A century later, after Dagor Bragollach, Thargelion was overrun by Orcs and deserted by the Noldor.

Thargelion was the name given the area by the Noldor, who approached it from the west. The Sindar called it Talath Rhúnen. Also called Dor Caranthir. (S 124, 143, 145-46, 153, 364; B 148, 171, 174-75, 184, 457)

THARKÛN (Kh.?) Dwarvish name for Gandalf (q.v.). (II 353)

THAURON (Q.: 'abominable') Early form of Sauron (q.v.). (S 364; B 457)

THELLAMIE A country, in Bilbo's poem *Errantry*. The name is an imitation of Elvish, and Thellamie was probably imaginary. (TB 8, 25)

THENGEL (TA 2905-80) Man, sixteenth King of Rohan (2953-80). From about 2925 to 2953 he lived in Gondor because he did not get on well with his father, King Fengel. During his reign Saruman first troubled Rohan.

Thengel married Morwen of Lossarnach in 2943, and she bore him five children, including Théoden and Théodwyn. (III 436)

THÉODEN (TA 2948-3019) Man, seventeenth King of Rohan (2980-3019). Under Saruman's spells, worked through Théoden's evil counsellor Gríma, Théoden decayed toward the end of his reign, but in 3019 he was healed by Gandalf. Théoden led the Rohirrim against Saruman in the Battle of the Hornburg and against Mordor in the Battle of the Pelennor Fields. In the latter battle he defeated an army of Haradrim, but was slain by the Lord of the Nazgûl.

He was known as Théoden the Renowned, and, because of his decline and recovery, as Théoden Ednew (tr. Roh.: 'renewed fortune'). (II 148 ff.; III 137-45, 314, 436, 437)

THÉODRED (TA 2978-3019) Man of Rohan, only child of King Théoden, the Second Marshal of the Mark. He was slain in the First Battle of the Fords of Isen during the WR. (II 149; III 437)

THÉODWYN (TA 2963-3002) Woman of Rohan, youngest child of King Thengel. In 2889 she married Eomund of Eastfold and bore him two children, Eomer and Eowyn. Théodwyn died soon after her husband was slain. (III 436, 437)

THINGOL (S.: 'greycloak') Elwë (q.v.). (I 260; S 56; B 58)

THIRD AGE The age of Middle-earth beginning with the first downfall of Sauron and the death of Gil-galad and ending with the War of the Rings, the second and final downfall of Sauron, and the Last Riding of the Keepers of the Rings, in which the greatest of the Eldar still in Middle-earth departed over Sea. In this Age the Elves and Dwarves remained in Middle-earth but did little new, while Men increased in power and numbers. The Dúnedain kingdoms of Arnor and Gondor prospered at first, but waned as the evils of the Second Age, especially the Nazgûl and Sauron, rose again. In the end, however, the desperate gamble of the Wise to preserve the Free Peoples succeeded and great evil was banished, but at the same time much good and beauty were lost to Middle-earth.

Called by Elves the Fading Years. (III 387, 452; S 299; B 371)

THIRD HOUSE OF THE EDAIN The last kindred of the Edain to enter Beleriand, probably the most numerous. Led by Marach, the Third House settled at first in Estolad near their kinsmen of the First House. Later they gathered in Dor-lómin under the lordship of Hador; there they enjoyed the greatest splendor of any of the Edain, and were commonly renamed the House of Hador.

The Third House was the most renowned in the Wars of Beleriand, in which it fought beside the House of Fingolfin. After the fall of Dorthonion the House absorbed many of the women of the First House. Despite the death of Hador in Dagor Bragollach, the warriors of the Third House held Eithel Sirion against Morgoth until the Nirnaeth Arnoediad, when the House was decimated on Anfauglith. The remnant, led by Húrin and Huor, covered the retreat of Turgon and the Gondolindrim. Then, in the most renowned of the deeds of war of the Edain, the warriors of the Third House refused to leave the North; they drew up their lines behind Rivil and, after killing hundreds of Orcs and trolls, were all slain, save for Húrin, who was taken prisoner.

In Dor-lómin many of the surviving women and children of the Third House were enslaved by the Easterlings or killed trying to flee. But a few survived in Hithlum and the Havens of Sirion, and among the heroes of the House are counted Túrin and Tuor, Eärendil and perhaps Elros.

The people of the Third House were tall and warlike, strong and quick in mind and spirit. They alone among the Edain had golden hair. In Dor-lómin they spoke both Sindarin and the Mannish tongue which formed the basis of Adûnaic.

Also called the people of Hador. (II 364; III 389; S 142, 143, 147-48, 155, 157, 158, 160, 190, 194, 195, 198-99, 227, 308; B 170, 171, 177, 187, 189, 190, 193-94, 232, 236, 238, 242-43, 280, 382)

THIRD LINE   The third group of the Kings of Rohan. The first King of the Third Line was Eomer, who acceded in TA 3019 after the deaths of Théoden and his only son Théodred in the WR. (III 437-38)

THIRD THEME OF ILÚVATAR   The last part of the Ainulindalë, conceived and uttered by Ilúvatar alone. Quiet but profound, the Third Theme encompassed and overcame the louder melody of the first two themes and the discord of Melkor. The Children of Ilúvatar were conceived in the Third Theme, which is why neither Melkor nor the Valar understand their being or their full destiny. (S 16-17, 18, 68; B 4-5, 7, 74)

THISTLE BROOK   Brook flowing into the Shirebourn near Willowbottom. Its source was in the Green Hill Country. (I 40)

THISTLEWOOL   Family of Men of Bree.
Also spelled Thistlewood. (I 212; RHM III 428)

THORIN I (TA 2035-2289)   Dwarf, King of Durin's Folk (2190-2289). He led a large number of Durin's Folk from Erebor to the Ered Mithrin. (III 440, 450)

THORIN II (TA 2746-2941)   Dwarf, King of Durin's Folk in exile (2845-2941). In his youth Thorin fought bravely in the Battle of Azanulbizar, and after that battle he went with his father Thráin II and their folk to the Ered Luin. In 2845, after the disappearance of Thráin, Thorin became the King of Durin's Folk. For a hundred years he slowly increased the numbers and wealth of his people in the Ered Luin, until in 2941, long troubled by thoughts of the wrongs done his house, he met Gandalf and decided to reclaim Erebor from Smaug. This expedition of Thorin and Company met with success, but Thorin was killed soon after in the Battle of the Five Armies.

He was known as Thorin Oakenshield, because in the Battle of Azanulbizar he used an oak-branch as a shield and club. (III 440, 443, 445, 447-48, 450; H 23, 25-26, 29, 49-50, 268-69, 272-73)

THORIN III (TA 2866-FO ?)   Dwarf, King of Durin's Folk in Erebor (3019-?). After the downfall of Sauron, Thorin and Bard II of Dale routed the army of Easterlings besieging Erebor.

He was known as Thorin Stonehelm. (III 450, 469)

THORIN AND COMPANY   Business concern and expedition, organized by Thorin II, which in TA 2941 planned to recover the hoard of Smaug in Erebor. The members of the expedition were Thorin, Balin, Dwalin, Fíli, Kíli, Dori, Ori, Nori, Oin, Glóin, Bifur, Bofur, Bombur, and Bilbo Baggins, their burglar. Gandalf accompanied them part of the way in an advisory capacity.

Although the hoard was recovered and Erebor restored, the expedition had other, even more important results. Bilbo stole the One Ring, Gandalf found Glamdring and killed the Great Goblin of the Misty Mountains, the Battle of the Five Armies was fought and Smaug was killed, removing the greatest evil force in that part of the world, thus enabling Dale and Erebor to withstand the Easterling invasion during the WR.

Since the entire *Hobbit* is concerned with Thorin and Company, a more complete description of the expedition seems out of place here. (III 447-48; H 41)

THORONDIR (S.: 'eagle-sight'?) (d. TA 2882) Dúnadan, twenty-second Ruling Steward of Gondor (2872-82). (III 395)

THORONDOR (S.: 'eagle-high') (FA-) Lord of the Eagles of the Crissaegrim, a staunch friend of the Noldor and Edain. Aside from the actions, such as the guarding of Gondolin, in which he led his flock, Thorondor performed many heroic deeds himself. He helped Fingon rescue Maedhros from Thangorodrim; he wounded Morgoth in the face and recovered the body of Fingolfin during Dagor Bragollach; he rescued Beren and Lúthien as they fled from Angband; and he led the birds against Morgoth's winged dragons during the Great Battle. It may be that Thorondor went West at the end of the First Age, for he is not mentioned after the Great Battle.

The Quenya form of his name was Sorontar. His titles, King of Eagles and Lord of Eagles, may be translations of his name. (III 278; S 110, 154, 158, 182, 240, 243, 252, 351, 365; B 129, 186, 191, 221, 297, 301, 312, 437, 457)

THORONGIL (S.: 'eagle of the star') The name by which Aragorn (q.v.) was known in Gondor when he served Ecthelion II. The name was given him because he was swift and keen-sighted and wore the star of the Rangers of the North on his cloak. (III 417-18)

THOUSAND CAVES Menegroth (q.v.). (S 201; B 246)

THRÁIN I (TA 1934-2190) Dwarf, King of Durin's Folk (1981-2190). He led his people from Khazad-dûm to Erebor, where he founded the Kingdom under the Mountain in 1999 and discovered the Arkenstone.

Called Thráin the Old by Thorin II. (III 439-40, 450; H 9, 34)

THRÁIN II (TA 2644-2850) Dwarf, King of Durin's Folk in exile (2790-2850). He led the Dwarves in the War of the Dwarves and Orcs, and lost an eye in the Battle of

Azanulbizar. In 2841 Thráin, restless with the greed for gold, left the Ered Luin with a few companions and resolved to go to Erebor. His journey was troubled by evil things, and in 2845 he was captured by Sauron and imprisoned in Dol Guldur. He was tormented for five years, and his Ring of Power was taken from him, but before he died he gave the key to the Side-door of Erebor to Gandalf. (I 351; III 440, 441, 442-45, 446-47; H 37)

THRANDUIL (FA-) Sindarin Elf, King of the Woodland Realm, father of Legolas. At the beginning of the Second Age, Thranduil lived in Lindon, but before SA 1000 he established a kingdom in Greenwood the Great. This kingdom survived, despite attacks by the great spiders and the Orcs and a war with the Dwarves, for more than two ages of Middle-earth. In TA 2941 Thranduil led the Elven forces in the Battle of the Five Armies, and during the WR he repulsed an attack from Dol Guldur. After the fall of Sauron in the WR Thranduil fixed the southern boundary of his realm as the Mountains of Mirkwood, and the Woodland Realm flourished well into the Fourth Age.

Thranduil had a great love for jewels and riches, and it may have been that this love led him to excesses, especially with the Dwarves.

Thranduil is the Elvenking of *The Hobbit*. (I 315; III 452, 467, 468; H 152, 165-66, 167-69; S 299; B 371)

THREE-FARTHING STONE Stone on the Great East Road marking the place where the Eastfarthing, Westfarthing, and Southfarthing met. The Three-Farthing Stone more or less marked the center of the Shire. (I 40; III 349, 374)

THREE HOUSES OF MEN The Edain (q.v.). (II 364)

THREE HOUSES OF THE ELF-FRIENDS The Three branches of the Edain (q.v.).

Also called the Ancient Houses and the Three Houses of Men. (II 127, 364; III 506)

THREE HUNTERS   The name given by Aragorn to himself, Legolas, and Gimli, when during the WR they followed the Orc-band that had captured Merry and Pippin across Rohan. (II 26 ff.)

THREE KEEPERS   The Keepers of the Three Rings (q.v.). (III 471)

THREE KINDREDS, THREE KINDREDS OF THE ELDAR   The Vanyar, Noldor, and Teleri, the three tribes into which the Eldar (q.v.) were divided. (III 519; S 53, 143; B 54, 171)

THREE RINGS   The Elven Rings of Power (q.v.). They were forged without Sauron's assistance, and thus his taint was not directly on them. However, they and their works could be controlled by the One, and their wielders would be revealed to Sauron if he had the One Ring. Unlike the other Rings, the Three gave power to build, understand, and heal, not to control or conquer.
   The Three were somehow successfully hidden through the Second Age and were used in secret in the Third. However, when the One was destroyed they became powerless, and the things wrought with them failed. The Rings were taken to the West with the Last Riding of their Keepers at the end of the Third Age.
   The Three Rings, each of which was a band set with a single gem, were Vilya, Nenya, and Narya (qq.v.). (I 318, 321, 330, 351-52, 472-73; III 308, 381-82, 456; S 288, 298; B 353, 370, 371)

THRIHYRNE   The three tall peaks of the Ered Nimrais behind the Hornburg. Helm's Deep wound into the Thrihyrne, and the Hornrock was an outlying northern spur of the mountains. (II 167, 169)

THRIMICH   See: Thrimidge. (III 483)

THRIMIDGE   The fifth month of the Shire Reckoning, corresponding roughly to our May. At the time of the WR the name was also spelled "Thrimich." An earlier form of the name was Thrimilch. (III 478, 483)

THRIMILCH Thrimidge (q.v.). (III 483)

THRONE OF MORGOTH The seat of Morgoth in the nethermost hall of Angband, a place of great dread.
Also used to indicate Morgoth himself. (S 180, 251; B 218, 311)

THRÓR (TA 2542-2790) Dwarf, King of Durin's Folk (2589-2790). In 2590 he led his people back to Erebor from the Ered Mithrin because of the danger of dragons. In 2770 he and his people were driven from Erebor by Smaug, and they wandered off to the south. In 2790 Thrór left his people and went wandering; when he returned to Khazad-dûm he was slain and his body defiled by Azog. (III 440-41, 450; H 32, 34)

THRUSHES Birds of Middle-earth. The thrushes of Erebor and Dale could understand Westron. They were friendly with the Men of Dale, who could understand their language and used them as messengers. These thrushes were very long-lived, and perhaps attained the same age as the ravens of Erebor. (H 217-18, 237, 243)

THULE (Q.: 'spirit') Name for the tengwa ᚻ (number 9), which had the value *th* in most systems. An alternate name was súle, since in Quenya *th* was usually pronounced *s*. (III 500)

THURINGWETHIL (S.: 'woman of secret shadow') Creature of evil, perhaps one of the corrupted Maiar. Thuringwethil was the messenger of Sauron in Tol-in-Gaurhoth, and she flew in the form of a vampire-bat with an iron claw at each joint of its wings.
Lúthien took the shaping-cloak of Thuringwethil from Tol-in-Gaurhoth when she joined Beren on the Quest of the Silmaril; she wore it into Angband, where she abandoned it. (S 178-81, 351; B 216-19, 437-38)

TIGHFIELD Village in the Shire, where the Gamwiches, Gammidges, and Ropers lived. A rope-walk, probably the one which the Ropers worked in or operated, was located in Tighfield. (II 276; III 477; L 193)

TILION (Q.: 'horned') Ainu, one of the Maiar of Oromë. A lover of silver and of the silver light of Telperion, Tilion became the pilot of the Moon. He was somewhat erratic, for he desired to approach Arien, guiding the Sun, but he was scorched by her fire.

It is unclear if the Man in the Moon, the subject of songs in Gondor and the Shire, is in any way modeled on Tilion. (S 99-100, 365; B 114, 457)

TIM Tom's "nuncle" in Sam Gamgee's poem *The Stone Troll,* a corpse whose shinbone was being gnawed on by the Troll. Tim was most probably imaginary and fictitious. (I 276; TB 39)

TIME One of the dimensions of the structure of Eä, the sequence of the chords of Ilúvatar sung in the Ainulindalë. Time began with the creation of Eä and the entry of the Valar, and presumably will end with the End.

See also: the Deeps of Time. (S 20, 25, 28, 74; B 10, 17, 21, 82)

TIMELESS HALLS The dwelling of Ilúvatar and the Ainur, as distinct from the Timeless Void and Eä (qq.v.). The Timeless Halls are without limit, stretching from the Abyss to the Firmament. (S 20; B 10)

TIMELESS VOID The Void (q.v.). (S 254; B 315)

TINCO (Q.: 'metal') Name for the tengwa $\textrm{p}$ (number 1), which had the value *t* in most systems. (III 500)

TINCOTÉMA (Q.: 't-series') Dental and alveolar series of the Tengwar, generally applied in the Third Age to Series I. (III 496-97, 500)

TINDÓMË (Q.: 'star-twilight') The period of the day near dawn when the stars faded.

Called minuial in Sindarin and morrowdim by the Hobbits. (III 485; S 365; B 457)

TINDÓMEREL (Q.: 'twilight-daughter') The Quenya form of Tinúviel (q.v.). (S 365; B 457)

TINDROCK Tol Brandir (q.v.). (I 483; L 194)

TINTALLË (Q.: 'kindler') One of the oldest names of Varda (q.v.). (I 489; R 61; S 48, 365; B 48, 457)

TINÚVIEL (S.: 'twilight-maiden') A poetic name for the lómelindë or nightingale, the name by which Beren called Lúthien when he first saw her singing in the evening in Neldoreth.

The Quenya equivalent was Tindómerel. (I 259; S 165, 351, 365; B 199, 438, 457)

TIRION (Q.: 'great watch-tower') The main city of Eldamar, built in the Calacirya on the hill of Túna. Tirion had white walls and crystal stairs; its highest tower was the Mindon Eldaliéva, at the base of which grew Galathilion.

Tirion was the first home of the Vanyar in Eldamar and was also the dwelling of the Noldor, ruled by Finwë and Finarfin.

Also called Tirion the Fair. (I 309, 482; II 260; R 65; S 59, 61, 248, 365; B 62, 64, 307, 457)

TIRITH AEAR (S.: 'watch sea') The Sea-ward Tower (q.v.). (TB 8)

TÎW (S.: 'letters') The Tengwar (q.v.). (III 493)

TOBOLD HORNBLOWER (fl. TA 2670) Hobbit of the Shire, a resident of Longbottom. He was the first to grow pipe-weed in the Shire.

Tobold was known as Old Toby. (I 28; II 208; III 459)

TODE Marsh in *The Mewlips,* on the other side of the Merlock Mountains. Although possibly fictitious, Tode may have been patterned on the marsh at the eastern end of the Old Forest Road. (TB 46)

TOGO GOODBODY (fl. TA 29th Cent.) Hobbit of the Shire. He married Lily Baggins. (III 474)

TOL BRANDIR (S.) Sheer-sided mountain-island jutting out of the waters at the southern end of Nen Hithoel. It was said that no man or beast had ever set foot on it.
Called in Westron the Tindrock. (I 483, 509-10; II 300; L 194; S 365; B 457)

TOL ERESSËA (Q.?: 'island lonely') A large island, created by the upheavals of the destruction of the Lamps of the Valar. Originally located in the middle of Belegaer, the island was uprooted by Ulmo and brought to the Bay of Balar to transport the Eldar to Aman. On its first mooring, during which the Vanyar and Noldor boarded it, a portion of the island grounded and broke off to form the Isle of Balar.
After conveying the Vanyar and Noldor to Aman, Ulmo returned for the Teleri. During the course of this second voyage Ossë begged Ulmo not to take these Elves away from his home in the Sea, and so Ulmo anchored the island in the Bay of Eldamar, where it received its name. The easternmost of the Undying Lands, Tol Eressëa, especially its western shore, was bathed in the light of the Two Trees, and here grew the first flowers outside Valinor. It may have been deserted when the Teleri moved ashore to Alqualondë, but at the end of the First Age many Eldar from Beleriand settled here, built Avallónë on the east coast, and received Celeborn, a seedling of Galathilion. During the Second Age these Eldar visited Númenor frequently until the rise of the King's Men.
Also called the Lost Isle, reflecting the meaning of the Eldarin name and the island's remoteness from Middle-earth, the Lonely Isle, the Isle of Eressëa, and Eressëa. (I

321; III 289, 390, 452; R 62; S 57, 58-59, 248, 254, 260, 279; B 59, 61-62, 306, 315, 320, 345)

TOLFALAS (S.: 'coastal island') Island on the Bay of Belfalas near the Ethir Anduin. (I 16-17)

TOL GALEN (S.: 'green island') Island in the River Adurant in Ossiriand. Beren and Lúthien dwelt here after their return from the Houses of the Dead, and Tol Galen was the heart of Dor Firn-i-Guinar. (S 123, 188, 234, 235; B 147, 229, 290, 291)

TOL - IN - GAURHOTH (S.: 'island-of-Werewolves') Name given to Tol Sirion (q.v.) between FA 457 and 467, when it was controlled by Sauron. (S 156, 174-75; B 188, 210-11)

TOLMA (gen. Hobb.) A Hobbit forename usually shortened to Tom. (III 517)

TOLMAN COTTON (TA 2941-FO 20) Hobbit of the Shire, a farmer of Bywater. At the time of the WR he was influential in his neighborhood.
Tolman was known as Tom or Farmer Cotton. (III 353, 354 ff., 477)

TOLMAN COTTON (b. TA 2980) Hobbit of the Shire, eldest son of Tolman Cotton. In FO 22 he acted as Deputy Mayor for a year while Sam traveled to Gondor.
At the time of the WR, Tolman was known as Young Tom to distinguish him from his father. (III 471, 477)

TOLMAN GAMGEE (b. FO 22) Hobbit of the Shire, youngest son of Samwise Gamgee.
Tolman was known as Tom. (III 477)

TOL MORWEN (S.: 'island of Morwen') Small island in Belegaer off the coast of Lindon, formed during the ruin of Beleriand at the end of the First Age. The center of Tol Morwen was the grave of Túrin and Morwen and the Stone of the Hapless. (S 230; B 284)

TOL SIRION (S.: 'island of Sirion') Fair, green island of the River Sirion in the Pass of Sirion. When the Noldor first returned to Middle-earth, Finrod dwelt here and built the strategic fortress of Minas Tirith (q.v.). Finrod and Orodreth held the island until FA 457, when it was taken by Sauron and renamed Tol-in-Gaurhoth. Lúthien cast Sauron out ten years later and broke the tower. Finrod was buried on Tol Sirion, which remained uninhabited and undefiled until the ruin of Beleriand. (S 114, 120, 156, 174-76; B 133, 141, 187, 211-13)

TOM (d. TA 2941) Troll of the Trollshaws, one of the three encountered by Thorin and Company. He was turned to stone through Gandalf's trick. (H 46-52)

TOM The protagonist of *The Stone Troll*. It is likely that Tom was to some extent modeled on Tom Bombadil, since Sam Gamgee composed the poem soon after meeting Bombadil. (I 276-78; III 517; TB 39-40)

TOMBA Genuine Hobbit forename, usually abbreviated as Tom. (III 517)

TOM BOMBADIL A being, lord and master of the Old Forest. His race is unknown, although it is possible that he was a Maia "gone native." Certainly his power, knowledge, and joy were great enough. Tom's power within the Old Forest was absolute, and even the Ring could not affect him, but he did not go beyond the boundaries of the Forest, save for occasional visits to the Barrow-downs and the Marish.

Tom called himself Eldest and claimed to have been alive since very early in the First Age. He looked like a Man, short and red-faced. He wore a pointed hat with a blue feather and large yellow boots. Tom was merry and blithe, good-hearted but unconcerned with the problems of the outside world.

Tom Bombadil was the name given him by the Hobbits of Buckland. He was called Iarwain Ben-adar and the First by the Elves, Forn by the Dwarves, and Orald (tr. Mannish: 'very old') by northern Men. (I 167-86, 196-204, 347-48; TB 9, 11-23)

TOMBS The Hallows (q.v.). (III 152)

TOM COTTON Tolman Cotton (q.v.). (III 353, 354)

TOM PICKTHORN (d. TA 3019) Man of the Bree-land, killed in the fight between the Bree-landers and Bill Ferny and his friends. (III 335, 517)

TONGUE The lawn at the southernmost tip of Lórien between Celebrant and Anduin. Celeborn and Galadriel's farewell feast for the Company of the Ring was held there. (I 480, 482)

TOOK Influential Hobbitish family, living in the Took-land in the Westfarthing. The Tooks, because of their Fallohide blood, were (for Hobbits) rather adventurous and tended to be leaders. The Thainship was hereditary in the Took family from the time of Isumbras I (TA 2340), and Tooks were from time to time known to go off on adventures and even to become sailors.
From the time of Isengrim II (fl. 2683), the Tooks closely related to the Thain lived in the Great Smials.
Took is an Anglicization of the actual Hobbitish name Tûk, of forgotten origin. (I 22; III 475, 516; H 16)

TOOK, THE The head of the Took family. (III 471)

TOOKBANK Village in the Westfarthing, in the western Green Hills. (I 40)

TOOKLAND Folkland of the Tooks, in the Southfarthing and Westfarthing in and around the Green Hills. Most of the Tooks still lived there at the time of the WR. (I 30; III 357)

TORECH UNGOL (S.: 'lair of the spider'?) Shelob's Lair (q.v.). (II 414 ff.)

TOROG (S.: 'troll') See: Trolls. (III 511)

TOWER HALL The great audience-hall of the White Tower of Minas Tirith, an awesome room with tall pillars, stone statues of the Kings of Gondor, and, behind the throne, a carven and gem-set image of a White Tree in flower.

Also called the Hall of the Kings; the Tower Hall was evidently the royal throne-room. (III 28, 95, 304)

TOWER HILLS Hills in western Eriador. Until the end of the Third Age a palantír was kept in Elostirion, the tallest of the White Towers (q.v.) built on the Hills. In FO 32 the Tower Hills were made the western boundary of the Shire, and in 35 Fastred of Greenholm and Elanor, daughter of Sam Gamgee, moved to the Hills at Under-towers, where their descendants, the Fairbairns of the Towers, lived for many generations.

Called in Sindarin Emyn Beraid. (I 26-27; II 259, 471; S 291; B 361)

TOWER OF AMON SÛL The watch-tower on Weather-top, built by Elendil in the Second Age. The chief palantír of the North-kingdom was kept in the Tower, and for this reason in the Third Age possession of the Tower, which was on the border of the three realms, was contested by Arthedain, Cardolan, and Rhudaur. In 1409 the combined forces of Rhudaur and Angmar took the Tower and burned it, killing King Arveleg I of Arthedain. At the time of the WR, all that remained of the Tower was an uneven ring of stones. (I 250; III 397; S 291; B 361)

TOWER OF AVALLÓNË The great white tower of Avallónë (q.v.) which could be seen from Númenor by the farsighted. The Master-stone of the palantíri was kept here. (III 390; S 260, 262, 292; B 320, 323, 362)

TOWER OF BARAD-DUR The Barad-dûr (q.v.). (S 267; B 329)

TOWER OF CIRITH UNGOL Tower near the crest of Cirith Ungol, originally built by Gondor to prevent any evil beings from entering Mordor early in the Third Age. The Tower was later deserted by Gondor and manned by Orcs.

The Tower was built in three tiers against a mountainside, and at the time of the WR the main gate was guarded by the Two Watchers. When Frodo and Sam escaped from the Tower, the Watchers were so shaken by the Phial of Galadriel that the gateway crumbled.

See also: the Undergate. (II 405-06; 446-47; III 214-15, 217-35, 248)

TOWER OF ECTHELION the White Tower (q.v.). (III 24)

TOWER OF INGWË Mindon Eldaliéva (q.v.). (S 59; B 62)

TOWER OF THE KING The tower of Turgon in Gondolin, containing shining fountains and Glingal and Belthil. When Gondolin was invaded, Turgon defended the Tower, but it was overthrown and he died in the wreck. (S 126, 240, 242; B 151, 296, 300)

TOWER OF THE STONE OF OSGILIATH The Dome of Stars (q.v.). (III 406)

TOWERS OF THE TEETH Two towers, Narchost and Carchost, built on either side of Cirith Gorgor by Gondor as a guard on Mordor. Deserted about TA 1636 and later reoccupied by Sauron, the Towers became strong Orc-holds, but they were ruined at the unmaking of the One Ring during the WR.

Also called the Teeth of Mordor. (II 308; III 200, 215, 279)

TOWN HOLE Building in Michel Delving where the Mayor resided. (I 214)

TRAHALD (gen. Mannish: 'burrowing') See: Gollum. (III 518)

TRANSLATIONS FROM THE ELVISH Book of lore by Bilbo Baggins, written between TA 3003 and 3018 at Rivendell, in which he incorporated all the Elvish lore and history of the First Age he could cull from living or written records. The *Translations*, which were written in Westron, formed three volumes of the Red Book of Westmarch, and very probably included the *Ainulindalë*, *Valaquenta*, and *Quenta Silmarillion*. (I 37-38; III 380)

TRAVELLERS Name given to Frodo, Sam, Merry, and Pippin by the Hobbits of the Shire after their return from their adventures during the WR. (III 374)

TREEBEARD Fangorn (q.v.). (II 84)

TREEGARTH OF ORTHANC Name given to Isengard by Fangorn after he landscaped it during the WR.
See also: the Watchwood. (III 317)

TREE OF THE HIGH ELVES The emblem of the Eldar, representing Galathilion. (I 397)

TREE OF TIRION Galathilion (q.v.). (S 291; B 361)

TREES OF VALINOR The Two Trees (q.v.). (S 233; B 288)

TREWESDEI The oldest recorded form of the name of the fourth day of the Hobbit week, a translation of the Quenya Aldëa. The form of the name at the time of the WR was Trewsday.
Called Tuesday in *LotR*. (III 484)

TREWSDAY Trewesdei (q.v.). (III 484)

TROLL A fictitious troll in Sam Gamgee's poem *The Stone Troll.* (I 276-78; TB 39-40)

TROLLS Evil race of Middle-earth. Trolls were origi-nally bred by Morgoth in the First Age from some un-known stock, perhaps in imitation of Ents. During the Nirnaeth Arnoediad Gothmog had a bodyguard of trolls, but otherwise they were not prominent in the Wars of Beleriand. In later ages Sauron used trolls, but their value was limited by their stupidity.

Trolls were very large (perhaps as large as Ents), strong, ugly, and stupid. They had thick skin and black blood, and most trolls (except the Olog-hai) turned to stone when exposed to sunlight. They hoarded treasure, killed for pleasure, and ate raw flesh of all kinds. Although they could never be really intelligent, Sauron increased their wits with wickedness, and toward the end of the Third Age some trolls became quite dangerous.

There seem to have been at least four strains of trolls: the Stone-trolls (q.v.) of the Trollshaws and other parts of Eriador, the cave-trolls of Moria, the hill-trolls of Gor-goroth and Eriador, and the Olog-hai. The Stone-trolls spoke a debased Westron and seem to have been the most human; Bert, Tom, and William Huggins were Stone-trolls. The cave-trolls and hill-trolls spoke a debased version of Orkish, when they spoke at all, and were scaled; the cave-trolls were greenish, and their feet were toeless. The Olog-hai, bred by Sauron toward the end of the Third Age, dwelt in southern Mirkwood and the mountains of Mordor. More agile and cunning than other trolls, they could endure the sun as long as Sauron controlled them. The Olog-hai used the Black Speech.

The Sindarin word for troll was *torog,* to which the Black Speech *olog* may have been related in some way. (I 274-78, 421-22; II 83, 113; III 207-08, 420, 511-12, 514; H 49-53; S 195; B 238)

TROLLSHAWS Woods in the Angle north of the Great East Road. Rhudaur had built castles there; although long deserted at the time of the WR, they and the entire area had an unpleasant feeling. The Trollshaws were infested with trolls. (I 17, 270-79; H 43-53)

TRUE-SILVER Mithril (q.v.). (I 413)

TUCKBOROUGH Town in the Westfarthing in the Green Hills, site of the Great Smials. (I 40; II 80)

TUILË (Q.: 'spring') The first season of the loa of the Calendar of Imladris, corresponding roughly to our spring. Tuilë was also one of the seasons in the Dúnedain calendars.
The Sindarin form of the name was ethuil. (III 480, 485)

TUILÉRË (Q.: 'spring-day') Holiday of the Stewards' Reckoning occurring between Súlimë 30 and Víressë 1. Tuilérë fell near the vernal equinox. (III 481)

TÛK (gen. Hobb.) See: Took. (III 516)

TULKAS (Q.) Ainu, the last of the Valar to enter Eä. Loving deeds of prowess, Tulkas came to Arda to oppose Melkor in the First War, and the Dark Lord fled before him. Later, as the champion of the Valar, Tulkas overthrew Melkor in the Battle of the Powers. With Oromë, Tulkas pursued Melkor after the poisoning of the Two Trees, but the Valar were confounded by the Unlight of Ungoliant.
The strongest of the Valar, Tulkas delights in wrestling; he is also a tireless runner. He is not a weighty thinker nor a good counsellor, but he is true, slow to anger and slow to forget, and he laughs as he fights. His fana has golden hair and beard and a ruddy complexion. Tulkas wed Nessa at the feast of the Spring of Arda.
Also called Tulkas Astaldo, the Valiant, and Tulkas the Strong. (S 25, 28-29, 35, 36, 51, 66, 70, 71, 73, 77; B 18, 22, 29, 31, 51, 70-71, 77, 79, 80, 85)

TUMHALAD (S.: 'valley—') Field in Nargothrond, located at the angle of the Rivers Ginglith and Narog. The disastrous Battle of Tumhalad was fought here in FA 496. (S 212; B 261)

TUMLADEN (S.: 'valley-wide') The broad, fertile plain hidden in the Echoriath, site of the kingdom of Gondolin. Tumladen seems to have been level, except for the ravine of Orfalch Echor and the hill of Amon Gwareth. (S 115, 125, 239, 351; B 135, 149, 296, 438)

TUMLADEN Valley in Gondor southwest of Minas Tirith, near Lossarnach. (III 41; PB)

TUMUNZAHAR (Kh.) The Dwarves' name for their city of Nogrod (q.v.). (S 91; B 104)

TÚNA (Q.) The high green hill raised in the Calacirya when Aman was prepared for the Eldar. Its western side lit by the Two Trees, Túna cast a shadow out into Eldamar and the Sea. The city of Tirion was built on Túna. (S 59, 61, 248, 278; B 62, 64-65, 307, 344)

TUNNELLY Surname used by Hobbits of Bree, and perhaps also in the Shire. (I 212)

TUOR (S.) (FA 473-?) Adan and hero of the Third House, only son of Huor and Rían. Conceived just before Huor died in the Nirnaeth Arnoediad, Tuor was fostered by Annael, a Sinda of Mithrim, for Rían died of grief soon after his birth. Tuor spent his childhood in the caves of Androth, but when he was sixteen the Sindar were captured while trying to flee to the Havens of Sirion. Tuor was enslaved by Lorgan the Easterling, but escaped in 492. For four years he dwelt alone in Androth as an outlaw, doing great harm to the Easterlings..
   Ulmo had long ago chosen Tuor as his instrument, and in 496 the Vala prompted him to go in secret to Nevrast, where he found the sword and armor left there nearly 400 years earlier by Turgon. Ulmo then instructed Tuor to go to Gondolin, giving him a cloak of shadow and a companion of the Gondolindrim, Voronwë. Bearing the

tokens of Ulmo, Tuor gained admittance to Gondolin, where he delivered the message of warning given him by Ulmo. But Turgon in his pride refused to flee from Gondolin, and Tuor also remained there, growing strong in body and wise in Elven-lore. In 503, in the second of the unions of Elda and Adan, Tuor married Idril, and the following spring their only child, Eärendil, was born.

When Gondolin was overrun by Morgoth, Tuor rescued Idril and Eärendil from Maeglin, whom he slew, and with Idril led the remnant of the Gondolindrim to the Havens of Sirion. Tuor had yearned for the Sea ever since being led to Nevrast by Ulmo, and in his old age he and Idril sailed to the West in his great ship Eärrámë. Their fate is unknown, but it is said that Tuor was admitted to Eldamar, the only mortal Man to be numbered among the Eldar. (III 388, 389; S 126, 148, 210, 238-45, 246, 305, 307, 308; B 150, 177, 258, 294-303, 304, 379, 381, 382)

TURAMARTH (S.: 'master-doom') Sindarin form of Turambar (q.v.). (S 355; B 445)

TURAMBAR (Q.: 'master of doom') The pseudonym adopted by Túrin (q.v.) in Brethil, and the epithet most commonly (if ironically) applied to him.
The Sindarin form was Turamarth. (S 217, 223, 226; B 266-67, 274, 278)

TURAMBAR (d. TA 667) Dúnadan, ninth King of Gondor (541-667). He won a great victory over the Easterlings and increased Gondor's eastern territory. (III 394, 403)

TURGON (S.: 'commander of power'?) (d. FA 511) Noldorin Elf, second son of Fingolfin and in Middle-earth King of Gondolin (c. 104-511) and High King of the Noldor (473-511). In Eldamar Turgon was friendly with the sons of Finarfin and opposed Fëanor's plan to pursue Morgoth after the theft of the Silmarils, but at last he became one of the Exiles. His wife Elenwë was lost crossing the Helcaraxë, but Turgon and his daughter Idril came to Nevrast, where he built Vinyamar and gathered to him one-third of the Noldor of Fingolfin and a large number of Sindar.

In 51 and 52, Turgon was instructed by Ulmo to prepare a secret kingdom and was shown the hidden valley of Tumladen. After 52 years of secret labor, Turgon led his people into Gondolin, where he ruled for over 500 years, largely ignoring the events of the Wars of Beleriand.

Aside from the misadventure of Eöl, the splendor of Turgon's reign in Gondolin was undisturbed until Dagor Bragollach, when Turgon was brought his father's body by Thorondor. Two years later Thorondor brought him Húrin and Huor, whom he fostered for a year and then allowed to return to Dor-lómin. At this time Turgon foresaw the doom of the Noldor, and he secretly sent mariners to try to obtain the mercy of the Valar. None of these missions was successful and only one of the mariners, Voronwë, survived the Shadowy Seas.

For some reason Turgon joined the Union of Maedhros and fought alongside Fingon in the Nirnaeth Arnoediad, but the sacrifice of Húrin, Hour, and the Third House of the Edain enabled him to retreat without revealing the location of Gondolin. When Tuor came to Gondolin in 496, Turgon welcomed him, but in his pride he refused to follow the advice of Ulmo to flee to the Havens of Sirion. But now the full malice of Morgoth was directed toward Turgon, last of the House of Finwë to control a realm in Middle-earth. At last, aided by the despair of Húrin and the treachery of Maeglin, Morgoth discovered the location of Gondolin, and Turgon was slain defending his Tower.

A wise and cautious ruler, aware of the Doom of the Noldor and the ultimate futility of direct opposition to Melkor, Turgon nonetheless fell into the pride of his kindred. But from his caution, and the friendship of Ulmo, came the extra years of survival that allowed the union of Tuor and Idril and the birth of Eärendil, Turgon's grandson, who at length obtained the aid by which Morgoth was defeated.

Turgon wrought Glingal and Belthil, the splendid images of the Two Trees. His sword was Glamdring, which was made for him. (III 388-89; H 61; S 60, 83, 113-15, 119, 125-26, 154, 158-60, 190-96 passim, 228, 240-42, 305, 360, 365; B 64, 93, 133-35, 140, 141, 149-51, 186, 191-93, 232-40 passim, 281-82, 296-300, 379, 452, 458)

TURGON (d. TA 2753)   Dúnadan, twenty-fourth Ruling Steward of Gondor (2914-53). (III 395, 416-17)

TÛR HARETHA (Q.: 'barrow of the lady')   The burial mound of Haleth in Brethil.
   Called in Sindarin Haudh-en-Arwen. (S 147; B 176)

TÚRIN (Q.?: 'mastery—')   (FA 465-501)   Adan of the Third House, son of Húrin and Morwen. After the Nirnaeth Arnoediad Morwen sent Túrin to safety in Doriath, where he was fostered by Thingol. Between 482 and 485 Túrin fought beside Beleg in the marches of Doriath, but on his return to Menegroth he had a quarrel with Saeros in which the latter was killed. This mischance, which may have been the first effect on Túrin of Morgoth's curse on the family of Húrin, caused Túrin needlessly to flee Doriath and become an outlaw leader south of the River Teiglin, where he assumed the name Neithan, the first of his many pseudonyms.
   After a year (486) Túrin was found by Beleg, who told him of the good will of Thingol, but he refused to return to Doriath. Soon after Túrin captured Mîm, who led him to the refuge of Bar-en-Danwedh on Amon Rûdh. That winter he was rejoined by Beleg, and in 487 the Two Captains cleared the area of Orcs. Túrin renamed himself Gorthol, for he wore the Dragon-helm of Dor-lómin which Beleg had brought him, and the land he patrolled was named Dor-Cúarthol after the Helm of Túrin and the Bow of Beleg. But the Helm betrayed Túrin's identity and Mîm betrayed his refuge, and late in 487 Túrin was captured by Orcs. He was soon rescued by Beleg and Gwindor, but unknowingly he slew Beleg. Stunned by grief, he was tended by Gwindor until he recovered at Eithel Ivrin.
   With Gwindor, Túrin entered Nargothrond, where he named himself Agarwaen, son of Umarth—the Blood-

stained, son of Ill-fate. But he reached his full manhood in Nargothrond, and between 488 and 496 he became a great warrior and trusted counsellor, inducing King Orodreth to oppose the Orcs openly in Talath Dirnen. During these years the Elves of Nargothrond named him Adanedhel, for his beauty and noble bearing, and the Mormegil, the Black Sword of Nargothrond, for the sword Gurthang (the reforged Anglachel of Beleg) which he bore. During these years Finduilas came to love him, but he did not return her love.

Túrin fought valiantly in the disastrous Battle of Tumhalad, but returning to Nargothrond, whose ruin his counsels of open war had ensured, he was ensnared by Glaurung. Released by the dragon, he went to Dor-lómin to seek his mother and unknown sister instead of following the Orcs who had captured Finduilas. When he discovered in Hithlum that he had been tricked, Túrin fell into a rage and slaughtered many Easterlings.

Returning toward Nargothrond, Túrin, naming himself Wildman of the Woods, learned of the death of Finduilas in Brethil. Again he sickened with grief, but being healed by Brandir he settled among the Haladin, renaming himself Turambar. For several years (497-501) Túrin lived obscurely, keeping the Crossings of Teiglin and Haudh-en-Elleth free from Orcs but using neither the Dragon-helm nor Gurthang. In 500 he married the maiden Níniel, who was actually his sister Nienor. The next year Glaurung menaced Brethil and Túrin slew him, but the dying dragon's malice caused Túrin to slay Brandir (who he thought was lying about Níniel's true identity) and then himself. He was buried beneath the Stone of the Hapless.

Túrin had the grey eyes and dark hair of his mother's people. A mighty warrior (probably with Húrin the mightiest of his line) and noble man, Túrin was marred by the griefs of his life (not the least of which was his lifelong uncertainty about his mother's welfare) and the curse of Morgoth, and he tended to be excessive in anger and sorrow. (I 355; TB 8, 54-56; S 148, 197, 198-226, 239, 307, 308; B 178, 241, 242-79, 296, 381, 382)

TÚRIN I (d. TA 2278)   Dúnadan, sixth Ruling Steward of Gondor (2244-78). (III 395)

TÚRIN II (d. TA 2914)   Dúnadan, twenty-third Ruling Steward of Gondor (2882-2914). An active ruler, he built refuges such as Henneth Annûn for the Rangers of Ithilien and refortified Cair Andros against the threat of Mordor. He also won a great victory, with the aid of Rohan, over the Haradrim in the Battle of the Crossings of Poros (2885). (III 395, 416)

TURTLE-FISH   A probably mythical race of fish of the Sea, whose last member was Fastitocalon (q.v.). (TB 49)

TWENTY-FIRST HALL OF THE NORTH-END   The Chamber of Mazarbul (q.v.). (I 419, 420)

TWILIGHT   Probably the period of the Sleep of Yavanna, when Morgoth's creatures (such as the trolls) were bred to live in darkness. (III 511, 512)

TWILIGHT   The state of the Elves at the end of the Third Age. The term is especially apt in *The Tale of Aragorn and Arwen* because of her epithet Undómiel.
    Cf. the Evening (III 313) and the Fading Years. (III 425)

TWILIGHT MERES   Aelin-uial (q.v.). (S 118, 164; B 139, 198)

TWO CAPTAINS   Túrin and Beleg (qq.v.) during the period when they hunted Orcs in Dor-Cúarthol. (S 205; B 252)

TWOFOOT   Family of Hobbits of the Shire, at least one branch of which lived in Hobbiton. At the time of the Farewell Party (TA 3001), Daddy Twofoot lived in Bagshot Row. (I 45)

TWO KINDREDS   Elves and Men, the Children of Ilúvatar. (S 187, 248, 249; B 227, 307, 308)

TWO TREES OF VALINOR White Telperion and Laurelin the Golden (qq.v.), one of the greatest creations of the Valar. Created by the song of power of Yavanna and the tears of Nienna, the Trees were born when Valinor was fully established. They grew on Ezellohar, outside the western gates of Valmar, whence their light illuminated Valinor, Eldamar, and later Tol Eressëa, while Varda collected their dews in great vats, the Wells of Varda.

The Two Trees inspired reverence and wonder in the Eldar; the greatest creation of the Children of Ilúvatar, the Silmarils of Fëanor, captured the light of the Trees. But Melkor coveted this light, and with the aid of Ungoliant he poisoned the Trees, drained the Wells, and stole the Silmarils. Yavanna and Nienna could not heal the Trees, but their last yield was fashioned into the Moon and Sun. It may be that the Trees will be renewed at the End.

The light of the Two Trees waxed and waned in a twelve-hour cycle, the day of the Years of the Trees (q.v.).

Also called the Two Trees of the Valar, the Trees of Valinor, the Trees of Silver and Gold, and the White Tree and Golden. (II 260, 319; III 388, 389; R 62; K 65; S 38, 46, 52, 67, 76, 78, 98-99; B 33-34, 44, 53, 72, 84, 86, 113)

TWO WATCHERS Evil sentient statues guarding the gate of the Tower of Cirith Ungol at the time of the WR. Each had three joined bodies and three heads, facing outward, inward, and across the gateway. They barred entry or exit to any enemy unless he had a stronger will than they, and gave an alarm if one did pass. During the Quest of Mount Doom, Sam Gamgee gained entry and exit by using the Phial of Galadriel.

The Two Watchers seem also to have given the Orcs of the Tower warning of intruders anywhere in the neighborhood.

Also called the Watchers and the Silent Watchers. (II 316, 441; III 218, 234-35)

TYELLER (Q.: 'grades'; sing. *tyelle*) The horizontal

divisions of the Tengwar, usually six in number, although theoretically eight tyeller were available. The tyeller in general represented different modes of articulation, and were differentiated by the shape of the telco and the number of lúvar. (III 495)

TYELPETÉMA (Q.: *'ty*-series') The palatalized consonants of Quenya, *ty, ndy, hy*, etc. These sounds were usually indicated by the sign for the simple consonant plus two underposed dots, the tehta for following *y*. (III 496-97, 500)

TYRN GORTHAD The Barrow-downs (q.v.). (III 398)

UDÛN (S.: 'un-west'? 'hell'?) The source of the dark flame of the Balrogs, possibly Utumno, possibly the darkness of the spirit of Melkor. (I 429; RHM III 436)

UDÛN (S.: 'not-valley'?) Utumno (q.v.). (S 365; B 458)

UDÛN The circular plain in Mordor between Isenmouthe and Cirith Gorgor. (III 251)

UFTHAK (d. TA ?) Orc of the Tower of Cirith Ungol. At some time, he was captured and bound by Shelob. He was seen by his fellow Orcs, but was not released becau e they feared to anger Shelob. (II 445)

UGLÚK (d. TA 3019) Uruk-hai of Isengard, captain of the band that captured Merry and Pippin. He was slain by Eomer of Rohan. (II 60-62 ff., 78)

UIAL (S.) The name for the twilight periods of morning and evening, which were very important to the Eldar.
See: tindómë, undómë. (III 485)

UILOS (S.)   The Sindarin form of Oiolossë (q.v.). (R 62)

UINEN (S.: 'ever-water'?)   Ainu, one of the Maiar of Ulmo, spouse of Ossë. With Ossë she rules the Inner Seas. Gentle and compassionate, Uinen brings calm waters and protects aquatic plants and creatures. She helped return Ossë to his allegiance and befriended the Teleri and Númenóreans; her weeping for the Teleri after the Kin-slaying caused the storm that foundered many Noldorin ships.

Called the Lady of the Seas. (S 30, 40, 58, 87; B 24, 36, 60, 98)

ÚLAIRI (Q.?: 'without—')   The Nazgûl (q.v.). (S 267; B 330)

ULDOR (d. FA 473)   Easterling, son of Ulfang. With his father and his brothers Ulfast and Ulwarth, Uldor took service with Caranthir about 457; he may already have been allied secretly with Morgoth. During the Union of Maedhros Uldor's false warnings of an attack from Ang-band delayed the march of the eastern army, under Maedhros. In the midst of the Nirnaeth Arnoediad Uldor's army, reinforced by Easterlings hidden nearby, attacked the eastern Noldorin army in the rear. Although this treachery cost the Elves the battle, Uldor was slain by Maglor.

Called Uldor the Accursed; he seems to have been the chief of the brothers. (S 157, 190, 193; B 189, 232, 235)

ULFANG (FA 5th Cent.)   Easterling, one of the chief-tains of the Men who entered Beleriand after Dagor Bragollach. With his sons Uldor, Ulfast, and Ulwarth, Ulfang took service with Caranthir, although he may al-ready have secretly served Morgoth. Ulfang apparently did not fight in the Nirnaeth Arnoediad.

Called Ulfang the Black. (S 157, 189; B 189, 231)

ULFAST (d. FA 473)   Easterling, son of Ulfang and brother of Uldor (q.v.). He followed Uldor in battle and treachery, and during the Nirnaeth Arnoediad he was slain by the sons of Bór. (S 157, 193; B 189, 235)

ULMO (Q.: 'pourer, rainer') Ainu, second greatest of the Lords of the Valar and one of the Aratar. A lover of water, Ulmo was one of the chief architects of Arda, always in close friendship with Manwë. In Arda he dwells in the Outer Ocean or in the waters under Middle-earth, governing the movement of all waters from the waves of Belegaer to the dews of dawn. Ulmo does not like to assume a fana, and he rarely comes on land, not even to the councils of the Valar.

Ulmo cares greatly for the Children of Ilúvatar, and in Beleriand he advised Elves and Men frequently, by direct appearances, by dreams, or through the music of waters. He conveyed the Eldar to Aman despite his objection to that policy. During the Wars of Beleriand Ulmo protected the Sirion and Gelion (and Ossiriand) as long as he could; advised Finrod and Turgon to found secret realms, revealing Tumladen to Turgon and hiding his movement thither; advised Turgon and Círdan; directed the career of Tuor; and saved Elwing.

Ulmo learned more of music from Ilúvatar than any other of the Ainur and was the instructor in music of the Teleri. His horns are the Ulumúri, and his music expresses both glory and sadness; his is the call of the Sea which drew the Eldar to Belegaer and Aman.

Called Lord of Waters and King of the Sea, which may be loose translations of his name. (S 19, 20, 25, 26-27, 29, 30, 40, 57, 66, 103, 114, 115, 123, 125, 158, 196, 209, 212, 238-39, 240, 243, 244, 247, 249, 352; B 9, 10, 18, 19-20, 24, 36, 59, 60, 70-71, 119, 133, 135, 147, 149, 150, 190, 240, 256, 260, 295-96, 297, 301, 302, 305-06, 308, 312)

ULUMÚRI (Q.: 'Ulmo's horns'?) The great horns of Ulmo, made of white shell by the Maia Salmar. The music of the Ulumúri cannot be forgotten. (S 27, 40, 57; B 19-20, 36, 59)

ULWARTH (d. FA 473) Easterling, son of Ulfang and brother of Uldor (q.v.). Ulwarth accompanied Uldor in service and treachery; he was slain by the sons of Bór during the Nirnaeth Arnoediad. (S 157, 193; B 189, 235)

ÚMANYAR (Q.: 'not of Aman') Those of the Eldar, a large part of the Teleri, who did not complete the Great Journey. The Umanyar became in Middle-earth the Nandor, Laiquendi, and Sindar (qq.v.), and (except for Elwë) were counted among the Moriquendi.
Also called the Forsaken Elves. (S 53, 309, 353; B 54, 383, 440)

ÚMARTH (S.: 'ill-fate') Name given by Túrin to his father when he named himself Agarwaen to the Elves of Nargothrond. (S 210; B 257)

UMBAR (Q.: 'fate') Name for the tengwa ᴪᴥ (number 6), used for *mb* in Quenya and *b* in most other languages. (III 500)

UMBAR Coastal area in Harad, consisting of a cape, firth, havens, and fortress, and also the surrounding land. An excellent natural harbor, Umbar was used by the Númenóreans, and by SA 2280 it was a great fortress and the chief Númenórean harbor in Middle-earth. In 3261 Ar-Pharazôn landed here to contest the power of Sauron. After the fall of Númenor (and perhaps before that time), the Dúnedain of Umbar fell under the influence of Sauron and became known as Black Númenóreans (q.v.).
In the Third Age, Gondor and the Corsairs of Umbar (q.v.) were frequently at war, and Umbar changed hands many times. King Eärnil I took Umbar in 933, and despite a lengthy siege (933-1050) it was held by Gondor until 1448, when the defeated rebels of the Kin-strife escaped from Pelargir and established themselves at Umbar. In 1810 Telumehtar recaptured the havens, but they were soon after lost to the Haradrim. In 2980, a small fleet of Gondor, led by Thorongil, attacked Umbar in a surprise raid and burned many of the ships of the Corsairs. During the WR a large

Corsair fleet attacked Pelargir but was defeated by Aragorn and the Dead, and in the Fourth Age Umbar was once more controlled by Gondor, under King Elessar.

The name *Umbar* was of pre-Númenórean origin. The city of Umbar was also known as the City of the Corsairs at the time of the WR. (I 16; II 339; III 42, 186, 392, 403, 406-07, 408, 417, 454, 456, 457, 508; S 270; B 334)

UMBARDACIL (Q.: 'Umbar-victor') King Telumehtar (q.v.) of Gondor. (III 408)

UNDEEPS Area south of the Brown Lands. (PB)

UNDERGATE The lower gate of the Tower of Cirith Ungol, entered by a tunnel going through Shelob's Lair. (II 438)

UNDERHARROW Hamlet in Rohan, located in Harrowdale. (III 91)

UNDER-HILL Neighborhood in Hobbiton comprising those holes which, like Bag End, were built in Hobbiton Hill. (H 28)

UNDERHILL A family of Hobbits with branches in the Shire and in Staddle. Underhill was Frodo's incognito on his flight to Rivendell in TA 3018. (I 97, 212-13)

UNDERTOWERS The home of the Fairbairns of the Tower, built on or in the Tower Hills by Warden Fastred in FO 35. The original of the Red Book of Westmarch was kept at Undertowers. (I 37; III 471)

UNDER-WAY Orc-path in Shelob's Lair, probably the tunnel between the Undergate and the stone door blocking Shelob from approaching the Tower of Cirith Ungol. (II 440)

UNDERWORLD Hell, in opposition to Middle-earth and Over-heaven.
Called in Sindarin Udûn. (III 124)

UNDÓMË (Q.: 'twilight') The period of the day near evening when the stars first began to shine. Called aduial in Sindarin and evendim by the Hobbits. (III 485)

UNDÓMIEL (Q.: 'evening-maiden') Name given Arwen because she was the most beautiful Elven-lady of the fading years of the Eldar in Middle-earth. (I 300)

UNDYING LANDS General name given to the lands of Arda west of Belegaer: Aman (comprising Valinor and mainland Eldamar) and Tol Eressëa. Despite the lies of Sauron and the wishes of the Númenóreans, the Undying Lands were not inherently immortal, but rather were hallowed by the Valar, Maiar, and Eldar, their deathless inhabitants.

Also called the Deathless Lands. Such terms as the West, the Far West, the Uttermost West, and the Isles of the West refer to the same area. (III 390, 392; S 249, 260, 263; B 308, 320, 324)

UNGOLIANT (S.: 'spider—') Spirit of evil. Ungoliant may have been one of the Maiar corrupted by Melkor, but in Arda she served only herself. A creature of darkness, Ungoliant assumed a huge spider form and dwelt in a dark ravine in Avathar. Yet she desired and hated light, and she agreed to help Melkor poison the Two Trees. Cloaked in her Unlight (q.v.), Ungoliant and Melkor came to Ezellohar, where she drained the Trees of their sap, poisoned them, and drank the Wells of Varda dry. The pursuit of Oromë and Tulkas was stymied by the Unlight, and Ungoliant and Melkor escaped to Middle-earth. There, in Lammoth, Ungoliant demanded the gems which Melkor had stolen from Formenos. She devoured them and grew larger and darker, and she attacked Melkor when he refused to give her the Silmarils. Driven off by the Balrogs, Ungoliant fled to Nan Dungortheb, where she bred with the creatures there to increase the evil and terror of the great spiders. It is said that she later went far south, where in her last hunger she devoured herself. (II 423; S 73-76, 80-81, 121; B 80-84, 88-90, 144)

UNGWË (Q.: 'spider's web') Name for the tengwa ᴄq (number 8). (III 500)

UNION OF MAEDHROS Military alliance formed by Maedhros in FA 473 to assail Morgoth. Because of the evil wrought by the Oath of Fëanor, many Eldar (notably Orodreth of Nargothrond and Thingol of Doriath) did not join the Union, but Maedhros obtained enough assistance to form two great armies. The western army, led by Fingon, included the Noldor of Hithlum; the Edain of the Third House dwelling in Dor-lómin, led by Húrin and Huor; the Haladin of Brethil, led by Haldir; a company of Falathrim; Gwindor and a small group of Elves from Nargothrond; Mablung and Beleg of Doriath; and Turgon with ten thousand Gondolindrim. In the east gathered Maedhros and the other sons of Fëanor; the Dwarves of Nogrod and Belegost; and the Easterlings, led by the sons of Bór and Ulfang.

In preliminary campaigning West Beleriand and Dorthonion were cleared of Orcs and evil creatures, but Maedhros revealed himself too soon, and Morgoth had time to prepare his forces. Maedhros planned to use the eastern army and some western forces on Midsummer's Day to draw out the armies of Morgoth on Anfauglith, where their right flank could be crushed by the hidden forces of Fingon. But Maedhros was delayed by the treachery of Uldor, Morgoth induced the army of Fingon to commit itself too early, and the armies of the Union were themselves outflanked in the disastrous battle of the Nirnaeth Arnoediad (q.v.), which crushed the hopes of the Noldor. (S 188-92; B 229-35)

UNLIGHT The power and emanation of Ungoliant, an impenetrable darkness which engulfed and destroyed all light.

Also called the Cloud of Ungoliant, the Shadow, the Dark, and the Darkness. (S 74-79 passim; B 81-87 passim)

UNNAMED   Sauron (q.v.), so called by the Men of Gondor. (II 354)

UNQUE (Q.: 'hollow') Name for the tengwa 𝕔𝕕 (number 16). (III 500)

UNSEEN   The spirit world, in opposition to the material world of the Seen. The lords of the Eldar have great power over the Unseen, but among Men only sorcerers do, or those of high Dúnadan birth. (I 294)

UPBOURN   Hamlet in Rohan, located on the Snowbourn between Dunharrow and Edoras.
   The proper (more archaic) form is Upburnan. (III 91; L 194)

ÚR (Q.: 'heat')   Name for the tengwa O (number 36). (III 500)

ÚRIMË (Q.: 'hot—')   The eighth month of the Kings' and Stewards' Reckonings, and the fifth of the New Reckoning, corresponding roughly to our August.
   The Sindarin form, used only by the Dúnedain, was Urui. (III 483)

URTHEL (S.) (d. FA 460)   Adan of the First House, one of the last twelve of Barahir's outlaw companions in Dorthonion. (S 155, 162-63; B 187, 196)

ÚRUI (S.: 'hot')   Urimë (q.v.). (III 483)

URUK, URUKS   See: the Uruk-hai. (III 511)

URUK-HAI (B.S.: 'Orc-race')   Strain of Orcs bred by Sauron in the Third Age in Mordor. The Uruk-hai first appeared about TA 2475, when they overran Ithilien and took Osgiliath. By the time of the WR, uruks were used by Sauron and Saruman as soldiers on all fronts; Gorbag, Shagrat, Uglúk, and perhaps Azog and Bolg were uruks.
   The Uruk-hai were used as soldiers more than other

strains because, unlike other Orcs, they were almost as tall as Men, had straight, strong legs, and did not weaken in sunlight. Uruks were black and slanty-eyed. They regarded themselves as superior to other Orcs.

Saruman's spies in Bree and the Chief's Men may have been Uruk-hai; they almost certainly had some uruk blood in them.

Uruk-hai was the generic name for the breed; the singular was *uruk* and the (Anglicized) plural *uruks*. They were also called the Great Orcs. (I 421; II 20, 61, 441; III 255, 414, 511)

URULÓKI (Q.: 'hot serpents') The first of the three kinds of dragons bred by Morgoth and Sauron. The Urulóki breathed fire, but they could not fly. Glaurung (q.v.) was the first and greatest of the Urulóki; the breed may not have survived the Great Battle and the fall of Morgoth.

Also called fire-drakes. (S 116-17, 361, 365; B 137, 453, 458)

USURPERS A name given to Men (q.v.) by the Eldar. (S 103; B 119)

UTTERMOST WEST The Undying Lands, especially Valinor. (I 321; III 389)

UTUMNO (Q.: 'not-valley'?) The first dwelling of Melkor in Arda, a great underground fortress built in northern Middle-earth during the Spring of Arda. Melkor gathered his Balrogs in Utumno, and he may have bred Orcs and the great spiders here. Utumno was besieged and destroyed during the Battle of the Powers. Although not all its pits were laid bare, Melkor did not return to Utumno.

Called in Sindarin Udûn. (S 36, 47, 51, 365; B 31, 46, 51, 52, 458)

VAIRË (Q.) Ainu, one of the Valier, the spouse of Mandos. She weaves the tapestries which cover the walls of the halls of Mandos and tell the story of all things within Time.

She is called Vairë the Weaver, which may be a translation of her name. (S 25, 28, 353; B 18, 21, 440)

VALA (Q.: 'angelic power') Name for the tengwa 𝌆 (number 22). (III 500)

VALACAR (Q.: 'Vala—') (d. TA 1432) Dúnadan, twentieth King of Gondor (1366-1432). In his youth (1250), Valacar was sent by his father Rómendacil II to the court of Vidugavia to improve relations between Gondor and the Northmen and to enable Valacar to learn the ways of these important allies. Valacar, however, went far beyond this, for he came to love the Northmen, and he married Vidumavi, Vidugavia's daughter. Their child, Eldacar, was thus only half Dúnadan; this favoritism toward the Northmen led to the Kin-strife. (III 395, 405)

VALACIRCA (Q.: 'sickle of the Valar') The constellation of seven stars shaped by Varda in preparation for the awakening of the Elves and placed in the northern sky as a challenge to Melkor and a sign of his fall. The Valacirca is our Great Bear.

Also called the Sickle of the Valar, the Seven Stars, the Sickle and the Wain (by Hobbits), and (probably) Durin's Crown (by the Dwarves). (S 48, 174; B 48, 211)

VALANDIL (Q.: 'Vala-lover') (b. SA 6th Cent.) Dúnadan of Númenor, son of Silmariën and first Lord of Andúnië. (III 391)

VALANDIL (SA 3430?-TA 249) Dúnadan, third King

519

of Arnor (TA 10-249). Born in Imladris, Valandil became King when his father Isildur and his three elder brothers were slain in the Battle of the Gladden Fields. He received the sceptre of Annúminas in TA 10 on reaching his majority. (III 394, 456)

VALANDOR (Q.: 'Vala-land') An early name of Valinor (q.v.). (S 357; B 448)

VALANDUR (Q.: 'Vala—') (d. TA 652) Dúnadan, eighth King of Arnor (602-52). He died a violent death. (III 394)

VALANYA (Q.: 'day of the Valar') The sixth day of the Eldarin week and the seventh in Dúnedain calendars, named for the Valar. It was the chief day of the week.

The Sindarin form was Orbelain. Alternate names were the Quenya Tárion and the Sindarin Rodyn. The Hobbitish name was Highdei. (III 484)

VALAQUENTA A short book of lore, discussing the identities and functions of the Valar, some of the Maiar, and some of the servants of Melkor. *Valaquenta* was closely associated with *Quenta Silmarillion*; it was probably based on accounts of the Noldorin Exiles and preserved through Bilbo Baggins' *Translations from the Elvish* in the Red Book of Westmarch. (S 8, 25-32, esp. 30; B 17-26, esp. 23-24)

VALAR (Q.: *'vala* + plural') The fourteen greatest (excluding Melkor) of the Ainur who chose to enter Eä to fulfill the Vision of Ilúvatar. Seven male and seven female, the Valar were ruled by Manwë and Varda. Although beings of pure spirit, the Valar in Eä usually assumed physical forms, fanar, of great beauty and majesty.

Within Eä, the Valar were concerned with the completion of Arda according to their individual knowledge of various portions of the Vision. Although Arda was Marred by Melkor, the Valar established stability among its substances and then turned their attention to light and growth. The

Spring of Arda began when the Valar created the two Lamps and settled in Almaren. Once again Melkor marred their work, casting down the Lamps and ruining Almaren. The Valar removed to Aman, where they raised the Pelóri, established Valinor (q.v.), and created the Two Trees to light their realm.

While Middle-earth rested in the Sleep of Yavanna, the Valar prepared for the awakening of the Elves by having Varda create new stars. After the Elves awoke, the Valar decided to protect them by capturing Melkor (which they had been afraid to do before because the turmoil of such a war might have destroyed the unknown sleeping-place of the Elves) and bringing the Elves to Aman. Although some of the Valar mistrusted the latter part of the plan, after the Battle of the Powers and the Great Journey Arda seemed secure.

But Manwë in his purity misunderstood the malice of Melkor, and the Valar were forced to endure the poisoning of the Two Trees and the revolt of the Noldor. Once again the Valar decided to suffer this defeat and permit evil to go free, but they created the light of the Sun and Moon to weaken Melkor and hearten the Elves and newly awakened Men.

During the five hundred years of the Wars of Beleriand the Valar felt powerless to intervene, for the Oath of Fëanor had invoked Ilúvatar, and the Valar did not fully understand the destiny of his Children. Yet their pity moved them all, even stern Mandos, from time to time, and such actions as Mandos' releasing Beren and Lúthien from the Houses of the Dead and Ulmo's manipulation of the career of Tuor set the stage for Eärendil's arrival in Aman with the Silmaril. At this point, when the Edain and Eldar had been virtually destroyed without loss of dignity or reverence for the Valar and Ilúvatar, and when their representatives (although not of the Oath-sworn House of Fëanor) were willing to relinquish a Silmaril, the Valar felt empowered to act, and in the Great Battle the Host of Valinor destroyed Morgoth's hordes and cast him out of Eä.

At the end of the First Age the traditional concerns of the Valar—light and the security of Elves and Men—

caused them to place the Silmaril of Eärendil in the heavens as a star, reward the Edain with Elenna, and forgive all the Exiles save Galadriel. It was the gift of Elenna to the Edain which led to the greatest crisis of the Valar, for in SA 3319 Ar-Pharazôn of Númenor, corrupted by Sauron, assaulted Valinor; the Valar laid down their guardianship for the moment and Eru destroyed Númenor. Sauron, however, survived into the Third Age, and so about TA 1000 the Valar sent the Wizards to Middle-earth, and with their aid the Free Peoples of Middle-earth eventually worked out their destiny and overthrew Sauron in the War of the Rings.

Since the Vision had ended before this point, the role of the Valar in later ages is uncertain. They probably retain their guardianship of Eä, but they intervene all too seldom in the affairs of Men.

In all of this the actions of the Valar seem tentative and not always successful, but it must be stressed that the Valar were merely the demiurges and guardians of Eä, preparing, according to their imperfect understanding of the Ainulindalë, the physical substance of Arda for the Children of Ilúvatar. Since the Children were created in the Third Theme, in which the Ainur did not participate, the Valar understood neither the natures nor the destinies of Elves and Men. Because of this, the Valar acted directly as little as possible, instead bolstering the wisdom, courage, and (if possible) virtue of the Children so that they could achieve their own destiny. Even so, the Valar acted as arbiters in many areas; for example, they interpreted and enforced the rules of the Riddle-game.

The Valar were known by many names. The Sindarin form was Belain, singular Balan. Also called the Great Ones, the Mighty, the Powers (all loose translations of Valar), the Powers of Arda, the Rulers of Arda, the Powers of the World, the Guardians of the World, the Lords, the Lords of Valinor, the Lords of the West, the Authorities, the Deathless (especially among the Númenóreans), the Gods (by Men, who sometimes ignorantly worshipped them), and the Enemies beyond the Sea (by Orcs of Angband). (I 33; II 341; III 388, 389, 390,

395; R 66; S passim, esp. 16-18, 21-28, 31, 37, 43-48, 70, 94, 230; B passim, esp. 5-8, 11-22, 26, 31-32, 40-47, 76, 107, 284)

VALARAUKAR (Q.: 'demons of might,' sing. *Valarauko*) The Balrogs (q.v.). (S 31, 318, 353; B 26, 396, 441)

VALARÓMA (Q.: 'Vala-horn') The great horn of Oromë. (S 29, 41 363; B 22, 37, 455)

VALE OF NAROG The valley of the River Narog in West Beleriand. (S 203; B 248)

VALE OF SIRION The valley of the River Sirion in Beleriand, especially the narrow valley between Ered Wethrin and the Echoriath known as the Pass of Sirion (q.v.). (S 54, 106, 115; B 56, 124, 135)

VALE OF THE GREAT RIVER The Vales of Anduin (q.v.). (S 94; B 107)

VALES OF ANDUIN The valley of the River Anduin, more usually the upper vales, the lands above Rauros. In this narrower sense, the Vales were the original home of the Hobbits and the Men of the Vales of Anduin. Although a fair and fertile land, by the time of the WR the Vales of Anduin were nearly deserted because of the dread of Dol Guldur; only the Beornings and the Stoors of the Gladden Fields are mentioned as living there.

Also called the Vale of the Great River. (I 21; III 404, 429; RHM III 436)

VALIER (Q.) The seven Queens of the Valar, in order of greatness Varda, Yavanna, Nienna, Estë, Vairë, Vána, and Nessa.

The singular is Valië. (S 25, 27, 29, 353; B 18, 25, 441)

VALIMAR (Q.: 'Vala-home') The city of the Valar in central Valinor. Valimar had silver domes, golden gates, and many bells, and near it were the Máhanaxar and Ezellohar, the mound of the Two Trees.

Also called Valmar. Valimar is also used to refer to Valinor as a whole. (I 489; R 62; S 38, 74; B 33, 82)

VALINOR (Q.) The land of the Valar in Aman, bounded on the north, south, and east by the curve of the Pelóri and on the west by Ekkaia. Established by the Valar after the destruction of Almaren, Valinor was the home of the Valar (except Ulmo), most of the Maiar, and, later, the Vanyar. Its only city is Valimar. Valinor was lighted by the Two Trees until their poisoning, and later by the Moon and Sun.

Mandos and Vairë dwell in his halls on the shores of Ekkaia, and Nienna dwells nearby. The woods of Oromë lie in southern Valinor, east of the fields and gardens of Yavanna. The mansions of Aulë are in central Valinor, while Manwë and Varda dwell on Taniquetil. The gardens of Vána and the gardens and pools of Lórien and Estë are also in Valinor.

The original form of the name was Valinórë, 'people of the Valar,' which was confused with Valandor, 'land of the Valar.' Valimar is also sometimes used to refer to the whole land, just as Valinor is used loosely to mean Aman. Also called Ever-eve and Evereven, at least before the creation of the Sun and Moon. (I 309, 489; III 311, 388, 452; R 60; S 28, 37-39, 74, 102, 262; B 21, 32-34, 82, 117, 323)

VALINÓRË (Q.: 'people of the Valar') The original form of Valinor (q.v.). (S 357; B 448)

VALINOREAN The language of Valinor. The only example of Valinorean given, *asëa aranion*, is almost certainly Quenya; the speaker is the rather small-minded Warden of the Houses of Healing.

As beings of spirit the Valar had little need for a spoken language, but one Quenya word, *miruvórë*, is said to be "derived from the language of the Valar," so Valinorean apparently is a tongue distinct from Quenya. (III 172; R 61)

VALMAR   An alternate form of Valimar (q.v.). (S 38; B 33)

VÁNA (Q.)   Ainu, one of the Valier, the younger sister of Yavanna and spouse of Oromë. She cares for flowers and birds, both of which rejoice when she is near, and grows golden flowers in Valinor.

Vána is called the Ever-young. (S 25, 29, 30, 99; B 18, 23, 24, 114)

VANIMELDË, TAR- (Q.: 'fair-friend'?) (fl. SA 2600) Dúnadan, sixteenth Ruler of Númenor and the third Ruling Queen. (III 390)

VANYAR (Q.: 'fair ones')   The first and smallest of the Kindreds of the Eldar. Under the leadership of Ingwë, the Vanyar were the first to set forth on the Great Journey and the first to reach the shores of Belegaer; they sailed to Aman on the first voyage of Tol Eressëa. In Aman the Vanyar first dwelt in Tirion. Later, they came to love the full light of the Trees and wandered in Valinor or settled on Taniquetil. Many of the Vanyar marched to the Great Battle with the Host of Valinor, but otherwise they remained content in Valinor, ruled by Ingwë.

The Vanyar were favored among the Eldar by Manwë and Varda and always distrusted Melkor. Their hair was golden and their banners white.

Also called the Fair Elves and the Light-elves. (H 164; S 40, 52-54, 57, 59, 61-62, 66, 98, 102, 251, 254, 309, 354; B 35, 53-55, 59, 62, 65, 71, 112, 117, 310, 315, 383, 441)

VARDA (Q.: 'the exalted')   Ainu, the mightiest of the Valier and one of the Aratar, the spouse of Manwë, with whom she lives in Ilmarin on the summit of Taniquetil. An ancient enemy of Melkor, Varda aids Manwë in the rule of Arda and the watching of Middle-earth. Varda is concerned with light. She made the stars, filled the Lamps of the Valar with light, collected the dews of the Two Trees in her Wells, fashioned the newer stars and constellations in preparation for the awakening of the Elves, hallowed the Silmarils, established the courses of the Moon and Sun, and set the star Eärendil in the sky.

Because of her creation of the stars, Varda was the dearest of the Valar to the Elves, who called to her for aid from Middle-earth. At times she answered their prayers, and also those of Men. During the WR, for example, she aided Sam through the Phial of Galadriel (which of course contained the light of Eärendil) during his struggle against Shelob. Varda was the most beautiful of the Valar.

In Middle-earth she was usually called Elbereth. Other titles given her as creator of the stars were Tintallë, Gilthoniel, Elentári, and Lady of the Stars. Because of the shining white fana in which she appeared in visions to the Elves of Middle-earth, she was also called Fanuilos and Snowwhite. (I 117, 265, 310, 312, 489; II 430; III 234; R 60, 61, 64, 66; S 25, 26, 29, 35, 37, 39, 40, 48, 67, 99, 354; B 18, 19, 23, 29, 32, 34, 36, 47-48, 73, 113, 441)

VARDAMIR (Q.: 'exalted jewel, jewel of Varda') (fl. SA 5th Cent.)   Dúnadan, second King of Númenor (442-?). (III 390)

VARIAGS   A race, probably of Men, dwelling in Khand. In the WR they were allied with Sauron. (III 148)

VÁSA (Q.: 'consumer')   An Eldarin name for the Sun, given because of its energy and because its rising marked the beginning of the waning of the Elves. (S 99, 354; B 114, 441)

VEIL OF ARDA   The atmosphere, the special domain of Manwë in Arda. (S 26; B 18)

VIDUGAVIA (fl. TA 13th Cent.)   Northman, self-styled King of Rhovanion. He was the most powerful Northern prince of his time; his realm lay between Mirkwood and the Celduin. Vidugavia was friendly with Rómendacil II of Gondor, whom he aided in his great victory over the Easterlings in 1248. (III 405)

VIDUMAVI (fl. TA 13th Cent.)   Northman, daughter of Vidugavia. She married Valacar of Gondor. (III 405)

VILYA (Q.: 'air, sky')   Later and more usual name for the tengwa **ʊ** (number 24). The earlier form was wilya, but this changed because of a change in the pronunciation of Quenya in Middle-earth. (III 500)

VILYA   The mightiest of the Three Rings of the Elves (q.v.). Vilya was originally worn by Gil-galad, but it was given by him to Elrond. Vilya was made of gold and was set with a great sapphire.
   Also called the Ring of Air and the Ring of Sapphire. (III 381, 456; S 288, 298; B 357, 370)

VINGILOT (Q.: 'foam-flower')   The ship of Eärendil, built of birchwood from Nimbrethil with the aid of Círdan. Vingilot had a swan-shaped prow, golden oars, and silver lanterns and sails. Vingilot bore Eärendil on all his voyages over Belegaer; hallowed by the Valar (but not made of mithril), it was the vessel that bore him through the heavens as a star.
   The full form of the name was Vingilótë. Called in Adûnaic Rothinzil. (I 308, 310; S 246, 250, 354, 365; B 304, 309, 441-42, 458)

VINGILÓTË   See: Vingilot. (S 354; B 441-42)

VINITHARYA   The name given Eldacar (q.v.) by the Northmen in his youth. (III 405)

VINYAMAR (Q.: 'new-home'?)   The city built by Turgon on his return to Middle-earth, located beneath Mount Taras in Nevrast, overlooking the Sea. Vinyamar was deserted about FA 104 when Turgon led his people to Gondolin, but on the advice of Ulmo he left a sword and armor here which were later claimed by Tuor. (S 115, 119, 238, 354; B 135, 141, 295, 442)

VINYARION (Q.) Hyarmendacil II (q.v.). (III 395)

VÍRESSË (Q.) The fourth month of the Kings' and Stewards' Reckonings and the first of the New Reckoning, corresponding roughly to our April.

The Sindarin name, used only by the Dúnedain, was Gwirith. (III 483, 486)

VISION OF ILÚVATAR The visual image of the Ainulindalë, made by Ilúvatar to show the Ainur the nature of their Music. Because many of the Ainur loved the Vision, Ilúvatar brought it into Being, thus creating Eä. While each of the Ainur knew that part of the Music which he or she had sung, only in the Vision could they perceive the whole pattern of Eä. Their knowledge of the Vision was thus very important to the Valar in their labors in Arda, but it is said that the Vision ceased before the end of the Third Age. (S 17, 20, 46, 47; B 6, 10, 44, 47)

VOID The absence of Ilúvatar and the Flame Imperishable. Melkor wandered in the Void looking for the Flame (of course in vain), and Eä was set amidst the Void but was not of it.

Also called the Outer Void, the Timeless Void (in contrast to the Timeless Halls and the Time of Eä), the Everlasting Dark, the Ancient Darkness, and perhaps nothingness (III 125) and Outside. (S 15, 16, 17, 25, 32, 260; B 4, 6, 17, 26, 320)

VORONDIL (Q.: 'faithful friend' or 'lover of steadfastness') (d. TA 2029) Dúnadan, Steward from 1998 to 2029 of Eärnil II of Gondor. Vorondil was a great hunter, which is why he was known as Vorondil the Hunter, and he made the Great Horn from the horn of one of the Kine of Araw which he slew. (III 29, 395)

VORONWË (Q.: 'steadfast') (fl. FA 500) Elf of Gondolin, son of Aranwë. Voronwë sailed on the last ship which Turgon sent West to seek aid from the Valar. While returning in 496 to announce its failure to penetrate the Shadowy Seas, his ship foundered off the coast of Nevrast. Saved by Ulmo, Voronwë was the only survivor. He was cast ashore at Vinyamar, where he met Tuor, whom he brought to Gondolin. (S 196, 239; B 240, 295)

WAIN The Sickle (q.v.). (H 185)

WAINRIDERS An Easterling people or confederacy. They first ventured west of the Sea of Rhûn in TA 1851. In 1856, stirred up by Sauron, they attacked Gondor, taking Rhovanion and killing King Narmacil II. In 1899, the enslaved Northmen of Rhovanion revolted against the Wainriders, and Gondor, under King Calimehtar, took advantage of this to defeat the Wainriders in a battle on Dagorlad. In fifty years, however, the Wainriders had recovered their strength, and in 1944, allied with Men of Khand and Near Harad, they launched a great two-pronged assault on Gondor from the east and south. Although the northern Wainrider force defeated the Northern Army of Gondor and killed King Ondoher and both his sons, the southern assault was defeated by Eärnil, who then brought his army north and crushed the main Wainrider force in the Battle of the Camp. The Wainriders were totally destroyed.

The Wainriders were so called because they traveled in large wagons. Their chieftains fought in chariots, and in general they were better armed than previous Easterling invaders. (III 408-09)

WALDA (TA 2780-2851)   Man, twelfth King of Rohan (2842-51). He was ambushed and slain by Orcs near Dunharrow. (III 435)

WALLS OF MORIA   The great cliffs rising above the West-gate of Moria. (I 393)

WALLS OF THE NIGHT   In the First and Second Ages, when Arda was flat, the Walls of the Night were the outer boundary of Arda, encircling Ekkaia.

The Walls were breached by the Doors of Night in the west and (perhaps) the Gates of Morning in the east.

Also called the walls of the world (not capitalized) and perhaps the Mountain Wall. (S 28, 36, 37; B 21, 31, 32)

WALLS OF THE WORLD   The boundary between Eä and the Void, breached by the Door of Night. (S 254; B 315)

WANDERING COMPANIES   Groups of Elves that had no permanent home in Middle-earth, but wandered about together. (I 117 ff., 124)

WANDERING DAYS   The period, lasting from about TA 1000 to 1630, during which the Hobbits gradually migrated from the Vales of Anduin to Bree or the Shire, prompted by the rise of Dol Guldur and Angmar. About 1050 the Harfoots came to Eriador, and the Fallohides followed about a century later, while the Stoors went to Dunland or the Angle. When Angmar rose, the Hobbits migrated farther west, many settling at Bree. Some Stoors, however, returned to the Gladden Fields. In TA 1600 the Shire was settled by a large number of Hobbits from Bree, and thirty years later the Stoors of Dunland moved there as well. (I 21; III 456, 457)

WANDLIMB   Fimbrethil (q.v.). (II 99)

WAR, THE   The Wars of Beleriand or the War of the Great Jewels (qq.v.). (S 95, 141; B 108, 169)

WARDEN OF WESTMARCH   Title created by Thain Peregrin in FO 35 for Fastred of Greenholm and held by his descendants, the Fairbairns of the Tower Hills. It is uncertain if any responsibilities accrued to this title. (I 37; III 471)

WARGS   Evil wolves of Rhovanion, allies of the Orcs and servants of Sauron.

The Wargs of I 388-91 do not seem to have been true Wargs, in that they were west of the Misty Mountains and weren't real. (I 388-91; H 103-09, 265, 268)

WAR OF THE DWARVES AND ORCS   War fought from TA 2793 to 2799 between the Orcs of the Misty Mountains and the Dwarves, especially Durin's Folk. The war was caused by the murder and mutilation of Thrór in 2790 by Orcs of Moria. After mustering their forces, in 2793 the Dwarves began sacking every Orc-hold they could find in the Misty Mountains, searching for Azog, Thrór's murderer. In 2799 all the surviving Orcs gathered in Moria, and the Dwarves met them in the Battle of Azanulbizar (q.v.). Most of the Orcs were killed in this War, and this made the Misty Mountains safer for a century and a half, but many Dwarves were also slain. A large number of Orcs fled across Rohan and settled in the Ered Nimrais, but they were killed by 2864. (III 416, 442-44)

WAR OF THE ELVES AND SAURON   War fought from SA 1693 to 1701 between the Eldar of Eregion and Lindon and Sauron and his allies. The War began after Celebrimbor discovered Sauron's treachery in the forging of the Rings of Power and Sauron decided to crush the now implacably hostile Elves. The Three Rings were hidden by the Eldar, but in 1697 Eregion was overrun and Celebrimbor slain. Elrond, who had been sent to Eregion by Gil-galad, fled with the remaining Noldor and founded Rivendell. In the next two years Sauron overran all of Eriador except for Rivendell. Gil-galad asked Tar-Minastir of Númenor for aid, and in 1700 the latter sent a navy to

Middle-earth with whose aid Sauron was defeated. In 1701 he was driven out of Eriador and the war ended.

Aside from greatly reducing the power and numbers of the Eldar, the War ended the only close link between the Elves and the Dwarves, the friendship between Khazad-dûm and Eregion. (III 454; S 267, 291; B 330, 361)

WAR OF THE GREAT JEWELS The major phase of the Wars of Beleriand (q.v.), fought between the Noldor, aided at times by the Sindar, Edain, Easterlings, and Dwarves, and the vast armies of Morgoth. The aim of the Noldor was to recover the Silmarils, while Morgoth desired to crush the hated Noldor and conquer Beleriand. The War began with Dagor-nuin-Giliath and ended with the intervention of the Valar and the overthrow of Morgoth in the Great Battle.

Also called the War of the Jewels. (III 388, 507; S passim; B passim)

WAR OF THE JEWELS The War of the Great Jewels (q.v.). (S 259; B 319)

WAR OF THE POWERS The Battle of the Powers (q.v.). (S 118; B 139)

WAR OF THE RING The great war fought at the end of the Third Age between Sauron and the Free Peoples, the subject of *LotR*. In the War Sauron was overthrown for the final time and the One Ring destroyed. (I 23, 291; III 371, 379; S 303; B 376)

WAR OF WRATH The Great Battle (q.v.). (S 251; B 311)

WARS OF BELERIAND The great conflicts of the First Age between the forces of Morgoth and the Eldar and their allies, the Edain and the Dwarves, marked by six major battles. During the third age of the captivity of Melkor, his creatures, especially Orcs and wolves, multiplied; they began to spy out Beleriand, but farther east they severely harassed the inhabitants of Eriador, causing Lenwë's group of Nandor to seek refuge in Beleriand. The Elves, however, did little; although Thingol built the defensible halls of Menegroth and bought arms from the Dwarves, and Círdan had fortifications of some kind in the Falas, most of the Sindar wandered in the forests of Beleriand, disorganized and defenseless.

As soon as Melkor had returned to Middle-earth and rebuilt Angband, he sent his Orcs against Beleriand. In the west, they moved down the Vale of Sirion, overrunning the country between Sirion and Narog and besieging Círdan in the Falas. In the east, Orcs ranged down the valley of the Gelion, but they were defeated in the first major battle of the Wars by the Elves of Region, led by Thingol, and of Ossiriand, led by Denethor. Crushed between these two armies, the surviving Orcs fled north, but they were intercepted and destroyed by the Dwarves of the Ered Luin. However, Denethor's forces were lightly armed, and he was slain on Amon Ereb before his attackers were taken in the rear by Thingol.

At this point the Noldor of Fëanor landed at Losgar, and as they reached Mithrim they were attacked by a third army of Morgoth in the Dagor-nuin-Giliath, the Second Battle. But Morgoth had underestimated the strength of the Noldor fresh from Aman, and his forces, including the Orcs besieging the Falas who hastened north to reinforce the third army, were defeated. Even though Fëanor was slain in the pursuit of the fleeing Orcs, the arrival of Fingolfin and the first rising of the Sun caused Morgoth's forces to retreat into Angband. The Noldor then established defensive positions to contain the strength of Morgoth: Fingolfin in Hithlum holding Barad Eithel and the other fortresses defending the eastern passes of the Ered Wethrin, Finrod at Tol Sirion guarding the Pass of Sirion, Aegnor and Angrod on the north slopes of Dorthonion, and the sons of Fëanor holding the hills and passes between Dorthonion and the Ered Luin. In addition, the cavalry of Fingolfin and Maedhros patrolled Ard-galen and Lothlann.

About FA 60 Morgoth staged another sudden attack, forcing the Pass of Sirion and Maglor's Gap to draw out the

Elves and then sending his major force to assault Dorthonion. But the Elves were prepared. The raiding Orcs in
Beleriand were hunted down and destroyed, and Fingolfin
and Maedhros, attacking Morgoth's main army on both
flanks, destroyed it on Ard-galen in Dagor Aglareb, the
Third Battle.

After this time the Noldor instituted the Siege of Angband, closely patrolling Ard-galen and watching for any
movement out of Angband toward the south. About 160
Morgoth attacked Hithlum from the north and west with
a small force, but the Orcs were observed in time and
destroyed. About 260 Glaurung issued forth from Angband,
but he was still immature and was driven back by the
arrows of Fingon's riders.

Then followed the Long Peace (c. 260-455), when
there were only minor forays on the marches of Beleriand.
Yet Morgoth gathered his forces, bred his monsters,
and tightened his control over Eriador, while the Elves
did nothing except ally themselves with the Edain and
strengthen their defenses. In the winter of 455 Morgoth
sent forth flames which burned all Ard-galen (renamed
Anfauglith) and the slopes of Dorthonion, killing or
driving away the Noldorin cavalry. With the Siege of
Angband broken, Morgoth began the Fourth Battle, Dagor
Bragollach. The Ered Wethrin and the Pass of Sirion were
held, but the Elves and Men of Dorthonion were decimated,
enabling Morgoth to take the plateau at his leisure, despite
the valiant defense of Barahir. In the east, Maedhros held
Aglon and Himring, but Maglor's Gap and Thargelion were
overrun and ravaged by Glaurung and an army of Orcs.
Maedhros and Maglor remained at Himring, but Celegorm
and Curufin fled to Nargothrond and the other brothers
retreated beyond the Andram.

In the next few years Morgoth sought to consolidate his
gains. Sauron seized Tol Sirion in 457; although he was
driven out ten years later, the Pass remained defended only
by the threat of a flank attack from Hithlum. After the
death of Barahir in 460 only Beren remained to contest
Dorthonion, but he too fled in late 464. In 462 Morgoth
attacked Hithlum from the east and north; once again the

Ered Wethrin, defended by the Edain, held fast, but Morgoth's northern army was defeated only with aid from Círdan. The only Eldarin gain during this period was the theft of a Silmaril by Beren and Lúthien.

Perceiving that Morgoth was not unassailable, but that in time the Eldarin defenses would be eroded, in 473 Maedhros formed his Union. His battle plan was designed to trick Morgoth into a defeat like that of Dagor Aglareb, but Morgoth's vast strength and the treachery of the Easterlings led the armies of the Union into the disastrous Nirnaeth Arnoediad, the Fifth Battle. The majority of the warriors of the Eldar and Edain were slain, Hithlum and Himring were lost, and Beleriand lay open to Morgoth. In 474 the Falas was overrun, and after this time Talath Dirnen was raided by Orcs.

Only in Ossiriand, Brethil, and the hidden realms of Nargothrond, Doriath and Gondolin, could the Eldar and Edain offer effective resistance, and in most of these places their strength depended on secrecy. For a few years the amazing exploits of Túrin seemed to halt Morgoth's advance in West Beleriand, but when Túrin persuaded Orodreth of Nargothrond to oppose Morgoth openly, the Noldor were destroyed at Tumhalad (496) and Nargothrond was sacked. After this the Haladin of Brethil did not venture beyond their woods, and Morgoth had overrun virtually all of West Beleriand. After Menegroth was ravaged twice, by the Dwarves of Nogrod and the sons of Fëanor, and Gondolin fell in 511, all of Beleriand lay open to Morgoth.

Deeming his victory complete, Morgoth rested his forces, not bothering to annihilate the weak Elves and Edain of Ossiriand, Brethil, the Havens of Sirion, Arvernien, and Balar. Yet at the last Eärendil managed to win through to the West and obtain the aid of the Valar. In the final struggle of the Wars of Beleriand, the Host of Valinor destroyed Morgoth's forces in the Great Battle, broke Angband, and cast Morgoth out of Eä. But Beleriand itself was broken and sank beneath the waves.

Also called the Goblin-wars. The War of the Great Jewels properly begins with the return of the Noldor and the Second Battle, but is otherwise identical. (H 61, 72; S passim, esp. 96, 106-07, 115, 116, 150-56, 160, 188-96, 211-15; B passim, esp. 109, 124, 135, 137, 180-88, 193-94, 229-40, 260-64)

WASTE Perhaps the Desolation of Smaug. (H 286)

WATCH The official name for the Shirriffs, the Shire police. There were three in each Farthing for Inside Work, which consisted mostly of catching stray animals, and a variable number of Bounders to keep undesirable outsiders from entering the Shire. The Watch was run by the Mayor of Michel Delving, who was First Shirriff.

During the WR, Saruman and Lotho greatly increased the Watch, and the Shirriffs were assigned to arrest those who broke the Rules. The hundreds of Shirriffs were organized into companies, of which only one, the First East-farthing Troop, is named in *LotR*.

The members of the Watch wore feathers in their caps to identify themselves. (I 31; III 346-48, 355-56)

WATCHER IN THE WATER A many-tentacled creature who guarded the West-gate of Moria at least between the years TA 2994 and 3019, perhaps related to the nameless things below Khazad-dûm. The Watcher was definitely evil, but it is unclear whether he was under the control of Sauron or the Balrog.

The Watcher lived in a lake created by his damming of the Sirannon. (I 402-03, 419)

WATCHERS The Rangers of the North (q.v.). (TB 21)

WATCHERS The Two Watchers (q.v.). (III 218)

WATCHFUL PEACE The period from TA 2063 to 2460, during which Sauron remained hidden in the East and the Nazgûl were quiet in Minas Morgul. The Watchful Peace began when Sauron fled from Dol Guldur to avoid identification by Gandalf, and ended with his return to the tower with increased strength. During this period the West was relatively peaceful, although Eriador was troubled by evil creatures, especially wolves. (III 401, 414, 459)

WATCHWOOD   Forest of Ents and Huorns in the Ring of Isengard during the WR, so named because it guarded Saruman, who was a prisoner in Orthanc. (II 245)

WATER   Stream in the Shire, running through Needlehole and Bywater and emptying into the Brandywine just above the Bridge of Stonebows. Rushock Bog and the Pool of Bywater were on the Water. (I 40, 106, 365; H 16)

WATER-VALLEY   The valley of the Water, in the Shire. Part of the Great East Road went through the Watervalley. (I 107)

WAYBREAD   Lembas (q.v.). (I 478)

WAYMEET   Village in the Westfarthing on the Great East Road, fifteen miles west of Bywater. Waymeet was so called because the main road from Sarn Ford joined the Great East Road at Waymeet. Waymeet was one of the headquarters of the Chief's Men during the WR.
Called Waymoot on the Shire-map. (I 40; III 356, 357)

WAYMOOT   Waymeet (q.v.). (I 40)

WAY OF ESCAPE   Probably the original main entrance to Gondolin, following the Dry River upstream through an arched gate into a subterranean course which led into Tumladen.
The Hidden Way, which may or may not be identical to the Way of Escape, was apparently constructed by Turgon and the Gondolindrim. Beginning near the outflow of the Dry River, the Hidden Way was barred first by the Outer Gate, watched by the Dark Guard. After this one went up the Orfalch Echor, guarded by the Seven Gates (one of these may have been the Outer Gate) and leading into Tumladen. (S 137-38, 228, 239; B 164, 281, 296)

WEATHER HILLS   Hills north of the Great East Road between Bree and Mitheithel, at one time the boundary between Arthedain and Rhudaur. Arthedain fortified the Hills against Angmar, but they were taken in TA 1409 and later recovered.

The chief peak of the Weather Hills was the southernmost, Weathertop. (I 16, 247, 249; III 397)

WEATHERTOP   The southernmost of the Weather Hills, on which was built the Tower of Amon Sûl (q.v.).

Called in Sindarin Amon Sûl. (I 16, 233, 247, 250-67, 346; TB 41)

WEDMATH   The eighth month of the Shire Reckoning, corresponding roughly to our August. (III 478, 483)

WELLINGHALL   A dwelling of Fangorn near the roots of Methedras and the source of the Entwash. Its walls and roof consisted of the branches and trunks of evergreen trees, and there was a little waterfall in the back of its single large room. (II 91-92, 216)

WELLS OF VARDA   The great vats in which Varda gathered the dews of the Two Trees, which were used by the inhabitants of Valinor for light and refreshment. The Wells were drunk dry by Ungoliant. (S 39, 76; B 34, 84)

WEREWOLVES   One of the breeds of Morgoth's monsters, especially favored by Sauron. The werewolves were dreadful spirits imprisoned in large wolf-bodies; the two greatest of the breed were Draugluin and Carcharoth (qq.v.).

The wolves ridden by Orcs in Beleriand may have been werewolves. The Wargs that attacked the Company of the Ring were not; werewolves had real and mortal bodies. (S 93, 156, 164, 174-75, 180; B 106, 188, 198, 210-11, 218)

WERE-WORMS   Probably mythical monsters of the far East of Middle-earth. (H 31)

WEST The Undying Lands (q.v.). (II 353; S 28, 51; B 22, 51)

WEST The realms and peoples opposed to Sauron and favoring virtue and the Dúnedain. (III 195, 280, 469)

WEST BELERIAND The portion of Beleriand west of Sirion, including Nargothrond, the Falas, Arvernien, Nivrim, Brethil, and perhaps Nevrast. (S 119, 120-21)

WEST-ELVES The Eldar (q.v.). (III 505)

WESTEMNET That portion of Rohan west of the Entwash. (I 17; II 42)

WESTERNESSE Westron name for Númenor (q.v.). (I 23; S 261, 270; B 321, 333)

WESTERN SEA, WESTERN SEAS Belegaer (q.v.), sometimes specifically the part near Aman. (I 117, 412; III 381; S 186, 254; B 226, 314)

WESTFARTHING One of the Four Farthings of the Shire, seemingly the most important. Michel Delving, the "capital" of the Shire, was in the Westfarthing, and the Free Fair was held here. Other places of note in the Westfarthing included Bywater and Hobbiton. (I 40)

WESTFOLD Area of Rohan, running along the Ered Nimrais from the Isen to the western boundary of the Folde. The defensive center of the Westfold was at Helm's Deep, and its master dwelt in the Hornburg. (II 168, 170; L 185)

WESTFOLD VALE Valley in the Westfold of Rohan through which ran the Deeping Stream. (II 169)

WEST-GATE OF MORIA Gate in Khazad-dûm built by Narvi in the Second Age to facilitate trade between the Dwarves and the Noldor of Eregion. The gate was controlled by the spell placed on it by Celebrimbor. When Sauron overran Eregion the West-gate was closed. Sometime after TA 1981, the gate was blocked by the Watcher in the Water, who in 2994 prevented Balin's Dwarf-colony from escaping by that route. When the Company of the Ring opened the West-gate in 3019, the Watcher closed the doors and barricaded them with boulders and holly trees.

The West-gate was made of ithildin, and only opened when it was visible and when the person desiring entry spoke the word *mellon.*

Also called the Elven Door, the Doors of Durin, and the Gate. (I 388, 394-403)

WESTMANSWEED   Pipe-weed (q.v.). (III 178)

WESTMARCH   Area added to the Shire in FO 32 by gift of King Elessar, lying between the Far Downs and the Tower Hills. In 35 Fastred and Elanor moved to Under-towers in Westmarch, and Fastred was named Warden of Westmarch. His descendants, the Fairbairns, retained that office and had in their possession the Red Book of West-march. (I 30; III 471)

WEST ROAD   The road leading from Minas Tirith to Edoras.

Also called the North-way and the Great West Road. (III 14-15, 93-94, 127-29, 193, 306)

WESTRON   The native language at the time of the WR of all those Men and Hobbits living in the old areas of Gondor and Arnor, and also of those inhabitants of the west bank of Anduin as far north as the Gladden Fields, with the exception of the Woses, the Dunlendings, and the Rohirrim. In addition, Westron was the common tongue for all inter-lingual meetings, and as such was known to some degree by everybody west of Rhûn. Westron was also the public language of the Dwarves and the base for many Orkish tongues.

Westron was in origin a mingling of Adûnaic and the languages of the coastlands of Middle-earth, developing in the third millennium of the Second Age with the establishment of Númenorean settlements in Middle-earth. With the coming of Elendil to Middle-earth, the language was enriched with many Sindarin words, and this was the form in which Westron spread throughout Middle-earth.

The use of Westron also defined a cultural area, as may be seen by the spread of the Gondor calendar systems, and the term "Westron area" has been used in this *Guide* with this sense.

Hobbitish was in part a rustic form of Westron. The languages of the Men of Rhovanion and the Rohirrim were distinctly related to Westron, since all descended from the languages of the Edain and their kin.

There are very few examples of genuine Westron given in *LotR*, as most Westron names have been translated into equivalent English forms.

Westron was also called the Common Speech. (I 23; III 487, 504, 505, 506-09, 511, 512, 513-20 passim.)

WETWANG Nindalf (q.v.). (I 483)

WHISKER-LAD A young otter of the Withywindle, in the poem *Bombadil Goes Boating*. (TB 18-19, 23)

WHITE COMPANY The guard of the Princes of Ithilien in the Fourth Age, formed by King Elessar after the WR to serve Faramir, the first Prince. Beregond was the first Captain of the White Company.

Also called the Guard of Faramir. (III 305)

WHITE COUNCIL Council of the Wise formed at the summons of Galadriel to plan the strategy to be used against Sauron. The White Council was composed of the Wizards, Galadriel, Elrond, Círdan, and others of the chief Eldar. Saruman was chosen as its head.

The first meeting of the Council was held in TA 2463, three years after the end of the Watchful Peace. The next important meeting was held in 2851, at which Saruman, who desired the One Ring, overruled Gandalf's plan to attack Dol Guldur. At the next meeting, in 2941, Saruman agreed to the attack, and the Council drove Sauron to Mordor. The last meeting of the Council was held in 2953 to discuss the Rings of Power. At this meeting Saruman lied about the fate of the One, saying it had gone into the Sea, and thus quieted Gandalf's suspicions about Bilbo's ring.

The Council as an organization seems to have been a formality, since the Wise and the Council were the same people. The reference to the Council on III 414 is incorrect, since the Wise, not the yet unformed Council, drove Sauron from Dol Guldur in 2063.

Also called the Council and the Council of the Wise. (I 77, 78, 462; II 95-96; III 414, 434, 459-62; H 280-81; S 300; B 373)

WHITE CROWN   The Silver Crown (q.v.). (III 304)

WHITE DOWNS   Downs in the Westfarthing, on which Michel Delving was built. The Free Fair was held on the White Downs. (I 31; III 383)

WHITE HAND   The emblem of Saruman. (II 20, 202, 246)

WHITE HORSE UPON GREEN   The emblem of Rohan, showing a meara running over a grassy plain. (III 438)

WHITE LADY   Epithet applied to Galadriel (q.v.) by Faramir. (II 365)

WHITE LADY OF GONDOLIN   Aredhel (q.v.). (S 135; B 162)

WHITE LADY OF ROHAN   Éowyn (q.v.). (III 297, 300)

WHITE LADY OF THE NOLDOR   Aredhel (q.v.). (S 60; B 64)

WHITE MOUNTAIN Taniquetil (q.v.). (S 282; B 349)

WHITE MOUNTAINS The Ered Nimrais (q.v.). (I 16, 321)

WHITE RIDER Gandalf (q.v.) while riding Shadowfax, in opposition to the Black Riders, the Nazgûl. (II 133; III 100)

WHITE SHIPS The ships built by the Elves to sail from Middle-earth to Eldamar. They had both oars and sails. The white ships sailed from Dol Amroth until about TA 2000, and also down Anduin and from the Grey Havens.

Also called Elven-ships and grey ships. (I 74, 441, 483; III 181, 383; TB 62-64)

WHITESKINS Name given to the Rohirrim (q.v.) by the Orcs of Isengard. (II 65)

WHITE-SOCKS (fl. WR) One of the ponies provided by Merry for Frodo's flight to Rivendell. Driven off in Bree, he was later recovered and claimed by Barliman Butterbur.

White-socks was named by Tom Bombadil. (I 155, 198, 199, 242)

WHITE TELPERION Telperion (q.v.). (S 291; B 361-62)

WHITE TOWER The tower in the Citadel of Minas Tirith, built by King Calimehtar in TA 1900. In 2698 it was rebuilt by Steward Ecthelion I. The White Tower seems to have been the site of the royal court from the time of its construction. The main room of the Tower was the Tower Hall (q.v.), and the palantír of Minas Anor was kept in a chamber under the dome of the Tower.

Also called the Tower of Ecthelion. (III 24, 25, 115, 458, 459)

WHITE TOWERS   Three towers on the Tower Hills, probably built by Gil-galad for Elendil after the founding of Arnor. A palantír was kept in Elostirion, the tallest of the towers, from which one could see the Sea. The Towers remained standing into the Fourth Age. (I 26-27, 74, 349; III 383; S 291, 292; B 360, 362)

WHITE TREE   Telperion (q.v.). (S 59; B 62)

WHITE TREE   Nimloth (q.v.). (S 268; B 330)

WHITE TREE OF GONDOR   Any of the descendants of Nimloth growing in Gondor. Isildur stole a fruit of Nimloth from the King's Court in Númenor and brought the resulting sapling to Middle-earth, where he planted it in Minas Ithil. Sauron burned this White Tree when he captured Minas Ithil in SA 3429, but Isildur took a seedling with him as he fled to Arnor.

After the overthrow of Sauron, Isildur planted this seedling in the Citadel of Minas Anor in memory of his brother Anárion. This Tree survived until the Great Plague of TA 1636, but soon after King Tarondor planted a seedling in the Court of the Fountain of the Citadel. This Tree died in 2852 with the death of Steward Belecthor II, and as no sapling could be found, the Withered Tree (q.v.) was left standing. After the WR, Aragorn found a sapling of the White Tree on the slopes of Mindolluin, and this was planted in the Citadel.

The White Tree had leaves dark on top and silver beneath and clusters of flowers with white petals. Also called the White Tree of the Eldar. (I 321, 331; II 258; III 26, 308, 311, 393, 408, 416, 454, 456, 457; S 273, 276, 291-92, 293, 294, 296, 304; B 337, 342, 361-62, 364, 365, 367-68, 377)

WHITE WOLVES   Animals of Middle-earth, found in the Northern Waste. In the Fell Winter of TA 2911 White Wolves came south and troubled the inhabitants of Eriador. (III 461)

WHITFOOT Family of Hobbits of the Shire, not of the upper class but of some prominence. (I 214)

WHITFURROWS Village in the Eastfarthing on the Great East Road. (I 40)

WHITWELL Village in the Shire near Tuckborough. Paladin Took owned farm lands in Whitwell. (III 47)

WIDE WORLD Middle-earth (q.v.). (H 164)

WIDFARA (fl. WR) Man of Rohan, from the Wold. He fought in the Battle of the Pelennor Fields. (III 135)

WILCOME COTTON (b. TA 2946) Hobbit of the Shire, second child of Holman Cotton.
He was usually called Will. (III 477)

WILCOME COTTON (b. TA 2984) Hobbit of the Shire, third child of Tolman Cotton.
He was usually called Jolly. (III 354, 477)

WILD The area east of the Ford of Bruinen, where nothing was as safe or dependable as it was in the Shire.
The Wild may be identical to Rhovanion. (I 225, 307; H 12, 65)

WILD The men of Darkness (q.v.). (II 364)

WILDERLAND Rhovanion (q.v.). (I 17, 330; H 14; L 196)

WILDMAN OF THE WOODS The name first given by Túrin when he encountered the Haladin of Brethil. He soon renamed himself Turambar. (S 216; B 265-66)

WILD MEN The Woses (q.v.). (III 505)

WILD WOOD The wood in Cuiviénen whence came the first Elf-children. (II 78)

WILIBALD BOLGER (b. c. TA 2900, d. before 3001) Hobbit of the Shire. He married Prisca Baggins. (III 474)

WILLIAM HUGGINS (d. TA 2941) Troll of the Trollshaws, one of the three encountered by Thorin and Company and turned to stone through Gandalf's trickery. He was usually called Bill. (H 44-52)

WILLIE BANKS (d. TA 3019) Hobbit of the Breeland, killed in the fight between Breelanders and Bill Ferny and his friends. (III 335)

WILLOWBOTTOM Village in the Eastfarthing, near the place where Thistle Brook flowed into the Shirebourn. (I 40)

WILLOW, OLD MAN (FA-FO) Evil-hearted willow tree in the Old Forest, standing near the Withywindle. Old man Willow had power over much of the Forest, although he was not as powerful as Tom Bombadil.
Also called Old Grey Willow-man and the Great Willow. (I 164-69, 180-81; TB 12, 17)

WILLOW-WREN Bird of the Old Forest, in the poem *Bombadil Goes Boating.* (TB 17, 23)

WILL WHITFOOT (fl. WR) Hobbit of the Shire, Mayor of Michel Delving from TA 3013 or earlier to FO 7. Will was the first Hobbit put in the Lockholes by the Chief's Men. Before his imprisonment he was the fattest Hobbit in the Westfarthing.
Will was known as old Will and old Flourdumpling. (I 214; III 347, 360, 372-73, 377, 471)

WILWARIN (Q.: 'butterfly') One of the constellations, perhaps the modern Cassiopeia, shaped by Varda in preparation for the awakening of the Elves. (S 48, 354; B 48, 442)

WILYA Older form of vilya (q.v.). (III 500)

WINDFOLA (fl. WR) Horse of Rohan, ridden by Éowyn and Merry to the Battle of the Pelennor Fields. (III 93, 141)

WINDING STAIR The second stairway in the ascent from Imlad Morgul to Cirith Ungol. The Winding Stair zigzagged up the face of the Ephel Dúath. (II 404-05)

WINDLE-REACH Straight portion of the lower Withywindle between Grindwall and the Withy-weir. (TB 19)

WINDOW-CURTAIN The waterfall behind which Henneth Annûn (q.v.) was built.
Also called the Curtain. (II 357-58, 370, 371)

WINDOW OF THE EYE The window high in the western side of Barad-dûr whence watched the Eye of Sauron. Although Sauron could look in many directions from the Window, the Window actually pointed directly at the Sammath Naur. (III 270)

WINDOW OF THE SUNSET, WINDOW ON THE WEST Henneth Annûn (q.v.). (II 358)

WINGED CROWN The Silver Crown (q.v.) of Gondor. (S 296; B 367)

WINGED MESSENGER One of the Nazgûl (q.v.), whose steed was shot by Legolas over Anduin during the Quest. (I 501; II 129)

WINTERFILTH The tenth month of the Shire Reckoning, corresponding to our October. The name in Bree was Wintring, but Winterfilth was claimed by Shire-hobbits to be the older name. The name referred to the completing (filling) of the days remaining before winter, and dated from the time before the adoption of the Kings' Reckoning when the Hobbit year began after the harvest. (III 478, 483)

WINTRING   See: Winterfilth. (III 483)

WISE   The Wizards and the chief Eldar, who in the Third Age acted together to face the menace of Dol Guldur. In TA 2463 the Wise formed the White Council (q.v.). (I 326, 327; III 420, 456; S 288, 298; B 357, 370)

WISEMAN GAMWICH (b. TA 2800)   Hobbit of the Shire, son of Hamfast of Gamwich. He moved to Tighfield, where he was probably a roper. (III 477)

WISE-NOSE (fl. WR)   One of the ponies provided by Merry for Frodo's flight to Rivendell. Driven off in Bree, Wise-nose was later recovered and claimed by Barliman Butterbur.
　　He was named by Tom Bombadil. (I 155, 198, 199)

WITCH-KING OF ANGMAR   The name by which the Lord of the Nazgûl (q.v.) was known in Angmar. (III 397, 398, 399, 411-12)

WITHERED HEATH   Area in the eastern Ered Mithrin whence came dragons and other evil creatures that plagued the Dwarves of the Ered Mithrin. (I 17; H 13, 32)

WITHERED TREE   The dead White Tree of Gondor which remained in the Court of the Fountain from TA 2852 to 3019, as no sapling could be found to replace it. In 3019, when Gandalf and Aragorn found a sapling, the Withered Tree was laid to rest in Rath Dínen. (III 26-27, 309, 416)

WITHY-WEIR   Weir   in   the   Withywindle   above Windle-reach, made most probably by the Hobbits of Buckland. (TB 19, 23)

WITHYWINDLE   River flowing from its source in the Barrow-downs through the Old Forest (q.v.) and into the Brandywine at the southern end of Buckland. In its valley, the Dingle, grew many willow trees, and this area was the center of the evil of the Old Forest.

Goldberry, Bombadil's wife, was the daughter of the River-woman (q.v.) of the Withywindle.

See also: the Withy-weir, Windle-reach. (I 40, 160, 163-71, 176; TB 8-9, 11-23 passim)

WIZARDS The Istari (q.v.). (I 32; H 19)

WIZARD'S VALE Nan Curunír (q.v.). (II 167)

WOLD OF ROHAN The grassy upland plain of north-eastern Rohan, lying between Anduin and the Entwash. (I 17, 493, 494; II 38)

WOLF Carcharoth (q.v.). (I 260; S 182; B 221)

WOLF (fl. WR) One of Farmer Maggot's guard-dogs. (I 133, 134)

WOLF-RIDERS Evil beings who rode wolves of some sort, first used by Morgoth in the First Age. In the Battle of the Five Armies the Wolf-riders were clearly Orcs mounted on Wargs, but the identity of the Wolf-riders serving Saruman in the WR is less certain. (II 48; H 265, 267; S 188; B 230)

WOLF-SAURON The form assumed by Sauron to fight Huan during the Quest of the Silmaril. Sauron did this to fulfill the prophecy of the death of Huan, but he was defeated by the hound and Lúthien. (S 175; B 211-12)

WOLVES See: Wargs, White Wolves, Wolf-riders, Werewolves.

WOOD-ELVES The Silvan Elves (q.v.). (H 164)

WOODHALL Village in the Eastfarthing on the northern eaves of the Woody End. (I 40)

WOODLAND REALM The Elven-realm of Thranduil (q.v.) in northern Mirkwood, founded early in the Second Age. Its boundaries were uncertain until the end of the Third Age, when they were fixed so as to include all of Eryn Lasgalen north of the Mountains of Mirkwood.

The Elves of the Woodland Realm were untroubled, except for a war with the Dwarves and their constant struggle (after TA 1000) with the Orcs and great spiders of Mirkwood. (II 342; H 165)

WOODMEN OF WESTERN MIRKWOOD Men, related to the Edain, who inhabited the western portion of central Mirkwood in the Third Age. Although troubled by Orcs, spiders, and other evils out of Dol Guldur, they survived until the end of the Third Age. When Mirkwood was cleansed after the WR, the Woodmen and the Beornings were given that portion of the forest between the Mountains and the Narrows. (III 429, 468, 508; H 13)

WOODY END Woods in the Eastfarthing of the Shire. (I 40, 107)

WORLD Eä (q.v.). The word is also used loosely to signify Arda, especially when uncapitalized. (S 17; B 6)

WORLD'S END The western boundary of Arda in the First Age, perhaps the Doors of Night, perhaps used loosely to signify Aman. (I 310)

WORLD THAT IS Eä (q.v.), as opposed to the image of the Vision of Ilúvatar. (S 20; B 10)

WORM OF MORGOTH Glaurung (q.v.). (S 222; B 274)

WORMTONGUE Gríma (q.v.). (II 149)

WOSES Primitive Men living in Druadan Forest at the time of the WR. They had lived there at least since the Second Age, and although they did not dare to oppose

Sauron openly, they hated and feared him. In the Third Age they seem occasionally to have been hunted for sport by the Rohirrim. During the WR, the Woses, under their chieftain, Ghân-buri-Ghân, led the Rohirrim through Druadan Forest so that they could avoid the Orc-army on the West Road. In return for this service, at the beginning of the Fourth Age King Elessar gave Druadan Forest to the Woses and forbade any outsider to enter it without their permission.

The Woses were culturally primitive, but were very woodcrafty; they used poisoned arrows. Their language was entirely alien to Adûnaic.

Also called the Wild Men of the Woods or of Druadan Forest. (III 128, 129, 313, 505, 508-09; L 175)

WULF (d. TA 2759) Man of Rohan, son of Freca. After his father's death in 2754, Wulf fled to Dunland, and in 2758 he invaded Rohan with a large army of Dunlendings. He easily overran the country and took Meduseld, killing Prince Haleth. During the Long Winter, Wulf's armies besieged Helm in the Hornburg and Fréaláf, Helm's nephew, in Dunharrow. Although Helm and his second son Háma perished during the Winter, in early spring Fréaláf surprised Wulf in Meduseld and slew him. (III 431-33)

YALE Lowland area in the Eastfarthing. The Yale was west of Stock. (I 114)

YANTA (Q.: 'bridge') Name for the tengwa λ (number 35), which usually represented consonantal *y* or (in the mode of Beleriand) *e*. (III 500)

YAVANNA (Q.: 'fruit-gift, giver of fruits') Ainu, one of the Aratar and the second greatest of the Valier, the elder sister of Vána and spouse of Aulë. Yavanna watches over the growing things of Arda, especially the olvar, and she planted the first seeds of all the plants of Arda. Yavanna's greatest creation was the Two Trees, but she held all trees dear and ordained the harvests; she also made Galathilion and brought forth the flower and fruit which became the Moon and Sun.

Yavanna came often to Middle-earth in the early days of Arda, and since the evils of Melkor perverted the kelvar and olvar under her protection, she strongly supported all plans by the Valar to attack him.

Her gardens in Valinor are the source of miruvórë. Her usual fana is tall and garbed in green, but sometimes she appears as a tree reaching to the heavens. She is surnamed Kementári, Queen of the Earth. (R 61; S 25, 27-28, 29, 35, 38, 39, 40-41, 45-46, 47, 74-75, 78, 98-99, 260, 358, 365; B 18, 20-21, 23, 29, 33, 35, 36, 43-45, 47, 82, 86, 113, 321, 449)

YAVANNIË (Q.: 'fruit—') The ninth month of the Kings' and Stewards' Reckonings and the sixth of the New Reckoning, corresponding roughly to our September.

The Sindarin name, used only by the Dúnedain, was Ivanneth. (III 483)

YÁVIË (Q.) The third of the seasons of the loa of the Calendar of Imladris, corresponding roughly to our August and September. The name was also used by Men for the season of autumn.

Called in Sindarin iavas. (III 480, 485)

YÁVIÉRË (Q.: 'autumn-day') In the Stewards' Reckoning, a holiday coming between Yavannië 30 and Narquelië 1, falling near the autumnal equinox. (III 481)

YEAR-BOOK OF TUCKBOROUGH Yellowskin (q.v.). (III 484)

YEAR OF LAMENTATION The year of the Nirnaeth Arnoediad, FA 473. (S 126, 198; B 151, 243)

YEARS OF THE SUN The coranar (q.v.), the unit of time used after the rising of the Sun. (S 103; B 119)

YEARS OF THE TREES   The units of time measured in Aman while the Two Trees bloomed. The Years of the Trees were longer than the later Years of the Sun, but otherwise their duration is not given nor are any divisions into months or weeks.

The day, however, consisted of twelve hours of unknown length; one day contained a complete cycle of the Trees. The Opening Hour in which Telperion first began to bloom was not counted in the First Day, and so each day began with the second level of blooming of Telperion. During the third hour Telperion reached his greatest bloom, and at the end of the sixth hour he ceased to bloom, although his light remained in the air for some time. Laurelin began to bloom at the beginning of the sixth hour, which thus marked the onset of the mingling of the lights. Laurelin reached her maximum bloom during the ninth hour and ceased shining at the end of the twelfth hour. Telperion, however, began to bloom again at the beginning of the twelfth hour, and so this hour marked the onset of another mingling of the lights. (S 38-39, 103; B 33-34, 119)

YELLOW FACE   Gollum's name for the Sun (q.v.). (II 289)

YELLOWSKIN   Book kept by the Tooks recording Took births, deaths, marriages, and land-sales, and also various Shire events. It was begun about TA 2000 and contained much information cited in the Red Book of Westmarch. Yellowskin was the most ancient document in the Shire at the end of the Third Age.

Also called the Year-book of Tuckborough. (III 484)

YÉN (Q.: 'year')   The long year of the Eldar in Middle-earth, equal to 144 solar years. (III 479; R 58)

YESTARE (Q.: 'first-day')   The first day of the year in the Calendar of Imladris and the three Dúnedain calendars. In the Kings' and Stewards' Reckonings it fell at the winter solstice, but in the Rivendell and New Reckonings it came near the vernal equinox, on our March 29 and 17, respectively.

Yestarë fell outside the months. (III 480, 481, 486)

YOUNGER CHILDREN OF ILÚVATAR Men (q.v.). (S 103, 210; B 119, 258)

YOUNGER DAYS The Fourth Age, the Age of Men, as opposed to the Elder and Middle Days of the Elves, so called by Saruman. (I 339)

YOUNG TOM COTTON Tolman Cotton (2) (q.v.). (III 354)

YULEDAYS The first and last days of the year in the Shire Reckoning, with the Lithedays the chief holidays of the year. The two Yuledays did not belong to any month. (III 478, 482)

YULEMATH The name given Foreyule (q.v.) in Bree and the Eastfarthing. (III 483)

YULETIDE The six-day winter holiday period in the Shire, lasting from 29 Foreyule to 2 Afteryule. (III 482)

⇜ ⇝

ZARAGAMBA (gen. Hobb.) The Oldbucks (q.v.). (III 520)

ZIMRAPHEL, AR- (Ad.) The name which Ar-Pharazôn forced Tar-Míriel (q.v.) to take. (S 270; B 333)

ZIMRATHÔN, AR- (Ad.) (fl. c. SA 3000) Dúnadan, twentieth King of Númenor. (III 390)

ZIRAK Zirak-zigil (q.v.). (I 370)

ZIRAK-ZIGIL (Kh.)   One of the three Mountains of Moria. In its pinnacle was built Durin's Tower, and here Gandalf threw down the Balrog.

Called in Sindarin Celebdil and in Westron Silvertine. Also called Zirak for short by the Dwarves. (I 370, 432; II 134)

Appendix A

A Chronology of the First Age

In preparing this Chronology (for reasons explained in the Introduction) I have encountered a number of difficulties. First, *Quenta Silmarillion* provides no quantitative indication of the passage of time before the creation of the Sun and the return of the Noldorin Exiles; indeed, before the creation of the Two Trees the Valar apparently did not concern themselves with the measurement of Time. Therefore, the seventeen sections of the Chronology marked by Roman numerals are sequential but definitely not isochronous. The three ages of the Chaining of Melkor were obviously vastly longer than the three periods between the poisoning of the Two Trees and the first rising of the Sun, "but of bliss and glad life there is little to be said, before it ends." [1]

The second problem has to do with the beginning of the Years of the Sun. I have assumed that FA 1 (or, more accurately, YS 1) began with the first rising of the Sun in the West. But the reform by which Varda returned night to Arda soon changed the direction of movement, and by the end of FA/YS 1 the Sun was probably moving from East to West. Since this realignment took some time to accomplish, FA/YS 1 probably lasted more than 365 days. If, however, the Years of the Sun should be counted from the first rising of the Sun in the East, then all these dates may need to be adjusted.

Incidentally, I have assumed that the year begins in the spring, following the example of the Eldarin loa in providing dates for these Eldarin accounts of the First Age. Thus, the birth of Tuor, which probably occurred in January (Rían conceived two months before Huor went to

[1] S 95; B 108.

557

the Nirnaeth Arnoediad at Midsummer), would be dated 473 in the Calendar of Imladris, but 474 in the Kings' Reckoning. Of course, if the birth of Nienor "in the first beginning of the year"[1] occurred in January instead of in March (both are possible), then her birth would remain dated 474, but Dagor Bragollach should be changed to 456 and the Fell Winter to 497.

The greatest difficulty, though, involves the establishment of firm dates for most events. The great majority of the references to time in *Quenta Silmarillion* date events in terms of time elapsed since other events. Unfortunately, these datings occur infrequently, and out of all of them no more than four refer to any single common event: Mereth Aderthad is held "when twenty years of the Sun had passed";[2] Dagor Bragollach begins in winter, "it being then four hundred years and five and fifty since the coming of Fingolfin";[3] Nargothrond falls in the same year that the messengers of Círdan deliver to Orodreth the warning of Ulmo, "when four hundred and ninety-five years had passed since the rising of the Moon, in the spring of the year";[4] Eärendil is born in the spring, "five hundred years and three since the coming of the Noldor to Middle-earth."[5] It is clear that Fëanor came to Losgar some time before Fingolfin crossed the Helcaraxë. The Moon rose as Fingolfin first entered Middle-earth, and it had crossed the sky seven times (days? months?) when Fingolfin entered Mithrim at the first rising of the Sun. I have dated Mereth Aderthad as FA/YS 21, since one Year of the Sun had passed at the beginning of FA/YS 2. Similarly with the messengers of Círdan (496, i.e., the *next* spring) and the birth of Eärendil (504, nearly eight years after Tuor's arrival in Gondolin). But I have dated Dagor Bragollach 455, assuming winter to occur at the end of the year and "the coming of Fingolfin" to refer to his crossing of the Helcaraxë a number of months earlier than his arrival in

[1] S 199; B 243.
[2] S 113; B 132.
[3] S 150; B 180-81.
[4] S 211; B 260.
[5] S 241; B 298.

Mithrim. (Incidentally, an indication of the considerable length of time involved in the return of the Noldor is that during this period Melkor returned to Middle-earth, quarreled with Ungoliant at Lammoth, rebuilt Angband, and overran Beleriand as far as Amon Ereb and the Falas.)

But even with this juggling of dates some problems remain. The events between Dagor Bragollach and the fall of Nargothrond can be dated fairly closely by examining the careers of Túrin (born in the year when Beren first saw Lúthien, and eight years old in the Year of Lamentation) and Tuor (born in the Year of Lamentation, and twenty-three—sixteen years of youth, three of slavery, and four of outlawry—when he journeyed to Gondolin during the Fell Winter that followed the autumn in which Nargothrond was sacked). This kind of narrative dating is somewhat unreliable; Tuor's three years of slavery could easily be thirty-one months—or thirty-nine. It is doubtless because of this imprecision that the dates given for Dagor Bragollach and the sack of Nargothrond seem two years too close. To reconcile this, I have removed two years from Barahir's outlawry in Dorthonion (according to the text, he is killed "in that time" [1] in which Galdor dies, seven years after Dagor Bragollach, i.e., about 462) and one from Tuor's enslavement in Hithlum.

In short, I must emphasize that the dates in this Chronology (and in the *Guide* as a whole) for the First Age depend totally on my interpretations of information that does not really warrant this kind of scrutiny. But while there may be errors in the absolute values of the dates, they can nonetheless be relied on as an accurate indication of the relative sequence of events and life-spans. If some of my conclusions seem those of some wayward pupil of Findegil the King's Writer, rather than of a careful scholar and Elf-friend like Bilbo Baggins, my only excuse is the poverty of this Age; I have been unable to ask the Wise to emend my eagerness with their knowledge.

    I.   The Creation of Eä. The Valar, the Maiar, and Melkor enter Eä.

[1] S 161; B 194.

II. The First War and the Marring of Arda. Tulkas enters Eä; Melkor retreats. The completion of Arda.

III. The Spring of Arda begins. The Valar create the Lamps and settle at Almaren. Tulkas weds Nessa.

IV. Melkor secretly returns to Arda, builds Utumno and the Ered Engrin, and partly blights the Spring.

V. Melkor overthrows the Lamps; Almaren is destroyed. End of the Spring of Arda; beginning of the Sleep of Yavanna.

VI. The Valar raise the Pelóri and settle in Aman.

VII. The Valar create the Two Trees, which begin to shine on the First Day. Beginning of the Count of Time.

VIII. Varda kindles new stars; the Elves awake in Cuiviénen. They are harassed by Melkor; the first breeding of Orcs.

IX. Oromë discovers the Elves. The Battle of the Powers and the Chaining of Melkor. The Great Journey begins. Thingol and Melian wed.

X. The first age of the Chaining of Melkor. The Sundering of the Elves. Some of the Eldar arrive in Aman; the Noontide of Valinor begins. The Sindar flourish in Beleriand. At the end of the age, Lúthien is born.

XI. The second age of the Chaining. Dwarves enter Beleriand and settle the Ered Luin. At the end of this age, Thingol builds Menegroth.

XII. The third age of the Chaining. Evil things begin to stir in Middle-earth. The Laiquendi come to Beleriand. Daeron invents the Cirth.

XIII. Melkor is unchained. He raises dissension among the sons of Finwë. Fëanor is banished for twelve years and Melkor vanishes from Valinor.

XIV. The Darkening of Valinor; end of the Noontide. Melkor and Ungoliant poison the Two Trees, kill Finwë, and steal the Silmarils.

XV. The Long Night. Melkor and Ungoliant flee

	across the Helcaraxë and quarrel at Lammoth. Melkor rebuilds Angband. The revolt of the Noldor, the Kinslaying, and the utterance of the Doom of Mandos. Melkor invades Beleriand; the first battle of the Wars of Beleriand. The Girdle of Melian is raised.
XVI.	The Long Night continues. Fëanor burns his ships at Losgar. Dagor-nuin-Giliath; Fëanor slain and Maedhros captured. Fingolfin marches to the Helcaraxë. The Valar prepare the Moon and Sun.
XVII.	The Moon rises. End of the Long Night (?) and the Sleep of Yavanna; the Second Spring of Arda. Fingolfin enters Middle-earth. The Moon crosses the sky seven times.
FA 1	The Years of the Sun begin; the Sun rises in the West. Men awaken. Fingolfin enters Mithrim. The Orcs flee into Angband. Fingon rescues Maedhros. Fingolfin is named High King of the Noldor. Varda causes the Sun to change direction.
21	Mereth Aderthad.
51	Ulmo appears to Finrod and Turgon in a dream. Finrod learns of the Caverns of Narog and begins to build Nargothrond, which is completed before Gondolin.
52	Ulmo reveals Tumladen to Turgon.
c. 60	Dagor Aglareb. The Siege of Angband begins.
c. 70	Thingol forbids the Sindar to speak Quenya.
104	The completion of Gondolin.
c. 160	Orcs attack Hithlum from Lammoth.
c. 260	Glaurung is defeated on Ard-galen. The Long Peace begins.
c. 304	Aredhel leaves Gondolin.
c. 306	Maeglin is born.
c. 310	Finrod meets the Edain in Ossiriand.
c. 311	Bëor enters the service of Finrod.
c. 330	Aredhel and Maeglin enter Gondolin. Death of Aredhel and Eöl.
c. 355	Death of Bëor.
c. 365	Bereg of the First House returns to Eriador.

c. 370   Haleth brings the Haladin to Brethil.

389   Birth of Hador.

c. 425   The House of Hador settles in Dor-lómin.

c. 441   Birth of Húrin.

444   Birth of Huor.

455   Winter: Dagor Bragollach; death of Hador and Fingolfin. End of the Siege of Angband and the Long Peace. Fingon becomes High King of the Noldor.

457   Sauron takes Tol Sirion. Beleg and Halmir hold the Crossings of Teiglin. Húrin and Huor spend a year in Gondolin. About this time the Easterlings enter Beleriand.

460   Autumn: Death of Barahir and the outlaws of Dorthonion. Beren remains in Dorthonion.

462   Orcs assault Hithlum from north and east; Galdor slain.

464   Winter: Beren flees Dorthonion.

465   Summer: Beren first sees Lúthien. In this year Túrin is born.

466   Spring: Lúthien returns Beren's love.
Summer: Beren is brought to Menegroth and undertakes the Quest of the Silmaril.
Autumn: Beren in Nargothrond.

466-68   The Quest of the Silmaril. Death of Finrod and Draugluin. Tol Sirion cleansed; Sauron flees to Taur-nu-Fuin. Beren recovers a Silmaril. The Hunting of the Wolf; death of Beren, Huan, Carcharoth, and Lúthien.

c. 470   Beren and Lúthien in Tol Galen; Dior is born.

473   The Year of Lamentation. The Union of Maedhros and the Nirnaeth Arnoediad; death of Fingon and Huor, capture of Húrin and Gwindor. Túrin is sent to Doriath. Tuor and Nienor are born. Turgon becomes High King of the Noldor.

474   Fall of the Falas; Círdan retreats to Balar and builds the Havens of Sirion.

482-85   Túrin fights with Beleg in the marches of Doriath.

485 Death of Saeros; Túrin flees Doriath and becomes an outlaw.

486 Beleg finds Túrin. Túrin settles at Amon Rûdh.

487 The Two Captains in Dor-Cúarthol. Amon Rûdh betrayed. Beleg and Gwindor free Túrin; death of Beleg. Túrin comes to Nargothrond.

490 Tuor enslaved by Lorgan.

492 Tuor escapes and becomes an outlaw in Mithrim.

496 Defeat of the Haladin. Glaurung invades West Beleriand; the Battle of Tumhalad and the sack of Nargothrond. Death of Orodreth, Gwindor, and Finduilas. Túrin ensnared by Glaurung. Tuor comes to Nevrast and Gondolin. The Fell Winter.

497 Túrin in Brethil.

500 Túrin and Nienor wed.

501 Death of Glaurung, Nienor, Brandir, and Túrin.

502 Húrin released from Thangorodrim. Death of Morwen. Húrin brings the Nauglamír to Thingol.

503 Wedding of Tuor and Idril. About this time Húrin dies.

504 Spring: Birth of Eärendil.

c. 505 Death of Thingol. The Dwarves sack Menegroth. Beren recovers the Nauglamír.

c. 509 Second death of Beren and Lúthien. The sons of Fëanor sack Menegroth; death of Dior and Nimloth. Elwing flees to the Havens of Sirion.

511 Midsummer: Fall of Gondolin. Death of Ecthelion, Gothmog, Turgon, Maeglin, and Glorfindel. Tuor, Idril, and Eärendil flee to the Havens of Sirion. Gil-galad named High King of the Noldor.

c. 543 Tuor and Idril sail West. Eärendil becomes lord of the people of the Havens and marries Elwing. Sometime after this Elrond and Elros are born.

NOTE: From this point dates must be figured backward from the end of the Age. Since Elros died in SA 442 at the age of 500, he was born 58 years before the end of the First Age. If Tuor began to feel old at age

70 (as I have assumed here), then the First Age ended after about 600 Years of the Sun. This is not to say, of course, that the First Age lasted six hundred years; the Sleep of Yavanna alone may have endured for the equivalent of tens of thousands of Years of the Sun.

THE FIRST HOUSE OF THE EDAIN

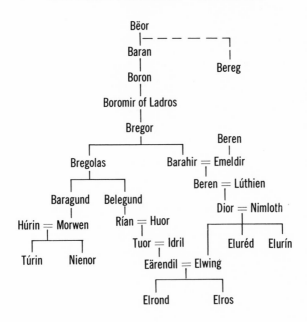

THE HALADIN   THE THIRD HOUSE OF THE EDAIN

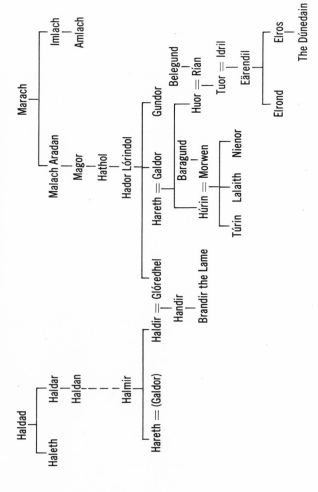

THE HOUSE OF ELROS: KINGS OF NÚMENOR AND LORDS OF ANDÚNIË

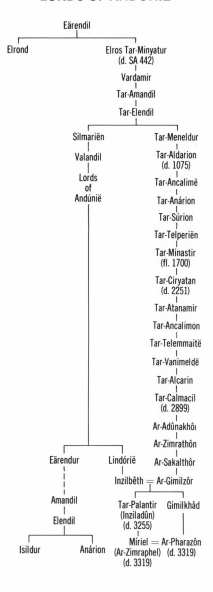

Eärendil

Elrond

Elros Tar-Minyatur
(d. SA 442)

Vardamir

Tar-Amandil

Tar-Elendil

Silmariën

Valandil

Lords
of
Andúnië

Tar-Meneldur

Tar-Aldarion
(d. 1075)

Tar-Ancalimë

Tar-Anárion

Tar-Súrion

Tar-Telperiën

Tar-Minastir
(fl. 1700)

Tar-Ciryatan
(d. 2251)

Tar-Atanamir

Tar-Ancalimon

Tar-Telemmaitë

Tar-Vanimeldë

Tar-Alcarin

Tar-Calmacil
(d. 2899)

Ar-Adûnakhôı

Ar-Zimrathôn

Eärendur

Lindórië

Ar-Sakalthôr

Inzilbêth = Ar-Gimilzôr

Amandil

Elendil

Tar-Palantir
(Inziladûn)
(d. 3255)

Gimilkhâd

Isildur

Anárion

Míriel = Ar-Pharazôn
(Ar-Zimraphel) (d. 3319)
(d. 3319)

LINES OF ISILDUR AND ANÁRION: KINGS OF ARNOR, ARTHEDAIN AND GONDOR

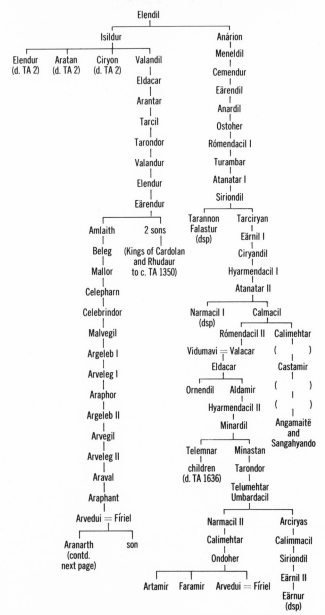

LINE OF ISILDUR (Contd.):
CHIEFTAINS OF THE DÚNEDAIN
AND
KINGS OF THE REUNITED KINGDOM

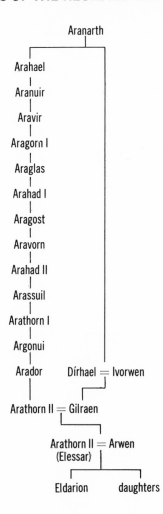

Aranarth

Arahael
|
Aranuir
|
Aravir
|
Aragorn I
|
Araglas
|
Arahad I
|
Aragost
|
Aravorn
|
Arahad II
|
Arassuil
|
Arathorn I
|
Argonui
|
Arador

Dírhael = Ivorwen

Arathorn II = Gilraen

Arathorn II = Arwen
(Elessar)

Eldarion   daughters

THE DESCENT OF THE PEREDHIL*

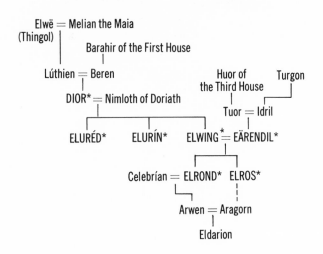

THE HOUSE OF HÚRIN
(THE HOUSE OF THE STEWARDS)

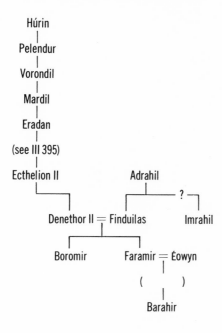

Húrin
|
Pelendur
|
Vorondil
|
Mardil
|
Eradan
|
(see III 395)
|
Ecthelion II   Adrahil

Denethor II = Finduilas   Imrahil

Boromir   Faramir = Éowyn

(   )

Barahir

THE ÉOTHÉOD AND THE ROHIRRIM

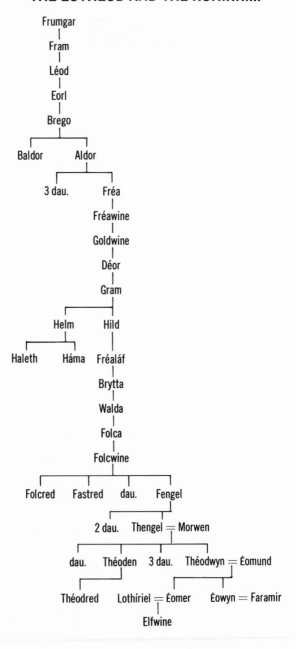

Frumgar
|
Fram
|
Léod
|
Eorl
|
Brego
|
Baldor — Aldor
|
3 dau. — Fréa
|
Fréawine
|
Goldwine
|
Déor
|
Gram
|
Helm — Hild
|
Haleth — Háma — Fréaláf
|
Brytta
|
Walda
|
Folca
|
Folcwine
|
Folcred — Fastred — dau. — Fengel
|
2 dau. — Thengel = Morwen
|
dau. — Théoden — 3 dau. — Théodwyn = Éomund
|
Théodred — Lothíriel = Éomer — Éowyn = Faramir
|
Elfwine

Appendix C
Conversion of Page References to
Houghton Mifflin Editions

In this era of pocket calculators, converting page references from one edition of a text to another is a fairly simple matter. The table below shows how to convert the page references in this *Guide,* which refer to Ballantine paperback editions, to references to the Houghton Mifflin hardback editions. Subtract the figure shown in Column 2 from the Ballantine page number, multiply the result by the number in Column 3, and add the number in Column 4. Results are usually accurate within a page. For example, to convert Ballantine I 489:

$$
\begin{array}{r}
489 \\
-18 \\
\hline
471 \\
\text{x.818} \\
\hline
385.278 \\
+9 \\
\hline
394
\end{array}
$$

1	2	3	4
Ballantine	Subtract	Multiply	Add
I 19 to I 526	18	.818	9
II 17 to II 447	16	.778	14
III 19 to III 385	18	.797	18
III 387 to III 520	386	.781	312
H 15 to 287	14	1.14	8

I vii equals HM I 3
I 17-18 equals HM I map
III 14-15 equals HM III map
H 10-11 equals HM H 6-7
H 12-13 equals HM H 318-19

About the Author

Robert Foster is an Assistant Professor of English at Rutgers College, New Brunswick, New Jersey. Born in Brooklyn, New York, he first encountered *Lord of the Rings* during a summer in his early teens. Several years later he began tracing the etymology of names used in Tolkien's works, a labor of love which eventually resulted in *The Complete Guide to Middle-earth,* a Ph.D. in English and Medieval Studies (University of Pennsylvania, 1974), and a scholarly career.

Mr. Foster likes cats, woodworking, and the outdoors.